THE PROPER STUDY

The Proper Study

ESSAYS ON WESTERN CLASSICS

EDITED BY

Quentin Anderson & Joseph A. Mazzeo

COLUMBIA UNIVERSITY

St Martin's Press   *New York*

PN
501
.A5

LIBRARY OF CONGRESS CATALOG CARD NUMBER 62-11703

DESIGNED BY ALFRED MANSO

MANUFACTURED IN THE UNITED STATES OF AMERICA BY THE
HADDON CRAFTSMEN, SCRANTON, PENNSYLVANIA.

P R E F A C E

IN 1936 THE FACULTY OF COLUMBIA COLLEGE VOTED TO INSTITUTE THE COURSE called Humanities A1-A2 and made it a requirement for all freshmen. It was taught for the first time—with a passion of enthusiasm—in the fall term of the following year. Few events in the history of American collegiate education have had so large an influence. Within a short time, faculties all over the country established courses of similar kind. They were certainly not drawn to do so by any mere spirit of emulation but rather out of their reasoned agreement with the idea upon which the Columbia College course was based. That idea was a very simple one, was simplicity itself. It consisted in the belief that no one could be thought educated who was ignorant of the chief works of the intellectual and artistic tradition of his own civilization. This single proposition comprised the whole "philosophy" of the new undertaking.

The simplicity of the originating idea of the course was matched by the simplicity of its method, which proposed to overcome the student's ignorance of the classical works of our tradition by one means only—the student was to read the books. So far as it was practicable for him to do so, he was to read them in their entirety. He would, to be sure, after he had read a work, discuss it with his teacher in the company of a relatively small group of his fellow students, but there were to be no "background" lectures or readings, no "guides," either in textbook or outline forms, no "secondary material" of any kind—all was to be primary.

This simplicity of method had not been arrived at without considerable difficulty and searching of the heart. The Columbia College faculty had come to its decision about the humanities course only after many years of debate, and the matter of the long disagreement had never been the purpose of the course—this was accepted out of hand—but only the method of teaching it.

The issue was made by those members of the faculty who doubted that a student might gain a correct or adequate understanding of a great book merely by reading it. And no doubt it was natural for seasoned scholars to wonder how, on a single and inevitably rapid reading, undergraduates, freshmen at that, might possibly comprehend books to whose study the scholars had devoted their professional lives. The students would not be able to look to their teachers for the help that scholarship gives, for, as the course was planned, the teaching staff was to be drawn from all the humanistic departments of the College, and this meant that what would be asked of any one instructor was the exercise not of his particular scholarly knowledge but only of his general intelligence and enlightenment. The member of the Department of Greek and Latin would be on firm scholarly ground during the early part of the course, which would begin with Homer and go on to St. Augustine, but he would have no special competence in dealing with Dante or Montaigne or Goethe. The teacher of English literature might be counted on to be knowledgeable about Shakespeare and Milton, but there was little in his professional training that equipped him to deal authoritatively with Spinoza. And so on, through the range of the humanistic disciplines.

The debate—it was not without its acrimony—was settled in favor of the party which believed that the purposes of the course and the needs of the students would be adequately served by the general intelligence and enlightenment of the teacher. The dominant opinion was surely a very reasonable one. The books that would make the substance of the course were to be chosen because they were no less pertinent now than when they had first been written, and also because their authors were men speaking to men, not to certain men who were especially trained to understand them, but to all men, so far as they were, in the French sense of the word, *honest* —that is to say, serious, fairminded, attentive. If a few of our authors were difficult, none was esoteric.* Some had even written for "popular" audiences. It seemed to us a denial of their nature to suppose that any sort of "secondary material" was needed to make them comprehensible.

The course, then, was conceived of as having but three elements—a book; a reader coming to it for the first time; a teacher who perhaps had no special scholarly knowledge but who, by reason of his experience of humanistic works in general, could see the book as a whole and help to bring its

---

* Spinoza is an exception. He said that he wrote his *Ethics* for a limited group of readers, scholars of strong mind, and that he did not think it appropriate for, and did not want it read by, the general public. The *Ethics,* it is worth noting, has always been especially liked and admired by the students of the Humanities course.

meanings and qualities to consciousness in the student. In short, the book was to be read by a young *honnête homme* with assistance and encouragement given by an older *honnête homme*. We who taught the course in its early years believed so strongly that there should be only the three elements that we made a point of urging our students not to consult works of scholarship and criticism. We felt that by their use some degree of the honesty would be lost. The situation seemed to us the more natural—perhaps we said more humanistic—if the special knowledge of the scholar and the highly instructed perception of the critic were excluded.

There was much in our attitude that was healthy and right. As every teacher knows, the formulations of a scholar or a critic about a great work sometimes have the effect upon the student of keeping him from confronting the work itself, from having an actual experience of it. Scholarship in the humanities proceeds on the hope of achieving an ideal reading of a work—one ought to read it, and with facility, in its own language; one ought to comprehend all its obscurities of reference; one ought to understand the tradition and the circumstances in which it was written, and so on. Criticism no less than scholarship—since the distinction between them must now be made, although once they were thought of as being the same thing—has also its imagination of a reading that is ideal. And, as so often happens in human affairs, the conception of the ideal may have the effect of nullifying what is good in the actual. We argued that the considerations appropriate to a developed familiarity with a work may be wholly inappropriate to a first reading, that they may stand in the way of its actuality, which is not necessarily the less worthy of respect because it has in it some confusion or inaccuracy of perception.

But if there was indeed healthiness and rightness in our attitude, how are we to account for the present volume? The editors, as I know, are especially committed to the essential principles of the Humanities course as it was first conceived. Yet they have prepared a collection of scholarly and critical essays on the great authors of the western tradition, intending the book for the use of students. What can have happened in the intervening years to justify their undertaking?

If I may try to answer the question from my own experience of teaching the humanities course, there came a time when the exclusion of all works of scholarship and criticism, so far from keeping the situation "natural," actually seemed to have the contrary effect. It was all very well to say of the books we read that they were written by men speaking to men and that they had as much meaning for men now as when they were written. This was a true thing to say, but one came to realize that its truth depended on how one said it. If one said it with the (perhaps unconscious) purpose of denying the significance of the time that had passed between *then* and *now,* if one tried to ignore or minimize the massive reality of history, then one was not saying a true thing. In the study of any literature of the past there are two propositions that must be given equal weight. One is that human nature is always the same. The other is that human nature changes, sometimes radically, with each historical epoch. The great charm—and one chief educative value—of reading works of the past lies in perceiving the truth of the two contradictory propositions and in seeing the sameness in the difference and the difference in the sameness. Some sense of the reality of the past—which is to say, its clear *otherness* in relation to the present— must enter into our comprehension of the works of the past. The consciousness of historicity must accompany all our other perceptions, such as the moral and the aesthetic. And I think I am reporting correctly when I say that in the pedagogic assumptions of those of us who taught the Humanities course during the early years, there was the impulse to deny, at least in some measure, the historicity of the books we read. In the interest of asserting the undiminished significance of the books, or perhaps, with some of us, in the interest of asserting the "eternality" of certain "values," we inclined to reduce the actuality of history. It was on this impulse, I think, that we excluded all scholarly or critical considerations of our books, for inevitably such considerations would force upon us the fact of the historicity of what we were dealing with.

No one will say that a lively sense of history is one of the intellectual virtues of the American people. Certainly it is not one of the intellectual virtues of the American undergraduate at the beginning of his college career, and we were wrong to try to exclude from our students' intellectual purview the concepts of historical thought as these relate to literature and philosophy. We did, of course, read our books in chronological order, and perhaps it can be said that the students could not help getting some sense of the past from this natural arrangement. Yet mere sequence in time can scarcely suggest the substance of the historical imagination.

There was, I believe, another and related mistake in that early purity of ours. To have made a point of excluding all scholarship and criticism from our course was to pretend that our great books existed in circumstances which were quite contrary to the fact. The great books do not have their being, as we seemed to imply, in splendid classic isolation or only in a kind of royal relation to each other. They exist in the lively *milieu* that is created by the responses that have long been given to them. For centuries they have been loved and admired and considered and interpreted and quarrelled over —and used, *used.* Some part of their reality consists in the way they have figured in the life of the world, certainly in the intellectual life of the world, a large part of which is constituted by what has been said about them. We can grant that the scholars and critics are not minds of the same stature and powers as those they undertook to study and praise—they themselves would be the first to say so—yet many among them have been fine minds and some have been great minds. In excluding them we were in effect excluding our students from the community of mind.* Even as we urged them toward discourse about the classic works of our tradition, we were in effect suggesting to them that all previous discourse was of no account, that in what they said and wrote about the great books there were no models to follow, no standards of cogency (except possibly those that were provided by their teachers!). This, surely, was not good pedagogy.

And if we speak of pedagogy, there was yet another reason why our entire exclusion of scholarship and criticism was ill-advised. Almost any teacher of a humanistic subject, if pressed to name the one thing that constitutes his pedagogic purpose, would say that it is to lead the student to become more active in his dealing with works of the imagination or intellect. A great work makes a kind of assault upon us, and it ought to be met with an appropriate counteraggression. It is in this activity that all the pleasure of humanistic study lies, and good scholarship and good criticism, no less than good teaching, have it as their intention to overcome the reader's passivity in relation to a work, to augment his active powers. It is no doubt true that a reader—perhaps especially a student reader—may be tempted to use a scholarly or critical essay about a work as a means of avoiding an actual, let alone an active, confrontation of the work itself. But this happens rather less often than is supposed, and in any case, there is really nothing that any teacher can do against wilful evasion. As for the common belief that the fresh innocence of our approach to a work is corrupted by becoming acquainted with someone else's ideas about it, I think that we give it too easy a credence. What we mean by a fresh innocence is often a bland passivity, and if it is, then how fortunate the fall from that Eden! Indeed, I would not even make a point of putting off the reading of the essay until the work itself is read. I think we should be simple and pragmatic about the conduct of the intellectual life—I am sure that if any teacher refers to his own experience as I refer to mine, he will join me in saying that our curiosity about a work is sharpened and our courage to encounter it is increased by reading something about it before we engage it in its own

* On this point I should like to refer the reader to Denys Hay's admirable article, "Learning and Literature," in *Cassell's Encyclopedia of World Literature.* Mr. Hay gives a lucid and comprehensive account of the relation that obtains between the great original genius and the minds that make up the general intellectual life. I would call especial attention to Mr. Hay's remarks on the revived tendency of scholars in relatively recent times to make their researches accessible to, that is, interesting to, the general public.

person, just as our interest in it and our realization of it are increased if we read something about it after we have finished it. And if we should happen further to corrupt our innocence by borrowing some of the scholar's or critic's ideas, what else are ideas for *except* to be borrowed—what else is meant by the community of mind by which the humanistic tradition sets so much store? And if this is true for us, why is it not true for our students?

LIONEL TRILLING

Columbia University

CONTENTS

[xi]

Contents

Contents

INTRODUCTION

THE EDITORS HAVE TRIED TO PUT TOGETHER A VOLUME OF ESSAYS, EACH ONE OF which offers a distinctive and commanding view of a classic in the western tradition. Those who know the works these essays are about will not mistake our intention (though they may quarrel with particular choices). But the general reader or student meeting these classics for the first time should perhaps be cautioned. This is not a handbook, nor a sufficient guide to intensive study of any one of the works discussed. As a text it enforces only one lesson: no single text is sufficient. But this collection points to what every reader may hope to achieve: a direct and broad relation to his cultural past. The essayists have not dreamed of "writing down" to any group of readers less accomplished than themselves; they are rather trying to answer the challenge of greatness in their own persons. If you are to meet them on their own level you must work too. In some cases these pieces are clearly the culmination of an enormous amount of scholarly labor; in others that labor, though required, is not displayed; still others seem to move without aids through the centuries to find in a great act of the imagination an image of our own times.

It was not our intention to pick certain essays as "background," although the reader will find a wealth of cultural and historical matter in many of them. Santayana's essay on Dante, for example, has a lucid and penetrating analysis of the nature of Greek cosmology and metaphysics, and of their transformations in medieval times. In this and other essays the reader will find much of the substance of what reference books contain, but he will find it shaped to the end of generating an understanding of a particular work or thinker. It ought also to be said that we do not aim at representing every "current" of western thought, or try to pick in every instance the most comprehensive essay from the scholar's viewpoint. Indeed, some of these essays

[1]

are idiosyncratic in their brilliance. To tell truth in one's own time one must often shock, distort, assume a mask. In short, the writer must prepare the reader for the reception of what he has to say.

It is especially important now to insist that the classics—either in the original sense (those works in Greek and Latin essential to an education), or in the modern sense that adds to the ancient canon works felt to have a comparable imaginative or philosophic authority—*do not* embody a single all-embracing humanistic world view. Those who purvey cultural salvation in units of one hundred books do much harm to what is called "general education." They err chiefly in denying that history has any meaning. This error the present book, so largely the record of relatively recent shifts in historical perspective, refutes. Finally, we disclaim the aim of the encyclopedist, that is, "coverage." Not every thinker has been fortunate enough to find his Matthew Arnold, nor every poet his Simone Weil; on some of the greatest of western authors there are no outstanding essays.

We have sought instances in which high talent or genius caught fire from its contact with genius itself, or examples of scholarship raised to the level of insight into the character and quality of a magisterial author of the past. These essays may be called "acts of reading"; they illustrate the inescapably dialectic character of live thought. Whether for the student or the inquiring general reader this is our only moral: genuine discussion, in the classroom, in the encounter of a living man with the living doctrine of an ancient work, or in the scholar's reseeing of the meanings of a body of historical material, is a personal affair. Whether in these encounters minds meet or clash is indifferent: what matters is that one should be assured of the presence of a thinking self, and not merely the impersonal exponent of a method of criticism or research.

To conclude, a word on the proper uses of such a book. We have tried to make a book that will be especially rewarding to study, whether in course or out. Obviously, the choice of method, and the emphases of each of our essayists, offer matter for inquiry. The reader will find that these essays range greatly in methods. They call our attention to the ways in which meaning is carried, through syntax, metaphor, structure, the representation of action, dialogue, and myth. Some center on the definition of a word or concept; others treat the significance of a literary form. Still others analyze the relations between different kinds of discourse. All of the essays are expository, but not one is merely so. They all reach beyond exposition to insight, and their varied rhetorical devices are of the sort that Plato would have approved: they are in the service of that highest form of communication which is synonymous with dialectic.

H O M E R

[*fl. c. 950–900* B.C.]

SIMONE WEIL DIED IN ENGLAND, IN EXILE FROM HER NATIVE FRANCE, IN 1943, when she was thirty-four. This essay first appeared in two installments, December 1940 and January 1941, in the *Cahiers du Sud,* under the pseudonym "Emile Novis," an anagram on her name. Written after the Nazi armies had overrun France, when she stood in the double jeopardy of being both French and Jewish, it nowhere mentions contemporary events, although it everywhere comments indirectly on the latest manifestation of force, which she saw as standing in the "very center of human history."

Her essay might have been written at any time, but it is doubtful that Weil's superb directness of vision would have reached its almost terrifying intensity had it not been exercised when the colossus of force had reduced itself to the same simplicities it had in the *Iliad.* She saw that Homer individualized the holocaust of war by having each man die to his own simile, that the apparently identical deaths of soldiers, the seeming uniformity of large-scale slaughter, is really the incalculable sum of unique, individual deaths, each with its own language and music.

Reprinted by permission of Dwight Macdonald. English translation by Mary McCarthy, originally published in *Politics,* November 1945.

SIMONE WEIL

The Iliad or
The Poem of Force

THE TRUE HERO, THE TRUE SUBJECT, THE CENTER OF THE *Iliad* IS FORCE. Force employed by man, force that enslaves man, force before which man's flesh shrinks away. In this work, at all times, the human spirit is shown as modified by its relations with force, as swept away, blinded, by the very force it imagined it could handle, as deformed by the weight of the force it submits to. For those dreamers who considered that force, thanks to progress, would soon be a thing of the past, the *Iliad* could appear as an historical document; for others, whose powers of recognition are more acute and who perceive force, today as yesterday, at the very center of human history, the *Iliad* is the purest and the loveliest of mirrors.

To define force—it is that x that turns anybody who is subjected to it into a *thing*. Exercised to the limit, it turns man into a thing in the most literal sense: it makes a corpse out of him. Somebody was here, and the next minute there is nobody here at all; this is a spectacle the *Iliad* never wearies of showing us:

> . . . the horses
> Rattled the empty chariots through the files of battle,

[4]

Longing for their noble drivers. But they on the ground
Lay, dearer to the vultures than to their wives.

The hero becomes a *thing* dragged behind a chariot in the dust:

All around, his black hair
Was spread; in the dust his whole head lay,
That once-charming head; now Zeus had let his enemies
Defile it on his native soil.

The bitterness of such a spectacle is offered us absolutely undiluted. No comforting fiction intervenes; no consoling prospect of immortality; and on the hero's head no washed-out halo of patriotism descends.

His soul, fleeing his limbs, passed to Hades,
Mourning its fate, forsaking its youth and its vigor.

Still more poignant—so painful is the contrast—is the sudden evocation, as quickly rubbed out, of another world: the faraway, precarious, touching world of peace, of the family, the world in which each man counts more than anything else to those about him.

She ordered her bright-haired maids in the palace
To place on the fire a large tripod, preparing
A hot bath for Hector, returning from battle.
Foolish woman! Already he lay, far from hot baths,
Slain by grey-eyed Athena, who guided Achilles' arm.

Far from hot baths he was indeed, poor man. And not he alone. Nearly all the *Iliad* takes place far from hot baths. Nearly all of human life, then and now, takes place far from hot baths.

Here we see force in its grossest and most summary form—the force that kills. How much more varied in its processes, how much more surprising in its effects is the other force, the force that does *not* kill, i.e., that does not kill just yet. It will surely kill, it will possibly kill, or perhaps it merely hangs, poised and ready, over the head of the creature it *can* kill, at any moment, which is to say at every moment. In whatever aspect, its effect is the same: it turns a man into a stone. From its first property (the ability to turn a human being into a thing by the simple method of killing him) flows another, quite prodigious too in its own way, the ability to turn a human being into a thing while he is still alive. He is alive; he has a soul; and yet—

he is a thing. An extraordinary entity this—a thing that has a soul. And as for the soul, what an extraordinary house it finds itself in! Who can say what it costs it, moment by moment, to accommodate itself to this residence, how much writhing and bending, folding and pleating are required of it? It was not made to live inside a thing; if it does so, under pressure of necessity, there is not a single element of its nature to which violence is not done.

A man stands disarmed and naked with a weapon pointing at him; this person becomes a corpse before anybody or anything touches him. Just a minute ago, he was thinking, acting, hoping:

> Motionless, he pondered. And the other drew near,
> Terrified, anxious to touch his knees, hoping in his heart
> To escape evil death and black destiny . . .
> With one hand he clasped, suppliant, his knees,
> While the other clung to the sharp spear, not letting go . . .

Soon, however, he grasps the fact that the weapon which is pointing at him will not be diverted; and now, still breathing, he is simply matter; still thinking, he can think no longer:

> Thus spoke the brilliant son of Priam
> In begging words. But he heard a harsh reply:
> He spoke. And the other's knees and heart failed him.
> Dropping his spear, he knelt down, holding out his arms.
> Achilles, drawing his sharp sword, struck
> Through the neck and breastbone. The two-edged sword
> Sunk home its full length. The other, face down,
> Lay still, and the black blood ran out, wetting the ground.

If a stranger, completely disabled, disarmed, strengthless, throws himself on the mercy of a warrior, he is not, by this very act, condemned to death; but a moment of impatience on the warrior's part will suffice to relieve him of his life. In any case, his flesh has lost that very important property which in the laboratory distinguishes living flesh from dead—the galvanic response. If you give a frog's leg an electric shock, it twitches. If you confront a human being with the touch or sight of something horrible or terrifying, this bundle of muscles, nerves, and flesh likewise twitches. Alone of all living things, the suppliant we have just described neither quivers nor trembles. He has lost the right to do so. As his lips advance to touch the object that is for him of all things most charged with horror, they do not draw back on his teeth—they cannot:

> No one saw great Priam enter. He stopped,
> Clasped the knees of Achilles, kissed his hands,
> Those terrible man-killing hands that had slaughtered so many of his
>   sons.

The sight of a human being pushed to such an extreme of suffering chills us like the sight of a dead body:

> As when harsh misfortune strikes a man if in his own country
> He has killed a man, and arrives at last at someone else's door,
> The door of a rich man; a shudder seizes those who see him.
> So Achilles shuddered to see divine Priam;
> The others shuddered too, looking one at the other.

But this feeling lasts only a moment. Soon the very presence of the suffering creature is forgotten:

> He spoke. The other, remembering his own father, longed to weep;
> Taking the old man's arm, he pushed him away.
> Both were remembering. Thinking of Hector, killer of men,
> Priam wept, abased at the feet of Achilles.
> But Achilles wept, now for his father,
> Now for Patroclus. And their sobs resounded through the house.

It was not insensibility that made Achilles with a single movement of his hand push away the old man who had been clinging to his knees; Priam's words, recalling his own old father, had moved him to tears. It was merely a question of his being as free in his attitudes and movements as if, clasping his knees, there were not a suppliant but an inert object. Anybody who is in our vicinity exercises a certain power over us by his very presence, and a power that belongs to him alone, that is, the power of halting, repressing, modifying each movement that our body sketches out. If we step aside for a passer-by on the road, it is not the same thing as stepping aside to avoid a billboard; alone in our rooms, we get up, walk about, sit down again quite differently from the way we do when we have a visitor. But this indefinable influence that the presence of another human being has on us is not exercised by men whom a moment of impatience can deprive of life, who can die before even thought has a chance to pass sentence on them. In their presence, people move about as if they were not there; they, on their side, running the risk of being reduced to nothing in a single instant, imitate nothingness in their own persons. Pushed, they fall. Fallen, they lie where they are, unless chance gives somebody the idea of raising them up again. But supposing that at long last they have been picked up, honored with cordial remarks, they still do not venture to take this resurrection seriously; they dare not express a wish lest an irritated voice return them forever to silence:

> He spoke; the old man trembled and obeyed.

At least a suppliant, once his prayer is answered, becomes a human being again, like everybody else. But there are other, more unfortunate creatures who have become things for the rest of their lives. Their days hold no pastimes, no free spaces, no room in them for any impulse of their own. It is not that their life is harder than other men's nor that they occupy a lower place in the social hierarchy; no, they are another human species, a compromise between a man and a corpse. The idea of a person's being a thing is a logical contradiction. Yet what is impossible in logic becomes true in life, and the contradiction lodged within the soul tears it to shreds. This thing is constantly aspiring to be a man or a woman, and never achieving it—here, surely, is death but death strung out over a whole lifetime; here, surely is life, but life that death congeals before abolishing.

This strange fate awaits the virgin, the priest's daughter:

> I will not give her up. Sooner shall old age come upon her
> In our house in Argos, far from her native land,
> Tending the loom and sharing my bed.

It awaits the young wife, the young mother, the prince's bride:

> And perhaps one day, in Argos, you will weave cloth for another,
> And the Messeian or Hyperian water you will fetch,
> Much against your will, yielding to a harsh necessity.

It awaits the baby, heir to the royal scepter:

> Soon they will be carried off in the hollow ships,
> I with them. And you, my child, will either go with me,
> To a land where you will work at wretched tasks,
> Laboring for a pitiless master. . . .

[8]

In the mother's eyes, such a fate is, for her child, as terrible as death; the husband would rather die than see his wife reduced to it; all the plagues of heaven are invoked by the father against the army that subjects his daughter to it. Yet the victims themselves are beyond all this. Curses, feelings of rebellion, comparisons, reflections on the future and the past, are obliterated from the mind of the captive; and memory itself barely lingers on. Fidelity to his city and his dead is not the slave's privilege.

And what does it take to make the slave weep? The misfortune of his master, his oppressor, despoiler, pillager, of the man who laid waste his town and killed his dear ones under his very eyes. This man suffers or dies; *then* the slave's tears come. And really why not? This is for him the only occasion on which tears are permitted, are, indeed, required. A slave will always cry whenever he can do so with impunity—his situation keeps tears on tap for him.

> She spoke, weeping, and the women groaned,
> Using the pretext of Patroclus to bewail their own torments.

Since the slave has no license to express anything except what is pleasing to his master, it follows that the only emotion that can touch or enliven him a little, that can reach him in the desolation of his life, is the emotion of love for his master. There is no place else to send the gift of love; all other outlets are barred, just as, with the horse in harness, bit, shafts, reins bar every way but one. And if, by some miracle, in the slave's breast a hope is born, the hope of becoming, some day, through somebody's influence, *someone* once again, how far won't these captives go to show love and thankfulness, even though these emotions are addressed to the very men who should, considering the very recent past, still reek with horror for them:

> My husband, to whom my father and respected mother gave me,
> I saw before the city transfixed by the sharp bronze.
> My three brothers, children, with me, of a single mother,
> So dear to me! They all met their fatal day.
> But you did not allow me to weep, when swift Achilles
> Slaughtered my husband and laid waste the city of Mynes.
> You promised me that I would be taken by divine Achilles,
> For his legitimate wife, that he would carry me away in his ships,
> To Pythia, where our marriage would be celebrated among the
>   Myrmidons,
> So without respite I mourn for you, you who have always been gentle.

To lose more than the slave does is impossible, for he loses his whole inner life. A fragment of it he may get back if he sees the possibility of changing his fate, but this is his only hope. Such is the empire of force, as extensive as the empire of nature. Nature, too, when vital needs are at stake, can erase the whole inner life, even the grief of a mother:

But the thought of eating came to her, when she was tired of tears.

Force, in the hands of another, exercises over the soul the same tyranny that extreme hunger does; for it possesses, and *in perpetuo,* the power of life and death. Its rule, moreover, is as cold and hard as the rule of inert matter. The man who knows himself weaker than another is more alone in the heart of a city than a man lost in the desert.

Two casks are placed before Zeus's doorsill,
Containing the gifts he gives, the bad in one, the good in the other . . .
The man to whom he gives baneful gifts, he exposes to outrage;
A frightful need drives across the divine earth;
He is a wanderer, and gets no respect from gods or men.

Force is as pitiless to the man who possesses it, or thinks he does, as it is to its victims; the second it crushes, the first it intoxicates. The truth is, nobody really possesses it. The human race is not divided up, in the *Iliad,* into conquered persons, slaves, suppliants, on the one hand, and conquerors and chiefs on the other. In this poem there is not a single man who does not at one time or another have to bow his neck to force. The common soldier in the *Iliad* is free and has the right to bear arms; nevertheless he is subject to the indignity of orders and abuse:

But whenever he came upon a commoner shouting out,
He struck him with his scepter and spoke sharply:
"Good for nothing! Be still and listen to your betters,
You are weak and cowardly and unwarlike,
You count for nothing, neither in battle nor in council."

Thersites pays dear for the perfectly reasonable comments he makes, comments not at all different, moreover, from those made by Achilles:

He hit him with his scepter on back and shoulders,
So that he doubled over, and a great tear welled up,

And a bloody welt appeared on his back
Under the golden scepter. Frightened, he sat down,
Wiping away his tears, bewildered and in pain.
Troubled though they were, the others laughed long at him.

Achilles himself, that proud hero, the undefeated, is shown us at the outset of the poem, weeping with humiliation and helpless grief—the woman he wanted for his bride has been taken from under his nose, and he has not dared to oppose it:

> . . . But Achilles
> Weeping, sat apart from his companions,
> By the white-capped waves, staring over the boundless ocean.

What has happened is that Agamemnon has deliberately humiliated Achilles, to show that he himself is the master:

> . . . So you will learn
> That I am greater than you, and anyone else will hesitate
> To treat me as an equal and set himself against me.

But a few days pass and now the supreme commander is weeping in his turn. He must humble himself, he must plead, and have, moreover, the added misery of doing it all in vain.

In the same way, there is not a single one of the combatants who is spared the shameful experience of fear. The heroes quake like everybody else. It only needs a challenge from Hector to throw the whole Greek force into consternation—except for Achilles and his men, and they did not happen to be present:

> He spoke and all grew still and held their peace,
> Ashamed to refuse, afraid to accept.

But once Ajax comes forward and offers himself, fear quickly changes sides:

> A shudder of terror ran through the Trojans, making their limbs weak;
> And Hector himself felt his heart leap in his breast.
> But he no longer had the right to tremble, or to run away. . . .

Two days later, it is Ajax's turn to be terrified:

[11]

Zeus the father on high, makes fear rise in Ajax.
He stops, overcome, puts behind him his buckler made of seven hides,
Trembles, looks at the crowd around, like a wild beast. . . .

Even to Achilles the moment comes; he too must shake and stammer with fear, though it is a river that has this effect on him, not a man. But, with the exception of Achilles, every man in the *Iliad* tastes a moment of defeat in battle. Victory is less a matter of valor than of blind destiny, which is symbolized in the poem by Zeus's golden scales:

Then Zeus the father took his golden scales,
In them he put the two fates of death that cuts down all men,
One for the Trojans, tamers of horses, one for the bronze-sheathed
   Greeks.
He seized the scales by the middle; it was the fatal day of Greece
   that sank.

By its very blindness, destiny establishes a kind of justice. Blind also is she who decrees to warriors punishment in kind. He that takes the sword, will perish by the sword. The *Iliad* formulated the principle long before the Gospels did, and in almost the same terms:

Ares is just, and kills those who kill.

Perhaps all men, by the very act of being born, are destined to suffer violence; yet this is a truth to which circumstance shuts men's eyes. The strong are, as a matter of fact, never absolutely strong, nor are the weak absolutely weak, but neither is aware of this. They have in common a refusal to believe that they both belong to the same species: the weak see no relation between themselves and the strong, and vice versa. The man who is the possessor of force seems to walk through a non-resistant element; in the human substance that surrounds him nothing has the power to interpose, between the impulse and the act, the tiny interval that is reflection. Where there is no room for reflection, there is none either for justice or prudence. Hence we see men in arms behaving harshly and madly. We see their sword bury itself in the breast of a disarmed enemy who is in the very act of pleading at their knees. We see them triumph over a dying man by describing to him the outrages his corpse will endure. We see Achilles cut the throats of twelve Trojan boys on the funeral pyre of Patroclus as naturally as we cut flowers for a grave. These men, wielding power, have no suspicion of the fact that the consequences of their deeds will at length come home to them—they too will bow the neck in their turn. If you can make an old man fall silent, tremble, obey, with a single word of your own, why should it occur to you that the curses of this old man, who is after all a priest, will have their own importance in the gods' eyes? Why should you refrain from taking Achilles' girl away from him if you know that neither he nor she can do anything but obey you? Achilles rejoices over the sight of the Greeks fleeing in misery and confusion. What could possibly suggest to him that this rout, which will last exactly as long as he wants it to and end when his mood indicates it, that this very rout will be the cause of his friend's death, and, for that matter, of his own? Thus it happens that those who have force on loan from fate count on it too much and are destroyed.

But at the time their own destruction seems impossible to them. For they do not see that the force in their possession is only a limited quantity; nor do they see their relations with other human beings as a kind of balance between unequal amounts of force. Since other people do not impose on their movements that halt, that interval of hesitation, wherein lies all our consideration for our brothers in humanity, they conclude that destiny has given complete license to them, and none at all to their inferiors. And at this point they exceed the measure of the force that is actually at their disposal. Inevitably they exceed it, since they are not aware that it is limited. And now we see them committed irretrievably to chance; suddenly things cease to obey them. Sometimes chance is kind to them, sometimes cruel. But in any case there they are, exposed, open to misfortune; gone is the armor of power that formerly protected their naked souls; nothing, no shield, stands between them and tears.

This retribution, which has a geometrical rigor, which operates auto-matically to penalize the abuse of force, was the main subject of Greek thought. It is the soul of the epic. Under the name of Nemesis, it functions as the mainspring of Aeschylus's tragedies. To the Pythagoreans, to Socrates and Plato, it was the jumping-off point of speculation upon the nature of man and the universe. Wherever Hellenism has penetrated, we find the idea of it familiar. In Oriental countries which are steeped in Buddhism, it is perhaps this Greek idea that has lived on under the name of Kharma. The Occident, however, has lost it, and no longer even has a word to express it in any of its languages: conceptions of limit, measure, equilibrium, which ought to determine the conduct of life are, in the West, restricted to a servile function in the vocabulary of technics. We are only geometricians of matter; the Greeks were, first of all, geometricians in their apprenticeship to virtue.

The progress of the war in the *Iliad* is simply a continual game of seesaw. The victor of the moment feels himself invincible, even though, only a few hours before, he may have experienced defeat; he forgets to treat victory as a transitory thing. At the end of the first day of combat described in the *Iliad*, the victorious Greeks were in a position to obtain the object of all their efforts, i.e., Helen and her riches—assuming of course as Homer did, that the Greeks had reason to believe that Helen was in Troy. Actually, the Egyptian priests, who ought to have known, affirmed later on to Herodotus that she was in Egypt. In any case, that evening the Greeks are no longer interested in her or her possessions:

> "For the present, let us not accept the riches of Paris;
> Nor Helen; everybody sees, even the most ignorant,
> That Troy stands on the verge of ruin."
> He spoke, and all the Achaeans acclaimed him.

What they want is, in fact, everything. For booty, all the riches of Troy; for their bonfires, all the palaces, temples, houses; for slaves, all the women and children; for corpses, all the men. They forget one detail, that *everything* is not within their power, for they are not in Troy. Perhaps they will be there tomorrow; perhaps not. Hector, the same day, makes the same mistake:

> For I know well in my entrails and in my heart,
> A day will come when Holy Troy will perish,
> And Priam, and the nation of Priam of the good lance.
> But I think less of the grief that is in store for the Trojans,
> And of Hecuba herself, and of Priam the king,
> And of my brothers, so numerous and so brave,
> Who will fall in the dust under the blows of the enemy,
> Than of you that day when a Greek in his bronze breastplate
> Will drag you away weeping and deprive you of your liberty.
>
> But as for me, may I be dead, and may the earth have covered
> me
> Before I hear you cry out or see you dragged away!

At this moment what would he not give to turn aside those horrors which he believes to be inevitable? But at this moment nothing he *could* give would be of any use. The next day but one, however, the Greeks have run away miserably, and Agamemnon himself is in favor of putting to the sea again. And now Hector, by making a very few concessions, could readily secure the enemy's departure; yet now he is even unwilling to let them go empty-handed:

Set fires everywhere and let the brightness mount the skies
Lest in the night the long-haired Greeks,
Escaping, sail over the broad back of ocean . . .
Let each of them take home a wound to heal
. . . thus others will fear
To bring dolorous war to the Trojans, tamers of horses.

His wish is granted; the Greeks stay; and the next day they reduce Hector and his men to a pitiable condition:

As for them—they fled across the plain like cattle
Whom a lion hunts before him in the dark midnight . . .
Thus the mighty Agamemnon, son of Atreus, pursued them,
Steadily killing the hindmost; and still they fled.

In the course of the afternoon, Hector regains the ascendancy, withdraws again, then puts the Greeks to flight, then is repulsed by Patroclus, who has come in with his fresh troops. Patroclus, pressing his advantage, ends by finding himself exposed, wounded and without armor, to the sword of Hector. And finally that evening the victorious Hector hears the prudent counsel of Polydamas and repudiates it sharply:

Now that wily Kronos's son has given me
Glory at the ships; now that I have driven the Greeks to the sea,
Do not offer, fool, such counsels to the people.
No Trojan will listen to you; nor would I permit it . . .
So Hector spoke, and the Trojans acclaimed him. . . .

The next day Hector is lost. Achilles has harried him across the field and is about to kill him. He has always been the stronger of the two in combat; how much the more so now, after several weeks of rest, ardent for vengeance and victory, against an exhausted enemy? And Hector stands alone, before the walls of Troy, absolutely alone, alone to wait for death and to steady his soul to face it:

Alas, were I to slip through the gate, behind the rampart,
Polydamas at once would heap dishonor on me . . .
And now that through my recklessness I have destroyed my people,
I fear the Trojans and the long-robed Trojan women,
I fear to hear from some one far less brave than I:
"Hector, trusting his own strength too far, has ruined his people." . . .
Suppose I were to down my bossed shield,

My massive helmet, and, leaning my spear against the wall,
Should go to meet renowned Achilles? . . .
But why spin out these fancies? Why such dreams?
I would not reach him, nor would he pity me,
Or respect me. He would kill me like a woman
If I came naked thus . . .

Not a jot of the grief and ignominy that fall to the unfortunate is Hector spared. Alone, stripped of the prestige of force, he discovers that the courage that kept him from taking to the shelter of the walls is not enough to save him from flight:

Seeing him, Hector began to tremble. He had not the heart
To stay . . .
. . . It is not for a ewe nor the skin of an ox,
That they are striving, not these ordinary rewards of the race;
It is for a life that they run, the life of Hector, tamer of horses.

Wounded to death, he enhances his conqueror's triumph by vain supplications:

I implore you, by your soul, by your knees, by your parents. . . .

But the auditors of the *Iliad* knew that the death of Hector would be but a brief joy to Achilles, and the death of Achilles but a brief joy to the Trojans, and the destruction of Troy but a brief joy to the Achaeans.

Thus violence obliterates anybody who feels its touch. It comes to seem just as external to its employer as to its victim. And from this springs the idea of a destiny before which executioner and victim stand equally innocent, before which conquered and conqueror are brothers in the same distress. The conquered brings misfortune to the conqueror, and vice versa:

A single son, short-lived, was born to him.
Neglected by me, he grows old—for far from home
I camp before Troy, injuring you and your sons.

A moderate use of force, which alone would enable man to escape being enmeshed in its machinery, would require superhuman virtue, which is as rare as dignity in weakness. Moreover, moderation itself is not without its perils, since prestige, from which force derives at least three quarters of its strength, rests principally upon that marvelous indifference that the strong feel toward the weak, an indifference so contagious that it infects the very people who are the objects of it. Yet ordinarily excess is not arrived at through prudence or politic considerations. On the contrary, man dashes to it as to an irresistible temptation. The voice of reason is occasionally heard in the mouths of the characters in the *Iliad*. Thersites' speeches are reasonable to the highest degree; so are the speeches of the angry Achilles:

> Nothing is worth my life, not all the goods
> They say the well-built city of Ilium contains. . . .
> A man can capture steers and fatted sheep
> But, once gone, the soul cannot be captured back.

But words of reason drop into the void. If they come from an inferior, he is punished and shuts up; if from a chief, his actions betray them. And failing everything else, there is always a god handy to advise him to be unreasonable. In the end, the very idea of wanting to escape the role fate has allotted one—the business of killing and dying—disappears from the mind:

> We to whom Zeus
> Has assigned suffering, from youth to old age,
> Suffering in grievous wars, till we perish to the last man.

Already these warriors, like Craonne's so much later, felt themselves to be "condemned men."

It was the simplest trap that pitched them into this situation. At the outset, at the embarkation, their hearts are light, as hearts always are if you have a large force on your side and nothing but space to oppose you. Their weapons are in their hands; the enemy is absent. Unless your spirit has been conquered in advance by the reputation of the enemy, you always feel yourself to be much stronger than anybody who is not there. An absent man does not impose the yoke of necessity. To the spirits of those embarking no necessity yet presents itself; consequently they go off as though to a game, as though on holiday from the confinement of daily life.

> Where have they gone, those braggadocio boasts
> We proudly flung upon the air at Lemnos,
> Stuffing ourselves with flesh of horned steers,

Drinking from cups brimming over with wine?
As for Trojans—a hundred or two each man of us
Could handle in battle. And now one is too much for us.

But the first contact of war does not immediately destroy the illusion that
war is a game. War's necessity is terrible, altogether different in kind from
the necessity of peace. So terrible is it that the human spirit will not submit
to it so long as it can possibly escape; and whenever it can escape it takes
refuge in long days empty of necessity, days of play, of revery, days arbitrary
and unreal. Danger then becomes an abstraction; the lives you destroy are
like toys broken by a child, and quite as incapable of feeling; heroism is but
a theatrical gesture and smirched with boastfulness. This becomes doubly
true if a momentary access of vitality comes to reinforce the divine hand that
wards off defeat and death. Then war is easy and basely, coarsely loved.

But with the majority of the combatants this state of mind does not persist.
Soon there comes a day when fear, or defeat, or the death of beloved comrades touches the warrior's spirit, and it crumbles in the hand of necessity.
At that moment war is no more a game or a dream; now at last the warrior
cannot doubt the reality of its existence. And this reality, which he perceives,
is hard, much too hard to be borne, for it enfolds death. Once you acknowledge death to be a practical possibility, the thought of it becomes unendur-
able, except in flashes. True enough, all men are fated to die; true enough
also, a soldier may grow old in battles; yet for those whose spirits have bent
under the yoke of war, the relation between death and the future is different
than for other men. For other men death appears as a limit set in advance on
the future; for the soldier death *is* the future, the future his profession assigns
him. Yet the idea of man's having death for a future is abhorrent to nature.
Once the experience of war makes visible the possibility of death that lies
locked up in each moment, our thoughts cannot travel from one day to the
next without meeting death's face. The mind is then strung up to a pitch it
can stand for only a short time; but each new dawn reintroduces the same
necessity; and days piled on days make years. On each one of these days the
soul suffers violence. Regularly, every morning, the soul castrates itself of
aspiration, for thought cannot journey through time without meeting death
on the way. Thus war effaces all conceptions of purpose or goal, including
even its own "war aims." It effaces the very notion of war's being brought to
an end. To be outside a situation so violent as this is to find it inconceivable;
to be inside it is to be unable to conceive its end. Consequently, nobody does
anything to bring this end about. In the presence of an armed enemy, what
hand can relinquish its weapon? The mind ought to find a way out, but the
mind has lost all capacity to so much as look outward. The mind is com-

pletely absorbed in doing itself violence. Always in human life, whether war
or slavery is in question, intolerable sufferings continue, as it were, by the
force of their own specific gravity, and so look to the outsider as though
they were easy to bear; actually, they continue because they have deprived
the sufferer of the resources which might serve to extricate him.

Nevertheless, the soul that is enslaved to war cries out for deliverance, but
deliverance itself appears to it in an extreme and tragic aspect, the aspect of
destruction. Any other solution, more moderate, more reasonable in character, would expose the mind to suffering so naked, so violent that it could
not be borne, even as memory. Terror, grief, exhaustion, slaughter, the
annihilation of comrades—is it credible that these things should not continually tear at the soul, if the intoxication of force had not intervened to
drown them? The idea that an unlimited effort should bring in only a
limited profit or no profit at all is terribly painful.

> What? Will we let Priam and the Trojans boast
> Of Argive Helen, she for whom so many Greeks
> Died before Troy, far from their native land?
> What? Do you want us to leave the city, wide-streeted Troy,
> Standing, when we have suffered so much for it?

But actually what is Helen to Ulysses? What indeed is Troy, full of riches
that will not compensate him for Ithaca's ruin? For the Greeks, Troy and
Helen are in reality mere sources of blood and tears; to master them is to
master frightful memories. If the existence of an enemy has made a soul
destroy in itself the thing nature put there, then the only remedy the soul
can imagine is the destruction of the enemy. At the same time the death of
dearly loved comrades arouses a spirit of somber emulation, a rivalry in
death:

> May I die, then, at once! Since fate has not let me
> Protect my dead friend, who far from home
> Perished, longing for me to defend him from death.
> So now I go to seek the murderer of my friend,
> Hector. And death shall I find at the moment
> Zeus wills it—Zeus and the other immortals.

It is the same despair that drives him on toward death, on the one hand, and
slaughter on the other:

> I know it well, my fate is to perish here,

[19]

Far from father and dearly loved mother;
  but meanwhile
I shall not stop till the Trojans have had their fill of war.

The man possessed by this twofold need for death belongs, so long as he
has not become something still different, to a different race from the race of
the living.

What echo can the timid hopes of life strike in such a heart? How can it
hear the defeated begging for another sight of the light of day? The threatened life has already been relieved of nearly all its consequence by a single,
simple distinction: it is now unarmed; its adversary possesses a weapon.
Furthermore, how can a man who has rooted out of himself the notion that
the light of day is sweet to the eyes respect such a notion when it makes its
appearance in some futile and humble lament?

I clasp tight your knees, Achilles. Have a thought, have pity for me.
I stand here, O son of Zeus, a suppliant, to be respected.
In your house it was I first tasted Demeter's bread,
That day in my well-pruned vineyard you caught me
And sold me, sending me far from father and friends,
To holy Lemnos; a hundred oxen was my price.
And now I will pay you three hundred for ransom.
This dawn is for me my twelfth day in Troy,
After so many sorrows. See me here, in your hands,
Through some evil fate. Zeus surely must hate me
Who again puts me into your hands. Alas, my poor mother, Laothoe,
Daughter of the old man, Altes—a short-lived son you have borne.

What a reception this feeble hope gets!

Come, friend, you too must die. Why make a fuss about it?
Patroclus, he too has died—a far better man than you are.
Don't you see how handsome I am, how mighty?
A noble father begat me, and I have a goddess for mother.
Yet even I, like you, must some day encounter my fate,
Whether the hour strikes at noon, or evening, or sunrise,
The hour that comes when some arms-bearing warrior will kill me.

To respect life in somebody else when you have had to castrate yourself of
all yearning for it demands a truly heartbreaking exertion of the powers of
generosity. It is impossible to imagine any of Homer's warriors being capable

of such an exertion, unless it is that warrior who dwells, in a peculiar way, at the very center of the poem—I mean Patroclus, who "knew how to be sweet to everybody," and who throughout the *Iliad* commits no cruel or brutal act. But then how many men do we know, in several thousand years of human history, who would have displayed such god-like generosity? Two or three?—even this is doubtful. Lacking this generosity, the conquering soldier is like a scourge of nature. Possessed by war, he, like the slave, becomes a thing, though his manner of doing so is different—over him too, words are as powerless as over matter itself. And both, at the touch of force, experience its inevitable effects: they become deaf and dumb.

Such is the nature of force. Its power of converting a man into a thing is a double one, and in its application double-edged. To the same degree, though in different fashions, those who use it and those who endure it are turned to stone. This property of force achieves its maximum effectiveness during the clash of arms, in battle, when the tide of the day has turned, and everything is rushing toward a decision. It is not the planning man, the man of strategy, the man acting on the resolution taken, who wins or loses a battle; battles are fought and decided by men deprived of these faculties, men who have undergone a transformation, who have dropped either to the level of inert matter, which is pure passivity, or to the level of blind force, which is pure momentum. Herein lies the last secret of war, a secret revealed by the *Iliad* in its similes, which liken the warriors either to fire, flood, wind, wild beasts, or God knows what blind cause of disaster, or else to frightened animals, trees, water, sand, to anything in nature that is set into motion by the violence of external forces. Greeks and Trojans, from one day to the next, sometimes even from one hour to the next, experience, turn and turn about, one or the other of these transmutations:

As when a lion, murderous, springs among the cattle
Which by thousands are grazing over some vast marshy field. . . .
And their flanks heave with terror; even so the Achaians
Scattered in panic before Hector and Zeus, the great father.

As when a ravening fire breaks out deep in a bushy wood
And the wheeling wind scatters sparks far and wide,
And trees, root and branch, topple over in flames;
So Atreus' son, Agamemnon, roared through the ranks
Of the Trojans in flight. . . .

[21]

The art of war is simply the art of producing such transformations, and its equipment, its processes, even the casualties it inflicts on the enemy, are only means directed toward this end—its true object is the warrior's soul. Yet these transformations are always a mystery; the gods are their authors, the gods who kindle men's imagination. But however caused, this petrifactive quality of force, two-fold always, is essential to its nature; and a soul which has entered the province of force will not escape this except by a miracle. Such miracles are rare and of brief duration.

The wantonness of the conqueror that knows no respect for any creature or thing that is at its mercy or is imagined to be so, the despair of the soldier that drives him on to destruction, the obliteration of the slave or the conquered man, the wholesale slaughter—all these elements combine in the *Iliad* to make a picture of uniform horror, of which force is the sole hero. A monotonous desolation would result were it not for those few luminous moments, scattered here and there throughout the poem, those brief, celestial moments in which man possesses his soul. The soul that awakes then, to live for an instant only and be lost almost at once in force's vast kingdom, awakes pure and whole; it contains no ambiguities, nothing complicated or turbid; it has no room for anything but courage and love. Sometimes it is in the course of inner deliberations that a man finds his soul: he meets it, like Hector before Troy, as he tries to face destiny on his own terms, without the help of gods or men. At other times, it is in a moment of love that men discover their souls—and there is hardly any form of pure love known to humanity of which the *Iliad* does not treat. The tradition of hospitality persists, even through several generations, to dispel the blindness of combat.

> Thus I am for you a beloved guest in the breast of Argos . . .
> Let us turn our lances away from each other, even in battle.

The love of the son for the parents, of father for son, of mother for son, is continually described, in a manner as touching as it is curt:

> Thetis answered, shedding tears,
> "You were born to me for a short life, my child, as you say . . ."

Even brotherly love:

> My three brothers whom the same mother bore for me,
> So dear. . . .

[22]

Conjugal love, condemned to sorrow, is of an astonishing purity. Imaging the humiliations of slavery which await a beloved wife, the husband passes over the one indignity which even in anticipation would stain their tenderness. What could be simpler than the words spoken by his wife to the man about to die?

> . . . Better for me
> Losing you, to go under the earth. No other comfort
> Will remain, when you have encountered your death-heavy fate,
> Only grief, only sorrow. . . .

Not less touching are the words expressed to a dead husband:

> Dear husband, you died young, and left me your widow
> Alone in the palace. Our child is still tiny,
> The child you and I, crossed by fate, had together.
> I think he will never grow up . . .
> For not in your bed did you die, holding my hand
> And speaking to me prudent words which forever
> Night and day, as I weep, might live in my memory.

The most beautiful friendship of all, the friendship between comrades-at-arms, is the final theme of The Epic:

> . . . But Achilles
> Wept, dreaming of the beloved comrade; sleep, all-prevailing,
> Would not take him; he turned over again and again.

But the purest triumph of love, the crowning grace of war, is the friendship that floods the hearts of mortal enemies. Before it a murdered son or a murdered friend no longer cries out for vengeance. Before it—even more miraculous—the distance between benefactor and suppliant, between victor and vanquished, shrinks to nothing:

> But when thirst and hunger had been appeased,
> Then Dardanian Priam fell to admiring Achilles.
> How tall he was, and handsome; he had the face of a god;
> And in his turn Dardanian Priam was admired by Achilles,
> Who watched his handsome face and listened to his words.
> And when they were satisfied with contemplation of each other . . .

These moments of grace are rare in the *Iliad,* but they are enough to make us feel with sharp regret what it is that violence has killed and will kill again.

However, such a heaping-up of violent deeds would have a frigid effect, were it not for the note of incurable bitterness that continually makes itself heard, though often only a single word marks its presence, often a mere stroke of the verse, or a run-on line. It is in this that the *Iliad* is absolutely unique, in this bitterness that proceeds from tenderness and that spreads over the whole human race, impartial as sunlight. Never does the tone lose its coloring of bitterness; yet never does the bitterness drop into lamentation. Justice and love, which have hardly any place in this study of extremes and of unjust acts of violence, nevertheless bathe the work in their light without ever becoming noticeable themselves, except as a kind of accent. Nothing precious is scorned, whether or not death is its destiny; everyone's unhappiness is laid bare without dissimulation or disdain; no man is set above or below the condition common to all men; whatever is destroyed is regretted. Victors and vanquished are brought equally near us; under the same head, both are seen as counterparts of the poet, and the listener as well. If there is any difference, it is that the enemy's misfortunes are possibly more sharply felt.

> So he fell there, put to sleep in the sleep of bronze,
> Unhappy man, far from his wife, defending his own people. . . .

And what accents echo the fate of the lad Achilles sold at Lemnos!

> Eleven days he rejoiced his heart among those he loved,
> Returning from Lemnos; the twelfth day, once more,
> God delivered him into the hands of Achilles,
> To him who had to send him, unwilling, to Hades.

And the fate of Euphorbus, who saw only a single day of war.

> Blood soaked his hair, the hair like to the Graces' . . .

When Hector is lamented:

> . . . guardian of chaste wives and little children. . . .

In these few words, chastity appears, dirtied by force, and childhood, delivered to the sword. The fountain at the gates of Troy becomes an object of poignant nostalgia when Hector runs by, seeking to elude his doom:

> Close by there stood the great stone tanks,
> Handsomely built, where silk-gleaming garments
> Were washed clean by Troy's lovely daughters and housewives
> In the old days of peace, long ago, when the Greeks had not come.
> Past these did they run their race, pursued and pursuer.

The whole of the *Iliad* lies under the shadow of the greatest calamity the human race can experience—the destruction of a city. This calamity could not tear more at the heart had the poet been born in Troy. But the tone is not different when the Achaeans are dying, far from home.

Insofar as this other life, the life of the living, seems calm and full, the brief evocations of the world of peace are felt as pain:

> With the break of dawn and the rising of the day,
> On both sides arrows flew, men fell.
> But at the very hour that the woodcutter goes home to fix his meal
> In the mountain valleys when his arms have had enough
> Of hacking great trees, and disgust rises in his heart,
> And the desire for sweet food seizes his entrails,
> At that hour, by their valor, the Danaans broke the front.

Whatever is not war, whatever war destroys or threatens, the *Iliad* wraps in poetry; the realities of war, never. No reticence veils the step from life to death:

> Then his teeth flew out; from two sides,
> Blood came to his eyes; the blood that from lips and nostrils
> He was spilling, open-mouthed; death enveloped him in its black cloud.

The cold brutality of the deeds of war is left undisguised; neither victors nor vanquished are admired, scorned, or hated. Almost always, fate and the gods decide the changing lot of battle. Within the limits fixed by fate, the gods determine with sovereign authority victory and defeat. It is always they who provoke those fits of madness, those treacheries, which are forever blocking peace; war is their true business; their only motives, caprice and malice. As for the warriors, victors or vanquished, those comparisons which liken them to beasts or things can inspire neither admiration nor contempt, but only regret that men are capable of being so transformed.

[25]

There may be, unknown to us, other expressions of the extraordinary sense of equity which breathes through the *Iliad;* certainly it has not been imitated. One is barely aware that the poet is a Greek and not a Trojan. The tone of the poem furnishes a direct clue to the origin of its oldest portions; history perhaps will never be able to tell us more. If one believes with Thucydides that eighty years after the fall of Troy, the Achaeans in their turn were conquered, one may ask whether these songs, with their rare references to iron, are not the songs of a conquered people, of whom a few went into exile. Obliged to live and die, "very far from the homeland," like the Greeks who fell before Troy, having lost their cities like the Trojans, they saw their own image both in the conquerors, who had been their fathers, and in the conquered, whose misery was like their own. They could still see the Trojan war over that brief span of years in its true light, unglossed by pride or shame. They could look at it as conquered and as conquerors simultaneously, and so perceive what neither conqueror nor conquered ever saw, for both were blinded. Of course, this is mere fancy; one can see such distant times only in fancy's light.

In any case, this poem is a miracle. Its bitterness is the only justifiable bitterness, for it springs from the subjections of the human spirit to force, that is, in the last analysis, to matter. This subjection is the common lot, although each spirit will bear it differently, in proportion to its own virtue. No one in the *Iliad* is spared by it, as no one on earth is. No one who succumbs to it is by virtue of this fact regarded with contempt. Whoever, within his own soul and in human relations, escapes the dominion of force is loved but loved sorrowfully because of the threat of destruction that constantly hangs over him.

Such is the spirit of the only true epic the Occident possesses. The *Odyssey* seems merely a good imitation, now of the *Iliad,* now of Oriental poems; the *Aeneid* is an imitation which, however brilliant, is disfigured by frigidity, bombast, and bad taste. The *chansons de geste,* lacking the sense of equity, could not attain greatness: in the *Chanson de Roland,* the death of an enemy does not come home to either author or reader in the same way as does the death of Roland.

Attic tragedy, or at any rate the tragedy of Aeschylus and Sophocles, is the true continuation of the epic. The conception of justice enlightens it, without ever directly intervening in it; here force appears in its coldness and hardness, always attended by effects from whose fatality neither those who use it nor those who suffer it can escape; here the shame of the coerced spirit is neither disguised, nor enveloped in facile pity, nor held up to scorn; here more than one spirit bruised and degraded by misfortune is offered for our admiration. The Gospels are the last marvelous expression of the Greek genius, as the *Iliad* is the first: here the Greek spirit reveals itself not only in the injunction given mankind to seek above all other goods, "the kingdom and justice of our Heavenly Father," but also in the fact that human suffering is laid bare, and we see it in a being who is at once divine and human. The accounts of the Passion show that a divine spirit, incarnate, is changed by misfortune, trembles before suffering and death, feels itself, in the depths of its agony, to be cut off from man and God. The sense of human misery gives the Gospels that accent of simplicity that is the mark of the Greek genius, and that endows Greek tragedy and the *Iliad* with all their value. Certain phrases have a ring strangely reminiscent of the epic, and it is the Trojan lad dispatched to Hades, though he does not wish to go, who comes to mind when Christ says to Peter: "Another shall gird thee and carry thee whither thou wouldst not." This accent cannot be separated from the idea that inspired the Gospels, for the sense of human misery is a pre-condition of justice and love. He who does not realize to what extent shifting fortune and necessity hold in subjection every human spirit, cannot regard as fellow-creatures nor love as he loves himself those whom chance separated from him by an abyss. The variety of constraints pressing upon man give rise to the illusion of several distinct species that cannot communicate. Only he who has measured the dominion of force, and knows how not to respect it, is capable of love and justice.

The relations between destiny and the human soul, the extent to which each soul creates its own destiny, the question of what elements in the soul are transformed by merciless necessity as it tailors the soul to fit the requirements of shifting fate, and of what elements can on the other hand be preserved, through the exercise of virtue and through grace—this whole question is fraught with temptations to falsehood, temptations that are positively enhanced by pride, by shame, by hatred, contempt, indifference, by the will to oblivion or to ignorance. Moreover, nothing is so rare as to see misfortune fairly portrayed; the tendency is either to treat the unfortunate person as though catastrophe were his natural vocation, or to ignore the effects of misfortune on the soul, to assume, that is, that the soul can suffer and remain unmarked by it, can fail, in fact, to be recast in misfortune's image. The Greeks, generally speaking, were endowed with spiritual force that allowed them to avoid self-deception. The rewards of this were great; they discovered how to achieve in all their acts the greatest lucidity, purity, and simplicity. But the spirit that was transmitted from the *Iliad* to the Gospels by way of the tragic poets never jumped the borders of Greek civilization; once Greece was destroyed, nothing remained of this spirit but pale reflections.

Both the Romans and the Hebrews believed themselves to be exempt from the misery that is the common human lot. The Romans saw their country as the nation chosen by destiny to be mistress of the world; with the Hebrews, it was their God who exalted them and they retained their superior position just as long as they obeyed Him. Strangers, enemies, conquered peoples, subjects, slaves, were objects of contempt to the Romans; and the Romans had no epics, no tragedies. In Rome gladiatorial fights took the place of tragedy. With the Hebrews, misfortune was a sure indication of sin and hence a legitimate object of contempt; to them a vanquished enemy was abhorrent to God himself and condemned to expiate all sorts of crimes —this is a view that makes cruelty permissible and indeed indispensable. And no text of the Old Testament strikes a note comparable to the note heard in the Greek epic, unless it be certain parts of the book of Job. Throughout twenty centuries of Christianity, the Romans and the Hebrews have been admired, read, imitated, both in deed and word; their masterpieces have yielded an appropriate quotation every time anybody had a crime he wanted to justify.

Furthermore, the spirit of the Gospels was not handed down in a pure state from one Christian generation to the next. To undergo suffering and death joyfully was from the very beginning considered a sign of grace in the Christian martyrs—as though grace could do more for a human being than it could for Christ. Those who believe that God himself, once he became man, could not face the harshness of destiny without a long tremor of anguish, should have understood that the only people who can give the impression of having risen to a higher plane, who seem superior to ordinary human misery, are the people who resort to the aids of illusion, exaltation, fanaticism, to conceal the harshness of destiny from their own eyes. The man who does not wear the armor of the lie cannot experience force without being touched by it to the very soul. Grace can prevent this touch from corrupting him, but it cannot spare him the wound. Having forgotten it too well, Christian tradition can only rarely recover that simplicity that renders so poignant every sentence in the story of the Passion. On the other hand, the practice of forcible proselytization threw a veil over the effects of force on the souls of those who used it.

In spite of the brief intoxication induced at the time of the Renaissance by the discovery of Greek literature, there has been, during the course of twenty centuries, no revival of the Greek genius. Something of it was seen in Villon, in Shakespeare, Cervantes, Molière, and—just once—in Racine. The bones of human suffering are exposed in *L'Ecole des Femmes* and in *Phèdre,* love being the context—a strange century indeed, which took the opposite view from that of the epic period, and would only acknowledge human suffering in the context of love, while it insisted on swathing with glory the effects of force in war and in politics. To the list of writers given above, a few other names might be added. But nothing the peoples of Europe have produced is worth the first known poem that appeared among them. Perhaps they will yet rediscover the epic genius, when they learn that there is no refuge from fate, learn not to admire force, not to hate the enemy, nor to scorn the unfortunate. How soon this will happen is another question.

H O M E R

[*fl. c. 950–900* B.C.]

UNTIL HIS DEATH IN 1957 ERICH AUERBACH WAS PROFESSOR OF FRENCH AND
Romance Philology at Yale University, a post he accepted in 1950 after a long
personal odyssey which took him from his native Germany to Turkey and
thence to the United States. His scholarship reflects a wide range of interests,
historical, philological, and critical; he was especially concerned with Italian,
French, and medieval Latin literature.

This essay considers a brief episode in the *Odyssey,* carefully analyzing its
linguistic and rhetorical features, of which even the most discerning reader,
caught up by the narrative, might not be aware. Then Auerbach compares
the style of Homer with that of Scripture, showing how each style expresses
a different grasp of reality. This remarkable essay helps the reader make
the primary act of the imagination, by which he comprehends style as the
ultimate carrier of meaning. It restructures his expectations of the narrative
and gives him entrance into the different cosmologies of both the *Odyssey*
and Scripture.

From *Mimesis* by Erich Auerbach. Translated by Willard Trask. Copyright 1953 by
Princeton University Press.

ERICH AUERBACH

Odysseus' Scar

R EADERS OF THE *Odyssey* WILL REMEMBER THE WELL-PREPARED AND TOUCHING scene in book 19, when Odysseus has at last come home, the scene in which the old housekeeper Euryclea, who had been his nurse, recognizes him by a scar on his thigh. The stranger has won Penelope's good will; at his request she tells the housekeeper to wash his feet, which, in all old stories, is the first duty of hospitality toward a tired traveler. Euryclea busies herself fetching water and mixing cold with hot, meanwhile speaking sadly of her absent master, who is probably of the same age as the guest, and who perhaps, like the guest, is even now wandering somewhere, a stranger; and she remarks how astonishingly like him the guest looks. Meanwhile Odysseus, remembering his scar, moves back out of the light; he knows that, despite his efforts to hide his identity, Euryclea will now recognize him, but he wants at least to keep Penelope in ignorance. No sooner has the old woman touched the scar than, in her joyous surprise, she lets Odysseus' foot drop into the basin; the water spills over, she is about to cry out her joy; Odysseus restrains her with whispered threats and endearments; she recovers herself and conceals her emotion. Penelope, whose attention Athena's foresight had diverted from the incident, has observed nothing.

All this is scrupulously externalized and narrated in leisurely fashion. The two women express their feelings in copious direct discourse. Feelings though they are, with only a slight admixture of the most general considerations upon human destiny, the syntactical connection between part and part is perfectly clear, no contour is blurred. There is also room and time for orderly, perfectly well-articulated, uniformly illuminated descriptions of implements, ministrations, and gestures; even in the dramatic moment of recognition, Homer does not omit to tell the reader that it is with his right hand that Odysseus takes the old woman by the throat to keep her from speaking, at the same time that he draws her closer to him with his left. Clearly outlined, brightly and uniformly illuminated, men and things stand out in a realm where everything is visible; and not less clear—wholly expressed, orderly even in their ardor—are the feelings and thoughts of the persons involved.

In my account of the incident I have so far passed over a whole series of verses which interrupt it in the middle. There are more than seventy of these verses—while to the incident itself some forty are devoted before the interruption and some forty after it. The interruption, which comes just at the point when the housekeeper recognizes the scar—that is, at the moment of crisis—describes the origin of the scar, a hunting accident which occurred in Odysseus' boyhood, at a boar hunt, during the time of his visit to his grandfather Autolycus. This first affords an opportunity to inform the reader about Autolycus, his house, the precise degree of the kinship, his character, and, no less exhaustively than touchingly, his behavior after the birth of his grandson; then follows the visit of Odysseus, now grown to be a youth; the exchange of greetings, the banquet with which he is welcomed, sleep and waking, the early start for the hunt, the tracking of the beast, the struggle, Odysseus' being wounded by the boar's tusk, his recovery, his return to Ithaca, his parents' anxious questions—all is narrated, again with such a complete externalization of all the elements of the story and of their interconnections as to leave nothing in obscurity. Not until then does the narrator return to Penelope's chamber, not until then, the digression having run its course, does Euryclea, who had recognized the scar before the digression began, let Odysseus' foot fall back into the basin.

The first thought of a modern reader—that this is a device to increase suspense—is, if not wholly wrong, at least not the essential explanation of this Homeric procedure. For the element of suspense is very slight in the Homeric poems; nothing in their entire style is calculated to keep the reader or hearer breathless. The digressions are not meant to keep the reader in suspense, but rather to relax the tension. And this frequently occurs, as in the passage before us. The broadly narrated, charming, and subtly fashioned story of the hunt, with all its elegance and self-sufficiency, its wealth of idyllic pictures, seeks to win the reader over wholly to itself as long as he is hearing it, to make him forget what had just taken place during the foot-washing. But an episode that will increase suspense by retarding the action must be so constructed that it will not fill the present entirely, will not put the crisis, whose resolution is being awaited, entirely out of the reader's mind, and thereby destroy the mood of suspense; the crisis and the suspense must continue, must remain vibrant in the background. But Homer—and to this we shall have to return later—knows no background. What he narrates is for the time being the only present, and fills both the stage and the reader's mind completely. So it is with the passage before us. When the young Euryclea sets the infant Odysseus on his grandfather Autolycus' lap after the banquet, the aged Euryclea, who a few lines earlier had touched the wanderer's foot, has entirely vanished from the stage and from the reader's mind.

Goethe and Schiller, who, though not referring to this particular episode, exchanged letters in April 1797 on the subject of "the retarding element" in the Homeric poems in general, put it in direct opposition to the element of suspense—the latter word is not used, but is clearly implied when the "retarding" procedure is opposed, as something proper to epic, to tragic procedure (letters of April 19, 21, and 22). The "retarding element," the "going back and forth" by means of episodes, seems to me, too, in the Homeric poems, to be opposed to any tensional and suspensive striving toward a goal, and doubtless Schiller is right in regard to Homer when he says that what he gives us is "simply the quiet existence and operation of things in accordance with their natures"; Homer's goal is "already present in every point of his progress." But both Schiller and Goethe raise Homer's procedure to the level of a law for epic poetry in general, and Schiller's words quoted above are meant to be universally binding upon the epic poet, in contradistinction from the tragic. Yet in both modern and ancient times, there are important epic works which are composed throughout with no "retarding element" in this sense but, on the contrary, with suspense throughout, and which perpetually "rob us of our emotional freedom"—which power Schiller will grant only to the tragic poet. And besides it seems to me undemonstrable and improbable that this procedure of Homeric poetry was directed by aesthetic considerations or even by an aesthetic feeling of the sort postulated by Goethe and Schiller. The effect, to be sure, is precisely that which they describe, and is, furthermore, the actual source of the conception of epic which they themselves hold, and with them all writers decisively influenced by classical antiquity. But the true cause of the impression of "retardation" appears to me to lie elsewhere—namely, in the need of the Homeric style to leave nothing which it mentions half in darkness and unexternalized.

The excursus upon the origin of Odysseus' scar is not basically different

from the many passages in which a newly introduced character, or even a
newly appearing object or implement, though it be in the thick of a battle, is
described as to its nature and origin; or in which, upon the appearance of a
god, we are told where he last was, what he was doing there, and by what
road he reached the scene; indeed, even the Homeric epithets seem to me in
the final analysis to be traceable to the same need for an externalization of
phenomena in terms perceptible to the senses. Here is the scar, which comes
up in the course of the narrative; and Homer's feeling simply will not permit
him to see it appear out of the darkness of an unilluminated past; it must be
set in full light, and with it a portion of the hero's boyhood—just as, in the
Iliad, when the first ship is already burning and the Myrmidons finally arm
that they may hasten to help, there is still time not only for the wonderful
simile of the wolf, not only for the order of the Myrmidon host, but also
for a detailed account of the ancestry of several subordinate leaders. To be
sure, the aesthetic effect thus produced was soon noticed and thereafter consciously sought; but the more original cause must have lain in the basic
impulse of the Homeric style: to represent phenomena in a fully externalized
form, visible and palpable in all their parts, and completely fixed in their
spatial and temporal relations. Nor do psychological processes receive any
other treatment: here too nothing must remain hidden and unexpressed.
With the utmost fullness, with an orderliness which even passion does not
disturb, Homer's personages vent their inmost hearts in speech; what they
do not say to others, they speak in their own minds, so that the reader is
informed of it. Much that is terrible takes place in the Homeric poems, but
it seldom takes place wordlessly: Polyphemus talks to Odysseus; Odysseus
talks to the suitors when he begins to kill them; Hector and Achilles talk
at length, before battle and after; and no speech is so filled with anger or
scorn that the particles which express logical and grammatical connections
are lacking or out of place. This last observation is true, of course, not only
of speeches but of the presentation in general. The separate elements of a
phenomenon are most clearly placed in relation to one another; a large
number of conjunctions, adverbs, particles, and other syntactical tools, all
clearly circumscribed and delicately differentiated in meaning, delimit persons, things, and portions of incidents in respect to one another, and at the
same time bring them together in a continuous and ever flexible connection;
like the separate phenomena themselves, their relationships—their temporal,
local, causal, final, consecutive, comparative, concessive, antithetical, and
conditional limitations—are brought to light in perfect fullness; so that a
continuous rhythmic procession of phenomena passes by, and never is there
a form left fragmentary or half-illuminated, never a lacuna, never a gap,
never a glimpse of unplumbed depths.

[34]

And this procession of phenomena takes place in the foreground—that is, in a local and temporal present which is absolute. One might think that the many interpolations, the frequent moving back and forth, would create a sort of perspective in time and place; but the Homeric style never gives any such impression. The way in which any impression of perspective is avoided can be clearly observed in the procedure for introducing episodes, a syntactical construction with which every reader of Homer is familiar; it is used in the passage we are considering, but can also be found in cases when the episodes are much shorter. To the word scar there is first attached a relative clause ("which once long ago a boar . . ."), which enlarges into a voluminous syntactical parenthesis; into this an independent sentence unexpectedly intrudes ("A god himself gave him . . ."), which quietly disentangles itself from syntactical subordination, until, with verse 399, an equally free syntactical treatment of the new content begins a new present which continues unchallenged until, with verse 467 ("The old woman now touched it . . ."), the scene which had been broken off is resumed. To be sure, in the case of such long episodes as the one we are considering, a purely syntactical connection with the principal theme would hardly have been possible; but a connection with it through perspective would have been all the easier had the content been arranged with that end in view; if, that is, the entire story of the scar had been presented as a recollection which awakens in Odysseus' mind at this particular moment. It would have been perfectly easy to do; the story of the scar had only to be inserted two verses earlier, at the first mention of the word scar, where the motifs "Odysseus" and "recollection" were already at hand. But any such subjectivistic-perspectivistic procedure, creating a foreground and background, resulting in the present lying open to the depths of the past, is entirely foreign to the Homeric style; the Homeric style knows only a foreground, only a uniformly illuminated, uniformly objective present. And so the excursus does not begin until two lines later, when Euryclea has discovered the scar—the possibility for a perspectivistic connection no longer exists, and the story of the wound becomes an independent and exclusive present.

The genius of the Homeric style becomes even more apparent when it is compared with an equally ancient and equally epic style from a different world of forms. I shall attempt this comparison with the account of the sacrifice of Isaac, a homogeneous narrative produced by the so-called Elohist. The King James version translates the opening as follows (Genesis 22: 1): "And it came to pass after these things, that God did tempt Abraham, and said to him, Abraham! and he said, Behold, here I am." Even this opening startles us when we come to it from Homer. Where are the two speakers? We are not told. The reader, however, knows that they are not normally to be found together in one place on earth, that one of them, God, in order to speak to Abraham, must come from somewhere, must enter the earthly realm from some unknown heights or depths. Whence does he come, whence does he call to Abraham? We are not told. He does not come, like Zeus or Poseidon, from the Aethiopians, where he has been enjoying a sacrificial feast. Nor are we told anything of his reasons for tempting Abraham so terribly. He has not, like Zeus, discussed them in set speeches with other gods gathered in council; nor have the deliberations in his own heart been presented to us; unexpected and mysterious, he enters the scene from some unknown height or depth and calls: Abraham! It will at once be said that this is to be explained by the particular concept of God which the Jews held and which was wholly different from that of the Greeks. True enough—but this constitutes no objection. For how is the Jewish concept of God to be explained? Even their earlier God of the desert was not fixed in form and content, and was alone; his lack of form, his lack of local habitation, his singleness, was in the end not only maintained but developed even further in competition with the comparatively far more manifest gods of the surrounding Near Eastern world. The concept of God held by the Jews is less a cause than a symptom of their manner of comprehending and representing things.

This becomes still clearer if we now turn to the other person in the dialogue, to Abraham. Where is he? We do not know. He says, indeed: Here I am—but the Hebrew word means only something like "behold me," and in any case is not meant to indicate the actual place where Abraham is, but a moral position in respect to God, who has called to him—Here am I awaiting thy command. Where he is actually, whether in Beersheba or elsewhere, whether indoors or in the open air, is not stated; it does not interest the narrator, the reader is not informed; and what Abraham was doing when God called to him is left in the same obscurity. To realize the difference, consider Hermes' visit to Calypso, for example, where command, journey, arrival and reception of the visitor, situation and occupation of the person visited, are set forth in many verses; and even on occasions when gods appear suddenly and briefly, whether to help one of their favorites or to deceive or destroy some mortal whom they hate, their bodily forms, and usually the manner of their coming and going, are given in detail. Here, however, God appears without bodily form (yet he "appears"), coming from some unspecified place—we only hear his voice, and that utters nothing but a name, a name without an adjective, without a descriptive epithet for the person spoken to, such as is the rule in every Homeric address; and of Abraham too nothing is made perceptible except the words in which he answers God: *Hinne-ni,* Behold me here—with which, to be sure, a most touching gesture expressive of obedience and readiness is suggested, but it is left to the reader to visualize it. Moreover the two speakers are not on the same level: if we conceive of Abraham in the foreground, where it might be possible to picture him as prostrate or kneeling or bowing with outspread arms or gazing upward, God is not there too: Abraham's words and gestures are directed toward the depths of the picture or upward, but in any case the undetermined, dark place from which the voice comes to him is not in the foreground.

After this opening, God gives his command, and the story itself begins: everyone knows it; it unrolls with no episodes in a few independent sentences whose syntactical connection is of the most rudimentary sort. In this atmosphere it is unthinkable that an implement, a landscape through which the travelers passed, the serving-men, or the ass, should be described, that their origin or descent or material or appearance or usefulness should be set forth in terms of praise; they do not even admit an adjective: they are serving-men, ass, wood, and knife, and nothing else, without an epithet; they are there to serve the end which God has commanded; what in other respects they were, are, or will be, remains in darkness. A journey is made, because God has designated the place where the sacrifice is to be performed; but we are told nothing about the journey except that it took three days, and even that we are told in a mysterious way: Abraham and his followers rose "early in the morning" and "went unto" the place of which God had told him; on the third day he lifted up his eyes and saw the place from afar. That gesture is the only gesture, is indeed the only occurrence during the whole journey, of which we are told; and though its motivation lies in the fact that the place is elevated, its uniqueness still heightens the impression that the journey took place through a vacuum; it is as if, while he traveled on, Abraham had looked neither to the right nor to the left, had suppressed any sign of life in his followers and himself save only their footfalls.

Thus the journey is like a silent progress through the indeterminate and the contingent, a holding of the breath, a process which has no present, which is inserted, like a blank duration, between what has passed and what lies ahead, and which yet is measured: three days! Three such days positively demand the symbolic interpretation which they later received. They began "early in the morning." But at what time on the third day did Abraham lift up his eyes and see his goal? The text says nothing on the subject. Obviously not "late in the evening," for it seems that there was still time enough to climb the mountain and make the sacrifice. So "early in the morning" is given, not as an indication of time, but for the sake of its ethical significance; it is intended to express the resolution, the promptness, the punctual obedience of the sorely tried Abraham. Bitter to him is the early morning in which he saddles his ass, calls his serving-men and his son Isaac, and sets out; but he obeys, he walks on until the third day, then lifts up his eyes and sees the place. Whence he comes, we do not know, but the goal is clearly stated: Jeruel in the land of Moriah. What place this is meant to indicate is not clear—"Moriah" especially may be a later correction of some other word. But in any case the goal was given, and in any case it is a matter of some sacred spot which was to receive a particular consecration by being connected with Abraham's sacrifice. Just as little as "early in the morning" serves as a temporal indication does "Jeruel in the land of Moriah" serve as a geographical indication; and in both cases alike, the complementary indication is not given, for we know as little of the hour at which Abraham lifted up his eyes as we do of the place from which he set forth—Jeruel is significant not so much as the goal of an earthly journey, in its geographical relation to other places, as through its special election, through its relation to God, who designated it as the scene of the act, and therefore it must be named.

In the narrative itself, a third chief character appears: Isaac. While God and Abraham, the serving-men, the ass, and the implements are simply named, without mention of any qualities or any other sort of definition, Isaac once receives an appositive; God says, "Take Isaac, thine only son, whom thou lovest." But this is not a characterization of Isaac as a person, apart from his relation to his father and apart from the story; he may be handsome or ugly, intelligent or stupid, tall or short, pleasant or unpleasant —we are not told. Only what we need to know about him as a personage in the action, here and now, is illuminated, so that it may become apparent how terrible Abraham's temptation is, and that God is fully aware of it. By this example of the contrary, we see the significance of the descriptive adjectives and digressions of the Homeric poems; with their indications of the earlier and as it were absolute existence of the persons described, they prevent the reader from concentrating exclusively on a present crisis; even when the most terrible things are occurring, they prevent the establishment of an overwhelming suspense. But here, in the story of Abraham's sacrifice, the overwhelming suspense is present; what Schiller makes the goal of the tragic poet—to rob us of our emotional freedom, to turn our intellectual and spiritual powers (Schiller says "our activity") in one direction, to concentrate them there—is effected in this Biblical narrative, which certainly deserves the epithet epic.

We find the same contrast if we compare the two uses of direct discourse. The personages speak in the Bible story too; but their speech does not serve, as does speech in Homer, to manifest, to externalize thoughts—on the contrary, it serves to indicate thoughts which remain unexpressed. God gives his command in direct discourse, but he leaves his motives and his purpose unexpressed; Abraham, receiving the command, says nothing and does what he has been told to do. The conversation between Abraham and Isaac on the way to the place of sacrifice is only an interruption of the heavy silence and makes it all the more burdensome. The two of them, Isaac carrying the wood and Abraham with fire and a knife, "went together." Hesitantly, Isaac ventures to ask about the ram, and Abraham gives the well-known answer. Then the text repeats: "So they went both of them together." Everything remains unexpressed.

It would be difficult, then, to imagine styles more contrasted than those of these two equally ancient and equally epic texts. On the one hand, externalized, uniformly illuminated phenomena, at a definite time and in a definite place, connected together without lacunae in a perpetual foreground; thoughts and feeling completely expressed; events taking place in leisurely fashion and with very little of suspense. On the other hand, the externalization of only so much of the phenomena as is necessary for the purpose of the narrative, all else left in obscurity; the decisive points of the narrative alone are emphasized, what lies between is nonexistent; time and place are undefined and call for interpretation; thoughts and feeling remain unexpressed, are only suggested by the silence and the fragmentary speeches; the whole, permeated with the most unrelieved suspense and directed toward a single goal (and to that extent far more of a unity), remains mysterious and "fraught with background."

I will discuss this term in some detail, lest it be misunderstood. I said above that the Homeric style was "of the foreground" because, despite much going back and forth, it yet causes what is momentarily being narrated to give the impression that it is the only present, pure and without perspective. A consideration of the Elohistic text teaches us that our term is capable of a broader and deeper application. It shows that even the separate personages can be represented as possessing "background"; God is always so represented in the Bible, for he is not comprehensible in his presence, as is Zeus; it is always only "something" of him that appears, he always extends into depths. But even the human beings in the Biblical stories have greater depths of time, fate, and consciousness than do the human beings in Homer; although they are nearly always caught up in an event engaging all their faculties, they are not so entirely immersed in its present that they do not remain continually conscious of what has happened to them earlier and elsewhere; their thoughts and feelings have more layers, are more entangled. Abraham's actions are explained not only by what is happening to him at the moment, nor yet only by his character (as Achilles' actions by his courage and his pride, and Odysseus' by his versatility and foresightedness),

[39]

but by his previous history; he remembers, he is constantly conscious of, what God has promised him and what God has already accomplished for him—his soul is torn between desperate rebellion and hopeful expectation; his silent obedience is multilayered, has background. Such a problematic psychological situation as this is impossible for any of the Homeric heroes, whose destiny is clearly defined and who wake every morning as if it were the first day of their lives: their emotions, though strong, are simple and find expression instantly.

How fraught with background, in comparison, are characters like Saul and David! How entangled and stratified are such human relations as those between David and Absalom, between David and Joab! Any such "background" quality of the psychological situation as that which the story of Absalom's death and its sequel (II Samuel 18 and 19, by the so-called Jahvist) rather suggests than expresses, is unthinkable in Homer. Here we are confronted not merely with the psychological processes of characters whose depth of background is veritably abysmal, but with a purely geographical background too. For David is absent from the battlefield; but the influence of his will and his feelings continues to operate, they affect even Joab in his rebellion and disregard for the consequences of his actions; in the magnificent scene with the two messengers, both the physical and psychological background is fully manifest, though the latter is never expressed. With this, compare, for example, how Achilles, who sends Patroclus first to scout and then into battle, loses almost all "presentness" so long as he is not physically present. But the most important thing is the "multilayeredness" of the individual character; this is hardly to be met with in Homer, or at most in the form of a conscious hesitation between two possible courses of action; otherwise, in Homer, the complexity of the psychological life is shown only in the succession and alternation of emotions; whereas the Jewish writers are able to express the simultaneous existence of various layers of consciousness and the conflict between them.

The Homeric poems, then, though their intellectual, linguistic, and above all syntactical culture appears to be so much more highly developed, are yet comparatively simple in their picture of human beings; and no less so in their relation to the real life which they describe in general. Delight in physical existence is everything to them, and their highest aim is to make that delight perceptible to us. Between battles and passions, adventures and perils, they show us hunts, banquets, palaces and shepherds' cots, athletic contests and washing days—in order that we may see the heroes in their ordinary life, and seeing them so, may take pleasure in their manner of enjoying their savory present, a present which sends strong roots down into social usages, landscape, and daily life. And thus they bewitch us and ingratiate themselves to us until we live with them in the reality of their lives; so long as we are reading or hearing the poems, it does not matter whether we know that all this is only legend, "make-believe." The oft-repeated reproach that Homer is a liar takes nothing from his effectiveness, he does not need to base his story on historical reality, his reality is powerful enough in itself; it ensnares us, weaving its web around us, and that suffices him. And this "real" world into which we are lured, exists for itself, contains nothing but itself; the Homeric poems conceal nothing, they contain no teaching and no secret second meaning. Homer can be analyzed, as we have essayed to do here, but he cannot be interpreted. Later allegorizing trends have tried their arts of interpretation upon him, but to no avail. He resists any such treatment; the interpretations are forced and foreign, they do not crystallize into a unified doctrine. The general considerations which occasionally occur (in our episode, for example, v. 360: that in misfortune men age quickly) reveal a calm acceptance of the basic facts of human existence, but with no compulsion to brood over them, still less any passionate impulse either to rebel against them or to embrace them in an ecstasy of submission.

It is all very different in the Biblical stories. Their aim is not to bewitch the senses, and if nevertheless they produce lively sensory effects, it is only because the moral, religious, and psychological phenomena which are their sole concern are made concrete in the sensible matter of life. But their religious intent involves an absolute claim to historical truth. The story of Abraham and Isaac is not better established than the story of Odysseus, Penelope, and Euryclea; both are legendary. But the Biblical narrator, the Elohist, had to believe in the objective truth of the story of Abraham's sacrifice—the existence of the sacred ordinances of life rested upon the truth of this and similar stories. He had to believe in it passionately; or else (as many rationalistic interpreters believed and perhaps still believe) he had to be a conscious liar—no harmless liar like Homer, who lied to give pleasure, but a political liar with a definite end in view, lying in the interest of a claim to absolute authority.

To me, the rationalistic interpretation seems psychologically absurd; but even if we take it into consideration, the relation of the Elohist to the truth of his story still remains a far more passionate and definite one than is Homer's relation. The Biblical narrator was obliged to write exactly what his belief in the truth of the tradition (or, from the rationalistic standpoint, his interest in the truth of it) demanded of him—in either case, his freedom in creative or representative imagination was severely limited; his activity was perforce reduced to composing an effective version of the pious tradition. What he produced, then, was not primarily oriented toward "realism" (if he succeeded in being realistic, it was merely a means, not an end); it was oriented toward truth. Woe to the man who did not believe it! One can perfectly well entertain historical doubts on the subject of the Trojan War or of Odysseus' wanderings, and still, when reading Homer, feel precisely the effects he sought to produce; but without believing in Abraham's sacrifice, it is impossible to put the narrative of it to the use for which it was written. Indeed, we must go even further. The Bible's claim to truth is not only far more urgent than Homer's, it is tyrannical—it excludes all other claims. The world of the Scripture stories is not satisfied with claiming to be a historically true reality—it insists that it is the only real world, is destined for autocracy. All other scenes, issues, and ordinances have no right to appear independently of it, and it is promised that all of them, the history of all mankind, will be given their due place within its frame, will be subordinated to it. The Scripture stories do not, like Homer's, court our favor, they do not flatter us that they may please us and enchant us—they seek to subject us, and if we refuse to be subjected we are rebels.

Let no one object that this goes too far, that not the stories, but the religious doctrine, raises the claim to absolute authority; because the stories are not, like Homer's, simply narrated "reality." Doctrine and promise are incarnate in them and inseparable from them; for that very reason they are fraught with "background" and mysterious, containing a second, concealed meaning. In the story of Isaac, it is not only God's intervention at the beginning and the end, but even the factual and psychological elements which come between, that are mysterious, merely touched upon, fraught with background; and therefore they require subtle investigation and interpretation, they demand them. Since so much in the story is dark and incomplete, and since the reader knows that God is a hidden God, his effort to interpret it constantly finds something new to feed upon. Doctrine and the search for enlightenment are inextricably connected with the physical side of the narrative—the latter being more than simple "reality"; indeed they are in constant danger of losing their own reality, as very soon happened when interpretation reached such proportions that the real vanished.

If the text of the Biblical narrative, then, is so greatly in need of interpretation on the basis of its own content, its claim to absolute authority forces it still further in the same direction. Far from seeking, like Homer, merely to make us forget our own reality for a few hours, it seeks to overcome our reality: we are to fit our own life into its world, feel ourselves to be elements in its structure of universal history. This becomes increasingly difficult the further our historical environment is removed from that of the Biblical books; and if these nevertheless maintain their claim to absolute authority, it is inevitable that they themselves be adapted through interpretative transformation. This was for a long time comparatively easy; as late as the European Middle Ages it was possible to represent Biblical events as ordinary phenomena of contemporary life, the methods of interpretation themselves forming the basis for such a treatment. But when, through too great a change in environment and through the awakening of a critical conscious-ness, this becomes impossible, the Biblical claim to absolute authority is jeopardized; the method of interpretation is scorned and rejected, the Biblical stories become ancient legends, and the doctrine they had contained, now dissevered from them, becomes a disembodied image.

As a result of this claim to absolute authority, the method of interpretation spread to traditions other than the Jewish. The Homeric poems present a definite complex of events whose boundaries in space and time are clearly delimited; before it, beside it, and after it, other complexes of events, which do not depend upon it, can be conceived without conflict and without diffi-culty. The Old Testament, on the other hand, presents universal history: it begins with the beginning of time, with the creation of the world, and will end with the Last Days, the fulfilling of the Covenant, with which the world will come to an end. Everything else that happens in the world can only be conceived as an element in this sequence; into it everything that is known about the world, or at least everything that touches upon the history of the Jews, must be fitted as an ingredient of the divine plan; and as this too became possible only by interpreting the new material as it poured in, the need for interpretation reaches out beyond the original Jewish-Israelitish realm of reality—for example to Assyrian, Babylonian, Persian, and Roman history; interpretation in a determined direction becomes a general method of comprehending reality; the new and strange world which now comes into view and which, in the form in which it presents itself, proves to be wholly unutilizable within the Jewish religious frame, must be so interpreted that it can find a place there. But this process nearly always also reacts upon the frame, which requires enlarging and modifying. The most striking piece of interpretation of this sort occurred in the first century of the Christian era, in consequence of Paul's mission to the Gentiles: Paul and the Church Fathers reinterpreted the entire Jewish tradition as a succession of figures prognosticating the appearance of Christ, and assigned the Roman Empire its proper place in the divine plan of salvation. Thus while, on the one hand, the reality of the Old Testament presents itself as complete truth with a claim to sole authority, on the other hand that very claim forces it to a con-stant interpretative change in its own content; for millennia it undergoes an incessant and active development with the life of man in Europe.

The claim of the Old Testament stories to represent universal history, their insistent relation—a relation constantly redefined by conflicts—to a single and hidden God, who yet shows himself and who guides universal history

[43]

by promise and exaction, gives these stories an entirely different perspective from any the Homeric poems can possess. As a composition, the Old Testament is incomparably less unified than the Homeric poems, it is more obviously pieced together—but the various components all belong to one concept of universal history and its interpretation. If certain elements survived which did not immediately fit in, interpretation took care of them; and so the reader is at every moment aware of the universal religio-historical perspective which gives the individual stories their general meaning and purpose. The greater the separateness and horizontal disconnection of the stories and groups of stories in relation to one another, compared with the *Iliad* and the *Odyssey,* the stronger is their general vertical connection, which holds them all together and which is entirely lacking in Homer. Each of the great figures of the Old Testament, from Adam to the prophets, embodies a moment of this vertical connection. God chose and formed these men to the end of embodying his essence and will—yet choice and formation do not coincide, for the latter proceeds gradually, historically, during the earthly life of him upon whom the choice has fallen. How the process is accomplished, what terrible trials such a formation inflicts, can be seen from our story of Abraham's sacrifice. Herein lies the reason why the great figures of the Old Testament are so much more fully developed, so much more fraught with their own biographical past, so much more distinct as individuals, than are the Homeric heroes. Achilles and Odysseus are splendidly described in many well-ordered words, epithets cling to them, their emotions are constantly displayed in their words and deeds—but they have no development, and their life-histories are clearly set forth once and for all. So little are the Homeric heroes presented as developing or having developed, that most of them— Nestor, Agamemnon, Achilles—appear to be of an age fixed from the very first. Even Odysseus, in whose case the long lapse of time and the many events which occurred offer so much opportunity for biographical development, shows almost nothing of it. Odysseus on his return is exactly the same as he was when he left Ithaca two decades earlier. But what a road, what a fate, lie between the Jacob who cheated his father out of his blessing and the old man whose favorite son has been torn to pieces by a wild beast! —between David the harp player, persecuted by his lord's jealousy, and the old king, surrounded by violent intrigues, whom Abishag the Shunnamite warmed in his bed, and he knew her not! The old man, of whom we know how he has become what he is, is more of an individual than the young man; for it it only during the course of an eventful life that men are differentiated into full individality; and it is this history of a personality which the Old Testament presents to us as the formation undergone by those whom God has chosen to be examples. Fraught with their development, sometimes

even aged to the verge of dissolution, they show a distinct stamp of individuality entirely foreign to the Homeric heroes. Time can touch the latter
only outwardly, and even that change is brought to our observation as little
as possible; whereas the stern hand of God is ever upon the Old Testament
figures; he has not only made them once and for all and chosen them, but
he continues to work upon them, bends them and kneads them, and, without destroying them in essence, produces from them forms which their
youth gave no grounds for anticipating. The objection that the biographical
element of the Old Testament often springs from the combination of several
legendary personages does not apply; for this combination is a part of the
development of the text. And how much wider is the pendulum swing of
their lives than that of the Homeric heroes! For they are bearers of the
divine will, and yet they are fallible, subject to misfortune and humiliation—
and in the midst of misfortune and in their humiliation their acts and words
reveal the transcendent majesty of God. There is hardly one of them who
does not, like Adam, undergo the deepest humiliation—and hardly one who
is not deemed worthy of God's personal intervention and personal inspiration. Humiliation and elevation go far deeper and far higher than in Homer,
and they belong basically together. The poor beggar Odysseus is only mas-
querading, but Adam is really cast down, Jacob really a refugee, Joseph
really in the pit and then a slave to be bought and sold. But their greatness,
rising out of humiliation, is almost superhuman and an image of God's
greatness. The reader clearly feels how the extent of the pendulum's swing
is connected with the intensity of the personal history—precisely the most
extreme circumstances, in which we are immeasurably forsaken and in
despair, or immeasurably joyous and exalted, give us, if we survive them, a
personal stamp which is recognized as the product of a rich existence, a rich
development. And very often, indeed generally, this element of development
gives the Old Testament stories a historical character, even when the subject
is purely legendary and traditional.

Homer remains within the legendary with all his material, whereas the
material of the Old Testament comes closer and closer to history as the
narrative proceeds; in the stories of David the historical report predominates.
Here too, much that is legendary still remains, as for example the story of
David and Goliath; but much—and the most essential—consists in things
which the narrators knew from their own experience or from firsthand
testimony. Now the difference between legend and history is in most cases
easily perceived by a reasonably experienced reader. It is a difficult matter,
requiring careful historical and philological training, to distinguish the true
from the synthetic or the biased in a historical presentation; but it is easy to
separate the historical from the legendary in general. Their structure is

different. Even where the legendary does not immediately betray itself by elements of the miraculous, by the repetition of well-known standard motives, typical patterns and themes, through neglect of clear details of time and place, and the like, it is generally quickly recognizable by its composition. It runs far too smoothly. All cross-currents, all friction, all that is casual, secondary to the main events and themes, everything unresolved, truncated, and uncertain, which confuses the clear progress of the action and the simple orientation of the actors, has disappeared. The historical event which we witness, or learn from the testimony of those who witnessed it, runs much more variously, contradictorily, and confusedly; not until it has produced results in a definite domain are we able, with their help, to classify it to a certain extent; and how often the order to which we think we have attained becomes doubtful again, how often we ask ourselves if the data before us have not led us to a far too simple classification of the original events! Legend arranges its material in a simple and straightforward way; it detaches it from its contemporary historical context, so that the latter will not confuse it; it knows only clearly outlined men who act from few and simple motives and the continuity of whose feelings and actions remains uninterrupted. In the legends of martyrs, for example, a stiff-necked and fanatical persecutor stands over against an equally stiff-necked and fanatical victim; and a situation so complicated—that is to say, so real and historical—as that in which the "persecutor" Pliny finds himself in his celebrated letter to Trajan on the subject of the Christians, is unfit for legend. And that is still a comparatively simple case. Let the reader think of the history which we are ourselves witnessing; anyone who, for example, evaluates the behavior of individual men and groups of men at the time of the rise of National Socialism in Germany, or the behavior of individual peoples and states before and during the last war, will feel how difficult it is to represent historical themes in general, and how unfit they are for legend; the historical comprises a great number of contradictory motives in each individual, a hesitation and ambiguous groping on the part of groups; only seldom (as in the last war) does a more or less plain situation, comparatively simple to describe, arise, and even such a situation is subject to division below the surface, is indeed almost constantly in danger of losing its simplicity; and the motives of all the interested parties are so complex that the slogans of propaganda can be composed only through the crudest simplification—with the result that friend and foe alike can often employ the same ones. To write history is so difficult that most historians are forced to make concessions to the technique of legend.

It is clear that a large part of the life of David as given in the Bible contains history and not legend. In Absalom's rebellion, for example, or in the scenes from David's last days, the contradictions and crossing of motives both in individuals and in the general action have become so concrete that it is impossible to doubt the historicity of the information conveyed. Now the men who composed the historical parts are often the same who edited the older legends too; their peculiar religious concept of man in history, which we have attempted to describe above, in no way led them to a legendary simplification of events; and so it is only natural that, in the legendary passages of the Old Testament, historical structure is frequently discernible —of course, not in the sense that the traditions are examined as to their credibility according to the methods of scientific criticism; but simply to the extent that the tendency to a smoothing down and harmonizing of events, to a simplification of motives, to a static definition of characters which avoids conflict, vacillation, and development, such as are natural to legendary structure, does not predominate in the Old Testament world of legend. Abraham, Jacob, or even Moses produces a more concrete, direct, and historical impression than the figures of the Homeric world—not because they are better described in terms of sense (the contrary is the case) but because the confused, contradictory multiplicity of events, the psychological and factual cross-purposes, which true history reveals, have not disappeared in the representation but still remain clearly perceptible. In the stories of David, the legendary, which only later scientific criticism makes recognizable as such, imperceptibly passes into the historical; and even in the legendary, the problem of the classification and interpretation of human history is already passionately apprehended—a problem which later shatters the framework of historical composition and completely overruns it with prophecy; thus the Old Testament, in so far as it is concerned with human events, ranges through all three domains: legend, historical reporting, and interpretative historical theology.

Connected with the matters just discussed is the fact that the Greek text seems more limited and more static in respect to the circle of personages involved in the action and to their political activity. In the recognition scene with which we began, there appears, aside from Odysseus and Penelope, the housekeeper Euryclea, a slave whom Odysseus' father Laertes had bought long before. She, like the swineherd Eumaeus, has spent her life in the service of Laertes' family; like Eumaeus, she is closely connected with their fate, she loves them and shares their interests and feelings. But she has no life of her own, no feelings of her own; she has only the life and feelings of her master. Eumaeus too, though he still remembers that he was born a freeman and indeed of a noble house (he was stolen as a boy), has, not only in fact but also in his own feeling, no longer a life of his own, he is entirely involved in the life of his masters. Yet these two characters are the only ones whom

Homer brings to life who do not belong to the ruling class. Thus we become conscious of the fact that in the Homeric poems life is enacted only among the ruling class—others appear only in the role of servants to that class. The ruling class is still so strongly patriarchal, and still itself so involved in the daily activities of domestic life, that one is sometimes likely to forget their rank. But they are unmistakably a sort of feudal aristocracy, whose men divide their lives between war, hunting, marketplace councils, and feasting, while the women supervise the maids in the house. As a social picture, this world is completely stable; wars take place only between different groups of the ruling class; nothing ever pushes up from below. In the early stories of the Old Testament the patriarchal condition is dominant too, but since the people involved are individual nomadic or half-nomadic tribal leaders, the social picture gives a much less stable impression; class distinctions are not felt. As soon as the people completely emerges—that is, after the exodus from Egypt—its activity is always discernible, it is often in ferment, it frequently intervenes in events not only as a whole but also in separate groups and through the medium of separate individuals who come forward; the origins of prophecy seem to lie in the irrepressible politico-religious spontaneity of the people. We receive the impression that the movements emerging from the depths of the people of Israel-Judah must have been of a wholly different nature from those even of the later ancient democracies—of a different nature and far more elemental.

With the more profound historicity and the more profound social activity of the Old Testament text, there is connected yet another important distinction from Homer: namely, that a different conception of the elevated style and of the sublime is to be found here. Homer, of course, is not afraid to let the realism of daily life enter into the sublime and tragic; our episode of the scar is an example, we see how the quietly depicted, domestic scene of the foot-washing is incorporated into the pathetic and sublime action of Odysseus' home-coming. From the rule of the separation of styles which was later almost universally accepted and which specified that the realistic depiction of daily life was incompatible with the sublime and had a place only in comedy or, carefully stylized, in idyl—from any such rule Homer is still far removed. And yet he is closer to it than is the Old Testament. For the great and sublime events in the Homeric poems take place far more exclusively and unmistakably among the members of a ruling class; and these are far more untouched in their heroic elevation than are the Old Testament figures, who can fall much lower in dignity (consider, for example, Adam, Noah, David, Job); and finally, domestic realism, the representation of daily life, remains in Homer in the peaceful realm of the idyllic, whereas, from the very first, in the Old Testament stories, the sublime, tragic, and problematic take shape precisely in the domestic and commonplace: scenes such as those between Cain

[48]

and Abel, between Noah and his sons, between Abraham, Sarah, and Hagar, between Rebekah, Jacob, and Esau, and so on, are inconceivable in the Homeric style. The entirely different ways of developing conflicts are enough to account for this. In the Old Testament stories the peace of daily life in the house, in the fields, and among the flocks, is undermined by jealousy over election and the promise of a blessing, and complications arise which would be utterly incomprehensible to the Homeric heroes. The latter must have palpable and clearly expressible reasons for their conflicts and enmities, and these work themselves out in free battles; whereas, with the former, the perpetually smouldering jealousy and the connection between the domestic and the spiritual, between the paternal blessing and the divine blessing, lead to daily life being permeated with the stuff of conflict, often with poison. The sublime influence of God here reaches so deeply into the everyday that the two realms of the sublime and the everyday are not only actually unseparated but basically inseparable.

We have compared these two texts, and, with them, the two kinds of style they embody, in order to reach a starting point for an investigation into the literary representation of reality in European culture. The two styles, in their opposition, represent basic types: on the one hand fully externalized description, uniform illumination, uninterrupted connection, free expression, all events in the foreground, displaying unmistakable meanings, few elements of historical development and of psychological perspective; on the other hand, certain parts brought into high relief, others left obscure, abruptness, suggestive influence of the unexpressed, "background" quality, multiplicity of meanings and the need for interpretation, universal-historical claims, development of the concept of the historically becoming, and preoccupation with the problematic.

Homer's realism is, of course, not to be equated with classical-antique realism in general; for the separation of styles, which did not develop until later, permitted no such leisurely and externalized description of everyday happenings; in tragedy especially there was no room for it; furthermore, Greek culture very soon encountered the phenomena of historical becoming and of the "multilayeredness" of the human problem, and dealt with them in its fashion; in Roman realism, finally, new and native concepts are added. We shall go into these later changes in the antique representation of reality when the occasion arises; on the whole, despite them, the basic tendencies of the Homeric style, which we have attempted to work out, remained effective and determinant down into late antiquity.

Since we are using the two styles, the Homeric and the Old Testament, as starting points, we have taken them as finished products, as they appear in the texts; we have disregarded everything that pertains to their origins, and thus have left untouched the question whether their peculiarities were theirs from the beginning or are to be referred wholly or in part to foreign influences. Within the limits of our purpose, a consideration of this question is not necessary; for it is in their full development, which they reached in early times, that the two styles exercised their determining influence upon the representation of reality in European literature.

A E S C H Y L U S

[525–456 B.C.]

RICHMOND LATTIMORE, PAUL SHOREY PROFESSOR OF GREEK AT BRYN MAWR College, is a distinguished American poet whose translations from the Greek have become famous throughout the English-speaking world. Indeed, his English version of Homer's *Iliad* has been called incomparably the best. This essay first appeared as an introduction to his equally distinguished translation of Aeschylus' *Oresteia*.

Few poetic works of antiquity have elicited more weighty comments of the historical, philological, and anthropological variety than the *Oresteia,* and our understanding of its great themes of guilt and retribution, the evolution of justice, has been clarified by such studies. Mr. Lattimore's essay, however, reminds us that Aeschylus was a poet, a lyric dramatist, who fused metaphorical texture with dramatic action to unfold the meaning of his trilogy. This elucidation of the art of Aeschylus blends the scholar's erudition with the insight of the critic who is himself a poet.

Reprinted from *The Complete Greek Tragedies* by David Grene and Richmond Lattimore by permission of The University of Chicago Press. Copyright 1953 by The University of Chicago.

RICHMOND LATTIMORE

Introduction to the Oresteia

THE LIFE OF AESCHYLUS

AESCHYLUS, THE SON OF EUPHORION, WAS BORN IN THE LAST QUARTER OF THE sixth century B.C., probably about 513 or 512 B.C. The great Persian Wars occurred during his early manhood, and he fought, certainly at Marathon (where his brother was killed in action) and probably also at Artemisium, Salamis, and Plataea. He is said to have begun at an early age to write tragedies; his first victory was in 484 B.C. In or about 476 B.C. he visted Sicily and, at the instance of Hieron of Syracuse, Pindar's friend, produced *The Women of Etna* at the new city of Etna which Hieron had founded. In 472 he produced his *Persians* at Athens, with Pericles as his choregus (or official sponsor) and re-produced it, presumably in the next year, in Sicily. Back in Athens in 468, he was defeated by the young Sophocles, but won again in 467 with a set of plays including *The Seven against Thebes*. In 458 he presented the *Oresteia* (*Agamemnon, The Libation Bearers, The Eumenides*). He died in Gela, Sicily, in 456 or 455 B.C., leaving behind him an epitaph which might be rendered as follows:

Under this monument lies Aeschylus the Athenian,
Euphorion's son, who died in the wheatlands of Gela. The grove

[52]

of Marathon with its glories can speak of his valor in battle.
The long-haired Persian remembers and can speak of it too.

He left behind more than seventy plays (the exact number is uncertain), of which seven have survived. They are *The Suppliants, The Persians, The Seven against Thebes, Prometheus Bound, Agamemnon, The Libation Bearers, The Eumenides.* He is said to have won first prize thirteen times while he lived, but after his death his tragedies were often produced again, and in competition with living poets he won more prizes still.

It would be interesting to know how old Aeschylus was when he wrote his known and dated plays. But the date of his birth is quite uncertain, though the year 525/4[1] is commonly given as if it were an established fact. It is true enough that apparently independent authorities give ages at the time of Marathon and at time of death which agree with this scheme. However, the birth date may very easily be accounted for by the rule-of-thumb method, favored by Greek chronologists, of taking an important event in a man's life and counting back forty years to an estimated date of birth. Thus the traditional birth date of Thucydides is 471 (from the outbreak of the war he recorded in 431); of Aristophanes, 445 (from the production of his masterpiece, *The Frogs,* in 405). Both these dates are bad (there are many parallels), and the one for Aeschylus is no more convincing. An age of forty at his first victory is suspect, not only because it tallies so neatly with a known method of reckoning, but because it is in itself unlikely that a man who utterly eclipsed his rivals in subsequent reputation, so that they are now very little more than bare names, should have had to wait so long before scoring his first success. A less popular but more attractive tradition would make him born in 513 or 512, but here also we may be dealing with estimates based on known and undated events, such as battles and dramatic productions.

Ancient authorities also tell us a few other things about Aeschylus which would be interesting if we could believe them. It is said that he left Athens for Sicily in chagrin because he was defeated by Simonides, the great lyric poet, in a competition for writing the epitaph of the dead at Marathon, or because he was defeated by Sophocles in dramatic competition, or because he disliked Athenian politics.[2] The defeats are real, but they do not tally,

---

[1] Athenian dates are generally fixed by the term of the *archon,* or titular chief magistrate. Since the archons changed over some time in the summer, not at our new year, such dates overlap those of our calendar. Since, however, plays came out in the spring before the change-over, a play dated to an archonship of, for instance, 485/4 will *always* fall in 484.

[2] Euripides, near the end of his life, left Athens in voluntary exile and died in Macedonia at the court of King Archelaus. There is reason to believe that he left because he had constantly failed to win critical approval in Athens and because he de-

chronologically, with the visits to Sicily; on the contrary, after losing to Sophocles, Aeschylus stayed in Athens and won first prize with *The Seven against Thebes* and its related dramas the next year, which is quite different from going off to Sicily in a huff. If one may guess at why he went to Sicily, it was because Sicily was the America of that day, the new Greek world, rich, generous, and young, with its own artists but without the tradition of perfected culture which Old Greece had built up, and it attracted Pindar, Bacchylides, Simonides, and Aeschylus much as America has attracted English men of letters from Dickens, Thackeray, and Wilde down to the present day. We do not know much about the personal character of Aeschylus and can make little critical use of what we do know. The epitaph shows he was proud of his military record, but this scarcely helps us to understand *The Persians, The Seven against Thebes,* or *Agamemnon.* We must approach Aeschylus, not from the biographies, but from his own plays.

EARLY TRAGEDY

From the time of the almost legendary Thespis, a full generation before the earliest tragedy we possess, dramatic performances of some sort had been regularly produced at Athens. In origin, they must have been a special local development of the choral lyric—sacred, occasional, provincial, public— which was alive in all the cities of Greece. But the early phases of the course by which dramatic lyric was transformed into lyric drama are now invisible to us. We can recognize certain ingredients, or essential features. Early drama was choral, and the life of Attic tragedy shows the indispensable chorus to the end, though the actors steadily invade the preserves of the chorus until, at the close of the fifth century, Euripides is using it sometimes in a most perfunctory manner, as if it were a convention he could not get rid of but might otherwise have preferred to do without. Early drama was sacred, having to do with the cult of divinities, and particularly with the cult of Dionysus: on the formal side, it was performed to the end on ground devoted to that god and before his priest; but developed tragedy did not have to be *about* Dionysus, and seldom was. Like most choral lyric, it was given through the medium of a formal competition. The early tragic poets drew, for narrative material and for metrical forms, on an already rich and highly developed tradition of nondramatic poetry, epic and lyric. They also drew, no

---

spaired of the hopeless course which his city had been following since the time of Pericles. The biographers doubtless applied the analogy of Euripides-Athens-Archelaus to Aeschylus-Athens-Hieron. But Euripides was a failure in his own lifetime, and it made him a defeatist and escapist. Of Aeschylus we can say with confidence that he was neither of these things.

doubt, on the unwritten and almost inarticulate experience of a living people, on folk memory and folklore, cult and ritual and ceremony and passion play and mystery play. But tragedy did not grow out of such elements. It was made. Concerning the makers, we know little indeed about Thespis, Pratinas, Choerilus, Phrynichus. Tragedy, for us, begins with Aeschylus.

By or during the career of Aeschylus, the features of Greek tragedy become fixed. At an Athenian festival, three player-groups, each consisting of two (later three) actors and chorus, act out competitively four-drama sets. The material is based on stories told or indicated in previous Greek legend. Tragedy is heroic. The costumes are formal, physical action restrained and without violence; naturalism is neither achieved nor desired. Aeschylus himself, and his older contemporary Phrynichus before him, experimented with dramatic stories taken from contemporary history, and of these we have *The Persians,* dealing with the repulse of Xerxes and his forces. This was a success, but circumstances in this case were favorable to special occasional drama, for the defeat of Persia was the proudest achievement of Greek history. And, even here, the play is *about* the Persians, not the Greeks, the setting is Persia, and only Persian individuals are named. Remoteness from the immediate here-and-now, required by tragedy and guaranteed by legendary material, is here to a great extent achieved by placing the scene in the heart of Persia, so far away and guarded from Greeks that to the audience it might have seemed almost as legendary as the Troy of Hector or the Thebes of Oedipus.[3] A drama dealing directly with Themistocles and Pericles or with the war between Athens and Aegina would have been neither desired by the poet nor tolerated by his audience.

The body of legend on which Aeschylus and the other tragic poets drew was composed of the epic poems of Homer and his successors and constituted a loose and informal, but fairly comprehensive, history of the world as the Greeks knew it. Typical sources in this complex were the *Iliad* and the *Odyssey;* the "Epic Cycle," or series of subsequent epics which filled out the story of Troy and dealt in detail with its occasions and aftereffects; the epics that told the story of Thebes; and numerous other narratives either written down or transmitted through unwritten oral tradition. The dramatist rarely worked directly from the main body of the *Iliad* or the *Odyssey;* the less authoritative minor texts were more popular. The dramatist seems not to have felt free to invent his material outright, but he could—in fact, he must— choose among variants, expand or deepen and interpret character, generally

---

[3] So Shakespeare drew on history and legend for his tragedies and romances, or, when these dealt with time not specifically antique, the place would be idealized by distance and the vagueness of his audience's information: Italy, Bohemia, Illyria, Arden.

shape the story on the trend of his own imagination. In the case of Aeschylus, this process can be best reconstructed in the *Oresteia*, the trilogy or sequence of three tragedies composed of *Agamemnon, The Libation Bearers,* and *The Eumenides*.

THE STORY OF THE HOUSE OF ATREUS

The version of the legend as Aeschylus used it runs as follows. Atreus and Thyestes, the sons of Pelops, quarreled because Thyestes had seduced his brother's wife, and disputed the throne of Argos. Thyestes, defeated and driven out, returned as a suppliant with his children, and Atreus in pretended reconciliation invited him and his children to a feast. There he slaughtered the children of Thyestes (all but one) and served them in a concealing dish to their father, who ate their flesh. When it was made known to him what he had been doing, Thyestes cursed the entire house and fled with his surviving son, Aegisthus. Agamemnon and Menelaus, the sons of Atreus, inherited the Kingdom of Argos, and married, respectively, Clytaemestra and Helen, the daughters of Tyndareus the Spartan. Clytaemestra bore Agamemnon three children—Iphigeneia, Electra, and Orestes. When Paris of Troy seduced Helen and carried her away, the brothers organized a great expedition to win her back. The armament, gathered at Aulis, was held there by wind and weather; Calchas the prophet divined that this was due to the anger of Artemis and, with the pressure of public opinion behind him, forced Agamemnon to sacrifice his daughter, Iphigeneia, in order to appease the goddess. Agamemnon with his forces sailed to Troy and in the tenth year captured it, destroyed the city and its temples, killed or enslaved the people, and set sail for home. On the sea, a great storm struck the fleet, and Agamemnon, with a single galley, made his way back to Argos, the rest of his ships being sunk or driven out of sight and knowledge. With him he brought his mistress, Cassandra, captive princess and prophetess of Troy.

Meanwhile, in Argos, Aegisthus had returned and Clytaemestra had taken him as her lover and sent Orestes out of the country. Warned of the king's approach by signal flares through which he had agreed to notify her of the fall of Troy, she made ready to receive him. She welcomed him into the house, but when he was unarmed in his bath, she pinioned him in a robe and stabbed him to death, and killed Cassandra as well. She defended her action before the people of Argos, who were helpless against Aegisthus and his bodyguard. But Orestes returned at last and was welcomed by his sister Electra, who had remained rebellious against her mother but without power to act. Orestes, disguised as a traveler and pretending to bring news of his own death, won access to the house and killed both Aegisthus and Clytaemestra. Portents and dreams had forewarned of this murder, and Orestes had been encouraged, even commanded, by Apollo to carry it through. Nevertheless, when he had displayed the bodies and defended his act, the Furies (Eumenides), or spirits of retribution, appeared to him and drove him out of Argos. Orestes took refuge with Apollo at Delphi and was at last purified of the murder, but the Furies refused to acknowledge any absolution and pursued him across the world until he took refuge on the rock of Athens before the statue of Athene. There, in the presence of Athene, Apollo and the Furies appealed to her for a decision, and she, thinking the case too difficult to be judged by a single person, even her divine self, appointed a court of Athenian jurors to hear the arguments and judge the case. When the votes of these resulted in a tie, Athene herself cast the deciding ballot in favor of Orestes. Orestes, deeply grateful to Athene and her city, returned to Argos, while Athene found it necessary to propitiate the angry Eumenides by inducing them to accept an honorable place as tutelary spirits in Athens. The law court of the Areiopagus, which had judged the case, was perpetuated as a just tribunal for homicide down through the history of man.

VARIATIONS OF THE LEGEND

Such are the bare facts of the story, the raw stuff out of which Aeschylus forged three massive tragedies. The story of the murder of Agamemnon had been told by Homer in the *Odyssey*[4] and by the cyclic successors of Homer in the *Nostoi* ("Returns"), while the early part of the story appears in the *Cypria*. Stesichorus, the Sicilian poet, had made the fortunes of Orestes the subject of a long narrative in lyric form; and Pindar in his *Eleventh Pythian* had summarized the tale and reflected on the motives of Clytaemestra; and others, too, had touched on the story. On all these Aeschylus doubtless drew, and he had numerous variations from which to pick and choose.[5] The main difference between Aeschylus and Homer is to be found, however, not in details but in the whole approach to the story, which, in turn, motivates se-

---

[4] Piecemeal: the plot is constantly referred to by analogy with the plot of the *Odyssey*. The principal references are: i. 29-43, Zeus calls the vengeance of Orestes an example of just retribution; i. 298-300, Athene uses it as an encouragement to Telemachus; iii. 254-312, Nestor tells Telemachus of the beguiling of Clytaemestra, the wanderings of Menelaus, and the vengeance of Orestes; iv. 514-37, Menelaus tells how he heard from Proteus about the death of Agamemnon; xi. 405-34, the ghost of Agamemnon tells Odysseus how his wife and Aegisthus murdered him and Cassandra.

[5] For example, Homer makes the scene of the murder (and consequently the palace of Agamemnon) Mycenae; Stesichorus and Simonides, Sparta; Pindar, Amyclae (which comes to the same thing); Aeschylus, Argos, doubtless for political reasons. Stesichorus called the nurse of Orestes Laodameia; Pindar, Arsinoë, Aeschylus, Cilissa; etc.

lection, addition, or omission of detail. It is to be noted that Homer does not tell the story consecutively; he really does not tell it at all, but he draws on it for example and illustration. The homecoming of Agamemnon is played against the homecoming of Odysseus; the situations are analogous, but the characters are different and bring different results out of similar materials. The murderous suitors lurk in the house of Odysseus as did Aegisthus in that of Agamemnon, but Penelope has not joined the enemy as Clytaemestra did. Nevertheless, when Odysseus comes home, he has his warning from the ghost of Agamemnon and goes warily so as not to fall into a similar trap. As for Telemachus, the resolute activity of Orestes is set as an example against his own indecision. The parts of the story that bear on such an apposition come out, and the tendency of it varies accordingly. The story is a domestic tragedy, but, since the house is a king's house, the tragedy becomes dynastic also. It begins with the betrayal of a king and the alienation of his kingdom and ends with the rewinning of dynastic power by the rightful heir. Therefore, though the death of Agamemnon is tragic, the deaths of Aegisthus and Clytaemestra are nothing of the sort; no tragedy adheres to Orestes, he merits no compassion, only praise. It is, I think, because of this *approach* that Homer fails to mention certain aspects of the story which are prominent in Attic tragedy. Iphigeneia does not appear; her slaughter would have suggested some motive of justice mixed into the treachery of Clytaemestra. Nor do we hear of the wrongs inflicted by Atreus on Thyestes and his sons, for this would have made the murder of Agamemnon in some measure defensible as an act of retribution. Nowhere in Homer do we hear of an Orestes pursued by the Furies of his mother, whether these might be actual spirits or the remorse in his own memory. Did Homer, then, know nothing of how Orestes murdered Clytaemestra? The lines in which he speaks of her death betray him (*Od.* iii. 304–10), for, while Menelaus was still on his travels,

> Seven years Aegisthus was lord in golden Mycenae,
> but in the eighth the evil came on him when great Orestes
> came back from Athens and killed his father's slayer, the crafty
> Aegisthus, who had murdered his glorious father. And after
> he had killed him, in the Argives' presence he held a funeral
> for his mother, who was hateful, and for the coward Aegisthus.

This unobtrusive notice is all we have, but it makes perfectly plain the fact that the matricide was in Homer's tradition, and he could not contradict it. But he was in a position to place the emphasis wherever he chose and to tell only as much of the story, or as little, as suited his purpose. It is surely no accident that the parts which he leaves out are those which would complicate and confuse his simple picture of Aegisthus as a conspiring villain, Orestes as an avenging hero, and Clytaemestra as a woman who yielded to her weakness.

Aeschylus, on the other hand, told the whole story. *Agamemnon* takes us from the news of Troy's fall to the murder of Agamemnon and the confirmation of his murderers as despots in Argos. *The Libation Bearers* begins with the return of Orestes and ends with his flight from Argos, pursued by the Furies, after the murder of Clytaemestra and Aegisthus. *The Eumenides* finds Orestes seeking sanctuary at Delphi, takes him to Athens for his acquittal and absolution, and ends with the establishment of the Furies in their new home at Athens. Further, particularly in the first play of the trilogy, there are constant cutbacks which sweep into the drama much of the foregoing material: the banquet of Thyestes, the sacrifice of Iphigeneia, the siege and fall of Troy. The simple narrative which we can reconstruct from notices in Homer could not have carried the weight of a tragic trilogy.

A G A M E M N O N

Agamemnon is, first of all, a domestic tragedy. The dominating figure, Clytaemestra, is a wife estranged through the wrong her husband committed on their daughter; love for Iphigeneia, acting through the murder of Agamemnon, is on its way toward driving her to fight her love for her surviving daughter and for her son. Her paramour and partner is her husband's cousin. Behind them all is the figure of Helen, Clytaemestra's sister, wife of Agamemnon's brother, whose treachery caused the Trojan War, Iphigeneia's death, and all the estrangement and broken faith that followed. The theme here is the *philo-aphilos* or hate-in-love; its drive is the dynamic force of contradiction.

Behind the domestic tragedy lies the tragedy of war. For the sake of Helen, whose beauty was unforgettable but whose worth could not be demonstrated by reason or defended by argument, Agamemnon drained Greece of its manhood and involved the innocent in the miseries of a bitter campaign. The Trojans welcomed Helen and her captor and so were guilty; but their punishment—the total destruction of their city, their temples, and their men; the enslavement and defiling of their women and children—was out of all proportion to any harm they had done to Greece. Neither Troy nor Greece deserved what the idea of Helen made Agamemnon do to them. For he destroyed his own country as well as Troy; many died in the years before Ilium, the survivors were drowned or scattered in the great storm on the way back; and the pomp of his entrance thinly disguises the fact that he brought home the crew of a single ship.

[59]

Because of this, with the war tragedy goes political tragedy as well. The means by which this is communicated is through the chorus, who, in so far as they function as characters in the play, represent the solid elders of Argos. These are king's men, since the king in the heroic period stands for lawful authority; they have seen that Agamemnon's expedition was wrong, and they tell him so (799–804), but they would still be loyal to him if he were a much worse man than he is. It is these sturdy citizens who tell how, as the death reports and the urns full of ashes came in from the front, the people at home began to mutter against the king and ask why the war was fought; and, though the chorus cannot take their part, they cannot deny that there is cause for such mutterings. But the people did find a champion, or so they thought, at least a leader, Aegisthus, the king's cousin. He took advantage of the disaffection among those who hated the king he hated, and so returned from exile; he won the throne by winning the queen, confirmed his seizure by contriving the murder of Agamemnon, and defended it with his tyrant's personal bodyguard.[6]

---

[6] The word *tyrannos* ("tyrant") was used by the Greek prose writers in a semi-technical sense, and it only gradually became a term of reproach. The tyrant was a self-appointed despot whose career was characteristic in various places at various times in Greek history, but especially in the seventh and sixth centuries B.C. The Athenian using the word would think at once of his own tyrants, Peisistratus and his son Hippias; the restoration of the latter was still a political issue when Aeschylus was a young man. The following may serve as a general description of the typical early tyrant. He was an aristocrat, but one who was likely not to be in power while the government remained stable. He posed as a representative of the underprivileged and won and used their support, but generally got his position by unconstitutional means. His policy was generally to hold more than royal power without assuming any formal title, through influence and threat. He nevertheless always attempted to found a permanent dynasty through his sons, but hardly ever succeeded. His championship of the poorer classes was generally more than a pose, and he frequently worked toward broadening the base of democracy. Thus his most persistent enemies were not the masses but his fellow-aristocrats, except for the few he could win over into his own personal following; but, because, in spite of all the good he might do, his very existence flouted all legality, those who loved law and liberty hated him too. He had to guard himself, and infallible signs of his presence were the bodyguard of professionals and the spy system. Tyranny was one of the great growing pains in the life of young democracy, and history has been unkind to the tyrant, but for solid reasons.

Tyranny actually came later than Homeric or heroic kingship, and Aeschylus probably knew very well that it was anachronistic to see in Aegisthus' usurpation a tyrant's *coup de main*. Yet he seems to have committed that anachronism. When the chorus hear Agamemnon's death cries and sense murder by the queen and her lover, one of them says (1354-55; see also 1365): "Anyone can see it, by these first steps they have taken, they purpose to be tyrants here upon our city." In speaking of tyranny (*tyrannis*) here, either Aeschylus is using the word strictly, or he is not. He might use "tyrant" loosely, as a synonym for *basileus,* "king" (Euripides does this). But then the statement would have no point whatever, for what could the chorus expect other than that the murderer would make himself king? Plainly, they fear life not only under the wrong

Thus we come about once more to the dynastic tragedy of Homer. But the interpretations of Agamemnon's murder do not exclude one another. Aeschylus can work on several levels at once. The war tragedy and the political tragedy do not contradict, they cohere with and deepen the tragedy of persons.

On the personal level, *Agamemnon* works through a complex of collisions, not so much right against wrong as right against right, each person insisting on his right with the force of passion. Agamemnon, the king, with a king's power and pride in arms, appears briefly and is relatively simple. Pride would have driven him without hesitation to undertake the recovery of Helen, and this decision sets in motion a chain of events which becomes increasingly inescapable. The sacrifice of Iphigeneia, the persistence in besieging Troy, even the intrigue with Cassandra, follow necessarily; his pride grows on its own acts, until just before death he is a swollen vanity. He himself began the series of acts which pile up to overwhelm him, but, looking back, one cannot see where a proud king could have chosen otherwise. Clytaemestra's motives are far more complex. Homer had made her act in simple surrender and consequent betrayal. But Pindar speculated on motives which would, if admitted by Homer, have spoiled the cast of his version:

> Was it Iphigeneia, who at the Euripos crossing
> was slaughtered far from home,
> that vexed her to drive in anger the hand of violence?
> Or was it couching in a strange bed
> by night that broke her will and set her awry—for young wives
> a sin most vile.[7]

Two motives to choose from: Iphigeneia or Aegisthus. But Pindar has already mentioned Cassandra and so implied a third alternative, mother-resentment, guilty love, or jealousy. After Pindar, we could choose A or B or C. Aeschylus ignores the "or" and takes them all. Clytaemestra has loved Agamemnon, Iphigeneia has made her hate him, she loves Aegisthus. But her love for Agamemnon was real, and enough of that love remains to waken

---

ruler but under the wrong kind of government. Historically, the tyrant overthrew a republic (the lawful constitution), but, in the heroic age on which tragedy drew, there was no republic; the lawful constitution was kingship; therefore, the tyrant overthrew this. When Aegisthus at last appears, he has his tyrant's bodyguard. It is impossible not to connect Aegisthus' *coup de main* with the rebellious murmuring of the masses against the king and his war. But the political pattern is a submotif, not fully worked out; its main effect is to shadow the character of Aegisthus—seducer, murderer, usurper already—with the dark memory of the hated historical tyrant.

[7] Pindar *Pyth.* II. 22-25, trans. Lattimore.

perfectly real jealousy at the sight of Agamemnon's lovely captive. This also moves her enormous pride, which amounts to unprecedented ambition for dynastic power. The women of the heroic age are represented as people of character, with will and temper of their own; but if their men insist, they must give way. Force them and they love. Cassandra, Clytaemestra's foil and rival, has seen her city and people wiped out by Agamemnon, her father and brothers butchered by his followers, but she clings to him. So Briseis in the *Iliad* clings to Achilles, who has personally killed her husband, and so Sophocles makes his Tecmessa protest to Aias that she loves him, for she has no one else, since he has destroyed her home.[8] Not so Clytaemestra, who, like Helen her sister, chooses her own loves. Again, the code obviously allowed the warlord, married or unmarried, to have the comforts of a captive mistress on campaign. But if Clytaemestra did not like a code, she would smash it. With her "male strength of heart in its high confidence," she steps boldly from the sphere of women's action into that of men;[9] like a king, she handles the city in her lord's absence, and to her the hostile and suspicious chorus turns with unwilling admiration. When the chorus doubts her intelligence, again when after the murder they openly challenge her, she faces them down and silences them; and it is only on the appearance of Aegisthus, whom they despise as they cannot despise Clytaemestra, that they break out rebelliously again. Even in deceit, as in shameless defiance, she is stately (855–88, 1667). She is the born aristocrat, heiress by birth as by marriage to the power and wealth of kings, and so contemptuous of the *nouveau riche* (1042–46). Everything she does and says is in the grand manner. The chain of beacon fires linking Argos and Troy, defeating distance and time, is a characteristically grand gesture, and worthy of it are the arrogant lines in which she concludes her story of relayed signal flares (315–16):

> By such proof and such symbol I announce to you
> my lord at Troy has sent his messengers to me.

Such is the spirit of her grandiose welcome to Agamemnon, the purple carpet on which he is forced to walk to his butchery, and the words in which such lavish outlay is defended, "the sea is there," with its plain implication that "the sea is ours."

---

[8] The most detailed Attic study of the womanly woman in the heroic age is Euripides' Andromache in the play named after her. It is she who says (213-14): "A wife, even if she is given to a worthless man, should cling to him, not set her will up against his." It is noteworthy that her definitions of a woman's duties occur in debate with her Spartan rival, Hermione, daughter of Menelaus and Helen.

[9] When she refers to herself as "a mere woman," it is with massive sarcasm (348, 590-97, 1661).

Such characteristics give Clytaemestra stature, but in no sense justify her. It is not only that, in asserting her right, or at least determination, to act as freely as a man, she has taken to her bed the "womanish" Aegisthus. The whole house has been wrong since the quarrel of Atreus and Thyestes. Atreus was hideous in murder, but this does not justify Aegisthus in murdering Agamemnon, any more than the sins of Agamemnon justified his murder by Clytaemestra, or the sins of Paris and Helen justified the obliteration of Troy. All the executioners plead that they act for just retribution, but the chain of murder has got out of hand and is perpetuating itself, until it seems no longer to come from personal purpose but has grown into a Curse, a Thing. Every correction is a blood-bath which calls for new correction.

> The truth stands ever beside God's throne
> eternal: he who has wrought shall pay; that is law.
> Then who shall tear the curse from their blood?
> The seed is stiffened to ruin.

Clytaemestra answers, over the corpse of Agamemnon, that she has been bloody but the house is clean. No more evil need be done. Orestes is to make the same claim over the corpse of Clytaemestra herself. Both are mistaken.

The tragedy is no simple matter of right or wrong, of pride and fall, though these enter in. It is a matter of love and hate working simultaneously to force distorted action, and the situation is given depth by cross-characterization. Clytaemestra imagines before the chorus the scene in captured Troy, opening with savage satisfaction in the thought of what is going on and closing with a prayer for peace, that her husband and his men may use their victory temperately, so that no fresh wrong may follow. As she speaks these words, she is herself plotting the fresh wrong she deprecates. There is surface contradiction, but under it lies not only the fact that Clytaemestra is intensely proud of the husband she is about to murder but also the lyric imagination, akin to the diviner's gift, by which the character's mind can transcend time and distance and penetrate to a sphere of objective truth which is beyond the character's own desire and prejudice. When she tells Agamemnon and the public of the torments she went through in his absence at Troy, she is flattering him and misleading all, but by means of truth, not fiction. This is the past, and this is real.

> It is evil and a thing of terror when a wife
> sits in the house forlorn with no man by.

Flattery, confession, reproach combine (through how much longing for the memory-ghost, as with Menelaus for Helen, might Clytaemestra have gone before she took Aegisthus as a lover; or even after?). Agamemnon, on the point of being entangled by flattery and dragged to his death, soberly describes himself as proof against flatterers. In a sense this is irony; it corresponds to his entrance full of the pride of capture on the heels of a warning by the chorus against pride; to the gloomy speculations of the chorus on sackers of cities that presages the return of the herald to tell of Troy's obliteration. But that is mainly a matter of timing; here the point is that Agamemnon's intelligence is partly engaged with the course he does not mean to take. He is proof against illusions except at the one point where they will be fatal to him. When Aegisthus, in the height of his dispute with the challenging chorus (1668), says of Orestes,

> Exiles feed on empty dreams of hope. I know it. I was one,

the jibe turns into a flash of instantly forgotten sympathy. The actors, in particular Clytaemestra and the chorus, do not collide with purely external forces but act always against a part of their own will or sympathy which is committed to the other side, and what they kill is what they love.

The action of the play in itself, of the trilogy as a whole, is thus bound inward upon itself. Its course is not logical, not even strictly dramatic sequence. After the fashion of choral lyric, it is both united to itself and given inward dimension through persistent ideas and a complex of symbols.

IDEA AND SYMBOL

By "idea" I mean motive, theme or subject, or type of situation which is dominant in the dramatic action. By "symbol" I mean a particular thing, usually material, which may be taken to represent the idea. And by a "complex of symbols" I mean a group of such objects which are related to one another in their nature or use.

The exhaustive study of this technique and the detailing of its uses is a proper study for a monograph, not for a segment of the introduction to a translation.[10] I will content myself with illustrating the principle through the symbol-complex of the net.

A central motive in the *Oresteia* is the idea of entanglement: the taming of wild things, the subjugation of the powerful, the involvement of innocent creatures as well. It is expressed in the *curb* forged to subdue Troy (132) or Cassandra (1066); the *bit* that gags Iphigeneia (234); the *yoke* of circum-

---

[10] Miss Barbara Hughes is at present working on such a monograph as a doctoral dissertation.

stance that forces Agamemnon to his crime; the *yoke* of slavery forced on Troy (529), on Cassandra (953, 1071, 1226), on the defiant citizens (1635), even the yoke of teammates (842); the *snare* of the huntsman, in which Agamemnon captures Troy (358, 821) and Cassandra (1048) and in which he is presently captured (1115, 1375, 1611).[11] Curb, yoke, snare—different objects for related purposes—might have been no more than persistent and thematic metaphor, but they have one embodiment which is not metaphorical, and this is the robe or shawl in which Clytaemestra actually entangles Agamemnon in order to strike him down and which is to be displayed on stage as a murder exhibit by Orestes in *The Libation Bearers* (980–84, 997–1004). Clytaemestra anticipates herself when she tells of her dreams and imaginations of terror in Agamemnon's long absence (866–68):

> Had Agamemnon taken all
> the wounds the tale whereof was carried home to me,
> he had been cut full of gashes like a fishing net,

and returns to her imagery in her challenging confession of murder (1382-83):

> as fishermen cast their huge circling nets, I spread
> deadly abundance of rich robes and caught him fast.

This is the idea seen in the thing and the thing embodying the idea, both in metaphor and in action. There are numerous other symbols and other ideas. Symbols are the snake (specially the viper) and the poison of the snake; the archer; the house; the ship; gold. Ideas are (in addition to entanglement) persuasion (flattery); recurrent sickness; hate-in-love; blood and sex; light in the dark; sound (of terror) in the night; dream and memory. The bare lists are not complete, and, in particular, neither symbols nor ideas are exclusive, nor does a given symbol stand toward a given idea in a one-to-one relation. The viper, who turns against his own family, whose mating is murder, stands principally for the idea of hate-in-love and, as such, might be called the prime symbol of the *Oresteia,* but its poison is involved also in the idea of recurrent sickness,[12] and its coils in the idea of entanglement (elsewhere signified by yoke, net, etc., as we have seen). So *The Libation Bearers,* 246–49:

---

[11] The idea of the manhunt appears in the retributive expedition against Troy (127, 695), and in *The Eumenides* it characterizes the Furies' pursuit of Orestes.

[12] The word *palinkotos* might signify a sickness or poisoning which lies hidden in the system, seemingly gone, then *re*curs; or the viper, which *re*-coils upon itself, or those so close to it that they form a part of itself.

Behold
the orphaned children of the eagle-father, now
that he has died entangled in the binding coils
of the deadly viper.

The spider web in which Agamemnon was trapped (1492) is one more
variation of entanglement, spun by another creature who murders in marriage. Entanglement may come by outright force or by seduction and surprise. Clytaemestra lures Agamemnon into it by flattery, persuasion, by her
sex (1116):

Or is the trap the woman there, the murderess?

Cross-binding and coherence of idea in symbol is seen where Agamemnon
recoils (he is soon to surrender) from stepping on the gorgeous robe Clytaemestra has spread at his feet (922–27)

Such state becomes the gods, and none beside.
I am a mortal, a man; I cannot trample down
these tinted splendors without fear thrown in my path.
I tell you, as a man, not god, to reverence me.
Discordant is the murmur at such treading down
of lovely things.

On the level of discourse, the speech is moral. The male rationalism is fighting against the irrational persuasion of the woman, the Greek defends his
code ("as if I were some Asiatic"), the king deprecates the subjects' disapproval; this is colored also by lyric memory. The "treading down of lovely
things" recalls Paris, who "trampled down the delicacy of things inviolable"
(371) and on whom Persuasion also worked (385). Agamemnon, who punished the barbarians, is being turned barbarian in order to be punished. He
is a victim of his wife's flattery and the magnificence of his own possessions.
Lastly, the robe itself on which he walks prefigures the robe in which he is
to be entangled and killed.

Cut anywhere into the play, and you will find such a nexus of intercross-
ing motives and properties. The system gives the play its inner dimension
and strength. An analogous but separable principle dominates the larger
structure.

DRAMATIC STRUCTURE AND LYRIC DIMENSION

As theater, *Agamemnon* and its companion pieces are simple. The scene
of *Agamemnon* is the familiar fixed position before the doors of a house,

which is, as most often in subsequent drama and in the nature of things, a palace. The same setting serves for *The Libation Bearers; The Eumenides* has one of those shifts of scene which are relatively rare in extant Greek tragedy, for we begin before the doors of Phoebus at Delphi and end before the doors of Athene in Athens, but this shift can easily be signified by addition or subtraction of a very few properties.

Characters are used sparingly. Aeschylus has at his disposal the three actors who were by now allotted to each poet or producer; but, far from reveling in this sober allowance, he is most reluctant to use all three at once in speaking action. Cassandra is on stage with Agamemnon and Clytaemestra, but does not speak until the other actors (not counting the chorus or chorus leader) have gone out.[13] Dialogue is, for the most part, just that, a passage between two persons, one of whom may be the chorus leader, at a time, not as in modern drama a complex in which three, four, or a dozen speaking persons participate. There are supernumeraries to be sure, handmaidens attending Clytaemestra and soldiers returning with Agamemnon, the significant bodyguard of Aegisthus; and at the close of *The Eumenides* the stage is quite full of people, and the exodus takes on the dignity of a processional. Agamemnon clearly must enter with Cassandra beside him in a horse-drawn chariot. The unrolling of the robe for Agamemnon's feet is an effective use of showy gesture. Yet, on the whole, the trilogy is physically

---

[13] Clytaemestra, apparently on stage at 83, does not respond to the chorus at that point and remains silent through their stasimon (ode); she speaks only when, 258-63, they address her again. In *The Libation Bearers* Pylades, present almost through the entire play, speaks only three lines (900-902); these have critical force in the action. In *Prometheus,* the titan is silent all through the first scene, where he is being fastened to the rock. We know also that Aeschylus exploited the silent character in many of his lost plays. On the silent characters of Aeschylus, see the scene in the *Frogs* of Aristophanes, where the ghost of Euripides challenges that of Aeschylus in the presence of Dionysus and Hades (911-22):

"EUR.   First of all he would cover a character's face and make him sit on the stage
there,
Achilles, maybe, or Niobe, but never show their features.
They made his tragedy look fine, but didn't mutter a syllable.
"DION.   By god, you know, they didn't at that.
"EUR.   The chorus would pound out long chains
of poetry, four one after another. The character said nothing.
"DION.   You know, I liked them quiet that way. They gave me as much pleasure
as the ones that gabble at us now.
"EUR.   Of course. You were a half-wit
and that's a fact.
"DION.   I know, I know. Tell me then, why did he do it?
"EUR.   To lead you on, and keep the audience in suspense. They were waiting
for Niobe to speak. Meanwhile his play was getting over.
"DION.   The dirty rat! So all that time he was cheating us out of our drama.
(*To Aesch.*) Why are you frowning and looking so cross?
"EUR.   I'm exposing him. He doesn't like it."

unpretentious, relying less on staging and properties than *Prometheus* appears to do. Also, it is physically static; not much physical activity or motion is called for. The use made of materials, of what might appeal to the eye, is measured and temperate.

There is a corresponding simplicity in plot. Considering the length of *Agamemnon,* there are few events that take place, nor are the major events displayed against any variety of subplot. It therefore takes dramatic time for these events to happen. The return of Agamemnon, assured from the watchman's opening speech (25), does not take place until line 782.[14] The only other *event* of the play is his murder, which does not take place until line 1344. Audience and actors occupy the times preceding these events in a growing strain of suspense, which gives the events redoubled impact when at last they do take place. The means by which the anomaly of many lines —little action is solved are the same as the means by which action and motive are deepened. The simplicity is on the surface. As, on its major plane, the action of the tragedy moves deliberately forward, in another dimension lyric memory and forecast take us, by association of ideas rather than in obedience to order in time, deep away into the past, the future, and the elsewhere.

Memory and forecast are a part of imagination, that divining spirit which

---

[14] Much unnecessary ingenuity has been wasted on the problem of "real" time in *Agamemnon.* By means of her beacons, Clytaemestra is understood to learn of Troy's capture just after the event, almost within the hour (320). The return voyage from Troy to Argos is a three or four days' sailing, hardly shortened by the hurricane that wrecked the fleet; and, further, Homer and the other sources on which tragedy drew make it plain that the Achaeans did not pick up and go home the moment Troy fell but understandably took some time getting off. Therefore, the arrival of the herald, followed by Agamemnon, comes days after the first scene of the play. This is true, but creates a problem only for those unduly preoccupied with the Aristotelian unities. "Tragedy tries as far as practicable to fall within the scope of a single day, or exceeds it by only a little" (*Poetics* v. 8). The statement of Aristotle is not made as if he meant to press it very hard. Also it should not be necessary, but apparently is, to point out that Aeschylus had never heard of Aristotle. To Aeschylus, the next thing that happened *in the plot,* after the arrival of the news, was the arrival of the Achaeans. It would have been, to him, as pointless as it would have been ugly to have the chorus solemnly quit the stage and return after the posting of a placard saying "six days later." What he does put in is a long choral lyric in which the choristers muse on the whole train of action (though not in chronological order) from the flight of Helen to the fall of Troy; thus giving in lyric form the illusion that far more time has passed than the real time it has actually taken them to deliver their ode. At l. 475, after the lyric closes, they begin to speak "in character." Their mood has changed; before the ode they were utterly convinced by Clytaemestra's beacons; now they are unconvinced and sarcastic. After the herald's speeches, they inform Clytaemestra that she has been right all along, and she tells them she has done *her* rejoicing *long ago.* By now, we are plainly meant to understand that a lapse of time has occurred, but *not* encouraged to figure out just how much, or how it could have happened.

takes men beyond the limits of what their senses can perceive. He who habitually, and under patronage of a god, so divines is the *mantis* or prophet. The prophet knew "all things that were, the things to come, and the things past" (*Iliad* i. 70); that is, he knew not only past and future, but *present,* what is occurring right now beyond that fragmentary point of space where he stands. Calchas the prophet of the Achaeans is remembered in the first ode, Cassandra the prophetess of Troy appears in person. But, apart from these formal prophets, the chorus assumes divining powers ("still by God's grace there surges within me singing magic": "why this strain unwanted, unrepaid, thus prophetic?"), and the imaginations of Clytaemestra, the herald, Agamemnon, and Aegisthus range far away. Calchas, in the memory of the chorus, goes deep into the past in order to make predictions which will be fulfilled, years away, in the subsequent action of the tragedy. Cassandra, who knows of a past she never witnessed, sees in its light the invisible network of treachery that waits for Agamemnon and her. The swan, who sings in the face of death and is helplessly dedicated to Apollo, is her symbol.

The choristers remember in their entrance chant the departure of the armament ten years ago (40–59), and it makes them see the struggle going on in Troy (60–68). They remember the portents that attended the gathering of the ships, the predictions of Calchas, and the sacrifice of Iphigeneia that was their sequel (104–257). Clytaemestra's living imagination follows the course of her beacon system, itself a device to defeat space and diminish time, as it breaks out from peak to peak on its way to her (281–316), and she sees the Achaeans in captured Troy, now, though far away (320–37). The chorus broods on the moral that Troy fallen conveys, but they think in pictures; of a man secure in wealth kicking over an altar (the audience will remember the golden Persians, their pride, sacrilege, and defeat); of Persuasion as a siren; of false fires and spurious metal gilded; of a greedy innocent child trying to catch a bird—the images, not the propositions, of delusion (367–95). This is Paris, and they fall at once to re-creating in imagination the flight of Helen (403–8). And there were *prophets* there, to be sure, who imagined the loneliness to follow for Menelaus with an empty bed and empty-eyed images of his wife, whose loveliness eluded him in dreams (408–26). But dream image is memory image, and there are others who remember too. The families of the common soldiers see brought back to them the ashes of their dead, transubstantiated by the money-changer, who is the god of war. They murmur against the king; their muttering is inarticulate and not clearly heard in high places but may be the symptom of a storm that waits for the returning king (427–74). *Te deum laudamus* has been transformed into foreboding, not through logical succession of ground and consequent but through a lyric succession of images whose forms melt into one another. Agamemnon's herald remembers the campaigning before Troy (551–81). At first, it is the dirty and brutal details of war-business that come out of the mist, but the sense of achievement infects him with Agamemnon's fatal pride, so that at the end the wings of his imagination take him out of the past across the present and far into the future and the days when the capture of Troy will be an antique glory of Argos. He is shaken out of this mood, however, by the questioning of the chorus leader, who wants to know what happened to the rest of the army and to Menelaus. He tells of the storm (650–70) in terms that make living things out of fire, wind, water, and rocks, and shows the wide seascape on which at dawn lay the wreckage of the Achaean fleet, torn flowers on the water.

The chorus, far now from the momentary exaltation they felt at news of the victory, now chant in terms of disaster: the sinister name of Helen, with the imagination once again of her flight to Troy (681–98); the lion's cub, the pet turned murderous (716–36), who is fatal Helen beguiling the Trojans (737–49). We remember Iphigeneia when Helen's eyes, like Iphigeneia's, sweep the beholder with soft arrows, and the victorious and guileful charmer recalls the innocent charmer who failed. The moralities which follow to prelude Agamemnon's entrance, the terms in which he is greeted, work again through images: houses gilded to hide dust, false coin, the smile of the charmer. Action follows in the public encounter of Clytaemestra and Agamemnon, but the wife's welcome brings back out of the past the fears that attended her during the years of separation (858–94). When he has gone into the house, the chorus turn uneasily from memory to forecast, and their gloom is abetted by Cassandra, who has vision on vision of the past, of the present (the intention behind Clytaemestra's face and words, the scene preparing behind closed doors), and the far future on the day when the avengers shall punish for the crime not yet committed (1069–1330). The death cry tells the chorus only what they already know. We do not see the murder take place, but we are told what happened (1381–92). In the scene that follows, where Clytaemestra faces the people, neither side can escape the memory of the hideous past which has forced these things to happen. Aegisthus' defense is a recounting of the crime of Atreus (1583–1611). At the end, Clytaemestra speaks as if all were over, but we know it is not, that the future holds more violence and it is the past which has made this so.

LYRIC TRAGEDY

The brief dramatic time of the play is a point of convergence for actions that come from deep in the past and project far into the future. The limited stage is a pivotal point from which we can be transported far away. The tragedy of Agamemnon, Cassandra, and Clytaemestra is involved with and opens into the tragedy of the children of Thyestes, of Iphigeneia, of Troy and all the Achaean army; and its action, in return, is partly dictated by the figures never enacted, remote but always present in memory, of Atreus, Iphigeneia, Paris, and Helen.[15]

This is the form of lyric tragedy, perfected here and never since so completely realized. Its manner is due partly to the historical accident in which two forms of fiction were combined: drama, still relatively primitive and naïve, with choral lyric, now, after generations of mature practice, brought to its highest point of development by Simonides and Pindar. But the direction taken by this form is due also to deliberate choice. The desire is to transcend the limitations of dramatic presentation, even before these limitations have been firmly established. The spirit is that of Shakespeare's chorus in *Henry V*:

> But pardon, gentles all,
> The flat unraised spirits that have dared
> On this unworthy scaffold to bring forth
> So great an object: can this cockpit hold
> The vasty fields of France? Or may we cram
> Within this wooden O the very casques
> That did affright the air at Agincourt?

It is true that Shakespeare intends to take us to the actual field of Agincourt, but principally he is aware of the impossibility of *staging* expeditions and battles adequately, and the appeal is to the imagination of the audience:

> For 'tis your thoughts that now must deck our kings,
> Carry them here and there; jumping o'er times,
> Turning the accomplishment of many years
> Into an hour-glass.

> Thus with imagined wing our swift scene flies
> In motion of no less celerity
> Than that of thought.

---

[15] We may compare *The Persians*. The cast of actors consists only of Darius, his queen, Xerxes, messenger, and chorus. The visible scene in Persia is static. But the scene of the action which the play is *about* is Salamis, and then all the water and land between; the persons of this action are all the vast army of the Persians, and all the Greeks. *The Persians* is the great messenger-play.

Shakespeare and Aeschylus alike forecast combinations which only the motion picture can realize visually—flashback, imaginary scene, pictorial dramatization of history, and messenger's account. Shakespeare's concern in this particular play with the fragmentary nature of staged action gives his chorus a brilliant part, but it is only a ghost of Aeschylus, for in Aeschylus the past and the elsewhere dominate present action.

But the direction in which he steered tragedy was not generally followed. Sophoclean drama prevailed, since Euripides, under protest, framed tragedy in accordance with Sophocles, not Aeschylus. Sophocles turned tragedy inward upon the principal actors, and drama becomes drama of character. His plays may open with public scenes, but, as they progress, the interest focuses hard on the hero. *Oedipus Tyrannus* begins with the plague in Thebes, but its ending is all Oedipus, and Thebes is as good as forgotten. It is true that the dead hand reaches out of the past to strike down Oedipus, Antigone, Aias, Heracles. But this is their tragedy, and theirs alone. *Agamemnon* is a play about the Trojan War, but *Antigone* is not a play about the Theban War, though that lies in the background. In Sophocles, the choruses are commentaries on the action, not part of the larger action, and their imagery is functional to the choruses themselves but not to the tragedy as a whole. Trilogy gives way to single drama. The enormous background becomes mainly irrelevant and is screened out. Lyric tragedy gives way to actor's tragedy.

Agamemnon is, in fact, the culmination of lyric tragedy, because the action narrows in *The Libation Bearers,* and when in *The Eumenides* it opens out again, it is with a new kind of meaning and composition.

THE LIBATION BEARERS

The second play of the trilogy takes place some years after the close of *Agamemnon.* The usurpers have grown secure in power. Orestes, sequestered in Phocis, is now a young man, and his sister Electra, resentful and bitter, awaits his return. The opening event is simple recognition, the identification of Orestes and the confirmation of the fact that, as Electra and the chorus hope, he means to avenge his father and regain his throne. Recognition is thus at once transformed into conspiracy. The children, with their faithful chorus, gather at Agamemnon's tomb, where Electra has gone on her mother's behalf, but without sympathy for her, to propitiate the dead king by reason of terrifying dreams which had shaken Clytaemestra in the night. The dead king is now a hero; his arrogance and his mistakes have been annulled by death, and his grave is a center of power. Therefore, the children with the chorus turn to him, invoke his ghost to anger against his murderers, with twofold driving intention: to enchant actual power out of the spirit and the grave and to incite themselves and arm themselves with the anger that will make them do what they must do. They then plot the means for assassination. Orestes poses as a traveling merchant who brings news of the death of Orestes; Clytaemestra, with archaic and stately courtesy, invites him in and sends for Aegisthus. As the messenger who is sent to summon him (she happens to be the slave who nursed Orestes when he was little) goes out on her errand, she encounters the chorus, who tell her not to suggest that Aegisthus should bring his bodyguard. Orestes and Pylades kill the king, and Clytaemestra stands at their mercy. She dares Orestes to kill her, and he stands irresolute until a word from Pylades solidifies his will. The bodies are brought out and displayed, with the robe in which Agamemnon had been entrapped, and Orestes declares publicly, as Clytaemestra had done, that this act is his own and that it is justice. But his wits are going, he sees the Furies, the avenging spirits of his mother (no one else can see them), and leaves in flight. This time, even before the play is over, the assassin knows that his act was not final but has created more suffering yet to come.

Once again the plot is simple, and the dramatic actions are few. Once again, despite these facts, the texture is saved from thinness, but the factors are different from those that give *Agamemnon* its coherence. First, this is a far shorter play. Second, the emphasis and direction have changed. We have, in a sense, more plot; there is intrigue, a practical problem. In *Agamemnon* the king's murder is felt by the witnessing chorus in their bones; it happens, is mourned, and defended. The problems of Clytaemestra, *whether* she can kill the husband she has loved and *how* she will do it, are implicit, but we are not present while she is solving them. But in *The Libation Bearers,* we are present at the deliberations of Orestes as he decides whether he can kill his mother, and how the assassination is to be effected. In recognition, decision, conspiracy, and climactic action we have, in fact, the mechanism, in naïve or even crude form, of that drama of revenge or play of successful action which we found in the Homeric story.

But *The Libation Bearers* is only superficially a drama of intrigue, and, in so far as it is one, it is hardly a significant specimen of its kind. The mechanism of the assassin's plot is simple, as the mechanism of recognition and identification is primitive. The emphasis lies on the mood in which the characters act.

For this is not a simple revenge play in which the young hero, long lost, returns to his sister and his kingdom to strike down the murderous and usurping villains. Orestes hardly gets a sight of his kingship before he must leave, haunted, driven, and alone. It is not until much later, near the close of *The Eumenides,* that he can speak as a king with subjects. Also, here the

emotions of Orestes and Electra are, like those of Clytaemestra, half-com-
mitted to the side against which they act; and Clytaemestra, in turn, loves
the son whom she fears, who kills her, and whom she would kill if she
could. It is the *philos-aphilos* still, or love-in-hate, the murder committed not
against an external enemy but against a part of the self.[16] The hate gains
intensity from the strength of the original love when that love has been
stopped or rejected. Electra ("the unmarried") has love to lavish, but her
mother has turned it aside. The chorus, like the captive women they are,
cling to the memory of Agamemnon, who enslaved them. Orestes, together
with the sense of outrage over the loss of his rightful inheritance (the
dynastic motive), nurses a deep sense of jealousy against his mother for
having sacrificed not only Agamemnon but *Orestes* to her love for Aegisthus.
The children were the price for which she bought herself this man (132–34).
It is the venom of such jealousy that spills out in the bitterly salacious
mockery of the dead lovers, and jealousy on his father's behalf and his own
is the theme of his last sharp dispute with his mother. Clytaemestra, when
she hears the false news of her son's death, is in a temper where relief and
sorrow cross, though relief wins. Her very dream of bearing and nursing
the snake (symbol of ingratitude), who fixes his poisonous fangs in her
breast, enacts terror through a gesture of love. Aegisthus, at the word that
Orestes is dead, goes soberly back to the image of the poison and the snake:

> For our house, already bitten
> and poisoned, to take this new load upon itself
> would be a thing of dripping fear and blood.

The chorus consider that both the tyrants are hypocrites, but even such
hypocrites know what they are doing, and to whom.

This mood of tangled motivation means that the conspirators must work
strongly upon themselves before they can act. Between the recognition and
the resolve to act comes a scene of incantation. Sister, brother, and chorus
turn to invoke dead Agamemnon. They implore his blessings and aid, they
set forth their grievances and his, they challenge and taunt him to action:

ORESTES   Think of that bath, father, where you were stripped of life.
ELECTRA   Think of the casting-net that they contrived for you.
ORESTES   They caught you like a beast in toils no bronzesmith made.

---

[16] So *Hamlet* is transformed from the vigorous revenge-intrigue drama it might
have been into the tragedy it is, because Hamlet is emotionally involved with the queen
and Ophelia, who are on the side of the enemy. Even the arch-enemy is close in blood
and perhaps once admired.

ELECTRA Rather, hid you in shrouds that were thought out in shame.
ORESTES Will you not waken, father, to these challenges?
ELECTRA Will you not rear upright that best beloved head?

But, while they are invoking a power and a tradition whose force is felt but only dimly believed, they are also lashing themselves into the fury of self-pity that will make them do what they have to do. So the theme of lyric prophecy which was at work in *Agamemnon* is altered here. There is dealing in both cases with what lies beyond the powers of perception, but there it was lyric memory and vision on the part of those who were to witness, and to suffer from, the ugly act; here those who are themselves about to commit the ugly act manipulate the unseen, in a mood more of witchcraft than of prophecy.

For this reason and because the drama focuses on the will to act, *The Libation Bearers* ties back to *Agamemnon,* but *Agamemnon* ties back to the whole world of action latent behind the beginning of the tragedy. The symbols of the earlier play are caught up and intensified, particularly viper and net. But the emphasis is changed, because we see things from the point of view of the murderers. In *Agamemnon,* vice was alluring, wearing all the captivating graces of Helen and her attendant symbols; in *The Libation Bearers,* duty becomes repulsive. Both tragedies are carried on a strong underdrift of sex, but in the second play the sex impulse, though it works, has lost its charm. Orestes at the end has done a brutal, necessary job.

Like Clytaemestra at the close of *Agamemnon,* Orestes defends his position in terms of: "I have cleared my house. It was bloody, but necessary. Now we can have peace." As for Clytaemestra, his claim is no better than a desperate challenge flung at circumstances. The blood-bath was no cleaning-out, and it means more blood. Clytaemestra had to reckon with resentment in the state and the younger generation to come. The enlightenment of Orestes, the defeat of his hollow optimism, comes without delay. "The house has been rid of snakes": and at once, on the heads of his mother's Furies, more snakes appear.

THE EUMENIDES (THE FURIES)

As we have seen (see above, p. 57), the last act of the trilogy finds Orestes cleared by Apollo but still pursued by the Furies. Is he clear, or not? Plainly, one divine decision has clashed with another decision which is also unquestionably divine. The fate of Orestes is referred to Athens and to a third divinity, Athene, who, reserving for herself the casting ballot, refers it to a jury of mortal men. When their vote is even and Athene has cast her deciding vote in his favor, the Furies must be propitiated by a new cult, as a new kind of goddess, in Athens. It is this episode that closes the play and the trilogy of the House of Atreus. The chorus has returned to its archaic part as chief character in the drama.

Who are the Furies, and what do they mean? And, since they stand up and identify themselves and protest their rights in the face of Apollo and Athene, we must also ask, What do these better-known Olympians represent for the purposes of Aeschylus?

As seen in the grand perspective, Agamemnon was only an unwilling agent in a chain of action far bigger than the fortunes of a single man. From the seduction of Atreus' wife, the murder of the children of Atreus, the sacrifice of Iphigeneia and the youth of Hellas, claim and counterclaim have been fiercely sustained, each act of blood has been avenged in a new act of blood. The problems of public good have been solved through private murder, which is no solution, until the situation has become intolerable to the forces that rule the world, and these must intervene to see that the contestants and the impulses in nature which drive the contestants become reconciled and find their places in a scheme that will be harmonious and progressive, not purely destructive.

Behind the personal motivations in the two first dramas of the trilogy, we can, if we choose, discern a conflict of related forces: of the younger against the elder generation; of male against female; of Greek against barbarian. As the gods step out of the darkness, where, before they could be reached only in fitful visions of the prophetic mind, and take their place on the stage, they personify these general forces, and, because they are divine and somewhat abstract, they can carry still further dimensions of meaning. The Furies are older than Apollo and Athene, and, being older, they are childish and barbarous; attached to Clytaemestra as mother, they are themselves female and represent the woman's claim to act which Clytaemestra has sustained from the beginning; in a Greek world they stand for the childhood of the race before it won Hellenic culture, the barbarian phase of pre-Hellenism, the dark of the race and of the world; they have archaic uprightness and strictness in action, with its attendant cruelty; they insist on the fact against the idea; they ignore the justifications of Orestes, for the blood on his hands means far more than the reasons why the blood is there. Apollo stands for everything which the Furies are not: Hellenism, civilization, intellect, and enlightenment. He is male and young. He despises cruelty for the fun of cruelty, and the thirst for blood, but he is as ruthless as the Furies. The commonwealth of the gods—therefore the universe—is in a convulsion of growth; the young Olympians are fighting down their own barbaric past.

[76]

But they must not fight it out of existence. In the impasse, Apollo uses every threat of arrogant force, but Athene, whose nature reconciles female with male, has a wisdom deeper than the intelligence of Apollo. She clears Orestes but concedes to the detested Furies what they had not known they wanted, a place in the affections of a civilized community of men, as well as in the divine hierarchy. There, gracious and transformed though they are, their place in the world is still made potent by the unchanged base of their character. The new city cannot progress by exterminating its old order of life; it must absorb and use it. Man cannot obliterate, and should not repress, the unintelligible emotions. Or again, in different terms, man's nature being what it is and Fury being a part of it, Justice must go armed with Terror before it can work.

Thus, through the dilemma of Orestes and its solution, the drama of the House of Atreus has been transformed into a grand parable of progress. Persuasion (flattery), the deadly magic of the earlier plays, has been turned to good by Athene as she wins the Furies to accept of their own free will a new and better place in the world. By the time Orestes leaves the stage, he has become an issue, a Dred Scott or Dreyfus, more important for what he means than for what he is; and, when he goes, the last human personality is gone, and with it vanish the bloody entanglements of the House of Atreus, as the anonymous citizens of Athens escort their protecting divinities into the beginning of a new world.

It is appropriate, and characteristic of Aeschylus, that this final parable, with its tremendous burden of thought, should be enacted on the frame of a naïve dramatic structure, where the basis of decision on matricide is as crude as the base of Portia's decision against Shylock. The magnificence of *The Eumenides* is different from that of *Agamemnon*. The imagery—the lyric imagination in memory and magic—is gone, because we are not now merely to see but to understand. The final act comes down into the present day and seals within itself the wisdom, neither reactionary nor revolutionary, of a great man. But in its own terms *The Eumenides* is the necessary conclusion of a trilogy whose special greatness lies in the fact that it transcends the limitations of dramatic enactment on a scale never achieved before or since.

S O P H O C L E S

[*496–406* B.C.]

THIS ESSAY IS DRAWN FROM KITTO'S *Greek Tragedy,* THE MOST IMPORTANT
modern critical study of the subject. The intensive study of Greek tragedy
involves so much philological, religious, and historical erudition that it is
perhaps no surprise that there are so few studies like this one, which treat
the ancient dramas as formally organized works of art. Professor Kitto reminds us that although the didactic element is strong in Greek tragedy, as
in all classical literature, the tragedians were artists, not pedagogues. As
syntax, style, and metaphor realize meaning, so does individual narrative or
dramatic structure. Professor Kitto's attention to the structure of each play
in Greek tragedy establishes the relation of the underlying tragic idea of
the single work to its own form and style.

H. D. F. Kitto is Professor of Greek at Bristol University. He is not only
a scholar and teacher of Greek literature, but has also directed modern
productions of Greek plays.

From *Greek Tragedy* by H. D. F. Kitto, published by Methuen & Co. Ltd., London,
1939, and Barnes & Noble Inc., New York.

[78]

H . D . F . K I T T O

Middle Tragedy: Sophocles

INTRODUCTION

AESCHYLUS IS A PROFOUND RELIGIOUS DRAMATIST, EURIPIDES A BRILLIANT, uneven representative of the new spirit which was so uncomfortable in the old forms, and Sophocles was an artist. We all know what an artist is: he is one who makes things which are beautiful or at least pretty, and if he is an artist of the right kind what he makes is good for us. Our public thinks like this, and so did the Greeks—with more excuse. Critics of the last century never ceased thanking Heaven that Sophocles believed in the Gods—their profound satisfaction lives on in the writings of examinees—and, assured that Sophocles was an artist of the right kind, they turned to the grateful and interesting task of examining and admiring his astonishing technique.

But an air of conventionality could be felt. Aeschylus has his religion, Euripides his views and his very tragic single-scenes; what was there to say about Sophocles except that his religion and politics were admirable and his art perfect? One concentrated on the art; indeed, when the *Electra* was mentioned one had to. The "happy ending" of this play and its avoidance of moral strife were a little puzzling. The poet who also wrote the *Antigone* has been accused of a certain complacency, of a bluntness of moral perception, and the *Electra* has been explained by the assumption that Sophocles

[79]

retired into the Homeric age to write it. It was said that Sophocles interested himself chiefly in the persons who did these things; he took the events for granted and studied the characters of the actors in them—as if one could study character in a moral vacuum.

This simple view of the artist brought other difficulties, and in spite of the close attention which Sophocles has received during the last twenty years some of them remain. The most troublesome, oddly enough, are structural. When Euripides fails to perform what is evidently the artist's first duty, to turn out a shapely play, we are not surprised; we may invent a series of special explanations, a different one for each offending play, or take refuge in a general theory of incompatibility or ineptitude, but we are not surprised. When Sophocles does the same thing we are perturbed; he did know better; yet the *Ajax* and the *Trachiniae* fall into two parts almost as badly as the *Andromache* and the *Hecuba,* and the end of the *Antigone* has been accused of throwing the play out of balance. Sophocles does not indeed descend to unrelated scenes, nor does he combine two distinct legends into one unsatisfactory plot, but the structure of the *Ajax* and the *Trachiniae,* since the plays were made by Sophocles, is at least as puzzling as that of the *Suppliant Women, Hecuba* or *Andromache,* which can plead the magic excuse "Euripides."

One way out of the difficulty was to say as little as possible about the *Antigone,* to think of special excuses for the *Ajax,* and to write off the *Trachiniae* as a total loss. Such criticism fails in all respects; especially does it fail to explain why the dichotomy is so unnecessarily absolute in the *Trachiniae.* A modern method is to call unsatisfactory plots diptychs or triptychs (which makes them sound better at once), and to suppose that there was a period in Sophocles' artistic career in which he thought that this was a reasonable, apparently the only reasonable, way of making drama. It is assumed that the *Trachiniae* belongs to the *Ajax-Antigone* period, *circa* 440, not to *circa* 420 as used to be thought, and the new date is supported, vainly, by stylo-statistical evidence.

The explanation that will be attempted here is that Sophocles, because he was a great artist, had something more important to do even than to make beautiful plays, namely to express as directly as his medium allowed certain tragic ideas which sprang out of a certain apprehension about human life. If he was only a technician with a bias towards beauty some of the "faults" are quite inexplicable. Being a great dramatic artist he must, like Aeschylus, have had a tragic way of thinking; from this his drama sprang, to express this his plays were shaped. When a critic can improve a play of Sophocles', he may be sure that he is only giving it a turn that Sophocles had already rejected. If then we can penetrate, however dimly, to this bed-rock of the dramatist's thought, we may hope to understand the plays more intimately.

We may hope for more. Aristotle says in his bald way: "Sophocles introduced the third actor and scene-painting." What explains the plays should explain too why Sophocles imposed on Greek Tragedy the form he did; questions of form and technique are fully resolved only when fully related to the mind of the artist who makes and uses them. What we should like to relate is Sophocles' introduction of the third actor, his interest in character and skill in drawing it, his marked leaning to irony in language and plot, his curtailment of the part of the Chorus, his typical tragic hero and plot— every element of his homogeneous art.

Before attempting this we may remove two obstacles. The first is to Sophoclean criticism what Aeschylus' religion is to Aeschylean; Sophocles' character-drawing is so important that it is often taken (not perhaps consciously, but in effect) to be the determinant thing. Thus one critic writes, in a blithe moment, "He even alters and manipulates the mythic material so that he may the more readily and brilliantly practise his hobby." This does indeed fall short of blasphemy, but it overlooks the essential difference between Sophocles and Dickens. It has been argued that the three Creons are portraits of the same character—which may be true. But it is not true that "it is hardly conceivable that so great an artist . . . primarily interested in the study and delineation of character, could have failed to see or could consciously have ignored the need for consistency in character." There is no such need: Sophocles was not creating a portrait-gallery. The only need is that each play should present as vividly as possible the tragic idea that lies behind it.

The other stumbling-block is the fact that most Greek theory of art is moral. The Greek theory of art is nothing to us, who are concerned exclusively with the Greek practice of art. There are as many possible theories of art as there are ways of regarding art; the Greeks regarded it from the moral point of view not because the Greek artist thought in a different way from any other but because their thought was predominantly political, and art, like drainage, undoubtedly performs some function in the state. Sophocles was no doubt aware that his plays were good for Athens (though the passage in the *Apology* suggests that he could not prove this to Socrates); he may have tried to make them such. But no amount of morals will make a good play, and no moral analysis will explain a play.

In this chapter we shall examine the content and structure of the *Ajax, Antigone, Electra* and *Tyrannus*. The *Philoctetes* and *Trachiniae*, for reasons which will appear later, we class as New Tragedy, and the *Coloneus* demands separate treatment.

H. D. F. KITTO

THE AJAX

It seems highly probable, though it is not certain nor even universally agreed, that the *Ajax* is Sophocles' earliest extant play, but at least fifteen and very likely twenty-five years separate it from his first victory. We are not therefore dealing with the work of a novice. The critical difficulty is that though Ajax kills himself at v. 865 the play goes on for another 550 verses, verses which are full of brilliant and hard wrangling about his burial, but which are not obviously a necessary continuation of the story. For a representative opinion of the play we might quote Dalmeyda: "Avec Ajax disparait l'interêt principal du drama, qui consistait surtout dans la peinture des émotions diverses d'une âme héroïque, confiante dans sa valeur jusqu'à l'excès, jusqu'à l'orgueil impie. Dans la seconde partie de la pièce Teucre prend la place de son frère." Or Bowra: "When he becomes sane he knows that he has lost his honour and therefore he kills himself. Our sympathies lie with Ajax, but true to the traditional outlook Sophocles makes it clear at the outset that the hero is guilty of presumption against the gods and is punished for it."

That is to say, it is the normal sort of tragedy of character, the tragedy of Ajax and his hybris, but for some reason a disproportionate amount of attention is devoted to the hero's burial.

But this is extremely odd, especially when one reflects that mastery of form was peculiarly Sophocles' gift. A scholiast (on v. 1123) can remark "Wishing to extend the drama he became frigid and dissipated the tragic emotion." The conclusion may be sound, but the reason given, "wishing to extend the play," is silly. Sophocles was not a dolt, and if he had only wished to extend the play he would have done it at the other end. There was no difficulty in making a play about Ajax. Sophocles could have begun with Ajax brooding over his wrongs, coming to his resolve, making his attack (messenger-speech), passing from exultation to despair, killing himself, and being allowed burial through the efforts of Teucer and the generosity of Odysseus. This would have made a unity, and would have served all the purposes which have been alleged in explanation of the plot as we have it. If this plot had been used before, exactly five minutes' reflection would produce another capable of showing Ajax as the victim of his own hybris without defying the elementary laws of construction.

We are reminded that the Greeks attached great importance to funeral rites. They did, but there was no need to spoil a play with them, and in fact the point would be better emphasized if it were an integral part of the whole. The importance of burial did but make Sophocles' "mistake" possible.

[82]

We need spend no time on the stock fantasies that the older critics used when in difficulties—such as that Iophon composed the second part; nor on the theory that Sophocles was interested in an Ajax-cult, for there is no suggestion of this in the play, and if it were in some sense a *pièce d'occasion,* why was it not made a better *pièce?* It is not true to say that the second part, like the second part of Julius Caesar, shows the greatness of Ajax. Caesar's spirit lives on, a giant among pygmies; Ajax is scorned by the Atreidae and not even defended by Odysseus. It is just as idle to talk of the "rehabilitation" of Ajax: Teucer is a match for the Atreidae in vituperation, not in argument. There is no attempt to palliate the crime of attempted treason and murder; even Odysseus' generosity stops short of that. Ajax was a hero, and he had done valiantly, but (as Agamemnon points out) he owes his burial to the enlightened self-interest of Odysseus. In fact, Sophocles is at pains to show that Ajax is buried because he is dead.

In the excuse that Greek plays preferred to end quietly there are points of interest. Since the difference is so wide between ending quietly and ending with two acts quite separate from the first three, the excuse is invalid; but how far is the general proposition true? The *Supplices, P.V., Agamemnon* and *Choephori* do not end quietly, but they are not independent plays. The *Eumenides* ends in peace, but the ending is the climax of the whole trilogy. The *Electra* ends on a climax which is not quiet, and the *Medea, Troades, Hecuba, Heracleidae* end with a most evident dramatic thrill, while all the quasi-melodramatic plays carefully pile up the excitement to the final tableau. This is not ending quietly. It is impossible to predicate any one thing of plays that vary so much in kind; all that we can say is that Greek taste preferred a play to follow its own logic. The lyrical ending of the *Septem* is not "quiet"; it is simply right; the same can be said of the *Tyrannus* and the *Antigone.*

None of these pleas helps the *Ajax* at all. We may agree with the scholiast that Sophocles made a gross error, but even then we are bound to try to find a more convincing explanation of the error than the one he thought of.

We must weigh the character of Ajax, not selecting from Sophocles' facts, but using all of them. It is of course impossible to transcribe these with the same colour and emphasis that Sophocles gives to them,[1] but it is fair to say that Ajax has virtually committed an atrocious and silly crime, which, when he emerges from his madness and despair, causes him no shame, only regret that he was thwarted. His vanity is extreme, and allows him to see no possible reason for Odysseus' success in the contest except dishonesty. Time

---

[1] A fact that Verrallians might remember when, having boiled down and fore-shortened a plot, they triumphantly ask, "Can anything be more absurd?"

after time Ajax refers to Odysseus, and he is always wrong. His sailors, although they are the chorus, are wrong too. The chorus is a dramatic one; and we have the advantage of seeing Odysseus for ourselves. This vanity is reinforced by the description (762–77) of Ajax' astonishing insolence to Athena; entirely consonant with it is his indifference to the danger of his men and of Tecmessa. But besides all this we have the soldierly greatness of Ajax and his spiritual daring; this, and the poetry which Sophocles entrusts to him, convince us that in spite of all he is a great man, but one completely lacking in *phronesis,* wisdom intellectual and moral. It is a bold but hardly a subtle character.

If we have any reason for confidence in Sophocles as a dramatist we must approach his structure not with preconceived ideas and excuses, but with a completely open mind. The structure differs from the conventional plot outlined above in its beginning and its end. It does not begin with Ajax brooding, or with Tecmessa lamenting, but with Odysseus. Why Odysseus? The play ends too with Odysseus, who, without trying to justify Ajax, does secure his burial. Why Odysseus? And if Odysseus, the clever speaker, why is he not made to "rehabilitate" Ajax? Let us look at him more closely.

In the prologue the most striking thing, even more striking than the appearance of Ajax mad, is Odysseus' attitude to him. Athena has so directed Ajax' thoughts as to bring out his especial hatred of Odysseus, but Odysseus' reply to her boasting, or tempting, shows such moral greatness and insight that it must seem to every reader the most significant thing that has yet happened:

ATHENA Seest thou, Odysseus, the power of the gods, how great it is? What man couldst thou have found more vigilant than he, better and more timely in action?

ODYSSEUS I know of none. Still, I pity him, enemy though he is, for he is yoked to an evil fate[2]—thinking of myself no less than of him: for I see that all of us mortals are nothing but shadows and insubstantial smoke.

Odysseus is represented as the preeminent enemy of Ajax; by this speech too we see him to be no ordinary man; by frequent references he is kept prominently before our notice, and nearly every reference shows that Ajax either cannot or will not understand him. At the close Odysseus appears, to win over Agamemnon. He secures burial for Ajax not because he prevails in argument but because Agamemnon is willing to grant an unusual favour to the great Odysseus (vv. 1370–4). So far as the official view goes, Ajax is still an outcast.

[2] *Atê:* "une fatalité mauvaise" (Masqueray); "infatuation."

In this last scene Odysseus shows the same characteristics as in the first; the same pity, the same insight. Pitying Ajax because of his evil fate he urges his burial "thinking of my own interests as much as his, for I too shall come to this." He admits freely that he is working for himself; he is, as the Chorus says, "sound in judgment." As in the prologue he shows prudence rather than romantic courage, so here he shows no altruism, no romantic generosity, but rather the large wisdom of a philosophic mind. As in the beginning he rose superior to Athena's temptations, so at the end he rises superior to the common morality of the Atreidae and gives burial honours to a dead foe and condemned criminal.

Odysseus therefore is no mere dramatic convenience: he does not merely give the play an external symmetry by appearing at the beginning and the end; he is, if not as prominent as the hero Ajax, at least as essential to the play, much more essential than Teucer. The unifying theme is the antagonism of Ajax and Odysseus, of physical, and, we may admit, of spiritual daring against intellectual greatness; an antagonism the more dramatic in that Ajax never understands Odysseus whereas Odysseus always understands Ajax. Ajax, lacking "wisdom," brings himself to ruin: Odysseus, rich in wisdom, not only is successful (as in the matter of the Arms), but also attains moral grandeur.

"Not the thick-set or broad of back are surest, but the wise prevail, everywhere."

So Agamemnon says, more profoundly than he suspects.

The scenes of wrangling now fall into line. There is here a complication followed by a denouement. Teucer and the Atreidae come to an *impasse*. We feel that Ajax is too great a man to be dishonoured in death; the Atreidae are too narrow to see this, and Teucer can only defy them, not rise above them. In these men there is no resolution of the antagonism; that comes only when the greatness of Odysseus recognizes the greatness of the defeated Ajax and above all the greatness of the fact of Death. The end is rather the triumph of Odysseus than the rehabilitation of Ajax. In the prologue he triumphs over Athena's suggestions of crude force and resentment: by the vote of the army his intellectual greatness has already overcome Ajax' soldierly greatness; now he brings the drama to a harmonious close by overcoming the moral violence of the Atreidae.

I do not suggest that this interpretation makes of the *Ajax* a perfect play, by Sophoclean standards of perfection. In many ways, notably in subtle control of dramatic rhythm, it falls short of what Sophocles was to do later; only in its poetry can it challenge comparison with anything. But this view does make of it a reasonable play, and the key-stone, the importance of

[85]

Odysseus, would be much more obvious in performance than it is in the reading. Moreover we shall see, I think, that the philosophic background is entirely consistent with that of Sophocles' other work in his middle period.

THE ANTIGONE

The *Antigone* is accused, though more gently, of the same fault as the *Ajax:* the heroine drops out half-way through and leaves us to do our best with Creon, Haemon, and their fortunes.[3]

We must recognize that if there is a fault it is a radical one, due to deliberate choice and not to oversight or to the inability of Sophocles to cope with a difficult situation. It is inevitable that Antigone should disappear, but it is not inevitable that so little should be said in the Exodus about her, that her lover's corpse but not hers is brought back, that Creon should at such length lament his own fate, least of all that Eurydice should be so unexpectedly introduced in order to kill herself immediately. Why Eurydice? Sophocles had no Elizabethan relish for corpses. She is relevant only to Creon. Clearly the close of the play is all Creon, deliberately so, for there is less of Antigone than might have been. Sophocles is not even making the best of a bad job.

The difficulty that we feel arises from our regarding Antigone as the chief character. If she is to this play what Oedipus and Electra are to theirs (and the *Antigone* is often criticized on this assumption), then the play is ill-balanced, but if the *Antigone* is more like the *Ajax* than the *Tyrannus,* the centre of gravity does not lie in one person, but between two. The *Ajax* is second-rate Sophocles until we feel the significance of Odysseus; the last part of the *Antigone* makes no sense until we realize that there is not one central character but two, and that of the two, the significant one to Sophocles was always Creon. It is simply a matter of looking at the dramatic facts.[4] The older criticism (for of late things have taken a turn for the

---

[3] A critic of a Glasgow production of the *Antigone* in 1922 objected to the impressive cortège which escorted Haemon's body back to the stage because, emphasizing the shift in the centre of gravity, it underlined this fault in construction.

[4] Purely formal criticism of Sophocles, by rule, is an impertinence. "All arts aspire to the condition of music"; what this means was illustrated by (I think) Schumann. He was once asked by a man who had just heard him play one of his compositions what it meant. "I will tell you," said Schumann, and he played it again. The form *was* the meaning; and so it is with Sophocles—until it is shown that he was incapable of expressing himself properly. Any fool could "improve" the *Ajax,* but only by making it mean something that Sophocles thought not worth saying. The disastrous notion that the artist is one who makes pretty things has been "the beginning of many evils to the Greeks."

better) assumed that of course the play was about Antigone, and then set about explaining away the last scenes. The most satisfactory proof is performance. Creon can dominate the play; in the Glasgow production he did, easily and naturally.[5] But even without performance, we may note that Creon's part is half as long again as Antigone's, a point which is less mechanical than it sounds, and that it is the more dynamic part. Hers is impressive and affecting enough, but his has the wider range and is the more elaborate. Her fate is decided in the first few verses and she can but go to meet it; most of the dramatic forces used in the play are deployed against Creon—the slight reserve with which the chorus receives his edict (211–14), the news that he has been defied, and that too by a woman, the opposition of Haemon, the disapproval of the city (691 ff.), the supernatural machinery of Teiresias, the desertion of the chorus (1098), the death of Haemon (foreshadowed), the death of Eurydice (unforeshadowed). Creon truly says

> Old sir, ye all like bowmen at a mark
> Let fly your shafts at me.

Antigone is indeed opposed, but not like this. Her tragedy is terrible, but it is foreseen and swift; Creon's grows before our eyes.

This must have been the balance that Sophocles designed; whether this reading saves the play from fault is not our business. Perhaps modern minds make more of Antigone than was intended (though as the argument of Sallustius explains why the play was called the *Antigone* we may perhaps infer that ancients felt the difficulty too), perhaps Antigone upset Sophocles' plans as Dido is held to have upset Vergil's; it is most likely that Sophocles did precisely what he set out to do, and that in this play, as in the *Ajax,* he built on a double foundation.

As to this double foundation, in the change from the bipartite structure of the *Ajax,* through the much less prominent double interest of the *Antigone,* to the splendid unity of the *Tyrannus* and the *Electra,* it is natural for us to see a technical development; but something much more important than technique is involved, and it is not in fact easy to picture a Sophocles learning the rudiments of his art at the age of forty-five. Between these two earlier plays and the next two there is a perceptible change of tragic emphasis. The *Ajax* and the *Antigone* are based on what we may call a purely

---

[5] This was interesting. It was produced (Harrower's translation) in a large circus; the ring became the orchestra and a narrow stage was erected at the back. Two choruses were used, one to dance, the other placed on either side of the stage, to sing. It ran for a week; on the first two nights the audience was all high-brow and paper, on the last two the populace was fighting to get in.

[87]

ethical conception; this way of life is right and that one is wrong: "Not the thick-set and broad-shouldered prevail, but the wise, everywhere"; "To be stiffnecked is folly." Such a general idea naturally takes dramatic shape in an opposition between one who takes the wrong view and another who takes the right. In the second pair of plays the tragic idea is more philosophical, without of course ceasing to be ethical. One hero, more complex, more delicately poised, less catastrophic than either Ajax or Creon, fights not a moral law but his own nature. The moral and dramatic issue does not lie between him and another, but between the various facets of his own nature, assisted by the complexities of circumstance. Thus the one hero stands out more clearly from the other personages and a higher degree of unity follows.[6] It is to some such fundamental change of outlook, not to the superficialities of dramatic technique, that we should turn if we wish to understand the development of Sophocles' form. Form, with him, is the same as thought;[7] he did not need lessons from Aristotle.

The *Antigone* has been variously interpreted. The transcendental philosophers, who, from Plato onwards, have never been at their ease with the tragic poets, have done their worst with it, and have been discomfited. It has been a problem-play, the poet's condemnation of contemporary statecraft, his confession of religious faith. What are the consequences of regarding it as primarily the tragedy of Creon?

First, I think we can afford to be reasonable about Antigone. Hegel had to assume that there was something seriously wrong with her; later critics, rejecting this preposterous view, were nevertheless careful to maintain (partly out of deference to Aristotle) that Antigone was not spotless. People are never spotless, especially heroes and heroines of tragedies. Antigone's hardness to Ismene therefore was exploited to the full—but this, surely, was no very striking blemish, hardly enough to spoil a perfect figure. We saw however in dealing with Pelasgus that the hamartia doctrine must either be interpreted reasonably or amended; Pelasgus had no fault in the *Supplices* not because he was a perfect man but because his character was irrelevant; equally we need not be assiduous in looking for saving faults in Antigone, because only part of her character comes into question here, the part which impels her to defy Creon; and where the blemish is there, only Hegel can tell us. The play is not a full-length portrait of Antigone, in which, let it be granted, perfection would be a little uninteresting. Her part is to suffer, and

---

[6] I believe that this represents a fundamental development in Sophocles' thought, but let it be said here once and for all that the difference may be accidental. We do not possess what a statistician would regard as a big enough sample of Sophocles' plays (though what we have, being among the best, have great significance).

[7] We all say this, but we do not always apply it.

there is no dramatic canon which demands that victims should have faults: hardness and decisiveness were given her to explain her rebellion and her suicide. The chief *agent* is Creon; his is the character, his the faults and merits, which are immediately relevant to the play. If Sophocles is really inviting us to watch Creon, Antigone becomes much more natural, relieved of the burden of Aristotelianism, no longer the standard-bearer of the Unwritten Laws. On this, the last day of her life, she can be spared faults, as she can be spared heroics. Why indeed does she defy Creon? From a sense of religious duty? To Ismene, in the prologue, she mentions religious duty once—in an attempt to shame her sister. Her real thought comes out in phrases like

> He has no right to touch what is *mine!*—
> Yes, my brother and—though you deny it—yours.

She has a passionate feeling of what is due to her brother, to her race. Face to face with Creon's legality she indeed answers legally, and nobly, inspired to her highest eloquence, but essentially she is doing much more than championing one code against another; she is giving her whole being for her brother's honour. This leads to the genuineness of vv. 911–30. The confrontation with Creon over, we hear little more of her religious faith; she protests her innocence indeed, but the burden of her defence is again that her brother is hers to honour. Her tone is noticeably more personal. As the end draws near her defences fail one by one, until, in that marvellously moving and tragic speech which was not to the taste of those who saw in Antigone chiefly a martyr to the Higher Law, she abandons everything except the fact that she did it and had to do it. Facing death, deserted by the Chorus, she has no confidence even in the gods, and doubts her own impulse. For a husband, she says, No; for a son, No; but for a brother—

"Since my mother and my father have both gone to the grave, there can be none henceforth that I can ever call my brother." A frigid sophism borrowed from Herodotus? Yes, the finest borrowing in literature. This is the final tragedy of Antigone: *novissima hora est*—and she can cling to nothing but a frigid sophism.

If Antigone is more interesting than a mere antithesis to Creon, he is more than the stubborn fool who kills her. Sophocles was interested in his fate. He is, if not cruel, at least insensitive; like a tyrant, he is quick to suspect, and he does not know how to yield. But he has his own honesty, his own justification, and his own sense of responsibility. But what Creon is is not the whole of the story. We have this clear-cut moral issue between him and Antigone—itself a little too elementary to serve as the sole background for so subtle a thinker as Sophocles. We have too the clear-cut personal clash; it is noteworthy that from the beginning of her confrontation Antigone shows her contempt for this court. She wastes no time in trying to bridge what she knows to be an impassable gap. But behind all this there is the evolving tragedy of Creon. Creon may be what you like, but he is neither unintelligent nor irresponsible. He has his own field of action and his own principles; impulse, unwritten laws, are, he feels, not for him; he cannot move in this ampler region, and he sincerely feels he has no business to. In his own field he has thought things out and is confident of himself. We feel his confidence as soon as we hear his

Citizens, for what concerns the State . . .

He has tradition and experience on his side, his maxims are sensible. True, a native stubbornness is given him, that he may defend his position to the dramatic end, but it is not from folly or wilfulness that he originally takes up his position. But his confident judgement was wrong; his reason betrays him. It is true that but for his obstinacy he could have escaped with a lighter penalty, but the bitterness is that his judgement was wrong, and that Antigone's instinct was right; and in the end he has less to cling to than she. She goes "in the sure and certain hope That dear to thee will be my coming, Father"; he can say only

Everything is turned to water in my hands.

"By far the biggest part of happiness," says the Chorus, "is Wisdom (*to phronein*)." And what is this? Not to behave impiously towards the Gods is part of it. And what is this? Creon was honouring the Gods after his fashion, Antigone after hers. How can you tell beforehand which is the right fashion? Alas! Piety is not an automatic thing; you may learn in time —*gera to phronein*. This is the tragedy of Creon.

THE ELECTRA

This is a play which has troubled Sophoclean criticism more than any. As in the *Oresteia,* the central problem is a problem of *dikê,* "justice": what are we to think of the matricide? Very different answers have been given. Jebb held that it is to be accepted as right and glorious, as it was commanded by the god; that from the very first scene, in which the birds are singing their morning songs, "it is the bright radiance of Apollo that prevails"; that Sophocles is inviting his audience to put itself at the Homeric standpoint, from which Orestes' act is seen to be one of simple merit.

This is quite impossible; all the dramatic facts are against it. The play does indeed open with dawn chasing away night, and with the cheerful songs of the birds, but from this point onwards it is sombre and unrelieved beyond any other play of Sophocles. The heroine, however much we may pity her, whatever her character may have been capable of, has become a harsh, unlovely woman, a credit to her own mother, as she herself says (v. 609). There is no sub-comic character, like Antigone's Guard, or the messenger from Corinth in the *Tyrannus*, to relieve or at least vary the tension. There is no ecstatic dance, nor any other sort of ode that gives relief. The only cheerful scene, the Recognition, has for its undertone the passionate cry for vengeance, and is clouded by the terrible deed to come. The heroine's part leads logically and implacably to her last scenes: she stands on guard outside the palace while Orestes is killing their mother within, and when Clytemnestra's death-cry is heard, she shouts "Strike her again, if you have the strength!" Then, when Aegisthus is confronted with his wife's dead body, and tries to parley, she cries "In god's name, let him say no more. Kill him at once! Throw his body to the dogs! Nothing less can compensate me for what I have endured." It is a grim and a bloody business, and Sophocles does not try to pretend that it is anything else.

This interpretation will not do—and those who respect Sophocles need not regret it; for had Sophocles, for once, nothing of importance to say to his fellow-citizens, that he should invite them to get into an archaic frame of mind, and pretend that the murder of a mother was a deed of simple merit, in order to enjoy some poetry, stage-craft, and character-drawing? We would rather suppose, if we can, that Sophocles once more had something of significance to say.

The exactly opposite view has been taken by Sheppard. He argues that Apollo did not approve of the vengeance; that Orestes, in asking him not whether he should do it, but how—presuming on the god's compliance—was falling into an elementary blunder, like Glaucus in Herodotus; and that the indignant god lets the impious man go ahead and take the consequences. But this view is obstructed by as many obstacles as the other. Bowra has mentioned several, but there is another which seems decisive—and just as decisive against the interpretation that was offered in the first edition of this book, that Sophocles carefully dissociates Apollo from the vengeance. Both of these interpretations disfigure what is perhaps the most important and exciting moment of the play.

Clytemnestra comes out of the palace to sacrifice to Apollo. She has been frightened, as we know, by a dream, the significance of which is perfectly plain: the rightful heir will recover his throne. This already shows how Sophocles is thinking; for if it does not mean that the gods are interested in the punishment of Clytemnestra, it is a mere coincidence—leading to nothing in particular, since its effect on the plot is slight. But if the gods are interested, then the dream and its results are momentous. For Clytemnestra comes out, intending to sacrifice to Apollo; but the harsh quarrel with Electra intervenes. "Cannot you even allow me to sacrifice in proper silence, after I have let you have your say?" Electra promises to keep the silence necessary for the rite. Clytemnestra, with her attendants, advances to the altar. The audience too must observe the reverent silence; and the holy rite begins. Clytemnestra places her offerings on the altar and puts fire to the incense. As she does so she prays—a prayer of unexampled blasphemy; for she prays that she may continue to enjoy what she won by murder and has protected by adultery, and that her son may never return to avenge his father, but may die first—though this is a prayer that she shrinks from putting into words. Such is the petition that she thinks fit to offer to the god of purity. There is a pause; we watch the incense rising to Heaven with this prayer. The silence is broken by the arrival of a man with news: Orestes is dead, killed in a chariot-race—and at Delphi. Unless we can persuade ourselves that this impressive scene and its immediate sequel were contrived by Sophocles only as a piquant turn in the plot—and that he was so pleased with it that he repeated it almost exactly in the *Tyrannus*—we must see in it, as the original audience must surely have seen, the hand of the god. Apollo has heard the terrible prayer, and swiftly sends the fitting answer, a false message, designed to lure Clytemnestra to her death.

But the messenger was coming anyhow; his coming was arranged by Orestes in the prologue. Similarly in the *Tyrannus:* the messenger's arrival at that precise moment, as if in answer to the prayer of Iocasta, the sceptic, seems to betray the agency of the god; yet Sophocles goes out of his way there to tell us that this man has come, post-haste from Corinth, entirely for his own profit. In both these plays, as elsewhere in Greek poetry, the action is seen on two planes at once, human and divine.

A satisfactory interpretation of the play, then, must explain convincingly several difficult points. Besides—as always—accounting logically for the general style of the play—for the elaborate character-drawing for instance— it must explain this dual plane on which the action seems to move. It must explain why an action which is necessarily shocking, and which is presented so starkly, such that even the hero doubts the propriety of it, can be countenanced by the god, and that too without any criticism or defence from the dramatist. It must also, if we are to regard the *Electra* as a first-rate play, make its religious or philosophical content something of importance, and not leave it a mere exercise in character-drawing and play-making. Finally, we would like our interpretation to explain the conspicuous detail on which Sheppard fastened, that Apollo does *not* command Orestes to kill Aegisthus and his mother.

Bowra's treatment of the play, valuable though it is in many ways, does not seem to satisfy these demands. It is, in brief, that justice must be done; that this is sometimes a painful task to him who has to do it; but that when it is done, in this play, and order is restored, a new force of love arises. But, in the first place, had Sophocles wished to show the re-establishment of order and of love, he could not have ended the *Electra* as he did, with these two grim scenes, with Electra crying "Strike her again, if you have the strength," and "Throw his body to the dogs." Surely somebody, at some time, must have told Sophocles that Greek tragedies end quietly, somewhere beyond the climax. Had he meant this, he must have added a quiet scene to show order and love gathering strength. A concluding tag from the chorus cannot possibly efface from our minds the grimness and horror of these final scenes. In the second place, though the punishment of crime may sometimes be painful, in no civilized society can it involve anything so hideous as matricide. With what intention then did Sophocles take this mythical situation, without either condemning it, as Euripides did, or explaining it, as Aeschylus did, as an unsatisfactory but transient phase in the struggle for justice?

Since the problem concerns a god, and Justice, we may remind ourselves that the word *theos* may have a very different complexion from the word "god," and that "justice" may be a very indifferent translation of the word *dikê*. Ares, to take an extreme case, was a *theos*, but he was often spoken of in terms that we reserve for the Devil. Certainly Apollo was no Ares, but for all that in thinking of "the god Apollo" we may unconsciously assume a degree of "godliness" which is not there, so ingrained in us is the idea of a personal, beneficent god. As Grube has pointed out, *theos* always implies "a power," and may imply no more than that. As for *dikê*, whatever the origin of the word may have been, an early meaning of it was simply "the way" of something, hence "the right way." In Aeschylus it is a moral and social word, "retributive justice" in the *Agamemnon*, mellowing into "justice" as things improve. But the Ionian philosophers could use *dikê* and its opposite, *adikia*, in an amoral sense, as when Anaximander said that "things are continually paying retribution (*tisis*) to each other," for their "injustice." Philosophers who did not make our sharp distinction between the physical and the moral could call *dikê* what we call "the balance of forces in Nature," "the law of averages," and the like. If there is too much wet now, there will be too much dry later on; wet will pay to dry retribution (*tisis*) for its encroachment; and so *dikê*, the proper balance, will be restored.

What if Sophocles' *dikê* has in it something of this conception? What if his *theoi*, and Apollo, their intermediary with men, are conceived as "the powers" who protect this *dikê*? We will assume—in order to see what happens—that in the *Electra dikê* means "the proper and natural order of things," not now in the physical universe, but in human affairs, moral and social. If the proper order is disturbed by some violence (*adikia*), it must, in the nature of things, restore itself, somehow; the restoration of the balance is an act of *dikê* because it re-establishes *dikê*. If so, we need not expect the act of *dikê* to be agreeable in itself; the deluge that ends a drought may itself do harm.

Clytemnestra, in murdering Agamemnon, violently disturbed the natural order. This was an action bound, in the nature of things, to provoke an equivalent reaction—unless indeed all concerned should acquiesce in the *adikia*. As the action was hideous, so there is no reason to expect that the reaction should be lovely. Why should it be? The *adikia* caused a wound; *dikê* may involve an amputation. To see that *dikê* is re-established is the concern of the gods, as well as of men. In the *Electra* it is re-established— and how? By a perfectly natural process. We have three people to consider, the three surviving children of Agamemnon. Chrysothemis is no impressive figure. She can acquiesce; so far as she is concerned, *adikia* can continue. The hero and heroine are not like this. Orestes cannot and will not spend his life living in exile, on charity; he is determined to recover his patrimony (as Sophocles is careful to tell us, even to the point, apparently, of showing us a view of this patrimony on his painted *periacti*). He asks Apollo how he is to set about it; and the reason why he is not commanded by the god, as he is in Aeschylus, is precisely that Sophocles wishes to represent the act of *dikê* as the natural, even inevitable, outcome of the original crime. A disinherited son *will* do this, unless he is a coward. Action provokes its reaction; this is *dikê,* and the act of *dikê* is conceived and carried out entirely by the human actors, from natural motives and by natural means. The third child, Electra, is like Orestes, unable to acquiesce; and in her we see a different aspect of this reaction. Her character, in her situation, makes it inevitable that she should live for vengeance; that is the reason why this character and situation must be described in such detail.

So, as these two are great enough to resent and resist *adikia,* the hour comes and *dikê* is achieved. We are not obliged to admire the deed—Orestes himself clearly does not—nor to see in it the institution of a new and better order of things—about which Sophocles is silent. A violent disturbance of *dikê* has been violently annulled. It is the nature of things, and Sophocles invites us to see in this the working of a natural law.

But what of Apollo, and the two planes? If the whole action is complete on the human plane, is not the god a superfluous addition? By no means. Apollo's part is of the utmost significance. He does not affect the action in the least; he neither commands nor assists Orestes; but he does, as it were, accompany the action on his own plane. When Orestes has at last decided to act, Clytemnestra has her dream—and it would be stultifying to suppose that this is mere coincidence. Orestes is an autonomous agent; but the gods are moving on a path parallel to his. Even more significant is the arrival of the Paedagogus at that particular moment. On the human plane, this is a move that we are expecting; but the fact that he comes just when he does, as if in answer to that prayer, suggests to our minds that Apollo is working here, independently of the Paedagogus and of Orestes. In other words, what Orestes and Electra are doing, though an action complete and intelligible in itself, is at the same time part of a larger design, the will of the gods, the principle of *dikê,* the universal law. It is not merely a private matter, a particular case.

Now we can see why Sophocles could take this, the most questionable part of the Pelopid legend, and present it, by itself, as an action that needed neither defence nor sequel. He is as far as possible from being "literary" and archaistic, asking us to make impossible assumptions for the sake of some trifling dramatic effects, like character-drawing and strong scenes. He is demonstrating a law in things, that violence must produce its recoil; and the fact that the *dikê* here is so grim and unrelieved is a measure of the hideousness of the original offence. That the actual form of the vengeance here is one that could not occur in civilized society is immaterial; the underlying law that it illuminates is true for all time.

One point remains, the explanation given by Electra of the sacrifice of Iphigeneia. It is conspicuously different from the explanation given by Aeschylus. In the *Agamemnon* Artemis holds up the fleet because, for pity, she objects to the expedition; she is "angry with the winged hounds of her father." She gives Agamemnon the choice between sacrificing his daughter and going home; if he is bent on playing the part of a devouring eagle, let him first devour an innocent child of his own, and take the consequences. In the *Electra* the position is entirely different. In the first place, Artemis is a Sophoclean, not an Aeschylean, deity; her motives are quite amoral. Agamemnon offends her by killing one of her stags and boasting about it. He was at fault, but the goddess hits back implacably and, by human standards, unreasonably. She acts as Athena does with Ajax, when he offends her; she acts as electricity does, if an incautious tinkerer makes a mistake. In the second place, Sophocles' Agamemnon had no choice at all, for we are told "There was no escape for the army, either homeward or to Troy" (vv. 573 f.). Agamemnon therefore was to be pitied much more than blamed, and Clytemnestra has much less justification than she had in the *Oresteia.* The reason for this difference of treatment is clear. Aeschylus wanted her crime to be the direct result of the similar crime of Agamemnon, its punishment and its continuation; Sophocles wanted it to be a wanton and unjustified disturbance of *dikê*, to be avenged, once and for all, by its inevitable recoil.

THE OEDIPUS TYRANNUS

The story of the *Tyrannus* is of a common Greek type; something unpleasant is predicted, the persons concerned try to avert it and think themselves safe, but in some natural though surprising fashion the prediction is fulfilled. Next to the *Tyrannus* itself, the most elaborate example is the story of Astyages and the infant Cyrus in Herodotus. What does Sophocles make of this ancient motif?

At the beginning of the play Oedipus is the great King who has saved Thebes in the past and is their only hope now; no one can compare with Oedipus in reading dark secrets. At the end, he is the polluted outcast, himself the cause of the city's distress, through crimes predicted by Apollo before he was born. Is this grim determinism? Is Sophocles telling us that Man is only the plaything of Fate? Or does he mean, as Bowra has recently suggested, that the gods have contrived this awful fate for Oedipus in order to display their power to man and to teach him a salutary lesson? Or is Sophocles simply making exciting drama, leaving the philosophical implications unexplored? There is only one way of finding out. Whatever Sophocles meant, he put his meaning into the play, and to get it out again we must contemplate the play—all of it, in all its aspects; not bits of it, and some of its aspects.

As in the *Electra,* the action shows a certain duality. In the foreground are autonomous human actors, drawn vividly, and complete. Oedipus himself, Tiresias, Creon, Iocasta, and the two shepherds, are all as lifelike as characters in a play can be; and so, in their degree, are the remoter characters who do not appear—the hot-tempered Laius at the cross-road, and the unknown Corinthian who insulted Oedipus when he was half-drunk. The circumstances too are natural, even inevitable, granted these characters. Oedipus, as we see him time after time, is intelligent, determined, self-reliant, but hot-tempered and too sure of himself; and an apparently malignant chain of circumstances combines now with the strong, now with the weak side of his character to produce the catastrophe. A man of poor spirit would have swallowed the insult and remained safe in Corinth, but Oedipus was resolute; not content with Polybus' assurance he went to Delphi and asked the god about it, and when the god, not answering his question, repeated the warning given originally to Laius, Oedipus, being a man of determination, never went back to Corinth. It was a coincidence, but not an unnatural one, that Laius was on his way from Thebes to Delphi. They met at the cross-road, and as father and son were of similar temper the disaster occurred. Even so, he could have arrived at Thebes safely, had he not been a man of high intelligence; for then he could not have read the riddle of the Sphinx. But again, though intelligent, he was blind enough to marry a woman old enough to be his mother, certain that his mother was in Corinth. The story is not moralized. Sophocles could have put Oedipus in the wrong at the cross-road; he could have suggested that blind ambition made him accept the crown and Queen of Thebes. He does neither of these things; Oedipus is not being given his deserts by an offended Heaven. What happens is the natural result of the weaknesses and the virtues of his character, in combination with other people's. It is a tragic chapter from life, complete in itself, except for the original oracle and its repetition. Sophocles is not trying to make us feel that an inexorable destiny or a malignant god is guiding the events.

But we are made to feel, as in the *Electra,* that the action is moving, at the same time, on a parallel and higher plane.

The presence of some power or some design in the background is already suggested by the continuous dramatic irony—which seems overdone, if it is regarded as only a dramatic effect. In the matter of the Plague this hidden power is definitely stated; and its presence is most imaginatively revealed, as in the *Electra,* in the scene containing Iocasta's sacrifice. She who has been so sceptical of oracles surprises us by coming out with sacrificial offerings. She lays them on Apollo's altar, puts fire to the incense, and prays for deliverance from fear. There is a moment of reverent silence, and this is broken by the arrival of the cheerful messenger from Corinth: Polybus is dead; fear is at an end; the prayer has been heard. But within the hour Iocasta has hanged herself.—And what of her offerings? Still there, on the altar, in full view of the audience; the incense, it may be, still carrying to the god a petition that he has so terribly answered.

This is no theatrical trick, but a revelation of the dramatist's thought. It is the action of the unseen god made manifest. But how does the god answer the pitiful prayer of Iocasta, the impious prayer of Clytemnestra? Not by any direct interposition. The Apollo of Sophocles is nothing like the Zeus of Aeschylus, who works his will by freezing the Strymon or by blasting a fleet. It was not Apollo who incited the Corinthian to come, but his own eagerness to be the first with the good news, and his own hopes (as Sophocles is careful to tell us) of standing well with the new King; for besides the news of his succession to the crown he has another and a much more exciting tale to tell—in his own good time. He, like the Paedagogus, is completely autonomous, yet in the coming of each the hand of the god is seen. The action moves on two planes at once.

Nevertheless, the whole texture of the play is so vividly naturalistic that we must be reluctant to interpret it as a bleak Determinism. These people are not puppets of higher powers; they act in their own right. Nor, I think, does this texture encourage us to accept Bowra's explanation.

In the first place, if Sophocles meant that the gods are displaying their power because they will, that they have ordained this life for Oedipus in order to read men a lesson, it was so easy for him to say so—to write an ode on the power and the mysterious ways of the gods. He conspicuously does not do this. Indeed, in the ode that immediately follows the catastrophe the chorus says not that the fate of Oedipus is a special display of divine power, but on the contrary that it is typical of human life and fortunes.

In the second place, although Oedipus is by far the greatest sufferer in the play he is not the only one. There are others who suffer, not by any means in the same degree, but in the same way; and we must take account of them too, not dismiss them as being parts of the dramatic economy but not of the thought. If we contemplate, as we should, the whole play and all its aspects, we see that Oedipus is not a special case, except in the degree to which he suffers; he is, as the Chorus says, typical; what has happened to him is part of the whole web of human life. Why for example does Sophocles introduce the children in the last act? Not simply because it is "natural"; a good play isn't "nature," but art. One reason must be that Oedipus may say to them what he does say: "What a life must yours be! Who will admit you to the festivals? Who will marry you—born as you were born?" Such is life, such are the gods. The innocent suffer with the guilty.

We must contemplate also two other characters who form no inconsiderable part of the play—the two shepherds. It was not merely to liven up his play, or to indulge his talents, that Sophocles drew them like this, with their motives, hopes, fears, so sharply presented. The Corinthian, like the Paedagogus, makes no bones about expecting a tip; not for the reason that Headlam so oddly gave, that it was the oriental custom to reward messengers (as if dramatists were only photographers), but because the point bears on the drama. The news that this man brings is great news indeed, but he has something much more astonishing in reserve and the moment for producing it soon comes. "Polybus? He was no more your father than I am. . . . Why, I gave you to him with my own hands. . . . A hired shepherd? Yes, my son; but that day I saved your life." A hired shepherd—but this is a great day for him; he began by addressing Oedipus as "My Lord," but now he can say "My son." "No, *that* I cannot tell you. . . . You must find the Theban who gave you to me. . . ." Iocasta's last despairing shriek does not disturb him, for, as Oedipus says, probably she is dismayed to find that her husband is of low birth. The chorus is happy and excited; and when the reluctant Theban is brought in, our friend becomes even more bland and helpful, as he works up to his climax:

> Here is the man, my friend, who was that baby!

And this is his last speech. No reward for him; no glory in Corinth—only bewilderment and utter dismay; for in a moment he hears, from his old companion,

> I pitied it, my lord. I thought to send
> The child abroad, whence this man came. And he
> Saved it, for utter doom. For if you are
> The man he says, then you were born for ruin.

He sees his new King rush into the palace; and then—the final ode? Not yet. These two actors have to make their exit, by the long side-passages, in full view of the audience; some forty yards of exit. And as we watch them stumbling out we have time to reflect that this is the outcome, for them, of their merciful interest in an abandoned baby.

Is not this too the work of Apollo? Here, as in the greater case of Oedipus, is that conjunction of well-meant action with a situation which makes it lead to disaster. An act of mercy, tinged with a perfectly honest shrewdness, leads the Corinthian to the verge of what is, for him, greatness; as he stretches out his hand, eagerly and with confidence, it turns into horror.

The other shepherd too is one who refused to kill a baby. Part of his reward comes years later, when he sees the man who killed Laius ascend his victim's throne and marry his Queen—an event which sends him, for his own safety, into half-exile;[8] the rest of his reward comes now, when a sudden command brings him back at last to the city, to learn what he learns here.

These minor tragedies, of the children and the shepherds, are all of a piece with the major one. This is Apollo; this is life. An awful sin is committed in all innocence; children are born to a life of shame; virtuous intentions go awry. What are we to think of it? Of course, moral and prudential lessons can be drawn from it—though Sophocles draws very few—but what do we think of it? Where is the explanation? What, in other words, is the catharsis? That Oedipus accepts his fate? But when you are knocked flat, you must

---

[8] For he, no bought slave, but reared in the palace (v. 1123), besought Iocasta to send him into the fields, as far as possible from the city (vv. 758 ff.).

accept it; and if you cannot get up again, you must be resigned. There is little illumination in this.

The catharsis that we are looking for is the ultimate illumination which shall turn a painful story into a profound and moving experience. It has been suggested by Professor Ellis-Fermor that the catharsis of plays like the *Tyrannus* and *Macbeth* lies in the perfection of their form, which, by implication, represents the forces of righteousness and beneficence, of which Aeschylus speaks directly, in his choric odes. This is manifestly true of the *Tyrannus*.

Let us go back to Iocasta's sacrifice, and Apollo's swift and devastating answer. In the corresponding passage of the *Electra* the point was clear. Clytemnestra prayed that injustice, *adikia,* might triumph, and she got the answer she deserved. What of Iocasta? She has been denying the truth of oracles. Was Sophocles then so fiercely orthodox that he could equate Iocasta's scepticism with Clytemnestra's wickedness? Of course not; this was not the size of Sophocles' mind. He means much more than this. Iocasta has said "Why should we fear oracles, when there is no such thing as foresight (*pronoia*)? Best live at random, as one may"—a doctrine which would deny the very basis of all serious Greek thought; for while Greek life was still healthy and stable, the Greek believed, as if by instinct, that the universe was not chaotic and "irrational," but was based on a *logos,* obeyed Law. The Ionian philosophers did not discover, but rather postulated, this *logos.*

The tragic poets too think in this way—as Whitehead saw, when he said that they, rather than the Ionians, were the first scientific thinkers. In the *Oresteia* we find moral laws which have the same sort of validity as physical and mathematical laws. The doer must suffer; hybris leads to Atê; the problem there—a problem for gods as well as for men—is to find a system of Justice that will fit into this framework without disastrously contravening these laws. To the mind of Sophocles this *logos* shows itself (as we shall see more fully in the next chapter) as a balance, rhythm, or pattern in human affairs. "Call no man happy until he is dead," for the chances of life are incalculable. But this does not mean that they are chaotic; if so they seem to us, it is because we are unable to see the whole pattern. But sometimes, when life for a moment becomes dramatic, we can see enough pattern to give us faith that there is a meaning in the whole. In the *Antigone,* when Creon is overwhelmed, it is by the natural recoil of his own acts, working themselves out through the minds and passions of Antigone and Haemon, and we can see in this a natural justice. In the *Electra,* the vengeance that at last falls on the assassins is linked to their crime by natural chains of cause and effect. In the *Tyrannus* we have a much more complex picture. The same *dikê* is at work, though this time the *adikia* which it avenges was involuntary and indeed innocent. Oedipus—to repeat our image—is blasted as a man may be who inadvertently interferes with the natural flow of electricity. *Dikê* here works through many apparently casual and unrelated actions—of the shepherds, of the charioteer who tried to push Oedipus off the road, of the man at the banquet. . . . Things fall out contrary to all expectation; life seems cruel and chaotic. Cruel, perhaps; chaotic, no—for if it were chaotic no god could predict, and Iocasta would be right. "If these oracles are not manifestly fulfilled, why should I join in the sacred dance?" Piety and purity are not the whole of the mysterious pattern of life, as the fate of Oedipus shows, but they are an important part of it, and the doctrine of chaos would deny even this. The pattern may harshly cut across the life of the individual, but at least we know that it exists, and we may feel assured that piety and purity are a large part of it.

Every detail in the *Tyrannus* is contrived in order to enforce Sophocles' faith in this underlying *logos;* that is the reason why it is true to say that the perfection of its form implies a world-order. Whether or not it is beneficent, Sophocles does not say.

E U R I P I D E S

[*480–406* B.C.]

THIS ESSAY IS ADDRESSED TO THE INTERPRETATION OF THAT ONE OF EURIPIDES'
plays which hardly fits the usual categories of Greek drama. Thomson's
solution to the problems presented by *Alcestis* rests on a careful examination
of the mythic and ritual background of the story, especially of the figure of
Heracles, in the light of Greek dramatic conventions. His justification of his
procedure might seem less necessary today than it did a generation ago, when
the work of the distinguished school of Cambridge classical anthropologists
was still uncritically resisted in the citadels of Greek scholarship. His essay
demonstrates what the judicious use of anthropological data can yield in the
solution of a literary problem. It might also be read as one of many attempts
to fill in the substance of the most tantalizing unreported conversation in
literary history, the one which we are told took place at the end of Plato's
Symposium, when Socrates was driving his audience to admit that the same
man could have the knowledge required for writing both comedy and
tragedy.

J. A. K. Thomson is best known for his studies of classical influences
on English literature.

From *The Greek Tradition* by J. A. K. Thomson, 1915, by permission of the publishers, George Allen & Unwin Ltd.

J. A. K. THOMSON

Alcestis and Her Hero

THE *Alcestis* OF EURIPIDES HAS CERTAIN PECULIARITIES OF THE KIND THAT attract discussion. For example, it has the structure and special diction of the Greek Tragedy; and in spirit also much of it is purely tragic. Yet— quite against the ancient rule and almost definition of a tragedy—it ends happily; while there are scenes in it which come near to be farcical. Is it then a tragedy or a comedy? Or is it neither, is it a satyr-play? These questions have vexed and divided scholars. The answer is that the *Alcestis* is none of these things; it is something new. The old scholar who wrote an *Argument* of our play says as much. The *Alcestis* is "rather of the satyric order"—not a satyr-drama, but something like it. We ascertain further that it came last in the series of four plays, the *tetralogy,* to which it belonged. Now, normally, the fourth play was satyric. The scholiast is clearly right: the *Alcestis* is not a satyr-drama but something like it. Professor Murray, who has been left to state the obvious facts of the case, suggests the term "pro-satyric."

It is as simple as that. Not that I would pay the reader with words; my very purpose being to meet the difficulty I fancy forming itself in his mind. I realize that "pro-satyric" may affect him much as the scientific names you see on little slips of wood in botanic gardens affect the man who has no botany; he disregards the Latin and looks at the flowers. The reader may

[103]

say: "Your *satyric* and *pro-satyric* are mere labels. To me they convey no meaning at all. And what do I lose? Take Shakespeare: I do not know what to call *The Tempest* or *As You Like It,* but my ignorance does not in the least interfere with my enjoyment of them. So you may give the *Alcestis* any of the titles in Polonius' list of possible varieties of drama. It does not matter."

It does matter.

This question involves one of those profound and fundamental differences between ancient and modern literature on which I have been perhaps wearisomely insisting. The whole character of a Greek play is determined by its classification. If it is a tragedy, if it is a comedy, if it is a satyr-play— in each case it must rigorously obey a different complex of traditional conventions. Modern literature has something analogous in its rondeaus and ballades and such things. If you write a ballade you must observe the rules of the game. If you break even the least of them, your poem may be very charming, but it will not be a ballade. So a Greek tragedy or comedy or satyric play had to be written according to its definite prescription. Now suppose we put the problem of the *Alcestis* in this way: "Did Euripides attempt to write a satyr-play and fail? Or did he invent for himself a new form of drama?" You see it does make a difference.

But there is more in it. In modern literature the spirit creates its appropriate form; in ancient literature the form is given and must be filled by its appropriate spirit. Now formally the *Alcestis* is a tragedy, or at least (to put ourselves on quite safe ground) much closer to a tragedy than a comedy. Let us restate the problem in these terms: "Did Euripides intend or did he not intend *Alcestis* for a tragedy?" If he did he has not filled the whole, but only a part of it, with the genuine tragic spirit; and there are whole scenes, like the altercation between Admetus and his father, which can only be explained if we suppose with Sir Richard Jebb that Euripides was devoid of any faintest sense of humour. But if Euripides did not mean the scene to be tragic at all—would that not make a difference? Of course it would; it makes all the difference between good art and bad.

To understand what "pro-satyric" might mean, we must know the meaning of "satyric." It is not very easy to know, for the evidence bearing on the satyr-play is really very slight, and some of it variously interpreted. There is one entire example: the *Cyclops* of Euripides. There have been discovered recently considerable fragments of the *Ichneutai* or *Trackers* of Sophocles. Beyond that our first hand evidence scarcely goes. We infer from it that in the time of Sophocles and Euripides the satyr-drama was of course comic, that it regularly had a chorus of satyrs, and that it was written—this is very surprising—in the set tragic diction. A very curious form, obviously, and (you would suppose) not a promising one. Nor do I think that very much can be said for the *Cyclops*. It is quite amusing if you do not go to it expecting something like the *Birds* or the *Frogs,* but accept it on its own terms, which are not those of a comedy at all, but rather of a burlesque of tragedy. But if the *Cyclops* is a typical satyr-play, it is certain that the *Alcestis* is none. It does not have the chorus of satyrs. The language almost never actually condescends—and never very far—but keeps its grace and dignity even in describing the feasting of Heracles. The *Alcestis* seems to be a new type of play, the invention—and a delightful and beautiful one—of Euripides himself. We are told that the subject had been treated before; and the power of tradition was so great upon the Greek stage that we may assume that Euripides had before him the model of Phrynichus' *Alcestis* (and perhaps of a number of plays on the same matter which have not been recorded) when he composed his own drama. The *Alcestis* of Phrynichus does not survive. If it did, we should be able to decide how far it influenced our *Alcestis.* The probability is that the play of the older dramatist was pure satyric. The reasons for thinking this will appear; they are reasons of tradition.

The story of Alcestis was itself traditional. We have seen that it was put on the stage long before Euripides; Phrynichus was writing before the Persian Wars. Phrynichus may have taken it either from some earlier poet or from the great mass of unwritten legend. The story is told in the *Bibliotheca* of mythology attributed to the scholar Apollodorus:

> When Admetus was king of Pherae, Apollo became his serf. Admetus was seeking to wife Alcestis the daughter of Pelias. When Pelias proclaimed that he would give his daughter in marriage to the man who should yoke lions and wild boars in a chariot, Apollo yoked them and gave them to Admetus, who brought them to Pelias; and so obtains Alcestis. But when he was sacrificing at his marriage he forgot to sacrifice to Artemis. Therefore, when he opened the marriage chamber, he found it full of coiling serpents. But Apollo, bidding him appease the goddess, made request of the Fates that, when Admetus was bound to die, he might be released from death, if someone freely consented to die for him. When the day came for his dying, Alcestis died in his stead, since both his father and his mother refused. And Persephone sent her back to upper air again, or (as some say) Heracles saved her after fighting with Hades.

To read "Apollodorus" is to wander in the Valley of Dry Bones. But he is useful to the student of mythology because he invents nothing and because he could draw from sources now sealed to us. In the case of this story of Alcestis the mythologist has an additional security; it is essentially identical with a hundred other stories he knows. They are all ritual stories or myths. The ritual which they express represents the death and resurrection of some sacred being. There must have been, to account for her myth, a ceremony in which the Passing and the Return of Alcestis were enacted. That form of rite was to be found everywhere in ancient Greece, as we know both from the written evidence and from the remains of Greek art, which frequently represent the resurrection of a Divine Woman literally being dug or hacked out of the ground by creatures inscribed "Satyrs." Her worshippers might call her here Korê, and Semelê there, and Alcestis somewhere else. At heart, under all these names, and in spite of local variations in her ritual, the *Rediviva* is everywhere one and the same, being in fact the Earth, who appears to die in winter and come to life again in the spring. In her resurrection aspect she was most widely known as Korê, "the Maiden," the young Earth (at least that is how we explain her; her actual worshippers very properly would not rationalize her) married to Pluto or Hades, the god of the underworld and the dead. The *Bibliotheca,* you remember, says that according to one account Alcestis was restored to life by Persephone. Persephone is the more familiar name of the goddess also named Korê. The Greek in fact says Korê here.

The Chorus, addressing Alcestis in Euripides' play, says:

> Minstrels many shall praise thy name
> With lyre full-strung and with voices lyreless,
> When Mid-Moon riseth, an orbéd flame,
> And from dusk to dawning the dance is tireless;
> And Carnos cometh to Sparta's call,
> And Athens shineth in festival;
> For thy death is a song, and a fullness of fame,
> Till the heart of the singer is left desireless.

This is to say, at the solemn feast of the *Carnea* at Sparta, and on some similar occasion at Athens, the legend of Alcestis was chanted, and probably in some way dramatically rendered. But Athens and Sparta are not Pherae; and Pherae (one is almost bound to suppose) must be the true home of her myth and of the rite with which the myth was associated. Was the story of Alcestis annually represented in song and action at Pherae? It looks as if it was. She had a known and conspicuous tomb there.

HERACLES Where lies the tomb?—Where shall I find her now?
SERVANT Close by the straight Larissa road. The tall
White marble showeth from the castle wall.

That it existed in Euripides' time, and was regarded as a holy monument, **is** implied in the following words of the Chorus:

> Let not the earth that lies upon her
> Be deemed a grave-mound of the dead.
> Let honour, as the Gods have honour,
> Be hers, till men shall bow the head,
> And strangers, climbing from the city
> Her slanting path, shall muse and say:
> "This woman died to save her lover,
> And liveth blest, the stars above her:
> Hail, Holy One, and grant thy pity!"
> So pass the wondering words away.

Nyn d'esti makaira daimōn—"Now is she a blessed Spirit" or Daemon; surely that is clear enough. She must have been worshipped at Pherae. That her cult was connected with the great prehistoric tomb on the road to Larissa is certain both from the nature of her legend (a death and resurrection myth) and from what Euripides says. Now from what we know of ceremonies held throughout Greece in honour of dead "Heroes" we may conjecture that athletic games were periodically celebrated in memory of Alcestis. If they were, it might explain a somewhat curious speech of Heracles in the play. When he comes back from the tomb with the veiled Alcestis, he pretends at first that she is a prize won by him at a wrestling, which has just been held somewhere near. These games, as Verrall saw, must have been in honour of Alcestis. And if this detail was not invented by Euripides, but was a part of the tradition as he received it, the games must have been traditional too. But it is a little matter, and there is no proof.

There are many undesigned correspondences which reveal the authenticity of the Alcestis myth. Korê was married to Pluto, "the Wealthy," lord of the dead: Alcestis was married to Admetus lord of Pherae in Thessaly. *Admetus,* "the Unsubdued," is one of the many names given to the god also called Pluto. Again, the wealth of Admetus was proverbial. He was especially rich in cattle. Naturally so, for in primitive times a man's wealth is mainly reckoned by the number of his cows. Now we find "the cows of Admetus" mentioned in terms which imply that they were identical with the cows of Hades—who is Pluto. Again, the hospitality of Admetus was proverbial; and the Hospitable—"He of the Many Guests"—is one of the surnames bestowed (without any original irony) on the god of the dead. The parallel will look less fanciful when we have penetrated deeper into the story.

One fixed element in the tradition (so far as it pertains to Admetus) is the sojourn with him of the god Apollo in guise of a herdsman. Apollo, to avenge the death of his son Asclepius, slew the Cyclôpes. Whereupon Zeus ordained that Apollo should pass a year in thraldom to a mortal. "And he came to Pheres' son Admetus in Pherae, and was a shepherd in his service, and caused all his cows to bear twins." That is the reduced prose of the *Bibliotheca*. The poetry is to be found in many places from the choral odes in the *Alcestis* to *Phoebus with Admetus*. So beautiful and famous a legend is explained by scholars as originating in this way: it mythically expresses the temporary obscuration of the Light-god or Sun-god, although of course, poetically, it expresses exactly as much as you are able to find in it. The early Greeks, watching the daily disappearance of the sun under the western horizon and his reappearance in the east, explained this to themselves by supposing that he passed through the underworld by night, shining to the dead. In the paradise of Pindar the dead have their sun and moon. The Sun, in Homer, threatens that, if he is not avenged upon the Companions of Odysseus, he will pass down into the house of Hades and shine among the dead. Hence (by a kind of paradox very strange to us but a commonplace of ancient religion) the Sun-god comes to be identified with the god of the dead. Helios is only the bright side of Hades. Now, the oxen of the Sun recur constantly in mythology; and they turn out to be really the same as the oxen of Hades or Admetus. That is why it is so natural for Apollo to keep the herds of Admetus. In one (only in one) aspect of his nature he *is* Admetus. The lions and the wild boars drawing the bridal car which brings Alcestis to her new home from Iolcus are the familiar beasts of Apollo, the same that gathered to his harping.

It was to Admetus in his shining aspect—as it were the Sun-god himself—that Alcestis was married on the day of that strange procession. In his other aspect she is the bride of Death. Both Admetus and Alcestis have this double nature like all these primitive nature spirits, who die to live again. But another belief has helped to mould her legend. The Greeks loved to represent the death of a maiden as her marriage to the god of the dead. And so Alcestis marrying Admetus is Alcestis dying. The mythopoeic imagination plays endless variations on a single theme. According to one variant of the myth (known to Euripides, as some words assigned to Heracles imply) it was Korê who restored Alcestis to the sunlight. And the Chorus pray that their queen may be *throned by the side of Hades' Bride,* that is Persephone or Korê. The Greek word—*paredrevois*—expresses a position of almost equal authority. And that is quite in order.

The other version of the myth said that Heracles wrestled with Death and forced Alcestis from his grasp. This is the version adopted by Euripides. It has certain obvious dramatic advantages over the other; but is it equally authentic? Has Heracles, as the most famous of Greek heroes, been brought into an older story and confused its original form? It looks probable enough, indeed it may be regarded as certain; for Heracles has no original connexion with Pherae, he comes from farther south. But he has not been thrust into the Alcestis legend without other recommendation than his popularity. He has taken the place (we must suppose) of some local Hero; taken it in virtue of a radical affinity which made identification easy.

But besides all this Alcestis has a special claim upon Heracles.

One of the most characteristic institutions of Greek life was the *Kômos* or Revelling Procession. It was so ancient, so twisted about the roots of Greek society, that it had become as complex and elusive as life itself. We know not whether to call it a religious or (in the restricted sense) a social custom; it was both. Nor can we justly call it either a dance or a procession or a choir or a revel-rout; it was all these things at once. As for the members of the Kômos, they usually carried torches—this for a religious reason. They often dressed up as animals—again no doubt for some religious or magical reason. They had naturally a leader to head the procession, to guide the steps and gestures of the dance, to strike up the Komos-song. This song was regularly of a festive or even a fescennine nature. A typical variety of it was the Marriage Song or *Hymenaeus*. Since this became a literary form, some exercises in which survive to us, we can guess at its original character from these, as: Catullus' poem on the marriage of Torquatus. It may remind us that the marriage procession was perhaps the most complete and representative form of the Kômos. The bride and bridegroom, amid flowers and music, were conducted in a chariot to his house. The evidence indicates that the bridegroom was regarded as in some sense a Victor or even a King, like the Beloved in the *Song of Solomon*. Conversely, the celebration of a victory was apt to take the form of a marriage of the victor; as at Olympia the victor in the Games, triumphing at the head of his Kômos, was regarded as the bridegroom of the winner in the women's race.

The confusion of thought seems complete. It is not really so; but, although there is a clue, it must be admitted that it cannot be unwound to the end. It is impossible to frame a set of words which shall not be at once too narrow and too wide to cover the emotions which created the Kômos; too narrow because they will confine those emotions to a single form of their expression, too wide in respect that this form will be of a definiteness that the sentiment of the Kômos never attained. The sentiment is like a cloud; capable of any shape and fixable in none. If one *must* try for a word to suggest it, the best I think is *Nikê,* which we translate Victory, but which means a great deal more than that. It was felt to bring increase of the power and numbers and wealth of the whole community to which the victor belonged, to bring luck, prestige, general "victoriousness" as I must lamely express it, to the state. Or we may say: it was something more than a personal distinction, or even a distinction reflected upon the community through one of its number; it was also a powerful charm. The whole end and purpose of a Kômos was simply to work this charm. It was a piece of magic. The people sought to make itself victorious by behaving as if it were. Nowadays the newspapers do this for us.

The Kômos ceremony evolved its hero, its typical legendary Victor, much as Father Christmas, for example, is the projection of our Christmas customs. The function of Kômos-leader, successively filled by an endless line of human functionaries stretching into the remotest past, begat the concept of an ideal functionary, relegated by hard facts to the misty time of the Heroic Age. This typical Victor is Heracles.

Everything about him can be explained on this view of his nature. He is the embodiment of Nikê, his constant epithet *Kallinikos* "winner of fair victory." Therefore tradition makes him the founder of the great Olympic Games and the first Olympic victor. At every celebration of the Games the victor of the occasion led the Kômos of his triumphant followers to the altar of Zeus, singing the hymn composed, it was said, by Archilochus:

> O Victor, hail, lord Heracles!
> Thyself and Iolaus, spearmen twain.

The victor in fact personated Heracles. Nothing helps us more to realize how much the conception of Heracles as the typical victor leading his rejoicing train dominated all others in the ancient mind than just this circumstance, that any human Kômos-leader at once suggested him. It was so in Greece, as the instance from Olympia and other instances show. It was so also at Rome, where the statue of Hercules *Victor* was dressed in triumphal robes whenever a general celebrated a triumph, which was essentially a Kômos.

Having remarked that the notion of victory was incomplete in the Greek mind without the thought of its celebration—as if a victory must be proclaimed before its full virtue could be extracted—what can we make of the apparent anomaly that it is not the Triumph of Heracles but his Labours that are the great theme of the literature concerned with him? It is explained when you reflect that literature could not help itself. The Triumph was a unique event; it was final, the conclusion. It was only the adventures that could be extended and developed in all directions. The arts that do not labour under this disability so much give in their predilection for the scene of the Triumph the right measure of its importance. We see Heracles entering Olympus in a triumphal car, renewed in youth and followed by a dancing and singing train of nymphs or satyrs or even gods. Nikê is a constant companion; sometimes he carries symbolically a little figure of her in his hand. He is also *Musagetes,* "Leader of the Muses"; and the Muses, as you may discover in the *Theogony* of Hesiod, are a singing and dancing company. The traveller Pausanias found a representation of *Heracles accompanied by the Muses* at Messana and at Sparta. The Roman general Fulvius Nobilior set up a statue of *Hercules Musarum* "because," Eumenius says, "when he was commanding in Greece, he had heard that Heracles was *Musagetes,* that is, the Companion and Leader of the Muses."

It is because Heracles was the projection of the Kômos, embodying and concentrating its qualities, that many *thiasi* or clubs at Athens were named after him; for a *thiasus* might be called a Kômos in permanence. It is because he comes of the Kômos that he possesses unmeasured strength, that he is such an enormous eater and drinker, that he has so many children, that he is (in the true and original sense) *comic.* He is all that the revellers desire their leader to be.

In an essay one can only touch on some of these points. But they are vital.

There is, for instance, what one might call the marriage motive. The ancient Kômos was apt to take the form of a marriage-pomp in which the Leader played the part of Bridegroom. There was a ritual wedding (*gamos*), which was of course a fertility charm. This aspect of the Kômos is reflected in the marriage of Heracles to Hebe, an essential part of his Triumph. There is evidence which makes it very probable that Heracles was worshipped in places as actually himself a marriage-god. It was customary to write over the door of a newly married man:

The Son of Zeus, Heracles the Victor, dwells here. Let nothing evil enter!

With the ancient marriage, and indeed probably with every Kômos, there went a certain amount of indecent badinage. Hence the "satyric" Heracles—the hero of so many satyr-plays. But the ribaldry of the Kômos has a double motive. It is incentive, but it is also apotropaic. The real intention of the insulting *carmina* in the Roman triumph (for instance) was to avert the evil which threatens the overproud. The *triumphator* might deem himself a god and provoke the jealousy of Olympus, unless he were effectively reminded of his human case. So in the service of Heracles we find the practice of ritual cursing. The myth or explanation of the rite is to be found in the *Bibliotheca.*

"When he was traversing Asia he landed at Thermydrae, a harbour of the Lindians. There he loosed from the wain one of the steers of an ox-driver, and sacrificed it, and feasted. And the driver, unable to help himself, stood upon a hill and cursed him. Wherefore to this day, when they sacrifice to Heracles, they do it with curses."

Heracles ate the whole ox at a sitting. The ritual abuse and cursing are thus brought into connexion with the *gluttony* of the hero. The leader of a Kômos was expected to eat and drink a great deal, that it might be a charm for the multiplying of food and wine. So Heracles was credited with a prodigious appetite—the subject of infinite jests. Even more expressive perhaps are the seriously bestowed cult-titles *Adêphagos,* "Glutton," *Epitrapezios,* "Who-sits-at-table." There was at Athens an association or charity of "Parasites," that is table-companions, of Heracles, who were maintained at the public expense. Many stories were told of his entertainment by mortals, as in our fable he is entertained by Admetus. Extraordinarily frequent in art is this subject of the *Feasting Heracles.* Alone, or in company, he reclines with a great goblet in his hand.

What economists call the "food supply" is the first need of a primitive, or indeed of any, community. But the insuring of an abundance of things to eat is only one part of the business incumbent on Heracles as representative of the Kômos. He produces all the things the Kômos dances for. He causes gardens to blossom and fertilizing springs to burst forth. His club was not originally a weapon, but a branch of blossoming wild olive, the wild olive whose leaves formed the victor's crown at Olympia. Such a branch was an emblem or magical instrument of fertility, capable also of scaring away spirits of blight and evil. Sometimes Heracles is represented wearing a garland of the white poplar, or holding in his hand a twig or a flower or an apple; very often with a cornucopia, which was a great horn brimmed with fruits. All these things were symbols of fruitfulness. Most significant perhaps of all, he was often carved in *herm* form, like the ithyphallic images of Hermes. Eros and he were frequently associated in worship. He was also reckoned one of the "Idaean Dactyls," the "eldest" of the Dactyls in fact; whose special function was the magical induction of fertility by a dance or procession which might fairly be called a Kômos.

It is a curious but (on reflection) quite natural consequence of the victor's position as leader of the Kômos that he often personated, or was thought to represent, the Sun, the father of magic and the evident fountain of light and life, and symbol of the victorious Summer. Thus at Olympia the victors in the men's and women's contests are thought to have personated, he the Sun, and she the Moon. The chariot of the victor or *triumphator* was drawn (when the ritual was perfect) by four horses, preferably white—the chariot and horses of the Sun. There is much to show that Heracles on one side of his nature came very near to Helios and Apollo. A great mass of his mythology has its roots in sun-worship. To deal with it here would involve too long an analysis; let me mention only the herds of Geryon and of Augeas, and the Cretan Bull—all cattle of the Sun. The meaning to the mythologist of these stories is that Heracles was, in the context they form, himself the Sun. He is the Sun when (according to another story) he sails across Oceanus in the golden cup of Helios. Like Helios, too, he is "unwearied" and full of labours.

> Surely the Sun hath labour all his days,
> And never any respite, steeds nor god,
> Since Eos first, whose hands are rosy rays,
> Ocean forsook, and Heaven's high pathway trod;
> All night across the sea that wondrous bed
> Shell-hollow, beaten by Hephaistos' hand,
> Of winged gold and gorgeous, bears his head
> Half-waking on the wave from eve's red strand
> To the Ethiop shore, where steeds and chariot are,
> Keen hearted, waiting for the morning star.

This aspect of Heracles affords us once more the opportunity of observing the curious and baffling, yet constantly repeated, phenomenon of the nature-religions. The characters of the myth dissolve and melt into one another, interchanging all but their names; for they are really one character viewed from different points or in different relations. Apollo, Admetus, Heracles are varying names for one divine being, a Power of light and life. And since in primitive religions the Power of light and life is at the same time the Power of darkness and death, Thanatos or Death, who seems in the play the enemy of all three, is in reality their double. Heracles fighting with Death in Pherae is like Heracles fighting with Hades at Pylos, like Heracles descending into the realm of Persephone. He received the cornucopia he often carries from Pluto, and the painters of vases are very fond of showing him in the underworld. He was worshipped along with Demeter and Korê —Korê with whom Alcestis is to be identified. But let us get this quite clear: when I say that Apollo, Admetus, and Heracles are at bottom identical, I mean in the Alcestis myth. Outside that context each developed new and comparatively alien phases of his nature. The phase they have in common happens to be particularly important for this legend; that is all. Or it may be put in this way: the legend has been created by their touching at a single point; and this touching was the result of a native affinity.

One other aspect of Heracles deeply concerns the Alcestis. The Kômos had a rite or traditional manner of behaviour, such as the Greeks called a

Drômenon. It was some kind of mimetic representation of the victory which the Kômos was celebrating. It has been recognized quite recently what this *Drômenon* really is. It is closely similar, it must indeed be the same as the Folk Play, of which many versions have been preserved, and which in a more or less degenerate form is still acted in certain of the less accessible parts of Europe. The essence of it is a combat between the Hero and an Enemy, and the ultimate marriage of the Hero to his Bride. The Enemy may be human, or he may take the form of some monster. Sometimes the Hero kills his antagonist, sometimes he is himself killed. In the latter case, after his death has been duly lamented by the Bride, appears a magician or doctor, who restores the Hero to life. Follows the consummation of the marriage.

Heracles is the leader of the Kômos, and therefore the Hero of the *Drômenon.* How much of his mythology is illustrated if we see that! All the Labours have this in common: the Hero disappears on some generally distant and always perilous adventure, and then suddenly reappears triumphant. A certain Istros of Alexandria wrote a book on these "Epiphanies of Heracles." Where a god or an immortal is in question, such disappearance and reappearance are mythologically equivalent to death and resurrection. A god cannot be supposed truly to die, even temporarily. He can only be exiled, like Apollo to the house of Admetus; or descend into Hades like Dionysus. Ultimately, there being no more labours for him to accomplish, Heracles does die; but only apparently. Zeus casts a thunderbolt on Oeta, the pyre is quenched, and Heracles enters Olympus in triumph.

The Hero or "Agonist" of the Folk Play is a pretty constant character; the "Antagonist" takes many forms. In the class of Plays of which "St. George and the Dragon" is the type the enemy is a dragon or a serpent or the like. To this class then belong the stories of Heracles strangling the serpents of Hera in his cradle, slaying the Hydra of Lerna, destroying the sea-monster in the Hesione-legend, smiting the snake of the Hesperides. The Antagonist is a lion in the stories of the Lion of Cithaeron and the Lion of Nemea. Often he is a bull—a formidable animal in antiquity, roaming half-wild over the unenclosed pastures. One of the Labours was the carrying off of the Cretan Bull. This Bull, who is "sacred to the Sun," reappears in the herds of Augeas and in the herds of Geryon.

Or the Antagonist may be human or semi-human: a Giant or an "Arab" or a Wild Man or the like. Well, Heracles fights with the Centaurs of Pelion and those of Pholoe. He is constantly engaged in putting down local tyrants, *hubristai.* One is mentioned, rather more than incidentally, in the *Alcestis:* Diomedes of Thrace. The story of Diomedes' fire-breathing, man-devouring horses reflects a ritual in the savage old Thracian religion; and in the other stories we should doubtless find in every case a native ritual accounting for the local legend, although it would be no longer possible in every case to reconstruct the ritual with any certainty. But observe that the myths, with whatever variety of detail, have all one plot: the Combat or *Agôn* with the Antagonist and the Victory of Heracles.—The Antagonist is a giant in the legends of Antaios, of Geryon, of Cacus, of Eurytion, of Eryx; in the *Alcestis* Death. So also at Pylus Heracles wounds Hades. He smites also *Old Age, Epiales* or Fever, a *Kêr* or demon imp—stories best explained as growing out of mimetic ceremonies comparable to the "Carrying out of Death" and similar customs described in the *Golden Bough*. Heracles with his leafy branch is leader of the Kômos which drives out Death and Winter.

Comedy is "the song of the Kômos," Heracles its leader; therefore Heracles is comic, *originally* comic, in this sense of the word. His history is pretty much the history of the Kômos itself. The comedy of literature, Aristotle tells us, had its source in the phallic songs sung by the Kômos under its leader or precentor; such a song as we find in the *Acharnians* of Aristophanes addressed to the god Phales, and accompanied by some kind of *Drômenon* or dramatic ritual, which it is possible partly to make out in the brief scene of the *Acharnians* where it occurs. Tragedy, again, developed *ek tou satyrikou,* from a satyric original; and the diction of Aeschylean tragedy was "elevated into seriousness" from its earlier ludicrous tone. If we let ourselves be convinced by these plain statements of Aristotle, we must conclude that the original forms of Greek comedy and tragedy (which, to begin with, was as much as comedy a choral performance) were singularly alike. Perhaps they were the same. Perhaps this original form survived under modification in the satyr-play. Recent investigation seems to point to that. Thus much is certain, tragedy underwent a long process of refinement and expurgation. Heracles shared in that development; the "tragic" Heracles is later than the satyric. For although the Agôn which precedes the Victory, the death which precedes the Resurrection of the Hero, hold the germs of tragedy, in Heracles' case the insistence was at first chiefly on the Victory and the Resurrection, joyous events to be celebrated in the antique manner.

It is not then surprising to find that many of the Heracles legends are comic. They are not late stories nor the inventions of poets. A whole series deals with Heracles' feats of eating and drinking; tales born of the Kômos-feast and as old as the hero himself. One remembers too the Battle with the Pygmies, as ancient at least as Epicharmus; the adventure with the Cercôpes, a very old story; the legend of Omphale, reflecting a primitive rite of the Saturnalian class involving an exchange of clothes between the sexes.

We learn from Aristophanes that the Glutton Heracles was a stock character in the popular or "vulgar" or "Megarian" comedy. Epicharmus introduced him time and again into his plays, notably *The Marriage of Hebe*. Of the Attic writers of comedy, Cratinus wrote a *Busiris*, in which Heracles on the point of being immolated in Egypt suddenly rends his bonds and slays his would-be sacrificers; Pherecrates a *Pseudo-Heracles;* Hermippus a *Cercôpes,* in which however it is not absolutely certain that Heracles appeared; Archippus a *Heracles Marrying.* As for the satyr-play, it was long ago pointed out that Heracles belonged to it in quite a special way. He was particularly at home among satyrs, art constantly representing him in their company, and literature making him the chief hero of the satyr-play, as may be gathered from the *Fragments* of the tragic poets. On the other hand the tragic Heracles is comparatively late. He appeared at the end of the *Prometheus Unbound* of Aeschylus, where his business was to release Prometheus from his rock; and he appears at the end of Sophocles' *Philoctêtes*. Both episodes are in the nature of Epiphanies, bringing a happy conclusion to a painful story. He is not a truly tragic character in *Alcestis*. It was not indeed till he wrote the *Heracles* that Euripides was ready to break finally with the satyric tradition and make Heracles the subject of a tragedy. The example was followed in the *Women of Trachis*. So far as our information goes, Heracles was the hero of only two, and these not early, tragedies.

His treatment in the epos is very curious. Homer barely mentions him—does not mention him at all, some scholars would say, who believe the passages where his name occurs to be interpolations. The reason seems clear: Heracles was still a somewhat grotesque figure of popular mythology with associations not at all consonant with the epic convention. True, the Madness of Heracles was touched upon in the *Cypria;* and he must have come into the *Taking of Oichalia* and the *Aegimius;* while we possess the *Shield of Heracles,* where the treatment is heavily serious. But how are we to date any part of these traditional poems? It is somewhat different with the *Heracleia*. We can date Panyassis. Before Panyassis, Pisander and a more shadowy Pisinous, both of Rhodes, worked at the poem. It was in fact the traditional Rhodian epic. For some reason, which we may only conjecture, Heracles became the national hero of the Dorians. Naturally therefore in the Dorian island of Rhodes the tendency would arise to represent him worthily and epically. It could be done by working in the spirit which has cleansed the Homeric Poems of all the gross and ugly and silly things in the old saga-material. Thereby, however, the traditional conception of Heracles was not one whit affected. And it is this conception which finds expression in the Drama, because the Drama holds closer than the Epic to the fixed *Drômenon* with its *Kômos*. And so the comic Heracles is not epic burlesque, although of course, after he became a figure of the heroic saga, a piquancy was added to the fun by travesty of the epic hero.

It is Heracles who chiefly gives the *Alcestis* its satyric colour. Euripides to be sure does not treat him in the mere spirit of farce; to regard the Heracles of *Alcestis* as purely farcical is to spoil the peculiar quality of its appeal. One fails to understand how exquisite a piece of art it is, until one grasps the nature of the problem Euripides proposed to himself. Suppose he had written a satyr-play of the traditional sort; what would it have been like? If we had the *Alcestis* of Phrynichus, very likely the question would be answered for us. As it is, the satyric form has certain characteristics so marked; and the comic possibilities of the story are so clear; that we can be almost sure of the main lines a satyric *Alcestis* would follow.

To begin with: we must assume that there would be a Chorus of satyrs. Heracles is the natural centre and leader of their band; compare the position of Silenus in the *Cyclops*. Taking this as given, we may so far follow the order of events in Euripides as to suppose a Prologue in which Apollo and Death appear and abuse one another *more satyrico*. Death—a grotesque figure like a great black bird—accuses Apollo of making the Fates drunk and then taking advantage of their drunken complaisance to procure for Admetus a conditional respite from death. Following the Prologue, the Chorus would come in, perhaps with Heracles at their head, and sing their first *ode*. What next? One can hardly suppose that the death of Alcestis would be represented in a satyr-play. The death scene (it is worth observing) is really quite short in Euripides; and this is what we should expect if it was an innovation in the traditional plot, Greek art always reducing innovation to a minimum. But the altercation between Admetus and his father must surely belong to the old plot, and must come in; and so must the scene in which Heracles drunkenly moralizes on human destiny. The gloomy servant too, complaining to the audience of Heracles' manners at table, is conceived quite in the spirit of Greek comedy. Ultimately Heracles, having learned the truth about Alcestis, sets out for her tomb to catch Death and squeeze the breath out of him till he surrenders his prey. The finale is the triumphant reappearance of the hero with Alcestis and the celebration of his victory by the Kômos of satyrs. Normally in this scene Heracles and Alcestis should appear as (what in a sense they are) Bridegroom and Bride. But perhaps even the satyric plot had come to accept the present ending, and Alcestis was restored to Admetus.

What Euripides does is to soften down the grotesque elements of the story until we just feel that they are there, lurking possibilities of laughter, giving a faintly ironic but extraordinarily human quality to the pathos of the central situation. Death remains a somewhat *macabre* figure and slightly ridiculous; yet, if you laugh, it is, as we say, with the wrong side of your mouth. Apollo's trick to beguile the Fates is no more than hinted at. The quarrel between Admetus and Pheres is characteristically seized to throw a vivid and rather merciless light on the psychology of father and son. The drunkenness of Heracles is a very mild affair. The Triumph of the Hero resolves itself into a somewhat protracted and curious scene in which Heracles appears with Alcestis veiled—it seems worth remarking that a Greek bride wore a concealing veil—and pretends to Admetus that she is a prize won at some games in the neighbourhood. I think the explanation may be that the scene was traditional, and originally comic; it is not without a humorous element even in Euripides, and one does not require much imagination to see the amount of comic "business" which could be imported into it. The Komos-procession, which in a satyr-play must have followed the reunion of husband and wife, has been quietly omitted. The satyrs have made way for a tragedy chorus of Elders.

But what makes the *Alcestis* so original is not a mere readjustment of emphasis; it is not even the treatment of a satyric subject in the form and spirit of Greek Tragedy, for this could have been no innovation (since only in this way could Tragedy progress at all); it is the unique commingling of two spirits. One is the characteristic Euripidean spirit, sad, disenchanted, subtle, rebellious, ironical, sympathetic, hungry for beauty, hungrier for justice. The other is the jovial, tolerant spirit of the satyric tradition. In all Euripides' work we observe the meeting of cross-currents. Nowhere out of the *Alcestis* do we find this undercurrent of a satirical humour; and nowhere else do the various streams flow together so quietly and, as it were, so naturally. It is perhaps the most human of all his dramas, though not the greatest. The characters approach more nearly the level of ordinary humanity. We can not only accept them, we know them, we have lived with them. It was just that slight relaxation of the tragic tension in *Alcestis* which enabled Euripides to get this effect by permitting him to dwell a little on the minor human weaknesses which are the proper subject of Comedy. It might indeed be argued without too much paradox that the method of the *Alcestis* in some ways resembles the method of Modern Comedy (as, for example, Meredith practised it) more closely than anything in Aristophanes.

Every character in the play is intensely realized. Admetus has the artistic temperament. The farewell scene between Alcestis and him always reminds me of *Any Wife to Any Husband*:

> I know that nature! Pass a festive day,
> Thou dost not throw its relic-flower away
> Nor bid its music's loitering echo speed. . . .

He is selfish in the way of a spoilt child or a spoilt artist. Impossible for him to exist without admiration. It is partly this need, one feels, which makes him yield hospitality to Heracles at a moment so trying for everybody. When the leader of the Chorus remonstrates, Admetus answers:

> And had I turned the stranger from my door,
> Who sought my shelter, hadst thou praised me more?
> I trow not, if my sorrow were thereby
> No whit less, only the more friendless I.
> And more, when bards tell tales, were it not worse
> My house should lie beneath the stranger's curse?

Heracles nor any one else would have "cursed" him for closing his doors under the circumstances. But Admetus sees the opportunity for a shining display of "magnanimity," sees himself in the poets—as it were in the newspapers. This, while Alcestis (who died for him) is being carried to her grave. Yet somehow one does not hate him; perhaps because Alcestis loved him, perhaps because his need of admiration is not greater than his need of affection, perhaps because he is a commoner type than the stronger sex cares to admit. One even gets a little sorry for him after Pheres (that very vital old man) has stripped him of all his comfortable pretences—a bitter experience for our egoist. The fine speeches grow rarer and rarer; and at last cease altogether.

It is difficult to say anything at all about Alcestis, she is so whole and single. If she had not done what she did, the temptation would have been to call her characterless. She is very instinctive and feminine, with none of a man's desire to act up to a situation imposing the ideal test of the professedly masculine virtues. Think of Admetus in her place; what "noble sentiments" we should have had! Never was a less stagey heroine. Considering that it is she who makes the play, it is astonishing how little she says; but her very inarticulateness expresses and endears her to us. She is conventional, practical, rooted in domesticities. One suspects that her children are more to her than her husband, although she loves him too in a protecting, maternal way. She is extraordinarily true to type, and her example shows of what the type is capable.

Heracles is a very attractive character. He is a big jovial man with a great deal of good sense and kindly feeling under that rough lion-skin of his. He is that at all times; but he is sometimes more. One of the finest things in the play is the revelation, at the call of an extreme danger, of the heroic strain in this unassuming son of the god. We are made to feel that the roystering mood of the feast was but the mask of a more permanent mood, a kind of cheerful stoicism, accepting, though fully conscious of, the burden of its duty. His few last words break a sort of supernatural light over his going, and we forget Alcestis for the moment as we watch the suffering, kindly hero fare onwards into the mists of the North to do battle with the Thracian savage.

Euripides has made us accept that transfiguration as natural, inevitable. This is great art. Yet it merely enforces the stroke of genius which created a new kind of drama, full of possibilities since realized, taking us into a region where laughter and tears and mockery and admiration familiarly mingle. We moderns have wandered much in that region, and so perhaps understand Euripides better here than the ancients themselves in general understood him. So vital a matter was it for their art to preserve the purity of the type, the continuity of the tradition. Whereas the *Alcestis* was an experiment.

THUCYDIDES

[*460–400* B.C.]

AT HIS DEATH IN 1943, F. M. CORNFORD HAD ACHIEVED PREËMINENCE AMONG the historians of Greek thought and culture in his generation. He was a brilliant student of the mythic origins of Greek metaphysics and of the religious antecedents of the scientific and philosophical concerns of ancient thinkers. This lifelong interest found expression in one degree or another in all of his works, in *Thucydides Mythistoricus,* in *From Religion to Philosophy: A Study in the Origins of Western Speculation* (1912), and in his commentaries on Plato.

No historian, no matter how "scientific"—and Thucydides claimed such objectivity—escapes from principles of organization, conscious or unconscious. Cornford's essay discloses the "tragic" and mythic pattern that Thucydides employed to select and order the mass of detail at his disposal, and discusses the complex realm of discourse where poetry and history, imagination and event, intersect and reinforce each other's truth.

From *Thucydides Mythistoricus* by F. M. Cornford, 1907, by permission of Edward Arnold (Publishers) Ltd.

F. M. CORNFORD

Mythistoria and the Drama

THE EPITHET "DRAMATIC" HAS OFTEN BEEN APPLIED TO THUCYDIDES' WORK;
but usually nothing more is meant than that he allows his persons to
speak for themselves, and presents their character with vividness. The dramatization which we have pointed out in the treatment of Cleon is a very different thing; it is a principle of construction which, wherever it operates, determines the selection of incidents to be recorded, and the proportions and
perspective assigned them. In this chapter we shall attempt to describe and
analyse the type of drama that we have to do with, and to trace the literary
influence under which Thucydides worked.

We ought first, perhaps, to meet a possible objection. It may be urged that
Thucydides in his preface expressly excludes anything of the nature of poetical construction from his literal record of what was said and what was done.
He criticizes the methods of poets and story-writers, and warns us that, at
the cost of making his story "somewhat unattractive," he intends to exclude
"the mythical" (to mythōdes). He cannot, therefore, it might be inferred,
have done what we have thought we found him doing. But we would ask

for a careful examination of the passage in question. What was in Thucydides' thoughts when he wrote it, and above all, what precisely did he mean to exclude when he banished "the mythical"?

The words occur towards the end of the introduction, which is designed to establish Thucydides' belief that the Peloponnesian war was the most memorable of all that had ever been in Greece. The possible rivals, he points out, are the Trojan war and the Persian invasion. For the first of these events the only literary evidence we have is that of the epic poets, and chiefly of Homer, whose record cannot be checked by direct observation, while much of his theme through the lapse of time has passed, or "won over," into the region of the mythical and incredible. The only tests we have are certain indications in the existing condition of Greece which seem inconsistent with the past state of things as represented by the literary authorities. With these indications we must be content; and they suffice to show that the epic poets embellished their tale by exaggeration. The story-writers, again, on whom we depend for the history of the Persian wars, were not bent upon accurate statement of truth;—witness the carelessness of Herodotus about points of detail. Their object was rather to make their recitations attractive and amusing to their audience; and if we discount their evidence accordingly, we shall find, going by ascertained facts alone, that the Peloponnesian war was the greatest ever seen.

Thucydides next passes abruptly to the formulation of his own method; he intends to record what was said and what was done as accurately and literally as possible. The result, he then remarks, will probably be somewhat unattractive to an audience at a recitation, because the facts recorded will have nothing "mythical" about them; he will be content, however, if they are judged useful by people who wish to know the plain truth of what happened.

The phrase "winning over into the mythical" is illuminating. It suggests the transformation which begins to steal over all events from the moment of their occurrence, unless they are arrested and pinned down in writing by an alert and trained observer. Even then some selection cannot be avoided— a selection, moreover, determined by irrelevant psychological factors, by the accidents of interest and attention. Moment by moment the whole fabric of events dissolves in ruins and melts into the past; and all that survives of the thing done passes into the custody of a shifting, capricious, imperfect, human memory. Nor is the mutilated fragment allowed to rest there, as on a shelf in a museum; imagination seizes on it and builds it with other fragments into some ideal construction, which may have a plan and outline laid out long before this fresh bit of material came to the craftsman's hand to be worked into it, as the drums of fallen columns are built into the rampart of an Acropolis. Add to this the cumulative effects of oral tradition. One ideal edifice falls into ruin; pieces of it, conglomerates of those ill-assorted and haphazard fragments, are carried to another site and worked into a structure of, perhaps, a quite different model. Thus fact shifts into legend, and legend into myth. The facts *work loose;* they are detached from their roots in time and space and shaped into a story. The story is moulded and re-moulded by imagination, by passion and prejudice, by religious preconception or aesthetic instinct, by the delight in the marvellous, by the itch for a moral, by the love of a good story; and the thing becomes a legend. A few irreducible facts will remain; no more, perhaps, than the names of persons and places—Arthur,[1] Caerleon, Camelot; but even these may at last drop out or be turned by a poet into symbols. "By Arthur," said Tennyson, "I always meant the soul, and by the Round Table the passions and capacities of man." The history has now all but won over into the mythical. Change the names, and every trace of literal fact will have vanished; the story will have escaped from time into eternity.

When we study this process, we seem to make out two phases of it, which, for the criticism of Thucydides, it is necessary to distinguish. The more important and pervasive of the two is the moulding of fact into types of myth contributed by traditional habits of thought. This process of *infigura-tion* (if we may coin the word) may be carried to any degree. Sometimes the facts happen to fit the mould, and require hardly any modification; mere unconscious selection is enough. In other cases they have to be stretched a little here, and patted down there, and given a twist before they will fit. In extreme instances, where a piece is missing, it is supplied by mythological inference from the interrupted portions which call for completion; and here we reach the other phase of the process, namely *invention.* This is no longer a matter of imparting a form to raw material; it is the creation of fresh material when the supply of fact is not sufficient to fill the mould. It leads further to the embroidery of fabulous anecdote, which not only has no basis in fact, but is a superfluous addition, related to fact as illustrations in a book are related to the text.

The process, in both its phases, can be illustrated from the version pre-served by Thucydides of the legend of Harmodius and Aristogeiton, the tyrant-slayers. Harmodius' sister, whom the tyrant insults, makes her first appearance in this account. She is superfluous, since the murderers had already a sufficient private motive arising out of the love-quarrel. That is

[1] We assume that Arthur was historic; but he may have been Arcturus for all we know.

not in itself an argument against her historical character, for superfluous people sometimes do exist; but other circumstances make it not improbable that she owes her existence to the mythical type which normally appears in legend when tyrants have to be slain. The two brothers, or lovers, and the injured sister, or wife—the relationships vary—are the standing *dramatis personae* on such occasions. Collatinus, Brutus, and Lucretia are another example from legend; while the purely mythical type which shapes such legends is seen in the Dioscuri and Helen.[2] The suggestion is that Harmodius and Aristogeiton were identified with the Heavenly Twins. If there is any truth in the story of how Peisistratus was conducted back to Athens by a woman dressed as Athena and accepted by the citizens as the goddess in person, it is not surprising that the next generation of Athenians should have recognized the Dioscuri in Harmodius and his friend. Given that identification, the injured sister is felt to be a desirable, if not indispensable, accessory; she is filled in by inference, and she becomes a candidate for the place of "basket-bearer" in the Panathenaic procession, at which the murder took place. Thus, the legend of Harmodius illustrates both the phases of the process we described: first, it is moulded on the mythical type of the Heavenly Twins, and then invention supplies the missing third figure.

Mythical types of this sort can be discovered and classified only after a wide survey of comparative Mythistoria; for we all take our own habits of thought for granted, and we cannot perceive their bias except by contrast. The Greek who knew only Greek legend could not possibly disengage the substance from the form; all he could do was to prune away the fabulous and supernatural overgrowths, and cut down poetry into prose. It is thus that Thucydides treats myths like the story of Tereus, Procne, and Philomela; he rationalizes them, thinking that he has reduced them to history when he has removed unattested and improbable accretions, such as the transformation of Tereus into a hoopoe. But history cannot be made by this process (which is still in use); all that we get is, not the original facts, but a mutilated legend; and this may very well be so mutilated that it is no longer possible to distinguish the informing element of fiction, which was discernible till we effaced the clues.

The phenomenon that especially concerns us now is something much wider than the mythical infiguration of a single incident here or there, such as the legend of the Tyrant-slayers. It is the moulding of a long series of

---

[2] Even aspirants to tyranny have to be killed on this pattern. Thus one version of Alcibiades' death was that the *brothers* of a woman with whom he was spending the night set fire to the house and cut him down as he leapt out through the flames. Plut. *vit. Alcib.* fin.

[125]

events into a plan determined by an *art form*. When we set the *Persians* of Aeschylus beside the history of Herodotus, we see at once that the tragedian in dramatizing the events of Xerxes' invasion, some of which he had personally witnessed, has also worked them into a theological scheme, preconceived and contributed by his own mind. Further we remark that Herodotus, although he is operating in a different medium and writing a saga about the glory of Athens, uses the same theological train of thought as a groundwork, and falls in with the dramatic conception of Aeschylus. This is a case of the infiguration of a whole train of events by a form which is mythical, in so far as it involves a theological theory of sinful pride punished by jealous divinity, and is also an art form, by which the action is shaped on dramatic principles of construction, involving such features as climax, reversal, catastrophe. The theory and the form together provide the setting of the whole story—the element which makes it a work of art. This element is so structural that it cannot be removed without the whole fabric falling to pieces, and at the same time so latent and pervasive, as not to be perceptible until the entire work is reviewed in its large outline. Even then it can be detected only by a critic who is on his guard and has not the same scheme inwrought into the substance of his own mind; for if he is himself disposed to see the events in conformity with the scheme, then the story will answer his expectation and look to him perfectly natural.

When Thucydides speaks of "the mythical," it seems probable from the context that he is thinking chiefly of *inventive* "embellishment." The accretions of fabulous anecdote are comparatively easy to detect; they often bring in the supernatural in the forms of vulgar superstition, and being for this reason improbable, they require better evidence than is forthcoming. Also, poets tend to *magnify* their theme for purposes of panegyric, flattering to their audience; they will, for instance, represent Agamemnon's expedition as much larger than it probably was. It is on these grounds that Thucydides objects to the evidence of Ionian Epos and Herodotean story-telling. He warns us against the faults which struck his notice; and he was on his guard against them, even more than against the popular superstition and dogmatic philosophy of the day, which he tacitly repudiates. But there was one thing against which he does not warn us, precisely because it was the framework of his own thought, not one among the objects of reflection,—a scheme contributed, like the Kantian categories of space and time, by the mind itself to whatever was presented from outside. Thucydides, like Descartes, thought he had stripped himself bare of every preconception; but, as happened also with Descartes, his work shows that there was after all a residuum wrought into the substance of his mind and ineradicable because unperceived. This residuum was his philosophy of human nature, as it is set forth in the speech

[126]

of Diodotus,—a theory of the passions and of their working which carried with it a principle of dramatic construction presently to be described. That he was not forearmed against this, he himself shows when, in attacking Herodotus, he accuses him of trivial errors of fact, and does not bring the one sweeping and valid indictment which is perfectly relevant to his own point about the embellishment of the Persian War. The dramatic construction of Herodotus' work, which stares a modern reader in the face, apparently escaped the observation of his severest ancient critic.

Another proof can be drawn from Thucydides' own account of a series of events which he evidently believed to be historical, the closing incidents, namely, of Pausanias' career. He shows us the Spartan king intriguing with the Persian, and "bent upon the empire of Hellas." Pausanias commits certain treacherous acts; boasts of his power to the Great King; "intends, if the king please, to marry his daughter"; is so "uplifted" by the king's answer that he can no longer live like ordinary men; behaves like an oriental; cannot keep silence about his larger designs; makes himself difficult of access, and displays a harsh temper. We know all these symptoms well enough, and we foresee the end. Pausanias is recalled, but the evidence against him is insufficient. He writes a letter betraying his designs and ending with an order for the execution of the bearer. The messenger, whose suspicions are aroused, opens the letter and shows it to the authorities at Sparta. The ephors arrange that they shall be concealed behind a partition and overhear a conversation between the king and his treacherous messenger, who contrives to draw from Pausanias a full and damning avowal. The end follows in the Brazen House.

This is not the sort of thing that Thucydides objects to as "mythical"; it is not "fabulous," not the embroidery of mere poetical invention; and so he reports it all in perfect good faith. What does not strike him, and what does strike us, is that the story is a drama, framed on familiar lines, and ready to be transferred to the stage without the alteration of a detail. The earlier part is a complete presentation of the "insolent" type of character. The climax is reached by a perfect example of "Recoil" (*peripeteia*), where the hero gives the fatal letter to the messenger, and thus by his own action precipitates the catastrophe. The last scene is staged by means of a theatrical property now so cheapened by use as to be barely respectable—a screen![3] The manner of the hero's death involved sacrilege, and was believed to bring a curse upon

---

[3] It is possible that in this scene we can just trace a dramatic motive, which is all but rationalized away,—the idea, namely, that Pausanias cannot fall till he has *committed himself by his own act*, to which act he must be tempted by the traitor.

his executioners. Could we have better proof that Thucydides was not on his guard against dramatic construction, and was predisposed to see in the working of events a train of "causes" which tragedy had made familiar?

When we are alive to the dramatic setting, we can infer with some certainty the stages through which the Thucydidean story of Pausanias has passed. The original stratum of fact must have been that Pausanias somehow misconducted himself, was recalled, and put to death in circumstances which were capable of being used by superstition and policy against the ephors. These facts worked loose into a legend, shaped by imagination on the model of preconceived morality and views of human nature. The mould is supplied by drama; and meanwhile fabulous invention is busy in many minds, embroidering the tale with illustrative anecdotes. Thucydides brushes away these extravagant and unattested accretions, and reduces the legend again to what seemed to him a natural series of events. It is only we who can perceive that what he has left is the dramatized legend, not the historical facts out of which it was worked up. It is not wildly paradoxical to think that the historian who accepted the legend of Pausanias might frame on the same pattern the legend of Cleon. Not that Thucydides invented anything; all that was needed was to select, half unconsciously, those parts of his life which of themselves composed the pattern.

We must now come to closer quarters with the epithet "dramatic." It is worth noting, at the outset, that in the mere matter of external form, the history seems to show the influence of tragedy,—a fact which need not surprise us, if we remember that Thucydides had no model for historical writing. The brief abstract of the annalist was a scaffold, not a building; and Thucydides was an architect, not a carpenter. Chroniclers and story-writers like Herodotus had chosen the lax form of epic, congenial to ramblers; but whatever the history was to be, it was not to be like Herodotus, and it was to draw no inspiration from the tradition of Ionian Epos. So Thucydides turned to drama—the only other developed form of literature then existing which could furnish a hint for the new type to be created. The severe outline and scrupulous limitations of this form satisfied his instinct for self-suppression. The epic poet stands before his audience and tells his own tale; but the dramatist never appears at all: the "thing done" (*drama*) works itself out before the spectators' eyes; the thing said comes straight from the lips of the actors.

Best of all, to Thucydides' thinking, if we, of after times, could ourselves have watched every battle as it was won and lost, and ourselves have heard every speech of envoy and statesman; we should then have known all, and much more than all, this history was designed to tell. But as this cannot be, we are to have the next thing to it; we shall sit as in a theatre, where the historian will erect his mimic stage and hold the mirror up to Nature. Himself will play the part of "messenger" and narrate "what was actually done" with just so much of vividness as the extent of his own information warrants. For the rest, the actors shall tell their own tale, as near as may be, in the very words they used, "as I heard them myself, or as others reported them."

Speeches are much more prominent in Thucydides' history than they are in that of Herodotus. The change seems partly due to the later historian's preference for setting forth motives in the form of "pretexts," instead of giving his own opinion; but it is also due to his being an Athenian. Plato similarly chose to cast his speculations in the dramatic form of dialogue, allowing various points of view to be expressed by typical representatives, without committing himself to any of them. Even oratory at Athens was dramatically conceived; the speech-writer did not appear as advocate in court; he wrote speeches in character to be delivered by his clients. It has often been remarked that the debates in Thucydides resemble in some points of technique the debates in a Euripidean play. There is moreover in one respect an intellectual kinship between Thucydides and the dramatist who was contemporaneously moulding the form of tragedy to the strange uses of realism, and working away from Aeschylus as Thucydides had to work away from Herodotus. The two men are of very different temperaments; but in both we seem to find the same sombre spirit of renunciation, the same conscious resolve nowhere to overstep the actual, but to present the naked thoughts and actions of humanity, just as they saw them. No matter how crude the light, how harsh the outline, so that the thing done and the thing said shall stand out as they were, in isolated sharpness, though

> Mist is under and mist above, . . .
> And we drift on legends for ever.[4]

These considerations, however, touch only the question of external form: they show why so much that we should state directly is stated indirectly by Thucydides, in speeches. The choice of this form is consistent with a complete absence of *plot* or of dramatic construction: otherwise Thucydides could not have chosen it at starting; for at that moment the plot lay in the unknown future. We mention the point only because evidently it was somewhat easier for an historian who consciously borrowed the outward form of tragedy, to take unconsciously the further step, and fall in with its inward form and principle of design. It is this which we now wish to define more closely. The type of drama we have detected in the history is not the

---

[4] Eurip. *Hippol.* 191 ff. Mr. Gilbert Murray's translation.

Euripidean type; it will be found, on examination, to show an analogy with the older form existing in the tragedies of Aeschylus.

The resemblances are reducible to two main points. The first is an analogy of technical construction, seen in the use and correlation of different parts of the work. The second is a community of psychological conceptions: a mode of presenting character, and also a theory of the passions which has a place not only in psychology, but in ethics. We shall begin by studying the structure; but we may bear in mind that this structure is closely involved with the psychological theory.

An art form, such as the Aeschylean drama, shapes itself as a sort of crust over certain beliefs which harden into that outline. When this has happened, the beliefs themselves—the content of the mould—may gradually be modified and transmuted in many ways. Finally, they may melt and almost fade away, leaving the type, which is preserved as a traditional form of art. This survival of an element of technical construction may be illustrated by the instance of "reversal" (*peripeteia*). A "reversal of fortune" is the cardinal point of primitive tragedy; and it originally means an overthrow caused by an *external* supernatural agency—Fate or an angry god. When the belief in such agencies fades, "reversal" remains as a feature in drama; but the change of situation is now caused by the hero's own act. The notion of "recoil" comes in: that is to say, the fatal action itself produces results just the opposite of those intended—a perfectly natural occurrence. In this way a piece of technique outlasts the belief which gave rise to it.

The Aeschylean drama appears to us to have gone through a process of this kind. The structure, as we find it, seems to imply an original content of beliefs in some respects more primitive than those explicitly held by Aeschylus himself, but surviving in his mind with sufficient strength to influence his work. Similarly, as we hope to show, in transmission from Aeschylus to Thucydides, the dramatic type has again outlasted much of the belief which informed it in the Aeschylean stage. It is the artistic structure which is permanent; the content changes with the advance of thought. Hence, if we point to Aeschylean technique in Thucydides, we are not necessarily attributing to him the creed of Aeschylus.

We must first attempt to describe the structure of Aeschylean tragedy.[5] In order to understand it we must try to imagine a yet more primitive stage

[5] The description which follows is based on an analysis of the impression made on the writer by an Aeschylean tragedy. It is of course not susceptible of demonstration; the only test is the reader's own impression. The description is not exhaustive, but is designed only to bring out a neglected aspect.

in the development of the drama than any represented in extant Greek literature, a stage which the earliest of Aeschylus' plays has already left some way behind. A glance at the development of modern drama may help us.

Certain features which survived in Greek tragedy suggest that we should look back to a type somewhat resembling the mediaeval mystery and some of the earliest modern dramas, such as *Everyman,* which are like the mystery in being religious performances and in the element of allegorical abstraction. Their effect, due in part to each of these features, may be described as *symbolic. Everyman* is a sermon made visible. To watch it is like watching the pastime called "living chess," in which the pieces are men and women, but the man who is dressed like a bishop is nothing more than a chessman who happens to be automatic. He has not the episcopal character; his dress is a disguise with nothing behind it; his words, if he spoke, would be the speech of a parrot. And so it is with *Everyman.* The persons are not persons at all, but *personae,* masks, symbols, the vehicles of abstract ideas. They do not exist, and could not be conceived as existing, in real space and time. They have no human characters, no inward motives, no life of their own. Everyman, as his name is meant to show, is in fact not *a* man, but Man, the universal.

The main development of modern drama shows, in one of its aspects, the process by which this symbolic method gives way to the realistic. The process consists in the gradual filling in of the human being behind the mask, till the humanity is sufficiently concrete and vital to burst the shell and step forth in solid flesh and blood. The symbol comes to contain a type of character; the type is particularized into a unique individual. The creature now has an independent status and behaviour of its own. Every gesture and every word must be such as would be used by an ordinary human being with the given character in the given situation. Once created, the personality is an original centre; it cannot be made to do what we please or to utter our thoughts. In some such terms as these a modern novelist or playwright will speak of his characters; and it is thus that they appear to us.

Now we can observe a certain intermediate stage in which these two methods, the symbolic and the realistic, are balanced in antagonism, so as to produce a curious effect of tension and incoherency. A good instance is Marlowe's *Faustus*. Faustus himself occupies the central plane; he is a living man, but still imprisoned in a symbolical type. The intrusion of humanity has gone far enough to disturb the abstract effect, and it reacts on some of the persons in the play who ought to be purely symbolic. Lucifer, it is true, is kept apart and remains non-human; but Mephistophilis oscillates in our imagination between the ideal and reality, with a distressing result. Again, on a lower level than Faustus there is yet another grade of persons, in contrast with whom he shows up as heroic and ideal. These are the vintner, the horse-courser, and other pieces of common clay picked out of a London alley; they belong to a different world, and we feel that they could no more communicate with the tragic characters than men can talk with angels.[6] Thus there are in this one play four sets or orders of persons: (1) the purely abstract and *symbolic,* such as Lucifer, who only appears on an upper stage at certain moments, and takes no part in the action; (2) the *intermediate,* for instance Mephistophilis, who ought to be symbolic, but treads the lower stage, a cowled enigma,[7] horrible because at moments he ceases to be symbolic without becoming human; (3) the *heroic* or tragic: Faustus, who is an ideal half realized, hanging together on its own plane; (4) the *real:* common mortals who would attract no attention in Fleet Street.

The Greek drama, although in the detail of historical development it started at a different point from the modern, and followed another course, seems, nevertheless, to pass through a phase analogous to that which we have just described. The original substance of the drama was the choral lyric; the actors (as they afterwards became) began as an excrescence. At a certain stage the actors are assimilated to the chorus and move in the same atmosphere. Thus in the earliest play of Aeschylus, the *Suppliants,* we find that the chorus of Danaids are actually the heroines of the action, which centres round them, so that they are not merely on the same plane with the actors, but themselves a complex actor, and the effect is simple, coherent, and uniform. In the *Prometheus,* again, the chorus belong to the same ideal world as the Titan hero, a world in which abstract symbols like Mastery and Violence can move without showing as unreal against the other persons. The whole drama is on the symbolic plane, the life in it being due to anthropomorphic imagination, not to the intrusion of realism.

But in the latest plays of Aeschylus, the beginning of a change is clearly marked: the actors are becoming human, while the lyric is rising above them, or else remains suspended in a rarer atmosphere from which they are sinking. This is a natural stage in the passage from pure symbolism to realism. The advance shows itself externally in the *drifting apart* of the

---

[6] We hope it is true that Marlowe did not write the comic scenes; but we are only concerned with the effect of the play as it stands.

[7] In the Elizabethan Stage Society's representation Mephistophilis is cowled and *his face is never seen.* The effect is indescribably horrible. At certain moments in Greek Tragedy the mask must have produced a somewhat similar effect, though the familiarity of the convention would make it much less in degree. The longing to see the actor's face, when his words are enigmatic, is almost enough to drive a modern spectator insane.

lyrical element from the dialogue,—a separation which, of course, widens in the later tragedians, till the choral ode, though still an indispensable and very beautiful feature, becomes in point of construction little more than an interlude, which relieves the concentrated intensity of the action. This change is commonly taken as a phenomenon which needs no explanation; but really it is caused inevitably by the *coming to life* of the persons in the drama. In proportion as these become more real, the lyric becomes more ideal and further removed from the action.

In the stage observable in Aeschylus' latest plays, the choral part is still *dramatic,* and of equal importance with the dialogue. The two elements are evenly balanced; but at the same time they have begun to occupy different worlds, so that we are sensible of the transition from one to the other. The result is a curious duplication of the drama which now has two aspects, the one universal and timeless, the other particular and temporal.

The nature of this phenomenon will, we hope, become clear, if we take as an illustration the *Agamemnon.* In this play, the visible presentation shows how the conqueror of Troy came home and was murdered by the queen. The events that go forward on the stage are *particular* events, located at a point of legendary time[8] and of real space. The characters are certain individuals, legendary or historic—there is to Aeschylus no difference here—who lived at that moment and trod that spot of earth. But in the choral odes the action is lifted out of time and place on to the plane of the universal. When the stage is clear and the visible presentation is for the time suspended, then, above and beyond the transient spectacle of a few suffering mortals caught, just there and then, in the net of crime, loom up in majestic distance and awful outline the truths established, more unchangeably than the mountains, in the eternal counsels of Zeus. The pulse of momentary passion dies down; the clash and conflict of human wills, which just now had held us in breathless concentration, sink and dwindle to the scale of a puppet-show; while the enduring song of Destiny unrolls the theme of blood-haunted Insolence lured by insistent Temptation into the toils of Doom. As though on a higher stage, uncurtained in the choral part, another company of actors concurrently plays out a more majestic and symbolic drama. On this invisible scene walk the figures of Hybris and Peitho, of Nemesis and Ate—not the bloodless abstractions of later allegory, but still clothed in the glowing lineaments of

---

[8] By legendary time we mean the time occupied by events which have worked so loose from real time that you can only date them within a century or so, and do not think of dating them at all, till challenged. They are near the stage in which the only date is "once-upon-a-time," the verge of mythical time which has no dates at all.

supernatural reality. The curtain lifts for a timeless moment on the spectacle of human life in an aspect known to the all-seeing eyes of Zeus; and when it drops again, we turn back to the mortal tragedy of Agamemnon and Clytemnestra, enlightened, purified, uplifted, calm.

Thus we find in Aeschylus something analogous to the hierarchy of persons we noted in *Faustus;* although, for various reasons, there is not the same crude effect of incoherency and tension. The supernatural characters—Zeus, supreme above all, and the demonic figures of Hybris, Nemesis, Ate, and the rest, are not *seen,* as Lucifer is seen on the upper stage of the Elizabethan theatre, but remain in the spiritual world to which lyrical emotion exalts the inward eye—the world where metaphor (as we call it) is the very stuff of reality, where Cassandra quickens and breathes, and whence she strays among mortal men like a fallen spirit, sweet-voiced, mad, and broken-winged. Hence the effect is far more awful and solemn than the actual apparition of Lucifer; and when Apollo and Athene and the spirits of vengeance take human shape in the *Eumenides,* a spell is broken, a veil rent, an impression shattered, for which not the most splendid symphony of poetical language can atone.

Here, however, we would confine our attention to the *Agamemnon.* At the lower end of the scale we find a further advance of realism in some minor characters, the watchman and the herald; the nurse in the *Choephori* is of the same order. These are allowed some wonderful touches of common humanity, below the heroic level; for they are not directly concerned in the central action, and a little irrelevant naturalism does no harm, if it is not carried far. But they are only just below the heroic standard, and are certainly not the sort of people you would have met in a walk to the Piraeus.

Thus, the two planes in the *Agamemnon* are divided by an interval less wide and less abrupt than the divisions in *Faustus.* In psychological conception also the union is very close, since the heroic characters are still so abstract and symbolic that they are barely distinguishable from the pure abstractions of the lyrical world. Agamemnon, for instance, is simply Hybris typified in a legendary person. He is a hero flown with "insolence" (the pride and elation of victory), and that is all that can be said of him. He is not, like a character in Ibsen, a complete human being with a complex personality,—a centre from which relations radiate to innumerable points of contact in a universe of indifferent fact. He has not a continuous history: nothing has ever happened to him except the conquest of Troy and the sacrifice of Iphigenia; nothing ever could happen to him except Pride's fall and the stroke of the axe. As we see him, he is not a man, but a single state of mind, which has never been preceded by other states of mind (except one, at the sacrifice in Aulis), but is isolated, without context, margin, or atmosphere. Every word he says, in so far as he speaks for himself and not for the poet, comes straight out of that state of mind and expresses some phase of it. He has a definite relation to Cassandra, a definite relation to Clytemnestra; but no relation to anything else. If he can be said to have a *character* at all, it consists solely of certain defects which make him liable to Insolence; if he has any *circumstances,* they are only those which prompt him to his besetting passion.

Now it is in some such way as this that Thucydides presents his principal characters. Cleon is a good instance. He is allowed no individuality, no past history, no atmosphere, no irrelevant relations. He enters the story abruptly from nowhere. A single phrase fixes his type, as though on a play-bill: "Cleon, the most violent of the citizens and first in the people's confidence"; that is all we know of him. There follows a speech in which the type reveals itself in a state of mind,—Violence in its several phases. Then he vanishes, to reappear, before Sphacteria, as Violence with one of its aspects ("covetousness") emphasized, and a sudden passion of ambitious self-confidence (*elpis*) added thereto. Finally, we see him wrecked by this passion at Amphipolis. Pericles is introduced in the same way, with a single epithet: "Pericles, the son of Xanthippos, a man at that time first among the Athenians, and *most powerful* (*dynatōtatos*) in action and in speech." His characteristic quality is wise foresight (*gnōmē*—the opening word of his first speech); and he stands also, in the Funeral Oration, for the glory (*timē*) of Athens. Alcibiades we shall study later. In every case the principal characters are nearly as far removed from realism, nearly as abstract and impersonal as the heroic characters in Aeschylus. Thucydides, in fact, learnt his psychology from the drama, just as we moderns (whether historians or not) learn ours, not by direct observation, but from the drama and the novel.

But we can carry the analogy further; it extends to minor points of Aeschylean technical construction, which follow naturally upon the drifting apart of lyric and dialogue. In the *Agamemnon* we note that the separation of the two planes has gone far enough to make it impossible for the members of the chorus to interfere with the action at its crisis. The elders, when they hear the death-cry, cannot enter the palace; not because the door is locked, nor yet because they are feeble old men. Rather they are old men because an impassable barrier of convention is forming between chorus and actors, and their age gives colour to their powerlessness. The need of a separate stage for the actors, though tradition may cling to the old orchestra, is already felt. The poet is half aware of the imaginative separation, and he bridges it by links of two kinds—formal links of technical device, and internal connexions of a psychological sort, which will occupy us in the next chapter.

The formal links are provided by what is called "tragic irony." The dialogue is so contrived that, instructed by the lyric, we can catch in it allusions to grander themes than any of which the speakers are conscious, and follow the action with eyes opened to a universal significance, hidden from the agents themselves. Tragic irony, however, is not a deliberately invented artifice; it arises of itself in the advance from the purely symbolic stage of drama. In that earliest stage the whole dialogue might be called "ironical," in the sense that it is the poet's message to the audience, not the expression of the persons' characters, for they have none. But it becomes ironical in the strict sense only when the persons begin to have elementary characters and minds, and so to be conscious of one meaning of their words, which is not the whole meaning or the most important. The effect is now no longer merely symbolic, but *hypnotic;* the speaker on the stage is like a somnambulist—alive, but controlled and occupied by an external personality, the playwright.

Tragic irony is used by Aeschylus with great freedom; because his persons are still so near to the symbolic, they have so little character and psychology of their own, that they do not mind serving as mouthpieces. Here and there we find instances of perfect irony, where the speaker's words bear both constructions equally well, and are at once the natural expression of the appropriate state of mind and also a message from the poet to the spectator, applying one of the lyrical themes. This is the only sort of irony admitted by Sophocles, whose characters have become so human that they will not speak merely for another. In Aeschylus, however, there are whole speeches which are hypnotic, and hardly in character at all. The effect is so unfamiliar to readers schooled in realism that it is often missed.

The first two speeches of Clytemnestra, for instance, seem to be of this kind; notably, the beacon speech. If we try to interpret this as a realistic revelation of Clytemnestra's character and thoughts, we shall not find that it helps us to much insight, because its main function has nothing to do with her character. The poet is speaking through her, and the thoughts are his. The early part of the play, down to the entrance of Agamemnon, is an overture, in which Aeschylus musters and marshals the abstract themes which are to be the framework of the trilogy. One of them is expressed in the beacon speech; and it is this. The fire of Idaean Zeus has fallen upon Troy, "neither before its season nor striking as an idle glancing shaft beyond the stars"; but that *same* fire, the symbol of Justice, speeds now to "strike the roof of the Atreidae." From mountain top it leaps and hastens across the sea to mountain top; and like the torch passed from hand to hand in the race, it is itself a runner and the only one which "running first and last reaches the goal." This description of the symbolic fire conducted along the beacon chain is given to Clytemnestra because it can be given to no one else, not because it is the best means of illustrating her psychology. The speech, by the way, also exhibits another artifice employed to link the two planes—the allusive verbal echo between dialogue and lyric. The symbol of the fire, in a slightly varied form, recurs at the beginning of the next chorus, and the keyword (*skēptein*) is reiterated to mark the correspondence.

Now the speeches in Thucydides can be roughly classed under four heads. There are, first, a few realistic speeches by minor characters; for instance, the short, sharp utterance of the Spartan ephor, which has the trick of the laconic practical man. Next, there are idealistic speeches, designed as direct expressions of character or of national ideals; the Funeral Oration will serve as an example. These shade off, through a class in which sketches of national character are introduced indirectly, with some strain upon dramatic probability, into a class where irony is openly employed in the tragic manner. Cleon's Mytilenean speech, for instance, is nearly all of the character-revealing sort, but it contains a passage about the evil results of exceptional prosperity which is without any true application to the position of Lesbos or to the history of the revolt. It runs as follows:

> Conceiving a reckless confidence in the future, and hopes that outran their strength though they fell short of their desires, they went to war; and they thought fit to prefer might to right, for where they thought they saw a chance of success, they set upon us when we were doing them no wrong. It is always so: when exceptional prosperity comes sudden and unexpected to a city, it turns to insolence: and, in general, good fortune is safer for mankind when it answers to calculation than when it surpasses expectation, and one might almost say that men find it easier to drive away adversity than to preserve prosperity. We were wrong from the first. We ought never to have put the Mytileneans above the rest by exceptional treatment; then their insolence would not have come to this height. It is a general rule that human nature despises flattery, and respects unyielding strength.

These words are patently inapplicable to the revolted island, whose exceptional position was notoriously a survival of the status originally enjoyed by every one of the allies, but now forfeited by all but a few; to speak of it as a sudden access of prosperity is simply meaningless. We are driven to see in the passage a use of tragic irony; Thucydides puts into Cleon's mouth the very moral which his own career is to illustrate. The device is unskillfully employed, since dramatic probability is too completely sacrificed. Sophocles would not have passed these sentences, which on the speaker's lips have not even a plausible meaning; but Aeschylus would have passed them, and after all Thucydides was only an amateur tragedian.

A fourth use of speeches is illustrated by the Spartan envoys' homily before Sphacteria. This is still further removed from realism, and resembles the beacon speech, which is but one degree below the lyric plane. The historian, reluctant to break silence in his own person, sets forth the theme and framework of his drama in the form of a solemn warning. He has already described the Athenians at Pylos as "wishing to follow up their present good fortune to the furthest point." This is a dangerous frame of mind, against which Themistocles had warned the Athenians after Salamis, when they wished to press forward and destroy the Persians' bridges over the Hellespont.[9] "I have often," says Themistocles, "myself witnessed occasions, and I have heard of many from others, where men who had been conquered by an enemy, having been driven quite to desperation, have renewed the fight and retrieved their former disasters. We have now had the great good luck (*heurēma heurēkamen*) to save both ourselves and all Greece by the repulse of this vast cloud of men; let us then be content and not press them too hard, now that they have begun to fly. Be sure that we have not done this by our own might. It is the work of gods and heroes, who were jealous that one man should be king at once of Europe and Asia. . . . At present all is well with us—let us then abide in Greece, and look to ourselves and to our families."

The warning of the Spartan envoys is conceived in the same spirit; but it is unheeded and unanswered. No answer, indeed, was possible; the speech is not an argument, but a prophecy. A reply from Cleon, a statement of the war party's policy, such as modern critics desiderate, would be as inappropriate as a reply from Clytemnestra to the Second Chorus in the *Agamemnon*. The stage is clear while this prophecy, addressed not to the actors but to the spectators, passes unheard by those who, could they have heard it, might have been saved.

One further point of formal resemblance between Aeschylus and Thucydides is the allusive echoing of significant phrases, which sustain the moral motive dominant in the plot. We have seen an instance of this device in the repetition of the words "coveting more" (*pleonos oregesthai*), which reappear at critical moments after the use of them in the envoys' speech; and we shall note other examples later. This completes the analogy with Aeschylean form, so far as concerns external peculiarities.

---

[9] Herod. viii. 109 Rawlinson trans.

A R I S T O P H A N E S

[*c. 448–c. 380* B.C.]

THE COMEDY OF ARISTOPHANES IS UNIQUE FOR ITS BLEND OF EXQUISITE LYRICISM with bawdry, its uninhibited mockery of things divine and human, its scathing and, in our view, sometimes unjust criticism of contemporary political and cultural figures, its permanence and universality, in spite of being so topical, so rooted in immediate events. Werner Jaeger's essay calls our attention to the singularity of this author in the history of literature and to his role in the great Hellenic dialogue over *paideia*.

Jaeger's book *Paideia: The Ideals of Greek Culture* is perhaps the indispensable work for the student of Greek culture. As he tells us in a brief prefatory note, the word *paideia* is difficult to define, and no English expression such as "civilization," "culture," "tradition," "literature," or "education" can express more than one of its aspects. It includes all of these English renderings simultaneously and in unity. The definition, indeed, is found only in the whole of Jaeger's magisterial work.

Professor Jaeger, University Professor at Harvard, died October 20, 1961.

From *Paideia: The Ideals of Greek Culture* by Werner Jaegar, 1939, by permission of the publishers, Basil Blackwell, Oxford.

WERNER JAEGER

The Comic Poetry of Aristophanes

No description of Greek civilization in the last quarter of the fifth century could pass over that strange but attractive phenomenon, Attic comedy. The ancients, in calling it "the mirror of life," meant that it reflected the eternal spectacle of human nature and its weaknesses. And yet it is also the most complete reflection of its own age, far surpassing any other type of literature or art in fullness and accuracy. If we wish to study the external appearance and habits of the Athenians, we can learn just as much from vase-painting, the epic of everyday life; but vivid, convenient, and varied as the vase-paintings are, they tell us nothing of the loftier spiritual activities which produced the greatest comic poetry now extant. One of the inestimable advantages that we owe to Attic comedy is that it shows us both philosophy and poetry and the state itself, in the heart of this living stream of activity, surrounded and inspired by it, so that they cease to look like isolated phenomena and the full power of their immediate influence can be appreciated within the frame of their own time. It is only in the period which we know through comedy that we can observe the development of the intellectual life of Athens as a continuous social process, instead of studying it as crystallized in complete and permanent works of literature, history, and philosophy. And what we observe makes it plain that the antiquarian method of writing the history of civilization by reconstructing separate periods from isolated historical details, picked up and fitted together, is a hopeless task, even when the evidence is far more copious than it is for ancient Greece. Poetry alone can make the life of its own time real and human to posterity. Hence the paradox—which is, after all, perfectly natural—that hardly any historical period, even our own immediate past, can be realized by us so vividly as the age of Attic comedy.

However, in this book we must study its artistic power (which inspired an astonishing number of authors of widely varied talents) not only as a source of evidence for the life of a vanished world, but also as one of the greatest manifestations of Greek poetic genius. More than any other art, comedy is tied to the realities of its own time and place. Although that fact makes it fascinating from a historical point of view, its sole purpose, in portraying ephemeral events and personalities, is to represent certain aspects of their eternal humanity which are overlooked by loftier types of poetry like epic and tragedy. The philosophy of poetry which was developed in the fourth century defined tragedy and comedy as fundamentally opposite and complementary expressions of the same primitive human instinct for imitation. It asserted that tragedy, and all the other types of high poetry which succeeded the epic, sprang from the inclination of noble minds to imitate great men, notable deeds and famous lives; while it explained the origin of comedy by the irresistible imitative urge of commoner natures—or, as we should put it, by the impulse of the ordinary man, with his realistic and critical outlook—to ape bad, blameworthy, and contemptible things. The famous scene in the *Iliad* which holds up the vulgar and hideous agitator Thersites to the malicious laughter of the mob—a rare comedy among the many tragedies in Homeric poetry—is a true piece of popular comedy, for it caters to the instincts of the mob. So also, in the divine farce which the enamoured Ares and Aphrodite are forced to play against their will, the Olympians themselves become a laughing audience at a comedy.

If even the mighty gods could laugh and be laughed at in this frankly comic way, the Greeks obviously felt that every human being, and every being with human attributes, had not only the power of feeling heroic emotion and serious dignity, but the ability and the need to laugh. Later Greek philosophy defined man as the only animal capable of laughter, though he was usually described as a talking or thinking animal; thereby they placed laughter on the same plane with thought and speech, as an expression of intellectual freedom. If we connect that philosophical conception of human nature with the laughing gods of Homer, we shall not readily believe that comedy had lower spiritual implications than tragedy, though its origin may have been meaner. Nothing shows the broad and deep humanity of Athenian culture so clearly as the differentiation and integration of the two genera, tragedy and comedy, in Attic drama. Plato was the first to point this out: at the end of *The Symposium* he makes Socrates say that the true poet must be both a tragedian and a comedian—a claim which Plato himself answered by writing *Phaedo* and *The Symposium*. All Athenian culture was aimed at realizing that ideal. Not only did it pit tragedy and comedy against each other in the same theatre, but it taught the Athenians (in Plato's words) to consider all human life as both a tragedy and a comedy. Its complete humanity is a mark of its classical perfection.

Modern critics were unable to apprehend the unique beauty of Aristophanic comedy until they abandoned the historical preconception that it was a crude but brilliant predecessor of the comedy of manners, studied its religious origins, and realized that it was an outpouring of the ecstatic Dionysian joy of life. It was necessary in fact to return to its psychical source in order to overcome the rationalist type of aesthetic criticism, which could not see the creative energy of nature in Attic comedy. But we must go a little further back if we are to see the pure spiritual heights to which the Dionysiac fervour soared in Aristophanes.

The history of comedy is the clearest possible example of the direct growth of a lofty artistic form from a root deep in the soil of Attica. Its origins were obscure—unlike those of tragedy, for the whole development of tragic poetry from the earliest dithyrambic choruses and dances to its climax in the art of Sophocles was perfectly familiar to the Greeks of that time. The reasons for this were not merely technical. Tragic poetry was from the very first the centre of serious public interest. It had always been the medium in which noble thoughts were expressed. But the drunken *kōmos* which marked the rustic festival of Dionysus, with the robust obscenity of its phallic songs, was not considered to be spiritual creation, *poiésis,* poetry in the full sense of the word. When comedy became literature, as in Aristophanes, it assimilated many very diverse elements which all originated from the old Dionysiac festival. It contained, of course, the spirit of the holiday revel, the kōmos, after which it was named. Another important feature was the parabasis, the procession in which the chorus gave free play to its mocking humour, taunting the audience (the gaping onlookers at the original festival) and frequently singling out individuals by name for a special shower of abuse. Equally ancient were the phallic costumes of the actors, and the disguises worn by the chorus—particularly the animal-masks of frogs, wasps, birds, and the like: for these features appeared even in the oldest comedians, who were still strongly bound to tradition and made few innovations of their own.

It is characteristic of the Athenian genius that it could blend these diverse elements into an artistic unity in comedy: the obvious parallel is Attic tragedy, which combined dance, choral song, and spoken poetry. It was that diversity in unity which made Attic comedy so much richer in scenic resources and intellectual energy than everything else of its kind produced independently of it elsewhere in the Greek world—the comedies of Epicharmus, for example, written in Dorian Sicily, and the mimes of Sophron. But the feature which had the greatest possibilities of dramatic development was its verse-form: the Ionian iambic line. It also had a Dionysiac origin, but had been raised to poetic form by Archilochus two centuries earlier. Nevertheless, the free structure of the comic trimeter proves that it did not develop from the literary iambus shaped by Archilochus, but directly from the primitive and probably improvised folk-metre of the same name, which had always been used for satiric poetry. It was only in the second generation and thereafter that the comic poets imitated the Archilochean lampoon, not in its rigid verse-structure, but in the higher craft of aiming bold satiric attacks at individuals of whom they disapproved, though they might be the greatest men in the state.

This technique had little significance until the time when comedy became politically important, and the state made it a privilege and a duty for rich citizens to pay the expenses of its production; for thereby the comic festival became a public occasion, and the comic "chorus" began to compete seriously with tragedy for the interest of the citizens. Although it could not pretend to the same prestige as tragedy, it now began to imitate it. The influence of tragedy upon the comic poets is shown in the many technical devices which they borrowed, and even more in their effort to give comedy a complete dramatic structure, though it was still impossible for them to trim away the luxuriant overgrowth of farcical episodes and reduce the plot to a rigid form. Similarly, the influence of tragedy was responsible for the introduction of a "hero" into comedy, and deeply affected the composition of its lyrics. And finally, at the height of its development, it was the inspiration of tragedy which raised it to the highest point by making it conscious of its noble educational mission: that consciousness pervades Aristophanes' whole conception of comedy, and makes his work both spiritually and technically a worthy rival to all the tragic poetry of his age.

This, it seems, is the explanation of the unique and predominant position among the writers of old comedy which was unanimously given to Aristophanes by the tradition which preserved his works alone, and a relatively large number of them. It can hardly be pure chance that he alone has survived out of the triad of comedians chosen as classical models by the Alexandrians—Cratinus, Eupolis, and Aristophanes. This canon, obviously meant for a parallel to the great triad of tragic poets, was only a literary historian's artificial selection, and did not reflect the true relative importance of these poets even in Hellenistic times. This is proved beyond cavil by the papyrus fragments of other comic poets which have recently been discovered. Plato was right to introduce Aristophanes in *The Symposium* as the comedian *par excellence*. Even at the time when comedies were being written by really important poets, like the dissolute genius Cratinus and the brilliantly inventive Crates, the art of comedy had nothing whatever to do with any noble cultural mission. Its only aim was to make the public laugh; like all clowns, even the most popular comedians were relentlessly hissed off the stage when they were old and lost the flowing wit which had been the real source of their effect. Wilamowitz in particular has entered a strong protest against the doctrine that comedy was intended to improve the morals of the audience; and in fact nothing seems more remote from it than didacticism in general, to say nothing of moral instruction. Still, his objection does not go far enough: it does not do justice to the actual history of comedy in the period known to us.

Cratinus—the old toper whom Aristophanes proposes the city should retire from the stage and keep honourably drunk in the Prytaneion till his death— seems to have excelled in relentless gibing at notoriously unpopular persons; and that was actually the essence of the old iambic, raised to the level of political satire. Eupolis and Aristophanes, the brilliant Dioscuri of the younger generation who began by writing comedies in friendly partnership and ended as bitter enemies accusing each other of plagiarism, followed him in delivering savage personal attacks on Cleon and Hyperbolus. But from the beginning of his career Aristophanes was conscious of being a higher kind of artist than others. The earliest of his extant plays, *The Acharnians,* is political lampoonery transformed into a brilliant fantasy, blending the usual coarse and vivid burlesque with the witty symbolism of an ambitious political Utopia, and enriching it by gay parodies of Euripidean tragedy. It is by combining these two primitive elements of the Dionysiac revel— grotesque fantasy and powerful realism—that Aristophanes creates the peculiar blend of actuality and unreality which was necessary before a higher form of comedy could come into being. Even in *The Acharnians* he alludes ironically to the coarse and obvious jokes with which Megarian farce-writers belaboured the witless mob, and to which in his own time comic poets still had recourse. No doubt the public taste had to be suited, and Aristophanes knew how to use the indispensable tricks of old-fashioned comedy when necessary—the stale gibes at bald members of the audience, the vulgar cordax-dance, and the whipping-scenes by which the actor disguised the stupidity of his material. Such were the jokes which (as Aristophanes says with hearty insolence in *The Knights*) old Crates wiped off his cabbage-eating mouth, still accustomed to the primitive Attic taste. In *The Clouds* he boldly asserts that he feels himself far superior to the technique of his predecessors (and not of them alone), and that he has full confidence in his own art and his own style. He is proud (he says) of producing new subjects every year—and thereby he emphasizes the artistic inventiveness of up-to-date comedy in contrast not only with the other type but even with tragedy, which always worked on traditional material. In the terrific competition of the annual dramatic festival, originality and novelty must have been at a premium. And original ideas could be made even more attractive if spiced with the boldness of a political attack like that which Aristophanes delivered on the omnipotent Cleon. By such a challenge a comedian could excite general interest, just as a rising politician could make a striking début as prosecutor in an important state trial. All that was needed was courage, and Aristophanes believed he had done a finer thing by "punching mighty Cleon in the belly" than his colleagues in pounding away year after year at the comparatively harmless demagogue Hyperbolus and his wretched mother.

All this has nothing to do with improving public morality. The spiritual transformation of comedy was worked by different means, and accompanied by a gradual change in its conception of its own critical function.

The iambic lampoon invented by Archilochus, though very largely personal invective, became to some extent the medium of public criticism in the new liberty of the Ionian city-state. But Attic comedy, the successor of the iambic, was the first critical poetry in the true and higher sense. It also had developed out of more or less harmless gibing at private individuals; but it found its true nature only when it entered the political arena. As known to us at the height of its achievement, it is a true product of democratic free speech. The Hellenistic historians of literature realized that the rise and fall of political comedy coincided with those of the Athenian democracy. It never flourished again (least of all in antiquity) after the Greeks had been driven—in Plato's phrase—from an excess of freedom to an excess of unfreedom. But it is not enough to consider comedy merely as an exponent of the free democratic spirit. Comedy was produced by democracy as an antidote to its own overdose of liberty, thereby outdoing its own excesses, and extending *parrhesia,* its vaunted freedom of speech, to subjects which are usually tabu even in a free political system.

More and more comedy assumed the function of expressing all kinds of public criticism. Not content with passing judgment on 'political affairs' in the narrow modern sense of the phrase, it discussed politics in the full Greek sense—that is, all questions of universal interest to the community. When it chose, it censured not only individuals, not only separate political acts, but the entire governmental system, the character and the weaknesses of the whole nation. It controlled the spirit of the people, and kept a constant watch on education, philosophy, poetry, and music. Thereby, these activities were for the first time regarded as expressing the culture of the nation, and as standards of its spiritual health. They were brought to judgment in the theatre before the whole Athenian people. This was a transference of the idea of responsibility, which is inseparable from liberty and which was realized in the democracy by the institution of the *euthyné,* to these supra-personal spiritual activities that serve or ought to serve the welfare of the community. Therefore the very democracy which so vaunted liberty was compelled by an inherent necessity to fix the limits of the liberty of the intellect.

On the other hand, it was part of the essence of Athenian democracy that this limitation should be done, not by officials, but by public opinion. Comedy was the censorship of Athens. That is what makes Aristophanes' wit so deadly serious despite its mask of outrageous laughter. Plato defines the principle of comedy as malicious laughter at the harmless failings and self-deceptions of our neighbours. Perhaps that definition suits the comedy of his day better than Aristophanes, whose gaiety sometimes touches tragedy, as in *The Frogs.* But we shall discuss that later. The fact that in spite of the dangers and crises of the war educational problems occupied an important, sometimes a predominant, place in comedy, shows the supreme importance which was attached to them in that period. It is only through comedy that we can study the violent passion with which the educational question was debated, and discover its causes. And comedy, by using its own peculiar powers to take over the leadership in that conflict, became one of the greatest cultural forces of its time. We shall demonstrate this in three of the principal spheres of communal life—politics, education, and art. It will not be necessary to analyse all Aristophanes' works, but each of these subjects will be discussed with reference to the plays which are particularly relevant to it.

As we have seen, *political* satire, which predominates in Aristophanes' earlier plays, originally had no lofty purpose. Often its freedom could hardly be distinguished from insolence. Even in democratic Athens it often came into conflict with the authorities. Again and again they attempted to abnegate its ancient privilege of delivering slanderous attacks on individual citizens by name. But the prohibitions never lasted long. They were against public sentiment; and even the spirit of the new constitutional state could not eradicate comic lampoonery, that scandalous survival of the primitive social sense. If it caricatured statesmen with anything like the nonchalant freedom of Aristophanes' portrait of Socrates in *The Clouds,* we can see why they attempted to use their power to protect themselves, while private citizens (like Socrates in Plato's account of his persecution by comic poetry) were defenceless in face of the public mockery and hatred which comedy encouraged. Cratinus did not shrink from attacking Pericles himself. In *The Thracian Women* he called him "the squillheaded Zeus," an allusion to the oddly shaped skull which he usually hid under a helmet. But even that harmless joke betrayed the poet's underlying respect for the great statesman, "the Olympian" who "flashed and boomed and mixed up Greece pell-mell."

Aristophanes' political attacks on Cleon were of a different type. His jokes were not the jokes of hearty frankness. He gave his victim no half-affectionate nicknames. He fought him with all the bitterness of principle. Cratinus had felt the superiority of Pericles, and laughed at him like the jester at the king. For Attic wit did not mix up great things with small, or belittle splendid things in a familiar way: it always kept its infallible sense of proportion. But Aristophanes had to stoop to attack this enemy. The descent to Cleon after the untimely death of Pericles was too abrupt and too sudden for him and others not to feel it as a symptom of the degeneration of the entire state. Athenians who were accustomed to the magnificent manners and intellectual nobility of Pericles turned with disgust from the common tanner whose vulgarity brought discredit on the whole nation.

It was not the lack of civic courage that silenced his critics in the assembly, when his policies were objectively discussed. There his undeniable ability and the practised energy of his oratory quelled his opponents. And yet he often showed weaknesses that disgraced not himself alone but the city which he governed. It was an act of incredible boldness for Aristophanes, scarcely out of his 'teens, to attack the all-powerful favourite of the demos, in his second comedy *The Babylonians* (unfortunately lost), and to expose his brutal treatment of the other members of the Delian League, on the public stage, before the representatives of these very states. The best commentary on Cleon's policy is provided by the speeches which Thucydides puts into his mouth at the time of the revolt of Mytilene, when he discusses the correct policy of Athens to the members of her alliance. Aristophanes depicted them as slaves in the treadmill. Cleon instantly prosecuted him. *The Knights* was his reply. He fell back on the support of the opposition party—the small but influential clique of feudal squires, the cavalry corps which had attained new importance since the invasion, the deadly enemies of Cleon. His chorus of knights embodied the defensive alliance of nobility and intellect against the growing power of barbarism and political terror.

It must be understood that this kind of criticism constituted a revolution in the history of comedy. It was fundamentally different from Cratinus' political jester's-tricks, just as Aristophanes' cultural persecution of Euripides and the sophists was poles apart from Cratinus' clowning parodies of the *Odyssey*. The revolution was caused by the change in the intellectual situation. At the very moment when, by the appearance of a poet of real genius, intelligence invaded comedy, intelligence was to be hunted out of Athens. The equilibrium which Pericles had established between politics and the new culture, and which he had typified in his own character, was now destroyed. If it were not restored, culture must disappear from Athens. But meanwhile intellectualism had acquired political influence. It was not the province of scholarly recluses, as in the Alexandrean era: it lived and worked in poetry, and through it had the ear of the public. So it took up the challenge. Aristophanes was not fighting against the state—he was fighting *for* the state against its temporary despot. Of course, writing comedy was not taking a regular share in political activity, and Aristophanes scarcely wished to support any particular person or party in winning power. But he could help to break the tension and to counteract the intolerable superiority of the brutal enemies of the intellect. In *The Knights* he did not support or oppose any definite policy, as he did in *The Babylonians* or *The Acharnians*: he merely scourged the people and its leader, and pilloried their alliance as unworthy of the Athenian state and its illustrious past.

He put this unholy alliance on the stage by means of a fantastic allegory— not a bloodless set of symbols as allegories usually are, but a visible embodiment of an invisible fact. To symbolize the condition of that abstract thing, the Athenian state, he showed the audience an ordinary household thoroughly upset. The pater-familias, deaf old Mr. Demos, always grumbling and always being cheated, images the manyheaded mob who govern Athens. He is completely under the influence of a new slave, a coarse brutal Paphlagonian, and his two older slaves are in constant trouble. The mask of the Paphlagonian conceals the face of the terrible Cleon, and his two miserable fellow-slaves are the generals Nicias and Demosthenes. The hero of the comedy, however, is not Cleon, but his adversary the Sausage-seller. He is an even more disgusting character than the Paphlagonian, and, through his shameless conduct and total lack of culture and moral standards, always comes out on top. In the competition to see which of them can do most good to Demos, Cleon is outwitted by the Sausage-seller, who produces a pair of slippers, a warm shirt, and a cushion for the old man to sit on at the assembly. Cleon breaks down like a tragic hero at the catastrophe. The chorus shouts applause to the victor, and rather emphatically asks him to show his gratitude for their help by giving them a nice public office. The next scene is more ambitious. The victor chooses as his first official act to rejuvenate old Demos, who is therefore boiled in a huge sauasage-kettle, and emerges when the magical ceremony is complete, to be presented to the jubilant audience, reborn and crowned with garlands. Once more he looks as he did in the spacious days of Miltiades and the wars of liberation: he is the living incarnation of the violet-crowned hymn-resounding Athens of old, wearing its honest old-fashioned costume, with his hair dressed in the antique fashion; and he is hailed as king of the Greeks. He is spiritually reborn too, and sadly confesses his shame for his old errors. His corruptor Cleon is condemned to peddle the sausages made of dog-meat and donkey-dung which his victorious successor used to sell.

Thus the apotheosis of the rejuvenated nation reaches its climax: the justice of heaven is fulfilled. The wildly impossible task of squaring the circle in politics—of driving out Cleon's vices by still greater vileness—has been easily solved by the poet's imagination. Few of his audience would ask whether the sausage-seller would really make a better successor to Pericles than the tanner. Aristophanes could leave the politicians to determine what they would make out of Athens reborn. He wanted only to hold up the mirror to the nation and to its leader, almost without hoping to change them. Cleon made a marvellous comic hero—a real hero reversed, distinguished by possessing all human faults and failings. It was a brilliant idea to bring him into conjunction with the Sausage-seller, his own "ideal," whom he never could equal or even approach, however hard he strove. The relentless savagery of Aristophanes' portrayal of Cleon makes a striking contrast to the patient tolerance with which he reveals the weaknesses of Demos, only to indulge them a little further. It would be a grave misunderstanding to imagine that he seriously believed Athens could return to the happiness of that bygone age, which he depicts with such nostalgic humour and such pure patriotic affection. In *Dichtung und Wahrheit* Goethe well describes the effect produced by that kind of poetic wishful thinking. "A poet can create universal pleasure by skillfully reminding a nation of its own past: it admires the virtues of its ancestors, and smiles at the faults which it believes it has surmounted long ago." The less one tries to interpret these magical fantasies, in which Aristophanes blends reality and fairyland, as straightforward political preaching, the more deeply one will understand his poetry.

Why is it that this type of comic poetry—which lives for one fleeting moment and expends all its force upon that moment—has been recognized more and more within the last century to be immortal? In Germany, the interest in Aristophanes' political comedies appeared when her political life began. But it is only in the last few decades that the problems of politics have been as urgent and absorbing in Germany as they were in Athens at the end of the fifth century. The fundamental facts are always the same—the polar oppositions between the individual and the community, the mob and the intellectual, the poor and the rich, liberty and oppression, tradition and progress. But there is another factor. Despite its passionate interest in politics, Aristophanic comedy contemplates its subject from such a height and with such intellectual liberty that it abolishes the irrelevant ephemeral aspects of even the most trivial fact. What the poet describes is eternal, because it is in Nietzsche's phrase the All-too-human Humanity; and he could not describe it unless he could stand at some distance from it. Again and again his picture of temporary reality dissolves into the timeless higher reality of imaginative or allegorical truth. The most impressive example of this is *The Birds,* where the poet gaily shakes off the pressing anxieties of the present, and makes a wish-picture of an ideal state, Cloud-Cuckoo-Land, where all the burdens of earth vanish and everything is winged and free, where only human follies and weaknesses may remain and flourish harmlessly, so that the finest of all delights may not be lacking, the delight whose absence would spoil even this paradise—immortal laughter.

From the first, Aristophanes was necessarily a critic not only of politics but of *culture.* This attitude appears in his first play, *The Banqueters,* which deals with the conflict between old and new ideals in education—the theme to which he returned in *The Clouds,* and which appears many times in other Attic comedians. Here he attacks the new ideal on what might seem to be a fairly inessential point—the eccentric and ill-bred conduct of its representatives. The Athenians, however, relished this keenly, because it added a new series of faults and follies to the rather hackneyed repertoire of comic subjects. In the same spirit, Eupolis wrote *The Flatterers* to deride the sophists who toadied to rich Athenians, and their parasitism seems to have been featured in Aristophanes' own comedy *The Fryers,* which made fun of the sophist Prodicus. The same comic motif reappears in Plato's *Protagoras;* but obviously none of the comedians saw the deeper implications of sophistic culture as Plato did. Still, Aristophanes in *The Banqueters* seems to have gone fairly deeply into the corrupting effects of sophistic teaching on young men. His chief characters are the two sons of an Athenian farmer, one of whom has been brought up at home in the old-fashioned way, while the other is sent to the city to enjoy the advantages of progressive education. The city-bred youth comes back completely transformed, morally corrupted, and spoilt for work on the farm, where his higher culture is useless. His father is grieved to find that he cannot sing the drinking-songs of the old poets, Alcaeus and Anacreon. Instead of the archaic words in Homer, he understands only the glosses on the text of Solon's legislation, for juristic training is now in fashion. The name of the rhetor Thrasymachus occurs in some argument about the meaning of words—a type of pedantry particularly repulsive to Athenians of the old school. But as a whole the play seems not to have passed beyond the bounds of harmless mockery.

However, *The Clouds,* produced a few years later, showed how profound and sincere was Aristophanes' dislike for the new intellectual movement, and resumed with greater vehemence the attack delivered in *The Banqueters.* He had now discovered a figure who seemed to be designed by nature for the hero of a comedy of intellectualism. This was Socrates of Alopeké, son of a stonemason and a midwife—a far more effective hero than any of the touring sophists who visited Athens at distant intervals, because he was known throughout the city and could easily be recognized on the stage. Nature herself in a fit of humour had made him a perfect comic mask, in the shape of a Silenus-face with a snub nose, protruding lips, and goggling eyes. All that was necessary was to exaggerate his character a little. Aristophanes decked his victim out with all the characteristics of the tribe to which he obviously belonged—the sophists, rhetors, and natural philosophers, or, as they were then called, meteorologists. And then—although the real Socrates spent almost the whole day walking about the market-place—Aristophanes gave this fantastically exaggerated figure a narrow mysterious Thinking-shop, where, suspended in a swing above the courtyard, he 'contemplated the sun' with his head tilted back, while his pale-faced pupils bent and scrutinized the sand, so as to fathom the underworld. Usually *The Clouds* is considered as if it were part of the history of philosophy, and is at best excused, never praised. *Summum ius, summa iniuria.* It is unfair to call the farcical Socrates of comedy to the bar of rigid historical truth. Plato himself, who reveals the important part which this caricature played in the condemnation of his master, never applies such a severe standard to it. In *The Symposium* he set his master, transfigured and glorified, beside the poet who had derided him; and he thought it no insult to the shade of Socrates to make Aristophanes play a leading part in the conversation. The comic Socrates has none of the moral energy which Plato and the other Socratics describe in their teacher. If Aristophanes knew that he really possessed this quality, he could not use it on the stage. He made his hero an eccentric and unworldly pioneer of progressive ideas, an atheistic scientist: the typical comic figure of the arrogant and oddly-behaved scholar, individualized by a few features borrowed from the character of the historical Socrates.

If we read the play with Plato's descriptions of Socrates in our mind it is impossible to find anything funny in the caricature. Real wit is the revelation of unexpected similarities; but there is practically no resemblance between the real and the comic Socrates. However, Aristophanes was not interested in the form and content of the Socratic conversations; and though there were significant differences between the intellectual attitude of Socrates and that of the sophists, differences which Plato was to work out with great care, Aristophanes ignored them and saw only the fundamental resemblance —both the sophists and Socrates analysed everything, and thought nothing was so great or so sacred that it was beyond discussion and did not need to be founded on a rational basis. In fact, Socrates with his passion for abstract ideas seemed to have beaten the sophists at their own game. We need not expect the poet, who felt that every form of this fashionable intellectualism was injurious, to draw any fine distinctions between one type and another. There were many who complained of this or that evil aspect of the new culture. Aristophanes was the first to describe it as a universal danger. He saw the destruction of all the traditions of the past, and it moved him to passionate protest. Personally, he would have been embarrassed if anyone had questioned him about his own attitude to the ancient gods; but as a comedian he thought it ludicrous for the "meteorologists" to call the aether divine, and he made the humour of the situation vivid and immediate by showing Socrates praying to the Vortex which he says formed Primal Matter, or to the Clouds, the shifting airy insubstantial forms which are so desperately like the misty doctrines of philosophy. After two hundred years of bold cosmological theorizing in which one system was constantly built on the ruins of its predecessor, the Greeks were too sceptical of the discoveries made by human intelligence to accept the arrogant assurance with which the advanced intellectuals confronted the ignorant mob. The only unshakable fact which emerged was that their pupils often made a disgraceful misuse of the unscrupulous verbal tricks they had learnt. So Aristophanes brought two allegorical figures on the stage to represent the Just and the Unjust Arguments which appeared in every sophistic discussion of every problem, and to show how the Unjust Argument conquered its opponent, as a comic tableau of the results of progressive education.

After the first skirmishes, in which these figures hurl the usual abuse at each other, the chorus invites them to fight an exhibition match as representatives of the old-fashioned and the new-fangled types of education. It is significant that the techniques of each system are not separately compared to prove which is superior. Instead, the Just Argument describes the old educational system as personified in a particular type of human character: for an educational system can prove its worth only by the complete character which it produces, not by any abstract merits. At the time when the Just Argument was still flourishing, and decent behaviour was obligatory, children were seen and not heard. They went quietly along the streets (says the

Just Argument) on their way to school, wearing no overcoats even when the snow fell thick as flour. There they learnt to sing old songs to traditional melodies. If one of them put in disgusting cadenzas and flourishes like modern musicians, he was flogged. That was how to bring up a generation of Marathon-warriors. But nowadays the children are weakened by being wrapped up in big coats, and it would make you choke with rage to see the young fellows awkwardly holding their shields in front of their bellies in the war-dance at the Panathenaea. The Just Argument promises to teach the young man who entrusts himself to its educational régime to hate the market-place and keep away from the baths, to be ashamed of disgraceful conduct and fire up when insulted, to rise and make room when older men come in, to keep pure the divine image of modesty, not to visit dancing-girls, and not to contradict his father. He must practise wrestling, oiled and muscular, in the gymnasium, instead of making stinging-nettle-sharp speeches in the market-place or letting himself be dragged into court to argue his head off about pettifogging trivialities. Under the olive-trees of the Academy, he will run races, crowned with reed, against decent companions, smelling of honeysuckle and poplar-leaves and gentlemanly leisure, and enjoying the spring season when the plane-tree whispers to the elm. The chorus calls these men happy who lived in the fine old days when that kind of education flourished, and admires the sweet perfume of sophrosyné which is wafted from the words of the Just Argument.

Now its opponent, the Unjust Argument, rises, almost choking with rage and eager to throw everything into confusion by its dialectic. It boasts of its ominous name—which it got for being the first to discover the art of making speeches to contradict the laws. To represent the worse cause and make it win, says the Unjust Argument, is a talent worth its weight in gold. It then attacks its adversary with the up-to-date method of cross-examination; and uses the new rhetorical trick of quoting noble mythological parallels to make its case seem respectable. The Homeric orators had always cited ancient instances to exemplify the ideal standards which they discussed, and early poets followed the same practice. The sophists had now adopted it, and collected all the mythological examples which they could utilize from their realistic and relativist standpoint to support them in destroying all accepted standards. Once upon a time a man defending himself in court had been content to show that his conduct was in accordance with the laws, but now he attacked the laws and the current morality, and tried to show that they were in the wrong. The Just Argument had said that warm baths weakened the physique: the Unjust Argument counters this by referring to the national hero Heracles, for Athena had created the warm springs at Thermopylae to refresh him. It then goes on to praise the custom of spending one's time in the market-place making speeches, which its opponent had condemned, and cites the eloquent Nestor and other Homeric heroes to prove its point. The Just Argument now adopts the same device, when it is cynically asked who was ever profited by sophrosyné. Once, when his virtue had brought him into dreadful danger, the gods sent Peleus a miraculous sword to defend himself with. But the Unjust Argument is not impressed by this "pretty present." To illustrate how much more profitable rascality is, it leaves mythology and cites a modern example, the demagogue Hyperbolus, who acquired "more than many talents" of gold by his underhand tricks. The other at once reminds him that the gods gave Peleus an even greater reward, for they married him to Thetis. The Unjust Argument replies that Thetis left him because he was rather poor company. And, turning to the youth for whose soul it is fighting with the representative of old-fashioned education, it warns him that to choose sophrosyné is to abandon all the joys of life. Not only that: if he does so, he will be helpless when the "necessities of nature" cause him to make a false step, for he will be unable to defend himself. "If you take my advice, you will give free rein to your nature, rollick and laugh, think nothing shameful. If you are caught in adultery, deny your guilt and appeal to Zeus, who was not strong enough to resist Eros and women. How can you, a mere mortal, be stronger than a god?" That is the same argument Euripides makes Helen, and the nurse in *Hippolytus,* employ to justify the faults of love. The climax of the discussion is that the Unjust Argument makes the audience burst into laughter by praising their own lax morality, and then explains that anything which is the practice of the vast majority of an honourable nation cannot possibly be a vice.

This attack on the old educational standards brings out the character produced by the new system. It need not be taken as evidence for the cultural ideals of the sophists; still, that is how they seemed to many contemporaries, and there must have been a number of exaggerated instances which made this kind of generalization easy. Which side did Aristophanes take in the dispute? It would be a mistake to believe that he was a wholehearted partisan of one side or the other. He himself had enjoyed the advantages of progressive education; and it is quite impossible to imagine that his comedy could have been written in the good old days. Much as he loved them, he would have been hissed off the stage. His sweet nostalgic picture of the past, with its springtime glamour, is the same kind of gay and melancholy fantasy as the rejuvenation of old Demos at the end of *The Knights.* Although he conjures up the spirit of the old paideia, he is not preaching a return to the past. In fact, he was not a rigidly dogmatic reactionary. But he was living in an age of transition, when thoughtful men shrank from being whirled along in a constant stream of innovations, seeing good old things destroyed before they were replaced by something equally good. They had none of our modern historical sense of change, still less our general belief in development, evolution, "progress." Thus, they could not help feeling that the historical process through which they were living meant the demolition of that firm structure of traditional values in which they had lived so long and so happily.

The Just Argument, personifying the old educational ideal, shows what the new ideal is *not*. In showing what it *is*, Aristophanes abandons his tone of hearty good humour for one of biting satire, for he considers the new system to be the complete antithesis of all that is right and healthy. His negative criticism of it is charged with the serious educational purpose which is unmistakably present throughout the play. He lays particular emphasis on the complete unscrupulousness of the clever modern intellectuals, with their abnegation of all moral standards. To us it must seem paradoxical that that point should be so stressed in a comedy whose hero is Socrates. And in the plan of the comedy as we have it there is little connexion between Socrates' character and the rivalry of the Just and Unjust Arguments: he is not even present at it. But the conclusion of *The Frogs* shows that Aristophanes considered Socrates to be the perfect type of the new intellectual spirit which was infuriating him and his contemporaries with its pretentiousness and its passion for hair-splitting abstract distinctions—and which moreover was abandoning the irreplaceable values of taste and neglecting the art of tragedy. With the unerring perception of a man who owed his own ideas and his own culture to these values, and now saw them endangered, Aristophanes instinctively turned away from an educational system whose greatest strength lay in cold rationalism; and his hatred for it was more than a personal matter—it was a symptom of a far-reaching historical tendency.

For this rationalist spirit had encroached on *literature* too. When Aristophanes defended tragedy against Socrates and the intellectuals, he had Euripides as an enemy at his back. It was through Euripides that the new movement had invaded high poetry. Therefore the central point of Aristophanes' fight to preserve the old cultural ideals was his defence of the old spirit of tragedy, and he showed the same uncompromising obstinacy in it as in his attack on the new education. He criticized every aspect of Euripides' poetry, including his modern music, until his criticism almost became a persecution. His political convictions were far less permanent and deep-seated than his poetic faith. Even his attack on Cleon or his advocacy of peace with the Peloponnesians—which were matters of principle with him—lasted only a few years. More and more he turned his attention from politics to culture. Certainly the cultural problem was the most important of those which could still be publicly discussed. Perhaps the decline of political comedy was due to the increasing dangers and tensions of the last years of the Peloponnesian War. Absolutely free discussion of public issues presupposes a good deal of surplus energy, which at that time the Athenian state no longer possessed. Political scepticism, though growing in volume, was forced to conceal itself in clubs and private assemblies. Not long before the collapse of Athens, within the same few months, Euripides and Sophocles died. The tragic stage was deserted. A historical epoch had come to an end. The miserable successors of the great dramatists—the tragedian Meletus, the dithyrambist Cinesias, and the comedian Sannyrion—appeared a few years later in Aristophanes' comedy *Gerytadés* as ambassadors sent to the underworld to get advice from their predecessors. Thus the age mocked its own weakness. *The Frogs,* written in the brief interval between the death of the two poets and the fall of Athens, is charged with a different and more tragic emotion. As the situation of Athens became more hopeless, and the pressure on the morale of her citizens increased to the breaking-point, they grew more eager for spiritual comfort and strength. Now at last we can see what tragedy meant to the Athenian people. Only comedy could express it; and it could do so just because of its objective view of tragedy, which was made possible through the vast difference separating the comic muse from her elder sister the muse of tragedy. And only comedy still had a poet worthy of the name. With the passage of the years, she had risen to a height from which she could warn, teach, and encourage the Athenians as tragedy once had done. It was her supreme moment.

In *The Frogs* Aristophanes conjures up the ghost of tragedy, which had died with Sophocles and Euripides. The memory of these poets was the strongest bond between the Athenian hearts which had been sundered by the furious quarrels of opposing parties. To renew and strengthen it was a task worthy of a statesman. Dionysus in person descends to the underworld —to bring back Euripides! Even his greatest enemy, Aristophanes, was forced to admit that that was what the public wanted. In the god Dionysus he typified the theatre-audience, with all its comical faults and peccadilloes. But he utilized its yearning for Euripides to make his last and most comprehensive attack on his art. He abandoned his usual Euripidean jokes— which had usually been incidental and would have been unsuitable at that crisis—and looked far more deeply into the problem of the function of tragedy. Therefore, he did not criticize Euripides by Euripides' own standards, although as a great artist he had a claim to such criticism; nor did he discuss him as a representative of his age. He contrasted him with Aeschylus, the noblest representative of the religious and moral dignity of tragic poetry. In the plot of *The Frogs,* this simple but highly effective conflict between the old and new ideals of tragedy plays the same important part as the *agon* of the old and new educational systems in *The Clouds.* But while the latter does not vitally affect the plot, the former carries the whole weight of the action. A descent to the underworld was a favourite theme in comedy. In that *The Frogs* resembles *The Wards* of Eupolis, where the old Athenian statesmen and generals were brought up from hell to help the state in its despair. Having connected that idea with the contest of the two great poets, Aristophanes arrives at an astonishingly apt solution: after descending to hell to bring back Euripides, Dionysus finds that his favourite is beaten by Aeschylus in a fair poetic competition, and takes back the elder poet to save the city.

It is not our task to assess the play as a work of art. We must, however, study it as the most authoritative piece of fifth-century evidence for the position of tragedy in the life of the polis. Therefore the most important scene is that section of the *agon* in which Euripides, while vaunting his own service to Athens, is asked by Aeschylus: "Tell me, why should a poet be admired?" Aeschylus' basically aesthetic criticisms of the prologues, choruses, and other elements of Euripidean tragedy, though brilliantly witty, and though so vivid and concrete that they alone can give life and reality to the whole play, do not require separate study and can therefore be neglected here. Of course, they are vitally important in dealing with the comic effect of the drama; for they serve to counterbalance the preceding discussion of the ethical purpose of all true poetry, which from time to time grows painfully, even tragically, serious, and needs some such relief. These contemporary definitions of the nature and function of poetry are specially important because we have very few direct discussions of the subject by great writers of the period. Even when we recollect that the theories of the name and nature of poetry which Aristophanes attributes to Aeschylus and Euripides had already been debated and formulated by contemporary sophists, they are invaluable as corroborating the impression which we receive from their extant tragedies.

Tell me, then, why should a poet be admired? Euripides gives the same answer as Aeschylus, though his phraseology would admit an interpretation peculiar to himself. "For cleverness and for the ability to teach others, because we make men better in the state." And if you have not done that, if you have taken decent men with noble natures and made them into rascals, what do you deserve? "Death!" interrupts Dionysus, "you need not ask him." And now, with a comical affectation of real emotion, Aeschylus describes how noble and martial the Athenians were until Euripides took them over from him. They coveted nothing, he says, except to beat the enemy. From the very beginning that has been the sole function of noble poets—to write what would benefit men. Orpheus showed them the mysteries, and taught them to abstain from murder; Musaeus explained how to cure the sick and foretell the future; Hesiod taught how to till the soil and know the seasons for ploughing and cropping; and the divine Homer won honour and glory by teaching men virtues like strategy, courage, and the equipment of warriors. Aeschylus says he has moulded many true heroes on that pattern—lion-hearted champions like Patroclus and Teucer—in order to inspire the citizens to emulate them when they hear the bugle sound the charge.

> And yet I made no whores, no Stheneboeas and Phaedras:
> no one can say that I ever wrote of a woman in love.

(By these gentle transitions from the minor to the major mode, Aristophanes often re-establishes the marvellous objectivity and balance which characterize his poetry.)

Euripides now appeals to the fact that the subjects of his feminine dramas were drawn straight from mythology. But Aeschylus asserts that a poet ought to conceal evil things rather than display them publicly as a lesson to others.

> For just as children
> have teachers to explain things, men are taught by poets—
> so our words must be noble.

Euripides accuses Aeschylus' mountainous words of lacking that very quality of nobility, because his style has ceased to be human. But his rival explains that a poet who has great thoughts and emotions must also use great language, and that demigods spoke in noble words just as they wore magnificent clothes. "But you have spoilt that, by making kings wear rags to look pathetic, and by teaching the rich Athenians to dress in rags too and to swear that they are poor, to avoid the expense of fitting out a warship. You have taught men to chatter and prate, and so emptied the gymnasiums, and incited sailors to mutiny against their officers." These words bring us back to the miserable state of Athenian politics, for which Euripides is made responsible, as he is for so many other Athenian misfortunes.

The wild comedy of Aeschylus' inverted homage to Euripides really comes out when we remember that the play was not performed to a theatre full of classical scholars taking every word literally and expecting to be infuriated by it, but to the Athenian public which adored Euripides like a god. Imperceptibly Aristophanes' subtle criticisms slide into fantastic caricatures, and the caricatures into outrageous exaggerations, so that the master of tragedy finally stands revealed as the incarnation of all the evils of the unhappy present day—the age of folly to which Aristophanes addresses words of encouragement and warning in the patriotic parabasis. But in every line we can hear his real inspiration—his dreadful anxiety for the future of Athens. He always thinks of the future of his city when he speaks of true and false poetry. Even though he knows very well that Euripides was not a charlatan, but an immortal genius, to whom he himself owes an immense debt, and with whom he really sympathizes more deeply than with his ideal Aeschylus, nevertheless he feels that the art of Euripides could not give Athens what Aeschylus had given to his fellow-countrymen in their sore need. And nothing else could save Athens at that critical moment. Therefore Dionysus is finally compelled to choose Aeschylus, and the king of the underworld dispatches the great poet to the light of day with these parting words:

> Farewell, then, Aeschylus: ascend,
> and save our country by your art.
> Give good advice, and educate
> the fools whose name is Legion.

Not for many years had tragedy dared to speak in such bold words as comedy now used. After all, comedy still lived by publicity and the oxygen of public discussion, whereas tragedy had quitted the open air and concentrated its interest on intimate psychological questions. Still, the public had never been compelled to pay such earnest attention to its spiritual problems as now; its political implications had never been realized so vividly as when Aristophanes stressed them by his lament for the disappearance of classical tragedy. At this critical juncture, the greatest of all comic poets once more emphasized the intimate connexion between the spirit and the future of the state, and the vast responsibility of creative genius to the community: and thereby comedy attained the climax of its great educational mission.

P L A T O

[*c. 427–347* B.C.]

PROFESSOR VOEGELIN's *Order and History* HAS BEEN CALLED THE MOST IMPOR-
tant historical work of the century, as well as "polemical, idiosyncratic, and
exciting." Whatever the reader's judgment, he cannot but be impressed by
the author's learning, which ranges from the ancient civilizations of the Near
East to modern times, and by his remarkable control of complex material.
The organizing principle of this work is the study of the symbolic forms—
myths, intellectual structures and institutions—through which a society reveals the more general pattern of order of which it conceives itself to be a
part. This essay, the introduction to Volume 3 of *Order and History,* prepares
the reader for a protracted consideration of the thought of Socrates and Plato
about the problems of their society. Professor Voegelin explains the political
character of the Socratic and Platonic effort, Platonic dialogue as a symbolic
form, the relation of Plato's philosophy to the problem of order and to the
great "limiting" states of death and love.

  Professor Voegelin is Boyd Professor of Government at the Louisiana State
University.

From *Plato and Aristotle* by Eric Voegelin. Copyright 1957 by Louisiana State University Press.

ERIC VOEGELIN

Plato and Socrates

ARISTOCLES THE SON OF ARISTON WAS BORN 428/27 B.C. FROM A NOBLE ATHE-
nian family. On his mother's side he could trace his lineage to Solon. The
name Plato he received, according to the various traditions, either from his
wrestling-master because of his robust figure, or from his friends because of
the breadth of his forehead; inevitably there were also less friendly suggestions which connected the name with the breadth of his style, and puns were
made on Plato and platitudes. His youth fell in the period of the Peloponnesian War (431–404); he was in his twenties when he witnessed the regime
of the Thirty Tyrants and their overthrow by the democratic party. The
years of his manhood were filled with the internecine wars of the Hellenic
poleis and their leagues; and in his last years he still could observe the rise
of Macedonia under Philip II. He died at the age of eighty-one, in 347. In
the year after his death the Third Sacred War was concluded with the Peace
of Philocrates, and Philip II became the chairman of the Amphictyonic
League. In 338 the battle of Chaeronea was followed by the congress of
Corinth and the foundation of an Hellenic League embracing all poleis except Sparta under the military command of Macedonia. In 337, ten years
after Plato's death, the League declared the war on Persia. The age of
Alexander and Empire had begun.

[161]

The motives which induced the young man of a well-connected family not to pursue his natural career in the politics of Athens but instead to become a philosopher, the founder of a school, and a man of letters, are revealed by Plato himself through an autobiographical passage of the *Seventh Letter* (324b–326b), written about 353, when he was in his seventies:

"When I was young I felt like so many others: as soon as I should become my own master, I thought, I would immediately enter public life. But my way was crossed by certain events in the affairs of the polis." The first opportunity seemed to have come with the revolution that led to the government of the Thirty. Some of the autocratic rulers were Plato's relatives, and they invited him to participate in the administration. In view of his inexperienced youth it was not surprising that he expected the new rulers to lead the polis from an unjust life to a just one; and he gave his mind diligently to them, to see what they would do. (Whether this phrase means actual participation in the regime, perhaps in a minor function, does not become clear.) Disillusion came soon. The former government looked like a golden age compared with the present one. And in particular he was shocked by the policy of the Tyrants, well-known in our own time, to consolidate their regime by involving citizens, among them Socrates, in criminal actions which would make them reliable supporters because a change of the regime would expose them to the vengeance of the victims. Socrates, "whom I would not hesitate to call the justest man at the time," resisted such involvement at the risk of unpleasant consequences; and Plato withdrew in disgust from the oligarchic regime. When the democratic revolution had abolished the Tyrants, Plato, though somewhat sobered about Athenian politics, again would have been willing to participate. The returned democrats, while marring their victory by many a personal revenge, were on the whole remarkably moderate. Still, they charged Socrates, of all people, with impiety (*asebeia*), prosecuted him, found him guilty, and slew him, the very man who had resisted criminal action against a democratic partisan at the time of the Tyrants.

As Plato considered all this, and observed the men who were active in politics, with their laws and customs, and as he advanced in age, it appeared to him ever more difficult to manage public affairs properly. For without friends and trusty companions one could not do anything at all; and they could not be found among old acquaintances because the polis was no longer managed according to the principles and customs of the forefathers. To acquire new friends, however, was impossible without great difficulties. Though at first he had felt the urgent desire to take part in politics, he became dazed by the spectacle of a general breakdown. He did not cease to contemplate means for improving the situation, but as regards action he continued to wait for the right moment. Finally, he arrived at the conclusion that only a deliberate effort of an almost miraculous kind could repair the bad state in which all poleis of the time found themselves, and then only under favorable circumstances. Thus, praising right philosophy, he was compelled to declare that it alone enabled one to discern what is right in the polis, as well as in the life of the individual. And the races of man would have no cessation from evils until either the race of the right and truly philosophizing gained political rule, or the race of rulers in the poleis, by some divine dispensation, began to philosophize truly. "With this conviction I came to Italy and Sicily, when I went there for the first time."

The autobiographical passage reports an evolution in the life of Plato that began when he was about twenty-three years old and reached its climax when he was about thirty-eight. Something like a crisis must have occurred around 390 B.C., for into this time falls the violent outburst of the *Gorgias,* perhaps in response to the attack of Polycrates on Socrates, with its transfer of authority from the statesmen of Athens to the new statesman Plato. Then followed the extended voyage to Italy and Sicily of 389/8 and, soon after the return, perhaps around 385, the foundation of the Academy. He had understood that participation in the politics of Athens was senseless if the purpose of politics was the establishment of just order; he had, furthermore, seen that the situation in the other Hellenic poleis was just as bad as in Athens, if not worse; and above all he had understood (what modern political reformers and revolutionaries seem to be unable to understand) that a reform cannot be achieved by a well-intentioned leader who recruits his followers from the very people whose moral confusion is the source of disorder. When he had gained those insights in the course of fifteen years, he did not fall, however, into despair or sullen resignation, but resolved on that "effort of an almost miraculous kind" to renew the order of Hellenic civilization out of the resources of his own love of wisdom, fortified by the paradigmatic life and death of the most just man, Socrates.

The autobiographical declaration will be our guide in the study of the "almost miraculous effort." We are not concerned with a "Platonic philosophy" or "doctrine" but with Plato's resistance to the disorder of the surrounding society and his effort to restore the order of Hellenic civilization through love of wisdom. His effort was a failure in so far as his dream of an Hellenic empire, in the form of a federation under an hegemonic polis, infused by the spirit of the Academy, could not be realized. The unification of Hellas came through the power of Macedonia. Nevertheless, it was a success, probably beyond any expectations entertained by Plato at the time when he founded the Academy, in as much as in his dialogues he created the symbols of the new order of wisdom, not for Hellas only, but for all mankind. In the following chapters we shall trace this effort from the *Gorgias,* in which Plato transferred the authority of Athenian order to himself, to its climax in the *Laws,* in which the order of wisdom became the analogue of cosmic order.

The present chapter has the nature of a preface to the study of the effort proper. Its first section will deal with the origin of the Platonic effort in the paradigmatic life and death of Socrates. Its second section will deal with Plato's participation in the politics of his time, as far as its character can be discerned in the *Letters*.

SOCRATES

Socrates the son of Sophroniscus was born in 469 B.C. and died from the hemlock in 399 B.C. Concerning his life the only primary source extant seems to be the affidavit sworn by his accuser Meletus, as reported by Diogenes Laertius II, 40: "Socrates is guilty, not to recognize the gods recognized by the polis, and to introduce other new divinities [*daimona*]; he is also guilty, to corrupt the youth. Penalty death." The reconstruction of an "historical" Socrates seems to be an impossible task, considering the lack of sources. The Socrates who formed Plato was the Socrates as seen by Plato.

We shall, first, circumscribe the central issue of the Socratic trial, as seen by Plato in the *Apology;* and, second, characterize the myth of the Socratic soul that unfolds in the work of Plato.

The Apology

The divine, regenerative force of order, transmitted by Socrates to Plato, had come to Socrates from the omphalos of Hellas, from Delphi.

A friend of Socrates, Chaerephon, had put to the oracle the question whether any man was wiser than Socrates, and the Pythia had answered that none was wiser than he. The answer was puzzling to Socrates who knew that he had no wisdom. And yet the god could not lie, for that was against his nature. Hence, Socrates began to test the answer by involving men renowned for their wisdom into conversation, in order to find one wiser than himself. Then he would go to the god, with the refutation in his hand. The first victim of Socratic examination into his wisdom was a well-known politician. He turned out to be not too wise, though he was thought of as wise by many and even more so by himself, and Socrates tried to impress on him that he was in error when he thought himself wise. Understandably he aroused the hatred of the politician as well as of several among those present. Still, he discovered on the occasion that he was wiser indeed than his victim, for while neither of them knew "anything really beautiful and good" he at least was aware of his ignorance and, thus, had a slight edge over the reputedly wise man. Further examinations of a similar nature had the same result, and increased the number of enemies.

The issue is joined between the pride of human wisdom that leads to disorder in the life of the individual, as well as of society, and the existence in obedience to the god. For "in truth, the god alone is wise, and by his answer he intended to show that human wisdom is worth little or nothing." Socrates goes about his task in obedience to the god. He tries to shake up the Athenians individually, and the most conceited among them first, to lead them back to true order. He is the gift of the god to Athens, given as a gadfly to the polis to stir it back into life. Recalling an Heraclitian phrase he admonishes his judges not to be out of temper, like a man suddenly awakened from sleep; they must spare him, for not easily will they find a successor to him to arouse and persuade and reproach them. The man who stands before them accused of *asebeia* is the true servant of divine order, sent by the Delphian god to save the impious accusers.

In the speeches of the defense three actions are going on at the same time: the trial of Socrates ending in his condemnation; the trial of Athens ending in the rejection of the savior; and the separation of Socrates from the polis ending in the solitude of his death.

The first speech is the defense speech proper. Socrates proves the accusation of *asebeia* unfounded, for he cannot be impious who tries to reform the polis under the order of the god of Delphi. Moreover, he refers to his Daimonion, well-known to everybody, that divine voice which made itself heard every time it wished to hold him back from an action. He assures the judges that the Daimonion had never counselled him to desist from his inquiry concerning the wisdom of other men. Somebody might argue that the proper way for him to save the community would have been to seek office and to use its power for the good of the polis. That way, however, he had to reject as futile, because the office-holders were so corrupt that they would not permit anybody to refrain from participating in their crimes. He would have found his death long ago if he had held an office of importance and tried to be honest. And again he was confirmed in his attitude by the Daimonion, as it raised its warning voice distinctly every time he considered this possibility.

The rottenness of the polis, described by Thucydides, had become the ultimate obstacle to a reform within constitutional forms; the direct appeal to the individual citizen had become necessary; and the pathos of the Periclean Funeral Oration had become the reforming will of the devoted citizen. Power and spirit had separated in the polis so far that a reunion through ordinary means of political action had become impossible. Socrates speaks as the representative of the divine power of Hellas; and he stresses the irony that he, the only Athenian who believes in the gods to such a degree that he follows their orders and risks his life, is accused of impiety by the very men whose disbelief in things divine is the reason for decay.

The atmosphere must have been tense. More than once Socrates had to admonish the large court not to break out in noisy demonstrations that would disturb his defense. One can imagine how incensed a considerable number among the Five Hundred must have been by the conduct of Socrates and his assurance that he would go on with his god-ordained task, even if they let him off lightly. Still, there were others who must have sensed the fatal hour, for the court divided almost evenly: only 281 of the 500 found him guilty.

The first speech had been technically the defense, in due legal form, against the accusation. After the verdict the trial of Athens overshadowed the trial of Socrates. The manifestation of the Delphian god in Socrates had been revealed, as well as his mission for the polis. Now the people had judged Socrates, and the gods had condemned the people.

With the second speech begins the separation of Socrates from the polis. According to procedural law the plaintiff had to propose a punishment, and the defendant, when found guilty, had to make a counter-proposal. The accuser had demanded the death penalty. On the level of the spiritual drama, however, the savior had been rejected and the man Socrates was now free. Hence, the second speech is a play of the free soul in the moment of suspense between the decision of fate and its fulfillment. He reconsiders his service to the city. What would be the proper reward for the man who is the benefactor of the polis and needs all his time to pursue his god-willed mission? It would seem most appropriate that he should be compensated with the highest honor granted to an Athenian citizen, a place at the public table in the Prytaneion. That honor would be much more fitting for him than for the victors at Olympia. His language is almost to the word that of Xenophanes a century earlier. Nevertheless, the situation has changed from the first insight into the order of wisdom and a reproach by the mystic-philosopher, to the inexorable call to duty by the savior who, facing death, acts as the instrument of God. The demand, however, is not blunt. The charm of Socrates, as always, lies in his superiority to the situation. His soul is quiet; and in his reflections he is the ironic onlooker while forces divine and human have chosen his earthly person as the field for their clash. His demand for a place in the Prytaneion is serious, for he should receive it as the man of the highest rank in the spiritual order of the polis; and it is not serious, for he knows that he will not receive it in the actual order of Athens. It serves as an ironical starting point for a reflection on practical alternatives. Socrates refuses to make a serious counterproposal, for that would be an admission of guilt. Fear of death would not induce him to make it, for death is not an evil while the other course would be an evil. And what should he suggest? Jail? But what should he do in jail? Or exile? That would only continue his troubles, for how could strangers be expected to tolerate him when even his fellow citizens could not stand his action? Hence, in obedience to the law, which requires him to make a proposition, he proposes an insignificant fine. After this proposal the court sentenced him to death.

The third speech is addressed to the judges, those who condemned him and those who acquitted him. First he reminds the judges who had voted for his death of the sad fame that is now theirs, to be the men who have killed Socrates. And he warns them that they will not escape the fate which they tried to avert by putting him to death, for others will arise and demand the account of their lives which they refused to him. Then he addresses himself to the judges who found him not guilty and reveals to them the secret order that had governed the proceedings of the day: At no point of the whole procedure had his Daimonion warned him; hence, the course taken by him was approved by the gods.

The *Apology* concludes with the great theme that will run through the work of Plato: "And now it is time for us to go, I to die, and you to live." The philosopher's life toward death and the judgment in eternity separates from the life of the dead souls. And then the pathos of the moment is relieved by the last irony of Socratic ignorance: "Who of us takes the better way, is hidden to all, except to the God."

Drama and Myth of the Socratic Soul

The drama of Socrates is a symbolic form created by Plato as the means for communicating, and expanding, the order of wisdom founded by its hero. We have to touch, therefore, the thorny question why the dialogue should have become the symbolic form of the new order. No final answer, however, can be intended with regard to a question of such infinite complexity. We shall do no more than modestly list a number of points which under all circumstances must be taken into consideration.

Plato was strongly influenced by Aeschylus. We are familiar with the Aeschylean problem of Peitho, the persuasive imposition of right order on unruly passion. In the *Prometheus* the personified forces of the soul were engaged in the struggle for the order of Dike, with the solution, suggested towards the end, of redemption through the representative suffering of Heracles. The drama of the soul proved, furthermore, to be the substance of the process of history in the *Oresteia,* as well as of constitutional procedure in the *Suppliants.* Tragedy in the Aeschylean sense was a liturgy of Dike, and in particular it was a cult of the political Dike. Tragedy as a political cult, however, will lose its meaning when the people for whom it is written and performed are no longer able to experience the drama of Dike as paradigmatic for the order in their own souls. The tension of order and passion that had been mastered by the cult of tragedy had broken into the open conflict between Socrates and Athens. The cult had become senseless because from now on tragedy had only one subject matter, the fate of Socrates. In so far as the Platonic dialogue was animated by the tension between Socrates and Athens, it was in the history of Hellenic symbolic forms the successor to Aeschylean tragedy under the new political conditions.

But why should there be tragedy at all, and in its succession the Platonic dialogue? The answer must be sought in the Aeschylean and Platonic understanding of society as an order of the soul, as well as in the understanding of the soul as a social order of forces. The order of the soul as the source of order in society and the parallel construction of the two orders will occupy us at greater length in the analysis of the *Republic*. For the present we shall only stress the conception of order as an Agon of forces that will not give way to a nondramatic conception until the victory for wisdom and justice is achieved. Only when the tension of conflict has subsided and the new order is established can its expression assume the form of a static dogma or a metaphysical proposition. Tendencies in this direction are to be observed in the late work of Plato; and the nondramatic form breaks through in the esoteric work of Aristotle. This victory of the new order has, however, the unsatisfactory consequence that the "bad man" of the dramatic play gets lost. We shall have to deal with that question again in the analysis of the *Republic* with its agonal pairs of concepts.

If the dialogue is understood as the successor to the public cult of tragedy, the question will arise to whom the new symbolic form is addressed, if the decisive public, the people of Athens, does not want to listen. One answer to this question is given by Plato in the Digression of the *Theaetetus*. Even the most stubborn politician or sophist, who in public will not listen to the philosopher, still is man and can be stirred up in private. The hard shell of his corruption can be pierced and the anxiety of existence can be touched. The dialogue is an exoteric literary work, accessible to everybody individually who wants to read it. The personal conversation between Socrates and the individual Athenian citizen is continued through the instrument of the dialogue.

The dialogue, however, can be conducted only if it does not degenerate into an exchange of rhetorical harangues without existential communication among the speakers. Decisive for this point are the scenes in *Protagoras* and *Gorgias* where Socrates threatens a walkout unless the sophistic partner stops his speechmaking and enters into the argument. The dialogue is the symbolic form of the order of wisdom, in opposition to the oration as the symbolic form of the disordered society. It restores the common order of the spirit that has been destroyed through the privatization of rhetoric.

In the concrete situation, among the living, however, the law of the dialogue cannot be enforced. The opponent will not listen at all, or he will respond with rhetoric and thereby break the possibility of communication, or he will enter the argument but not be moved existentially even when he is beaten intellectually. The order of Athens was not regenerated either by Socrates or Plato. Socrates had to die in the attempt. And Dike achieved no victory. Is the dialogue a futile gesture after all?

In answer to this question Plato lets stream into the dialogue the force of Thanatos, of the Socratic death. In the *Phaedo* Thanatos becomes the cathartic power that cures the soul of the sickness of the earth. Life is comparable to a submarine existence with only a glimmer of the world above. Death is the liberating force. It enables the soul to live free of the denseness of the lower atmosphere; and when the end has come, it brings the reconvalescence from the illness of life. The last word of the dying Socrates to his friend is: "Crito, I owe a cock to Asclepios." Thanatos is the force that orders the soul of the living, for it makes them desirous of stripping themselves of everything that is not noble and just. The soul is immortal; and death is the incision in its existence which permits the readjustment of station after the earthly period has given the soul its chance for development. Hence, the situation of the dialogue does not end with life. It continues into the beyond; and the speaker of the dialogue in the beyond is an eternal judge who has sanctions at his disposal. The inconclusive situation among the living is made conclusive by the Myth of Judgment in the *Gorgias* and the *Republic*. Moreover, the myth of the judgment developed as a content of the dialogue affects the substance of the dialogue itself. In the *Apology* we have seen the multiple levels of action. On the political level Socrates is condemned by Athens; on the mythical level, Athens has been condemned by the gods. The dialogue is itself a mythical judgment. The Socrates of the *Apology* leaves his judges in no doubt that others will ask them the questions which they tried to escape by sentencing him to death. The "others" have come. And the dialogue is the continuation of the trial.

The situation is quite different when the dialogue is conducted with success in the circle of Socrates, Plato, and their friends. Then the positive force of the Socratic soul, its Eros, comes into play. To create existential community through developing the other man's true humanity in the image of his own—that is the work of the Socratic Eros. It is a force closely related to Thanatos. To the desire for Death and its catharsis corresponds the erotic *enthousiasmos*. Thanatos orients the soul toward the Good by relieving it from the sickness of appearance; Eros is the positive desire for the Good. Man has to die, and in his desire to make the best in himself a perpetually living force, he tries to rejuvenate himself through procreation. He has re-

[169]

ceived life once through his birth and he wishes to continue it through rebirth in his children. Those in whom the desire is only bodily have physical
children. Those in whom it is spiritual rejuvenate themselves through procreation in the souls of young men, that is, through loving, tending, and
developing the best in them. That is the force which animates the world of
the Platonic dialogue. The older man, Socrates, speaks to the younger man
and, through the power of his soul, awakens in him the echoing desire for
the Good. The Idea of the Good, evoked in the communion of the dialogue,
fills the souls of those who participate in the evocative act. And thus it becomes the sacramental bond between them and creates the nucleus of the
new society.

Death and Love are intimately related as orienting forces in the soul of
Socrates. In the *Phaedo* philosophy is the practice of dying; in the *Sympo-
sion* and *Phaedrus* it is the eroticism of the soul for the Idea which creates
the procreative community among men. Eros dominates his life because it is
a life towards death; and his Eros is powerful because existence in the expectation of catharsis through death gives the proper distance to the incidents
of earthly life. The nobility of the soul, which manifests itself in the pursuit
of the good and the avoidance of the ignoble in personal conduct, endows
him with the power over other men who are willing to open their souls to
the influence of the noble. Eros, thus, becomes an ordering force in social
relations. Only the noble souls are attracted to the erotic, evocative communion; the lesser souls remain indifferent or resist. The erotic attraction
and indifference, the power and response in the erotic relation, create the
ranks of the spiritual hierarchy. The force of Eros shades off into the force
of Dike, as did the force of Thanatos.

EROS AND THE WORLD

We have spoken of the crisis in Plato's life that occurred about 390 B.C.
If the *Gorgias* be taken as the expression of his mood at the time, the situation in Athens must indeed have seemed unbearable to him. In 389 he embarked on the extended travel that led him to Italy and Sicily. In Syracuse
he formed the friendship with Dion, the brother-in-law of Dionysius I. After
the death of the tyrant, in 367, Dion thought the time propitious to use his
influence with his nephew, Dionysius II, for a reform of government. He
appealed to Plato to come to Syracuse and to support the attempt with his
presence. Plato, who at the time was sixty years of age, followed the request
with many hesitations. This was the beginning of his involvement in Sicilian
affairs which outlasted the murder of Dion in 354.

Plato and Socrates

Plato and Sicily

While in the nineteenth century it had been the habit among scholars to underrate the importance of Plato's intervention in Sicilian politics, and even to doubt the authenticity of Plato's letters, we are faced more recently with the danger of exaggeration in the opposite direction. The mere numbering of the Sicilian travels as the first (389/8), the second (366/5), and the third (361/60), is apt to create the impression of a continuity of political effort, running through a period of perhaps forty years. As a matter of fact, after the first journey nothing happened at all for more than twenty years. Plato's efforts went into the foundation and management of the Academy, and for all practical purposes he considered it the final field of action in his life. The revival of an active interest in Sicily was induced from the outside, and the necessity was accepted with reluctance. This revival came, furthermore, after the *Republic* had been finished, at a time when, in the literary field, Plato was occupied with the great trilogy of *Theaetetus-Sophist-Statesman.* Hence the problems of Sicily have no immediate bearing on the formation of Plato's ideas before the *Laws.* And even with regard to the *Laws* we have to use some caution in weighing the influence of the Sicilian situation. It is tempting, of course, to see in the *Laws* a code for the Sicilian reform, and the *Seventh Letter* leaves no doubt about the close connection of the *Laws* with the task of drafting a model code for the reform intended by the party of Dion. Nevertheless, we shall see that the *Laws* is definitely more than a political *livre de circonstance,* even if the Sicilian problems furnished the momentum of an occasion.

When all these reservations are made there remains, however, the fact that the participation in Sicilian politics left deep traces in the formation of Plato's ideas. The *Seventh Letter* which assesses, on occasion of the Sicilian problems, the relation between Plato's ideas and the reality of his age, ranks equal in importance with the *Republic* and the *Laws* for the understanding of Platonic politics. It is not a piece of private correspondence; it has the character of an open letter. Its occasion was the request of Dion's friends for advice in constitutional matters and it is, indeed, addressed to the "companions and friends of Dion." The advice itself, however, fills only a comparatively small part of the document (330c–337e); the larger part consists of an account of Plato's relations with the rulers of Syracuse. This larger part has the character of an apology for Dion and for Plato himself. Intrinsically it is addressed to the general public and its connection with the advice is rather loose. Moreover, it is quite possible that the apologetic part was written in the years preceding the publication of the *Letter* itself. The need for the publication of the various parts in the form of the *Letter* arose through the unfortunate end of Dion's attempt to reform the constitution of Syracuse. Dion was murdered by the opposition and in the actual killing were involved two men who, while not belonging to the Academy, were sufficiently close to the Platonic circle that for the general public the Academy was connected in an unsavory manner with the murderous plot. To dispel somewhat the shadow that had fallen on the Academy was probably the principal reason for the publication of the *Letter* in its ultimate form in 353.

In Syracuse, at the court of Dionysius I, Plato met Dion. At the time Plato was forty Dion was probably twenty years of age. Of the relationship between Plato and Dion we know little beyond an occasional hint. The realm of Eros is not open to the public. The *Seventh Letter* reveals only that Dion responded to the discourse of Plato more keenly and more enthusiastically than any other young man whom Plato had ever met (327a–b). Nevertheless, this meeting was "the beginning of everything" (327a). Under the influence of Plato, Dion embarked on the new life, "preferring Arete to pleasure and luxury"; and he persisted in it, much to the disapproval of the court. After the death of the tyrant in 367, it seemed possible that the group of Dion's friends in Syracuse could win over the young successor to the Platonic way of life. Dion requested the presence of Plato because now if ever seemed to arise the hope of having the ruler of a great polis become a philosopher (328a). Plato finally accepted the invitation, though with great misgivings, for a young man like the tyrant might have an impulse one day and a contradictory one the next—an apprehension that was amply justified by the events (328b). The relation with Dionysius II, however, we shall discuss later.

From the *Letters* we can conclude that the bond which united Plato with Dion was a most intimate union of heart and mind. In the opening paragraph of the *Seventh Letter,* Plato reminds the recipients of their assurance that their convictions (*dianoia*) are the same as Dion's; only if this is true will Plato assist them with advice. And what were Dion's convictions? No conjecture is necessary because they were the convictions that had been formed through the discourse with Plato. Dion's policy was Plato's; the latter can speak in the name of the dead friend because the union between them was so close that it left no room for differences (323e–324b). In the formula which precedes the advice of the *Eighth Letter,* Plato expressly designates what he has to say as his and Dion's "joint counsel." "I shall interpret" this counsel as Dion himself would pronounce it if he were alive (355a).

In the *Seventh Letter* Plato elaborates in a more general manner the conditions which the patient has to fulfill if he is desirous of Platonic advice (330d–331d). If a physician has to advise a sick man who lives in a way injurious to his health, he first will demand of him "to turn his life around." If the patient consents, then the advice may extend to other points; if he does not consent, then a self-respecting physician will not continue his treatment. The same principle is valid for political counsel. If a polis does not want advice, or if quite obviously it would not take it, Plato will not approach it self-invited; and certainly he will not use constraint. With regard to Athens, in particular, he clarifies his attitude by stating that he would consider it sinful to use constraint against "father or mother." Neither would he estrange them by useless admonitions, nor would he play the flatterer and counsel them to satisfy desires which he himself "would rather die than be addicted to." If a man considers the constitution of his country imperfect he ought to speak, provided the admonition is not obviously useless or would lead to his own death as in the case of Socrates. Under no circumstances, however, must he ferment violence and revolution in his fatherland. All he can do is pray for the best for himself and his polis.

The condition for advice is an existential community on the terms of Plato. Under this condition he is willing to advise the companions of Dion, as he has advised Dion himself and later Dionysius II; and perhaps the God will grant that the third time salvation will result from the counsel (334d). No doubt, however, should exist about the meaning of the terms. Plato reminds the recipients of the *Letter* that the same advice is valid for them that had been formerly extended by Dion and Plato to the tyrant. They had counselled him to lead a life of daily discipline that would result in self-control. A personality, thus, would be built that would attract loyal friends and companions (331d–e). The formation of a group would be the next step; the bond of this group would have to consist in *philia* and harmony with regard to *arete* (332d). But no such group could be formed for further action unless he had first produced in himself an intelligent and temperate character (*emphron, sophron*) (332e). If we translate these conditions into a modern terminology, we might say that Plato demanded, as the condition of his advice, a conversion to Platonism and the formation of something like an order. This order would be the nucleus for the regeneration of the polis.

The admonitions to the recipients of the *Seventh Letter* reveal in part the nature of the union between Plato and Dion—though no more of it than can enter into a general formulation. Quite possibly, however, we find a clearer reflection of it in the description of the erotic experience in the *Phaedrus* (particularly 252–256). In pre-existence the souls of the lovers follow in the train of a god. When they have fallen to earth each is in search of the beloved companion who carries in his soul the nature of the god whom they had formerly followed. The followers of Zeus desire that the soul of the beloved have the nature of Zeus; and they inquire, therefore, whether he has the nature of a philosopher and ruler. When they have found him and fallen in love with him they do what they can to strengthen this nature in him. They search their own souls; and they find their own divine nature in their fascinated gaze at the nature of the god in the beloved. Thus they become possessed of him and form their own character, as far as that is possible for man, into participation in the god. And since they believe the beloved to be the cause of this transformation, they love him all the more; and what they receive from Zeus, like the Bacchae, that they stream back into him to make him as like to their god as possible.

The erotic union has sacramental character, for the nature of the god becomes incarnate in the community of the erotic souls as in its mystical body. Not all souls, however, have followed the same god in their pre-existence. And only those who have followed Zeus are the chosen instruments for actualizing the god of political order in society. The symbol of the "Sons of Zeus" has its experiental basis in the eroticism of the philosopher-rulers. One can go perhaps even a step further, as Hildebrandt does in his *Platon,* where he suggests that the passage in *Phaedrus* seems deliberately to avoid the nominative *Zeus;* the name of the god appears always in the genitive *Dios.* In particular the construction *Dios dion* in 252e, however, makes it probable that these stylistic peculiarities are meant as a hint that Dion is the partner of the relationship which Plato celebrates in the dithyramb of the *Phaedrus.* The suggestion gains in probability if we consider the epitaph which Plato wrote for his friend, with the closing line: "Dion, thou, who made rage with Eros my heart."

The intimacy of the erotic relationship, though not beyond words, is beyond the written word. The wisdom of the soul which is engendered through Eros cannot and must not be put down on paper as a teachable doctrine. In the *Phaedrus* Socrates-Plato says that it would be simplicity to leave or receive an art (*techne*) in writing, under the belief that the written word would be reliable and clear. Writing is like painting; the creation of the painter has the likeness of life, but when you would ask it a question it would remain silent. Words, when they are written down, will fall into the hands of those who cannot understand them; and when they are abused they cannot defend themselves (275c-e). There is another word, however, the word graven with understanding into the soul of the learner, that can defend itself and knows when to speak and when to be silent. And Phaedrus answers: "It is the idea-word that you mean, living and with a soul, of which the written word justly is called no more than an image" (276a). The idea-word (*tou eidotos logos*) is the medium in which the tenderness and strength of the erotic mania express themselves; it is the vehicle of communication by means of which the erotic souls attune one another to the harmony of the cosmos; and it is the fragile vessel in which the god becomes incarnate in community.

The attempt to formulate the intimacy of the erotic community as a doctrine is worse than futile: it is the desecration of a mystery. That is the personal insult which Plato had to suffer at the hands of Dionysius II. We have seen that Plato had his misgivings about the seriousness of the tyrant's desire to become a convert to philosophy. As soon as he arrived in Syracuse and saw that his apprehensions were justified, he submitted therefore the seriousness of the tyrant to the infallible test (*peira*). He mapped out for him the course of study which a man, if he is truly desirous, will follow with zeal in spite of its hardships; while the man who is only tempted by some vanity will soon find the course impossible because it entails a change in his way of life. Dionysius did not pass this test. He was vain enough, however, to consider himself a philosopher and to put down in writing, and to circulate, what he had learned from the discourse with Plato and from secondary sources. That breach of confidence gave Plato the occasion to express himself, in the *Seventh Letter,* more distinctly on the problem of written publication of his doctrine.

Those who publish what they have learned, whether from direct instruction, or through other information, or through their own discovery, certainly have understood nothing. He himself has never written directly on the core of his philosophy, and never will, for it cannot be put into words like other knowledge. Understanding can come only after the long preparatory period of studies and discipline. And then it will be generated in the soul like a blaze by a leaping spark; and once this fire of understanding is lighted it will never burn down. Besides, if he thought that the doctrine could be written down, he would do it himself. But even if it were possible, it would hardly be advisable. For those who are able to understand, the very few, will surmise the truth anyway and discover it at the merest hint. The others who cannot understand it would despise the revelation and expose it to contempt; while still others, because nothing is touched in them existentially, would be filled with vanity and high hopes as if now they were in the possession of some sacred knowledge (341b–342). Hence no serious man will write of the really serious things for the many. Therefore, "when there comes anything before your eyes, for instance of a legislator on laws, it cannot have been the most serious matter to him, if he is a serious person himself, but that will

[175]

still lie in the most beautiful and noble place of his mind" (344c). To these explanations should be added the warnings to Dionysius himself, in the *Second Letter,* written perhaps ten years earlier than the *Seventh.* The best safeguard against misunderstandings is to learn by heart and not to write at all. "Therefore I have never written anything on it [*i.e.,* on the essence of philosophy], and that is the reason why there is not and never will be any writings by Plato himself, but those which go by his name, are by Socrates who has become beautiful and young." The warning is followed by the request to read the letter repeatedly and then to burn it (314c). Publication is the unforgivable insult to the "leader and lord" (*hegemon kai kyrios*) in these matters (345c).

The endeavors of the Platonists were no more than a brief episode in the disastrous Sicilian history. The spirit of the Platonic reform was revived in the reorganization of the island by Timoleon, beginning in 344, but the civil war flared up again, in 323, and this formerly most promising area of Hellenic colonization fell in the end to the Carthaginians and to their successors, the Romans.

The Letter to Hermias of Atarneus

Of a quite different historical importance was the expansion of Platonism in the East. By the Peace of Antalcidas in 387/6 the Greek cities in Anatolia had passed under Persian administration. Within this administration, however, it was possible for a skilful leader to attain a status of semi-autonomy for his territory. One Hermias, a man of lowly origin, was able to achieve control over some mountain places in the Troad. He could extend his domain over the coastal cities, at least down to Assos; he received public recognition from the Persian satrap and was allowed the title of prince. The capital of his realm was Atarneus.

In the expansion of Hermias, two Platonists, Erastus and Coriscus of Scepsis, were of decisive influence. Having completed their course in the Academy, they had returned to Scepsis. They seem to have advised Hermias to temper somewhat the form of his tyranny, with the result that the coastal cities joined voluntarily the dominion of Hermias. What Plato had planned for Sicily, that is, a reform of the government in Syracuse that would induce the other cities to enter into a hegemonic federation, succeeded on a smaller scale in Anatolia. The organization of the government under Hermias and the Platonists is not known in detail. We only know that Hermias allotted to Erastus and Coriscus the city of Assos as their special domain and that a treaty with the city of Erythrae was concluded in the name of "Hermias and the companions." Around Erastus and Coriscus there existed quite probably a Platonic circle, for in 347, when Aristotle and Xenocrates left the Academy, they went to Assos; during the next few years something like a daughter Academy developed in the city. Among the pupils of Aristotle at this time was Callisthenes, his nephew, the later campaign historiographer in the suite of Alexander. For the close relationship among the members of the ruling group of Platonists there is further evidence in the fact that Aristotle married the niece of Hermias.

The rule of Hermias came to an unfortunate end as a consequence of his Hellenic policy. He considered his realm a bridgehead for the impending war of Macedonia against Persia. His negotiations with Philip were betrayed to the Persians; and the satrap who conducted the subsequent campaign against Atarneus got hold of the person of Hermias. Under torture he did not betray the plans of Philip and, finally, he was crucified. When he was asked for the last grace that he requested, he answered: "Tell my friends and companions that I have done nothing unworthy of philosophy or weak." The message was delivered to Aristotle and the friends at Assos. In his commemorative hymn to the dead friend, Aristotle praised Arete for whom to die is an envied fate in Hellas; Hermias went to Hades for her sake like Achilles.

The motif of Achilles, the protagonist of the Hellenes against Asia, is more than a poetic ornament. Hermias died in 341. The military alliance with Philip in preparation for the Persian war has to be dated probably in 342. This is the year in which Aristotle went to Pella to become the educator of Alexander. The romantic picture of the King of Macedonia searching Hellas for the greatest philosopher (who at that time was not the distinguished public figure) for his great son (who at that time was not the Great), must be somewhat tempered by the reality of the political link between Atarneus and Macedonia and the probability that Aristotle's mission in Pella was in part diplomatic. The tutor of Alexander was not only the great philosopher, he was also the son-in-law of Hermias, engaged in political negotiations that would lead to the Hellenic conquest of Asia. This was the atmosphere in which Alexander grew up and was formed. And we see, indeed, the motif of Achilles reappear in the early years of Alexander's campaigns, which were conducted in the *imitatio Achillis.*

The chain of human relations, which ends with the second Achilles setting out for the conquest of Asia, begins with Plato's *Sixth Letter,* the founding document of the union between the three men who organized the realm of Atarneus. It has to be dated somewhere in the last years of Plato's life, that is, between 350 and 347. The *Letter* is addressed to the three men in common, that is, to "Hermias and Erastus and Coriscus." It has the character of a sacred constitution. A god seemed to have good fortune in store for them when he brought them together; for their company will be to each other of mutual benefit. Nothing could add more to the strength of Hermias than the acquisition of loyal and uncorrupt friends; and nothing is more necessary for Erastus and Coriscus than to add the worldly wisdom of an experienced ruler to their wisdom of the Idea. "What then have I to say?" To Hermias, that he can assure him of the trustworthiness of the two Platonists, and advise him to cling to their friendship by all means. To Coriscus and Erastus, that they should cling to Hermias and be bound with him in the one bond of *philia*. Such a bond, however well knit, may become strained. In this case they should submit their difficulty to Plato; his counsel, rendered with justice and reverent restraint, will heal the friendship and community surer than any charm. Having thus recommended the friends to each other, and having made himself the partner in their community as its guardian and arbiter, Plato reflects on the Letter itself: "This Letter all three of you must read; the best would be all three together, otherwise at least two; as much in communion [*koinê*] as possible, and as often as possible. You must recognize it as a contract and binding law, as it is just. And you must swear to it with a not a-music seriousness as well as with the playfulness that is the brother of earnestness. You must swear to it by the God who is the guide in all things, present and future; and by the lordly father of the guide and author; whom we shall see in his clearness, if we are truly philosophers, as far as it is possible to men who are blessed."

The document is so clear that it hardly requires interpretation. The philosophers and the king have, indeed, entered into the existential communion of *philia*. Their bond is the faith that was kindled by Plato. In his name they should cling to each other; and to his healing power they should refer any strains on their bond. We see emerging in outline the conception of an Hellenic theocratic empire of federated communities of Platonists with its center in the Academy. The sacred symbol of the union between the companions is the Letter, to be read and re-read in communion. The rite of reading it and swearing to it should be celebrated in that mood of suspense between seriousness and play which is the appropriate mood toward a myth. And they should swear by the guiding god as well as by the father of the guide and author—a theological symbolism which at this period of Plato's life probably signifies the divine forces of the *Timaeus,* that is, nous-in-psyche and the Demiurge.

A R I S T O T L E

[*384–322* B.C.]

THE INFLUENCE OF "THE PHILOSOPHER," AS HE WAS CALLED IN THE MIDDLE ages, on the history of western civilization has been incalculably great, too great according to his critics. Nevertheless, it is astonishing how vital some of his works have proved to be. *The Poetics,* of all of Aristotle's works, has perhaps been least affected by the passage of time. From the time of its re-discovery in the Renaissance it has never lost its relevance and its power to enrich our understanding of literature. The work has fathered many off-spring, some of which would have astonished its author. It has been the point of departure for moral and structural theories of literature, for analyses of "aesthetic distance," for long and acrimonious debates on truth in litera-ture, for the study of the relations among literature, philosophy, and history, indeed, for virtually all major literary problems.

The present essay is a study of an important and controversial word in *The Poetics—catharsis,* a word whose ambiguities have generated much of the most original thinking on the drama.

S. H. Butcher was for many years Professor of Greek at the University of Edinburgh. His edition of *The Poetics,* with an elaborate apparatus and numerous supplementary essays, has held its distinguished place in the literature on Aristotle since its final revision, completed shortly before his death in 1910. The following essay is taken from Butcher's *Theory of Poetry and Fine Arts,* first published in 1894.

S. H. BUTCHER

The Function of Tragedy

ARISTOTLE'S DEFINITION OF TRAGEDY RUNS THUS: "TRAGEDY IS AN IMITATION of an action that is serious, complete, and of a certain magnitude; in language embellished with each kind of artistic ornament, the several kinds being found in separate parts of the play; in the form of action, not of narrative; through pity and fear effecting the proper *katharsis,* or purgation, of these emotions." The "several kinds of embellishment" are in the next paragraph explained to be verse and song; verse without music being employed in the dialogue, lyrical song in the choral parts. Tragedy is hereby distinguished from Nomic and Dithyrambic poetry, which use the combined embellishments throughout.

From this definition it appears first, that the *genus* of tragedy is Imitation. This it has in common with all the fine arts.

Next, it is differentiated from comedy as being a *mimēsis praxeōs spoudaias,* an imitation of an action that is neither *geloia* nor *phaulē,* neither ludicrous nor morally trivial. It is concerned with a serious end, namely *eudaimonia*—that well-being which is the true end of life. It is a picture of human destiny in all its significance. No one English word completely renders *spoudaias.* The translation "noble," which has the merit of applying to the characters as well as to the action, yet suggests too much a purely moral quality, while at the same time it does not adequately bring out the implied antithesis to comedy. *Grave* and *great*—these are the two ideas contained in the word. Many of the older critics, missing the true import of *spoudaias,* transfer the meaning which they ought to have found here to the later words, *megethos echousēs,* of the definition. These—as is plain from Aristotle's explanation in ch. vii.—refer to the actual length of the poem. Addison,[1] who does not stand alone in this view, includes under them the greatness or significance of the action (which is in fact denoted by *spoudaias*) and also the internal length or duration of the action, of which Aristotle here says nothing.

Further, tragedy is differentiated in form from Epic poetry as being dramatic, not narrative.

The remainder of the definition describes the specific effect, the proper function (*ergon*) of tragedy,—namely, to produce a certain kind of *katharsis.* It would be a curious study to collect the many and strange translations that have been given of this definition in the last three hundred years. Almost every word of it has been misinterpreted in one way or another. But after all it contains only two real difficulties. The one lies in the clause concerning the 'several kinds of embellishment.' Fortunately, however, Aristotle has interpreted this for us himself; otherwise it would doubtless have called forth volumes of criticism. The other and more fundamental difficulty relates to the meaning of the *katharsis.* Here we seek in vain for any direct aid from the *Poetics.*

A great historic discussion has centred round the phrase. No passage, probably, in ancient literature has been so frequently handled by commentators, critics, and poets, by men who knew Greek, and by men who knew no Greek. A tradition almost unbroken through centuries found in it a reference to a moral effect which tragedy produces through the "purification of the passions." What the precise effect is, and what are the passions on which tragedy works, was very variously interpreted. Corneille, Racine, Lessing, each offered different solutions, but all agreed in assuming the purely ethical intention of the drama. Goethe protested; but his own most interesting theory is for linguistic reasons quite impossible, nor does it accord with much else that is contained in the *Poetics.* In 1857 a pamphlet by Jacob Bernays reopened the whole question, and gave a new direction to the argument. His main idea had been forestalled by Italian critics of the

---

[1] *Spectator* No. 267: "Aristotle by the greatness of the action does not only mean that it should be great in its nature but also in its duration, or in other words that it should have a due length in it, as well as what we properly call greatness."

Renaissance; afterwards it fell into oblivion; a similar theory was independently struck out by H. Weil in 1847, but it attracted little notice till Bernays set it forth in detail.

Bernays, with equal learning and literary skill, maintained that *katharsis* here is a medical metaphor,[2] "purgation," and denotes a pathological effect on the soul analogous to the effect of medicine on the body. The thought, as he interpreted it, may be expressed thus. Tragedy excites the emotions of pity and fear—kindred emotions that are in the breasts of all men—and by the act of excitation affords a pleasurable relief. The feelings called forth by the tragic spectacle are not indeed permanently removed, but are quieted for the time, so that the system can fall back upon its normal course. The stage, in fact, provides a harmless and pleasurable outlet for instincts which demand satisfaction, and which can be indulged here more fearlessly than in real life.

Plato, it must be remembered, in his attack upon the drama had said that "the natural hunger after sorrow and weeping" which is kept under control in our own calamities, is satisfied and delighted by the poets. "Poetry feeds and waters the passions instead of starving them." Through its tearful moods it enfeebles the manly temper; it makes anarchy in the soul by exalting the lower elements over the higher, and by dethroning reason in favour of feeling. Aristotle held that it is not desirable to kill or to starve the emotional part of the soul, and that the regulated indulgence of the feelings serves to maintain the balance of our nature. Tragedy, he would say, is a vent for the particular emotions of pity and fear. In the first instance, it is true, its effect is not to tranquillise but to excite. It excites emotion, however, only to allay it. Pity and fear, artificially stirred, expel the latent pity and fear which we bring with us from real life, or at least, such elements in them as are disquieting. In the pleasurable calm which follows when the passion is spent, an emotional cure has been wrought.[3]

It is worth noting, as has been pointed out by Bernays, and before him by Twining, that Milton had already apprehended something of the true import of Aristotle's words. In adopting the pathological theory of the effect of tragedy he was, as has been more recently shown, following in the wake of Italian criticism. In his preface to *Samson Agonistes* he writes:

---

[2] The three chief meanings of the word, (1) the medical, (2) the religious or liturgical, "lustratio" or "expiatio," and (3) the moral, "purificatio," are sometimes difficult to keep apart. In Plato *Soph.* 230 c the medical metaphor is prominent.

[3] Zeller (*Phil. der Gr.*) thinks it unimportant whether the medical or the religious use of the *katharsis* is primarily intended, as in either case the word bears a sense far removed from the original metaphor. But the distinctive method of relief is different in the two cases. The medical *katharsis* implies relief following upon previous excitation.

The Function of Tragedy

Tragedy, as it was anciently composed, hath been ever held the gravest, moralest, and most profitable of all other poems; therefore said by Aristotle to be of power, by raising pity and fear, or terrour, to purge the mind of those and such-like passions; that is to temper or reduce them to just measure with a kind of delight stirred up by reading or seeing those passions well imitated. Nor is Nature herself wanting in her own effects to make good his assertion, for so, in physick, things of melancholick hue and quality are used against melancholy, sour against sour, salt to remove salt humours.

In other words tragedy is a form of homeopathic treatment, curing emotion by means of an emotion like in kind, but not identical.[4]

Aristotle, it would seem, was led to this remarkable theory by observing the effect of certain melodies upon a form of religious ecstasy, or, as the Greeks said, "enthusiasm," such as is rarely seen in this country, and whose proper home is in the East. The persons subject to such transports were regarded as men possessed by a god, and were taken under the care of the priesthood. The treatment prescribed for them was so far homeopathic in character, that it consisted in applying movement to cure movement, in soothing the internal trouble of the mind by a wild and restless music. The passage in the *Politics* in which Aristotle describes the operation of these tumultuous melodies is the key to the meaning of *katharsis* in the *Poetics*. Such music is expressly distinguished by Aristotle from the music which has a moral effect or educational value (*paideias heneken*). It differs, again, from those forms of music whose end is either relaxation (*pros avapausin*) or the higher aesthetic enjoyment (*pros diagōgēn*). Its object is *katharsis*. It is a physical stimulus which provides an outlet for religious fervour. Patients, who have been subjected to this process, "fall back," to quote Aristotle's phrase, "into their normal state, as if they had undergone a medical or purgative treatment." The emotional result is a "harmless joy."

The homeopathic cure of morbid "enthusiasm" by means of music, was, it may be incidentally observed, known also to Plato. In a passage of the *Laws,* where he is laying down rules for the management of infants, his advice is that infants should be kept in perpetual motion, and live as if they were always tossing at sea. He proceeds to compare the principle on which religious ecstasy is cured by a strain of impassioned music with the method of nurses, who lull their babies to sleep not by silence but by singing, not

---

[4] Cf. the closing lines of *Samson Agonistes*:
>His servants he, with new acquist
>Of true experience, from this great event
>With peace and consolation hath dismissed,
>And calm of mind, all passion spent.

by holding them quiet but by rocking them in their arms. Fear, he thinks, is in each case the emotion that has to be subdued,—a fear caused by something that has gone wrong within. In each case the method of cure is the same; an external agitation (*kinēsis*) is employed to calm and counteract an internal. But Plato recognised the principle only as it applied to music and the useful art of nursing. Aristotle, with his generalising faculty and his love of discovering unity in different domains of life, extended the principle to tragedy and hints at even a wider application of it. In the *Politics,* after explaining the action of the musical *katharsis,* he adds that "those who are liable to pity and fear, and, in general, persons of emotional temperament pass through a like experience; . . . they all undergo a *katharsis* of some kind and feel a pleasurable relief."

The whole passage of the *Politics* here referred to is introduced by certain important prefatory words: "What we mean by *katharsis* we will now state in general terms (*haplōs*); hereafter we will explain it more clearly (*eroumen saphesteron*) in our treatise on Poetry." But in the *Poetics,* as we have it, the much desired explanation is wanting; there appears to be a gap in the text at this most critical point. We are therefore driven back upon the *Politics* itself as our primary authority. The tone of the passage and particular expressions show two things plainly—first, that there the term is consciously metaphorical; secondly, that though its technical use in medicine was familiar, the metaphorical application of it was novel and needed elucidation. Moreover, in the words last quoted,—"all undergo a *katharsis* of some kind,"—it is pretty plainly implied that the *katharsis* of pity and fear in tragedy is analogous to, but not identical with, the *katharsis* of "enthusiasm."

Now, Bernays transferred the *katharsis* of the *Politics* almost without modification of meaning to the definition of tragedy. He limited its reference to the simple idea of an emotional relief, a pleasurable vent for overcharged feeling.[5] This idea, no doubt, almost exhausts the meaning of the phrase as it is used in the *Politics*. It also expresses, as has been above ex-

---

[5] Keble's theory of poetry—of the "vis medica poeticae," as he calls it—may well be compared. It is expounded in his *Praelectiones Academicae,* and also in a review of Lockhart's *Life of Scott,* which has been republished in Keble's *Occasional Papers and Reviews.* The most important pages of the review are quoted in Prickard (*Aristotle on the Art of Poetry*), pp. 102 sqq. Dr. Lock (*Biography of Keble*) sums up the theory thus: "Poetry is essentially for him a relief to the poet, a relief for overcharged emotion. It is the utterance of feelings which struggle for expression, but which are too deep for perfect expression at all, much more for expression in the language of daily life." Having pointed out that Keble's theory rests mainly on the *Poetics* he adds: "But Aristotle writes as a critic and is thinking of the effect upon the readers; Keble, as a poet, dwells primarily on the effect upon the poet, and secondarily on that upon the readers."

plained, one important aspect of the tragic *katharsis*. But the word, as taken up by Aristotle into his terminology of art, has probably a further meaning. It expresses not only a fact of psychology or of pathology, but a principle of art. The original metaphor is in itself a guide to the full aesthetic significance of the term. In the medical language of the school of Hippocrates it strictly denotes the removal of a painful or disturbing element from the organism, and hence the purifying of what remains, by the elimination of alien matter. Applying this to tragedy we observe that the feelings of pity and fear in real life contain a morbid and disturbing element. In the process of tragic excitation they find relief, and the morbid element is thrown off. As the tragic action progresses, when the tumult of the mind, first roused, has afterwards subsided, the lower forms of emotion are found to have been transmuted into higher and more refined forms. The painful element in the pity and fear of reality is purged away; the emotions themselves are purged. The curative and tranquillising influence that tragedy exercises follows as an immediate accompaniment of the transformation of feeling. Tragedy, then, does more than effect the homeopathic cure of certain passions. Its function on this view is not merely to provide an outlet for pity and fear, but to provide for them a distinctively aesthetic satisfaction, to purify and clarify them by passing them through the medium of art.

But what is the nature of this clarifying process? Here we have no direct reply from Aristotle. He has, however, left us some few hints, some materials, out of which we may perhaps reconstruct the outlines of his thought.

The idea of *katharsis* implies, as we have seen, the expulsion of a painful and disquieting element,—*ta lypounta*. Now pity and fear in their relation to real life are by Aristotle reckoned among *ta lypounta*. Each of them is, according to the definition in the *Rhetoric,* a form of pain (*lypē tis*). Fear Aristotle defines to be "a species of pain or disturbance arising from an impression of impending evil which is destructive or painful in its nature." Moreover, the evil is near not remote, and the persons threatened are ourselves. Similarly, pity is "a sort of pain at an evident evil of a destructive or painful kind in the case of somebody who does not deserve it, the evil being one which we might expect to happen to ourselves or to some of our friends, and this at a time when it is seen to be near at hand." Pity, however, turns into fear where the object is so nearly related to us that the suffering seems to be our own. Thus pity and fear in Aristotle are strictly correlated feelings. We pity others where under like circumstances we should fear for ourselves. Those who are incapable of fear are incapable also of pity.

Thus in psychological analysis fear is the primary emotion from which pity derives its meaning. Its basis is a self-regarding instinct; it springs from the feeling that a similar suffering may happen to ourselves. It has in it a latent and potential fear. But it is a wrong inference to say, as Lessing does,[6] that fear is always an ingredient in pity,—that we fear for ourselves whenever we feel pity for another. The Aristotelian idea simply is that we would fear for ourselves if we were in the position of him who is the object of our pity. The possible fear may never become actual, but the strength of the pity is not thereby impaired. Still the tacit reference to self makes pity, as generally described in the *Rhetoric,* sensibly different from the pure instinct of compassion, the unselfish sympathy with others' distress, which most modern writers understand by pity.

The conditions of dramatic representation, and above all the combined appeal which tragedy makes to both feelings, will considerably modify the emotions as they are known in actual reality. Pity in itself undergoes no essential change. It has still for its object the misfortunes of "one who is undeserving" (*ho anaxios*); which phrase, as interpreted by Aristotle (*Poet.* ch. xiii.), means not a wholly innocent sufferer, but rather a man who meets with sufferings beyond his deserts. The emotion of fear is profoundly altered when it is transferred from the real to the imaginative world. It is no longer the direct apprehension of misfortune impending over our own life. It is not caused by the actual approach of danger. It is the sympathetic shudder we feel for a hero whose character in its essentials resembles our own.

The tragic sufferer is a man like ourselves (*homoios*); and on this inner likeness the effect of tragedy, as described in the *Poetics,* mainly hinges. Without it our complete sympathy would not be enlisted. The resemblance on which Aristotle insists is one of moral character. His hero (*Poet.* ch. xiii) is not a man of flawless perfection, nor yet one of consummate villainy; by which we must not understand that he has merely average or mediocre qualities. He rises, indeed, above the common level in moral elevation and dignity, but he is not free from frailties and imperfections. His must be a rich and full humanity, composed of elements which other men possess, but blended more harmoniously or of more potent quality. So much human nature must there be in him that we are able in some sense to identify ourselves with him, to make his misfortunes our own. At the same time he is raised above us in external dignity and station. He is a prince or famous man who falls from a height of greatness. Apart from the impressive effect of the contrast so presented, there is a gain in the hero being placed at an ideal distance from the spectator. We are not confronted with outward conditions of life too like our own. The pressure of immediate reality is

---

[6] Lessing, *Hamb. Dram.* Trans. (Bohn) pp. 409, 415, 436. The view that the mention of fear in the definition is superfluous, fear being implicit in pity, is strangely inconsistent with the position he takes up against Corneille, that pity and fear are the tragic emotions, pity alone being insufficient.

[186]

removed; we are not painfully reminded of the cares of our own material existence. We have here part of the refining process which the tragic emotions undergo within the region of art. They are disengaged from the petty interests of self, and are on the way to being universalised.

The tragic fear, though modified in passing under the conditions of art, is not any languid emotion. It differs, indeed, from the crushing apprehension of personal disaster. In reading or witnessing the *Oedipus Tyrannus* we are not possessed with a fear that we may be placed in circumstances similar to those of Oedipus, or be overtaken by the same calamities.[7] Yet a thrill runs through us, a shudder of horror or of vague foreboding. The feeling is immediate and unreflective. The tension of mind, the agonised expectation with which we await the impending catastrophe, springs from our sympathy with the hero in whose existence we have for the time merged our own. The events as they pass before us seem almost as if we were directly concerned. We are brought into a mood in which we feel that we too are liable to suffering. Yet the object of dread is not a definite evil threatening us at close quarters. In the spectacle of another's errors or misfortunes, in the shocks and blows of circumstance, we read the "doubtful doom of human kind." The vividness with which the imagination pictures unrealised calamity produces the same intensity of impression as if the danger were at hand. The true tragic fear becomes an almost impersonal emotion, attaching itself not so much to this or that particular incident, as to the general course of the action which is for us an image of human destiny. We are thrilled with awe at the greatness of the issues thus unfolded, and with the moral inevitableness of the result. In this sense of awe the emotions of fear and pity are blended.

We can now see that the essential tragic effect depends on maintaining the intimate alliance between pity and fear. According to Aristotle, not pity alone should be evoked by tragedy, as many moderns have held;[8] not pity *or* fear, for which Corneille argued; not pity and "admiration," which is the modification under which the Aristotelian phrase finds currency in the

---

[7] Corneille (Discours ii. *De la Tragédie*) argues from the absence of any such dread that the *Oedipus Tyrannus* excites pity only, and not fear. But if fear is rightly understood, it is *par excellence* a tragedy of fear.

[8] e.g. Schiller in his essay *On Tragic Art*. Elsewhere in his letters and other writings he sometimes speaks of fear as well as pity; but his fear is not the Aristotelian fear; it is merely the apprehension felt while the terrible event is still in the future, a fear which becomes pity after the event.

In ancient tragedy fear was a powerful and necessary factor. In modern tragedy— with the exception of Shakespeare—pity predominates over fear. In the eighteenth century fear was almost entirely eliminated.

Elizabethan writers.[9] The requirement of Aristotle is pity *and* fear. He would no doubt allow that in some tragedies the primary and predominant impression is fear, in others pity. He would probably go farther and say that an inferior tragedy may excite one only of the two emotions generally called tragic. But the full tragic effect requires the union of the two, nor can the distinctive function of tragedy as *katharsis* be discharged otherwise.

In the phrase of the anonymous fragment, "On Comedy," which appears to contain some genuine Aristotelian tradition, "tragedy seeks to blend fear with pity in due proportion" (*hē tragōidia symmetrian thelei echein tou phobou*). Pity, as Bernays explains, through its kinship with fear, is preserved from eccentricity and sentimentalism. Fear, through its alliance with pity, is divested of a narrow selfishness, of the vulgar terror which is inspired by personal danger.[10] A self-absorbed anxiety or alarm makes us incapable of sympathy with others. In this sense "fear casts out pity." Tragic fear, though it may send an inward shudder through the blood, does not paralyse the mind or stun the sense, as does the direct vision of some impending calamity. And the reason is that this fear, unlike the fear of common reality, is based on an imaginative union with another's life. The spectator is lifted out of himself. He becomes one with the tragic sufferer, and through him with humanity at large. One effect of the drama, said Plato, is that through it a man becomes many, instead of one; it makes him lose his proper personality in a pantomimic instinct, and so prove false to himself. Aristotle might reply: True; he passes out of himself, but it is through the enlarging power of sympathy. He forgets his own petty sufferings. He quits the narrow sphere of the individual. He identifies himself with the fate of mankind.

We are here brought back to Aristotle's theory of poetry as a representation of the universal. Tragedy exemplifies with concentrated power this highest function of the poetic art. The characters it depicts, the actions and fortunes of the persons with whom it acquaints us, possess a typical and universal value. The artistic unity of plot, binding together the several parts of the play in close inward coherence, reveals the law of human destiny, the causes and effects of suffering. The incidents which thrill us are intensified in their effect, when to the shock of surprise is added the discovery that each

---

[9] e.g. Sir Philip Sidney, *An Apologie for Poetrie*: "The high and excellent Tragedy . . . that with stirring the affects of admiration and commiseration teacheth the uncertainty of the world. . . ."

[10] Voltaire quotes with approval the observation of Saint-Evremont that in French tragedy tenderness takes the place of pity and surprise the place of fear. "It cannot be denied," he says, "that Saint-Evremont has put his finger on the secret sore of the French theatre." The idea of fear, again, was frequently that of mere terror. Thus in France in the seventeenth century the conception of the tragic had come to be the union of the sentimental and the horrible.

thing as it has happened could not be otherwise; it stands in organic relation to what has gone before. There is a combination of the inevitable and the unexpected. Pity and fear awakened in connexion with these larger aspects of human suffering, and kept in close alliance with one another, become universalised emotions. What is purely personal and self-regarding drops away. The spectator who is brought face to face with grander sufferings than his own experiences a sympathetic ecstasy, or lifting out of himself. It is precisely in this transport of feeling, which carries a man beyond his individual self, that the distinctive tragic pleasure resides. Pity and fear are purged of the impure element which clings to them in life. In the glow of tragic excitement these feelings are so transformed that the net result is a noble emotional satisfaction.

The *katharsis,* viewed as a refining process, may have primarily implied no more to Aristotle than the expulsion of the disturbing element, namely, the pain, which enters into pity and fear when aroused by real objects. The mere fact of such an expulsion would have supplied him with a point of argument against Plato, in addition to the main line of reply above indicated. In the *Philebus* Plato had described the mixed (*michtheisai*) or impure (*achathartoi*) pleasures as those which have in them an alloy of pain; and the pleasure of tragedy was stated to be of the mixed order. The Aristotelian theory asserts that the emotions on which tragedy works do indeed in real life contain a large admixture of pain, but that by artistic treatment the painful element is expelled or overpowered.

In the foregoing pages, however, we have carried the analysis a step farther, and shown how and why the pain gives way to pleasure. The sting of the pain, the disquiet and unrest, arise from the selfish element which in the world of reality clings to these emotions. The pain is expelled when the taint of egoism is removed. If it is objected that the notion of universalising the emotions and ridding them of an intrusive element that belongs to the sphere of the accidental and individual, is a modern conception, which we have no warrant for attributing to Aristotle, we may reply that if this is not what Aristotle meant, it is at least the natural outcome of his doctrine; to this conclusion his general theory of poetry points.

Let us assume, then, that the tragic *katharsis* involves not only the idea of an emotional relief, but the further idea of the purifying of the emotions so relieved. In accepting this interpretation we do not ascribe to tragedy a direct moral purpose and influence. Tragedy, according to the definition, acts on the feelings, not on the will. It does not make men better, though it removes certain hindrances to virtue. The refining of passion under temporary and artificial excitement is still far distant from moral improvement. Aristotle would probably admit that indirectly the drama has a moral influence in enabling the emotional system to throw off some perilous stuff, certain elements of feeling, which, if left to themselves, might develop dangerous energy and impede the free play of those vital functions on which the exercise of virtue depends. The excitation of noble emotions will probably in time exert an effect upon the will. But whatever may be the indirect effect of the repeated operation of the *katharsis,* we may confidently say that Aristotle in his definition of tragedy is thinking, not of any such remote result, but of the immediate end of the art, of the aesthetic function it fulfils.

It is only under certain conditions of art that the homeopathic cure of pity and fear by similar emotions is possible. Fear cannot be combined with the proper measure of pity unless the subject-matter admits of being universalised. The dramatic action must be so significant, and its meaning capable of such extension, that through it we can discern the higher laws which rule the world. The private life of an individual, tragic as it may be in its inner quality, has never been made the subject of the highest tragedy. Its consequences are not of far-reaching importance; it does not move the imagination with sufficient power. Within the limited circle of a *bourgeois* society a great action is hardly capable of being unfolded. A parochial drama, like that of Ibsen, where the hero struggles against the cramping conditions of his normal life, sometimes with all the ardour of aspiring hope, more often in the spirit of egoistic self-assertion which mistakes the measure of the individual's powers, can hardly rise to tragic dignity. We are conscious of a too narrow stage, of a confined outlook, and of squalid motives underlying even conduct which is invested with a certain air of grandeur. The play moves on the flat levels of existence. The characters are unequal to the task imposed on them; and though we may find room for human pity in witnessing failure and foiled hopes, still it is commonplace and gloomy failure. No one can question the skill in dramatic construction and the stirring interest of Ibsen's plays, but the depressing sense of the trivial cannot be shaken off, and the action always retains traces of an inherent littleness which hinders the awakening of tragic fear,—still more of that solemnity and awe which is the final feeling left by genuine tragedy. Some quality of greatness in the situation as well as in the characters appears to be all but indispensable, if we are to be raised above the individual suffering and experience a calming instead of a disquieting feeling at the close. The tragic *katharsis* requires that suffering shall be exhibited in one of its comprehensive aspects; that the deeds and fortunes of the actors shall attach themselves to larger issues, and the spectator himself be lifted above the special case and brought face to face with universal law and the divine plan of the world.

In order that an emotion may be not only excited but also allayed,—that the tumult of the mind may be resolved into a pleasurable calm,—the emotion stirred by a fictitious representation must divest itself of its purely selfish and material elements, and become part of a new order of things. It is perhaps for this reason that love in itself is hardly a tragic motive. The more exclusive and self-absorbed a passion is, the more does it resist *kathartic* treatment. The feelings excited must have their basis in the permanent and objective realities of life, and be independent of individual caprice or sentiment. In the ordinary novel the passion of love in its egoistic and self-centred interest does not admit of being generalised, or its story enlarged into a typical and independent action. The rare cases where a love story is truly tragic go to prove the point which is here enforced. In *Romeo and Juliet* the tragedy does not lie merely in the unhappy ending of a tale of true love. Certain other conditions, beyond those which contribute to give a dramatic interest, are required to produce the tragic effect. There is the feud of the two houses, whose high place in the commonwealth makes their enmity an affair of public concern. The lovers in their new-found rapture act in defiance of all external obligations. The elemental force and depth of their passion bring them into collision with the fabric of the society to which they belong. Their tragic doom quickly closes in upon them. Yet even in death the consequences of their act extend beyond the sphere of the individual. Over the grave of their love the two houses are reconciled.

Tragedy, as it has been here explained, satisfies a universal human need. The fear and pity on and through which it operates are not, as some have maintained, rare and abnormal emotions. All men, as Aristotle says, are susceptible to them, some persons in an overpowering measure. For the modern, as for the ancient world, they are still among the primary instincts; always present, if below the surface, and ready to be called into activity. The Greeks, from temperament, circumstances, and religious beliefs, may have been more sensitive to their influence than we are, and more likely to suffer from them in a morbid form. Greek tragedy, indeed, in its beginnings was but a wild religious excitement, a bacchic ecstasy. This aimless ecstasy was brought under artistic law. It was ennobled by objects worthy of an ideal emotion. The poets found out how the transport of human pity and human fear might, under the excitation of art, be dissolved in joy, and the pain escape in the purified tide of human sympathy.

VERGIL

[*70–19* B.C.]

VERGIL, BY TEMPERAMENT AND CIRCUMSTANCE, CONFRONTED TRADITION IN ALL ITS weight and power, as perhaps only Milton did subsequently. Both were compelled to be what, in our contemporary passion for "originality," we refer to as "derivative" authors. Vergil, the possessor of a romantic sensibility, was called upon to write an epic of Empire and Roman *gravitas* at a time when austerity hardly prevailed in Rome. He had to describe a hero who embodied *pietas,* conscientiousness about his duties to gods and men, a hero that is by definition incapable of heroic excesses. He had to do all this within unquestioned assumptions concerning the normative character of the models created by his epic predecessors. The result is a very beautiful and very "literary" poem, a combination of terms which much contemporary taste would not admit.

This essay can be read as a study of the poet who gives literature itself a central place in his experience. Mr. Knight is reader in Classical Literature in University College of the South West, Exeter, England.

From *Roman Vergil* by W. F. Jackson Knight. Published 1944 by Faber and Faber Ltd., London.

W. F. JACKSON KNIGHT

Tradition and Poetry

A LL WHO THINK MUCH ABOUT VERGIL ARE NEARLY CERTAIN TO BECOME IN-
volved in the question of his derivations from earlier poets. The attractive
force which this question exerts is surprising, until we recognize that it is a
necessary result of Vergil's greatness. In the discussions of this subject, one
side usually argues that Vergil copies other writers, and is therefore a plagiarist, and a bad poet, while the other side contends either that Vergil does not
precisely depend on derivations from other writers, or that if he does he is
yet so great that he can do so without spoiling his poetry. In the present state
of knowledge, it is possible to see that the question is more important even
than has been supposed, but that the discussions of it have usually taken
wrong directions, and have often been conducted with wrong motives. It
should soon become hard to believe that there could ever have been surprise
at Vergil's method, or any talk about plagiarism in connexion with him.

There seems to have been current for centuries the false assumption that
a poet can either write down his own sentiments in his own words, which is
praiseworthy, or he can derive his words, and therefore his thoughts, from
other writers, which is certainly suspicious, and probably quite enough to
condemn him. The facts which contradict this assumption are obvious

enough, and there would be no need to revive the controversy, if it were not that the present position of it is enlightening, and that there is further progress to be made.

The most obvious fact is the excellence of the poetry written by the derivative poets. Even Voltaire said that, if Homer made Vergil, Vergil was the best thing that ever he did make. Father Aurelio Espinosa has lately explained that if it is clear, as indeed it is, that Vergil depends verbally on an immense number of literary reminiscences, that does not prove that his poetry is dead, since it is just as clear that his poetry is very much alive. Domenico Comparetti is among those who have used a similar argument. Father Espinosa firmly asserts that imitation, as he calls it, is the universal law of poetry; and that is the right place to start. He explains that even the supposedly original Homer was just as dependent on his sources as Vergil himself. Yet not many generations ago Dr. Johnson held that all the stories in the world were derived from the uniquely original Homer; and still more recently Mr. Gladstone believed, that when Homer's descriptions of works of art correspond with objects that have been actually found, that is because Homer first imagined them and described what his imagination saw, and the Greek artists simply copied the Homeric descriptions.

Father Espinosa's warning was greatly needed, since respected scholars regularly express surprise that Vergil should have been able to improve what he borrowed, and even copy several originals at once. He "copied" Lucretius, according to two different computations, once in every twelve or even every seven lines; but he "improved on" Lucretius regularly. He depended still more on Homer; he "copied" both the beginning of the *Iliad* and the beginning of the *Odyssey* for the beginning of the *Aeneid;* and to the surprise of many made the result great.

There is, meanwhile, a frequent assertion, not from scholars but from poets, of the importance of tradition, whatever that may mean. Goethe is particularly insistent; and Shelley, followed by Mr. T. S. Eliot, went some of the way towards explaining it. Artists, to be artists, says Mr. Eliot, must explicitly place themselves in their true relation to the dead artists; they must feel and shew their presence within the whole coherent sequence of world art, which is altered for ever by the new work of each new artist. That does not explain everything. But it reveals that derivation is rather essential to the arts than accidental and unfortunate.

Mr. E. E. Kellett has observed that the best poets are also the best borrowers. Chaucer, Shakespeare, Milton, Gray, Coleridge, Tennyson, and Eliot are among English poets most distinguished for borrowing. But why poets should want to borrow is still left obscure. However, there is now an instructive theory of Mlle. A.-M. Guillemin for the "borrowing" of Latin poets. She regards them as following a convention which would not nowadays be understood, and pitting their brains against each other, to say the same thing more and more exactly and beautifully. The poets, according to Professor R. B. Steele, were in search of the matchless word or phrase, and trying to improve on the work of their predecessors. They were not trying to say anything that had never been said before.

There is much truth in this. Still, it is not always easy to distinguish the saying of the same thing in a new way and the saying of something different. Nor is it always a question of what the poet intends. Landor, in so many words, and other poets regularly in their different ways, have recorded that that is the question least worth considering about poetry. But Mlle. Guillemin is right to say, as she does, that the Latin poets were in "competition," *agōn,* to reach perfection, by a rehandling, *retractatio,* of the same idea with slight changes of words again and again. She cites Horace, Seneca, and Pliny as explicitly saying this happened; Seneca explaining that Vergil's "thefts" were of a special kind, since he wanted them to be recognized. Perhaps it was a new and wrong kind of just this emulation that Agrippa blamed Vergil for inventing.

Common sense, however, with help from detailed examination of poetry, shews that all derivations are not due to conscious competition. Possibly poets trained themselves that way; Horace implies it. But they hardly stopped there; though much of their conscious thought may have been directed to the ambition to excel each other with similar words, and that was anyhow a healthy discipline, if not carried too far. And there is meanwhile the probability that Latin poets quoted each other, without change of words, as a compliment; not to excel, but to shew admiration.

Besides these views, there are also "allusive" theories, perhaps going back to Aristotle's observation that recognition gives pleasure. According to the "allusive" theories poets refer openly to earlier poetry, because the recognition of the allusion gives pleasure. Familiarity and recognition may be effective either for their own sake, or because the context gives added point to familiar words or thoughts. Allusive theories are certainly true sometimes, but they are not, except in a much elaborated form, applicable always, since in the great poets by far the greater number of the allusions are unlikely to be noticed. Donatus reports that Quintus Octavius Avitus compiled eight volumes of Vergilian parallels, and Perellius Faustus an anthology of his "thefts."

All the theories work towards the recognition that, somehow, available earlier poetry helps the poets, and should help them to create new poetry. The derivations clearly help the poet to write quite as much as they help the reader to enjoy, or more; and they help the poet not to evade but to discharge his responsibilities. The ordinary theories are, however, insufficient. Still, each of them is true of some poetic passages. Much poetry is conscious retractation, much is allusion meant to be recognized, and some even unsuccessful, deplorable copying, for there is such a thing, even if it is rare. But these conceptions are only approaches to the real problem, which is not so simple as any one of them implies.

The real question has been opened and partly solved by Professor E. K. Rand, who has applied to Vergil the results of Professor John Livingston Lowes' work on Coleridge. Vergil's method is seen to be characteristic of many of the greatest poets; he could not help remembering words, sounds, and rhythms from earlier poetry, and letting them start new poetic complexes in his own mind, subtly different from the poetry which he remembered. That is how Coleridge worked also.

Professor Lowes proved from Coleridge's notebooks that countless ideas and words derived from his reading, mainly in poetry and in the literature of travel, were accepted by Coleridge, and retained by him in the part of the mind called by William James "the deep well of unconscious cerebration." They were like "hooked atoms," as M. Henri Poincaré, the French mathematician, described such fragments of reminiscence; and they gradually coalesced in the unconscious mind into new expressive wholes, till one day, quite suddenly, they emerged into consciousness as poetry. The process does not apply to poetry only, but to all discoveries. M. Poincaré described his own mathematical discoveries as made in this way. It is the same in classical scholarship; problems are consciously stated, and stored, apparently forgotten, in the unconscious; and it may be twenty years after that the answer, having pieced itself together unseen, appears in the conscious mind.

Professor Lowes considers that the acceptance of "hooked atoms" of experience, from life or from books, and their self-combination into new wholes, are in varying degrees normal to everyone. For Lowes, the peculiarities of the poet are his shaping will and intelligence, by which he organizes into a larger scheme the units delivered to his conscious mind. Coleridge himself spoke of "the shaping spirit of imagination," and also of the "esemplastic imagination," that is, the imagination "which shapes into one." It seems that Coleridge himself supposed that a larger part of the process is unconscious than Professor Lowes assumes it to be.

This leaves something to be said. There is a theory of Dr. I. A. Richards that the poet is distinguished by his greater psychological vigilance, that is, readiness to accept impressions, a readiness which he has the power to communicate. Further, *Kubla Khan* was delivered to Coleridge's consciousness ready made; it is well known that he composed it in his sleep, and, when he woke up again, wrote down as much as he could, before he was interrupted.

Conscious organization had nothing to do with it whatever. And, as Professor G. Wilson Knight has shewn, the poem is a perfect whole, fully organized, and intensely and profoundly significant; it is not in the least the meaningless fragment which it was once supposed to be. Further, discoveries in other branches than poetry, such as mathematics or botany, are also given in this way, ready made; though of course much conscious thought is used to express them, afterwards. It is to be noticed, too, that ordinary people do not make great discoveries. The hooked atoms in their minds combine to form a dream world, which they may certainly know in sleep; but normally the dream world does not produce material of importance to waking life, such as great poetry, or scientific discoveries.

I suggest, therefore, that the shaping will and intelligence that are characteristic of genius, poetic or other, may operate consciously or unconsciously. There may or may not be much left for the conscious mind to do; sometimes the units delivered by the unconscious are already comprehensive and fully organized. The large structural lines of an epic may conceivably be unconsciously invented, no less than small phrases may be, through the combination of remembered elements; though there is sure to be at least some conscious work in the organization of long poems.

The poets who mainly "integrate"—a word is needed for the process and this one will do—from literary originals appear to be awakened to the productive poetic mood by the effect of earlier poetry on them. In that mood they create their own poetry, and it is likely to contain words and thoughts from earlier work, which reappear more or less altered. Coleridge might fuse and blend a dozen memories of various books in one stanza of *The Ancient Mariner,* scarcely a phrase being quite new, but scarcely a phrase being exactly what he had read.

All poets do not depend preponderantly on literary derivation. Some take inspiration from the common ideas and talk of a group, as Pindar, Catullus in most of his colloquial lyrics, Donne, Auden, and Day Lewis. Among the poets who depend on literary derivation are Homer, perhaps Sappho, Vergil, more than any, most of the great English poets, and now Ezra Pound and Eliot, who are unusually conscious in their derivations. The method of the ancient poets was developed naturally from the endless repetitions, with gradual slight changes, through centuries of Greek epic poetry; with a new start in the loose kind of translation which began literary work in Latin. After the great periods of Latin poetry, the later Latin poets depended too literally on former work, saying too nearly the same thing in only slightly different ways. An extreme was reached in the *centones,* poems entirely made by the redistribution of old lines. This may have helped to set the fashion for the Middle Ages, which in ballad, epic, and court poetry were inclined to go on doing the same thing with increasing elaboration. Mediaeval epic, at first fresh with a new inspiration, declined into repetitions and expansions. Then, out of the Middle Ages, grew the more constructive integration, comparable to Vergil's, of Dante and Chaucer. The other tradition, of statement according to words and thoughts current not in literature but in the talk of a social group, might be said to emerge most noticeably in the informal work of Skelton, which is in contrast to his more traditional poems, and to appear again, after a gap, in Elizabethan lyrics and sonnets. The tradition might be said to pass through Donne, Wordsworth, and Browning to several of the moderns.

Vergil's integration could be called inspiration from former poetry, which might equally be the poetry of others, or poetry of his own. He probably tried direct colloquial lyric, following Catullus, but poems of that kind in the *Appendix* are not certainly his. Of course, Vergil and the "new poets" or "moderns" made close contact with the Alexandrians; and the true derivative method, then as at other historical moments, grew out of attempts at reproduction, and translation. It became a habit to try to say what had been already said, but if possible with improvements; and eventually, almost by mistake, to create poetry of the best and most original kind, in which numerous reminiscences are fused and blended.

The exact truth about this process is elusive; but it is now quite clear that in integrative method Vergil was like, but not exactly like, Coleridge. Vergil used all methods, but the integrative tendency nearly always conditioned the others. The process worked apparently as follows.

Vergil read something. The emotional charge, in the sound, the rhythm, the words, the ideas, the sequence of events, the grand structure—anything, in fact, on whatever scale—communicated itself to him, never to be dispelled altogether from his conscious or at least his unconscious memory. The impulse was to say the verse or tell the story over and over again, partly because there was a mysterious, self-sufficient delight in the poetry, and partly because it fitted Vergil's own feelings, expressed them, clarified them, and made them acceptable and friendly to himself. These feelings were strong, and ever developing. They exerted force on what had at first seemed the perfect expression of similar feelings, in the poetry of Theocritus, or Euphorion, or Hesiod, or any of the others. The scheme and structure might remain; or the sounds and rhythms; but everything could not remain; and in general, as with Coleridge, nothing at all was ever reproduced entirely without alteration. Everything went into the dream world, into the "deep well"; the "hooked atoms" parted and recombined. Vergil's supposed mistranslations of Greek are characteristic. Superficially, the process of getting poetry right is almost indistinguishable from the process of getting anything else wrong; but, though the poetic process may resemble hallucination, really it is a discovery of truth, like other sorts of discovery.

The process declares itself with unusual clarity in Mr. Ezra Pound's poem, *Homage to Sextus Propertius*. Pound lets Propertius suggest ideas. But, as Mr. Martin Gilkes has shewn in detail, there is nothing in the poem obviously like Propertius. The mistakes in Latin, if they are mistakes, are perhaps the most glaring on record anywhere. *Canere,* "sing," will reappear as if it were *canis,* "dog"; and so on, in countless instances. The spirit, also, is quite different, and so is everything else. The truth is that the poem is a poem and not a translation. It has travelled perhaps a little further than Vergil's *Eclogues* along the way that started with the loose, active renderings of Greek works by Livius, Plautus, Ennius, and the rest.

The natural human tendency towards forgetfulness and confusion normally produces error, but in poets it may produce poetic truth. Their unconscious mind is full, not only of imaginative impressions, but also of a latent reason. The "hooked atoms" combine according to it. The reason in it all is missed, because it is too quick, and too compressed and elliptic. Poets seem to talk nonsense because they talk so much truth all at the same time.

The poetry of ancient Italy, and Europe since, was fortunate in that Naevius, Plautus, and Terence combined, or "contaminated," plots of different Greek works. It was fortunate, too, that Vergil combined different *Idylls* of Theocritus into one *Eclogue.* Vergil remembered everything but the organization of details; and his personal feelings provided a new organization, which was, however, not too new to allow their expression to be generalized, in touch with tradition, and so artistic.

Donatus in his *Life of Vergil,* which seems to go back to Suetonius, explained how Vergil worked, and Professor Rand has shewn how Donatus is to be understood.

Vergil wrote each morning a large number of lines. He spent the day, as he himself is recorded by Donatus to have said, licking them into shape, as a she-bear is supposed to lick her cubs. In the evening he had just a few perfect lines—perhaps an average, for his writing life, of well under twenty a day; less than one finished line a day was the pace of the *Georgics.*

Possibly following Vergil himself, Donatus used the word *retractatio* to mean the process of polishing and improving verses already roughly made. The other sense, which was emphasized by Mlle. Guillemin, is also legitimate; the word can mean the act of rehandling, and either improving, or merely changing for use in a different context, verses or parts of verses used already either by the same poet or by one or more other poets.

Vergil's practice as Donatus describes it looks at first sight like very conscious work. So does the further fact recorded by Donatus that Vergil wrote the *Aeneid* in a prose draft, with the sequence of events divided into twelve books. But he adds that Vergil created the poetry as the fancy took him, any passage at any time; and that when the right line did not come readily, he invented any kind of line, however bad, temporarily, "so that nothing might stop the flow of creation." Vergil called such a line a *tibicen* or "prop," something to hold up the edifice for a time. Sometimes, too, he might leave a line uncompleted, where the inspiration stopped, intending to fill in the rest of it later.

How he filled the gaps is one of the most significant facts about his method. Donatus also records that Vergil had left uncompleted a line in the Sixth *Aeneid*—. . . *ut venere, vident indigna morte peremptum Misenum Aeoliden . . .* "they saw, when they came, lifeless, of a death unfair, Misenus, of Aeolid line . . ." Eros, Vergil's secretary, was reading the passage to him one day. Suddenly the answer came, and Vergil told Eros to write down . . . *quo non praestantior alter aere ciere viros . . .,* "than whom no second had been more supreme, to wake the heart of fighting men with notes of bronze . . ." Apparently, though here the interpretation is uncertain, the inspiration stopped again, and was renewed later in exactly the same way; as Eros was reading, the final completion suddenly occurred to Vergil, and he told him to write down, *Martemque accendere cantu,* "and light the fire of battle with his music." There is no need to doubt that the story contains the truth about the completion of at least one of the two lines.

As Vergil read, and thought, and watched, and felt, impressions from life and letters sank into his memory and combined, unseen. Meanwhile he worked and planned, and decided at least what he thought that he wanted to do, however much the wayward poetic drive might distort his human planning. But the planning itself was contributing to the unconscious integration. "Take care of the conscious," is a psychologist's advice, "and the unconscious will look after itself." It is not all mad, mysterious, automatic, or fortuitous. Hard thinking, facing facts, planning, and reasoning, were just as important in the unconscious centre of Vergil's creation as old heard melodies, not understood, but caught and held; lovely, but with little meaning that we, or Vergil either, could have defined.

The unconscious process, therefore, was not independent of the conscious processes of thinking and planning and choosing—even down to the mere choice of what to read; and it was also followed by a conscious process, of judging, criticizing and correcting what the unconscious mind had delivered. There is something unconscious still in such criticism and correction. Taste is involved. Sometimes, it is a matter of consciously applying truth, which has been acquired from the unconscious in another mood. There is little doubt, either, that Vergil, like living poets whom I have known, consciously

[200]

planned to make, or to let, the unconscious mind work for him; though he would not have described it like that.

There are, of course, difficulties. It is hard to say, sometimes—Plato thought, always—what is inspiration, and what is just madness. W. B. Yeats was careful to leave his early poems unaltered in his first collected volume, "fearing," he said, "some stupidity of my later years." Coleridge, in a footnote to a passage of splendid poetry which was never understood till the other day, wrote, with apology, that he printed it because it was clearly good, though he himself could see no meaning in it.

Vergil also misunderstood himself sometimes. For example, according to Servius in his *Life,* the famous passage in the Second *Aeneid,* where Aeneas sees Helen in burning Troy and wants to kill her, was rejected by Vergil's editors, clearly according to his known wishes, but not less clearly to the disadvantage of the poem. There is scarcely anything finer than the passage, or more necessary to the *Aeneid.* Poets, at dull moments, make mistakes. Coleridge refused to publish *Kubla Khan* for years till Byron made him, and he persuaded Wordsworth to remove very necessary lines from the *Ode on Intimations of Immortality.*

According to Shelley, the greatest poet cannot create poetry just when he wishes. The poetry comes "from whence 'tis nourished," in the words of Shakespeare, . . . "like a gum which oozes," not like "the fire i' the flint," which "shews not till it be struck." So Noel Essex, a contemporary writer of unusual power, says that the poetry "does not seem to go through my head at all"; and that its meaning sometimes only becomes clear, for the first time, weeks after it is written. Of the same writer it can be observed that impressions, sometimes acquired years before, are integrated into poetry when they are consciously forgotten.

But there are times when inspiration does not come; and, in a long poem especially, it may be necessary to make poetry by effort of thought. This process can be called composition. Vergil, as he knew himself, "composed" the *tibicines,* the "prop" lines. He may or may not have known that he "composed" longer passages. But it is fairly safe to say that he did, and we can sometimes decide, tentatively, which they are.

The word "integration" might reasonably be used to mean the integration of impressions from life. Vergil's true integration, however, preponderantly works on literary reminiscences, large or small. To integrate well, Vergil needed literary reminiscences, and they had to be stored for a long time in his mind. Professor Rand observed that a less successful passage of Vergil may mean that the impressions had not been stored long enough. Sometimes at least Vergil was hampered by having none to store. Macrobius says that Vergil used a weak motive for the start of the war in Latium, the misfortune of Iulus in shooting Silvia's pet stag, because there was no Homeric precedent available. Macrobius was wrong. The motive is not weak, but touching and powerful, characteristically Vergilian in sympathy. And there was a precedent for it, which he missed, not actually in Homer, but in the Cyclic epic. In the *Cypria* Agamemnon shot a sacred stag at Aulis. Macrobius was right, however, to suggest that Vergil is the better for a precedent. He might have said that Vergil needs literary reminiscences in large numbers, if he is to write his best; the best passages usually prove, on examination, to have the largest number of such reminiscences at their root. Strangely, Mr. David Gurney recently made the same remark, and rightly, about Coleridge.

Vergil also integrated from himself, not from others only. It was convenient and natural, and also helpful for the best results, for him to rehandle his former work until he had a newly enriched and softly toned version of it for a new passage. The recognition of this habit, its integrative nature, and its valid utility, is of immense importance for all Vergilian criticism.

The poets reveal each other's ways. Some general remarks of Mr. T. S. Eliot are as revelatory for Vergil as the psychological comments of Coleridge himself. Writing of Kipling, Mr. Eliot says—"Most of us are interested in the form for its own sake—not apart from the content, but because we aim at making something which shall first of all *be,* something which in consequence will have the capability of exciting, within a limited range, a considerable variety of responses from different readers. For Kipling the poem is something which is intended to *act*—and for the most part his poems are intended to elicit the same response from all readers, and only the response which they can make in common. For other poets—at least, for some other poets—the poem may begin to shape itself in fragments of musical rhythm, and its structure will first appear in terms of something analogous to musical form; and such poets find it expedient to occupy their conscious mind with the craftsman's problems, leaving the deeper meaning to emerge, if there, from a lower level. It is a question then of what one chooses to be conscious of, and of how much of the meaning, in a poem, is conveyed direct to the intelligence and how much is conveyed indirectly by the musical impression upon the sensibility—always remembering that the use of the word 'musical' and of musical analogies, in discussing poetry, has its dangers if we do not constantly check its limitations; for the music of verse is inseparable from the meanings and associations of words. If I say then, that this musical concern is secondary and infrequent with Kipling, I am not implying any inferiority of craftsmanship, but rather a different order of values from that which we expect to determine the structure of poetry." Here, it might be said, Vergil's method, and especially its audially-delivered construction, is most precisely defined, by reference both to Kipling's method, the opposite to it, and to Mr. Eliot's own, which is often, I believe, almost exactly the same as Vergil's. But perhaps this quotation will only seem fully clear and relevant at a later stage of the argument.

When true integration stops, composition may have to begin. It may prove very useful; the attempt to think out a solution may lead to new and good integration, as if by luck, since "chance" as Agathon said, is "the friend of art"; a more probable reason is that something in the unconscious has been released for consciousness by thinking. But it is equally possible that the result of composition may be poetry that is weak and strained.

When the inspiration of the unconscious mind failed, Vergil might tell a straight story, derived from some single source such as a handbook of mythology. He might make up a story in an obvious way, and attempt to decorate it. And he might read or say to himself his own poetry from elsewhere, trusting it to start the required process.

We see the results. The boat race in the Fifth *Aeneid* was new. No other boat race in any ancient poem is known. It was conscious invention, to replace Homer's land racing. We find it forced, and unintentionally humorous. Vergil may be parodying himself, or, as so often, he may be too deep for us. The passage is quite likely, also, to be very early work. But provisionally we must be dissatisfied, on the standard that Vergil has set. So it is with much of the Ninth *Aeneid*. Vergil has a real emotion, and a picture in his own mind to transmit, not in all the book, but in parts of it; especially the part concerning Nisus and Euryalus, the attached friends who try to find their way through the besiegers of the camp to Aeneas, but are killed. Even here, the only literary foundation was in the Tenth *Iliad,* where Odysseus and Diomedes at night raid the Trojans; and of course the feeling in Homer is very different. Vergil can be watched attempting to integrate his own earlier work, sometimes with rather unnatural and forced developments. Pathos possessed him, and, very interestingly, he reproduces again and again in the Ninth *Aeneid,* in the right and in the wrong places, one of his specially pathetic rhythms, a pause with an elision within the third foot of the hexameter.

True integration works otherwise and is infinitely flexible. It can be classified according to scale. On the smallest scale there are words and phrases; and on the largest scale there is the story, with parts of it often growing out of at least two passages of Homer, with several Greek tragedies helping, and subordinate suggestions from countless other works. Partly by thinking and planning, and partly by letting impressions coalesce of themselves, Vergil would contrive a new form for a story, compounded of all earlier forms, and packed with all the valuable meanings of the past, and reaching, in the blend, quite new meanings too.

It is not impossible to get the impression that Vergil would always use an

[203]

existing legend faithfully, if he could, inventing only when he must. On the contrary, Vergil, who, like most great poets scarcely ever invented anything, equally rarely, and probably never, followed any legend faithfully. Like Coleridge, he fused the stories and characters, as he fused remembered phrases. Servius partly understood. He observed that Vergil regularly transferred actions and characteristics from one personality to another; as, elsewhere, he observed that Vergil could allude to history, which to Servius included legends, but could not express it directly, because that was against the artistic principles of poetry.

On all the different scales of integration Vergil's poetic process was on the whole homogeneous, and steadily guided by his unconscious mind, in the development of new poetry out of old. It was equally by integration that Vergil built phrases out of words, lines out of phrases, incidents out of other incidents, by isolating and reassembling the attributes and actions of former characters, and, next, large dramatic situations, and finally whole books and poems, all from older elements, redistributed and recombined.

The integration of words, phrases, and lines is a continuous thread, delicately and infinitely complex, running from Homer through Greek and Latin poets to Vergil, then all through Vergil's own work, and onwards to the successors who learnt from him. A phrase may start in some Greek poem, and by combinations and alterations live on until it starts a new history in Vergil's mind, and a sequence of developing appearances in his work, gathering power and depth of meaning on its way. Sometimes, of course, the history of Vergil's expressions might be said to start in Vergil's own mind, for he may be the first to associate together, into a new complex, sounds, thoughts, and words never put together before. But often, and probably most often, the history and ancestry goes back to earlier poetry, sometimes old, and sometimes almost or quite contemporary, as when Vergil exchanges reminiscences with Horace, or adopts and adapts, from Messalla perhaps, or Catullus, or Lucretius, pairs of words, groups of words, and occasionally a whole line. Vergil treats Ennius in the same way; and, in so far as the difference of language allows, Greek poetry also. Sometimes the conscious, and sometimes the unconscious, processes predominate.

It has proved possible to analyse and to classify, according to the different kinds of changes in the adaptation, Vergil's reminiscences of Ennius and Lucretius.

One kind of change which Vergil seems to have sought was in the sound. This is specially noticed by Macrobius and by Servius. Vergil's words are nearly always more musical. For this purpose according to Servius Vergil changed the line of Ennius, *at tuba terribili sonitu taratantara dixit,* "hark, the trumpet with its alarming note, has cried 'taratantara,'" to *at tuba terribilem sonitum procul aera canoro increpuit,* "hark, the distant trumpet has crashed its dreadful note with music of the bronze." Vergil had many other such fastidious motives. He might think a verbal or metrical usage of Ennius incorrect. Concurrently, he might seek to make words of Ennius more figurative and forcible. Ennius wrote of a fighter's head wrenched from him, and his "eyes still flickering, half-living yet, longing to find the light again." Vergil transferred the ideas to a hand cut off, and "fingers still flickering, half-living yet, trying to clutch the blade again." He kept many of the words of Ennius; others he characteristically used again in other passages also. Characteristically, too, he had a ready reason for applying the verb "flicker," *micare,* to fingers. It was a colloquial usage, applied to a game in which players suddenly shewed their fingers, and their opponents had to guess how many would be shewn. Many derivations are multiple. Ennius, like Vergil, rehandled in "retraction," or "reintegrated," his own earlier lines. Vergil might remember each occurrence of a word-group in Ennius, and apply it himself more than once, with new changes, in his own work. Even then, so sharp is his economy, there might still remain some element, unused, and available for unexpected exploitation in some very different context.

Vergil consciously improved the rhythm and harmony of old lines, by simply applying his fastidious aesthetic conscience. It was, of course, hardly possible for him to be entirely satisfied with any older line, and it was most unlikely, anyway, that it would exactly express his own mood, even if its literal sense needed no alteration. Yet all the time an old line might appeal to him unforgettably, and start his own imagination working. It is usually possible to see some of the reasons why an old line attracted Vergil and why he altered it as he did; even if the possibilities, and the kinds of conscious and unconscious motive, are too many to allow any exhaustive account.

Vergil's most obvious and famous adoption from Ennius is probably the line about Quintus Fabius Maximus Cunctator, who saved Rome from Hannibal in the Second Punic War by *cunctatio,* "dilatoriness." Ennius wrote *unus homo nobis cunctando restituit rem,* literally, "one man, alone, restored to us our whole fortune by dilatory action." Vergil makes Anchises, in Elysium where beyond death, and before life, the Roman heroes of the future are awaiting their time on earth, address Fabius, and describe him as *unus qui nobis cunctando restituis rem,* "you who alone restore . . . ." A series of Roman heroes, seen and described, has been working up to an intense moment, a climax after which thought, emotion, and rhythm come for an instant to rest. The steady, inexorable pace of the Sixth *Aeneid* depends on these periodic rests, enforced by a sudden coincidence of word accent and metrical ictus—of which there will be more to say later—in the fourth foot.

Here the coincidence comes at the middle syllable of *cunctándo*. This coincidence in this place, as will appear later, is characteristic of all Latin hexameter poetry before Vergil, but Vergil himself mitigated its application. It is
old-fashioned, and suggests the rugged, hardy past. Words of three long
syllables in this part of the line always have a kind of resolute muscularity,
suggesting a determination to force a way through a terrible or difficult task.
So Vergil has *compéllat,* "addresses," in this place, when in tragic situations
one character forces himself to speak to another while his heart is breaking.
It is tempting to call words of this form in this place in the line "will-power
words." And to Vergil, and perhaps to all Romans who had been brought up
at school on Ennius, there was something Ennian about a will-power word.
Accordingly, at this point in the Sixth *Aeneid,* just where a strong punctuation finished a long, steady period of lines, the impact of an unexpected line
from Ennius himself, reproduced almost unchanged, must have been terrific
to Romans. To them the thought of Fabius, and the tones of Ennius, had
great depth of meaning and strong, evocative association; and the impact
can be almost as terrific for us, if we use our imagination just a little. And
Vergil, according to his way, apparently by doing nothing at all, lets an
overpowering new contrast emerge. The immense weight on *cunctándo,*
more than any that Ennius laid on the word, starts thoughts. Fabius saved
Rome from Hannibal, by not being afraid to seem weak and slow, and not
putting rumour before safety, as Ennius also said; and so might Julius and
Pompeius, addressed with deprecation by Anchises near this very place, have
saved Rome from itself, if they had forborne. Vergil allowed much of his
political philosophy to emerge from this Ennian word.

The changes that Vergil made in the line of Ennius are obvious and simple. The second person, not the third, is needed in the context, and it makes
the line more dramatic. So does the present tense which that change also involves, for Fabius is made to seem a kind of eternal principle of restraint.
Vergil elsewhere writes of a gift which Dido had given. It is after her death,
but he writes a present tense, *dat;* it is a gift which Dido "gives," or of which
Dido "is the giver." Perhaps that is because Dido's influence is permanent in
the *Aeneid*; in a sense she haunts Aeneas, and haunts Vergil, and us too.
There are similar presents in Old Latin, which so uses the same word *dat,*
and in other writers. It would be possible to adduce Greek present tenses also
for comparison, but the parallels, for once, might not prove sufficiently exact.

Vergil is enabled by his first change to make another change too. To fit
the line to the passage, he must have a relative, *qui,* "who." That displaces
homo, "man," a word normally used in a very general and not very dignified
sense. By Vergil's time Fabius had gathered sanctity, and would probably
have to be called not *homo,* but *vir,* a word of greater dignity.

[206]

Tradition and Poetry

That is only a rough account of circumstances, which need fuller statement, and various qualifications; but perhaps it is enough for now.

This particular derivation from Ennius is conscious, on the whole, and not one of Vergil's more unconscious acts of integration. Vergil's unconscious mind might be said to have delivered the line of Ennius to him; but the rest was mainly conscious, obviously enough. The theory of allusion and intended recognition might fit this instance of derivation; as perhaps the theory of retractation might fit the line about Atlas, soon to be mentioned, which Vergil developed from Ennius and Lucretius.

Much simpler is Vergil's alteration, already met, of another line of Ennius, *at tuba terribili sonitu taratantara dixit,* "but the trumpet, with its dreaded note, said 'taratantara,'" or, perhaps, in English, "'tarántaráh.'" Vergil could hardly accept *taratantara,* but that was really the only interesting part of the line. Still, he took the line without its last two words, substituting for them *aere canoro,* "with the music of its bronze." He thus took from Ennius not much more than the idea of onomatopoeia, and chose onomatopoetic words for himself, without help from him.

The derivations from Lucretius are similar, but this time it is clearer how many small expressions Vergil consciously or unconsciously owed to him. The motives for change are often fastidiously delicate. There are many things in Lucretius which Vergil does not normally admit to his repertory, for example his long, old-fashioned, compound adjectives, and other old-fashioned forms. Ideas in Lucretius suggest different ideas to Vergil. In three lines Lucretius wrote of kids, and lambs that butt. Vergil uses two of the words, compressed into a reference to kids that butt. Lucretius says that the sun unravels the texture of water with rays, *radiisque retexens,* from *texo,* "weave." Vergil twice says that the sun uncovered the world from darkness with his rays, *radiisque retexerit orbem,* the verb being now, however, *retego,* "uncover." He kept the sound, but changed the sense, as he did elsewhere, again and again. The influences exerted by Lucretius on Vergil, and Vergil's ways of reacting to them, are too many to assess in full. But however often they are examined, they remain fascinating and revealing too.

There are examples of lines adopted and adapted from Ennius by Lucretius, and by Vergil from both; especially, perhaps, Vergil's *axem umero torquet stellis adentibus aptum,* "upon his shoulder twists the pole, ablaze with its fitted stars," of Atlas, one of the lines whose subtle and complex history Dr. C. M. Bowra succinctly gives. Even so, this is a very simple case of Vergil's method. Habitually, in large things and in small, he holds contact with the tradition through the centuries, going back often as far as he can, but not sacrificing what has intervened. Elsewhere I have given instances. Hundreds of years of poetic history can leave their signs in a single line.

[207]

An unusual example of a simple derivation is a line adopted from Catullus. In his poem *The Lock of Berenice* a hair says to the Queen *invita, o
regina, tuo de vertice cessi,* "Queen, against my will I departed from your
head." Vergil took this comic line for an intensely tragic moment. His
Aeneas, in Hades, says to Dido, whom he had loved and left, *invitus, regina,
tuo de litore cessi,* "Queen, against my will I departed from your coast." Vergil may have forgotten the comic associations; or perhaps, with a characteristic and subtle inversion, he has made his tragic line of the inherently solemn
rhythm which helps by contrast to make the line of Catullus a comic success.

From his own earlier poems, and from the *Ciris,* which is possibly one of
them, Vergil took not merely single lines, but groups of lines, to incorporate
without change in his later poetry. His practice in this has been established.
So he took four charming lines on Nisus and his daughter Scylla, both
changed to birds, from the *Ciris,* and set them in the Second *Georgics.* So,
too, he took from the Fourth *Georgics* to use in the Sixth *Aeneid* the famous
lines on the dead waiting, like migrating birds, to cross the waters of death
to their last home, "stretching out hands in yearning for the further shore."
And he took from the Fourth *Georgics* a description of Cyclopes at work,
and applied it again in the Eighth *Aeneid* with four changes, which might
be overlooked. This is the link between Vergil's normal self-integration and
self-retractation, and his derivations from others. Except in the last line of
the last book, the *Georgics* never copy the *Eclogues* verbally. Occasionally,
Vergil uses twice within the *Aeneid* a single line, and still more rarely a
group of lines, as of the fleeting ghost of both Creusa and Anchises. Otherwise, these repetitions, from the *Ciris,* from an earlier certainly Vergilian
poem, or from within the same poem, are the only known instances of older
lines used by Vergil completely without change.

That is a very short account, with the fewest possible examples, but, if we
went on, it would be hard to know where to stop, and the enterprise might
seem endless.

According to the different computations, Vergil reflects Lucretius either
once in every twelve lines, or once in every seven. Some of the reminiscences
consist of pairs of words, coming together in an obvious and perhaps inevitable conjunction, so that they might be called fortuitous. It is not important
to decide whether they are fortuitous, or whether Vergil would have used
some of these phrases if he had never read Lucretius. It is sufficiently certain
that the work of Lucretius had sunk so deeply into his mind that it guided
his expression almost as much as the general quality of the whole Latin language guided it; and yet Vergil's lines and Vergil's Latin are very different
from any other, all the time.

There is, however, some importance in the question how much of this particular process was conscious. Here the truth seems to be, that in general, and all the time, Vergil retained much, or most, of the poetry of Lucretius in his memory, and could hardly help integrating it unconsciously every day for much of his life. But he might sometimes consciously think of a passage of Lucretius, and make of it, not merely a way of saying things, but something to say. He might contemplate a Lucretian complex of words and sounds and thoughts, and take that complex as his subject, or, more exactly, as a reality to form one term of an antagonism. Another reality would then come under contemplation as the other term. The result is Vergilian poetry, about Lucretius; but also, perhaps, about the old country gods of Italy. That is a simple outline of the process by which Vergil created the great passage in the Second *Georgics* in which he counts happy the scientists and philosophers who know the origins of the universe and have no fear of death and the dark; but happy also the country men, who know their own country gods. There may always be a Vergilian transference or inversion to help; so that the words of Lucretius recur, meaning in the context just what Lucretius would not have had them mean—or perhaps what he had, in spite of himself, given them the power to mean, in the mind of the Vergil whom he helped to make.

This more conscious contemplation of former poetry, as the subject of Vergil's own poetry rather than its inevitable medium, can be understood from an example which Professor E. K. Rand has discussed in his sensitive way. Vergil wrote of the moon, *at si virgineum suffuderit ore ruborem, ventus erit*; *vento semper rubet aurea Phoebe,* "but next, if she sheds a colour of red over her maiden face, there will be wind; for with a wind will Phoebe ever go golden red." That is made from the contemplation of a passage of Aratus, "You can judge by a moon, all reddened, that the wind is on its ways." Vergil thought hard about the words of Aratus, and their picture. He meanwhile let his own experience of the moon, and nights before the coming of windy days, strengthen and qualify his contemplation of the Greek words. And there came too a memory of lyric repetition, perhaps from Catullus, or some older Latin poet, with the thought of the maiden, lyric moon; so that lyric repetition of words helped to make the thought and the picture of Aratus what it could be.

There is, I suppose, in the making of the best poetry, at least often, if not always, a triple beginning—the thing, the thought, and the tradition in poetry already existing. Vergil normally needs direct observation and literary antecedent, and when they coalesce, his poetry is made. The late Professor Charles Knapp expressed this very well in an inaccessible article which deserves to be reprinted.

The Vergilian systems of integration can be compared to a set of concentric circles, like ripples made by a stone falling into a pond. Nearest to the centre are systems of words, phrases, and lines. Next nearest are incidents, and other short statements of imagined realities. A character is described in a few words or a few lines as acting in a certain way. How the character and the action came to be evolved is sometimes a surprisingly long and complicated process.

Questions are always being asked about the origins of Vergil's characters, and whether he invented them. In one sense he always invented them, and in another sense he never did.

A fascinating example is Camilla. In Vergil she is a maiden of the Volscians, who lived on the borders of Latium. She was unmarried, and had always lived in the wilds; and now she led a party of her friends to war. Camilla is unknown in literature before Vergil. Her name existed; a *camillus* was a boy who attended a priest or *flamen*, and the Furii Camilli, a great family in early Rome, used the word as a family name. Vergil derives it from "Casmilla," which, he says, was the name of Camilla's mother. Perhaps Casmilla was invented to connect the name Camilla with the Greek god Casmilus. Camilla may possibly have been a local nymph. But mainly she is Vergil's creation.

Camilla's lonely upbringing in the wilds has an antecedent in the upbringing of Harpalyce, the Thracian maiden of Greek myth, whose name and quality Vergil uses elsewhere, in a description of Dido. Camilla runs so lightly that she could travel over standing corn without harming the ears. The description is from Homer's lines on the horses of Erichthonius, and, still more closely, lines of a lost Hesiodic poem describing Iphiclus. The conception belongs to folk-lore, and something like it is known in Scotland, for example. Perhaps in the Volscian country the corn blown by the wind was thought to betray the presence of some spirit of the corn, and perhaps Vergil took the Greek forms of expression to help him enrich an Italian thought.

But the clearest antecedents of all are in the Amazons of Greek poetry, especially the old Cyclic epic, about the last days of Troy, which is now lost; and among the Amazons especially their leader Penthesilea, whom Achilles slew, and too late loved, and whom Vergil used in his description of Dido, as he used Harpalyce. But it is hard to think that any Amazon of Greek poetry had Camilla's boyish grace, like the grace of Vergil's Venus, disguised as a huntress; or even perhaps Camilla's feminine, tragic weakness, which caused her death for love of a bright garment that a foeman wore.

But Camilla lived on in poetry, in Dante and in Tasso; and in history too, for a distinguished Dante scholar of the Renaissance, Benvenuto da Imola, tells the story of a fighting Volscian maiden from Privernum of his own times, whom he calls a new Camilla.

A complicated and instructive system of integration started with old stories of the fall of Troy. I have investigated it elsewhere.

From various Greek poems Vergil derived some attributes and actions of Cassandra, the Trojan prophetess who was never believed, and used them in his characteristic way. She violently denounced the wooden horse in which Greeks were entering Troy. She tried to burn it with a torch; and, torch in hand, danced madly like a bacchanal. Later, during the sack of Troy, she was torn by the lesser Ajax from the temple of Athena. Soon after, Helen was captured in the house of Deiphobus, whom she married after the death of Paris, and who was "weighted with wine" on the last night of Troy, by Menelaus, who wanted to kill her, but was warned by Aphrodite to consult his own future happiness by letting her live. Earlier in the story, Sinon, the Greek sent in, disguised, to deceive the Trojans into accepting the wooden horse, shone a beacon to guide the other Greeks, returning from Tenedos, where they had been hiding. In a much later different part of the story, related in the *Odyssey,* Odysseus, having returned to Ithaca, removed the arms from the hall of his own house, so that the suitors could not use them when he started shooting them. He was helped by his son Telemachus, and Athena, who shewed a miraculous light.

Vergil redistributes all those actions. In the Second *Aeneid* Cassandra prophesies very shortly, but her denunciation of the wooden horse and attack on it are transferred to the priest Laocoon, who throws a spear at it. Cassandra is dragged from the temple of Athena-Minerva, but not much is said of that. The traditions of Cassandra and Helen are entwined; for Aeneas sees Helen hiding in the temple of Vesta, who is a perfect translation of the Trojan Athena, goddess of the city's defence. There Aeneas wants to kill her; but he is restrained by his divine mother, Venus, with a far higher plea than the plea of Aphrodite to Menelaus. For instead of saying, as in the old Greek tradition Aphrodite said, "Not Helen but Paris is to blame" for the fall of Troy, Venus says, "Not Helen, nor Paris is to blame," but the will of gods. Vergil is so close to a Greek original that he strains Latin, and says *non tibi . . . culpatus,* "not blamed by you," instead of "not to be blamed by you"; however, he has a slight extenuation, in the old Latin usage, by which the perfect participle was sometimes tinged with a gerundive meaning, so that it connotes the idea of necessity, not fact only.

Venus tells Aeneas to forbear, appearing to him as Aphrodite appeared to Menelaus, and, as her parallel appearance in the First *Aeneid* with its further suggestions shews, as Artemis revealed herself to the dying Hippolytus in Euripides. But the Venus of Vergil is infinitely higher, almost Christian; she rescues her son with her touch, as Vergil's own mother used to rescue him; and starts hope again.

That is not all about Vergil's Helen. In the Sixth *Aeneid* she behaves differently. She is in the house of Deiphobus, who is sleeping "weighted," as in the Greek tradition, not however with drink but with anxiety, *cura,* the same word which Vergil substituted in the account of Aeneas, sleepless, in the Eighth *Aeneid,* to differentiate him from sleepless Dido, of whom in the Fourth similar phrases are used. Of this there will be more to say. In Greek poetry on the fall of Troy, the Trojans were drunk. The drunken sleep of the Trojans, barely hinted in the Second *Aeneid,* is boldly transferred from them to the enemies of Aeneas, the Rutulians killed by Euryalus and Nisus, raiding the enemy at night in the Ninth.

Helen, meanwhile, was also developed. Like Odysseus in the Eighteenth *Odyssey,* removing arms from his hall, she removes the sword of Deiphobus, from under his pillow, as he sleeps. Like Athena in the *Odyssey,* Helen shews a light; but it is a torch, and she shews it in bacchic revelry, having acquired these actions from Cassandra. Helen, however, only pretends to revel. Actually she is signalling to the Greeks, having gained this motive from Sinon, the treacherous Greek who deceived the Trojans, and, helping the other Greeks to enter Troy, signalled to them with beacons. The revelry of Cassandra, partly attributed to Helen in the sixth book, is used much more fully in the seventh for the behaviour of the Latin queen, Amata, maddened by the strain which she undergoes, and by the malignance of gods.

These are a few examples of Vergil's redistribution of actions and attributes to create new characters and new incidents. Everything is both old and new.

The integration of Camilla and Helen is on a small scale, involving comparatively few lines of poetry. There is a sense in which integration can be simpler still, as when Vergil developed an *Eclogue* primarily from the combination of two *Idylls* of Theocritus. That was early in the development of his process. An example on a large scale, with greater complexity, is the tragedy of Dido in the First and Fourth *Aeneid.*

In creating the tragedy of Dido's love, Vergil wrote under strong emotional pressure, which made his integration very pervasive and powerful. From his own feminine intensity, and from who knows what secret and tragic event of his own life, he knew the conflict, and knew the heart of the Dido whom he created. That was within himself. Outside, and in the experience of his own times, he knew the heartlessness with which politicians made and broke marriages. There was Octavia herself, married to Antonius, and set aside. Vergil's scheming goddesses, Juno and Venus, who plotted Dido's love, are like those politicians. Outside, too, there was the lure and danger of eastern luxury, which Vergil had contemplated in the *Georgics,* and contrasted with simple Italian life. The conflicts between love and duty, the moment and the future, are familiar; they have become familiar through Vergil.

But Vergil could not imagine out of nothing, for that would not be imagination. He had to inherit a focal point.

Naevius, in a fragment from the introduction of his long poem called *The Punic War,* says that someone "asked how Aeneas had left Troy." Who asked is not known; most probably it was Dido herself, who, with Anna her sister, was mentioned elsewhere by Naevius. Possibly enough, Vergil owed her name and her association with Aeneas to Naevius. This is the more likely, since it is recorded that the first book of Naevius is the original of the magnificent storm at sea in the First *Aeneid,* when Aeneas is about to reach Africa and Dido. But the storm in Naevius may have come in a different part of the story.

There were other legends of Dido. Servius says that her name meant "brave maiden" in Phoenician, and was given to her after her death. Her other name, Elissa, is Elath, the feminine of the Semitic El, which means Lord or God. Her brother's name, Pygmalion, and hers are both thought Phoenician. Partly she was a Phoenician fertility goddess, as Mr. G. A. Wainwright first explained to me. For that reason, but not only for that, her death on the pyre in Vergil was appropriate; fertility kings were sacrificed by burning, especially in Libya. But long before Vergil Dido had become a real personality. In the third century the Greek historian Timaeus had told the story of her tragic death, before any one associated her with Aeneas. His version is lost, but it was followed by Pompeius Trogus, a writer of the Augustan age, and an abridgement of his account has been preserved by Justinus.

In this legend there was a real motive, lacking in the *Aeneid,* for Dido's conviction that impurity, or marrying again, was for her wrong. Vergil even leaves in his verse a phrase that belonged to the older story; Dido says, "I was not allowed to live my life, without marriage, without blame, like a beast of the wild"—*more ferae.* But beasts are not "without marriage," and so the words are not strictly right in their place. However, in Justinus they are also found, and there they fit the context. For there Elissa, as he always calls her, was being compelled to marry Iarbas the African to preserve her people, and saved herself at the last by suicide, that she might not live "like a beast of the wild." The phrase remains, with its meaning mysteriously reversed. As Vergil uses it, he is thinking of the unspoilt freedom of the wild country, and perhaps of his heroine, the soldier maiden Camilla, who, devoted like Hippolytus to Diana, had there spent in purity her life. After Vergil, the old tradition revived, and Dido lived on in a pattern of pure fidelity. Perhaps it is characteristic of Vergil to have made of her a heroine of passion.

The tragedy of Dido begins with a storm and shipwreck in the First *Aeneid.* The mood and description come from storms in the *Odyssey,* especially in the fifth book. Aeolus, god of the winds, is involved in both the Tenth *Odyssey* and the First *Aeneid,* but for Odysseus he puts the winds safely in a bag for him to take, a bag later untied by the sailors, whereas in the *Aeneid* he releases all the winds to harm Aeneas, at the request of Juno. It is another characteristic inversion. The storm itself is from the Fifth *Odyssey* mainly, with echoes of the Twelfth. No doubt it is from Naevius also, and also from the lost Cyclic epic poem, the *Nosti,* "Homeward Journey"; to the contents of which the first *Aeneid* refers in a mention of the fate of Ajax, destroyed by lightning on the Caphyrean rocks.

After the shipwreck in the Fifth *Odyssey,* Odysseus lands in Scheria. But the landing at Carthage is at a place like Homer's lovely cave of the nymphs, in the Thirteenth *Odyssey,* when Odysseus is reaching Ithaca. Aeneas, however, having landed at Carthage, meets his divine mother, disguised as a young huntress. This is in part a memory of the meeting between Odysseus and his protectress, Athena, also disguised, on his arrival in Scheria, in the Sixth *Odyssey.* Next, Odysseus meets Nausicaa, a princess. She befriends him, and he goes to the city, enveloped by Athena in a cloud. So, too, Aeneas goes to Carthage, enveloped by Venus in a cloud. He has not yet met his Nausicaa. In Homer's source, as Professor W. J. Woodhouse shewed, Odysseus fell in love with the princess, and she with him—as she still does, perhaps, in the *Odyssey,* at least a little. But Homer has another tale to tell. There is the wife of Odysseus, Penelope, waiting patiently for him; and, accordingly, Nausicaa is forgotten. Vergil restored Homer's broken tale. Aeneas meets Dido not on the beach but in the city. They fall in love; and Aeneas stays, more nearly as Odysseus stayed with Calypso, the lonely goddess, than as he stayed in Scheria.

Dido, however, is a queen, and partly recalls Arete, mother of Nausicaa; and to her, as Odysseus to Arete and to Alcinous the king, Aeneas tells his story. The story begins in the second book, about the fall of Troy; it is not from Homer, but from many other sources, mainly Greek plays and, probably, the lost Cyclic epic. In the third book the story goes on, about the journey from Troy to Sicily by way of Thrace, Delos, Crete, Buthrotum, and a place near Etna, a narrative of which the sources are more obscure, possibly more numerous, and probably more general, including prose works and verbal information. Of the travels there will be more to say.

The love story in the Fourth *Aeneid* is a complex unit. Dido is no longer only Nausicaa, but, at least in slenderest outline, the mythical queen of the Punic story. More really, she is some secret of Vergil's own life; she is also a type of ladies in the Roman world subdued to power, and even, possibly, to a tiny degree, Cleopatra. More than all these, however, her heart, at first, is the heart of Medea in Apollonius Rhodius, of the third century, who is supposed to have been the first to treat delicate feelings "romantically." To Medea's first love, Apollonius applies a strange simile of light flickering as it is reflected from a cauldron. The simile is used by Vergil, but not for Dido's love. Most significantly, he detaches it, to be applied, altered, to Aeneas in the eighth book, where he worries, sleepless, as Dido had worried sleepless through him. So Dido for a time is this Medea; but only for a time, even though Servius says that Vergil wholly "transferred" Dido from Apollonius. For soon there is another change; and Dido, if she is still a Medea, is nearer to the Medea of the play by Euripides than to the Medea of Apollonius, even in her fiercer moods.

From Euripides and Apollonius, though hardly from them only, Vergil learnt that a poet might, and should, look closely into the feminine heart, which Vergil himself anyway knew so well. The echoes of Medea continue in the story. Strangely, the god Mercurius, warning Aeneas to go, tells him that there is danger; the fleet may be attacked and burnt. Dido has not thought of doing that. But when Aeneas has sailed she thinks of it; she cries for an attack on the fleet, and afterwards she wishes that she had attacked it. That is how Vergil partly obliterated and then half revived the threat of the Colchians in Apollonius to burn Jason's fleet. The thought of that threat gives to Dido perhaps the supreme expression of her hate, where Vergil allows a peculiar freedom to his power over words and sounds.

Dido talks to her sister Anna, revealing her thoughts, as Phaedra, in the *Hippolytus* of Euripides, talking to her nurse, reveals hers. It is from Phaedra, or some other Euripidean heroine, as prototype, that Dido's love turns to hate, but Vergil makes Dido's hate go beyond the earthly life. Anna, however, is not a nurse, though Dido has with her the nurse of Sychaeus; the only other nurse in Vergil is Caieta, nurse of Aeneas, who gave her name to Caieta, on the Italian coast, and who perhaps recalls the nurse of Augustus, to whom he was much attached. Anna is, however, many other people also. She has a Semitic name, and may well be a mythical figure from Syria originally. Her name is however Latin too. She is Anna Perenna, the functional goddess of the ritual conclusion of the year, *annus*. So a quaint combination was evolved, known to Cato; Anna had fallen in love with Aeneas, and followed him to Latium. It was known to Ovid, and Vergil also; Vergil hints at it, when Dido asks Anna to appeal to Aeneas on the ground of his special friendship with her, almost as if Aeneas thought more of her than of Dido. Meanwhile, Vergil's story is entering the world of Sophocles. Dido and Anna recall his pairs of sisters, Antigone and Ismene in the *Antigone,* and Electra and Chrysothemis in the *Electra.* Like the weaker sisters in Sophocles, Anna does not understand the emotional depth and moral stature of her sister, Dido.

The "marriage" of Aeneas and Dido seems to be outside the tradition of dramatic poetry. It is in a cave, amid storm and lightning. It is really the old mythic marriage between earth and sky, that makes the fields flower again and the world go on. Lingering yet in our minds are traces of the old awe, and we know in that scene how momentous the union is, and how tremendous the result will be.

Mercurius, sent from Heaven, tells Aeneas to leave Dido, as in the *Odyssey* Hermes was sent to tell Calypso that Odysseus must go. After that, it is still more exactly the world of Sophocles, whose play, *Ajax,* strongly guided Vergil in the Fourth *Aeneid.* The connexion, long ago observed, is incontestable, and only at first sight hard to believe. Dido, like Ajax who killed the sheep of the Greeks in mad mistake for the Greek leaders, is furious with herself, and hopeless, and resolves to die. In the end, as Ajax falls on the sword of Hector his foe, so Dido falls on the sword of Aeneas, once her dearest, crying to the sun that sees all; they both pray for vengeance, Ajax to the Erinyes, the Furies, and Dido to "Angels of Dido at her death"; and Dido's long curse is, like the curse of Ajax, half a prophecy. But her curse reaches down Roman history, to Hannibal.

There is still more Sophocles than that. Vergil translated the old Phoenician fertility sacrifice that lingered round Dido into a corresponding Greek fertility sacrifice, which was remembered in the *Trachiniae* of Sophocles, where Heracles dies on a pyre at Oeta's crest. For Dido has her pyre. It belongs to her, but Vergil could have let her die without it. Ostensibly, the motive for it is that Anna should think the pyre a magical plan to destroy, not Dido herself, but her love for Aeneas, and so never suspect the real intention. The plain story does not really need the pyre. But in the version known to Justinus Dido used such a device to save her life from love. Vergil wastes nothing; but it would take a long time to relate the poignancy of the implied contrasts, in a poem where nothing is lost that is still in the stories, and little that has been in them ever before.

Then there is Catullus too, for Dido is his deserted Ariadne, and speaks in some of her tones. Catullus wrote hexameters with a monotonous rhythm, having a nearly regular stress accent on the fifth syllable from the end of each line. He did not think of restricting it, as Vergil did. However, Vergil restored the rhythm of Catullus for Dido's speeches, turning it into a monotony of extremest poetry, hot hate and misery, and all that desecrated love can be.

The largest of all the schemes of integration, the integration of the whole *Aeneid,* is an immense subject for analysis. There is layer on layer of thought and emotion, coinciding marvellously in the end. The chief layers are the forms and contents of Greek poems, old and new, many books in prose, the current thought and feeling and symbolism of Vergil's own time, much of it not yet written, the Roman tradition of history guided by destiny, and lastly, or firstly, the historical or legendary conditions and events of the Mediterranean world at the end of the age of bronze, and of Italy in the earlier centuries of Rome. These conditions and events offered an outline of story which Vergil adopted as a start, and adapted. Some slight hint of how he adopted and adapted them can be got from comparing the *Aeneid* with two other extant versions of the voyage of Trojans to Latium, and their contribution to the start of Rome.

According to Vergil, Aeneas, in the winter or spring following the fall of Troy, which traditionally happened in the late autumn, set sail with a party of survivors on a fleet which they had themselves built. The numbers are vague; in one place, which belongs to an early conception of the *Aeneid,* Vergil says that there were twenty ships, though elsewhere he seems to imagine a larger expedition.

Aeneas was not the only Trojan to lead an expedition of refugees. Antenor also led such an expedition, and settled in north-east Italy at the mouth of the Timavus, near Vergil's first home.

Aeneas and his Trojans first went to Thrace, but soon sailed south to the island of Delos, sacred to Apollo, where his priest Anius was king. A voice from the temple commanded the Trojans to continue their way, and "seek their ancient mother." Anchises thought that this meant Crete, and they sailed there, but there was a plague, and the Penates, gods of his ancestors and his home, appeared to Aeneas in a vision of bright light, to warn him that Crete was not his new home, and he must sail onwards.

On the advice of Anchises they now sailed towards Italy, rounding the south of the Peloponnese and then going north, up the east coast of the Ionian Sea. They landed at Actium, where they celebrated "Actian Games," and then at Buthrotum in Chaonia. There, to their great surprise, they found Trojans living, ruled by Helenus, a Trojan prince, and Andromache, Hector's widow. They had been captured, but had afterwards been released, and married. Helenus was a prophet, and he gave Aeneas prophetic warnings. Aeneas dedicated in the temple a shield captured from Greeks with an inscription on it. The Trojans at Buthrotum gave to the expedition presents and guides.

Warned by Helenus, Aeneas and his people did not land till they reached south Italy, and then only to sacrifice to Juno. They saw on the coast, in particular, temples of Athena and Juno, and the land of Iapygians and Sallentini. They avoided the Straits of Messina, where Scylla and Charybdis were, and sailed westwards. They landed in Sicily, at a point near Mount Etna. Then they sailed round to the north-west of the island, where some remained, at or near Egesta. In Sicily Anchises, father of Aeneas, died. From there they set sail for Italy, but were driven by a storm to a place on the north African coast near Carthage. There they stayed for the winter. The ships needed repair, the men needed rest, and Aeneas and Dido, queen of Carthage, were in love. In the spring the expedition sailed to Sicily again, and met the Trojans who had already settled there. Aeneas celebrated the death of Anchises which had occurred just a year before, with funeral ritual and games. By a plot of Juno, some women of the party, tired of travel, started to burn the ships. Most of the ships were saved; but the less active members of the expedition settled in Sicily with other Trojans there already, and Aeneas founded the city of Egesta for them. The rest went on to Cumae in Campania, south of Latium, and there Aeneas visited the world of the dead below the earth. He was led by the Sibyl, priestess, there, of Apollo and Diana, who prophesied the future to him, and brought him to Elysium, a heaven below the earth, where the spirit of Anchises shewed him a vision of great Romans to be. After the return to the upper world, the expedition sailed up the coast and landed in Latium.

They were guided by signs which had been foretold to them. One prophecy was that they would have to eat their tables; and it happened that they put their food on flat cakes, during a meal in the open air; Iulus exclaimed that they were eating their tables, and the fulfilment of the prophecy, probably meaning the end of their journey, was recognized. Having landed the Trojans built a kind of camp, or possibly a city, for Vergil does not make it quite clear which it was. They gained the permission of Latinus, king of the Latins, to occupy a strip of land. Latinus knew of an oracle which required him to marry his daughter Lavinia to a foreign prince. She was engaged to Turnus, chief of the Rutulians; but Latinus, helped by a further oracle, now saw that Aeneas must really be the prince of destiny, and engaged his daughter to him. Inspired by Juno, Turnus, with the sympathy of Amata, the queen of Latium, rebelled, and gathered many tribes in his support. Aeneas was now at war with all Italians near. He went for help to Evander, an Arcadian Greek settled on the site of Rome, and that was his first sight of the place where his descendants were to rule. Before he arrived, the god of the river Tiber appeared to Aeneas in a dream, and promised him success; telling him that he would immediately see a sign which had been foretold to him, a white sow with thirty young. The sign meant that the Trojans had already reached the end of their journey; the number thirty signifying either the number of the old Latin cities, or else the years to elapse before Alba Longa was founded.

When Aeneas arrived, Evander quickly made friends, and shewed him round the place which was later to be Rome. He told him of a visit of Her-

cules, on the way back from Spain where he had captured the cattle of
Geryon, and how he had killed a fiery monster Cacus, who lived on the
Aventine hill, and had stolen some of the cattle. Evander lent Aeneas an
army, under his own son Pallas, and he also suggested that Aeneas should
get help from Tarchon, king of the Etruscans, north of the Tiber. He did;
and returning by sea found his camp in Latium heavily attacked. He repelled
the attack, and killed Lausus son of Mezentius, the exiled king of the Etruscans, and Mezentius himself; but Turnus had first killed Evander's son,
Pallas. There was a truce, to bury the dead, and a chance of reconciliation;
but the enemies of Aeneas, under Juno's power, broke the truce. The war
started again. Aeneas began to win. Amata, the queen of Latinus, killed herself. Finally Juno gave way, and consented with Jupiter that Aeneas and
Latinus should rule together. Aeneas finally defeated Turnus, and killed him
in revenge for Pallas. It is implied that afterwards Aeneas, married to
Lavinia, was going to share the sovereignty with Latinus, and found the
city of Lavinium; that Aeneas would die three years afterwards, and that
thirty years afterwards either his son Iulus or, according to anther version
also recognized, his posthumous son by Lavinia, Aeneas Silvius, having inherited the kingdom, would found Alba Longa. From Alba Longa, Romulus and Remus, descendants of Aeneas, were to found Rome.

In Livy's version, which he wrote probably a few years after Vergil wrote
the *Aeneid,* two Trojans, Aeneas and Antenor, were purposely spared by
the Greeks. Antenor, with Trojans and Eneti from Paphlagonia, east of
Troy, sailed to north-east Italy and settled near the mouths of the Po and the
Timavus, where later the Eneti gave their name to the Veneti, whose name
appears in Venice. Aeneas with his Trojans went to Macedonia, and then to
Sicily; and from Sicily to the Laurentian country in Latium, where they
were resisted by Latinus, king of the people of the country, called the
Aborigines. Livy then recognizes two variants. In one, Aeneas overcame
Latinus, made peace, and married into his family. In the other, the battle
was just going to begin when Latinus walked out in front, questioned
Aeneas, and, pleased with the account of himself which he gave, made peace
with him instead of fighting, and gave him his daughter Lavinia in marriage. They founded a city Lavinium, called after Lavinia; and had a son,
Ascanius—who was not, in this passage at least, the son of Aeneas and
Creusa, as he is in Vergil. Next, Turnus king of the Rutuli, who had been
engaged to Lavinia before, attacked Aeneas and Latinus. They defeated
Turnus, but Latinus was killed. Turnus appealed successfully to the Etruscans, especially Mezentius, king of the city of Caere in south Etruria. In face
of this threat, Aeneas conciliated his allies by combining the Trojans with
them under the joint name of Latins. There was a battle. The Latins won,

but Aeneas was killed; he was buried near the river Numicius, and called "Jupiter Indiges," a mysterious name under which he was canonized as a 'hero' or saint. Ascanius was still young, but his mother helped him, and he retained his kingdom. Who he was, Livy is not sure; he was certainly the son of Aeneas, but possibly his mother was not Lavinia, but—as in Vergil—Creusa, the first wife of Aeneas. Anyway, he left Lavinium in his mother's charge, and founded the city of Alba Longa, thirty years after Lavinium had been founded. The Latins prospered; even Mezentius and his Etruscans did not dare to attack them, and there was peace between the two nations, the river Tiber, then called Albula, being the frontier. The monarchy descended in the direct male line from Ascanius to Silvius, from him to Aeneas Silvius, and then to Latinus Silvius, who founded the thirty cities of the "Ancient Latins," and after whom all later kings of Alba were called Silvius, besides their other names. Of them Livy mentions several, before he comes to the foundation of Rome by Romulus and Remus, sons of Rhea Silvia, a princess in the direct line, and, according to a usual tradition, of the war god Mars. Livy relates that the Palatine Hill, where Romulus founded the earliest Rome, was formerly called Pallantium, after the city of Pallanteum in Arcadia, part of southern Greece; and that long before the foundation of Rome Evander had come from Arcadia and lived on the Palatine, where he had instituted the worship of the Arcadian wolf-god Pan, later to become the Roman wolf-cult of the Lupercalia.

Dionysius of Halicarnassus lived in Rome in the time of Augustus and Livy, and wrote a history of earliest Rome in Greek. He gives a long account of Aeneas, and the legendary background, and details, of his arrival.

The site of Rome, he says, was occupied first by Sicels, and then by Aborigines. They lived in unwalled village settlements on the hills. Then Pelasgian and other Greeks came, and helped them to secure for themselves, against the Sicels, the country between the two rivers, the Tiber, to the north, and the Liris, to the south, a distance given as a hundred miles. Later, at the time of the Trojan war, Latinus ruled this political unit, and it began to be called Latin. That was sixteen generations before Romulus founded Rome (? 753 B.C.); that is perhaps four hundred and eighty to five hundred years, which gives a fairly early but not improbable date for the Trojan War, in the third quarter of the thirteenth century B.C.

Dionysius cites "the most learned Roman historians," among whom he mentions Porcius Cato and Gaius Sempronius, for the view that there was a strong Greek element in the population of Italy, and that it had come from Achaea many generations before the Trojan War. Dionysius thinks that they were Arcadians, who crossed the Ionian Gulf led by Oenotrus, son of Lycaon, fifth in descent from Aezeius, son of Phoroneus, dated seventeen generations before the Trojan War. Phoroneus, king of Argos at the beginning of the second millennium B.C., is perhaps the earliest Greek mentioned by any tradition. The brother of Oenotrus, Peucetius, settled with his followers in Iapygia in the extreme south of Italy, and gave their name to the later Peucetii. Oenotrus himself, with the larger half of immigrants, settled on the west coast of Italy. "Oenotri" came almost to mean "Italians" and "Oenotria" "Italy." Dionysius cites Antiochus of Syracuse, of the third century, and Pherecydes, of the sixth century, for these movements; so that though they are legendary the authority is good and early. He goes on to say that other Greeks who came to Italy, Pelasgians and Cretans, came afterwards; and to identify places in Italy where there were supposed to be traces of very ancient Greek occupation. The Pelasgians came from Thessaly in north Greece, though they also had an origin further to the south. They and the Aborigines, more or less combined, occupied cities of central Italy later to become Etruscan. The Siceli were driven out, and went to Sicily, about eighty years before the Trojan War. The name Tyrrhenian or Etruscan now appears. It is sometimes made almost synonymous with the Pelasgian name. But in another legend Tyrrhenus was a leader who came with followers to Italy, after the Pelasgians; Dionysius does not believe in the identification of Etruscans, or Tyrrhenians, with either Pelasgians or Lydians. Soon after, and about sixty years before the Trojan War, according to Roman tradition, Arcadians from Palantium, led by Evander son of Hermes and an Arcadian nymph, called Themis in Greek but Carmenta in Latin, came to Italy; they were welcomed by Faunus, king of the Aborigines, and allowed to settle on the Palatine Hill, called first Palantium and then Palatium; but there was also a story that the Palatine was named after a young man called Palas, son of Heracles, who died and was buried there. The Romans owed to them their cults of Carmenta, and of Lycaean Pan, the Lupercalia.

Soon after, more Greeks came, led by Heracles on his way from Spain, and some settled near the Palatine, with some Trojans among them, whom Heracles captured in the earlier Trojan war, against Laomedon's Troy. Before he left, Heracles killed the giant Cacus who lived on the Aventine and had stolen some of the cows of Geryon which Heracles was driving back to Argos. Dionysius recognizes also different details of the visit of Heracles. He was sometimes said to have left a son Palas, by Evander's daughter Launa, or Lavinia, and another son Latinus, by a maiden from the far north. Palas died young; Latinus became king of the Aborigines, and was killed in battle by the Rutulians. As he had no sons, Aeneas, having married his daughter, became king. This, Dionysius adds, happened afterwards.

Aeneas, with Trojans who had escaped from Troy, landed at Laurentum near the mouth of the Tiber. With permission from the Aborigines, they built a city called Lavinium, and soon after they and the Aborigines together came to be called Latins. Later again they founded Alba Longa and other cities of the Ancient Latins, and sixteen generations after the Trojan War sent a colony to the Palatine and the neighbouring settlement called Saturnia, where the Arcadians already were.

At the fall of Troy, Aeneas had held out in the citadel, where were the sanctities and the treasure. Then, by agreement with the attackers, he had escaped, with all that he could take, to Ida. His eldest son Ascanius settled for a time in the neighbouring Dascylitis, and then, with sons of Hector, returned to Troy. Aeneas with his other sons sailed to Thrace. Dionysius continues that, according to Hellanicus and Sophocles, Aeneas left Troy for Ida at the order of his father Anchises, who followed the command either of Aphrodite or of Venus. There were stories also that Aeneas betrayed Troy and so escaped. When Aeneas left Thrace, in one version he settled at Orchomenos in Arcadia. Then he moved on to Italy, where, according to Agathyllus, an Arcadian poet, he had a son Romulus.

In the usual version, according to Dionysius, Aeneas and his men founded a temple to Aphrodite in Thrace, on the promontory of Pallene. Then they came to Delos, and from there to Cythera, where they founded another temple to Aphrodite. The next visits were at Cinaethium in Arcadia, and at Zacynthus, an island west of Greece, where the settlement had been founded by a hero called Zacynthus, descended like Aeneas from Dardanus. They sacrificed to Aphrodite, and held games in the place known as "the race track of Aeneas and Aphrodite." They moved on to the next island, Leucas, and here again founded a temple to Aphrodite, called Aphrodite Aeneas. They sailed to Actium further north, and founded another temple to her there. Anchises went on to Buthrotum with the ships, and Aeneas inland to Dodona, where he found Trojans with Helenus, a Trojan prince and prophet who had been captured. Aeneas there dedicated inscribed bronze bowls, of which Dionysius says that some were extant in his day. The party joined together again, and founded another temple of Aphrodite further along the coast.

Taking local guides, they now crossed to Italy, and landed in Iapygia, some at the promontory of the Sallentini, and Aeneas himself at a place called Athenaeum, or the temple of Athena, where the harbour was afterwards called the harbour of Aphrodite. They sailed on, here and there leaving traces of themselves, such as an inscribed bowl, with the name of Aeneas, in a temple of Hera.

They continued west, and landed in Sicily near Drepana, and met Trojans, under Elymus and Aegestus, or Acestes, settled near the river Crimisus; for there had been a former migration from Troy, when Laomedon reigned.

Aeneas now helped them by founding the cities of Aegesta or Egesta and Elyma, and leaving there some members of his expedition, either because they were tired of traveling, or because some women burnt some of the ships. Aeneas left traces in an altar to Aphrodite at Elyma and a temple to himself at Aegesta.

Aeneas then went to Italy, anchoring first at Palinurus, called after a helmsman of Aeneas who died there, and putting in at an island called Leucasia, where a female cousin of Aeneas died, and then at Misenum and Prochyta, where another relative of Aeneas, and his old nurse, died. At last they reached Laurentum, where they founded a settlement. This, says Dionysius, is the truth, though there were other versions; that Aeneas never came at all; that it was some other Aeneas; or that Aeneas came, but went back to Troy, and left Ascanius to rule in Italy. He adds that the existence of many graves of Aeneas in many places is no argument against the truth of the legend, since this is a usual phenomenon with important characters.

Two altars erected by Aeneas were shewn near the first settlement. After the first sacrifice, the Trojans ate food off parsley or cakes, used as plates, and one said, "Why, our own table is already eaten," fulfilling a prophecy, given either at Dodona, or at Erythrae in Asia Minor where there was a Sibyl or prophetess, that the Trojans must sail west till they ate their tables, and must then follow a four-footed guide, and found their city where it rested. They now began to offer sacrifice. A sow was the victim. It broke loose and ran away, for about three miles. Then it rested; and Aeneas decided to found the city there. It was not a good place; but a divine voice from a wood warned him to obey the sign. Another version was that Aeneas saw a vision of his ancestral gods in sleep, giving him the warning. Next day the sow bore a litter of thirty young; the meaning was that in thirty years another city should be founded. Aeneas sacrificed the sow and the litter to the Ancestral Gods.

Latinus, the king of the country, was fighting the Rutulians. He now left them, and came to oppose the Trojans. But before they fought, in the night Latinus was warned by a spirit and Aeneas by the Ancestral Gods to come to terms. They came to terms. The Trojans were to have land, and help the Aborigines against the Rutulians or other enemies. They in turn helped the Trojans to build their city Lavinium, called, according to the Romans, after Launa, daughter of Latinus, and, according to some Greeks, after Launa, daughter of Anius, king of Delos who had come with the Trojans, and lately died. Aeneas now married Launa, or Lavinia, daughter of Latinus. Dionysius then traces the lineage of Dardanus founder of Troy to Zeus in Arcadia by way of Samothrace, to prove that the Trojans were akin to the Greeks.

Latinus died three years later. The Rutulians had revolted again under

Turnus, a cousin of Amata queen of Latinus, and a deserter from Latinus. In the fighting the enemy were beaten, but Latinus was killed, and Aeneas ruled over his subjects as well as his own. Three years later, however, the Rutulians had their revenge, for, helped by Mezentius king of the Etruscans, they killed Aeneas in battle. His body could not be found. A shrine was built to him, inscribed to him as "Father God of the Earth Below, who controls the stream of the River Numicius"—an expansion of the title "Jupiter Indiges."

Opinions may well differ about the general interest of these legends. Criticism has traced their history in part, but it cannot fully extricate their entanglements, or trace the history of their development. Nor can it get very far in the search for some underlying historical facts. Too many unknown quantities are involved for very much certain progress to be made; not that it is impossible to reach some limited results, by long and highly specialized researches.

But there is a particular interest in the legends, especially as they are given by Dionysius. His version is clearly very much like the material on which Vergil worked. Of that, though no one can give a full account of the immense mass of tradition that Vergil had before him, there can be no doubt at all.

It would be possible to make a long and instructive comparison. A very short comparison, though, is enough to shew how Vergil applied his characteristic method here, as elsewhere. He seems to try to neglect tradition as little as he can, but to take every chance to alter it and combine versions together.

Vergil, thus, alters the account of the fighting given by Livy. Latinus, in Vergil, was unwillingly on the side of Turnus, and he survived; in Livy he fought for Aeneas, and he was killed in battle. Vergil combines Livy's variants about the meeting of Aeneas and Latinus. In Livy, either they began by fighting, or made peace at the start and did not quarrel. In Vergil, they made peace at first, and a quarrel came afterwards, followed by peace again.

The comparison with Dionysius is far more complicated, and only a few examples can be given. Vergil seems to have known the versions followed by Dionysius of the fighting in Latium, and to have introduced changes into them as he did into the accounts reproduced by Livy. Latinus, Turnus, Pallas, and Mezentius all appear, but there are changes in the parts which they play, and in the chronology. Hardly anything is exactly the same.

Less obvious but still more interesting are the contrasts in the versions of the travels. In Vergil, the Penates appear to Aeneas in Delos; in Dionysius they appear to him in Italy. In Vergil, Aeneas celebrates Actian games near

Actium; in Dionysius he seems to have established a cult, with athletic games, in the island of Zacynthus. In Vergil, Aeneas met Helenus at Buthrotum, and dedicated an inscribed shield at Actium; in Dionysius he met him at Dodona, and there, and afterwards in Italy, dedicated inscribed bowls. The Aeneas of Vergil seems to land for a very short time, on the coast of Italy, but he explicitly sees the very places which the Aeneas of Dionysius visits. In Sicily, according to Dionysius, there have been Trojans for years; according to Vergil, Trojans seem to arrive now for the first time, or else Aeneas has been forestalled by Acestes only recently. The Greek element in Italy is elaborately analysed by Dionysius; Vergil uses Evander, following tradition more closely than usual, but referring to the rest, if at all, mainly in hints scattered about the second half of the *Aeneid*. The vision of the Tiber god in Vergil seems to owe something to various different visions in the tradition. The portents of the tables that were eaten and the white sow are just slightly different; in particular, Vergil does not make the sow lead the Trojans, and he seems not to have finally decided exactly what he meant the sow to signify. The voice from the wood in Dionysius which warned Aeneas in Italy seems to have been transferred by Vergil to Delos, where it is the warning voice from the shrine of Apollo.

These are only a very few of the examples which could be found. Everything is entirely characteristic. Vergil chooses and uses everything for the imaginative value which it has, or can be made to have. He clearly began with some version or versions very much like the story in Dionysius. Most interestingly, the Third *Aeneid* is closest to such a version, but there are already Vergilian changes. As the *Aeneid* grew, Vergil's imagination led him farther away and onwards. The patterns of the *Iliad* and *Odyssey,* and the tale of Dido, and facts and passions of his own day, and also his own patient researches into ancient Italian tradition, varied the outlines more and more.

Vergil is not totally unlike all other poets in his process of creation. Perhaps he is supreme in the accuracy and precision with which his deeper mind delivered poetry in the most authentically poetic way. Perhaps somewhere in the secret of the Vergilian process of creation lies the secret of the Vergilian power and appeal, reaching far on to the future because it reaches far back into the past, and ranges across the living world into the rhythms which make mankind akin.

MARCUS AURELIUS

[*121–180* A.D.]

No AGE MADE OF THE REVIEW SUCH A SERIOUS INSTRUMENT OF FRESH THOUGHT OR found such great reviewers as the nineteenth century. The serious review is now addressed to a much narrower audience than Macaulay, Mill, or Arnold entertained and has become in large part simply a way of bringing new books to our attention. This famous essay, a review of George Long's translation of Marcus Aurelius' *Meditations,* does not insistently label itself a review. The publication of Long's book becomes the point of departure for reflections on Marcus Aurelius, which in turn serve to examine the differences between morality and religion. The essay contrasts the austere *apathia,* or passionless tranquility, of the Stoic Emperor with the joyous religious emotion expressed in the most exalted sayings of Jesus. Arnold's essay is intensely personal, although it is also somehow quite proper and reserved. We know that Arnold achieved a spiritual state like that of the dutiful, conscientious, almost reluctant, Emperor. For Arnold, "The Sea of Faith"—that once authoritative blend of high aspiration, poetry, morality, magic, and superstition—had indeed receded, and he could only hear

> Its melancholy, long, withdrawing roar,
> Retreating to the breath
> Of the night-wind down the vast edges drear
> And naked shingles of the world.

Stoicism had become a living option, if not the only one.

First published in *Essays in Criticism,* First Series, in 1865.

MATTHEW ARNOLD

An Essay on Marcus Aurelius

MR. MILL SAYS, IN HIS BOOK ON LIBERTY, THAT "CHRISTIAN MORALITY IS IN great part merely a protest against paganism; its ideal is negative rather than positive, passive rather than active." He says that, in certain most important respects, "it falls far below the best morality of the ancients." Now, the object of systems of morality is to take possession of human life, to save it from being abandoned to passion or allowed to drift at hazard, to give it happiness by establishing it in the practice of virtue; and this object they seek to attain by prescribing to human life fixed principles of action, fixed rules of conduct. In its uninspired as well as in its inspired moments, in its days of languor and gloom as well as in its days of sunshine and energy, human life has thus always a clue to follow, and may always be making way towards its goal. Christian morality has not failed to supply to human life aids of this sort. It has supplied them far more abundantly than many of its critics imagine. The most exquisite document after those of the New Testament, of all the documents the Christian spirit has ever inspired,—the *Imitation,*—by no means contains the whole of Christian morality; nay, the disparagers of this morality would think themselves sure of triumphing if one agreed to look for it in the *Imitation* only. But even the *Imitation* is full of passages like these:

> *"Vita sine proposito languida et vaga est;"*—*"Omni die renovare debemus propositum nostrum, dicentes: nunc hodiè perfectè incipiamus, quia nihil est quod hactenus fecimus;"*—*"Secundum propositum nostrum est cursus profectûs nostri;"*—*"Raro etiam unum vitium perfectè vincimus, et ad quotidianum profectum non accendimur;" "Semper aliquid certi proponendum est;"*—*"Tibi ipsi violentiam frequenter fac:"*

(A life without a purpose is a languid, drifting thing;—Every day we ought to renew our purpose, saying to ourselves: This day let us make a sound beginning, for what we have hitherto done is naught;—Our improvement is in proportion to our purpose;—We hardly ever manage to get completely rid even of one fault, and do not set our hearts on daily improvement;—Always place a definite purpose before thee;—Get the habit of mastering thine inclination.)

These are moral precepts, and moral precepts of the best kind. As rules to hold possession of our conduct, and to keep us in the right course through outward troubles and inward perplexity, they are equal to the best ever furnished by the great masters of morals—Epictetus or Marcus Aurelius.

But moral rules, apprehended as ideas first, and then rigorously followed as laws, are, and must be, for the sage only. The mass of mankind have neither force of intellect enough to apprehend them clearly as ideas, nor force of character enough to follow them strictly as laws. The mass of mankind can be carried along a course full of hardship for the natural man, can be borne over the thousand impediments of the narrow way, only by the tide of a joyful and bounding emotion. It is impossible to rise from reading Epictetus or Marcus Aurelius without a sense of constraint and melancholy, without feeling that the burden laid upon man is well-nigh greater than he can bear. Honour to the sages who have felt this, and yet have borne it! Yet, even for the sage, this sense of labour and sorrow in his march towards the goal constitutes a relative inferiority; the noblest souls of whatever creed, the pagan Empedocles as well as the Christian Paul, have insisted on the necessity of an inspiration, a joyful emotion, to make moral action perfect; an obscure indication of this necessity is the one drop of truth in the ocean of verbiage with which the controversy on justification by faith has flooded the world. But, for the ordinary man, this sense of labour and sorrow constitutes an absolute disqualification; it paralyses him; under the weight of it, he cannot make way towards the goal at all. The paramount virtue of religion is, that it has *lighted up* morality; that it has supplied the emotion and inspiration needful for carrying the sage along the narrow way perfectly, for carrying the ordinary man along it at all. Even the religions with most dross in them have had something of this virtue; but the Christian religion manifests it with unexampled splendour. "Lead me, Zeus and Destiny!" says the prayer of Epictetus, "withersoever I am appointed to go; I will follow without wavering; even though I turn coward and shrink, I shall have to follow all the same." The fortitude of that is for the strong, for the few; even for them the spiritual atmosphere with which it surrounds them is bleak and gray. But, "Let thy loving spirit lead me forth into the land of righteousness;"—"The Lord shall be unto thee an everlasting light, and thy God thy glory;"—"Unto you that fear my name shall the sun of righteousness arise with healing in his wings," says the Old Testament; "Born, not of blood, nor of the will of the flesh, nor of the will of man, but of God;"—"Except a man be born again, he cannot see the kingdom of God;"—"Whatsoever is born of God, overcometh the world," says the New. The ray of sunshine is there, the glow of a divine warmth;—the austerity of the sage melts away under it, the paralysis of the weak is healed; he who is vivified by it renews his strength; "all things are possible to him;" "he is a new creature."

Epictetus says: "Every matter has two handles, one of which will bear taking hold of, the other not. If thy brother sin against thee, lay not hold of the matter by this, that he sins against thee; for by this handle the matter will not bear taking hold of. But rather lay hold of it by this, that he is thy brother, thy born mate; and thou wilt take hold of it by what will bear handling." Jesus, being asked whether a man is bound to forgive his brother as often as seven times, answers: "I say not unto thee, until seven times, but until seventy times seven." Epictetus here suggests to the reason grounds for forgiveness of injuries which Jesus does not; but it is vain to say that Epictetus is on that account a better moralist than Jesus, if the warmth, the emotion, of Jesus's answer fires his hearer to the practice of forgiveness of injuries, while the thought in Epictetus's leaves him cold. So with Christian morality in general: its distinction is not that it propounds the maxim, "Thou shalt love God and thy neighbour," with more development, closer reasoning, truer sincerity, than other moral systems; it is that it propounds this maxim with an inspiration which wonderfully catches the hearer and makes him act upon it. It is because Mr. Mill has attained to the perception of truths of this nature, that he is,—instead of being, like the school from which he proceeds, doomed to sterility,—a writer of distinguished mark and influence, a writer deserving all attention and respect; it is (I must be pardoned for saying) because he is not sufficiently leavened with them, that he falls just short of being a great writer.

That which gives to the moral writings of the Emperor Marcus Aurelius their peculiar character and charm, is their being suffused and softened by something of this very sentiment whence Christian morality draws its best power. Mr. Long has recently published in a convenient form a translation of these writings, and has thus enabled English readers to judge Marcus Aurelius for themselves; he has rendered his countrymen a real service by so doing. Mr. Long's reputation as a scholar is a sufficient guarantee of the general fidelity and accuracy of his translation; on these matters, besides, I am hardly entitled to speak, and my praise is of no value. But that for which I and the rest of the unlearned may venture to praise Mr. Long is this; that he treats Marcus Aurelius's writings, as he treats all the other remains of Greek and Roman antiquity which he touches, not as a dead and dry matter of learning, but as documents with a side of modern applicability and living interest, and valuable mainly so far as this side in them can be made clear; that as in his notes on Plutarch's *Roman Lives* he deals with the modern epoch of Caesar and Cicero, not as food for schoolboys, but as food for men, and men engaged in the current of contemporary life and action, so in his remarks and essays on Marcus Aurelius he treats this truly modern striver and thinker not as a Classical Dictionary hero, but as a present source from which to draw "example of life, and instruction of manners." Why may not a son of Dr. Arnold say, what might naturally here be said by any other critic, that in this lively and fruitful way of considering the men and affairs of ancient Greece and Rome, Mr. Long resembles Dr. Arnold?

One or two little complaints, however, I have against Mr. Long, and I will get them off my mind at once. In the first place, why could he not have found gentler and juster terms to describe the translation of his predecessor, Jeremy Collier,—the redoutable enemy of stage plays,—than these: "a most coarse and vulgar copy of the original"? As a matter of taste, a translator should deal leniently with his predecessor; but putting that out of the question, Mr. Long's language is a great deal too hard. Most English people who knew Marcus Aurelius before Mr. Long appeared as his introducer, knew him through Jeremy Collier. And the acquaintance of a man like Marcus Aurelius is such an imperishable benefit, that one can never lose a peculiar sense of obligation towards the man who confers it. Apart from this claim upon one's tenderness, however, Jeremy Collier's version deserves respect for its genuine spirit and vigour, the spirit and vigour of the age of Dryden. Jeremy Collier too, like Mr. Long, regarded in Marcus Aurelius the living moralist, and not the dead classic; and his warmth of feeling gave to his style an impetuosity and rhythm which from Mr. Long's style (I do not blame it on that account) are absent. Let us place the two side by side. The impressive opening of Marcus Aurelius's fifth book, Mr. Long translates thus:

> In the morning when thou risest unwillingly, let this thought be present: I am rising to the work of a human being. Why then am I dissatisfied if I am going to do the things for which I exist and for which I was brought into the world? Or have I been made for this, to lie in the bedclothes and keep myself warm?—But this is more pleasant.—Dost thou exist then to take thy pleasure, and not at all for action or exertion?

Jeremy Collier has:

> When you find an unwillingness to rise early in the morning, make this short speech to yourself: 'I am getting up now to do the business of a man; and am I out of humour for going about that which I was made for, and for the sake of which I was sent into the world? Was I then designed for nothing

but to doze and batten beneath the counterpane? I thought action had been the end of your being.'

In another striking passage, again, Mr. Long has:

No longer wonder at hazard; for neither wilt thou read thy own memoirs, nor the acts of the ancient Romans and Hellenes, and the selections from books which thou wast reserving for thy old age. Hasten then to the end which thou hast before thee, and, throwing away idle hopes, come to thine own aid, if thou carest at all for thyself, while it is in thy power.

Here his despised predecessor has:

Don't go too far in your books and overgrasp yourself. Alas, you have no time left to peruse your diary, to read over the Greek and Roman history: come, don't flatter and deceive yourself; look to the main chance, to the end and design of reading, and mind life more than notion: I say, if you have a kindness for your person, drive at the practice and help yourself, for that is in your own power.

It seems to me that here for style and force Jeremy Collier can (to say the least) perfectly stand comparison with Mr. Long. Jeremy Collier's real defect as a translator is not his coarseness and vulgarity, but his imperfect acquaintance with Greek; this is a serious defect, a fatal one; it rendered a translation like Mr. Long's necessary. Jeremy Collier's work will now be forgotten, and Mr. Long stands master of the field; but he may be content, at any rate, to leave his predecessor's grave unharmed, even if he will not throw upon it, in passing, a handful of kindly earth.

Another complaint I have against Mr. Long is, that he is not quite idiomatic and simple enough. It is a little formal, at least, if not pedantic, to say *Ethic* and *Dialectic,* instead of *Ethics* and *Dialectics,* and to say "*Hellenes* and Romans" instead of "*Greeks* and Romans." And why, too,—the name of Antoninus being preoccupied by Antoninus Pius,—will Mr. Long call his author Marcus *Antoninus* instead of Marcus *Aurelius?* Small as these matters appear, they are important when one has to deal with the general public, and not with a small circle of scholars; and it is the general public that the translator of a short masterpeice on morals, such as is the book of Marcus Aurelius, should have in view; his aim should be to make Marcus Aurelius's work as popular as the *Imitation,* and Marcus Aurelius's name as familiar as Socrates's. In rendering or naming him, therefore, punctilious accuracy of phrase is not so much to be sought as accessibility and currency; everything which may best enable the Emperor and his precepts *volitare per ora virûm.* It is essential to render him in language perfectly plain and unprofessional, and to call him by the name by which he is best and most distinctly known. The translators of the Bible talk of *pence* and not *denarii,* and the admirers of Voltaire do not celebrate him under the name of Arouet.

But, after these trifling complaints are made, one must end, as one began, in unfeigned gratitude to Mr. Long for his excellent and substantial reproduction in English of an invaluable work. In general the substantiality, soundness, and precision of Mr. Long's rendering are (I will venture, after all, to give my opinion about them) as conspicuous as the living spirit with which he treats antiquity; and these qualities are particularly desirable in the translator of a work like that of Marcus Aurelius, of which the language is often corrupt, almost always hard and obscure. Any one who wants to appreciate Mr. Long's merits as a translator may read, in the original and in Mr. Long's translation, the seventh chapter of the tenth book; he will see how, through all the dubiousness and involved manner of the Greek, Mr. Long has firmly seized upon the clear thought which is certainly at the bottom of that troubled wording, and, in distinctly rendering this thought, has at the same time thrown round its expression a characteristic shade of painfulness and difficulty which just suits it. And Marcus Aurelius's book is one which, when it is rendered so accurately as Mr. Long renders it, even those who know Greek tolerably well may choose to read rather in the translation than in the original. For not only are the contents here incomparably more valuable than the external form, but this form, the Greek of a Roman, is not exactly one of those styles which have a physiognomy, which are an essential part of their author, which stamp an indelible impression of him on the reader's mind. An old Lyons commentator finds, indeed, in Marcus Aurelius's Greek, something characteristic, something specially firm and imperial; but I think an ordinary mortal will hardly find this: he will find crabbed Greek, without any great charm of distinct physiognomy. The Greek of Thucydides and Plato has this charm, and he who reads them in a translation, however accurate, loses it, and loses much in losing it; but the Greek of Marcus Aurelius, like the Greek of the New Testament, and even more than the Greek of the New Testament, is wanting in it. If one could be assured that the English Testament were made perfectly accurate, one might be almost content never to open a Greek Testament again; and, Mr. Long's version of Marcus Aurelius being what it is, an Englishman who reads to live, and does not live to read, may henceforth let the Greek original repose upon its shelf.

The man whose thoughts Mr. Long has thus faithfully reproduced, is perhaps the most beautiful figure in history. He is one of those consoling and hope-inspiring marks, which stand for ever to remind our weak and easily discouraged race how high human goodness and perseverance have once been carried, and may be carried again. The interest of mankind is peculiarly attracted by examples of signal goodness in high places; for that testimony to the worth of goodness is the most striking which is borne by those to whom all the means of pleasure and self-indulgence lay open, by those who had at their command the kingdoms of the world and the glory of them. Marcus Aurelius was the ruler of the grandest of empires; and he was one of the best of men. Besides him, history presents one or two sovereigns eminent for their goodness, such as Saint Louis or Alfred. But Marcus Aurelius has, for us moderns, this great superiority in interest over Saint Louis or Alfred, that he lived and acted in a state of society modern by its essential characteristics, in an epoch akin to our own, in a brilliant centre of civilisation. Trajan talks of "our enlightened age" just as glibly as the *Times* talks of it. Marcus Aurelius thus becomes for us a man like ourselves, a man in all things tempted as we are. Saint Louis inhabits an atmosphere of mediaeval Catholicism, which the man of the nineteenth century may admire, indeed, may even passionately wish to inhabit, but which, strive as he will, he cannot really inhabit. Alfred belongs to a state of society (I say it with all deference to the *Saturday Review* critic who keeps such jealous watch over the honour of our Saxon ancestors) half barbarous. Neither Alfred nor Saint Louis can be morally and intellectually as near to us as Marcus Aurelius.

The record of the outward life of this admirable man has in it little of striking incident. He was born at Rome on the 26th of April, in the year 121 of the Christian era. He was nephew and son-in-law to his predecessor on the throne, Antoninus Pius. When Antoninus died, he was forty years old, but from the time of his earliest manhood he had assisted in administering public affairs. Then, after his uncle's death in 161, for nineteen years he reigned as emperor. The barbarians were pressing on the Roman frontier, and a great part of Marcus Aurelius's nineteen years of reign was passed in campaigning. His absences from Rome were numerous and long. We hear of him in Asia Minor, Syria, Egypt, Greece; but, above all, in the countries on the Danube, where the war with the barbarians was going on,—in Austria, Moravia, Hungary. In these countries much of his *Journal* seems to have been written; parts of it are dated from them; and there, a few weeks before his fifty-ninth birthday, he fell sick and died. The record of him on which his fame chiefly rests is the record of his inward life,—his *Journal,* or *Commentaries,* or *Meditations,* or *Thoughts,* for by all these names has the work been called. Perhaps the most interesting of the records of his outward life is that which the first book of his work supplies, where he gives an account of his education, recites the names of those to whom he is indebted for it, and enumerates his obligations to each of them. It is a refreshing and consoling picture, a priceless treasure for those, who, sick of the "wild and dreamlike trade of blood and guile," which seems to be nearly the whole of what history has to offer to our view, seek eagerly for that substratum of right thinking and well-doing which in all ages must surely have somewhere existed, for without it the continued life of humanity would have been impossible. "From my mother I learnt piety and beneficence, and abstinence not only from evil deeds but even from evil thoughts; and further, simplicity in my way of living, far removed from the habits of the rich." Let us remember that, the next time we are reading the sixth satire of Juvenal. "From my tutor I learnt" (hear it, ye tutors of princes!) "endurance of labour, and to want little, and to work with my own hands, and not to meddle with other people's affairs, and not to be ready to listen to slander." The vices and foibles of the Greek sophist or rhetorician— the *Graeculus esuriens*—are in everybody's mind; but he who reads Marcus Aurelius's account of his Greek teachers and masters, will understand how it is that, in spite of the vices and foibles of individual *Graeculi,* the education of the human race owes to Greece a debt which can never be overrated. The vague and colourless praise of history leaves on the mind hardly any impression of Antoninus Pius: it is only from the private memoranda of his nephew that we learn what a disciplined, hard-working, gentle, wise, virtuous man he was; a man who, perhaps, interests mankind less than his immortal nephew only because he has left in writing no record of his inner life,—*caret quia vate sacro.*

Of the outward life and circumstances of Marcus Aurelius, beyond these notices which he has himself supplied, there are few of much interest and importance. There is the fine anecdote of his speech when he heard of the assassination of the revolted Avidius Cassius, against whom he was marching; *he was sorry,* he said, *to be deprived of the pleasure of pardoning him.* And there are one or two more anecdotes of him which show the same spirit. But the great record for the outward life of a man who has left such a record of his lofty inward aspirations as that which Marcus Aurelius has left, is the clear consenting voice of all his contemporaries,—high and low, friend and enemy, pagan and Christian,—in praise of his sincerity, justice, and goodness. The world's charity does not err on the side of excess, and here was a man occupying the most conspicuous station in the world, and professing the highest possible standard of conduct;—yet the world was obliged to declare that he walked worthily of his profession. Long after his death, his bust was to be seen in the houses of private men through the wide Roman empire. It may be the vulgar part of human nature which busies itself with the semblance and doings of living sovereigns, it is its nobler part which busies itself with those of the dead; these busts of Marcus Aurelius, in the homes of Gaul, Britain, and Italy, bear witness, not to the inmates' frivolous curiosity about princes and palaces, but to their reverential memory of the passage of a great man upon the earth.

Two things, however, before one turns from the outward to the inward life of Marcus Aurelius, force themselves upon one's notice, and demand a word of comment; he persecuted the Christians, and he had for his son the vicious and brutal Commodus. The persecution at Lyons, in which Attalus and Pothinus suffered, the persecution of Smyrna, in which Polycarp suffered, took place in his reign. Of his humanity, of his tolerance, of his horror of cruelty and violence, of his wish to refrain from severe measures against the Christians, of his anxiety to temper the severity of these measures when they appeared to him indispensable, there is no doubt: but, on the one hand, it is certain that the letter, attributed to him, directing that no Christian should be punished for being a Christian, is spurious; it is almost certain that his alleged answer to the authorities of Lyons, in which he directs that Christians persisting in their profession shall be dealt with according to law, is genuine. Mr. Long seems inclined to try and throw doubt over the persecution at Lyons, by pointing out that the letter of the Lyons Christians relating it, alleges it to have been attended by miraculous and incredible incidents. "A man," he says, "can only act consistently by accepting all this letter or rejecting it all, and we cannot blame him for either." But it is contrary to all experience to say that because a fact is related with incorrect additions and embellishments, therefore it probably never happened at all; or that it is not, in general, easy for an impartial mind to distinguish between the fact and the embellishments. I cannot doubt that the Lyons persecution took place, and that the punishment of Christians for being Christians was sanctioned by Marcus Aurelius. But then I must add that nine modern readers out of ten, when they read this, will, I believe, have a perfectly false notion of what the moral action of Marcus Aurelius, in sanctioning that punishment, really was. They imagine Trajan, or Antoninus Pius, or Marcus Aurelius, fresh from the perusal of the Gospel, fully aware of the spirit and holiness of the Christian saints, ordering their extermination because he loved darkness rather than light. Far from this, the Christianity which these emperors aimed at repressing was, in their conception of it, something philosophically contemptible, politically subversive, and morally abominable. As men, they sincerely regarded it much as well-conditioned people, with us, regard Mormonism; as rulers, they regarded it much as Liberal statesmen, with us, regard the Jesuits. A kind of Mormonism, constituted as a vast secret society, with obscure aims of political and social subversion, was what Antoninus Pius and Marcus Aurelius believed themselves to be repressing when they punished Christians. The early Christian apologists again and again declare to us under what odious imputations the Christians lay, how general was the belief that these imputations were well-grounded, how sincere was the horror which the belief inspired. The multitude, convinced that the Christians were atheists who ate human flesh and thought incest no crime, displayed against them a fury so passionate as to embarrass and alarm their rulers. The severe expressions of Tacitus, *exitiabilis superstitio—odio humani generis convicti,* show how deeply the prejudices of the multitude imbued the educated class also. One asks oneself with astonishment how a doctrine so benign as that of Jesus Christ can have incurred misrepresentation so monstrous. The inner and moving cause of the misrepresentation lay, no doubt, in this,—that Christianity was a new spirit in the Roman world, destined to act in that world as its dissolvent; and it was inevitable that Christianity in the Roman world, like democracy in the modern world, like every new spirit with a similar mission assigned to it, should at its first appearance occasion an instinctive shrinking and repugnance in the world which it was to dissolve. The outer and palpable causes of the misrepresentation were, for the Roman public at large, the confounding of the Christians with the Jews, that isolated, fierce, and stubborn race, whose stubbornness, fierceness, and isolation, real as they were, the fancy of a civilised Roman yet further exaggerated; the atmosphere of mystery and novelty which surrounded the Christian rites; the very simplicity of Christian theism. For the Roman statesman, the cause of mistake lay in that character of secret assemblages which the meetings of the Christian community wore, under a State-system as jealous of unauthorised associations as is the State-system of modern France.

A Roman of Marcus Aurelius's time and position could not well see the Christians except through the mist of these prejudices. Seen through such a mist, the Christians appeared with a thousand faults not their own; but it has not been sufficiently remarked that faults really their own many of them assuredly appeared with besides, faults especially likely to strike such an observer as Marcus Aurelius, and to confirm him in the prejudices of his race, station, and rearing. We look back upon Christianity after it has proved what a future it bore within it, and for us the sole representatives of its early struggles are the pure and devoted spirits through whom it proved this; Marcus Aurelius saw it with its future yet unshown, and with the tares among its professed progeny not less conspicuous than the wheat. Who can doubt that among the professing Christians of the second century, as among the professing Christians of the nineteenth, there was plenty of folly, plenty of rabid nonsense, plenty of gross fanaticism? Who will even venture to affirm that, separated in great measure from the intellect and civilisation of the world for one or two centuries, Christianity, wonderful as have been its fruits, had the development perfectly worthy of its inestimable germ? Who will venture to affirm that, by the alliance of Christianity with the virtue and intelligence of men like the Antonines—of the best product of Greek and Roman civilisation, while Greek and Roman civilisation had yet life and power,—Christianity and the world, as well as the Antonines themselves, would not have been gainers? That alliance was not to be. The Antonines lived and died with an utter misconception of Christianity; Christianity grew up in the Catacombs, not on the Palatine. And Marcus Aurelius incurs no moral reproach by having authorised the punishment of the Christians; he does not thereby become in the least what we mean by a *persecutor*. One may concede that it was impossible for him to see Christianity as it really was;—as impossible as for even the moderate and sensible Fleury to see the Antonines as they really were; —one may concede that the point of view from which Christianity appeared something anti-civil and anti-social, which the State had the faculty to judge and the duty to suppress, was inevitably his. Still, however, it remains true that this sage, who made perfection his aim and reason his law, did Christianity an immense injustice and rested in an idea of State-attributes which was illusive. And this is, in truth, characteristic of Marcus Aurelius, that he is blameless, yet, in a certain sense, unfortunate; in his character, beautiful as it is, there is something melancholy, circumscribed, and ineffectual.

For of his having such a son as Commodus, too, one must say that he is not to be blamed on that account, but that he is unfortunate. Disposition and temperament are inexplicable things; there are natures on which the best education and example are thrown away; excellent fathers may have, without any fault of theirs, incurably vicious sons. It is to be remembered, also, that Commodus was left, at the perilous age of nineteen, master of the world; while his father, at that age, was but beginning a twenty years' apprenticeship to wisdom, labour, and self-command, under the sheltering teachership of his uncle Antoninus. Commodus was a prince apt to be led by favourites; and if the story is true which says that he left, all through his reign, the Christians untroubled, and ascribes this lenity to the influence of his mistress Marcia, it shows that he could be led to good as well as to evil. But for such a nature to be left at a critical age with absolute power, and wholly without good counsel and direction, was the more fatal. Still one cannot help wishing that the example of Marcus Aurelius could have availed more with his own only son. One cannot but think that with such virtue as his there should go, too, the ardour which removes mountains, and that the ardour which removes mountains might have even won Commodus. The word *ineffectual* again rises to one's mind; Marcus Aurelius saved his own soul by his righteousness, and he could do no more. Happy they who can do this! But still happier, who can do more! Yet, when one passes from his outward to his inward life, when one turns over the pages of his *Meditations,*—entries jotted down from day to day, amid the business of the city or the fatigues of the camp, for his own guidance and support, meant for no eye but his own, without the slightest attempt at style, with no care, even, for correct writing, not to be surpassed for naturalness and sincerity,—all disposition to carp and cavil dies away, and one is overpowered by the charm of a character of such purity, delicacy, and virtue. He fails neither in small things nor in great; he keeps watch over himself both that the great springs of action may be right in him, and that the minute details of action may be right also. How admirable in a hard-tasked ruler, and a ruler, too, with a passion for thinking and reading, is such a memorandum as the following:

> Not frequently nor without necessity to say to any one, or to write in a letter, that I have no leisure; nor continually to excuse the neglect of duties required by our relation to those with whom we live, by alleging urgent occupation.

And, when that ruler is a Roman emperor, what an "idea" is this to be written down and meditated by him:

> The idea of a polity in which there is the same law for all, a polity administered with regard to equal rights and equal freedom of speech, and the idea of a kingly government which respects most of all the freedom of the governed.

And, for all men who "drive at practice," what practical rules may not one accumulate out of these *Meditations*:

> The greatest part of what we say or do being unnecessary, if a man takes this away, he will have more leisure and less uneasiness. Accordingly, on every occasion a man should ask himself: 'Is this one of the unnecessary things?' Now a man should take away not only unnecessary acts, but also unnecessary thoughts, for thus superfluous acts will not follow after.

And again:

> We ought to check in the series of our thoughts everything that is without a purpose and useless, but most of all the over-curious feeling and the malignant; and a man should use himself to think of those things only about which if one should suddenly ask, 'What hast thou now in thy thoughts?' with perfect openness thou mightest immediately answer, 'This or That;' so that from thy words it should be plain that everything in thee is simple and benevolent, and such as befits a social animal, and one that cares not for thoughts about sensual enjoyments, or any rivalry or envy and suspicion, or anything else for which thou wouldst blush if thou shouldest say thou hadst it in thy mind.

So, with a stringent practicalness worthy of Franklin, he discourses on his favourite text, *Let nothing be done without a purpose*. But it is when he enters the region where Franklin cannot follow him, when he utters his thoughts on the ground-motives of human action, that he is most interesting; that he becomes the unique, the incomparable Marcus Aurelius. Christianity uses language very liable to be misunderstood when it seems to tell men to do good, not, certainly, from the vulgar motives of worldly interest, or vanity, or love of human praise, but "that their Father which seeth in secret may reward them openly." The motives of reward and punishment have come, from the misconception of language of this kind, to be strangely overpressed by many Christian moralists, to the deterioration and disfigurement of Christianity. Marcus Aurelius says, truly and nobly:

One man, when he has done a service to another, is ready to set it down to his account as a favour conferred. Another is not ready to do this, but still in his own mind he thinks of the man as his debtor, and he knows what he has done. A third in a manner does not even know what he has done, *but he is like a vine which has produced grapes, and seeks for nothing more after it has once produced its proper fruit.* As a horse when he has run, a dog when he has caught the game, a bee when it has made its honey, so a man when he has done a good act, does not call out for others to come and see, but he goes on to another act, as a vine goes on to produce again the grapes in season. Must a man, then, be one of these, who in a manner acts thus without observing it? Yes.

And again:

What more dost thou want when thou hast done a man a service? Art thou not content that thou hast done something conformable to thy nature, and dost thou seek to be paid for it, *just as if the eye demanded a recompense for seeing, or the feet for walking?*

Christianity, in order to match morality of this strain, has to correct its apparent offers of external reward, and to say: *The kingdom of God is within you.*

I have said that it is by its accent of emotion that the morality of Marcus Aurelius acquires a special character, and reminds one of Christian morality. The sentences of Seneca are stimulating to the intellect; the sentences of Epictetus are fortifying to the character; the sentences of Marcus Aurelius find their way to the soul. I have said that religious emotion has the power to *light up morality:* the emotion of Marcus Aurelius does not quite light up his morality, but it suffuses it; it has not power to melt the clouds of effort and austerity quite away, but it shines through them and glorifies them; it is a spirit, not so much of gladness and elation, as of gentleness and sweetness; a delicate and tender sentiment, which is less than joy and more than resignation. He says that in his youth he learned from Maximus, one of his teachers, "cheerfulness in all circumstances as well as in illness; *and a just admixture in the moral character of sweetness and dignity:*" and it is this very admixture of sweetness with his dignity which makes him so beautiful a moralist. It enables him to carry even into his observation of nature, a delicate penetration, a sympathetic tenderness, worthy of Wordsworth; the spirit of such a remark as the following has hardly a parallel, so far as my knowledge goes, in the whole range of Greek and Roman literature:

Figs, when they are quite ripe, gape open; and in the ripe olives the very circumstance of their being near to rottenness adds a peculiar beauty to the fruit. And the ears of corn bending down, and the lion's eyebrows, and the foam which flows from the mouth of wild boars, and many other things,—though they are far from being beautiful, in a certain sense,—still, because they come in the course of nature, have a beauty in them, and they please the mind; so that if a man should have a feeling and a deeper insight with respect to the things which are produced in the universe, there is hardly anything which comes in the course of nature which will not seem to him to be in a manner disposed so as to give pleasure.

But it is when his strain passes to directly moral subjects that his delicacy and sweetness lend to it the greatest charm. Let those who can feel the beauty of spiritual refinement read this, the reflection of an emperor who prized mental superiority highly:

Thou sayest, 'Men cannot admire the sharpness of thy wits.' Be it so; but there are many other things of which thou canst not say, 'I am not formed for them by nature.' Show those qualities, then, which are altogether in thy power,—sincerity, gravity, endurance of labour, aversion to pleasure, contentment with thy portion and with few things, benevolence, frankness, no love of superfluity, freedom from trifling, magnanimity. Dost thou not see how many qualities thou art at once able to exhibit, as to which there is no excuse of natural incapacity and unfitness, and yet thou still remainest voluntarily below the mark? Or art thou compelled, through being defectively furnished by nature, to murmur, and to be mean, and to flatter, and to find fault with thy poor body, and to try to please men, and to make great display, and to be so restless in thy mind? No, indeed; but thou mightest have been delivered from these things long ago. Only, if in truth thou canst be charged with being rather slow and dull of comprehension, thou must exert thyself about this also, not neglecting nor yet taking pleasure in thy dulness.

The same sweetness enables him to fix his mind, when he sees the isolation and moral death caused by sin, not on the cheerless thought of the misery of this condition, but on the inspiriting thought that man is blest with the power to escape from it:

> Suppose that thou hast detached thyself from the natural unity,—for thou wast made by nature a part, but now thou hast cut thyself off,—yet here is this beautiful provision, that it is in thy power again to unite thyself. God has allowed this to no other part,—after it has been separated and cut asunder, to come together again. But consider the goodness with which he has privileged man; for he has put it in his power, when he has been separated, to return and to be united and to resume his place.

It enables him to control even the passion for retreat and solitude, so strong in a soul like his, to which the world could offer no abiding city:

> Men seek retreat for themselves, houses in the country, seashores, and mountains; and thou, too, art wont to desire such things very much. But this is altogether a mark of the most common sort of men, for it is in thy power whenever thou shalt choose to retire into thyself. For nowhere either with more quiet or more freedom from trouble does a man retire than into his own soul, particularly when he has within him such thoughts that by looking into them he is immediately in perfect tranquillity. Constantly, then, give to thyself this retreat, and renew thyself; and let thy principles be brief and fundamental, which, as soon as thou shalt recur to them, will be sufficient to cleanse the soul completely, and to send thee back free from all discontent with the things to which thou returnest.

Against this feeling of discontent and weariness, so natural to the great for whom there seems nothing left to desire or to strive after, but so enfeebling to them, so deteriorating, Marcus Aurelius never ceased to struggle. With resolute thankfulness he kept in remembrance the blessings of his lot; the true blessings of it, not the false:

> I have to thank Heaven that I was subjected to a ruler and a father (Antoninus Pius) who was able to take away all pride from me, and to bring me to the knowledge that it is possible for a man to live in a palace without either guards, or embroidered dresses, or any show of this kind; but that it is in such a man's power to bring himself very near to the fashion of a private person, without being for this reason either meaner in thought or more remiss in action with respect to the things which must be done for public interest. ... I have to be thankful that my children have not been stupid nor deformed in body; that I did not make more proficiency in rhetoric, poetry, and the other studies, by which I should perhaps have been completely engrossed, if I had seen that I was making great progress in them; ... that I knew Apol-

lonius, Rusticus, Maximus; . . . that I received clear and frequent impressions about living according to nature, and what kind of a life that is, so that, so far as depended on Heaven, and its gifts, help, and inspiration, nothing hindered me from forthwith living according to nature, though I still fall short of it through my own fault, and through not observing the admonitions of Heaven, and, I may almost say, its direct instructions; that my body has held out so long in such a kind of life as mine; that though it was my mother's lot to die young, she spent the last years of her life with me; that whenever I wished to help any man in his need, I was never told that I had not the means of doing it; that, when I had an inclination to philosophy, I did not fall into the hands of a sophist.

And, as he dwelt with gratitude on these helps and blessings vouchsafed to him, his mind (so, at least, it seems to me) would sometimes revert with awe to the perils and temptations of the lonely height where he stood, to the lives of Tiberius, Caligula, Nero, Domitian, in their hideous blackness and ruin; and then he wrote down for himself such a warning entry as this, significant and terrible in its abruptness:

A black character, a womanish character, a stubborn character, bestial, childish, animal, stupid, counterfeit, scurrilous, fraudulent, tyrannical.

Or this:

About what am I now employing my soul? On every occasion I must ask myself this question, and enquire, What have I now in this part of me which they call the ruling principle, and whose soul have I now?—that of a child, or of a young man, or of a weak woman, or of a tyrant, or of one of the lower animals in the service of man, or of a wild beast?

The character he wished to attain he knew well, and beautifully he has marked it, and marked, too, his sense of shortcoming:

When thou hast assumed these names,—good, modest, true, rational, equalminded, magnanimous,—take care that thou dost not change these names; and, if thou shouldst lose them, quickly return to them. If thou maintainest thyself in possession of these names without desiring that others should call thee by them, thou wilt be another being, and wilt enter on another life. For to continue to be such as thou hast hitherto been, and to be torn in pieces and defiled in such a life, is the character of a very stupid man, and one overfond of his life, and like those half-devoured fighters with wild beasts, who though covered with wounds and gore still entreat to be kept to the following day, though they will be exposed in the same state to the same claws and bites.

Therefore fix thyself in the possession of these few names; and if thou art able to abide in them, abide as if thou wast removed to the Happy Islands.

For all his sweetness and serenity, however, man's point of life "between two infinities" (of that expression Marcus Aurelius is the real owner) was to him anything but a Happy Island, and the performances on it he saw through no veils of illusion. Nothing is in general more gloomy and monotonous than declamations on the hollowness and transitoriness of human life and grandeur: but here, too, the great charm of Marcus Aurelius, his emotion, comes in to relieve the monotony and to break through the gloom; and even on this eternally used topic he is imaginative, fresh, and striking:

Consider, for example, the times of Vespasian. Thou wilt see all these things, people marrying, bringing up children, sick, dying, warring, feasting, trafficking, cultivating the ground, flattering, obstinately arrogant, suspecting, plotting, wishing for somebody to die, grumbling about the present, loving, heaping up treasure, desiring to be consuls or kings. Well then that life of these people no longer exists at all. Again, go to the times of Trajan. All is again the same. Their life too is gone. But chiefly thou shouldst think of those whom thou hast thyself known distracting themselves about idle things, neglecting to do what was in accordance with their proper constitution, and to hold firmly to this and to be content with it.

Again:

The things which are much valued in life are empty, and rotten, and trifling; and people are like little dogs, biting one another, and little children quarrelling, crying, and then straightway laughing. But fidelity, and modesty, and justice, and truth, are fled

'Up to Olympus from the wide-spread earth.'

What then is there which still detains thee here?

And once more:

Look down from above on the countless herds of men, and their countless solemnities, and the infinitely varied voyagings in storms and calms, and the differences among those who are born, who live together, and die. And consider too the life lived by others in olden time, and the life now lived among barbarous nations, and how many know not even thy name, and how many will soon forget it, and how they who perhaps now are praising thee will very soon blame thee, and that neither a posthumous name is of any value, nor reputation, nor anything else.

[243]

He recognised, indeed, that (to use his own words) "the prime principle in man's constitution is the social;" and he laboured sincerely to make not only his acts towards his fellow-men, but his thoughts also, suitable to this conviction:

> When thou wishest to delight thyself, think of the virtues of those who live with thee; for instance, the activity of one, and the modesty of another, and the liberality of a third, and some other good quality of a fourth.

Still, it is hard for a pure and thoughtful man to live in a state of rapture at the spectacle afforded to him by his fellow-creatures; above all it is hard, when such a man is placed as Marcus Aurelius was placed, and has had the meanness and perversity of his fellow-creatures thrust, in no common measure, upon his notice,—has had, time after time, to experience how "within ten days thou wilt seem a god to those to whom thou art now a beast and an ape." His true strain of thought as to his relations with his fellow-men is rather the following. He has been enumerating the higher consolations which may support a man at the approach of death, and he goes on:

> But if thou requirest also a vulgar kind of comfort which shall reach thy heart, thou wilt be made best reconciled to death by observing the objects from which thou art going to be removed, and the morals of those with whom thy soul will no longer be mingled. For it is no way right to be offended with men, but it is thy duty to care for them and to bear with them gently; and yet to remember that thy departure will not be from men who have the same principles as thyself. For this is the only thing, if there be any, which could draw us the contrary way and attach us to life, to be permitted to live with those who have the same principles as ourselves. But now thou seest how great is the distress caused by the difference of those who live together, so that thou mayest say: 'Come quick, O death, lest perchance I too should forget myself.'

O faithless and perverse generation! how long shall I be with you? how long shall I suffer you? Sometimes this strain rises even to passion:

> Short is the little which remains to thee of life. Live as on a mountain. Let men see, let them know, a real man, who lives as he was meant to live. If they cannot endure him, let them kill him. For that is better than to live as men do.

It is remarkable how little of a merely local and temporary character, how little of those *scoriae* which a reader has to clear away before he gets to the precious ore, how little that even admits of doubt or question, the morality of

Marcus Aurelius exhibits. Perhaps as to one point we must make an exception. Marcus Aurelius is fond of urging as a motive for man's cheerful acquiescence in whatever befalls him, that "whatever happens to every man *is for the interest of the universal"*; that the whole contains nothing *which is not for its advantage;* that everything which happens to a man is to be accepted, "even if it seems disagreeable, *because it leads to the health of the universe."* And the whole course of the universe, he adds, has a providential reference to man's welfare: *"all other things have been made for the sake of rational beings."* Religion has in all ages freely used this language, and it is not religion which will object to Marcus Aurelius's use of it; but science can hardly accept as severely accurate this employment of terms *interest* and *advantage.* To a sound nature and a clear reason the proposition that things happen "for the interest of the universal," as men conceive of interest, may seem to have no meaning at all, and the proposition that "all things have been made for the sake of rational beings" may seem to be false. Yet even to this language, not irresistibly cogent when it is thus absolutely used, Marcus Aurelius gives a turn which makes it true and useful, when he says: "The ruling part of man can make a material for itself out of that which opposes it, as fire lays hold of what falls into it, and rises higher by means of this very material;"—when he says: "What else are all things except exercises for the reason? Persevere then until thou shalt have made all things thine own, as the stomach which is strengthened makes all things its own, as the blazing fire makes flame and brightness out of everything that is thrown into it;"—when he says: "Thou wilt not cease to be miserable till thy mind is in such a condition, that, what luxury is to those who enjoy pleasure, such shall be to thee, in every matter which presents itself, the doing of the things which are conformable to man's constitution; for a man ought to consider as an enjoyment everything which it is in his power to do according to his own nature,—and it is in his power everywhere." In this sense it is, indeed, most true that "all things have been made for the sake of rational beings;" that "all things work together for good."

In general, however, the action Marcus Aurelius prescribes is action which every sound nature must recognise as right, and the motives he assigns are motives which every clear reason must recognise as valid. And so he remains the especial friend and comforter of all clear-headed and scrupulous, yet pure-hearted and upward-striving men, in those ages most especially that walk by sight, not by faith, but yet have no open vision. He cannot give such souls, perhaps, all they yearn for, but he gives them much; and what he gives them, they can receive.

Yet no, it is not for what he thus gives them that such souls love him most! It is rather because of the emotion which lends to his voice so touching an accent, it is because he too yearns as they do for something unattained by him. What an affinity for Christianity had this persecutor of the Christians! The effusion of Christianity, its relieving tears, its happy self-sacrifice, were the very element, one feels, for which his soul longed; they were near him, they brushed him, he touched them, he passed them by. One feels, too, that the Marcus Aurelius one reads must still have remained, even had Christianity been fully known to him, in a great measure himself; he would have been no Justin;—but how would Christianity have affected him? In what measure would it have changed him? Granted that he might have found, like the *Alogi* of modern times, in the most beautiful of the Gospels, the Gospel which has leavened Christendom most powerfully, the Gospel of St. John, too much Greek metaphysics, too much *gnosis;* granted that this Gospel might have looked too like what he knew already to be a total surprise to him: what, then, would he have said to the Sermon on the Mount, to the twenty-sixth chapter of St. Matthew? What would have become of his notions of the *exitiabilis superstitio,* of the "obstinacy of the Christians"? Vain question! Yet the greatest charm of Marcus Aurelius is that he makes us ask it. We see him wise, just, self-governed, tender, thankful, blameless; yet, with all this, agitated, stretching out his arms for something beyond,— *tendentemque manus ripae ulterioris amore.*

S T. A U G U S T I N E

[*354–430* A.D.]

ADOLPH HARNACK BELONGED TO THE LAST GENERATION OF THE GREAT NINETEENTH-century German scholars and scientists, men who, like Theodore Mommsen, Max Weber, Count Willamowitz Von Moellendorf, and Sigmund Freud, worked on a prodigious scale. When he died in 1930, Harnack left behind him a library of distinguished theological and historical scholarship, as well as many devoted and brilliant students. His great work, *The History of Dogma,* is characterized by massive erudition, a liberal spirit, and the high moral purpose of revealing what he felt was truly living in Christianity, its moral core and its message of love and forgiveness.

If such a book can be said to have a hero, it is St. Augustine, whom Harnack admired not for his contributions to dogma, but for the way in which his varied and even contradictory thought grew out of a profound moral and religious experience. This selection from his own one-volume abridgment of the longer history is a remarkable distillation of the thought and significance of a complex and voluminous thinker. It could have been produced only by a lifetime of study, reflection, and deep personal conviction.

English translation by Edwin Knox Mitchell, first published in 1893.

ADOLPH HARNACK

The World-Historical Position
of Augustine as Teacher of
the Church

THE ANCIENT CHURCH EXPOUNDED ITS THEOLOGY FROM THE CENTRES OF Christology and the doctrine of freedom (doctrine of morals); Augustine drew the two centres together. *The good became to him the axis for the contemplation of all blessings.* Moral good and redemptive good should include each other (*ipsa virtus et praemium virtutis*). He brought dogmatics down from the heavens; yet did not discard the old conception but amalgamated it with the new. In his interpretations of the symbol this union is most clearly manifest. Through his præ-Catholic development and conversion, then through his conflict with Donatism and Pelagianism, Christianity appeared to him in a new form; but inasmuch as he considered the symbol as the essence of doctrine, his conception of doctrine necessarily became complicated—a union of the old Catholic theology and of the old ecclesiastical scheme with his new thoughts on the doctrine of faith compressed into the frame of the symbol. This mixture of elements, which the Occidental Church has preserved until this day, subsequently caused contradictions and rendered the old dogma impressionless.

In detail the following discrepancies in the theology of Augustine are especially to be noted: (1) The discrepancies between symbol and Scripture.

Those who place Scripture above the symbol, as well as those who prescribe the opposite order, can refer to him. Augustine strengthened Biblicism and at the same time also the position of those ecclesiastics who with Tertullian refuted the Biblicists. (2) The discrepancy between the principle of Scripture and the principle of salvation. Augustine taught, on the one hand, that only the *substance* (*i.e.* salvation) is of importance in the Scriptures; yes, he advanced as far sometimes as that spiritualism which skips over the Scriptures; on the other hand, he could not rid himself of the thought that every word of the Scriptures is absolute revelation. (3) The discrepancy between his conceptions of the essence of religion; on the one hand, it is faith, love, hope; yet, on the other, knowledge and super-terrestrial, immortal life; it should aim to secure blessedness through grace, and again through the *amor intellectualis*. Faith as conceived by Paul and a non-cosmic mysticism contend for the primacy. (4) The discrepancy between the doctrine of predestined grace and a doctrine of grace that is essentially an ecclesiastical and sacramental doctrine. (5) Discrepancies within the principal lines of thought. Thus in the doctrine of grace the thought of the *gratia per (propter) Christum* not infrequently conflicts with the conception of a grace flowing independently from Christ out of the original being of God as the *summum bonum* and *summum esse*. Thus, in his ecclesiastical doctrine, the hierarchical-sacramental basal element is not reconciled with a liberal, universal view, such as originated with the apologists.

One can distinguish three planes in the theology of Augustine: The predestinarian, the soteriologic, and the plane of the authority and of the sacraments of the Church; but one would not do him justice, if one should describe these evaluations separately, for in his summary of the whole they are united. Just because his rich spirit embraced all these discrepancies and characteristically represented them as experiences, has he become *the father* of the Church of the Occident. He is the father of the Roman Church and of the Reformation, of Biblicists and of mystics; yes, even the Renaissance and modern empirical philosophy (psychology) are indebted to him. New *dogmas,* in the strict sense, he did not introduce. It was left to a very much later period to formulate strictly definite dogmas out of the transformation wrought by him in the old dogmatic material, *i.e.* the condemnation of Pelagianism and the new doctrine of the sacraments.

AUGUSTINE'S DOCTRINE OF THE FIRST AND LAST THINGS

The fear of the Lord is the beginning of wisdom: With the life of prayer Augustine united an inward contemplation which led him, the pupil of the Neo-Platonists and of Paul, to a new psychology and theology. He became the *"alter Aristoteles"* in making the inner life the starting-point for thoughts concerning the world. He first absolutely put away the näive-objective frame of mind and with it the antique-classical, at the same time, however, the remnants of the polytheistic view also. He was the first monotheistic theologian (in the strict sense of the word) among the Church fathers, since he lifted the Neo-Platonic philosophy above himself. Not unfamiliar with the realm of knowledge of the objective world, he yet wished to know but two things, *God* and the *soul;* for his skepticism had dissolved the world of external phenomena, but in the flight of these phenomena the facts of the inner life had, after painful struggles, remained to him as *facts*. Even if there exists no evil and no God, there still exists unquestionably the fear of evil. Out of this, *i.e.* through psychological analysis, one can find the soul and God and sketch a picture of the world. Hence the skeptic can arrive at the knowledge of truth, for which the marrow of the soul sighs.

The fundamental form of the life of the soul is the desire for happiness (*cupido, amor*) as a desire for blessedness. All inclinations are only developments of this fundamental form (as receptivity and as activity) and they are valid for the sphere of the spiritual life as well as for that of the sensuous. The will is connected with these inclinations, nevertheless it is a power rising above sensuous nature (Augustine is an indeterminist). *In concreto* it is indeed bound to the sensuous instincts, *i.e.* not free. Theoretical freedom of election becomes real freedom only when the *cupiditas* (*amor*) *boni* has become the ruling motive for the will, *i.e. only the good will is free.* Moral goodness and freedom of will coincide. The truly free will has its freedom in the impulse of the good (*beata necessitas boni*). This bondage is freedom, because it withdraws the will from the dominion of the lower instincts and realizes the destiny and disposition of man to be filled with true existence and life. In attachment to the good, therefore, is realized the higher *appetitus,* the true instinct of self-preservation in man; while he gradually brings about his own destruction, if he follows his lower instincts. For these lines of thought Augustine claimed strict validity, for he knew that every man, meditating about himself, must affirm them. With them Augustine united the results of the Neo-Platonic cosmological speculation; but the simple greatness of his living conception of God worked powerfully upon them and coerced the artificially gained elements of the doctrine of God again and again into the simplest confession: "The Lord of heaven and earth is love; he is the salvation of the soul; whom should ye fear"?

Through the Neo-Platonic speculation (through proof of the nothingness of phenomena and through progressive elimination of the lower spheres of the sensuous and conceivable) Augustine arrived at the conception of the one, unchangeable, eternal Being (*incorporea veritas, spiritalis substantia, lux incommutabilis*). At the same time this *summum esse* alone corresponds to the simplicity of the highest object of the soul's desire. This *summum esse* alone is in reality *the Being,* since every other being has the quality of non-being, and can indeed not exist but really perishes. But, on the other hand, it can also be conceived as the development of the sole Substance, as the radiant artistic expression of the latter, and in this conception the metaphysically dissolved phenomena and the interest therein recur in an æsthetic form. Yet this natural feeling is still only the establishing of the Augustinian conception. He does not surrender himself to it, but rather passes over at once to the observation, that the soul strives for this highest Being and seeks it in all lower good with indestructible, noble concupiscence; *yet after all it hesitates to seize the same.* Here a dreadful paradox presented itself to him, which he designates as *"monstrum,"* viz., *that the will does not actually want, what it wants, or rather what it seems to want.* Together with the whole weight of man's individual responsibility Augustine conceived this state of the case, which was ameliorated by no æsthetic consideration, yet at times was so smooth to him (the cosmos with light and shadow as the *"pulchrum,"* as the simile of the fulness of life of the universal One). *Hence metaphysics was transformed for him into ethics.* Through the feeling of responsibility, God (the *summum esse*) appeared to him as the *summum bonum;* and the selfish, individual life, which determines the will, as *the evil.* This *summum bonum* is not only the constant resting-place for the restless thinker, and the intoxicating joy of life for the life-loving mortal, but it is also an expression for the *shall-be,* for that which shall become the ruling fundamental motive of the will, for that which shall give to the will its freedom and therewith for the first time its power over the sphere of the natural, for that which shall free the indestructible inclination of man toward the good from the *misera necessitas peccandi*—expression of the *good.* Thus for him all inferences of the intellect and all eudemonistic wrappings dropped from the conception of the good to the ground. For this line of thought also he claimed general validity.

But still another experience now followed and it scorned all analysis. Yonder *good* not only confronted him as the "shall be," but he felt himself seized by it as *love* and lifted out of the misery of the monstrous contradiction of existence. Accordingly the conception of God received an entirely new meaning: The good which is able to do this, the Almighty, is Person, is Love. The *summum esse* is the holy good in Person, working upon the will as almighty Love. *Metaphysics and ethics are transformed into religion.* Evil is not only *privatio substantiae* and therefore not mere *privatio boni,* but godlessness (*privatio Dei*); the ontological defect in the creature existence and the moral defect in the good is a defect in the attitude of love toward God; but to possess God is everything, is being, good being, free-will and peace. Henceforth a stream of Divine thought flowed forth freely from Augustine. It is just as inherently natural to God to be *gratia,* imparting himself in love, as to be *causa causatrix non causata; man however lives by the grace of love.* That he—embarrassed by a monstrous existence, which points back to a serious fall into sin—can live only by grace, may still be explained; but that the grace of love really exists is a transcendent fact. Man does not arrive at freedom through independence as regards God, but through dependence upon him: Only that love which has been bestowed upon him by God renders man blessed and good.

In the detailed deductions of Augustine respecting God and the soul the notes of metaphysics, ethics and of the deepest Christian experience vibrate within one another. God is the only *"res,"* which may be enjoyed (*frui= alicui rei amore inhaerere propter se ipsam*), other things may only be used. This sounds Neo-Platonic, but it is resolved in a Christian sense into the thought: *fide, spe et caritate colendum deum.* God is *Person,* whom one can trust above all other things and whom one should love. The *fides quae per dilectionem operatur* becomes the sovereign expression of religion. The æsthetically grounded optimism, the subtle doctrine of emanation, the idea of the sole agency of God (doctrine of predestination), the representation of evil as the "non-existent" which limits the good, do not indeed entirely disappear, but they are joined in a peculiar manner with the representation of God as the Creator of mankind which has through its own fault become a *massa perditionis,* and of God as the Redeemer and *ordinator peccatorum.* The striving also after absolute knowledge and the conception of the Christian religion in accordance with the scheme of the apologists (rationalistic) never failed in Augustine, and the love of God which he felt was secure to him only under the authority of outward revelation, to which he obediently submitted; but in his religious thinking, in which the appreciation of the importance of history was indeed not so well developed as the capacity for psychological observation, the Christian spirit nevertheless ruled.

From his youth up Christ was the silent guiding principle of his soul. And the apparently purely philosophical deductions were in many ways influenced by the thought of him. All of Augustine's attempts to break through the iron plan of the immutability of God, and to discriminate between God, the world and the *ego,* are to be explained by the impression of history upon him, *i.e.* of Christ. Thus Christ appeared to him, the religious philosopher, more and more plainly as the *way,* the *power* and the *authority.* How often did he speak of revelation in general and mean only him! How often did he speak of Christ where his predecessors spoke of revelation in general! The speculative representation of the idea of the good and of its agency as love became a certainty to him only through the vision of Christ and through the authoritative proclamation of the Church respecting him. The *vision of Christ* was a new element, which he first (after Paul and Ignatius) again introduced. Just as his doctrine of the trinity received a new form through the conviction, experienced through faith, of the unity of God, although he adopted the old formulas, so also did his Christology, in spite of all adherence to tradition (rigid combating of Apollinaris), receive a new content through the preaching of Ambrose and his own experience. (1) In the first place as regards Christ the representation of his sublimity in his humility was of decisive importance to him, the actual verifying of the sentence, *omne bonum in humilitate perficitur* (the incarnation also he represented from this point of view); in this he began to strike the mediæval key-notes of Christology, (2) He laid the whole stress upon the possibility now won, that man, lying in the dust, can apprehend God since he has come near us in our lowliness (the Greek waits for an exaltation to be able to grasp God in Christ), (3) He construed not infrequently the personality of Christ also from the human soul of the Redeemer and he saw in the endowments of the same the great example of the *gratia praeveniens,* which made the man Jesus what he became, (4) He conceived the *man* Jesus as Mediator, as Sacrifice and Priest, through whom we have been reconciled to the Deity and redeemed, whose death, as the Church proclaims it, is the surest foundation of our faith in redemption. In all these respects Augustine introduced new ideas into the old dogma, joining them thereto indeed only insecurely and artificially. A new Christological formula he did not create; to him Christ became the rock of faith, since he knew that the influence of this Person had broken his pride and given him strength to believe in the love of God and to let himself be found by it. The living Christ is the truth, and he who is proclaimed by the Church, is the way and the authority.

The soul is guided by the *quae per dilectionem operatur* unto the *vita beata*. This is the blessed peace in the *vision* of God. Therefore *knowledge* still remains the aim of man. It is not the will that holds the primacy, but the intellect. Finally Augustine retained the vulgar Catholic form of thought which confines man in the hereafter to an adoring knowledge; in this life asceticism and contemplation answers to it (hence Augustine's defence of monasticism as against Jovinian). The kingdom of God, so far as it is earthly, is also perishable. The soul must be freed from the world of appearances, of similitudes and compulsory conduct. Nevertheless Augustine exerted indirectly a powerful influence upon the current eschatological ideas: (1) Virtue is not the highest good, but dependence upon God (in the representation of the decisive significance of the *merita* this point of view was indeed abandoned), (2) The priestly ascetic life should be a *spiritual* one; the magico-physical elements of Greek mysticism recede entirely (no cultus

mysticism), (3) In the thought, *"mihi adhaerere deo bonum est,"* intellectualism was broken down; the will received its due position, (4) Love remains
even the same in eternity as that which we possess in this life; therefore this
world and the other are still closely united, (5) If love remains also in the
other world, then intellectualism reappears in a modified form, (6) Not the
earthly life, but the earthly Church has a higher meaning; the latter is, so to
speak, the holy above all that is most holy, and it is a duty to build it up;
not a religion of a second order supersedes the religion, but ecclesiasticism,
the service of the Church as a moral agency for reforming society, as an
organism of the sacramental powers of love, of the good and of the right in
which Christ works, (7) Higher than all monasticism stand *fides, spes* and
caritas; hence the scheme of a dreary and egotistical contemplation is broken.
To be sure, Augustine succeeded in uniting in all directions, although indeed
with contradictions, the new lines of thought with the old.

D A N T E

[*1265–1321*]

THE LITERATURE ON DANTE IS EQUALED OR EXCEEDED ONLY BY THAT ON SHAKE-speare, and both range in quality from work of the highest excellence to strange productions by cipher experts and devotees of odd cults. It would be difficult to find a more beautifully written, sensitive introduction to Dante than this classic essay, which holds its place after more than fifty years. Santayana scarcely needs identification. His gifts as a thinker and master stylist particularly equipped him to discuss a great philosophical poet. His essay is rich in what the reader of Dante needs to know. It discusses Greek metaphysics, which in its medieval version provides the frame for the *Divine Comedy,* touches on symbolism and allegory, and raises a central problem of literary criticism: the nature and function of philosophical ideas in literature. This last problem has proved a formidable stumbling block to modern readers of Dante, for time has rendered his thought and belief perhaps more remote than that of any other poet of equal stature. This essay helps the reader understand the *Comedy* and penetrate through the surface to its enduring literary value.

From *Three Philosophical Poets* by George Santayana. Copyright 1910 by Harvard University Press, Cambridge, Mass., 1938 by George Santayana.

Dante

IN THE *Phædo* OF PLATO THERE IS AN INCIDENTAL PASSAGE OF SUPREME IN-
terest to the historian. It foreshadows, and accurately defines, the whole
transition from antiquity to the middle age, from naturalism to superna-
turalism, from Lucretius to Dante. Socrates, in his prison, is addressing
his disciples for the last time. The general subject is immortality; but
in a pause in the argument Socrates says: "In my youth . . . I heard
some one reading, as he said, from a book of Anaxagoras, that Reason was
the disposer and cause of all, and I was delighted at this notion, which appeared quite admirable, and I said to myself: 'If Reason is the disposer,
Reason will dispose all for the best, and put each particular in the best
place;' and I argued that if any desired to find out the cause of the generation
or destruction or existence of anything, he must find out what . . . was best
for that thing. . . . And I rejoiced to think that I had found in Anaxagoras
a teacher of the causes of existence such as I desired, and I imagined that he
would tell me first whether the earth is flat or round; and whichever was
true, he would proceed . . . to show the nature of the best, and show that
this was best; and if he said that the earth was in the centre [of the universe],
he would further explain that this position was the best, and I should be satis-

fied with the explanation given, and not want any other sort of cause. . . .
For I could not imagine that when he spoke of Reason as the disposer of
things, he would give any other account of their being, except that this was
best. . . . These hopes I would not have sold for a large sum of money, and I
seized the books and read them as fast as I could, in my eagerness to know
the better and the worse.

"What expectations I had formed and how grievously was I disappointed!
As I proceeded, I found my philosopher altogether forsaking Reason or any
other principle of order, but having recourse to air, and ether, and water,
and other eccentricities. . . . Thus one man makes a vortex all round, and
steadies the earth by the heaven; another gives the air as a support to the
earth, which is a sort of bread trough. Any power which in arranging them
as they are arranges them for the best never enters into their minds; and
instead of finding any superior strength in it, they rather expect to discover
another Atlas of the world who is stronger and more everlasting and more
containing than the good; of the obligatory and containing power of the
good they think nothing; and yet this is the principle which I would fain
learn if anyone would teach me."

Here we have the programme of a new philosophy. Things are to be
understood by their uses or purposes, not by their elements or antecedents;
as the fact that Socrates sits in his prison, when he might have escaped to
Euboea, is to be understood by his allegiance to his notion of what is best,
of his duty to himself and to his country, and not by the composition of his
bones and muscles. Such reasons as we give for our actions, such grounds as
might move the public assembly to decree this or that, are to be given in
explanation of the order of nature. The world is a work of reason. It must be
interpreted, as we interpret the actions of a man, by its motives. And these
motives we must guess, not by a fanciful dramatic mythology, such as the
poets of old had invented, but by a conscientious study of the better and the
worse in the conduct of our own lives. For instance, the highest occupation,
according to Plato, is the study of philosophy; but this would not be possible
for man if he had to be continually feeding, like a grazing animal, with its
nose to the ground. Now, to obviate the necessity of eating all the time, long
intestines are useful; therefore the cause of long intestines is the study of
philosophy. Again, the eyes, nose, and mouth are in the front of the head,
because (says Plato) the front is the nobler side,—as if the back would not
have been the nobler side (and the front side) had the eyes, nose, and
mouth been there! This method is what Molière ridicules in *Le Malade
Imaginaire,* when the chorus sings that opium puts people to sleep because it
has a dormitive virtue, the nature of which is to make the senses slumber.

All this is ridiculous physics enough; but Plato knew—though he forgot sometimes—that his physics were playful. What it is important for us now to remember is rather that, under this childish or metaphorical physics, there is a serious morality. After all, the use of opium is that it is a narcotic; no matter why, physically, it is one. The use of the body *is* the mind, whatever the origin of the body may be. And it seems to dignify and vindicate these uses to say that they are the "causes" of the organs that make them possible. What is true of particular organs or substances is true of the whole frame of nature. Its use is to serve the good—to make life, happiness, and virtue possible. Therefore, speaking in parables, Plato says with his whole school: Discover the right principle of action, and you will have discovered the ruling force in the universe. Evoke in your rapt aspiration the essence of a supreme good, and you will have understood why the spheres revolve, why the earth is fertile, and why mankind suffers and exists. Observation must yield to dialectic; political art must yield to aspiration.

It took many hundred years for the revolution to work itself out; Plato had a prophetic genius, and looked away from what he was (for he was a Greek) to what mankind was to become in the next cycle of civilization. In Dante the revolution is complete, not merely intellectually (for it had been completed intellectually long before, in the Neoplatonists and the Fathers of the Church), but complete morally and poetically, in that all the habits of the mind and all the sanctions of public life had been assimilated to it. There had been time to reinterpret everything, obliterating the natural lines of cleavage in the world, and substituting moral lines of cleavage for them. Nature was a compound of ideal purposes and inert matter. Life was a conflict between sin and grace. The environment was a battle-ground between a host of angels and a legion of demons. The better and the worse had actually become, as Socrates desired, the sole principles of understanding.

Having become Socratic, the thinking part of mankind devoted all its energies henceforward to defining good and evil in all their grades, and in their ultimate essence; a task which Dante brings to a perfect conclusion. So earnestly and exclusively did they speculate about moral distinctions that they saw them in almost visible shapes, as Plato had seen his ideas. They materialized the terms of their moral philosophy into existing objects and powers. The highest good—in Plato still chiefly a political ideal, the aim of policy and art—became God, the creator of the world. The various stages or elements of perfection became persons in the Godhead, or angelic intelligences, or aerial demons, or lower types of the animal soul. Evil was identified with matter. The various stages of imperfection were ascribed to the grossness of various bodies, which weighted and smothered the spark of divinity that animated them. This spark, however, might be released; then it would fly up again to its parent fire and a soul would be saved.

This philosophy was not a serious description of nature or evolution; but it was a serious judgment upon them. The good, the better, the best, had been discerned; and a mythical bevy of powers, symbolizing these degrees of excellence, had been first talked of and then believed in. Myth, when another man has invented it, can pass for history; and when this man is a Plato, and has lived long ago, it can pass for revelation. In this way moral values came to be regarded as forces working in nature. But if they worked in nature, which was a compound of evil matter and perfect form, they must exist outside: for the ideal of excellence beckons from afar; it is what we pine for and are not. The forces that worked in nature were accordingly supernatural virtues, dominations, and powers; each natural thing had its supernatural incubus, a guardian angel, or a devil that possessed it. The supernatural—that is, something moral or ideal regarded as a power and an existence—was all about us. Everything in the world was an effect of something beyond the world; everything in life was a step to something beyond life.

Into this system Christianity fitted easily. It enriched it by adding miraculous history to symbolic cosmology. The Platonists had conceived a cosmos in which there were higher and lower beings, marshalled in concentric circles, around this vile but pivotal lump of earth. The Christians supplied a dramatic action for which the stage seemed admirably fitted, a story in which the whole human race, or the single soul, passed successively through these higher and lower stages. There had been a fall, and there might be a salvation. In a sense, even this conception of descent from the good, and ascent towards it again, was Platonic. According to the Platonists, the good eternally shed its vital influence, like light, and received (though unawares and without increase of excellence to itself) reflected rays that, in the form of love and thought, reverted to it from the ends of the universe. But according to the Platonist this radiation of life and focusing of aspiration were both perpetual. The double movement was eternal. The history of the world was monotonous; or rather the world had no significant history, but only a movement like that of a fountain playing for ever, or like the circulation of water that is always falling from the clouds in rain and always rising again in vapour. This fall, or emanation of the world from the deity, was the origin of evil for the Platonists; evil consisted merely in finitude, materiality, or otherness from God. If anything besides God was to exist, it had to be imperfect; instability and conflict were essential to finitude and to existence. Salvation, on the other hand, was the return current of aspiration on the part of the creature to revert to its source; an aspiration which was expressed in various types of being, fixed in the eternal,—types which led up, like the steps of a temple, to the ineffable good at the top.

In the Christian system this cosmic circulation became only a figure or symbol expressing the true creation, the true fall, and the true salvation; all three being really episodes in a historical drama, occurring only once. The material world was only a scene, a stage-setting, designed expressly to be appropriate for the play; and this play was the history of mankind, especially of Israel and of the Church. The persons and events of this history had a philosophic import; each played some part in a providential plan. Each illustrated creation, sin, and salvation in some degree, and on some particular level.

The Jews had never felt uncomfortable at being material; even in the other world they hoped to remain so, and their immortality was a resurrection of the flesh. It did not seem plausible to them that this excellent frame of things should be nothing but a faint, troubled, and unintended echo of the good. On the contrary, they thought this world so good, intrinsically, that they were sure God must have made it expressly, and not by an unconscious effluence of his virtue, as the Platonists had believed. Their wonder at the power and ingenuity of the deity reached its maximum when they thought of him as the cunning contriver of nature, and of themselves. Nevertheless the work seemed to show some imperfections; indeed, its moral excellence was potential rather than actual, a suggestion of what might be, rather than an accomplished fact. And so, to explain the unexpected flaws in a creation which they thought essentially good, they put back at the beginning of things an experience they had daily in the present, namely, that trouble springs from bad conduct.

The Jews were intent watchers of fortune and of its vicissitudes. The careers of men were their meditation by day and by night; and it takes little attention to perceive that frivolity, indifference, knavery, and debauchery do not make for well-being in this world. And like other hard-pressed peoples, the ancient Jews had a pathetic admiration for safety and plenty. How little they must have known these things, to think of them so rapturously and so poetically! Not merely their personal prudence, but their corporate and religious zeal made them abhor that bad conduct which defeated prosperity. It was not mere folly, but wickedness and the abomination of desolation. With the lessons of conduct continually in mind, they framed the theory that all suffering, and even death, were the wages of sin. Finally they went so far as to attribute evil in all creation to the casual sin of a first man, and to the taint of it transmitted to his decendants; thus passing over the suffering and death of all creatures that are not human with an indifference that would have astonished the Hindoos.

The imperfection of things, in the Hebraic view, was due to accidents in their operation; not, as in the Platonic view, to their esential separation from their source and their end. It is in harmony with this that salvation too should come by virtue of some special act, like the incarnation or death of Christ. Just so, the Jews had conceived salvation as a revival of their national existence and greatness, to be brought about by the patience and fidelity of the elect, with tremendous miracles supervening to reward these virtues.

Thus their conception of the fall and of the redemption was historical. And this was a great advantage to a man of imagination inheriting their system; for the personages and the miracles that figured in their sacred histories afforded a rich subject for fancy to work upon, and for the arts to depict. The patriarchs from Adam down, the kings and prophets, the creation, Eden, the deluge, the deliverance out of Egypt, the thunders and the law of Sinai, the temple, the exile—all this and much more that fills the Bible was a rich fund, a familiar tradition living in the Church, on which Dante could draw, as he drew at the same time from the parallel classic tradition which he also inherited. To lend all these Biblical persons and incidents a philosophical dignity he had only to fit them, as the Fathers of the Church had done, into the Neoplatonic cosmology, or, as the doctors of his own time were doing, into the Aristotelian ethics.

So interpreted, sacred history acquired for the philosopher a new importance besides that which it had seemed to have to Israel in exile, or to the Christian soul conscious of sin. Every episode became the symbol for some moral state or some moral principle. Every preacher in Christendom, as he repeated his homily on the gospel of the day, was invited to rear a structure of spiritual interpretations upon the literal sense of the narrative, which nevertheless he was always to hold and preserve as a foundation for the others. In a world made by God for the illustration of his glory, things and events, though real, must be also symbolical; for there is intention and propriety behind them. The creation, the deluge, the incarnation, crucifixion, and resurrection of Christ, the coming of the Holy Ghost with flames of fire and the gift of tongues, were all historical facts. The Church was heir to the chosen people; it was an historic and political institution, with a destiny in this world, in which all her children should share, and for which they should fight. At the same time all those facts were mysteries and sacraments for the private soul; they were channels for the same moral graces that were embodied in the order of the heavenly spheres, and in the types of moral life on earth. Thus the Hebrew tradition brought to Dante's mind the consciousness of a providential history, a great earthly task,—to be transmitted from generation to generation,—and a great hope. The Greek tradition brought him natural and moral philosophy. These contributions, joined together, had made Christian theology.

Although this theology was the guide to Dante's imagination, and his general theme, yet it was not his only interest; or rather he put into the framework of orthodox theology theories and visions of his own, fusing all into one moral unity and one poetical enthusiasm. The fusion was perfect between the personal and the traditional elements. He threw politics and love into the melting-pot, and they, too, lost their impurities and were refined into a philosophic religion. Theology became, to his mind, the guardian of patriotism, and, in a strangely literal sense, the angel of love.

The political theory of Dante is a sublime and largely original one. It suffers only from its extreme ideality, which makes it inapplicable, and has caused it to be studied less than it deserves.

A man's country, in the modern sense, is something that arose yesterday, that is constantly changing its limits and its ideals; it is something that cannot last for ever. It is the product of geographical and historical accidents. The diversities between our different nations are irrational; each of them has the same right, or want of right, to its peculiarities. A man who is just and reasonable must nowadays, so far as his imagination permits, share the patriotism of the rivals and enemies of his country,—a patriotism as inevitable and pathetic as his own. Nationality being an irrational accident, like sex or complexion, a man's allegiance to his country must be conditional, at least if he is a philosopher. His patriotism has to be subordinated to rational allegiance to such things as justice and humanity.

Very different was the situation in Dante's case. For him the love of country could be something absolute, and at the same time something reasonable, deliberate, and moral. What he found claiming his allegiance was a political body quite ideal, providential, and universal. This political body had two heads, like the heraldic eagle,—the pope and the emperor. Both were, by right, universal potentates; both should have their seat in Rome; and both should direct their government to the same end, although by different means and in different spheres. The pope should watch over the faith and discipline of the Church. He should bear witness, in all lands and ages, to the fact that life on earth was merely a preliminary to existence in the other world, and should be a preparation for that. The emperor, on the other hand, should guard peace and justice everywhere, leaving to free cities or princes the regulation of local affairs. These two powers had been established by God through special miracles and commissions. An evident providential design, culminating in them, ran through all history.

To betray or resist these divine rights, or to confound them, was accordingly a sin of the first magnitude. The evils from which society suffered were the consequence of such transgressions. The pope had acquired temporal power, which was alien to his purely spiritual office; besides, he had become a tool of the French king, who was (what no king should be) at war with the emperor, and rebellious against the supreme imperial authority; indeed, the pope had actually been seen to abandon Rome for Avignon,—an act which was a sort of satanic sacrament, the outward sign of an inward disgrace. The emperor, in his turn, had forgotten that he was King of the Romans and Caesar, and was fond of loitering in his native Germany, among its forests and princelings, as if the whole world were not by right his country, and the object of his solicitude.

And here the larger, theoretical patriotism of Dante, as a Catholic and a Roman, passed into his narrower and actual patriotism as a Florentine. Had Florence been true to its duties and worthy of its privileges, under the double authority of the Church and the Empire? Florence was a Roman colony. Had it maintained the purity of its Roman stock, and a Roman simplicity and austerity in its laws? Alas, Etruscan immigrants had contaminated its blood, and this taint was responsible, Dante thought, for the prevalent corruption of manners. All that has made Florence great in the history of the world was then only just beginning,—its industry, refinements, arts, and literature. But to Dante that budding age seemed one of decadence and moral ruin. He makes his ancestor, the crusader Cacciaguida, praise the time when the narrow circuit of the walls held only one-fifth of its later inhabitants. "Then the city abided in peace, sober and chaste." The women plied the distaff, or rocked the cradle, and prattled to their children of the heroic legends of Troy, Fiesole, and Rome. A woman could turn from her glass with her face unpainted; she wore no girdle far more deserving of admiration than her own person. The birth of a daughter did not frighten a good burgher; her dowry would not have to be excessive, nor her marriage premature. No houses were empty, their masters being in exile; none were disgraced by unmentionable orgies. This was not all; for if luxury was a great curse to Florence, faction was a greater. Florence, an imperial city, far from assisting in the restitution of the emperors to their universal rights, had fought against them traitorously, in alliance with the French invader and the usurping pontiff. It had thus undermined the only possible foundation of its own peace and dignity.

These were the theoretical sorrows that loomed behind the personal sorrows of Dante in his poverty and exile. They helped him to pour forth the intense bitterness of his heart with the breath of prophetic invective. They made his hatred of the actual popes and of the actual Florence so much fervid zeal for what the popes and Florence ought to have been. His political passions and political hopes were fused with a sublime political ideal; that fusion sublimated them, and made it possible for the expression of them to rise into poetry.

Here is one iron string on which Dante played, and which gave a tragic strength to his music. He recorded the villainies of priests, princes, and peoples. He upbraided them for their infidelity to the tasks assigned to them by God,—tasks which Dante conceived with a Biblical definiteness and simplicity. He lamented the consequences of this iniquity, wasted provinces, corrupted cities, and the bodies of heroes rolling unburied down polluted streams. These vigorous details were exalted by the immense significance that Dante infused into them. His ever-present definite ideal quickened his eye for the ebb and flow of things, rendered the experience of them singly more poignant, and the vision of them together more sustained and cumulative. Dante read contemporary Italy as the Hebrew prophets read the signs of their times; and whatever allowance our critical judgment may make for generous illusions on the part of either, there can be no doubt that their wholeness of soul, and the prophetic absoluteness of their judgments, made their hold on particular facts very strong, and their sense for impending weal or woe quite overpowering.

Nor does it seem that at bottom Dante's political philosophy, any more than that of the Hebrew prophets, missed the great causes and the great aims of human progress. Behind mythical and narrow conceptions of history, he had a true sense for the moral principles that really condition our well-being. A better science need subtract nothing from the insight he had into the difference between political good and evil. What in his day seemed a dream—that mankind should be one great commonwealth—is now obvious to the idealist, the socialist, the merchant. Science and trade are giving, in a very different form, to be sure, a practical realization to that idea. And the other half of his theory, that of the Catholic Church, is maintained literally by that church itself to this day; and the outsider might see in that ideal of a universal spiritual society a symbol or premonition of the right of the mind to freedom from legal compulsions, or of the common allegiance of honest minds to science, and to their common spiritual heritage and destiny.

On the other hand, the sting of Dante's private wrongs, like the enthusiasm of his private loves, lent a wonderful warmth and clearness to the great objects of his imagination. We are too often kept from feeling great things greatly for want of power to assimilate them to the little things which we feel keenly and sincerely. Dante had, in this respect, the art of a Platonic lover: he could enlarge the object of his passion, and keep the warmth and ardour of it undiminished. He had been banished unjustly—*Florentinus exul immeritus,* he liked to call himself. That injustice rankled, but it did not fester, in his heart; for his indignation spread to all wrong, and thundered against Florence, Europe, and mankind, in that they were corrupt and perfidious. Dante had loved. The memory of that passion remained also, but it did not degenerate into sentimentality; for his adoration passed to a larger object and one less accidental. His love had been a spark of that "love which moves the sun and the other stars." He had known, in that revelation, the secret of the universe. The spheres, the angels, the sciences, were henceforth full of sweetness, comfort, and light.

Of this Platonic expansion of emotion, till it suffuses all that deserves to kindle it, we have a wonderful version in Dante's *Vita Nuova*. This book, on the surface, is an account of Dante's meeting, at the age of nine, with Beatrice, a child even a little younger; of another meeting with her at the age of eighteen; of an overwhelming mystic passion which the lover wished to keep secret, so much so that he feigned another attachment as a blind; of a consequent estrangement; and of the death of Beatrice, whereupon the poet resolved not to speak publicly of her again, until he could praise her in such wise as no woman had ever been praised before.

This story is interspersed with poems of the most exquisite delicacy, both in sentiment and in versification. They are dreamlike, allegorical, musical meditations, ambiguous in their veiled meanings, but absolutely clear and perfect in their artful structure, like a work of tracery and stained glass, geometrical, mystical, and tender. A singular limpidity of accent and image, a singular naïveté, is strangely combined in these pieces with scholastic distinctions and a delight in hiding and hinting, as in a charade.

The learned will dispute for ever on the exact basis and meaning of these confessions of Dante. The learned are perhaps not those best fitted to solve the problem. It is a matter for literary tact and sympathetic imagination. It must be left to the delicate intelligence of the reader, if he has it; and if he has not, Dante does not wish to open his heart to him. His enigmatical manner is his protection against the intrusion of uncongenial minds.

Without passing beyond the sphere of learned criticism, I think we may say this: the various interpretations, in this matter, are not mutually exclusive. Symbolism and literalness, in Dante's time, and in his practice, are simultaneous. For instance, in any history of mediaeval philosophy you may read that a great subject of dispute in those days was the question whether universal terms or natures, such as man, or humanity, existed before the particulars, in the particulars, or after the particulars, by abstraction of what was common to them all. Now, this matter was undoubtedly much disputed about; but there is one comprehensive and orthodox solution, which represents the true mind of the age, above the peculiar hobbies or heresies of individuals. This solution is that universal terms or natures exist before the particulars, *and* in the particulars, *and* after the particulars: for God, before he made the world, knew how he intended to make it, and had eternally in his mind the notions of a perfect man, horse, etc., after which the particulars were to be modelled, or to which, in case of accident, they were to be restored, either by the healing and recuperative force of nature, or by the ministrations of grace. But universal terms or natures existed also *in* the particulars, since the particulars illustrated them, shared in them, and were what they were by virtue of that participation. Nevertheless, the universals existed also after the particulars: for the discursive mind of man, surveying the variety of natural things, could not help noticing and abstracting the common types that often recur in them; and this *ex post facto* idea, in the human mind, is a universal term also. To deny any of the three theories, and not to see their consistency, is to miss the mediaeval point of view, which, in every sense of the word, was Catholic.

Just such a solution seems to be natural in the case of Beatrice. We have it on independent documentary evidence that in Dante's time there actually lived in Florence a certain Bice Portinari; and there are many incidents in the *Vita Nuova* and in the *Commedia* which hardly admit of an allegorical interpretation; such as the death of Beatrice, and especially that of her father, on which occasion Dante writes a sympathetic poem. I can see no reason why this lady, as easily as any other person, should not have called forth the dreamful passion of our poet. That he had loved some one is certain. Most people have; and why should Dante, in particular, have found the language of love a natural veil for his philosophy, if the passion and the language of love had not been his mother-tongue? The language of love is no doubt usual in the allegories of mystics, and was current in the conventional poetry of Dante's time; but mystics themselves are commonly crossed or potential lovers; and the troubadours harped on the string of love simply because it was the most responsive string in their own natures, and that which could most easily be made to vibrate in their hearers. Dante was not less sensitive than the average man of his generation; and if he followed the fashion of minstrels and mystics, it was because he had shared their disposition. The beautiful, the unapproachable, the divine, had passed before him in some visible form; it matters nothing whether this vision came once only, and in the shape of the actual Beatrice, or continuously, and in every shape through which a divine influence may seem to come to a poet. No one would deserve this name of poet—and who deserves it more than Dante?—if real sights and sounds never impressed him; and he would hardly deserve it either, if they impressed him only physically, and for what they are in themselves. His sensibility creates his ideal.

If to deny the existence of an historical Beatrice seems violent and gratuitous, it would be a much worse misunderstanding not to perceive that Beatrice is *also* a symbol. On one occasion, as we read in the *Vita Nuova,* Dante found himself, in a church, in the presence of Beatrice. His eyes were inevitably fixed upon her; but as he wished to conceal his profound passion from the gossiping crowd, he chose another lady, who happened to stand in the direct line of vision between him and Beatrice, and pretended to be gazing at her, in reality looking beyond her to Beatrice. This intervening lady, *la donna gentile,* became the screen to his true love. But his attentions to her were so assiduous that they were misinterpreted. Beatrice herself observed them, and thinking he was going too far and not with an honourable purpose, showed her displeasure by refusing to greet him as he passed. This sounds real and earthly enough: but what is our surprise when we read expressly, in the *Convito,* that the *donna gentile,* the screen to Dante's true love, is philosophy. If the *donna gentile* is philosophy, the *donna gentilissima,* Beatrice, must be something of the same sort, only nobler. She must be theology, and theology Beatrice undoubtedly is. Her very name is played upon, if not selected, to mean that she is what renders blessed, what shows the path of salvation.

Now the scene in the church becomes an allegory throughout. The young Dante, we are given to understand, was at heart a religious and devout soul, looking for the highest wisdom. But intervening between his human reason and revealed truth (which he really was in love with, and wished to win and to understand) he found philosophy or, as we should say, science. To science he gave his preliminary attention; so much so that the mysteries of theology were momentarily obscured in his mind; and his faith, to his great sorrow, refused to salute him as he passed. He had fallen into materialistic errors; he had interpreted the spots on the moon as if they could be due to physical, not to Socratic, causes; and his religious philosophy had lost its warmth, even if his religious faith had not actually been endangered. It is certain, then, that Beatrice, besides being a woman, was also a symbol.

But this is not the end. If Beatrice is a symbol for theology, theology itself is not final. It, too, is an avenue, an interpretation. The eyes of Beatrice reflect a supernal light. It is the ineffable vision of God, the beatific vision, that alone can make us happy and be the reason and the end of our loves and our pilgrimages.

A supreme ideal of peace and perfection which moves the lover, and which moves the sky, is more easily named than understood. In the last canto of the *Paradiso,* where Dante is attempting to describe the beatific vision, he says many times over that our notion of this ideal must be vague and inadequate. The value of the notion to a poet or a philosopher does not lie in what it contains positively, but in the attitude which it causes him to assume towards real experience. Or perhaps it would be better to say that to have an ideal does not mean so much to have any image in the fancy, any Utopia more or less articulate, but rather to take a consistent moral attitude towards all the things of this world, to judge and coördinate our interests, to establish a hierarchy of goods and evils, and to value events and persons, not by a casual personal impression or instinct, but according to their real nature and tendency. So understood, an ultimate ideal is no mere vision of the philosophical dreamer, but a powerful and passionate force in the poet and the orator. It is the voice of his love or hate, of his hope or sorrow, idealizing, challenging, or condemning the world.

It is here that the feverish sensibility of the young Dante stood him in good stead; it gave an unprecedented vigour and clearness to his moral vision; it made him the classic poet of hell and of heaven. At the same time, it helped to make him an upright judge, a terrible accuser, of the earth. Everything and everybody in his day and generation became to him, on account of his intense loyalty to his inward vision, an instance of divine graciousness or of devilish perversity. Doubtless this keenness of soul was not wholly due to the gift of loving, or to the discipline of love; it was due in part also to pride, to resentment, to theoretical prejudices. But figures like that of Francesca di Rimini and Manfred, and the light and rapture vibrating through the whole *Paradiso,* could hardly have been evoked by a merely irritated genius. The background and the starting-point of everything in Dante is the *intelletto d'amore,* the genius of love.

Everybody has heard that God is love and that love makes the world go round; and those who have traced this latter notion back to its source in Aristotle may have some notion of what it means. It means, as we saw in the beginning, that we should not try to explain motion and life by their natural antecedents, for these run back *in infinitum.* We should explain motion and life rather by their purpose or end, by that unrealized ideal which moving and living things seem to aspire to, and may be said to love. What justifies itself is not any fact or law; for why should these not have been different? What justifies itself is what is good, what is as it ought to be. But things in motion, Aristotle conceived, declare, as it were, that they are not satisfied, and ought to be in some different condition. They look to a fulfilment which is as yet ideal. This fulfilment, if it included motion and life, could include them inwardly only; it would consist in a sustained activity, never lapsing nor suffering change. Such an activity is the unchanging goal towards which life advances and by which its different stages are measured. But since the purpose of things, and not their natural causes, is that which explains them, we may call this eventual activity their reason for being. It will be their unmoved mover.

But how, we may ask,—how can the unchanging, the ideal, the eventual, initiate anything or determine the disposition and tendency of what actually lives and moves? The answer, or rather the impossibility of giving an answer, may be expressed in a single word: magic. It is magic when a good or interesting result, because it would prove good or interesting, is credited with marshalling the conditions and evoking the beings that are to realize it. It is natural that I should be hungry, and natural that there should be things suitable for me to eat—for otherwise I should not be hungry long; but if my hunger, in case it is sharp enough, should be able of itself to produce the food it calls for, that would be magic. Nature would be evoked by the incantations of the will.

I do not forget that Aristotle, with Dante after him, asserts that the goal of life is a separate being already existing, namely, the mind of God, eternally realizing what the world aspires to. The influence of this mind, however, upon the world is no less magical than would be that of a non-existent ideal. For its operation is admittedly not transitive or physical. It itself does not change in working. No virtue leaves it; it does not, according to Aristotle and Plotinus, even know that it works. Indeed, it works only because other things are disposed to pursue it as their ideal; let things keep this disposition, and they will pursue and frame their ideal no less if it nowhere has an actual existence, than if by chance it exists elsewhere in its own person. It works only in its capacity of ideal; therefore, even if it exists, it works only by magic. The matter beneath feels the spell of its presence, and catches something of its image, as the waves of the sea might receive and reflect tremblingly the light shed by the moon. The world accordingly is moved and vivified in every fibre by magic, by the magic of the goal to which it aspires.

But this magic, on earth, bore the name of love. The life of the world was a love, produced by the magic attraction of a good it has never possessed and, so long as it remains a world, is incapable of possessing. Actual things were only suggestions of what the elements in that ulterior existence ought to be: they were mere symbols. The acorn was a mere prophecy—an existing symbol —for the ideal oak; because when the acorn falls into good ground it will be corrupted, but the idea of the oak will arise and be manifested in its place. The acorn was a sort of reliquary in which the miraculous power of the idea was somehow enshrined. In the vulgar attribution of causes we, like Anaxagoras, resemble a superstitious relic-worshipper who should forget that the intercession and merits of the saint really work the miracle, and should attribute it instead to the saint's bones and garments in their material capacity. Similarly, we should attribute the power which things exerted over us, not to the rarer or denser substance, but to the eternal ideas that they existed by expressing, and existed to express. Things merely localized—like the saint's relics—the influences which flowed to us from above. In the world of values they were mere symbols, accidental channels for divine energy; and since divine energy, by its magic assimilation of matter, had created these things, in order to express itself, they were symbols altogether not merely in their use, but in their origin and nature.

A mind persuaded that it lives among things that, like words, are essentially significant, and that what they signify is the magic attraction, called love, which draws all things after it, is a mind poetic in its intuition, even if its language be prose. The science and philosophy of Dante did not have to be put into verse in order to become poetry: they were poetry fundamentally and in their essence. When Plato and Aristotle, following the momentous precept of Socrates, decreed that observation of nature should stop and a moral interpretation of nature should begin, they launched into the world a new mythology, to take the place of the Homeric one which was losing its authority. The power the poets had lost of producing illusion was possessed by these philosophers in a high degree; and no one was ever more thoroughly under their spell than Dante. He became to Platonism and Christianity what Homer had been to Paganism; and if Platonism and Christianity, like Paganism, should ever cease to be defended scientifically, Dante will keep the poetry and wisdom of them alive; and it is safe to say that later generations will envy more than they will despise his philosophy. When the absurd controversies and factious passions that in some measure obscure the nature of this system have completely passed away, no one will think of reproaching Dante with his bad science, and bad history, and minute theology. These will not seem blemishes in his poetry, but integral parts of it.

A thousand years after Homer, Alexandrian critics were expounding his charming myths as if they were a revealed treatise of physics and morals. A thousand years after Dante we may hope that his conscientious vision of the universe, where all is love, magic, and symbolism, may charm mankind exclusively as poetry. So conceived, the *Divine Comedy* marks high noon in that long day-dream of which Plato's dialogues mark the beginning: a pause of two thousand years in the work of political reason, during which the moral imagination spun out of itself an allegorical philosophy, as a boy, kept at home during a rainy day with books too hard and literal for his years, might spin his own romance out of his father's histories, and might define, with infantile precision, his ideal lady-love, battles, and kingdoms. The middle age saw the good in a vision. It is for the new age to translate those delightful symbols into the purposes of manhood.

In a letter which tradition assigns to Dante, addressed to his protector, Cangrande della Scala, lord of Verona and Vicenza, are these words about the *Divine Comedy:* "The subject of the whole work, taken merely in its literal sense, is the state of souls after death, considered simply as a fact. But if the work is understood in its allegorical intention, the subject of it is man, according as, by his deserts and demerits in the use of his free will, he is justly open to rewards and punishments." This by no means exhausts, however, the significations which we may look for in a work of Dante's. How many these may be is pointed out to us in the same letter, and illustrated by the beginning of the one hundred and fourteenth Psalm: "When Israel went out of Egypt, the house of Jacob from a people of strange language; Judah was his sanctuary, and Israel his dominion." Here, Dante tells us, "if we look to the *letter* only, what is conveyed to us is the deliverance of the children of Israel out of Egypt in the time of Moses; if we look to the *allegory* of it, what is signified is our redemption accomplished through Christ; if we consider the *moral sense,* what is signified is the conversion of the soul from her present grief and wretchedness to a state of grace; and if we consider the *anagogical sense* [that is, the revelation contained concerning our highest destiny], what is signified is the passing of the sanctified soul from the bondage of earthly corruption to the freedom of everlasting glory."

When people brooded so much over a simple text as to find all these meanings in it, we may expect that their own works, when meant to be profound, should have stage above stage of allegorical application. So in the first canto of the *Inferno* we find a lion that keeps Dante from approaching a delectable mountain; and this lion, besides what he is in the landscape of the poem, is a symbol for pride or power in general, for the king of France in particular, and for whatever political ambitions in Dante's personal life may have robbed him of happiness or distracted him from faith and from piety. Thus, throughout the *Divine Comedy,* meaning and meaning lurk beneath the luminous pictures; and the poem, besides being a description of the other world, and of the rewards and punishment meted out to souls, is a dramatic view of human passions in this life; a history of Italy and of the world; a theory of Church and State; the autobiography of an exile; and the confessions of a Christian, and of a lover, conscious of his sins and of the miracle of divine grace that intervenes to save him.

The subject-matter of the *Divine Comedy* is accordingly the moral universe in all its levels,—romantic, political, religious. To present these moral facts in a graphic way, the poet performed a double work of imagination. First he chose some historical personage that might plausibly illustrate each condition of the soul. Then he pictured this person in some characteristic and symbolic attitude of mind and of body, and in an appropriate, symbolic environment. To give material embodiment to moral ideas by such a method would nowadays be very artificial, and perhaps impossible; but in Dante's time everything was favourable to the attempt. We are accustomed to think of goods and evils as functions of a natural life, sparks struck out in the chance shock of men with things or with one another. For Dante, it was a matter of course that moral distinctions might be discerned, not merely as they arise incidentally in human experience, but also, and more genuinely, as they are displayed in the order of creation. The Creator himself was a poet producing allegories.

The material world was a parable which he had built out in space, and ordered to be enacted. History was a great charade. The symbols of earthly poets are words or images; the symbols of the divine poet were natural things and the fortunes of men. They had been devised for a purpose; and this purpose, as the Koran, too, declares, had been precisely to show forth the great difference there is in God's sight between good and evil.

In Platonic cosmology, the concentric spheres were bodies formed and animated by intelligences of various orders. The nobler an intelligence, the more swift and outward, or higher, was the sphere it moved; whence the identification of "higher" with better, which survives, absurdly, to this day. And while Dante could not attribute literal truth to his fancies about hell, purgatory, and heaven, he believed that an actual heaven, purgatory, and hell had been fashioned by God on purpose to receive souls of varying deserts and complexions; so that while the poet's imagination, unless it reëchoed divine revelation, was only human and not prophetic, yet it was a genuine and plausible imagination, moving on the lines of nature, and anticipating such things as experience might very well realize. Dante's objectification of morality, his art of giving visible forms and local habitations to ideal virtues and vices, was for him a thoroughly serious and philosophical exercise. God had created nature and life on that very principle. The poet's method repeated the magic of Genesis. His symbolical imagination mirrored this symbolical world; it was a sincere anticipation of fact, no mere laboured and wilful allegory.

This situation has a curious consequence. Probably for the first and last time in the history of the world a classification worked out by a systematic moralist guided the vision of a great poet. Aristotle had distinguished, named, and classified the various virtues, with their opposites. But observe: if the other world was made on purpose—as it was—to express and render palpable those moral distinctions which were eternal, and to express and render them palpable in great detail, with all their possible tints and varieties; and if Aristotle had correctly classified moral qualities, as he had—then it follows that Aristotle (without knowing it) must have supplied the ground-plan, as it were, of hell and of heaven. Such was Dante's thought. With Aristotle's *Ethics* open before him, with a supplementary hint, here and there, drawn from the catechism, and with an ingrained preference (pious and almost philosophic) for the number three and its multiples, he needed not to voyage without a chart. The most visionary of subjects, life after death, could be treated with scientific soberness and deep sincerity. This vision was to be no wanton dream. It was to be a sober meditation, a philosophical prophecy, a probable drama,—the most poignant, terrible, and consoling of all possible truths.

The good—this was the fundamental thought of Aristotle and of all Greek ethics,—the good is the end at which nature aims. The demands of life cannot be radically perverse, since they are the judges of every excellence. No man, as Dante says, could hate his own soul; he could not at once be, and contradict, the voice of his instincts and emotions. Nor could a man hate God; for if that man knew himself, he would see that God was, by definition, his natural good, the ultimate goal of his actual aspirations. Since it was impossible, according to this insight, that our faculties should be intrinsically evil, all evil had to arise from the disorder into which these faculties fall, their too great weakness or strength in relation to one another. If the animal part of man was too strong for his reason, he fell into incontinence,—that is, into lust, gluttony, avarice, wrath, or pride. Incontinence came from an excessive or ill-timed pursuit of something good, of a part of what nature aims at; for food, children, property, and character are natural goods. These sins are accordingly the most excusable and the least odious. Dante puts those who have sinned through love in the first circle of hell, nearest to the sunlight, or in the topmost round of purgatory, nearest to the earthly paradise. Below the lovers, in each case, are the gluttons,—where a northern poet would have been obliged to place his drunkards. Beneath these again are the misers,— worse because less open to the excuse of a merely childish lack of self-control.

The disorder of the faculties may arise, however, in another way. The combative or spirited element, rather than the senses, may get out of hand, and lead to crimes of violence. Violence, like incontinence, is spontaneous enough in its personal origin, and would not be odious if it did not inflict, and intend to inflict, harm on others; so that besides incontinence, there is malice in it. Ill-will to others may arise from pride, because one loves to be superior to them, or from envy, because one abhors that they should seem superior to oneself; or through desire for vengeance, because one smarts under some injury. Sins of these kinds are more serious than those of foolish incontinence; they complicate the moral world more; they introduce endless opposition of interests, and perpetual, self-propagating crimes. They are hateful. Dante feels less pity for those who suffer by them: he remembers the sufferings these malefactors have themselves caused, and he feels a sort of joy in joining the divine justice, and would gladly lash them himself.

Worse still than violence, however, is guile: the sin of those who in the service of their intemperance or their malice have abused the gift of reason. *Corruptio optimi pessima;* and to turn reason, the faculty that establishes order, into a means of organizing disorder, is a perversity truly satanic: it turns evil into an art. But even this perversity has stages; and Dante distinguishes ten sorts of dishonesty or simple fraud, as well as three sorts of treachery.

Besides these positive transgressions there is a possibility of general moral sluggishness and indifference. This Dante, with his fervid nature, particularly hates. He puts the Laodiceans in the fringe of his hell; within the gate, that they may be without hope, but outside of limbo, that they may have torments to endure, and be stung by wasps and hornets into a belated activity.

To these vices, known to Aristotle, the Catholic moralist was obliged to add two others: original sin, of which spontaneous disbelief is one consequence, and heresy, or misbelief, after a revelation has been given and accepted. Original sin, and the paganism that goes with it, if they lead to nothing worse, are a mere privation of excellence and involve in eternity merely a privation of joy: they are punished in limbo. There sighs are heard, but no lamentation, and the only sorrow is to live in desire without hope. This fate is most appropriately imputed to the noble and clear-sighted in the hereafter, since it is so often their experience here. Dante was never juster than in this stroke. Heresy, on the other hand, is a kind of passion when honest, or a kind of fraud when politic; and it is punished as pride in fiery tombs, or as faction by perpetual gaping wounds and horrible mutilations.

So far, with these slight additions, Dante is following Aristotle; but here a great divergence sets in. If a pagan poet had conceived the idea of illustrating the catalogue of vices and virtues in poetic scenes, he would have chosen suitable episodes in human life, and painted the typical characters that figured in them in their earthly environment; for pagan morality is a plant of earth. Not so with Dante. His poem describes this world merely in retrospect; the foreground is occupied by the eternal consequences of what time had brought forth. These consequences are new facts, not merely, as for the rationalist, the old facts conceived in their truth; they often reverse, in their emotional quality, the events they represent. Such a reversal is made possible by the theory that justice is partly retributive; that virtue is not its own sufficient reward, nor vice its own sufficient punishment. According to this theory, this life contains a part of our experience only, yet determines the rest. The other life is a second experience, yet it does not contain any novel adventures. It is determined altogether by what we have done on earth; as the tree falleth so it lieth, and souls after death have no further initiative.

The theory Dante adopts mediates between two earlier views; in so far as it is Greek, it conceives immortality ideally, as something timeless; but in so far as it is Hebraic, it conceives of a new existence and a second, different taste of life. Dante thinks of a second experience, but of one that is wholly retrospective and changeless. It is an epilogue which sums up the play, and is the last episode in it. The purpose of this epilogue is not to carry on the play indefinitely: such a romantic notion of immortality never entered Dante's mind. The purpose of the epilogue is merely to vindicate (in a more unmis-

takable fashion than the play, being ill acted, itself could do) the excellence
of goodness and the misery of vice. Were this life all, he thinks the wicked
might laugh. If not wholly happy, at least they might boast that their lot was
no worse than that of many good men. Nothing would make an overwhelming difference. Moral distinctions would be largely impertinent and remarkably jumbled. If I am a simple lover of goodness, I may perhaps put up with
this situation. I may say of the excellences I prize what Wordsworth says of
his Lucy: there may be none to praise and few to love them, but they make
all the difference to me.

Dante, however, was not merely a simple lover of excellence: he was also a
keen hater of wickedness, one that took the moral world tragically and
wished to heighten the distinctions he felt into something absolute and infinite. Now any man who is enragé in his preferences will probably say, with
Mohammed, Tertullian, and Calvin, that good is dishonoured if those who
contemn it can go scot-free, and never repent of their negligence; that the
more horrible the consequences of evil-doing, the more tolerable the presence
of evil-doing is in the world; and that the everlasting shrieks and contortions
of the damned alone will make it possible for the saints to sit quiet, and be
convinced that there is perfect harmony in the universe. On this principle, in
the famous inscription which Dante places over the gate of hell, we read that
primal love, as well as justice and power, established that torture-house;
primal love, that is, of that good which, by the extreme punishment of those
who scorn it, is honoured, vindicated, and made to shine like the sun. The
damned are damned for the glory of God.

This doctrine, I cannot help thinking, is a great disgrace to human nature.
It shows how desperate, at heart, is the folly of an egotistic or anthropocentric
philosophy. This philosophy begins by assuring us that everything is obviously created to serve our needs; it then maintains that everything serves our
ideals; and in the end, it reveals that everything serves our blind hatreds and
superstitious qualms. Because my instinct taboos something, the whole universe, with insane intensity, shall taboo it for ever. This infatuation was inherited by Dante, and it was not uncongenial to his bitter and intemperate
spleen. Nevertheless, he saw beyond it at times. Like many other Christian
seers, he betrays here and there an esoteric view of rewards and punishments,
which makes them simply symbols for the intrinsic quality of good and evil
ways. The punishment, he then seems to say, is nothing added; it is what the
passion itself pursues; it is a fulfilment, horrifying the soul that desired it.

For instance, spirits newly arrived in hell require no devil with his prong
to drive them to their punishment. They flit towards it eagerly, of their own
accord. Similarly, the souls in purgatory are kept by their own will at the
penance they are doing. No external force retains them, but until they are

quite purged they are not able, because they are not willing to absolve themselves. The whole mountain, we are told, trembles and bursts into psalmody
when any one frees himself and reaches heaven. Is it too much of a gloss to
say that these souls change their prison when they change their ideal, and that
an inferior state of soul is its own purgatory, and determines its own duration? In one place, at any rate, Dante proclaims the intrinsic nature of punishment in express terms. Among the blasphemers is a certain king of Thebes,
who defied the thunderbolts of Jupiter. He shows himself indifferent to his
punishment and says: "Such as I was alive, such I am dead." Whereupon
Virgil exclaims, with a force Dante had never found in his voice before: "In
that thy pride is not mortified, thou are punished the more. No torture, other
than thy own rage, would be woe enough to match thy fury." And indeed,
Dante's imagination cannot outdo, it cannot even equal, the horrors which
men have brought upon themselves in this world. If we were to choose the
most fearful of the scenes in the *Inferno,* we should have to choose the story
of Ugolino, but this is only a pale recital of what Pisa had actually witnessed.

A more subtle and interesting instance, if a less obvious one, may be found
in the punishment of Paolo and Francesca di Rimini. What makes these
lovers so wretched in the Inferno? They are still together. Can an eternity of
floating on the wind, in each other's arms, be a punishment for lovers? That
is just what their passion, if left to speak for itself, would have chosen. It is
what passion stops at, and would gladly prolong for ever. Divine judgement
has only taken it at its word. This fate is precisely what Aucassin, in the well-
known tale, wishes for himself and his sweetheart Nicolette,—not a heaven to
be won by renunciation, but the possession, even if it be in hell, of what he
loves and fancies. And a great romantic poet, Alfred de Musset, actually
upbraids Dante for not seeing that such an eternal destiny as he has assigned
to Paola and Francesca would be not the ruin of their love, but the perfect
fulfilment of it. This last seems to be very true; but did Dante overlook the
truth of it? If so, what instinct guided him to choose just the fate for these
lovers that they would have chosen for themselves?

There is a great difference between the apprentices in life, and the masters,
—Aucassin and Alfred de Musset were among the apprentices; Dante was
one of the masters. He could feel the fresh promptings of life as keenly as any
youngster, or any romanticist; but he had lived these things through, he
knew the possible and the impossible issue of them; he saw their relation to
the rest of human nature, and to the ideal of an ultimate happiness and
peace. He had discovered the necessity of saying continually to oneself: Thou
shalt renounce. And for this reason he needed no other furniture for hell than
the literal ideals and fulfilments of our absolute little passions. The soul that
is possessed by any one of these passions nevertheless has other hopes in

abeyance. Love itself dreams of more than mere possession; to conceive happiness, it must conceive a life to be shared in a varied world, full of events and activities, which shall be new and ideal bonds between the lovers. But unlawful love cannot pass out into this public fulfilment. It is condemned to be mere possession—possession in the dark, without an environment, without a future. It is love among the ruins. And it is precisely this that is the torment of Paolo and Francesca—love among the ruins of themselves and of all else they might have had to give to one another. Abandon yourself, Dante would say to us,—abandon yourself altogether to a love that is nothing but love, and you are in hell already. Only an inspired poet could be so subtle a moralist. Only a sound moralist could be so tragic a poet.

The same tact and fine feeling that appear in these little moral dramas appear also in the sympathetic landscape in which each episode is set. The poet actually accomplishes the feat which he attributes to the Creator; he evokes a material world to be the fit theatre for moral attitudes. Popular imagination and the precedents of Homer and Virgil had indeed carried him halfway in this symbolic labour, as tradition almost always carries a poet who is successful. Mankind, from remotest antiquity, had conceived a dark subterranean hell, inhabited by unhappy ghosts. In Christian times, these shades had become lost souls, tormented by hideous demons. But Dante, with the Aristotelian chart of the vices before him, turned those vague windy caverns into a symmetrical labyrinth. Seven concentric terraces descended, step by step, towards the waters of the Styx, which in turn encircled the brazen walls of the City of Dis, or Pluto. Within these walls, two more terraces led down to the edge of a prodigious precipice—perhaps a thousand miles deep—which formed the pit of hell. At the bottom of this, still sinking gently towards the centre, were ten concentric furrows or ditches, to hold ten sorts of rogues; and finally a last sheer precipice fell to the frozen lake of Cocytus, at the very centre of the earth, in the midst of which Lucifer was congealed amongst lesser traitors.

Precision and horror, graphic and moral truth, were never so wonderfully combined as in the description of this hell. Yet the conception of purgatory is more original, and perhaps more poetical. The very approach to the place is enchanting. We hear of it first in the fatal adventure ascribed to Ulysses by Dante. Restless at Ithaca after his return from Troy, the hero had summoned his surviving companions for a last voyage of discovery. He had sailed with them past the Pillars of Hercules, skirting the African shore; until after three months of open sea, he saw a colossal mountain, a great truncated cone, looming before him. This was the island and hill of purgatory, at the very antipodes of Jerusalem. Yet before Ulysses could land there, a squall overtook him; and his galley sank, prow foremost, in that untraversed sea, within sight of a new world. So must the heathen fail of salvation, though some oracular impulse bring them near the goal.

How easy is success, on the other hand, to the ministers of grace! From the mouth of the Tiber, where the souls of Christians congregate after death, a light skiff, piloted by an angel, and propelled only by his white wings, skims the sea swiftly towards the mountain of purgatory, there deposits the spirits it carries, and is back at the mouth of the Tiber again on the same day. So much for the approach to purgatory. When a spirit lands it finds the skirts of the mountain broad and spreading, but the slope soon becomes hard and precipitous. When he has passed the narrow gate of repentance, he must stay upon each of the ledges that encircle the mountain at various heights, until one of his sins is purged, and then upon the next ledge above, if he has been guilty also of the sin that is atoned for there. The mountain is so high as to lift its head into the sphere of the moon, above the reach of terrestrial tempests. The top, which is a broad circular plain, contains the Garden of Eden, watered by the rivers Lethe and Eunoe, one to heal all painful memories, and the other to bring all good thoughts to clearness. From this place, which literally touches the lowest heaven, the upward flight is easy from sphere to sphere.

The astronomy of Dante's day fell in beautifully with his poetic task. It described and measured a firmament that would still be identified with the posthumous heaven of the saints. The whirling invisible spheres of that astronomy had the earth for their centre. The sublime complexities of this Ptolemaic system were day and night before Dante's mind. He loves to tell us in what constellation the sun is rising or setting, and what portion of the sky is then over the antipodes; he carries in his mind an orrery that shows him, at any given moment, the position of every star.

Such a constant dragging in of astronomical lore may seem to us puerile or pedantic; but for Dante the astronomical situation had the charm of a landscape, literally full of the most wonderful lights and shadows; and it also had the charm of a hard-won discovery that unveiled the secrets of nature. To think straight, to see things as they are, or as they might naturally be, interested him more than to fancy things impossible; and in this he shows, not want of imagination, but true imaginative power and imaginative maturity. It is those of us who are too feeble to conceive and master the real world, or too cowardly to face it, that run away from it to those cheap fictions that alone seem to us fine enough for poetry or for religion. In Dante the fancy is not empty or arbitrary; it is serious, fed on the study of real things. It adopts their tendency and divines their true destiny. His art is, in the original Greek sense, an imitation or rehearsal of nature, an anticipation of fate. For this reason curious details of science or theology enter as a matter of course into

[278]

his verse. With the straightforward faith and simplicity of his age he devours these interesting images, which help him to clarify the mysteries of this world.

There is a kind of sensualism or aestheticism that has decreed in our day that theory is not poetical; as if all the images and emotions that enter a cultivated mind were not saturated with theory. The prevalence of such a sensualism or aestheticism would alone suffice to explain the impotence of the arts. The life of theory is not less human or less emotional than the life of sense; it is more typically human and more keenly emotional. Philosophy is a more intense sort of experience than common life is, just as pure and subtle music, heard in retirement, is something keener and more intense than the howling of storms or the rumble of cities. For this reason philosophy, when a poet is not mindless, enters inevitably into his poetry, since it has entered into his life; or rather, the detail of things and the detail of ideas pass equally into his verse, when both alike lie in the path that has led him to his ideal. To object to theory in poetry would be like objecting to words there; for words, too, are symbols without the sensuous character of the things they stand for; and yet it is only by the net of new connections which words throw over things, in recalling them, that poetry arises at all. Poetry is an attenuation, a rehandling, an echo of crude experience; it is itself a theoretic vision of things at arm's length.

Never before or since has a poet lived in so large a landscape as Dante; for our infinite times and distances are of little poetic value while we have no graphic image of what may fill them. Dante's spaces were filled; they enlarged, to the limits of human imagination, the habitations and destinies of mankind. Although the saints did not literally inhabit the spheres, but the empyrean beyond, yet each spirit could be manifested in that sphere the genius of which was most akin to his own. In Dante's vision spirits appear as points of light, from which voices also flow sometimes, as well as radiance. Further than reporting their words (which are usually about the things of earth) Dante tells us little about them. He has indeed, at the end, a vision of a celestial rose; tier upon tier of saints are seated as in an amphitheatre, and the Deity overarches them in the form of a triple rainbow, with a semblance of man in the midst. But this is avowedly a mere symbol, a somewhat conventional picture to which Dante has recourse unwillingly, for want of a better image to render his mystical intention. What may perhaps help us to divine this intention is the fact, just mentioned, that according to him the celestial spheres are not the real seat of any human soul; that the pure rise through them with increasing ease and velocity, the nearer they come to God; and that the eyes of Beatrice—the revelation of God to man—are only mirrors, shedding merely reflected beauty and light.

These hints suggest the doctrine that the goal of life is the very bosom of

God; not any finite form of existence, however excellent, but a complete absorption and disappearance in the Godhead. So the Neo-platonists had thought, from whom all this heavenly landscape is borrowed; and the reservations that Christian orthodoxy requires have not always remained present to the minds of Christian mystics and poets. Dante broaches this very point in the memorable interview he has with the spirit of Piccarda, in the third canto of the *Paradiso*. She is in the lowest sphere of heaven, that of the inconstant moon, because after she had been stolen from her convent and forcibly married, she felt no prompting to renew her earlier vows. Dante asks her if she never longs for a higher station in paradise, one nearer to God, the natural goal of all aspiration. She answers that to share the will of God, who has established many different mansions in his house, is to be truly one with him. The wish to be nearer God would actually carry the soul farther away, since it would oppose the order he has established.

Even in heaven, therefore, the Christian saint was to keep his essential fidelity, separation, and lowliness. He was to feel still helpless and lost in himself, like Tobias, and happy only in that the angel of the Lord was holding him by the hand. For Piccarda to say that she accepts the will of God means not that she shares it, but that she submits to it. She would fain go higher, for her moral nature demands it, as Dante—incorrigible Platonist—perfectly perceived; but she dare not mention it, for she knows that God, whose thoughts are not her thoughts, has forbidden it. The inconstant sphere of the moon does not afford her a perfect happiness; but, chastened as she is, she says it brings her happiness enough; all that a broken and a contrite heart has the courage to hope for.

Such are the conflicting inspirations beneath the lovely harmonies of the *Paradiso*. It was not the poet's soul that was in conflict here; it was only his traditions. The conflicts of his own spirit had been left behind in other regions; on that threshing-floor of earth which, from the height of heaven, he looked back upon with wonder, surprised that men should take so passionately this trouble of ants, which he judges best, says Dante, who thinks least of it.

In this saying the poet is perhaps conscious of a personal fault; for Dante was far from perfect, even as a poet. He was too much a man of his own time, and often wrote with a passion not clarified into judgement. So much does the purely personal and dramatic interest dominate us as we read of a Boniface or an Ugolino that we forget that these historical figures are supposed to have been transmuted into the eternal, and to have become bits in the mosaic of Platonic essences. Dante himself almost forgets it. The modern reader, accustomed to insignificant, wayward fictions, and expecting to be entertained by images without thoughts, may not notice this lack of perspective, or may

rejoice in it. But, if he is judicious, he will not rejoice in it long. The Boni-
faces and the Ugolinos are not the truly deep, the truly lovely figures of the
Divine Comedy. They are, in a relative sense, the vulgarities in it. We feel
too much, in these cases, the heat of the poet's prejudice or indignation. He
is not just, as he usually is; he does not stop to think, as he almost always
does. He forgets that he is in the eternal world, and dips for the moment into
a brawl in some Italian market-place, or into the council-chamber of some
factious *condottiere*. The passages—such as those about Boniface and Ugolino
—which Dante writes in this mood are powerful and vehement, but they are
not beautiful. They brand the object of their invective more than they reveal
it; they shock more than they move the reader.

This lower kind of success—for it is still a success in rhetoric—falls to the
poet because he has abandoned the Platonic half of his inspiration and has
become for the moment wholly historical, wholly Hebraic or Roman. He
would have been a far inferior mind if he had always moved on this level.
With the Platonic spheres and the Aristotelian ethics taken out, his *Comedy*
would not have been divine. Persons and incidents, to be truly memorable,
have to be rendered significant; they have to be seen in their place in the
moral world; they have to be judged, and judged rightly, in their dignity
and value. A casual personal sentiment towards them, however passionate,
cannot take the place of the sympathetic insight that comprehends and the
wide experience that judges.

Again (what is fundamental with Dante) love, as he feels and renders it, is
not normal or healthy love. It was doubtless real enough, but too much restrained and expressed too much in fancy; so that when it is extended
Platonically and identified so easily with the grace of God and with revealed
wisdom, we feel the suspicion that if the love in question had been natural
and manly it would have offered more resistance to so mystical a transformation. The poet who wishes to pass convincingly from love to philosophy (and
that seems a natural progress for a poet) should accordingly be a hearty and
complete lover—a lover like Goethe and his Faust—rather than like Plato and
Dante. Faust, too, passes from Gretchen to Helen, and partly back again; and
Goethe made even more passages. Had any of them led to something which
not only was loved, but deserved to be loved, which not only could inspire a
whole life, but which ought to inspire it—then we should have had a genuine
progress.

In the next place, Dante talks too much about himself. There is a sense in
which this egotism is a merit, or at least a ground of interest for us moderns;
for egotism is the distinctive attitude of modern philosophy and of romantic
sentiment. In being egotistical Dante was ahead of his time. His philosophy
would have lost an element of depth, and his poetry an element of pathos, had

he not placed himself in the centre of the stage, and described everything as his experience, or as a revelation made to himself and made for the sake of his personal salvation. But Dante's egotism goes rather further than was requisite, so that the transcendental insight might not fail in his philosophy. It extended so far that he cast the shadow of his person not only over the terraces of purgatory (as he is careful to tell us repeatedly), but over the whole of Italy and of Europe, which he saw and judged under the evident influence of private passions and resentments.

Moreover, the personality thrust forward so obtrusively is not in every respect worthy of contemplation. Dante is very proud and very bitter; at the same time, he is curiously timid; and one may tire sometimes of his perpetual tremblings and tears, of his fainting fits and his intricate doubts. A man who knows he is under the special protection of God, and of three celestial ladies, and who has such a sage and magician as Virgil for a guide, might have looked even upon hell with a little more confidence. How far is this shivering and swooning philosopher from the laughing courage of Faust, who sees his poodle swell into a monster, then into a cloud, and finally change into Mephistopheles, and says at once: *Das also war des Pudels Kern!* Doubtless Dante was mediaeval, and contrition, humility, and fear of the devil were great virtues in those days; but the conclusion we must come to is precisely that the virtues of those days were not the best virtues, and that a poet who represents that time cannot be a fair nor an ultimate spokesman for humanity.

Perhaps we have now reviewed the chief objects that peopled Dante's imagination, the chief objects into the midst of which his poetry transports us; and if a poet's genius avails to transport us into his enchanted world, the character of that world will determine the quality and dignity of his poetry. Dante transports us, with unmistakable power, first into the atmosphere of a visionary love; then into the history of his conversion, affected by this love, or by the divine grace identified with it. The supreme ideal to which his conversion brought him back is expressed for him by universal nature, and is embodied among men in the double institution of a revealed religion and a providential empire. To trace the fortunes of these institutions, we are transported next into the panorama of history, in its great crises and its great men; and particularly into the panorama of Italy in the poet's time, where we survey the crimes, the virtues, and the sorrows of those prominent in furthering or thwarting the ideal of Christendom. These numerous persons are set before us with the sympathy and brevity of a dramatist; yet it is no mere carnival, no *danse macabre:* for throughout, above the confused strife of parties and passions, we hear the steady voice, the implacable sentence, of the prophet that judges them.

Thus Dante, gifted with the tenderest sense of colour, and the firmest art of design, has put his whole world into his canvas. Seen there, that world becomes complete, clear, beautiful, and tragic. It is vivid and truthful in its detail, sublime in its march and in its harmony. This is not poetry where the parts are better than the whole. Here, as in some great symphony, everything is cumulative: the movements conspire, the tension grows, the volume re-doubles, the keen melody soars higher and higher; and it all ends, not with a bang, not with some casual incident, but in sustained reflection, in the sense that it has not ended, but remains by us in its totality, a revelation and a resource for ever. It has taught us to love and to renounce, to judge and to worship. What more could a poet do? Dante poetized all life and nature as he found them. His imagination dominated and focused the whole world. He thereby touched the ultimate goal to which a poet can aspire; he set the standard for all possible performance, and became the type of a supreme poet. This is not to say that he is the "greatest" of poets. The relative merit of poets is a barren thing to wrangle about. The question can always be opened anew, when a critic appears with a fresh temperament or a new criterion. Even less need we say that no greater poet can ever arise; we may be confi-dent of the opposite. But Dante gives a successful example of the *highest species* of poetry. His poetry covers the whole field from which poetry may be fetched, and to which poetry may be applied, from the inmost recesses of the heart to the uttermost bounds of nature and of destiny. If to give imaginative value to something is the minimum task of a poet, to give imaginative value to all things, and to the system which things compose, is evidently his greatest task.

Dante fulfilled this task, of course under special conditions and limitations, personal and social; but he fulfilled it, and he thereby fulfilled the conditions of supreme poetry. Even Homer, as we are beginning to perceive nowadays, suffered from a certain conventionality and one-sidedness. There was much in the life and religion of his time that his art ignored. It was a flattering, a euphemistic art; it had a sort of pervasive blandness, like that which we now associate with a fashionable sermon. It was poetry addressed to the ruling caste in the state, to the conquerors; and it spread an intentional glamour over their past brutalities and present self-deceptions. No such partiality in Dante; he paints what he hates as frankly as what he loves, and in all things he is complete and sincere. If any similar adequacy is attained again by any poet, it will not be, presumably, by a poet of the supernatural. Henceforth, for any wide and honest imagination, the supernatural must figure as an idea in the human mind,—a part of the natural. To conceive it otherwise would be to fall short of the insight of this age, not to express or to complete it. Dante, however, for this very reason, may be expected to remain the supreme poet of the supernatural, the unrivalled exponent, after Plato, of that phase of thought and feeling in which the supernatural seems to be the key to nature and to happiness. This is the hypothesis on which, as yet, moral unity has been best attained in this world. Here, then, we have the most complete idealization and comprehension of things achieved by mankind hitherto. Dante is the type of a consummate poet.

MACHIAVELLI

[*1469–1527*]

MACHIAVELLI HAD BEEN IDENTIFIED WITH POLITICAL OPPRESSION, BRUTALITY, AND deceit for more than two centuries when the young Macaulay published this brilliant essay in 1827. The future Member of Parliament and Secretary for War overturned the conventional attitudes toward Machiavelli by showing that he had dealt with the realities of political power. In later years Macaulay was anxious to be remembered as the author of his *History of England,* and set far less store by his essays. But it is hard to match the freshness and authority of Macaulay's discovery, at the age of twenty-seven, that *The Prince* was about the very political world in which he lived. He does not admire the means Machiavelli recommends, but he makes his author's high political genius clear.

A modern essayist would be likely to give more attention to Machiavelli's commentary on the Roman historian, Livy, which serves to correct some of the distortions which arise out of reading *The Prince* alone. It is in commenting on that part of Livy's work which deals with the remarkable endurance of the Roman republic that Machiavelli comes closest to American experience. He argues that it was by representing all the interests in the state that the republic lasted eight hundred years, and this has lately been held to be the distinguishing characteristic of American political parties.

THOMAS BABINGTON MACAULAY

Machiavelli

THOSE WHO HAVE ATTENDED TO THE PRACTICE OF OUR LITERARY TRIBUNAL ARE well aware that, by means of certain legal fictions similar to those of Westminster Hall, we are frequently enabled to take cognisance of cases lying beyond the sphere of our original jurisdiction. We need hardly say, therefore, that in the present instance M. Périer is merely a Richard Roe, who will not be mentioned in any subsequent stage of the proceedings, and whose name is used for the sole purpose of bringing Machiavelli into court.

We doubt whether any name in literary history be so generally odious as that of the man whose character and writings we now propose to consider. The terms in which he is commonly described would seem to import that he was the Tempter, the Evil Principle, the discoverer of ambition and revenge, the original inventor of perjury, and that, before the publication of his fatal *Prince,* there had never been a hypocrite, a tyrant, or a traitor, a simulated virtue, or a convenient crime. One writer gravely assures us that Maurice of Saxony learned all his fraudulent policy from that execrable volume. Another remarks that since it was translated into Turkish, the Sultans have been more addicted than formerly to the custom of strangling their brothers. Lord Lyttelton charges the poor Florentine with the manifold treasons of the house of Guise, and with the massacre of St. Bartholomew. Several authors have hinted that the Gunpowder Plot is to be primarily attributed to his doctrines, and seem to think that his effigy ought to be substituted for that of Guy Faux, in those processions by which the ingenious youth of England annually commemorate the preservation of the Three Estates. The Church of Rome has pronounced his works accursed things. Nor have our own countrymen been backward in testifying their opinion of his merits. Out of his surname they have coined an epithet for a knave, and out of his Christian name a synonym for the Devil.

It is indeed scarcely possible for any person, not well acquainted with the history and literature of Italy, to read without horror and amazement the celebrated treatise which has brought so much obloquy on the name of Machiavelli. Such a display of wickedness, naked yet not ashamed, such cool, judicious, scientific atrocity, seemed rather to belong to a fiend than to the most depraved of men. Principles which the most hardened ruffian would scarcely hint to his most trusted accomplice, or avow, without the disguise of some palliating sophism, even to his own mind, are professed without the slightest circumlocution, and assumed as the fundamental axioms of all political science.

It is not strange that ordinary readers should regard the author of such a book as the most depraved and shameless of human beings. Wise men, however, have always been inclined to look with great suspicion on the angels and dæmons of the multitude: and in the present instance, several circumstances have led even superficial observers to question the justice of the vulgar decision. It is notorious that Machiavelli was, through life, a zealous republican. In the same year in which he composed his manual of King-craft, he suffered imprisonment and torture in the cause of public liberty. It seems inconceivable that the martyr of freedom should have designedly acted as the apostle of tyranny. Several eminent writers have, therefore, endeavoured to detect in this unfortunate performance some concealed meaning, more consistent with the character and conduct of the author than that which appears at the first glance.

One hypothesis is that Machiavelli intended to practise on the young Lorenzo de Medici a fraud similar to that which Sunderland is said to have employed against our James the Second, and that he urged his pupil to violent and perfidious measures, as the surest means of accelerating the moment of deliverance and revenge. Another supposition which Lord Bacon seems to countenance, is that the treatise was merely a piece of grave irony, intended to warn nations against the arts of ambitious men. It would be easy to show that neither of these solutions is consistent with many passages in *The Prince* itself. But the most decisive refutation is that which is furnished by the other works of Machiavelli. In all the writings which he gave to the public, and in all those which the research of editors has, in the course of three centuries, discovered, in his Comedies, designed for the entertainment of the multitude, in his Comments on Livy, intended for the perusal of the most enthusiastic patriots of Florence, in his History, inscribed to one of the most amiable and estimable of the Popes, in his public despatches, in his private memoranda, the same obliquity of moral principle for which *The Prince* is so severely censured is more or less discernible. We doubt whether it would be possible to find, in all the many volumes of his compositions, a single expression indicating that dissimulation and treachery had ever struck him as discreditable.

After this, it may seem ridiculous to say that we are acquainted with few writings which exhibit so much elevation of sentiment, so pure and warm a zeal for the public good, or so just a view of the duties and rights of citizens, as those of Machiavelli. Yet so it is. And even from *The Prince* itself we could select many passages in support of this remark. To a reader of our age and country this inconsistency is, at first, perfectly bewildering. The whole man seems to be an enigma, a grotesque assemblage of incongruous qualities, selfishness and generosity, cruelty and benevolence, craft and simplicity, abject villainy and romantic heroism. One sentence is such as a veteran diplomatist would scarcely write in cipher for the direction of his most confidential spy; the next seems to be extracted from a theme composed by an ardent schoolboy on the death of Leonidas. An act of dexterous perfidy, and an act of patriotic self-devotion, call forth the same kind and the same degree of respectful admiration. The moral sensibility of the writer seems at once to be morbidly obtuse and morbidly acute. Two characters altogether dissimilar are united in him. They are not merely joined, but interwoven. They are the warp and the woof of his mind; and their combination, like that of the variegated threads in shot silk, gives to the whole texture a glancing and ever-changing appearance. The explanation might have been easy, if he had been a very weak or a very affected man. But he was evidently neither the one nor the other. His works prove, beyond all contradiction, that his understanding was strong, his taste pure, and his sense of the ridiculous exquisitely keen.

This is strange: and yet the strangest is behind. There is no reason whatever to think, that those amongst whom he lived saw anything shocking or incongruous in his writings. Abundant proofs remain of the high estimation in which both his works and his person were held by the most respectable among his contemporaries. Clement the Seventh patronised the publication of those very books which the Council of Trent, in the following generation, pronounced unfit for the perusal of Christians. Some members of the democratical party censured the Secretary for dedicating *The Prince* to a patron who bore the unpopular name of Medici. But to those immoral doctrines which have since called forth such severe reprehensions no exception appears to have been taken. The cry against them was first raised beyond the Alps, and seems to have been heard with amazement in Italy. The earliest assailant, as far as we are aware, was a countryman of our own, Cardinal Pole. The author of the Anti-Machiavelli was a French Protestant.

It is, therefore, in the state of moral feeling among the Italians of those times that we must seek for the real explanation of what seems most mysterious in the life and writings of this remarkable man. As this is a subject which suggests many interesting considerations, both political and metaphysical, we shall make no apology for discussing it at some length.

During the gloomy and disastrous centuries which followed the downfall of the Roman Empire, Italy had preserved, in a far greater degree than any other part of Western Europe, the traces of ancient civilisation. The night which descended upon her was the night of an Arctic summer. The dawn began to reappear before the last reflection of the preceding sunset had faded from the horizon. It was in the time of the French Merovingians and of the Saxon Heptarchy that ignorance and ferocity seemed to have done their worst. Yet even then the Neapolitan provinces, recognising the authority of the Eastern Empire, preserved something of Eastern knowledge and refinement. Rome, protected by the sacred character of her Pontiffs, enjoyed at least comparative security and repose. Even in those regions where the sanguinary Lombards had fixed their monarchy, there was incomparably more of wealth, of information, of physical comfort, and of social order, than could be found in Gaul, Britain, or Germany.

That which most distinguished Italy from the neighbouring countries was the importance which the population of the towns, at a very early period, began to acquire. Some cities had been founded in wild and remote situations, by fugitives who had escaped from the rage of the barbarians. Such were Venice and Genoa, which preserved their freedom by their obscurity, till they became able to preserve it by their power. Other cities seem to have retained, under all the changing dynasties of invaders, under Odoacer and Theodoric, Narses and Alboin, the municipal institutions which had been conferred on them by the liberal policy of the Great Republic. In provinces which the central government was too feeble either to protect or to oppress, these institutions gradually acquired stability and vigour. The citizens, defended by their walls, and governed by their own magistrates and their own by-laws, enjoyed a considerable share of republican independence. Thus a strong democratic spirit was called into action. The Carlovingian sovereigns were too imbecile to subdue it. The generous policy of Otho encouraged it.

It might perhaps have been suppressed by a close coalition between the Church and the Empire. It was fostered and invigorated by their disputes. In the twelfth century it attained its full vigour, and, after a long and doubtful conflict, triumphed over the abilities and courage of the Swabian princes.

The assistance of the Ecclesiastical power had greatly contributed to the success of the Guelfs. That success would, however, have been a doubtful good, if its only effect had been to substitute a moral for a political servitude, and to exalt the Popes at the expense of the Cæsars. Happily the public mind of Italy had long contained the seeds of free opinions, which were now rapidly developed by the genial influence of free institutions. The people of that country had observed the whole machinery of the Church, its saints and its miracles, its lofty pretensions and its splendid ceremonial, its worthless blessings and its harmless curses, too long and too closely to be duped. They stood behind the scenes on which others were gazing with childish awe and interest. They witnessed the arrangement of the pulleys, and the manufacture of the thunders. They saw the natural faces and heard the natural voices of the actors. Distant nations looked on the Pope as the Vicegerent of the Almighty, the oracle of the All-wise, the umpire from whose decisions, in the disputes either of theologians or of kings, no Christian ought to appeal. The Italians were acquainted with all the follies of his youth, and with all the dishonest arts by which he had attained power. They knew how often he had employed the keys of the Church to release himself from the most sacred engagements, and its wealth to pamper his mistresses and nephews. The doctrines and rites of the established religion they treated with decent reverence. But though they still called themselves Catholics, they had ceased to be Papists. Those spiritual arms which carried terror into the palaces and camps of the proudest sovereigns excited only contempt in the immediate neighbourhood of the Vatican. Alexander, when he commanded our Henry the Second to submit to the lash before the tomb of a rebellious subject, was himself an exile. The Romans apprehending that he entertained designs against their liberties, had driven him from their city; and though he solemnly promised to confine himself for the future to his spiritual functions, they still refused to readmit him.

In every other part of Europe, a large and powerful privileged class trampled on the people and defied the Government. But in the most flourishing parts of Italy, the feudal nobles were reduced to comparative insignificance. In some districts they took shelter under the protection of the powerful commonwealths which they were unable to oppose, and gradually sank into the mass of burghers. In other places they possessed great influence; but it was an influence widely different from that which was exercised by the aristocracy of any Transalpine kingdom. They were not petty princes, but eminent citizens. Instead of strengthening their fastnesses among the mountains, they embellished their palaces in the market-place. The state of society in the Neapolitan dominions, and in some parts of the Ecclesiastical State, more nearly resembled that which existed in the great monarchies of Europe. But the Governments of Lombardy and Tuscany, through all their revolutions, preserved a different character. A people, when assembled in a town, is far more formidable to its rulers than when dispersed over a wide extent of country. The most arbitrary of the Cæsars found it necessary to feed and divert the inhabitants of their unwieldy capital at the expense of the provinces. The citizens of Madrid have more than once besieged their sovereign in his own palace, and extorted from him the most humiliating concessions. The Sultans have often been compelled to propitiate the furious rabble of Constantinople with the head of an unpopular Vizier. From the same cause there was a certain tinge of democracy in the monarchies and aristocracies of Northern Italy.

Thus liberty, partially indeed and transiently, revisited Italy; and with liberty came commerce and empire, science and taste, all the comforts and all the ornaments of life. The Crusades, from which the inhabitants of other countries gained nothing but relics and wounds, brought to the rising commonwealths of the Adriatic and Tyrrhene seas a large increase of wealth, dominion, and knowledge. The moral and geographical position of those commonwealths enabled them to profit alike by the barbarism of the West and by the civilisation of the East. Italian ships covered every sea. Italian factories rose on every shore. The tables of Italian money-changers were set in every city. Manufactures flourished. Banks were established. The operations of the commercial machine were facilitated by many useful and beautiful inventions. We doubt whether any country of Europe, our own excepted, have at the present time reached so high a point of wealth and civilisation as some parts of Italy had attained four hundred years ago. Historians rarely descend to those details from which alone the real state of a community can be collected. Hence posterity is too often deceived by the vague hyperboles of poets and rhetoricians, who mistake the splendour of a court for the happiness of a people. Fortunately, John Villani has given us an ample and precise account of the state of Florence in the early part of the fourteenth century. The revenue of the Republic amounted to three hundred thousand florins; a sum which, allowing for the depreciation of the precious metals, was at least equivalent to six hundred thousand pounds sterling; a larger sum than England and Ireland, two centuries ago, yielded annually to Elizabeth. The manufacture of wool alone employed two hundred factories and thirty thousand workmen. The cloth annually produced sold, at an average, for twelve hundred thousand florins; a sum fully equal in exchangeable value to two millions and a half of our money. Four hundred thousand florins were annually coined. Eighty banks conducted the commercial operations, not of Florence only but of all Europe. The transactions of these establishments were sometimes of a magnitude which may surprise even the contemporaries of the Barings and the Rothschilds. Two houses advanced to Edward the Third of England upwards of three hundred thousand marks, at a time when the mark contained more silver than fifty shillings of the present day, and when the value of silver was more than quadruple of what it now is. The city and its environs contained a hundred and seventy thousand inhabitants. In the various schools about ten thousand children were taught to read; twelve hundred studied arithmetic; six hundred received a learned education.

The progress of elegant literature and of the fine arts was proportioned to that of the public prosperity. Under the despotic successors of Augustus, all the fields of intellect had been turned into arid wastes, still marked out by formal boundaries, still retaining the traces of old cultivation, but yielding neither flowers nor fruit. The deluge of barbarism came. It swept away all the landmarks. It obliterated all the signs of former tillage. But it fertilised while it devastated. When it receded, the wilderness was as the garden of God, rejoicing on every side, laughing, clapping its hands, pouring forth, in spontaneous abundance, everything brilliant, or fragrant, or nourishing. A new language, characterised by simple sweetness and simple energy, had attained perfection. No tongue ever furnished more gorgeous and vivid tints to poetry; nor was it long before a poet appeared who knew how to employ them. Early in the fourteenth century came forth the *Divine Comedy*, beyond comparison the greatest work of imagination which had appeared since the poems of Homer. The following generation produced indeed no second Dante: but it was eminently distinguished by general intellectual activity. The study of the Latin writers had never been wholly neglected in Italy. But Petrarch introduced a more profound, liberal, and elegant scholarship, and communicated to his countrymen that enthusiasm for the literature, the history, and the antiquities of Rome, which divided his own heart with a frigid mistress and a more frigid Muse. Boccaccio turned their attention to the more sublime and graceful models of Greece.

From this time, the admiration of learning and genius became almost an idolatry among the people of Italy. Kings and republics, cardinals and doges, vied with each other in honouring and flattering Petrarch. Embassies from rival States solicited the honour of his instructions. His coronation agitated the Court of Naples and the people of Rome as much as the most important political transaction could have done. To collect books and antiques, to found professorships, to patronise men of learning, became almost universal fashions among the great. The spirit of literary research allied itself to that of commercial enterprise. Every place to which the merchant princes of Florence extended their gigantic traffic, from the bazars of the Tigris to the monasteries of the Clyde, was ransacked for medals and manuscripts. Architecture, painting, and sculpture, were munificently encouraged. Indeed it would be difficult to name an Italian of eminence, during the period of which we speak, who, whatever may have been his general character, did not at least affect a love of letters and of the arts.

Knowledge and public prosperity continued to advance together. Both attained their meridian in the age of Lorenzo the Magnificent. We cannot refrain from quoting the splendid passage, in which the Tuscan Thucydides describes the state of Italy at that period. *"Ridotta tutta in somma pace e tranquillità, coltivata non meno ne' luoghi più montuosi e più sterili che nelle pianure e regioni più fertili, nè sottoposta ad altro imperio che de' suoi medesimi, non solo era abbondantissima d' abitatori e di ricchezze; ma illustrata sommamente dalla magnificenza di molti principi, dallo splendore di molte nobilissime e bellissime città, dalla sedia e maestà della religione, fioriva d' uomini prestantissimi nell' amministrazione delle cose pubbliche, e d' ingegni molto nobili in tutte le scienze, ed in qualunque arte preclara ed industriosa."* When we peruse this just and splendid description, we can scarcely persuade ourselves that we are reading of times in which the annals of England and France present us only with a frightful spectacle of poverty, barbarity, and ignorance. From the oppressions of illiterate masters, and the sufferings of a degraded peasantry, it is delightful to turn to the opulent and enlightened States of Italy, to the vast and magnificent cities, the ports, the arsenals, the villas, the museums, the libraries, the marts filled with every article of comfort or luxury, the factories swarming with artisans, the Apennines covered with rich cultivation up to their very summits, the Po wafting the harvests of Lombardy to the granaries of Venice, and carrying back the silks of Bengal and the furs of Siberia to the palaces of Milan. With peculiar pleasure, every cultivated mind must repose on the fair, the happy, the glorious Florence, the halls which rang with the mirth of Pulci, the cell where twinkled the midnight lamp of Politian, the statues on which the young eye of Michael Angelo glared with the frenzy of a kindred inspiration, the gardens in which Lorenzo meditated some sparkling song for the May-day dance of the Etrurian virgins. Alas for the beautiful city! Alas for the wit and the learning, the genius and the love!

> Le donne, e i cavalier, gli affanni, e gli agi,
> Che ne 'nvogliava amore e cortesia
> Là dove i cuor son fatti sì malvagi.

A time was at hand, when all the seven vials of the Apocalypse were to be poured forth and shaken out over those pleasant countries, a time of slaughter, famine, beggary, infamy, slavery, despair.

In the Italian States, as in many natural bodies, untimely decrepitude was the penalty of precocious maturity. Their early greatness, and their early decline, are principally to be attributed to the same cause, the preponderance which the towns acquired in the political system.

In a community of hunters or of shepherds, every man easily and necessarily becomes a soldier. His ordinary avocations are perfectly compatible with all the duties of military service. However remote may be the expedition on which he is bound, he finds it easy to transport with him the stock from which he derives his subsistence. The whole people is an army; the whole year a march. Such was the state of society which facilitated the gigantic conquests of Attila and Tamerlane.

But a people which subsists by the cultivation of the earth is in a very different situation. The husbandman is bound to the soil on which he labours. A long campaign would be ruinous to him. Still his pursuits are such as give to his frame both the active and the passive strength necessary to a soldier. Nor do they, at least in the infancy of agricultural science, demand his uninterrupted attention. At particular times of the year he is almost wholly unemployed, and can, without injury to himself, afford the time necessary for a short expedition. Thus the legions of Rome were supplied during its earlier wars. The season during which the fields did not require the presence of the cultivators sufficed for a short inroad and a battle. These operations, too frequently interrupted to produce decisive results, yet served to keep up among the people a degree of discipline and courage which rendered them, not only secure, but formidable. The archers and billmen of the middle ages, who, with provisions for forty days at their backs, left the fields for the camp, were troops of the same description.

But when commerce and manufactures begin to flourish a great change takes place. The sedentary habits of the desk and the loom render the exertions and hardships of war insupportable. The business of traders and artisans requires their constant presence and attention. In such a community there is little superfluous time; but there is generally much superfluous money. Some members of the society are, therefore, hired to relieve the rest from a task inconsistent with their habits and engagements.

The history of Greece is, in this, as in many other respects, the best commentary on the history of Italy. Five hundred years before the Christian era, the citizens of the republics round the Aegean Sea formed perhaps the finest militia that ever existed. As wealth and refinement advanced, the system underwent a gradual alteration. The Ionian States were the first in which commerce and the arts were cultivated, and the first in which the ancient discipline decayed. Within eighty years after the battle of Platæa, mercenary troops were everywhere plying for battles and sieges. In the time of Demosthenes, it was scarcely possible to persuade or compel the Athenians to enlist for foreign service. The laws of Lycurgus prohibited trade and manufactures. The Spartans, therefore, continued to form a national force long after their neighbours had begun to hire soldiers. But their military spirit declined with their singular institutions. In the second century before Christ, Greece contained only one nation of warriors, the savage highlanders of Aetolia, who were some generations behind their countrymen in civilisation and intelligence.

All the causes which produced these effects among the Greeks acted still more strongly on the modern Italians. Instead of a power like Sparta, in its nature warlike, they had amongst them an ecclesiastical state, in its nature pacific. Where there are numerous slaves, every freeman is induced by the strongest motives to familiarise himself with the use of arms. The commonwealths of Italy did not, like those of Greece, swarm with thousands of these household enemies. Lastly, the mode in which military operations were conducted during the prosperous times of Italy was peculiarly unfavourable to the formation of an efficient militia. Men covered with iron from head to foot, armed with ponderous lances, and mounted on horses of the largest breed, were considered as composing the strength of an army. The infantry was regarded as comparatively worthless, and was neglected till it became really so. These tactics maintained their ground for centuries in most parts of Europe. That foot-soldiers could withstand the charge of heavy cavalry was thought utterly impossible, till, towards the close of the fifteenth century, the rude mountaineers of Switzerland dissolved the spell, and astounded the most experienced generals by receiving the dreaded shock on an impenetrable forest of pikes.

The use of the Grecian spear, the Roman sword, or the modern bayonet, might be acquired with comparative ease. But nothing short of the daily exercise of years could train the man-at-arms to support his ponderous panoply, and manage his unwieldy weapon. Throughout Europe this most important branch of war became a separate profession. Beyond the Alps, indeed, though a profession, it was not generally a trade. It was the duty and the amusement of a large class of country gentlemen. It was the service by which they held their lands, and the diversion by which, in the absence of mental resources, they beguiled their leisure. But in the Northern States of Italy, as we have already remarked, the growing power of the cities, where it had not exterminated this order of men, had completely changed their

[295]

habits. Here, therefore, the practice of employing mercenaries became universal, at a time when it was almost unknown in other countries.

When war becomes the trade of a separate class, the least dangerous course left to a government is to force that class into a standing army. It is scarcely possible, that men can pass their lives in the service of one State, without feeling some interest in its greatness. Its victories are their victories. Its defeats are their defeats. The contract loses something of its mercantile character. The services of the soldier are considered as the effects of patriotic zeal, his pay as the tribute of national gratitude. To betray the power which employs him, to be even remiss in its service, are in his eyes the most atrocious and degrading of crimes.

When the princes and commonwealths of Italy began to use hired troops, their wisest course would have been to form separate military establishments. Unhappily this was not done. The mercenary warriors of the Peninsula, instead of being attached to the service of different powers, were regarded as the common property of all. The connection between the State and its defenders was reduced to the most simple and naked traffic. The adventurer brought his horse, his weapons, his strength, and his experience, into the market. Whether the King of Naples or the Duke of Milan, the Pope or the Signory of Florence, struck the bargain, was to him a matter of perfect indifference. He was for the highest wages and the longest term. When the campaign for which he had contracted was finished, there was neither law nor punctilio to prevent him from instantly turning his arms against his late masters. The soldier was altogether disjoined from the citizen and from the subject.

The natural consequences followed. Left to the conduct of men who neither loved those whom they defended, nor hated those whom they opposed, who were often bound by stronger ties to the army against which they fought than to the State which they served, who lost by the termination of the conflict, and gained by its prolongation, war completely changed its character. Every man came into the field of the battle impressed with the knowledge that, in a few days, he might be taking the pay of the power against which he was then employed, and fighting by the side of his enemies against his associates. The strongest interests and the strongest feelings concurred to mitigate the hostility of those who had lately been brethren in arms, and who might soon be brethren in arms once more. Their common profession was a bond of union not to be forgotten even when they were engaged in the service of contending parties. Hence it was that operations, languid and indecisive beyond any recorded in history, marches and countermarches, pillaging expeditions and blockades, bloodless capitulations and equally bloodless combats, make up the military history of Italy during the course of nearly two centuries. Mighty armies fight from sunrise to sunset. A great victory is won. Thousands of prisoners are taken; and hardly a life is lost. A pitched battle seems to have been really less dangerous than an ordinary civil tumult.

Courage was now no longer necessary even to the military character. Men grew old in camps, and acquired the highest renown by their warlike achievements, without being once required to face serious danger. The political consequences are too well known. The richest and most enlightened part of the world was left undefended to the assaults of every barbarous invader, to the brutality of Switzerland, the insolence of France, and the fierce rapacity of Arragon. The moral effects which followed from this state of things were still more remarkable.

Among the rude nations which lay beyond the Alps, valour was absolutely indispensable. Without it none could be eminent; few could be secure. Cowardice was, therefore, naturally considered as the foulest reproach. Among the polished Italians, enriched by commerce, governed by law, and passionately attached to literature, everything was done by superiority and intelligence. Their very wars, more pacific than the peace of their neighbours, required rather civil than military qualifications. Hence, while courage was the point of honour in other countries, ingenuity became the point of honour in Italy.

From these principles were deduced, by processes strictly analogous, two opposite systems of fashionable morality. Through the greater part of Europe, the vices which peculiarly belong to timid dispositions, and which are the natural defence of weakness, fraud, and hypocrisy, have always been most disreputable. On the other hand, the excesses of haughty and daring spirits have been treated with indulgence, and even with respect. The Italians regarded with corresponding lenity those crimes which require self-command, address, quick observation, fertile invention, and profound knowledge of human nature.

Such a prince as our Henry the Fifth would have been the idol of the North. The follies of his youth, the selfish ambition of his manhood, the Lollards roasted at slow fires, the prisoners massacred on the field of battle, the expiring lease of priestcraft renewed for another century, the dreadful legacy of a causeless and hopeless war bequeathed to a people who had no interest in its event, everything is forgotten but the victory of Agincourt. Francis Sforza, on the other hand, was the model of Italian heroes. He made his employers and his rivals alike his tools. He first overpowered his open enemies by the help of faithless allies; he then armed himself against his allies with the spoils taken from his enemies. By his incomparable dexterity, he raised himself from the precarious and dependent situation of a military adventurer to the first throne of Italy. To such a man much was forgiven,

[297]

hollow friendship, ungenerous enmity, violated faith. Such are the opposite errors which men commit, when their morality is not a science but a taste, when they abandon eternal principles for accidental associations.

We have illustrated our meaning by an instance taken from history. We will select another from fiction. Othello murders his wife; he gives orders for the murder of his lieutenant; he ends by murdering himself. Yet he never loses the esteem and affection of Northern readers. His intrepid and ardent spirit redeems everything. The unsuspecting confidence with which he listens to his adviser, the agony with which he shrinks from the thought of shame, the tempest of passion with which he commits his crimes, and the haughty fearlessness with which he avows them, give an extraordinary interest to his character. Iago, on the contrary, is the object of universal loathing. Many are inclined to suspect that Shakespeare has been seduced into an exaggeration unusual with him, and has drawn a monster who has no archetype in human nature. Now we suspect that an Italian audience in the fifteenth century would have felt very differently. Othello would have inspired nothing but detestation and contempt. The folly with which he trusts the friendly professions of a man whose promotion he had obstructed, the credulity with which he takes unsupported assertions, and trivial circumstances, for unanswerable proofs, the violence with which he silences the exculpation till the exculpation can only aggravate his misery, would have excited the abhorrence and disgust of the spectators. The conduct of Iago they would assuredly have condemned; but they would have condemned it as we condemn that of his victim. Something of interest and respect would have mingled with their disapprobation. The readiness of the traitor's wit, the clearness of his judgment, the skill with which he penetrates the dispositions of others and conceals his own, would have ensured to him a certain portion of their esteem.

So wide was the difference between the Italians and their neighbours. A similar difference existed between the Greeks of the second century before Christ, and their masters the Romans. The conquerors, brave and resolute, faithful to their engagements, and strongly influenced by religious feelings, were, at the same time, ignorant, arbitrary, and cruel. With the vanquished people were deposited all the art, the science, and the literature of the Western world. In poetry, in philosophy, in painting, in architecture, in sculpture, they had no rivals. Their manners were polished, their perceptions acute, their invention ready; they were tolerant, affable, humane; but of courage and sincerity they were almost utterly destitute. Every rude centurion consoled himself for his intellectual inferiority, by remarking that knowledge and taste seemed only to make men atheists, cowards, and slaves. The distinction long continued to be strongly marked, and furnished an admirable subject for the fierce sarcasms of Juvenal.

The citizen of an Italian commonwealth was the Greek of the time of Juvenal and the Greek of the time of Pericles, joined in one. Like the former, he was timid and pliable, artful and mean. But, like the latter, he had a country. Its independence and prosperity were dear to him. If his character were degraded by some base crimes, it was, on the other hand, ennobled by public spirit and by an honourable ambition.

A vice sanctioned by the general opinion is merely a vice. The evil terminates in itself. A vice condemned by the general opinion produces a pernicious effect on the whole character. The former is a local malady, the latter a constitutional taint. When the reputation of the offender is lost, he too often flings the remains of his virtue after it in despair. The Highland gentleman who, a century ago, lived by taking blackmail from his neighbours, committed the same crime for which Wild was accompanied to Tyburn by the huzzas of two hundred thousand people. But there can be no doubt that he was a much less depraved man than Wild. The deed for which Mrs. Brownrigg was hanged sinks into nothing, when compared with the conduct of the Roman who treated the public to a hundred pair of gladiators. Yet we should greatly wrong such a Roman if we supposed that his disposition was as cruel as that of Mrs. Brownrigg. In our own country, a woman forfeits her place in society by what, in a man, is too commonly considered as an honourable distinction, and, at worst, as a venial error. The consequence is notorious. The moral principle of a woman is frequently more impaired by a single lapse from virtue than that of a man by twenty years of intrigues. Classical antiquity would furnish us with instances stronger, if possible, than those to which we have referred.

We must apply this principle to the case before us. Habits of dissimulation and falsehood, no doubt, mark a man of our age and country as utterly worthless and abandoned. But it by no means follows that a similar judgment would be just in the case of an Italian of the middle ages. On the contrary, we frequently find those faults which we are accustomed to consider as certain indications of a mind altogether depraved, in company with great and good qualities, with generosity, with benevolence, with disinterestedness. From such a state of society, Palamedes, in the admirable dialogue of Hume, might have drawn illustrations of his theory as striking as any of those with which Fourli furnished him. These are not, we well know, the lessons which historians are generally most careful to teach, or readers most willing to learn. But they are not therefore useless. How Philip disposed his troops at Chæronea, where Hannibal crossed the Alps, whether Mary blew up Darnley, or Siquier shot Charles the Twelfth, and ten thousand other questions of the same description, are in themselves unimportant. The inquiry may amuse us, but the decision leaves us no wiser. He alone reads history aright who, observing how powerfully circumstances influence the feelings and opinions of men, how often vices pass into virtues and paradoxes into axioms, learns to distinguish what is accidental and transitory in human nature from what is essential and immutable.

In this respect no history suggests more important reflections than that of Tuscan and Lombard commonwealths. The character of the Italian states-man seems, at first sight, a collection of contradictions, a phantom as monstrous as the portress of hell in Milton, half divinity, half snake, majestic and beautiful above, grovelling and poisonous below. We see a man whose thoughts and words have no connection with each other, who never hesitates at an oath when he wishes to seduce, who never wants a pre-text when he is inclined to betray. His cruelties spring, not from the heat of blood, or the insanity of uncontrolled power, but from deep and cool medita-tion. His passions, like well-trained troops, are impetuous by rule, and in their most headstrong fury never forget the discipline to which they have been accustomed. His whole soul is occupied with vast and complicated schemes of ambition: yet his aspect and language exhibit nothing but philo-sophical moderation. Hatred and revenge eat into his heart: yet every look is a cordial smile, every gesture a familiar caress. He never excites the suspicion of his adversaries by petty provocations. His purpose is disclosed only when it is accomplished. His face is unruffled, his speech is courteous, till vigilance is laid asleep, till a vital point is exposed, till a sure aim is taken; and then he strikes for the first and last time. Military courage, the boast of the sottish German, of the frivolous and prating Frenchman, of the romantic and arrogant Spaniard, he neither possesses nor values. He shuns danger, not be-cause he is insensible to shame, but because, in the society in which he lives, timidity has ceased to be shameful. To do an injury openly is, in his estima-tion, as wicked as to do it secretly, and far less profitable. With him the most honourable means are those which are the surest, the speediest, and the dark-est. He cannot comprehend how a man should scruple to deceive those whom he does not scruple to destroy. He would think it madness to declare open hostilities against rivals whom he might stab in a friendly embrace, or poison in a consecrated wafer.

Yet this man, black with the vices which we consider as most loathsome, traitor, hypocrite, coward, assassin, was by no means destitute even of those virtues which we generally consider as indicating superior elevation of char-acter. In civil courage, in perseverance, in presence of mind, those barbarous warriors, who were foremost in the battle or the breach, were far his inferiors. Even the dangers which he avoided with a caution almost pusillanimous never confused his perceptions, never paralysed his inventive faculties, never wrung out one secret from his smooth tongue, and his inscrutable brow.

Though a dangerous enemy, and a still more dangerous accomplice, he could be a just and beneficent ruler. With so much unfairness in his policy, there was an extraordinary degree of fairness in his intellect. Indifferent to truth in the transactions of life, he was honestly devoted to truth in the researches of speculation. Wanton cruelty was not in his nature. On the contrary, where no political object was at stake, his disposition was soft and humane. The susceptibility of his nerves and the activity of his imagination inclined him to sympathise with the feelings of others, and to delight in the charities and courtesies of social life. Perpetually descending to actions which might seem to mark a mind diseased through all its faculties, he had nevertheless an exquisite sensibility, both for the natural and the moral sublime, for every graceful and every lofty conception. Habits of petty intrigue and dissimulation might have rendered him incapable of great general views, but that the expanding effect of his philosophical studies counteracted the narrowing tendency. He had the keenest enjoyment of wit, eloquence, and poetry. The fine arts profited alike by the severity of his judgment, and by the liberality of his patronage. The portraits of some of the remarkable Italians of those times are perfectly in harmony with this description. Ample and majestic foreheads, brows strong and dark, but not frowning, eyes of which the calm full gaze, while it expresses nothing, seems to discern everything, cheeks pale with thought and sedentary habits, lips formed with feminine delicacy, but compressed with more than masculine decision, mark out men at once enterprising and timid, men equally skilled in detecting the purposes of others, and in concealing their own, men who must have been formidable enemies and unsafe allies, but men, at the same time, whose tempers were mild and equable, and who possessed an amplitude and subtlety of intellect which would have rendered them eminent either in active or in contemplative life, and fitted them either to govern or to instruct mankind.

Every age and every nation has certain characteristic vices, which prevail almost universally, which scarcely any person scruples to avow, and which even rigid moralists but faintly censure. Succeeding generations change the fashion of their morals, with the fashion of their hats and their coaches; take some other kind of wickedness under their patronage, and wonder at the depravity of their ancestors. Nor is this all. Posterity, that high court of appeal which is never tired of eulogising its own justice and discernment, acts on such occasions like a Roman dictator after a general mutiny. Finding the delinquents too numerous to be all punished, it selects some of them at hazard, to bear the whole penalty of an offence in which they are not more deeply implicated than those who escape. Whether decimation be a convenient mode of military execution, we know not; but we solemnly protest against the introduction of such a principle into the philosophy of history.

In the present instance, the lot has fallen on Machiavelli, a man whose public conduct was upright and honourable, whose views of morality, where they differed from those of the persons around him, seemed to have differed for the better, and whose only fault was, that, having adopted some of the maxims then generally received, he arranged them more luminously, and expressed them more forcibly, than any other writer.

Having now, we hope, in some degree cleared the personal character of Machiavelli, we come to the consideration of his works. As a poet he is not entitled to a high place; but his comedies deserve attention.

The *Mandragola,* in particular, is superior to the best of Goldoni, and inferior only to the best of Molière. It is the work of a man who, if he had devoted himself to the drama, would probably have attained the highest eminence, and produced a permanent and salutary effect on the national taste. This we infer, not so much from the degree, as from the kind of its excellence. There are compositions which indicate still greater talent, and which are perused with still greater delight, from which we should have drawn very different conclusions. Books quite worthless are quite harmless. The sure sign of the general decline of an art is the frequent occurrence, not of deformity, but of misplaced beauty. In general Tragedy is corrupted by eloquence, and Comedy by wit.

The real object of the drama is the exhibition of human character. This, we conceive, is no arbitrary canon, originating in local and temporary associations, like those canons which regulate the number of acts in a play, or of syllables in a line. To this fundamental law every other regulation is subordinate. The situations which most signally develop character form the best plot. The mother tongue of the passions is the best style.

This principle rightly understood, does not debar the poet from any grace of composition. There is no style in which some man may not under some circumstances express himself. There is therefore no style which the drama rejects, none which it does not occasionally require. It is in the discernment of place, of time, and of person, that the inferior artists fail. The fantastic rhapsody of Mercutio, the elaborate declamation of Antony, are, where Shakspeare has placed them, natural and pleasing. But Dryden would have made Mercutio challenge Tybalt in hyperboles as fanciful as those in which he describes the chariot of Mab. Corneille would have represented Antony as scolding and coaxing Cleopatra with all the measured rhetoric of a funeral oration.

No writers have injured the Comedy of England so deeply as Congreve and Sheridan. Both were men of splendid wit and polished taste. Unhappily, they made all their characters in their own likeness. Their works bear the same relation to the legitimate drama which a transparency bears to a painting. There are no delicate touches, no hues imperceptibly fading into each other: the whole is lighted up with an universal glare. Outlines and tints are forgotten in the common blaze which illuminates all. The flowers and fruits of the intellect abound; but it is the abundance of a jungle, not of a garden, unwholesome, bewildering, unprofitable from its very plenty, rank from its very fragrance. Every fop, every boor, every valet, is a man of wit. The very butts and dupes, Tattle, Witwould, Puff, Acres, outshine the whole Hotel of Rambouillet. To prove the whole system of this school erroneous, it is only necessary to apply the test which dissolved the enchanted Florimel, to place the true by the false Thalia, to contrast the most celebrated characters which have been drawn by the writers of whom we speak with the Bastard in *King John* or the Nurse in *Romeo and Juliet*. It was not surely from want of wit that Shakspeare adopted so different a manner. Benedick and Beatrice throw Mirabel and Millamant into the shade. All the good sayings of the facetious houses of Absolute and Surface might have been clipped from the single character of Falstaff, without being missed. It would have been easy for that fertile mind to have given Bardolph and Shallow as much wit as Prince Hal, and to have made Dogberry and Verges retort on each other in sparkling epigrams. But he knew that such indiscriminate prodigality was, to use his own admirable language, "from the purpose of playing, whose end, both at the first and now, was, and is, to hold, as it were, the mirror up to Nature."

This digression will enable our readers to understand what we mean when we say that in the *Mandragola*, Machiavelli has proved that he completely understood the nature of the dramatic art, and possessed talents which would have enabled him to excel in it. By the correct and vigorous delineation of human nature, it produces interest without a pleasing or skillful plot, and laughter without the least ambition of wit. The lover, not a very delicate or generous lover, and his adviser the parasite, are drawn with spirit. The hypocritical confessor is an admirable portrait. He is, if we mistake not, the original of Father Dominic, the best comic character of Dryden. But old Nicias is the glory of the piece. We cannot call to mind anything that resembles him. The follies which Molière ridicules are those of affectation, not those of fatuity. Coxcombs and pedants, not absolute simpletons, are his game. Shakspeare has indeed a vast assortment of fools; but the precise species of which we speak is not, if we remember right, to be found there. Shallow is a fool. But his animal spirits supply, to a certain degree, the place of cleverness. His talk is to that of Sir John what soda water is to champagne. It has the effervescence though not the body or the flavour. Slender and Sir Andrew Aguecheek are fools, troubled with an uneasy consciousness of their folly, which in the latter produces meekness and docility, and in the former, awkwardness, obstinacy, and confusion. Cloten is an arrogant fool, Osric a fop-

pish fool, Ajax a savage fool; but Nicias is, as Thersites says of Patroclus, a
fool positive. His mind is occupied by no strong feeling; it takes every character, and retains none; its aspect is diversified, not by passions, but by faint
and transitory semblances of passion, a mock joy, a mock fear, a mock love,
a mock pride, which chase each other like shadows over its surface, and
vanish as soon as they appear. He is just idiot enough to be an object, not of
pity or horror, but of ridicule. He bears some resemblance to poor Calandrino,
whose mishaps, as recounted by Boccaccio, have made all Europe merry for
more than four centuries. He perhaps resembles still more closely Simon da
Villa, to whom Bruno and Buffalmacco promised the love of the Countess
Civillari. Nicias is, like Simon, of a learned profession; and the dignity with
which he wears the doctoral fur, renders his absurdities infinitely more grotesque. The old Tuscan is the very language for such a being. Its peculiar
simplicity gives even to the most forcible reasoning and the most brilliant
wit an infantine air, generally delightful, but to a foreign reader sometimes
a little ludicrous. Heroes and statesmen seem to lisp when they use it. It becomes Nicias incomparably, and renders all his silliness infinitely more silly.

We may add, that the verses with which the *Mandragola* is interspersed,
appear to us to be the most spirited and correct of all that Machiavelli has
written in metre. He seems to have entertained the same opinion; for he has
introduced some of them in other places. The contemporaries of the author
were not blind to the merits of this striking piece. It was acted at Florence
with the greatest success. Leo the Tenth was among its admirers, and by his
order it was represented at Rome.

The *Clizia* is an imitation of the *Casina* of Plautus, which is itself an imitation of the lost *Klēroumenoi* of Diphilus. Plautus was, unquestionably, one of
the best Latin writers; but the *Casina* is by no means one of his best plays;
nor is it one which offers great facilities to an imitator. The story is as alien
from modern habits of life, as the manner in which it is developed from the
modern fashion of composition. The lover remains in the country and the
heroine in her chamber during the whole action, leaving their fate to be
decided by a foolish father, a cunning mother, and two knavish servants.
Machiavelli has executed his task with judgment and taste. He has accom-
modated the plot to a different state of society, and has very dexterously
connected it with the history of his own times. The relation of the trick put
on the doting old lover is exquisitely humorous. It is far superior to the corresponding passage in the Latin comedy, and scarcely yields to the account
which Falstaff gives of his ducking.

Two other comedies without titles, the one in prose, the other in verse, appear among the works of Machiavelli. The former is very short, lively enough,
but of no great value. The latter we can scarcely believe to be genuine.

Neither its merits nor its defects remind us of the reputed author. It was first printed in 1796, from a manuscript discovered in the celebrated library of the Strozzi. Its genuineness, if we have been rightly informed, is established solely by the comparison of hands. Our suspicions are strengthened by the circumstance, that the same manuscript contained a description of the plague of 1527, which has also, in consequence, been added to the works of Machiavelli. Of this last composition the strongest external evidence would scarcely induce us to believe him guilty. Nothing was ever written more detestable in matter and manner. The narrations, the reflections, the jokes, the lamentations, are all the very worst of their respective kinds, at once trite and affected, threadbare tinsel from the Rag Fairs and Monmouth Streets of literature. A foolish schoolboy might write such a piece, and, after he had written it, think it much finer than the incomparable introduction of the *Decameron.* But that a shrewd statesman, whose earliest works are characterised by manliness of thought and language, should, at near sixty years of age, descend to such puerility, is utterly inconceivable.

The little novel of *Belphegor* is pleasantly conceived and pleasantly told. But the extravagance of the satire in some measure injures its effect. Machiavelli was unhappily married; and his wish to avenge his own cause and that of his brethren in misfortune, carried him beyond even the license of fiction. Jonson seems to have combined some hints taken from this tale, with others from Boccaccio, in the plot of *The Devil is an Ass,* a play which, though not the most highly finished of his compositions, perhaps that which exhibits the strongest proofs of genius.

The *Political Correspondence* of Machiavelli, first published in 1767, is unquestionably genuine, and highly valuable. The unhappy circumstances in which his country was placed during the greater part of his public life gave extraordinary encouragement to diplomatic talents. From the moment that Charles the Eighth descended from the Alps, the whole character of Italian politics was changed. The governments of the Peninsula ceased to form an independent system. Drawn from their old orbit by the attraction of the larger bodies which now approached them, they became mere satellites of France and Spain. All their disputes, internal and external, were decided by foreign influence. The contests of opposite factions were carried on, not as formerly in the senate-house or in the marketplace, but in the antechambers of Louis and Ferdinand. Under these circumstances, the prosperity of the Italian States depended far more on the ability of their foreign agents, than on the conduct of those who were intrusted with the domestic administration. The ambassador had to discharge functions far more delicate than transmitting orders of knighthood, introducing tourists, or presenting his brethren with the homage of his high consideration. He was an advocate to whose management the dearest interests of his clients were intrusted, a spy clothed with an inviolable character. Instead of consulting, by a reserved manner and ambiguous style, the dignity of those whom he represented, he was to plunge into all the intrigues of the Court at which he resided, to discover and flatter every weakness of the prince, and of the favourite who governed the prince, and of the lacquey who governed the favourite. He was to compliment the mistress and bribe the confessor, to panegyrise or supplicate, to laugh or weep, to accommodate himself to every caprice, to lull every suspicion, to treasure every hint, to be everything, to observe everything, to endure everything. High as the art of political intrigue had been carried in Italy, these were times which required it all.

On these arduous errands Machiavelli was frequently employed. He was sent to treat with the King of the Romans and with the Duke of Valentinois. He was twice ambassador at the Court of Rome, and thrice at that of France. In these missions, and in several others of inferior importance, he acquitted himself with great dexterity. His despatches form one of the most amusing and instructive collections extant. The narratives are clear and agreeably written; the remarks on men and things clever and judicious. The conversations are reported in a spirited and characteristic manner. We find ourselves introduced into the presence of the men who, during twenty eventful years, swayed the destinies of Europe. Their wit and their folly, their fretfulness and their merriment, are exposed to us. We are admitted to overhear their chat, and to watch their familiar gestures. It is interesting and curious to recognise, in circumstances which elude the notice of historians, the feeble violence and shallow cunning of Louis the Twelfth; the bustling insignificance of Maximilian, cursed with an impotent pruriency for renown, rash yet timid, obstinate yet fickle, always in a hurry, yet always too late; the fierce and haughty energy which gave dignity to the eccentricities of Julius; the soft and graceful manners which masked the insatiable ambition and the implacable hatred of Cæsar Borgia.

We have mentioned Cæsar Borgia. It is impossible not to pause for a moment on the name of a man in whom the political morality of Italy was so strongly personified, partially blended with the sterner lineaments of the Spanish character. On two important occasions Machiavelli was admitted to his society; once, at the moment when Cæsar's splendid villainy achieved its most signal triumph, when he caught in one snare and crushed at one blow all his most formidable rivals; and again when, exhausted by disease and overwhelmed by misfortunes, which no human prudence could have averted, he was the prisoner of the deadliest enemy of his house. These interviews between the greatest speculative and the greatest practical statesman of the age are fully described in the *Correspondence,* and form perhaps the most interesting part of it. From some passages in *The Prince,* and perhaps also from some indistinct traditions, several writers have supposed a connection between those remarkable men much closer than ever existed. The Envoy has even been accused of prompting the crimes of the artful and merciless tyrant. But from the official documents it is clear that their intercourse, though ostensibly amicable, was in reality hostile. It cannot be doubted, however, that the imagination of Machiavelli was strongly impressed, and his speculations on government coloured, by the observations which he made on the singular character and equally singular fortunes of a man who under such disadvantages had achieved such exploits; who, when sensuality, varied through innumerable forms, could no longer stimulate his sated mind, found a more powerful and durable excitement in the intense thirst of empire and revenge; who emerged from the sloth and luxury of the Roman purple the first prince and general of the age; who, trained in an unwarlike profession, formed a gallant army out of the dregs of an unwarlike people; who, after acquiring sovereignty by destroying his enemies, acquired popularity by destroying his tools; who had begun to employ for the most salutary ends the power which he had attained by the most atrocious means; who tolerated within the sphere of his iron despotism no plunderer or oppressor but himself; and who fell at last amidst the mingled curses and regrets of a people of whom his genius had been the wonder, and might have been the salvation. Some of those crimes of Borgia which to us appear the most odious would not, from causes which we have already considered have struck an Italian of the fifteenth century with equal horror. Patriotic feeling also might induce Machiavelli to look with some indulgence and regret on the memory of the only leader who could have defended the independence of Italy against the confederate spoilers of Cambray.

On this subject Machiavelli felt most strongly. Indeed the expulsion of the foreign tyrants, and the restoration of that golden age which had preceded the irruption of Charles the Eighth, were projects which, at that time, fascinated all the master-spirits of Italy. The magnificent vision delighted the great but ill-regulated mind of Julius. It divided with manuscripts and sauces, painters, and falcons, the attention of the frivolous Leo. It prompted the generous treason of Morone. It imparted a transient energy to the feeble mind and body of the last Sforza. It excited for one moment an honest ambition in the false heart of Pescara. Ferocity and insolence were not among the vices of the national character. To the discriminating cruelties of politicians, committed for great ends on select victims, the moral code of the Italians was too indulgent. But though they might have recourse to barbarity as an expedient, they did not require it as a stimulant. They turned with loathing from the atrocity of the strangers who seemed to love blood for its own sake, who, not content with subjugating, were impatient to destroy, who found a fiendish pleasure in razing magnificent cities, cutting the throats of enemies who cried for quarter, or suffocating an unarmed population by thousands in the caverns to which it had fled for safety. Such were the cruelties which daily excited the terror and disgust of a people among whom, till lately, the worst that a soldier had to fear in a pitched battle was the loss of his horse and the expense of his ransom. The swinish intemperance of Switzerland, the wolfish avarice of Spain, the gross licentiousness of the French, indulged in violation of hospitality, of decency, of love itself, the wanton inhumanity which was common to all the invaders, had made them objects of deadly hatred to the inhabitants of the Peninsula. The wealth which had been accumulated during centuries of prosperity and repose was rapidly melting away. The intellectual superiority of the oppressed people only rendered them more keenly sensible of their political degradation. Literature and taste, indeed, still disguised with a flush of hectic loveliness and brilliancy the ravages of an incurable decay. The iron had not yet entered into the soul. The time was not yet come when eloquence was to be gagged, and reason to be hoodwinked, when the harp of the poet was to be hung on the willows of Arno, and the right hand of the painter to forget its cunning. Yet a discerning eye might even then have seen that genius and learning would not long survive the state of things from which they had sprung, and that the great men whose talents gave lustre to that melancholy period had been formed under the influence of happier days, and would leave no successors behind them. The times which shine with the greatest splendour in literary history are not always those to which the human mind is most indebted. Of this we may be convinced, by comparing the generation which follows them with that which had preceded them. The first fruits which are reaped under a bad system often spring from seed sown under a good one. Thus it was, in some measure, with the Augustan age. Thus it was with the age of Raphael and Ariosto, of Aldus and Vida.

Machiavelli deeply regretted the misfortunes of his country, and clearly discerned the cause and the remedy. It was the military system of the Italian people which had extinguished their value and discipline, and left their wealth an easy prey to every foreign plunderer. The Secretary projected a scheme alike honourable to his heart and to his intellect, for abolishing the use of mercenary troops, and for organising a national militia.

The exertions which he made to effect this great object ought alone to rescue his name from obloquy. Though his situation and his habits were pacific, he studied with intense assiduity the theory of war. He made himself master of all its details. The Florentine Government entered into his views. A council of war was appointed. Levies were decreed. The indefatigable minister flew from place to place in order to superintend the execution of his design. The times were, in some respects, favourable to the experiment. The system of military tactics had undergone a great revolution. The cavalry was no longer considered as forming the strength of an army. The hours which a citizen could spare from his ordinary employments, though by no means sufficient to familiarise him with the exercise of a man-at-arms, might render him an useful foot-soldier. The dread of a foreign yoke, of plunder, massacre, and conflagration, might have conquered that repugnance to military pursuits which both the industry and the idleness of great towns commonly generate. For a time the scheme promised well. The new troops acquitted themselves respectably in the field. Machiavelli looked with parental rapture on the success of his plan, and began to hope that the arms of Italy might once more be formidable to the barbarians of the Tagus and the Rhine. But the tide of misfortune came on before the barriers which should have withstood it were prepared. For a time, indeed, Florence might be considered as peculiarly fortunate. Famine and sword and pestilence had devastated the fertile plains and stately cities of the Po. All the curses denounced of old against Tyre seemed to have fallen on Venice. Her merchants already stood afar off, lamenting for their great city. The time seemed near when the sea-weed should overgrow her silent Rialto, and the fisherman wash his nets in her deserted arsenal. Naples had been four times conquered and reconquered by tyrants equally indifferent to its welfare, and equally greedy for its spoils. Florence, as yet, had only to endure degradation and extortion, to submit to the mandates of foreign powers, to buy over and over again, at an enormous price, what was already justly her own, to return thanks for being wronged, and to ask pardon for being in the right. She was at length deprived of the blessings even of this infamous and servile repose. Her military and political institutions were swept away together. The Medici returned, in the train of foreign invaders, from their long exile. The policy of Machiavelli was abandoned; and his public services were requited with poverty, imprisonment, and torture.

The fallen statesman still clung to his project with unabated ardour. With the view of vindicating it from some popular objections and of refuting some prevailing errors on the subject of military science, he wrote his seven books on *The Art of War*. This excellent work is in the form of a dialogue. The opinions of the writer are put into the mouth of Fabrizio Colonna, a powerful nobleman of the Ecclesiastical State, and an officer of distinguished merit in the service of the King of Spain. Colonna visits Florence on his way from Lombardy to his own domains. He is invited to meet some friends at the house of Cosimo Rucellai, an amiable and accomplished young man, whose early death Machiavelli feelingly deplores. After partaking of an elegant entertainment, they retire from the heat into the most shady recesses of the garden. Fabrizio is struck by the sight of some uncommon plants. Cosimo says that, though rare, in modern days, they are frequently mentioned by the classical authors, and that his grandfather, like many other Italians, amused himself with practising the ancient methods of gardening. Fabrizio expresses his regret that those who, in later times, affected the manners of the old Romans should select for imitation the most trifling pursuits. This leads to a conversation on the decline of military discipline and on the best means of restoring it. The institution of the Florentine militia is ably defended; and several improvements are suggested in the details.

The Swiss and the Spaniards were, at that time, regarded as the best soldiers in Europe. The Swiss battalion consisted of pikemen, and bore a close resemblance to the Greek phalanx. The Spaniards, like the soldiers of Rome, were armed with the sword and the shield. The victories of Flamininus and Aemilius over the Macedonian kings seem to prove the superiority of the weapons used by the legions. The same experiment had been recently tried with the same result at the battle of Ravenna, one of those tremendous days into which human folly and wickedness compress the whole devastation of a famine or a plague. In that memorable conflict, the infantry of Arragon, the old companions of Gonsalvo, deserted by all their allies, hewed a passage through the thickest of the imperial pikes, and effected an unbroken retreat, in the face of the gendarmerie of De Foix, and the re-nowned artillery of Este. Fabrizio, or rather Machiavelli, proposes to combine the two systems, to arm the foremost lines with the pike for the purpose of repulsing cavalry, and those in the rear with the sword, as being a weapon better adapted for every other purpose. Throughout the work, the author expresses the highest admiration of the military science of the ancient Romans, and the greatest contempt for the maxims which had been in vogue amongst the Italian commanders of the preceding generation. He prefers infantry to cavalry, and fortified camps to fortified towns. He is inclined to substitute rapid movements and decisive engagements for the languid and dilatory operations of his countrymen. He attaches very little importance to the invention of gunpowder. Indeed he seems to think that it ought scarcely to produce any change in the mode of arming or of disposing troops. The general testimony of historians, it must be allowed, seems to prove that the ill-constructed and ill-served artillery of those times, though useful in a siege, was of little value on the field of battle.

Of the tactics of Machiavelli we will not venture to give an opinion: but we are certain that his book is most able and interesting. As a commentary on the history of his times, it is invaluable. The ingenuity, the grace, and the perspicuity of the style, and the eloquence and animation of particular passages, must give pleasure even to readers who take no interest in the subject.

The Prince and the *Discourses on Livy* were written after the fall of the Republican Government. The former was dedicated to the Young Lorenzo di Medici. This circumstance seems to have disgusted the contemporaries of the writer far more than the doctrines which have rendered the name of the work odious in later times. It was considered as an indication of political apostasy. The fact however seems to have been that Machiavelli, despairing of the liberty of Florence, was inclined to support any government which might preserve her independence. The interval which separated a democracy and a despotism, Soderini and Lorenzo, seemed to vanish when compared with the difference between the former and the present state of Italy, between the security, the opulence, and the repose which she had enjoyed under her native rulers, and the misery in which she had been plunged since the fatal year in which the first foreign tyrant had descended from the Alps. The noble and pathetic exhortation with which *The Prince* concludes shows how strongly the writer felt upon this subject.

The Prince traces the progress of an ambitious man, the *Discourses* the progress of an ambitious people. The same principles on which, in the former work, the elevation of an individual is explained, are applied in the latter, to the longer duration and more complex interest of a society. To a modern statesman the form of the *Discourses* may appear to be puerile. In truth Livy is not an historian on whom implicit reliance can be placed, even in cases where he must have possessed considerable means of information. And the first Decade, to which Machiavelli has confined himself, is scarcely entitled to more credit than our Chronicle of British Kings who reigned before the Roman invasion. But the commentator is indebted to Livy for little more than a few texts which he might as easily have extracted from the *Vulgate* or the *Decameron*. The whole train of thought is original.

On the peculiar immorality which has rendered *The Prince* unpopular, and which is almost equally discernible in the *Discourses,* we have already given our opinion at length. We have attempted to show that it belonged rather to the age than to the man, that it was a partial taint, and by no means implied general depravity. We cannot, however, deny that it is a great blemish, and that it considerably diminishes the pleasure which, in other respects, those works must afford to every intelligent mind.

It is, indeed, impossible to conceive a more healthful and vigorous constitution of the understanding than that which these works indicate. The qualities of the active and the contemplative statesman appear to have been blended in the mind of the writer into a rare and exquisite harmony. His skill in the details of business had not been acquired at the expense of his general powers. It had not rendered his mind less comprehensive; but it had served to correct his speculations and to impart to them that vivid and practical character which so widely distinguishes them from the vague theories of most political philosophers.

Every man who has seen the world knows that nothing is so useless as a general maxim. If it be very moral and very true, it may serve for a copy to a charity-boy. If, like those of Rochefoucault, it be sparkling and whimsical, it may make an excellent motto for an essay. But few indeed of the many wise apophthegms which have been uttered, from the time of the Seven Sages of Greece to that of Poor Richard, have prevented a single foolish action. We give the highest and the most peculiar praise to the precepts of Machiavelli when we say that they may frequently be of real use in regulating conduct, not so much because they are more just or more profound than those which might be culled from other authors, as because they can be more readily applied to the problems of real life.

There are errors in these works. But they are errors which a writer, situated like Machiavelli, could scarcely avoid. They arise, for the most part, from a single defect which appears to us to pervade his whole system. In his political scheme, the means had been more deeply considered than the ends. The great principle, that societies and laws exist only for the purpose of increasing the sum of private happiness, is not recognised with sufficient clearness. The good of the body, distinct from the good of the members, and sometimes hardly compatible with the good of the members, seems to be the object which he proposes to himself. Of all political fallacies, this has perhaps had the widest and the most mischievous operation. The state of society in the little commonwealths of Greece, the close connection and mutual dependence of the citizens, and the severity of the laws of war, tended to encourage an opinion which, under such circumstances, could hardly be called erroneous. The interests of every individual were inseparably bound up with those of the State. An invasion destroyed his corn-fields and vineyards, drove him from his home, and compelled him to encounter all the hardships of a military life. A treaty of peace restored him to security and comfort. A victory doubled the number of his slaves. A defeat perhaps made him a slave himself. When Pericles, in the Peloponnesian war, told the Athenians, that, if their country triumphed, their private losses would speedily be repaired, but, that, if their arms failed of success, every individual amongst them would probably be ruined, he spoke no more than the truth. He spoke to men whom the tribute of vanquished cities supplied with food and clothing, with the luxury of the bath and the amusements of the theatre, on whom the greatness of their country conferred rank, and before whom the members of less prosperous communities trembled; to men who, in case of a change in the public fortunes, would, at least, be deprived of every comfort and every distinction which they enjoyed. To be butchered on the smoking ruins of their city, to be dragged in chains to a slave-market, to see one child torn from them to dig in the quarries of Sicily, and another to guard the harams of Persepolis, these were the frequent and probable consequences of national calamities. Hence, among the Greeks, patriotism became a governing principle, or rather an ungovernable passion. Their legislators and their philosophers took it for granted that, in providing for the strength and greatness of the state, they sufficiently provided for the happiness of the people. The writers of the Roman empire lived under despots, into whose dominion a hundred nations were melted down, and whose gardens would have covered the little commonwealths of Phlius and Platæa. Yet they continued to employ the same language, and to cant about the duty of sacrificing everything to a country to which they owed nothing.

Causes similar to those which had influenced the disposition of the Greeks operated powerfully on the less vigorous and daring character of the Italians. The Italians, like the Greeks, were members of small communities. Every man was deeply interested in the welfare of the society to which he belonged, a partaker in its wealth and its poverty, in its glory and its shame. In the age of Machiavelli this was peculiarly the case. Public events had produced an immense sum of misery to private citizens. The Northern invaders had brought want to their boards, infamy to their beds, fire to their roofs, and the knife to their throats. It was natural that a man who lived in times like these should overrate the importance of those measures by which a nation is rendered formidable to its neighbours, and undervalue those which make it prosperous within itself.

Nothing is more remarkable in the political treatises of Machiavelli than the fairness of mind which they indicate. It appears where the author is in the wrong, almost as strongly as where he is in the right. He never advances a false opinion because it is new or splendid, because he can clothe it in a happy phrase, or defend it by an ingenious sophism. His errors are at once explained by a reference to the circumstances in which he was placed. They evidently were not sought out; they lay in his way, and could scarcely be avoided. Such mistakes must necessarily be committed by early speculators in every science.

In this respect it is amusing to compare *The Prince* and the *Discourses* with the *Spirit of Laws*. Montesquieu enjoys, perhaps, a wider celebrity than any political writer of modern Europe. Something he doubtless owes to his merit, but much more to his fortune. He had the good luck of a Valentine. He caught the eye of the French nation, at the moment when it was waking from the long sleep of political and religious bigotry; and, in consequence, he became a favourite. The English, at that time, considered a Frenchman who talked about constitutional checks and fundamental laws as a prodigy not less astonishing than the learned pig or the musical infant. Specious but shallow, studious of effect, indifferent to truth, eager to build a system, but careless of collecting those materials out of which alone a sound and durable system can be built, the lively President constructed theories as rapidly and as slightly as card-houses, no sooner projected than completed, no sooner completed than blown away, no sooner blown away than forgotten. Machiavelli errs only because his experience, acquired in a very peculiar state of society, could not always enable him to calculate the effect of institutions differing from those of which he had observed the operation. Montesquieu errs, because he has a fine thing to say, and is resolved to say it. If the phæ-nomena which lie before him will not suit his purpose, all history must be ransacked. If nothing established by authentic testimony can be racked or chipped to suit his Procrustean hypothesis, he puts up with some monstrous fable about Siam, or Bantam, or Japan, told by writers compared with whom Lucian and Gulliver were veracious, liars by a double right, as travellers and as Jesuits.

Propriety of thought, and propriety of diction, are commonly found together. Obscurity and affectation are the two greatest faults of style. Obscurity of expression generally springs from confusion of ideas; and the same wish to dazzle at any cost which produces affectation in the manner of a writer, is likely to produce sophistry in his reasonings. The judicious and candid mind of Machiavelli shows itself in his luminous, manly, and polished language. The style of Montesquieu, on the other hand, indicates in every page a lively and ingenious, but an unsound mind. Every trick of expression, from the mysterious conciseness of an oracle to the flippancy of a Parisian coxcomb, is employed to disguise the fallacy of some positions, and the triteness of others. Absurdities are brightened into epigrams; truisms are darkened into enigmas. It is with difficulty that the strongest eye can sustain the glare with which some parts are illuminated, or penetrate the shade in which others are concealed.

The political works of Machiavelli derive a peculiar interest from the mournful earnestness which he manifests whenever he touches on topics connected with the calamities of his native land. It is difficult to conceive any situation more painful than that of a great man, condemned to watch the lingering agony of an exhausted country, to tend it during the alternate fits of stupefaction and raving which precede its dissolution, and to see the symptoms of vitality disappear one by one, till nothing is left but coldness, darkness, and corruption. To this joyless and thankless duty was Machiavelli called. In the energetic language of the prophet, he was "mad for the sight of his eyes which he saw," disunion in the council, effeminacy in the camp, liberty extinguished, commerce decaying, national honour sullied, an enlightened and flourishing people given over to the ferocity of ignorant savages. Though his opinions had not escaped the contagion of that political immorality which was common among his countrymen, his natural disposition seems to have been rather stern and impetuous than pliant and artful. When the misery and degradation of Florence and the foul outrage which he had himself sustained recur to his mind, the smooth craft of his profession and his nation is exchanged for the honest bitterness of scorn and anger. He speaks like one sick of the calamitous times and abject people among whom his lot is cast. He pines for the strength and glory of ancient Rome, for the fasces of Brutus, and the sword of Scipio, the gravity of the curule chair, and the bloody pomp of the triumphal sacrifice. He seems to be transported back to the days when eight hundred thousand Italian warriors sprung to arms at the rumour of a Gallic invasion. He breathes all the spirit of those intrepid and haughty senators who forgot the dearest ties of nature in the claims of public duty, who looked with disdain on the elephants and on the gold of Pyrrhus, and listened with unaltered composure to the tremendous tidings of Cannæ. Like an ancient temple deformed by the barbarous architecture of a later age, his character acquires an interest from the very circumstances which debase it. The original proportions are rendered more striking by the contrast which they present to the mean and incongruous additions.

The influence of the sentiments which we have described was not apparent in his writings alone. His enthusiasm, barred from the career which it would have selected for itself, seems to have found a vent in desperate levity. He enjoyed a vindictive pleasure in outraging the opinions of a society which he despised. He became careless of the decencies which were expected from a man so highly distinguished in the literary and political world. The sarcastic bitterness of his conversation disgusted those who were more inclined to accuse his licentiousness than their own degeneracy, and who were unable to conceive the strength of those emotions which are concealed by the jests of the wretched, and by the follies of the wise.

The historical works of Machiavelli still remain to be considered. The *Life of Castruccio Castracani* will occupy us for a very short time, and would scarcely have demanded our notice, had it not attracted a much greater share of public attention than it deserves. Few books, indeed, could be more interesting than a careful and judicious account, from such a pen, of the illustrious Prince of Lucca, the most eminent of those Italian chiefs who, like Pisistratus and Gelon, acquired a power felt rather than seen, and resting, not on law or on prescription, but on the public favour and on their great personal qualities. Such a work would exhibit to us the real nature of that species of sovereignty, so singular and so often misunderstood, which the Greeks denominated tyranny, and which, modified in some degree by the feudal system, reappeared in the commonwealths of Lombardy and Tuscany. But this little composition of Machiavelli is in no sense a history. It has no pretensions to fidelity. It is a trifle, and not a very successful trifle. It is scarcely more authentic than the novel of *Belphegor,* and is very much duller.

The last great work of this illustrious man was the history of his native city. It was written by command of the Pope, who, as chief of the house of Medici, was at that time sovereign of Florence. The characters of Cosmo, of Piero, and of Lorenzo, are, however, treated with a freedom and impartiality equally honourable to the writer and to the patron. The miseries and humiliations of dependence, the bread which is more bitter than every other food, the stairs which are more painful than every other ascent, had not broken the spirit of Machiavelli. The most corrupting post in a corrupting profession had not depraved the generous heart of Clement.

The *History* does not appear to be the fruit of much industry or research. It is unquestionably inaccurate. But it is elegant, lively, and picturesque, beyond any other in the Italian language. The reader, we believe, carries away from it a more vivid and a more faithful impression of the national character and manners than from more correct accounts. The truth is, that the book belongs rather to ancient than to modern literature. It is in the style, not of Davila and Clarendon, but of Herodotus and Tacitus. The classical histories may almost be called romances founded in fact. The relation is, no doubt, in all its principal points, strictly true. But the numerous little incidents which heighten the interest, the words, the gestures, the looks, are evidently furnished by the imagination of the author. The fashion of later times is different. A more exact narrative is given by the writer. It may be doubted whether more exact notions are conveyed to the reader. The best portraits are perhaps those in which there is a slight mixture of caricature, and we are not certain that the best histories are not those in which a little of the exaggeration of fictitious narrative is judiciously employed. Something is lost in accuracy; but much is gained in effect. The fainter lines are neglected; but the great characteristic features are imprinted on the mind for ever.

The *History* terminates with the death of Lorenzo de' Medici. Machiavelli had, it seems, intended to continue his narrative to a later period. But his death prevented the execution of his design; and the melancholy task of recording the desolation and shame of Italy devolved on Guicciardini.

Machiavelli lived long enough to see the commencement of the last struggle for Florentine liberty. Soon after his death monarchy was finally established, not such a monarchy as that of which Cosmo had laid the foundations deep in the institutions and feelings of his countryman, and which Lorenzo had embellished with the trophies of every science and every art; but a loathsome tyranny, proud and mean, cruel and feeble, bigoted and lascivious. The character of Machiavelli was hateful to the new masters of Italy; and those parts of his theory which were in strict accordance with their own daily practice afforded a pretext for blackening his memory. His works were misrepresented by the learned, misconstrued by the ignorant, censured by the Church, abused with all the rancour of simulated virtue by the tools of a base government, and the priests of a baser superstition. The name of the man whose genius had illuminated all the dark places of policy, and to whose patriotic wisdom an oppressed people had owed their last chance of emancipation and revenge, passed into a proverb of infamy. For more than two hundred years his bones lay undistinguished. At length, an English nobleman paid the last honours to the greatest statesman of Florence. In the church of Santa Croce a monument was erected to his memory, which is contemplated with reverence by all who can distinguish the virtues of a great mind through the corruptions of a degenerate age, and which will be approached with still deeper homage when the object to which his public life was devoted shall be attained, when the foreign yoke shall be broken, when a second Procida shall avenge the wrongs of Naples, when a happier Rienzi shall restore the good estate of Rome, when the streets of Florence and Bologna shall again resound with their ancient war-cry, *Popolo; popolo; muoiano i tiranni!*

M O N T A I G N E

[*1533–1592*]

THE TERM "ESSAY" SPRINGS FROM MONTAIGNE'S DESCRIPTION OF HIS WRITINGS
as attempts (*essais*) to come to grips with experience. No man has been
more honest in dealing with himself or his age. Montaigne as a rule begins
an essay with a personal anecdote or incident, and then, like a composer of
themes and variations, explores its implications. He has been called a skeptic,
but he is a particular kind of skeptic, one who sees the possibility of believing everything, rather than nothing. His skepticism does not comfortably
exclude the diverse or the unusual, but encompasses it; all oppositions and
contradictions are resolved within the large unities of nature and the self.

It may be objected that Lüthy does not touch on Montaigne's ability to
make his language convey the cadences of his thought. He does not talk in
the conventional terms of "style." But the attentive reader will discover that
"the *art* of being truthful" is an art of representation in words; the result is
a completely realized style.

Herbert Lüthy is a distinguished historian, and has translated Montaigne
into German.

Reprinted from *Encounter,* November 1953.

HERBERT LÜTHY

Montaigne, or the Art of Being Truthful

Reader, here is a truthful book. It warns you, even as you first enter it, that I have set myself only a familiar and private end. I have taken no thought in it either for your needs or my glory. My powers are not equal to such a task. I wish to be seen in it without art or affectation, but simply and naturally: for it is myself I portray. My faults will be found here as they are; also my plain nature, so far as decorum will allow. Had I lived among those peoples of whom it is said they dwell still under the sweet freedom of nature's first laws, I assure you I would have willingly pictured myself wholly naked. Thus, reader, I myself am the only content of my book; there is no reason for you to employ your leisure on so idle and frivolous a subject. Farewell then! From *Montaigne,* the first of March, 1580.

THIS WAS MONTAIGNE'S OWN FOREWORD TO THE READER WHEN HE FIRST SET before the public the book, written "for few people and few years," which has since stood fast against the centuries. What remains to be said after this? Montaigne and his book say frankly everything that they have to say about each other: Montaigne about his book and the book about him; and both go to extraordinary lengths to guard against misunderstanding. "Montaigne is neighbour to us all," and the most openhearted, even gossipy neighbour we could wish for. He hides nothing from us, or nothing essential; and if he, who hardly conceals from us a single peculiarity of his diet or his digestion, forgets to speak of other things—completely of his mother, who survived him by nearly ten years, almost completely of his wife, whose existence he mentions once in passing, and of his children, of whom "two or three" died in childhood—then we can conclude only that these were things that touched him little; and that fact, too, rounds out his portrait.

In the same way, what he has to say about God, the world, and his own times is without shadow or mystery: the absolutely straight-forward, unconnected, and changeable opinions of a landed nobleman of middle-class temperament and extraction, opinions born more out of his experience and the common judgement of mankind than of any definite *Weltanschauung,* and quite without pretensions to anything higher or more universal. For he is much less concerned to present the results of his thinking, or even to arrive at results at all, than to follow his thought itself in its playful movement, and to carry us with him. We can, indeed, follow him effortlessly, without breathing heavily, for this thought of his never goes very far, it undertakes only little sauntering strolls and always turns back before getting out of sight. Each one of his essays, like the book itself, begins without a purpose; if he sets an object before his mind it is only to put it in motion, as one throws a stone ahead of a dog, not to have him bring it back but to have him run, and is content if he brings back not the stone but an odd piece of wood or a dead mouse.

So it is possible to leaf through the Essays, reading a few pages and turning away at pleasure, as Montaigne himself read, as all his best readers have read him, without fear of losing the thread, for there is none. One learns to know him through his book as one would learn to know one's neighbour in life, through accidental meetings, and the more common the meetings, the more unimportant and unconnected the strokes, the more truthful does the portrait finally become. The best introduction to his book might be simply: Take it and read! or better still: read it and take!—for everyone is free to take what suits him, as Montaigne himself took whatever suited him, in order to make it his own, as, according to his own account, he plucked out of his Plutarch, whenever he picked it up, now a wing and now a leg.

Still, almost everyone who has read Montaigne in this way has mistaken the leg or the wing he brought away for the whole of Montaigne. There have been almost as many different Montaignes as there have been readers of him. For the pious, he was a man of piety, and for the free-thinking, a free-thinker; for the pagan, a pagan, and for Christians, a Christian. For the descendants of the Stoa, he was a Stoic moralist, for Epicureans of the higher or lower variety, he was an Epicurean of their variety; the men of the Enlightenment quoted his judgements on witchcraft and miracles with untiring enthusiasm, their adversaries pointed just as enthusiastically to the long essay called "Apology for Raymond Sebond" and its dethronement of reason. Conservatives found in him a defender of tradition, and the inherited order; the advocates of natural rights saw him as a critic of positive law and of the conventions and veneers of civilisation. The list could be extended endlessly, and just as long a list might be drawn up of what his opponents found to reproach him with.

But, in view of all this, how do things stand with his truthfulness? Is it possible to have so many faces without disguising oneself, and so many truths without being a liar?

Montaigne said everything there was to be said about this too, but it has not helped him much. His foreword to the reader is to be taken quite literally—yet that is exactly what almost no one has done. So that if the Essays hardly require an introduction they do perhaps require some advice: not to look in them for what they do not contain—that is, truths about anything or anyone except Michel de Montaigne. His thoughts and opinions may be wrong or right; they are true only insofar as they are *his* thoughts. Their truth does not lie in where they tend, for they tend everywhere, but in the place from which they depart and to which they return. *"Ramener à soi"* is one of the key phrases of the Essays, untranslatable in its full range of meaning; it means to draw back on oneself, to draw to oneself, to take to oneself, but it contains also the logical meaning of a movement of thought from the object to oneself, and the physical gesture of picking up, holding, or embracing. So Montaigne draws to himself what would escape him: his life, his feelings, his thoughts, his book, his very self; and his reproach against the "licentiousness of thought" is nothing else but that it wishes to pass beyond him and his limitations in order to fix itself in the objective, the absolute, and the unlimited. He, Montaigne, wishes to remain with himself.

For this reason his excursions into the more abstruse matters of philosophy remain, even measured by the standards of his time, scanty and negligent, a mere careless gesture of warding off; he does not care about knowledge of things, only about knowledge of himself. Even when he does for once come to grips with the question of how man can know the truth, as in the "Apology for Raymond Sebond," his epistemology remains a kind of shaking of the head: how can man know anything when he cannot even grasp himself? All his philosophic arguments are such arguments *ad hominem,* as unphilosophic as they can be. What has the objective truth of a philosophic proposition to do with the philosopher who propounds it, his indigestion, his passions, and his personal truthfulness?

These are frivolous arguments for anyone who is seeking knowledge of things. But Montaigne has another purpose, for which he wishes never to lose sight of himself, and another frame of reference, which measures truth not by what is said, but by the sayer—which prefers, in other words, subjective truthfulness to objective truth. Every discipline, from physics to theology, can advance step by step from once-given premises to conclusions that pass far beyond the insight and imaginative power of the investigator, and lose all connection with him. Such knowledge, which cuts itself loose from the knower and cleaves to the object, has nothing more to say to him, Michel de Montaigne; it is of no use for self-knowledge. It is for this reason that the disconnectedness, wilfulness, and apparent purposelessness of his essays, the sauntering, tentative, and unpredictable movement of his thought, are not mere wilfulness or incapacity. A thought or a style which submitted itself to any discipline would cease, immediately or wholly, to be his own. He seems always careful to let no structure of thought arise which might stand by itself without his intervention, to let no method intrude between him and his fancies. He prefers, rather, looking on ironically, to let his mind build little houses of cards which he blows down again before they grow too large.

And yet these "mental exercises" reach a greatness, a truth and a profundity, when he follows himself into the twilight borderlands of his consciousness, on the edge of sleep, dreams, distraction, torpor, and death—in those corners where consciousness, Montaigne's consciousness, first becomes fully realised, that is, detached from every connection with the extraneous. These are the places in which he reaches furthest, and we can learn from them not to content ourselves too lightly with Montaigne's seeming superficiality; for much of the dawdling and dallying of the Essays amid the banal and the trivial is, in the same way, a kind of half-sleep of the unconsciousness, in which it permits itself, unknowingly, to be observed. To be sure, many thoughts are brought to light in this way whose interest and even greatness is in themselves; but they are by-products of a thought directed to other ends. For Montaigne, it is not a question of taking the measure of his eyes. The way in which he sees things, now so, now otherwise, leads to no conclusions about the things, only about himself.

"Montaigne against miracles; Montaigne for miracles," Pascal noted. Montaigne is both at once. He brought together tirelessly and indiscriminately a whole chamber of curiosities, full of all the possible conclusions of his own and all other philosophies, not to play them off against each other, but to display the range and possibility of human thought, and with a little prompting he would accept them all—and the most unusual with the most alacrity. They contradict each other?—yes, but all together they mark out the borders of human awareness, with all its manifold possibilities. "Truth is the whole." To the Essays, too, Hegel's dictum applies, but altered: Michel de Montaigne's truth is the sum of his contradictions. And this truth of his he demonstrates in his book as Dionysus the Cynic demonstrated motion by walking: there he stands, a whole man, in whom all these contradictions come to harmony.

Truth of another, general, superpersonal kind he does not possess and is not looking for. "I do not see the whole of anything," he says, and adds, smiling: "Nor do those who promise to show it to us." This renunciation troubles him so little that almost every general opinion passes as equally valid with him; rather than worry his head over it, he prefers to hold fast to those opinions customary in his land and his family, certainly as good as any other. He is at pains to set them outside the reach of all human possibility of knowing—this is the whole content of the "Apology for Raymond Sebond"—the better to put them at a distance. They are unattainable, and they do not trouble him. His essays, those little strolls of thought, never set out in search of such truths, but always and only, in search of Montaigne. The whole, which he calls God or Nature, Fate or Order, almost without distinction, gets along very well without him, and he without it: or rather, he is embedded and hidden in it, like the mole or the plant louse, who also knows nothing of how things stand with the universe.

It is this placid, unquestioning taking of things for granted which roused Pascal to indignation. "There are only three types of men: those who serve God, having found Him; those who exert themselves to seek Him, not having found Him; and those who live without seeking Him and without having found Him." It is plain to which of these categories of Pascal's Michel de Montaigne belongs. Whatever he was, a god-seeker he was not. He fulfilled his religious obligations as he fulfilled those of his rank, his marriage, and his public office, and there is no reason to doubt that he fulfilled them honourably and earnestly. But it was not as something of his own, not out of personal conviction, or as an expression of his own essence; it was rather as something expected of him, in the station allotted him by birth and heredity. The separation is astonishingly clear through the Essays, and it requires gross bias not to see it: where Montaigne is speaking in general and about generalities he seldom neglects to weave into his discourse the rhetoric of orthodoxy which was especially advisable in his age of religious persecution; when he speaks of his external behaviour, his morals and habits, he takes pains to note his crossing of himself, his saying of grace, and his attendance at Mass; but when he really turns to himself, when he is no longer speaking of mankind, life and death in general, but of himself, his life and his death, then faith is left behind, as habit and philosophy are left behind, and he is alone with himself.

This then is Montaignean scepticism. But the philosophic label does not really suit him. Certainly, the description of sceptical thought given by Hegel in the *Phenomenology of the Spirit* sounds word for word as if it were meant for Montaigne; it is perfectly true that he "only deals with the particular and wallows in the accidental," that his style of thought is "this senseless drivel alternating from one extreme of undifferentiated self-awareness to the other of chance awareness, confused and confusing," and "it perceives its freedom sometimes as a revolt against all the confusion and accidentalness of being and at other times as a falling back into the unessential and a frolicking about in it." It is, too, "only . . . a musical thinking which never arrives at . . . the objective concept" and "so we see only a personality restricted to, and brooding on, itself and its own little activities, as unfortunate as it is unhappy. . . ." How well-aimed this description of the sceptical mind is—and how widely it misses Montaigne! The man who steps before us in the Essays is as little a representative of Hegel's "unhappy consciousness" as he is the damned and despairing figure of Pascal. And just this is perhaps the scandal of Montaigne: to be so aware of that limitation which does not allow him to grasp "the whole," to content himself with the imperfect and the fragmentary, and yet to be so wholly untragic. His scepticism, philosophic as well as religious, is no sorrowful renunciation, because it is not a philosophy, but a form of spiritual hygiene; a device to help hold off the extraneous and give room for what is his own. His truthfulness applies other, but no less stringent, criteria to truth: is it mine? does it fit me? does it remain mine even in sickness, in pain, and in death?

One can only speak of Montaigne in contradictions, and as he himself rambled on from one thing to another, so one can ramble on in speaking of him, for his subject is himself, in which all other subjects are mirrored. He imposed no method on himself, not even a method for self-knowledge, and there is no such method except unconditional honesty with oneself. Those astonishing journeys of exploration he made on the frontiers of the unconscious were only possible because through long acquaintance with himself he had found the right distance to keep, in order—as he says once—to consider himself impartially "like a neighbour, or a tree." One can follow precisely this process through the development of the Essays, the process by which Montaigne wins that distance from himself, that lack of a *parti pris,* which is the hardest part of truthfulness.

The first two books of the Essays, in their earlier form, are full of the general truths of Stoic wisdom; these are the essays of which Montaigne later said that they "smelt a little of the property of others." But then that spiritual hygiene begins to operate, the sceptical questioning of his own wisdom—how do I come to it, I, Michel de Montaigne, landed nobleman of Perigord, fifty years old, a little below average height, afflicted with incipient kidney-stones? What does it mean to *me?* This is the beginning of Montaigne's marvellous truthfulness, this return to self, this limitation of truth to his personal measure; and the Essays have remained unique in the consistency with which they follow the path of honesty—the most personal book in world literature. Unique, perhaps, because they took this path not *a priori* but artlessly and unintentionally at first, then with a growing joy of discovery. For the personal belongs also to things one does not achieve by a purposeful striving after them; the self that, without long detours, at once reaches itself, has in reality gone no distance at all and remains empty. To take the measure of one's eyes it is necessary to seek first the measure of things.

Montaigne reflected very earnestly on things outside himself, on the nature and destiny of man, on the state, on law, virtue, marriage and education, on belief in miracles, on the passions, and, over and over, on the possibility of objective knowledge, always with reference to himself but never with reference only to himself. So this book of self-knowledge is no confession, no autobiography, no self-justification or self-accusation, no *Ecce Homo.* Montaigne does not start from himself, he comes to himself quite simply, as one comes to the point.

In Montaigne all the usual motives for self-description are lacking. He did not write out of a sense of his own uncommonness, his "otherness" or his exemplary quality, either for good or evil; on the contrary, his experiment was all the more valid because of his ordinariness, and one often senses that he is emphasising this ordinariness, that he is making himself more ordinary than he is. In this way he escaped all the dangers of conscious self-description, the danger of self-enchantment and the perhaps even greater danger of self-abasement, that "sly humility" of confessionals, whose authors tread themselves into the dust in order to demonstrate how high they have raised themselves above themselves. There is no *Weltschmerz,* remorse, rebellion, accusation, inner strife, grief against others or against himself, nothing of all of that which since Rousseau has driven so many failures to spit in the world's face, so many beaten people to write their *De Profundis,* so many sinners to summon the world to a last judgement on themselves. This is the unusual thing: here a rich, healthy, and fairly happy man makes himself known, one who has thoroughly mastered his life and played his part with honour in the public affairs of his city and his countryside. He does not write in order to create a role for himself, but to lay one aside, and come to himself.

"Mundus universus exercet histrioniam";—the word "person" itself, is etymologically, "mask." In this comedy where all must act a role chosen or imposed, in character-masks which everyone finally accepts as his real visage, with commitments, articles of faith, and dogmas which we "believe we believe" and to which we must adhere out of loyalty to ourselves, without much knowing how we really came to them: in this comedy Montaigne's role was thoroughly in order. To set himself at a distance from the mere "making of books," he underlines, rather emphatically on occasion, the man-of-the-world element in himself. He surrounded his ancestry with an aura of old warrior nobility it was not at all entitled to; he notes with pride that as the mayor of his city he had a marshal to precede him and another to follow him; and, with a vanity full of imperceptible self-irony, he quotes the entire Latin text of his Roman patent of nobility. These traits, too, noted by his Jansenist critics with bitter derision, are essential to him, and they are mirrored in the Essays without dissimulation. He did not renounce the world in order to find himself: he sought to find himself in the world.

But what is left now of the personality he is seeking? Everything that holds it together, ancestry, education, milieu, habit, convention, principles, relations, beliefs, rank, name, and position comes to it from outside, they are allotted, accidental roles, and yet they make up almost the whole conscious "I." The more closely he considers himself the more his contours blur, the more individuality is dissolved into that many-coloured, unstable, iridescent and fleeting chaos he never, in his contradictoriness, grows tired of describing. Yes, one should play one's role fitly, he says—but always as a role, without identifying oneself with it or losing oneself in it. And this attitude can be followed on the title pages of the early editions of the Essays; if the first two editions, conforming to the custom of the period, still display the full splendour of the titles possessed by the royal knight, councillor, and mayor, Michel de Montaigne, there is left on the title page of the last edition, supervised by Montaigne himself, only his name.

For the stepping out of his role in which the actor betrays himself, a special ear for the undertones of consciousness is needed. All the splendid life of the Essays springs from this keen listening of Montaigne's to his relaxed and outward-turned self. It is true that this kind of thinking goes in circles. But the circle grows smaller and smaller until at last it circles only around the one point at which Montaigne finds himself alone—death. Here all acting ends; "that is a business for one man alone." The thought of death engaged him early, and we can follow the process of his self-discovery in nothing so clearly as in his relation to death. In death he found the ultimate test of truthfulness. To come to terms with it was what Montaigne sought, in the beginning, from philosophy. *Hic Rhodus, hic salta!* "To philosophise is to learn to die," he titled the long chapter on death in the first book, written when he was still full of the wisdom of the ancients about life and death; and all the consolations of Stoicism are here summoned up. Montaigne always understood as philosophy this spiritual elevation of man in the face of his sad, confused, and ephemeral humanity, and that was what he still meant by it when he said later, of himself, "I am no philosopher." He has reached the end of the way when, considering the calm and natural death of the simplest men in the plague year 1585, he rejects Cicero's phrase about the philosophic preparation for death as idle boasting: What is it, to be able to do what every fool and every beast can and must do? to strike a pose in order to endure what everyone must endure anyway? If philosophising is to learn to die, "well then, let us go to school with stupidity." To learn to live, not die, is wisdom. The essays of his first and last period can be endlessly contrasted, for with the change in his attitude towards death all the perspectives and measuring-rods of life change too.

Yet the last judgements do not cancel the first; nothing is taken back, only added to and deepened. In the beginning it is man, life, and death that occupy him, in the end it is only "my life" and "my death," and he is no longer dealing with a philosophic allegory of death, but experiencing and enduring his own slow dissolution. He, Michel de Montaigne, can no longer push death out of his consciousness, for it is he himself who is dying, together with his consciousness, and no speculation can prevail against this. Here he no longer grants himself the doubt that makes everything else, even miracles, possible; death is the end, and whatever may be on the other side, he, Michel de Montaigne, remains on this side. The consolations of philosophy, like those of religion, he never denies, he leaves them undecided; he accepts extreme unction and the sympathy of friends, but they do not concern him; these are the last actions of a life lived according to custom and usage, since it was not granted him to die unmolested—"quite alone"—journeying and far from home. A man must act his role in life to the last instant.

The Stoic, like the Christian, contempt for death is grounded in the contempt for physical life, but the more Montaigne feels himself disappearing the more deeply he feels that this life is all he has, and that it is much and precious. Now he finds in all contempt for life the overweening pride of the human spirit, the will to lift itself over and beyond itself towards the absolute, a revolt against the unbearable thought of existing today and ceasing to exist tomorrow—against the natural order that embraces both life and death. His last essay, already full of the presence of death and the readiness for it, closes with a hymn to this existence. *"C'est une absolue perfection, et comme divine. . . ."* In the presence of death Montaigne learned to love life, to "hold it fast with tooth and claw," to savour it to the last drop. Life is earthly, but not therefore void; transitory but not therefore despicable; losable, but not absurd; precious beyond words in its very fragility and unsureness.

In these last dialogues with old age, sickness, and death, there is no more art and no more cleverness, only obedience and assent to the riddling laws of life and death—*amor fati.* But if this is wisdom, then it is wisdom of the humblest and most unassuming kind, the wisdom of all creation, which goes hence unquestioning, without puzzling over the universe in which it lives and dies; the wisdom of the obedient. And if such thankful obedience to the unknowable is piety, then this is piety—but a piety that is wholly of this world. How much of the beauty of the Essays is due to the fact that their movement so truly describes the curve of life through ripeness and to death —the whole of life!

Why did Montaigne write them? He himself posed the question over and over, without finding an answer. Yet we must believe his foreword: he did not write them for us. He wrote them for himself, for his own sake, out of inner necessity; and yet he needed the unknown reader in order to reveal himself to himself. Self-description was the instrument of his self-discovery. For, and this is the last contradiction, there is no self-knowledge which does not make itself known, and no truthfulness without communication. "Whoever does not live a little for others hardly lives for himself." The consciousness of self that remains mute and unexpressed cannot attain self-knowledge. Perhaps there lay, at the source of Montaigne's decision to write down his thoughts, the death of his friend, Etienne de la Boëtie, who shared with him common ideas and ideals. The Essays are the continuation of a broken-off conversation. The whole first period of the Essays is an echo of this intimate association of two humanistic minds, both in love with antique greatness and the wisdom of Stoicism. Now Montaigne was alone, bereft of that "other I" who "alone possessed my true image, and took it with him," and it was "as if I had been cut in half." But this lost image of himself which he tried to reconstruct was hardly the one that emerges in the Essays; the undertaking led him further than he had intended.

We can infer Montaigne's image from the portrait he sketches of La

Boëtie; how impersonal, how declamatory in spite of all its real emotion, this essay is! We sense the humanistic enthusiasm for antique greatness "as our century no longer knows it" in which these two come together, the spirit of emulation of the Scipios and Catos which one finds also in La Boëtie's posthumous *Contr'un*. It was only slowly that Montaigne freed himself from the spell of that image of ideal manhood proposed by the Stoa, which was embodied for him in Etienne de la Boëtie. He cannot maintain himself on such heights—in such a role—alone, and the great generalities of virtue, truth, and freedom remain empty, for they find no echo. Hesitantly, in a few tentative thrusts, whose keenness for a late-Renaissance mind still filled with the spirit of antiquity we are hardly able to measure any more, he begins to question not mankind itself but these standards for mankind, and to seek the criteria of judgement within himself. And in shaping this new and quite personal image of man he attained his full reality. His book was the triumphant bursting loose of the free man from late-Humanistic epigonism. And through it, Montaigne himself became what he was. Montaigne noted finely the reciprocal process in which he and his book were engaged: "And even if no one were to read me, should I have wasted my time? I no more made my book than it has made *me*. . . ." His book has become a true collaborator, and through it the reader becomes one too—"my book," Montaigne says, as he would say "my friend," and, reading his book, we are drawn into this intimacy too. Whence the inexhaustible freshness which speaks to us from this book across more than three and a half centuries, as from no other book of his time, and few of all time.

In the end the richness of this book is the richness of the personality which shared itself with it, wholly and without holding back. It is not the monologue of a crank in his library, brooding over himself. The man who wrote this lived open-eyed among men caught up in the most merciless of civil and religious wars; he stood in his time with both feet, at the end of that colossal century in which the new world was discovered and the world of antiquity rediscovered, which saw the Christian church tottering on its foundations, and the anthropocentric model of the universe overturned, the century of the conquistadors and the great rebels: Cortez and Copernicus, Luther and Machiavelli, Calvin, Loyola, and Giordano Bruno.

The book, too, is of this time—and what a time! Montaigne began to write his essays in the year of the St. Bartholomew massacre, which gave the signal for slaughter throughout France, and entered history as the ineradicable symbol of betrayal, baseness, and murder in the name of the highest certainties of faith; the night of butchery in Paris, and of the thanksgiving mass with which it was greeted in Rome. All his life Montaigne saw religious war smouldering or blazing all around him, in his city, in his own family, and among his brothers and sisters, three of whom adhered to Calvinism. The twenty years during which he wrote the Essays were twenty years of civil war, hardly interrupted by the worthless peace treaties and edicts of toleration, broken before they came into force. Montaigne's retreat in 1571 "to the lap of the learned Muses, where he will pass in calm and security the days left him to live," was of short duration; the next year he was with the royal army in Poitou sent against rebellious La Rochelle, then bearer of the king's commands to the Parliament of Bordeaux, and in the following year we meet him again and again as agent and mediator between the warring camps. The news of his election as mayor of Bordeaux reached him on his "extended journey" in Italy, and King Henry III wrote to him in Rome to summon him to the immediate and pressing assumption of his office—a difficult one in a city torn by outer and inner quarrels, and become a storm-centre of the Huguenot wars.

But the Michel de Montaigne faithful to church and king was also the confidant and adviser of Henry of Navarre, the chief of the Protestant party, who visited him in his castle and appointed him, already chamberlain to Henry III, to be his own *ex officio* chamberlain too. An unelevating role, and one hard to understand, like the role of all those who issue no calls to battle and wage no wars, but seek to make peace instead; suspect, like all moderation; dangerous, like all will to balance in times of fanaticism. So Montaigne also passed, as he once complains, "for Guelf among the Ghibellines and Ghibelline among the Guelfs"—for a Papist among the Calvinists, and a heretic, or, what was almost the same thing, a lukewarm believer, among the Catholic zealots.

He has been called with justice, if also with some exaggeration, the philosopher of Henry IV, who brought peace and order to the French state, and to whom Montaigne, in one of his last essays, dedicated the verses Virgil wrote for Augustus. But if he was the philosopher of Henry IV, it was before the latter's victory, which he did not live to see. Montaigne had party loyalty, but it was not to the party of a dogma. His loyalty was to the old order, embodied in the monarchy which fell to pieces under the blows of both religious parties, the Calvinists as well as the Catholic League. If one wishes to range him with a party then it must be with the *"parti des politiques,"* as his contemporaries called that "third force" made up of moderate and tolerant spirits which—hence its designation as "political"—drew a distinction between religious conviction and political practice.

When hereditary succession made the Protestant Bourbon, Henry of Navarre, heir to the throne of the weak and degenerate Valois, the split became open; while the Catholic League sought to deliver the crown of France into the hands of the Spanish Hapsburg, Philip II, or the Lothringian Duke of Guise, the legitimist party of "the politicals" became simply the patriotic party. But it was only by going over to the religious faith of the majority of his people that Henry IV could finally become the "prince of peace," the "good king" who has entered legend. For those sick alike of the oligarchic city-republics of the Calvinists and the caricature of democracy created in Paris by the League through the long reign of terror enforced by a fanaticised mob, the monarchy appeared as salvation. That the paternal and tolerant régime of Henry IV prepared the way for the absolute monarchy which less than a century later began to destroy his work, is part of the history of another epoch, which had gone on to new problems; for history knows no "solutions" by which everything works out as smoothly as in the arithmetic books and ideological primers, only the triumph of new formulations of a problem over the old ones, the replacement of the religious formulation by the political, and the political by the social—all of them, however, only new forms of the old. What Montaigne says of the political problems of his time is spoken out of that time and his personal experience: it is uncontemporary to us. And yet, in a far deeper sense, it *is* contemporary.

Nowhere is politics the subject of this book. Nowhere does Montaigne draft an ideology or a programme of even the most modest kind; here too it is a question solely of *his* relation to politics and ideology. He was involved in these disorders as a citizen and an official, not as Michel de Montaigne, and the self-contemplation of the Essays is once again the means, in a time of ideological murder and carnage, to gain distance from the struggle, to come to himself, in the full sense of the phrase, to win the inner freedom that the party follower loses. In politics, too, it is a book of spiritual hygiene.

Here again scepticism above all fulfills its cleansing function. In the blackest impasse of the civil war, sharpened to ultimate bitterness by the betrayal of St. Bartholomew's Night, while the unity of the kingdom itself was for the first time put in jeopardy, and the "natural right" to rebellion and to execute kings was seized on in turn by Calvinist theoreticians and the zealots of the Catholic League, Montaigne read Sextus Empiricus' "Outline of Pyrrhonism," struck off his philosophical coat-of-arms, showing the arms of a scale poised in wavering equilibrium and the motto *"Que sais-je?";* and began to set down his "Apology for Raymond Sebond," the only really polemic essay in his work. All certainties are overturned here, with a true lust for destruction and an undiscriminating insatiability, all dogmas reduced to mere opinion, illusion, and conjecture, one as good as the next and each a mere curiosity in the cabinet of human fantasy. Everything is reduced to one level, man and beast, wise man and fool, intellect and instinct, belief and delusion, science, speculation and old wives' tales, and every supposed certainty cancelled by mere confrontation with a dozen contradictory and just as evident certainties. Montaigne notes sarcastically that two hundred and eighty-eight sects arose in antiquity out of the dispute over the highest good alone, and Pascal later copied this remark into his *Pensées*. Religion too is brought into this sphere of mere human supposition, for "it is clear and distinct that we accept our beliefs only in our own fashion and from our own hands, just as other religions have been accepted," according to the accidents of place, birth, and education: "A different latitude, different parents, similar promises and threats, could have produced in the same way a quite contrary belief. We are Christian in the same sense that we are German or Perigordian. . . ." Curious defence of the good Sebond, who wished "to demonstrate the truth of our religion by the conclusions of reason!"

No one, probably, will ever succeed entirely in clarifying the strange labyrinth of this polemical piece, for Montaigne himself has taken pains to make sure that no one will be able to pin him down to anything—not even doubt. Perhaps such a mock battle, with reversed weapons, in which Montaigne undertakes to defend Sebond's proof of religion by reason while pushing reason (and all human certainties with it) into the void, was the only way in which a free spirit of that age could create room for itself to breathe between inexorably hostile dogmas—one thinks of the quite otherwise motivated, but very similarly constructed, *Defense of Herodotus* by Henri Estienne, which undertook to prove the credibility of the wildest fables of the ancient Greeks by assembling a selection of the even more grotesque miracle stories and fairy tales which the priests of his time had imposed on a credulous people. . . . Yet one need not therefore impute to Montaigne a case of plain fraud. Here, as everywhere in the Essays, the occasion and point of departure for the essay, Sebond's "natural theology," turns quickly into a mere pretext for following Montaigne's own thoughts down every sideway and bypath. Nor is it a question of simple enlightened denial or doubt of an article of faith. The possibility of divine revelation remains open to rare and chosen spirits; but it is clear that it is not these spirits who are drowning France in fire, murder, and warfare, while they battle for the mastery of the country. By themselves the genuinely religious would hardly be numerous enough to form a troop of militia. The others—and are these others not, in reality, all?—are possessed, not by the truth, but by blood-frenzy, greed, and hunger for power. If they weighed truly the fragility of their convictions, the uncertainty of their murderous certainties, if they were in possession of, instead of beside, themselves, would they not sheath their swords?

He too, Michel de Montaigne, belongs not at all to the graced who have received the light of holy truth; he too is a Christian like the multitude, as he is a Perigordian, by heredity and habit. It is for just this reason that he stands fast; precisely because he cannot decide by himself what the truth is, he holds to that truth which is his by birth—"and since I am in no position to choose, I follow the choice of others, and remain in the rut in which God has set me. For otherwise I would roll and roll without end. . . ." With this he contents himself, to this he clings, but modestly; it is a personal, historically limited faith, which makes no claim to be binding on those whom God has set in another track. "What sort of truth is it that ends on this side of the mountains and is a lie for the world beyond?" It is a rule of behaviour, a "local ordinance," to which Montaigne submits himself in his ignorance; blind, but conscious of his blindness.

So he rejects the Reformation, not as sin and error, but as disorder and a sectarian arrogance of spirit which presumes to pass personal judgement on what is ultimate truth; not because his certainty is better but because he knows the questionableness of all certainties. It would take passionate conviction to change his faith, but it requires only mild conviction to hold to the old one. All the more because Calvin's Genevan papacy was both more demanding and less tolerant than pre-Tridentine Catholicism—and the introduction of the Tridentine creed into France had long been successfully resisted by the Gallican *politiques*—which contented itself with external submission to churchly usage, and gave its approval to the Essays as a tract written in defence of the old faith, until a new wave of fanaticism, two generations later, repudiated as anti-Christian both the Essays and, characteristically, the religious tolerance of the Edict of Nantes. Of course, the zealots were not wrong. Montaigne was indeed, in Sainte-Beuve's pointed phrase, a good Catholic in the exact measure that he was a lukewarm Christian. He, personally, was prepared to let pass every belief and every superstition, "to light one candle to St. Michael and another to the dragon," and with Socrates he held that "the truest opinion of the supernatural is to have no opinion."

Montaigne's loyalty to the old faith does not therefore contradict his scepticism, it is grounded in it. He defended the hereditary church as a conservative, not as a fighter for the true faith; as a *politique,* not as a crusader against heresy. He did not put the light on one side and the darkness on the other, he reserved the freedom to look around him, and to see what became of his convictions in the fists and mouths of their defenders, "who believe they believe because they do not know what belief is," and to recognise the human qualities and virtues of their opponents. He speaks often, in the Essays, with curiosity and astonishment, of the strange phenomenon of party passion, that human loss of self in a "role" thanks to which men work them-selves up over things which do not in the least concern them. *"Je m'engage difficilement"* is a key sentence of the Essays; he is "not easily inclined to belief nor to disbelief"; and the essay in which he reports how he exercised his mayoral office bears the magnificent title, "On the Management of the Will." His political ethos is the rejection of passion.

He refuses to be passionate even about the tradition he upholds. Every traditional form of order is an inheritance, and nothing else. Church, crown, state, law, family, and marriage are institutions which earn the esteem of a citizen in his role as citizen, but only in that role; they can claim no com-pulsion over his way of thinking or his conscience. What exists is neither holy, nor good, nor even reasonable; it has no other virtue but that it exists. Order, the state, law and justice are nothing else but disorder, lawlessness and violence, established and grown venerable by age, and often enough laughable, inhuman, and absurd. "The laws are not law, because they are just, but because they are laws." All human order is non-rational, neither derivable from, nor justifiable by, reason; every schoolboy is able to demon-strate its senselessness, but he had better let it stand: he knows nothing better.

For there is no rational order. Society has grown not out of the test tubes of reason but the disorder of history, not as an abstract logical construction for abstract logical men, but as an empirically discovered form of the living-together of human beings. For the state too, what is truth this side of the Pyrenees is a lie on the other. Like all historical reality it cannot withstand the scrutiny of reason, for it is grounded not on truth but on custom; and yet it is infinitely superior to reason, for it is actual. And the older and more customary it is, the better, for it has survived its violent birth pangs and found its inner equilibrium, it has shown its usefulness and vitality by its survival, and grown to be the normal state of affairs with which everyone is familiar, because he is born to them, and which therefore allow the high-est measure of freedom. Whoever assails it risks a relapse into the rule of the fist. Montaigne's whole polemic against the "innovators" is an indictment of the power-pretensions of abstract reason in its attempt to create an order outside historical contingency, and he has only scorn for the ideal states of philosophy, which have no place and no time. Every idea which presents itself as an ideology and claims power over men as a universally valid prin-ciple of order, is *hubris* and folly, arrogant transgression.

But even to the existing order he did not concede the right to impair his private freedom: "If the laws I serve threatened me even with their little finger I would go immediately in search of others, wherever they might be. . . . I am so greedy for freedom that I would feel hemmed-in if I were denied access to no matter what corner of the Indies." He acquiesced in the external order precisely for the sake of this freedom: freedom, too, he drew to himself as *his* freedom, not as a public postulate; and practical conformity seemed to him a small price to pay in order to defend it. He played the part that was allotted him, in a bad time, as Frenchman, Catholic, Perigordian, citizen, and mayor of Bordeaux, dutifully and without passion, with calm acceptance of his historic "contingency," and thereby preserved the inner freedom to remain Michel de Montaigne, sceptic and citizen of the world. Thus this political attitude flows back into the self-knowledge from which it issued, into the open-eyed acceptance of that contradiction of freedom and obligation, individuality and conformity, in which Montaigne found his own nature—"So I am."

The best fruit of this self-possession is its absolute openness to other things and other men. This deeply liberal spirit was tolerant without that tinge of sufferance, of the magnanimous concession granted by Truth to Error, that so often clings to the word—a word Montaigne does not even know. This enemy of all ideology had an insatiable, unprejudiced curiosity about all ideas, this scorner of all pretensions to special knowledge had an unbounded readiness for learning, this sceptic in regard to every dogma was open to the whole endless variety of spiritual possibilities, the life-forms and life-truths of other men and other peoples, and he treated with respect even those possibilities which were closed to him. Willingly, playfully, he tests his capacity to assume another opinion and seek its justification, and it often happens that the game turns to earnest in the process, and he abandons his own to adopt the opinion he began by combatting.

To be sure, a great deal also escaped this mind, which grasped so much in the attempt to grasp itself. The soaring lights of inspiration, the mystic vision of the world, the passion for knowledge and perhaps passion itself he sensed only by imaginative intuition, without really experiencing them: the border forms of human existence, the seer, the hero, and the saint, like the radically evil, were foreign to him. The psychic phenomena of transport and ecstasy he traced in himself and others again and again, with a mixture of curiosity and aversion; but his whole effort is in the opposite direction: to come to himself, not to allow himself to be transported, to possess himself, not to be possessed. He found this way to himself not by negating, but by affirming what was outside his nature, by the affirmation even of what was to him foreign, mysterious, and incomprehensible.

This rare and precious faculty for setting himself in the place of another being and respecting its inner laws as equal to his own he pushed to its utmost reach: "When I play with my cat who knows if she does not amuse

[335]

herself more with me than I with her?" All of Montaigne lies in that casual sentence.

Truthfulness is not only a great, it is a difficult, virtue. It demands not merely an open character but a clear head, and that, for a man of Montaigne's time, as for our own, was difficult indeed to achieve. Every time of disorder is also a time of dishonored minds who know all about God and the world, the cause of things and their background, the meaning of history and the destiny of man—all about everything except themselves. And in such times nothing is more necessary than to come, in the spiritual and even in the clinical sense, to oneself. That is the spiritual hygiene Montaigne practised as his joyful wisdom, and his only teaching. "With him I would live," Nietzsche wrote, "if the task were set me to make myself at home on earth." It is just this task, perhaps, that we have all been set again.

SHAKESPEARE

[1564–1616]

The Idea of a Theater HAS INFLUENCED OUR THINKING ABOUT THE DRAMA MORE than any other book of the last twenty years. In his book, Francis Fergusson considers the theater as a mirror of life, from the comprehensive picture offered by Sophocles to the more limited perspectives afforded by modern dramatists. His analysis not only illuminates the dramatic structure of particular plays, but also shows how those plays grew out of their cultures. Fergusson in this essay examines the "direct, profoundly histrionic dramaturgy" of *Hamlet,* which, though rooted in ritual and in Renaissance ideas of order, nevertheless expresses Shakespeare's modern skeptical intelligence. He shows how the many analogies knit together the diverse strands of the plot, and how each strand furthers the central theme of the play, the "hidden imposthume" that ravages Denmark. Thus the play is more than a revelation of Prince Hamlet's character; unity underlies its often bewildering richness.

Francis Fergusson is University Professor of Comparative Literature at Rutgers.

FRANCIS FERGUSSON

Hamlet, Prince of Denmark:
The Analogy of Action

THOUGH *Hamlet* WAS WRITTEN LONG BEFORE *Bérénice,* OR *Tristan,* MODERN
readers are more at ease with it than with either of the others. We may
admire the masterpiece of Racine, or be genuinely "sunk" by *Tristan,* but
compared with *Hamlet* they are artificial, limited, and arbitrary. Shakespeare's mysterious play has, even in our day, a directness and an intimacy
which the others lack.

That is because *Hamlet* was formed in a Theater which was close to the
root of drama itself—that art which is both more primitive and more subtle
than Philosophy. Since the destruction of the great "mirror" of the Elizabethan theater, it has been necessary to restore or invent the theater; and
modern drama has been a succession of more limited *genres,* based upon
more limited postulates about human life, like Racine's "action as rational,"
or Wagner's "action as passion." These sharp perspectives may seem to their
own times to reveal the essence of life but to the next generation they may
appear partial or even depraved. But *Hamlet,* like *Oedipus* and the *Purga-
torio,* can take myth and ritual as still alive. Its imitation of human action
"undercuts" or precedes all theory. If it is "the" modern play, it is also very

ancient, the heir of the great tradition in its completeness. Thus it is necessary to examine *Hamlet* (mysterious though it is) in order to complete the study of the idea of a theater in our tradition.

This view of *Hamlet* has been emerging slowly since the end of the eighteenth century. Every generation has regarded it in the light of its own taste which was formed by the then regnant form of drama. The critics have been fascinated with it, but they have made it over in their own image: as Hamlet himself tells Ophelia, "the power of beauty will sooner transform honesty from what it is to a bawd than the force of honesty can translate beauty into his likeness: this was sometime a paradox, but now the time gives it proof." The beauty of *Hamlet,* its endless suggestiveness, the iridescent play of the analogical relationships within it, will no doubt continue to seduce, and then show up its well-intentioned lovers. But this process, as I say, has been going on for a hundred and fifty years at least; the efforts of Hamlet's critics to some extent correct each other; and in our time, with modern drama almost dead, it may be possible to get a little closer to the play itself.

For this purpose, the first step is to become aware of certain preconceptions, certain instinctive demands which the modern theater has taught us to make of all drama. The most common complaint made of *Hamlet* is that in spite of its vitality it is not intelligible; it is fascinating but an artistic failure. Is this criticism based upon an understanding of Shakespeare's dramaturgy or does it judge him on the basis of alien standards?

Hamlet as an Artistic Failure

Robertson's essay on *Hamlet* together with Mr. Eliot's essay, which was apparently inspired by a reading of Robertson, may be taken as typical of the objections which many critics make to the play: they cannot find that it has any unity, or intellectual consistency, as a whole. Thus Robertson, while he admits that it makes superb entertainment and that it is full of brilliant characterization and passages of wonderful poetry, reports that it leaves the critical intellect unsatisfied. He suggests that Shakespeare may have intended nothing more than an entertainment and never bothered about the deeper unity or wider meaning of the whole: "If Shakespeare could be recreated and asked why he managed here and there so oddly, he might with an unanswerable effect open eyes of wonder and ask what should make us thus put his mechanism to the rack. 'Do you want an absolute,' he might ask, 'as a stage entertainment?' . . . But the critical intellect too has its right: its concern is simply conceptual truth."

Robertson, and after him Mr. Eliot, seek in *Hamlet* conceptual truth, and do not find it. They wish to be able to reduce *Hamlet* to terms which the reason can accept; and, in the attempt to satisfy this demand, they make an interpretation of the play which certainly makes it appear confused, form-less, and, in short, a failure. "Mr. Robertson is undoubtedly correct," Mr. Eliot writes, "in concluding that the essential emotion of the play is the feel-ing of a son toward a guilty mother." He then shows that there are many elements and several entire scenes in the play which have nothing to do with the feeling of a son toward a guilty mother. He shows that on this interpreta-tion, Hamlet himself is incomprehensible; and he concludes that Shakespeare failed to find "objective equivalents" for Hamlet's feeling: "Hamlet (the man) is dominated by an emotion which is inexpressible, because it is in excess of the facts as they appear. And the supposed identity of Hamlet with his author is genuine to this point: that Hamlet's bafflement at the absence of objective equivalent to his feelings is a prolongation of the bafflement of his creator in the face of his artistic problem."

I am not sure that I understand Mr. Eliot's famous formula of the objec-tive equivalent of a feeling, at least in its application to this play. Does Mr. Eliot mean that the many objects, facts, and chains of events which Shake-speare presents to make us share and understand Hamlet's feeling, do not work for us? In other words, that as we read or see the play we cannot sym-pathize with Hamlet's feeling? Or does he mean that we cannot understand Hamlet's psychology? Hamlet is full of feeling—much more so than Polo-nius, for example; but is this feeling "in excess"? One may hazard the guess that what troubles Mr. Eliot here is not that the character fails to live drama-tically—his stage vitality, his fascination for many and varied audiences proves the contrary—but rather that neither he nor his author explains his situation in the clear and univocal terms of reason. Hamlet is presented di-rectly, in his concrete and many-sided setting, in his complex situation as prince, son, and lover. If we are to understand him, we must take him thus directly, and not try to simplify and reduce the picture Shakespeare offers.

The view that "the essential emotion of the play is the feeling of a son to-ward a guilty mother" is a drastic reduction of the play as Shakespeare wrote it. Hamlet's feeling toward his guilty mother is certainly essential, but not more essential than his dismay at the loss of a father. Stephen Daedalus in *Ulysses* builds up an interpretation of the play on this basis, which reveals at least as much as the Eliot-Robertson interpretation. And Mr. Dover Wilson offers an explanation of Hamlet's feeling which is perhaps still more fruitful: Hamlet has lost a throne, and he has lost thereby a social, publicly acceptable *persona:* a local habitation and a name. It is for this reason that he haunts the stage like the dispossessed of classical drama: like an Electra, who has lost the traditional life which was her due as daughter, wife, and mother—

or even like the ghost of Polyneikes, who cannot rest because the ritual order of society which might have provided such a place has been destroyed. And Mr. Wilson assures us that an Elizabethan audience (more or less aware of such implications as these) would have accepted the loss of the throne as sufficient explanation for Hamlet's dismay.

It is not necessary to rule out the Eliot-Robertson, or the Joycean interpretation, merely because one accepts Mr. Dover Wilson's: on the contrary, the various critics should be taken as Jamesian "reflectors," each lighting a facet of the whole from his own peculiar angle. Mr. Dover Wilson's "angle," however, has a special value, for it enables one to see beyond the plight of Hamlet as an individual to certain traditional values of society which underlie the play as a whole. And one of the chief objections to the type of criticism which Mr. Eliot brings to bear, is that it does not distinguish clearly between the story of Hamlet the individual and the story of the play as a whole. He objects to the criticism of Hamlet abstracted from the work in which he appears; but his own essay deals with "Hamlet without the Prince of Denmark"—i.e., the character without reference to the society in which he endeavors to realize himself. Hence he cannot understand the relevance of the minor characters, nor the significance of certain scenes which do not bear directly upon Hamlet's individual fate.

"There are unexplained scenes," he writes, "the Polonius-Laertes and the Polonius-Reynaldo scene—for which there is little excuse." There is no explanation and no excuse for them if Shakespeare was merely trying to convey the feeling of a son toward a guilty mother. If he was also picturing the relation of a son to his father, then the whole Polonius-Laertes-Reynaldo sequence makes sense as a comic-pathetic sub-plot, with many ironic parallels to the story of Hamlet and his father's Ghost. If to this we add Mr. Dover Wilson's suggestions, we see that the welfare of Denmark—the traditional order of society, with its father-king upon whom depend "the lives of many" —is the matter of the play as a whole, rather than Hamlet's individual plight. In the welfare of Denmark, Polonius, Laertes and Reynaldo have a stake also. The postulate upon which the entire action is based (from the first scene on the parapet, with the soldiers peering through the darkness to discern what danger may threaten the body politic) is that "the times are out of joint." It is Hamlet's misfortune that, as Prince, and as a man of profound insight, he especially should have been "born to set them right."

The Eliot-Robertson reading of *Hamlet* makes it clear that none of the characters, and none of the plots or narrative sequences, is intended to convey the meaning of the play as a whole. Nor does the play offer, even in the meditations of Hamlet, the finality of conceptual truth wherein the reason could find its satisfaction and its rest. This reading has the value of showing what

Hamlet is not, rather than throwing light upon its actual complexity. It has also the value of summing up a sense of the theater and of drama which has largely prevailed since the Elizabethan theater ceased to exist. The demands and the criticism which Robertson and Eliot make would have been approved by the critics of the age of reason from Corneille to Voltaire. They are, in principle, very much like those that William Archer made in his book on Elizabethan drama, *The Old Drama and the New.* Archer demanded naturalistic psychology like that of Ibsen and his structural principles were the rationalistic ones of the well-made play. Therefore he too found the drama of Shakespeare's theater unsatisfying. It is our habit to insist on literal unity and conceptual truth; the value of the Eliot-Robertson reading is that it does so with such clarity as to show what we are doing. Once we understand that, the way is clear, and we may inquire whether Shakespeare was not composing on a different principle altogether.

For such an inquiry there is plenty of material available. There are studies of that characteristic device of the Elizabethans, the double plot. And there are the many recent works which show the Elizabethan theater not from our contemporary standpoint but as the heir of the Middle Ages and, behind that, even of classical antiquity. In their light one can see, if not the unity of *Hamlet,* at least the kind of "oneness by analogy" which Shakespeare's dramaturgy aimed at.

HAMLET AS MULTIPLE PLOT

It has been well established by now that the Elizabethan "double plot," at its best, is more than a device for resting the audience. The comic sequences which are woven through the tragedies are not to be dismissed as mere "comic relief," or as punctuation for the main story, like the music that Corneille used between the acts. In Shakespeare, and in the best of his contemporaries, the minor plots are essential parts of the whole composition. This much is, I think, generally recognized. But there is little agreement about the nature of these relationships: we lack a generally accepted critical vocabulary for describing them.

Thus Moulton, in his *Shakespeare the Dramatic Artist,* studied the plots themselves as intelligible chains of events, and showed (for *Lear* and *The Merchant of Venice,* for example) that the various narrative strands depend causally upon each other; that their climaxes, coming together, reinforce each other; and that their denouements are interdependent. Moulton was thinking of the objections of rationalistic critics like Robertson, and answering them in their own terms. But Mr. William Empson, in his extremely illuminating study, *Some Versions of Pastoral,* is interested, not in the logical concatenation of the stories, but in the ironic parallels between them: the tragi-comic parallel between the motivations of love and war, as in *Troilus and Cressida;* between the lives of "clowns" and the lives of "heroes" in the whole tradition of British drama to the middle of the eighteenth century.

Henry James's technical concept of the "reflector" is akin to the notion of the double plot as Mr. Empson explains it. The "occasions," or the more or less peripheral intelligences which James used to mirror his action, serve to reveal it from various (ironically different) angles. Neither the author nor the protagonist is to be allowed to break down and "tell all": that would not be truly dramatic; it would not be "objective" in the realist sense. The situation, the moral and metaphysical "scene" of the drama, is presented only as one character after another sees and reflects it; and the action of the drama as a whole is presented only as each character in turn actualizes it in his story and according to his lights. This is as much as to say that the various stories with their diverse casts of characters are analogous, and that the drama as a whole is therefore "one by analogy" only. It does not have the literal and rational unity of the single logically and causally connected chain of events or story. And if we are to grasp a novel of Henry James or a play by Shakespeare, we must be prepared to follow these shifting perspectives, as we move from character to character and from story to story, trying, as we go, to divine the supreme analogue, the underlying theme, to which they all point in their various ways.

This "supreme analogue" or "underlying theme" is the main action of the play, as Aristotle explains in a neglected passage of the *Poetics.* Aristotle knew plays with a double plot-thread, one of which issues "happily," the other tragically; and he did not like them—they are "less perfect," he says, than pure tragedy; a concession to popular taste. But in his few remarks on the *Odyssey* he comes closer to describing a multiple plot as Shakespeare employed it. The *Odyssey* has neither the literal unity of the one cast of characters, nor the rational unity of the single plot-line. There is the story of Telemachus's search for his father, the *Telemacheia.* There is the intrigue between Penelope and the suitors. There are the many smaller stories of Odysseus' adventures on the islands and the sea; and at last his conflict with the suitors. The stories are many but they are analogous: they are all "actualizations" of the one general action, which is the attempt "to return home." The Odyssey (*hoi nostoi*) sets forth, in many figures, this basic action, this quest for home.

In considering the structure of *Hamlet,* all of these studies of the properties of the double plot are useful. The stories of the play—the struggle between Hamlet and Claudius; between Hamlet, Polonius and Laertes; between Fortinbras and Claudius' regime—are tightly woven together, causally and logically interdependent, in the manner Moulton demonstrates for *The Merchant of Venice.* At the same time the various stories are presented as ironically parallel in the ways Mr. Empson describes. Polonius, for instance, plays the "clown" to Hamlet's "hero," to use Mr. Empson's words; at the same time Hamlet frequently feels himself in the role of clown in relation to Fortinbras and even Laertes. Or, taking Henry James's phrase, you may put it that we are continually shifting from reflector to reflector throughout the play: from the simple soldiers of Scene 1 to the smoothly hypocritical Claudius of Scene 2; from the myopic shrewdness of Polonius, to the troubled but profound intuitions of Ophelia. The action is illumined from so many angles that we have an embarrassment of riches; the problem is not to demonstrate that the play moves in ironic parallels but rather to show that they add up to something—are intended to convey (with however rich a profusion) an underlying unity of theme. For this purpose Aristotle's notion of analogous actions is the most useful.

The main action of Hamlet may be described as the attempt to find and destroy the hidden "imposthume" which is poisoning the life of Claudius' Denmark. All of the characters—from Polonius with his "windlasses" and "assays of bias," to Hamlet with his parables and symbolic shows—realize this action, in comic, or evil, or inspired ways. And the organic parts of the plot—the movement of the play as a whole—show forth the beginning, middle, and end of this action according to the traditional scheme.

The Prologue includes approximately the first three scenes of Act 1. Scene 1, Act 1 (the parapet) makes the simplest and most general statement of the main theme or action of the play. The soldiers, in the cold and darkness of the night, are watching for the hidden danger (the physical or metaphysical malady) which may threaten the present Danish regime. Is it war—and thus connected with young Fortinbras in neighboring Norway? Or something less natural, and thus connected with Hamlet's father's ghost, who appears but will not speak? The soldiers' peering-through-the-dark constitutes a sort of overture, in sensuous terms, to their speculations about the Ghost and his meanings.

Act 1, scene 2 (Claudius' Court) restates the main theme, this time from the point of view of Claudius and his regime. What possible ill is threatening his rule? His marriage to Gertrude on the heels of the death of Hamlet's father has been accepted by all, so that cannot be the danger. But three young men, unaccountable quantities, all with the restlessness of youth, are potential sources of trouble. Fortinbras, who wishes to avenge his father for the loss of lands to Denmark, is threatening war in nearby Norway. Laertes is asking his father, Polonius, for permission to travel; and Hamlet, in black, moody, seems not to have accepted Claudius' regime with good grace—perhaps because of the loss of *his* father. Claudius deals with Fortinbras through his uncle, the present king of Norway; satisfies Laertes by giving permission for the traditional fling in Paris; but fails to appease Hamlet, who thus begins to appear to him as the most dangerous center of infection. When Claudius departs, with his glittering court, and Hamlet, in his solemn black, is left alone on-stage, we get his sharply different version of Denmark's trouble: "Things rank and gross in nature possess it merely." And then, when Horatio and the soldiers come to report the Ghost, we are led to connect this apparition with Hamlet's sense that the body politic is sick.

Act I, scene 3 (Polonius' house) is a comic variation on the main theme. Laertes is warning his sister Ophelia about the dangers of youth, particularly Hamlet's youth—for Laertes, with his simple-minded conventionality, instinctively thinks of Hamlet as the source of infection, much as Claudius does, though for less specific reasons. When Polonius appears, he gives Laertes the same advice that Laertes had given Ophelia. We see that Laertes is a chip off the old block; and that for this family there is no hidden malady which ordinary prudence and the experience of the aged cannot find and cure. But Ophelia, with her love for Hamlet, throws doubt on Polonius' simple diagnosis. (Ophelia, like Gertrude, has great symbolic value in the economy of the play as a whole. Both women base their very beings upon their men; and both of them are attached at once to Hamlet and to Claudius' regime. Thus they are at once touching reminders of what might have been —the unity and health of the whole state—and victims of its actual illness and disunity.)

The Agons, or conflicts of the play, are developed in scenes 4 and 5 of Act I, in Act II, and in the first scene of Act III. It is established that all of the characters are seeking to identify and to destroy the actual or potential malady of Claudius' Denmark; but they interpret it differently, and hence conflicts and contrasts develop between their various lines of action. Because the "malady" is so mysterious, and because it would be perilous to trouble the smooth surface of Claudius' regime, the characters all act secretly, indirectly, and in mutual mistrust. Hamlet does not even trust the Ghost; he cannot tell whether it is a "spirit of health or goblin damned"; and thus there is contrast and conflict even in this relationship. Polonius is endeavoring to serve Claudius' regime; but Claudius does not trust Polonius' diagnosis of the trouble; he summons Rosencrantz and Guildenstern as a check. Thus the struggles which develop in this part of the play are all struggles in the dark, as though the antagonists, waiting and listening, could not find each other, and fought only briefly and desperately when they happened to bump together.

But by the first scenes of Act III the main lines of the many-sided conflict which the Prologue prepared, are visible. Claudius, having satisfied Laertes with his trip to Paris, and having diverted the dutiful Fortinbras from Denmark to Poland, has decided that Hamlet is the source of his dis-ease, and must be rendered harmless. Polonius agrees with him, and is now beginning to feel a little out of his depth: he is no longer sure that Hamlet's malady is merely thwarted love for Ophelia. As for Hamlet, he sees Claudius as the chief plague-spot, and his main antagonist though, at the same time, the spreading disease has vitiated his every relationship.

I have said that the agon shows conflicts *and contrasts*. The contrasts between the visions and the lines of action of the various characters are more important than their overt struggles, and reveal far more about the real malady of Denmark and the attempt to find and destroy it. These *contrasts* are brought out by the order of the scenes, as we shift from comic to tragic versions of the main action. This may be illustrated by considering the alternation of the Polonius story and the Hamlet story in Acts I and II—the scenes for which Mr. Eliot says there is no explanation or excuse.

The last scene of the Prologue, Polonius' house (Act I, scene 3) is at once a comic version of the opening statement of the main action, and the prologue to the story of Polonius and Laertes which is closely analogous in many respects to the story of Hamlet's "father" (the Ghost *and* Claudius) and Hamlet. The clownish and comic father-son relationship of Polonius and Laertes throws ironic lights upon the tragic relationship of Hamlet to his anomalous parent. Thus as soon as we have seen Polonius attempting to guide and advise Laertes in preparation for his trip to Paris, we are shifted to the dark parapet with Hamlet awaiting word from his Ghost-father and hearing, below, the roaring and the booming which Claudius, his other "father," is making at his drunken celebration. The Ghost appears, and speaks to Hamlet; but, from the other side of the grave, he can convey little to his son—and that only in hints and metaphors. He is definite enough about the fact that Claudius killed him; but Hamlet does not know what to make even of that:

> O all you host of heaven! O earth! What else?
> And shall I couple hell? O fie!

After this we return to Polonius who is sending Reynaldo to Paris to watch over Laertes. It is another father trying to reach and guide his son—who is not on the other side of the grave, this time, but on the other side of the sea; yet as absurdly remote as Hamlet from the Ghost. We can be sure that when Reynaldo gets to Paris, and tries to apply to Laertes the "bait of falsehood," the "indirections" and "windlasses and assays of bias" which father Polonius devised to reach him, Laertes will also reply "O fie!"

Thus these three scenes are closely parallel, yet sharply contrasted: the divided world of Polonius-Laertes is incommensurable with the divided world of the Ghost-Hamlet; and this incommensurability is deeper than any overt conflict, and shows more about Hamlet's problem and the true malady of Denmark than any fact, or any explicit issue, could do. And when Ophelia appears on Reynaldo's exit, torn and frightened by her sight of Hamlet, we have before us the most pathetic victim of this division within the sick society; and with this vision, the Hamlet-Ghost, Laertes-Polonius sequence ends.

The Climax, Peripety and Recognition are presented in Act III, scenes 2, 3, and 4—the players' scene, and the two scenes following. In the first of these scenes which follow the players' scene (scene 3) Claudius, convicted of the crime, attempts to pray, and Hamlet rejects his chance to kill him. In the next (scene 4) Hamlet faces his mother with her guilt, and inadvertently kills Polonius.

Hamlet's presentation of his play to the Danish Court is both a direct attack on Claudius, as his chief antagonist, and an attempt to resolve the deeper "contrasts," the divided counsels, the incommensurable visions, which constitute the malady of Denmark—or at least its chief symptom. By hinting broadly at Claudius' crime Hamlet, of course, shakes Claudius' whole position, for that depends upon concealment. At the same time he convicts all of the supporters of the regime, even including Ophelia and Gertrude, of a share in the guilt.

The further meanings of Hamlet's play are considered at more length below. At this point I merely wish to point out that the presentation of the play is the peripety: it puts the King and his regime on the defensive, and justifies the most hidden intuitions of Hamlet and the most secret messages of the Ghost. The two scenes following the players' scene merely drive home its effects: Claudius becomes in his own eyes an outlaw; Gertrude's heart is "cleft in twain" and, as a sort of absurd and pathetic parenthesis, Polonius is destroyed. The "hidden imposthume," in all its ramifications, is opened; and from this point the action, beyond anyone's control, runs down to its fated end.

The Pathos and/or Sparagmos coincides with Act IV. Both the state and the individuals that compose it "suffer" the results of Hamlet's opening the "hidden imposthume." Laertes, hearing of his father's death, comes back to avenge him, and starts a rebellion; and the scenes which show this overt social disorder alternate with Ophelia's mad scenes: "Schism in the State and Schism in the soul," in Toynbee's phrase. Meanwhile Hamlet, on his trip to England and his return, and Fortinbras, at the head of his troops, approach for the kill. The King (who conceals Hamlet's murder of Polonius, minimizes Ophelia's tragedy, and corrupts Laertes' demand for justice) is trying to "skin and film the ulcerous place." But his efforts do not re-establish his regime; they make at most a horrible simulacrum of a healthy state; smooth on the surface but dead within.

The Epiphany or Collective Revelation is shown in Act v. It is Shakespeare's habit to wind up his complicated plots at the very end; and the big killings do not occur until the last scene. But these sensational events tell us little that is new; they seem to be only minor corollaries of the great peripety in Act iii. The substance of Act v is chiefly what Hamlet, the "chief reflector," sees, when he returns, spent, nervously exhausted, but clear-eyed, from England. He sees the fatal illness of Denmark: the literal bones in the graveyard; the many details of social disorder (the Prince, for instance, on a level with the grave-digging clowns); the "maimèd rite" of Ophelia's funeral, and the death-trap of Claudius' last court assembled for his duel with Laertes. The widespread malady of Denmark is clear at last; and with the end of Claudius and his regime it is gone like a bad dream. Fortinbras appears at last in Denmark: a new hope for a new, purged state.

The purpose of this sketch, of course, is not to exhaust the analogical relationships among the narrative strands in *Hamlet,* but only to suggest, by means of a few illustrations, that they are there, and that they are an all-important element in the structure of the play. They point, I think, to the main action, and to the concern for the welfare of Denmark which all the characters share.

Ernest Jones has an interpretation of the play also based upon analogies between its stories and characters, but reducing them all to the machinery of the Oedipus complex: "The main theme of this story," Dr. Jones writes, "is a highly elaborated and disguised account of a boy's love for his mother, and consequent jealousy of and hatred toward his father." Dr. Jones's study is very suggestive and, while confirming what might be called the analogical texture of the play, it raises important questions about the essential nature of these analogical relationships and the underlying theme to which they all point. I have no doubt that the father-son relationships are there: I have suggested it in my remarks on the Polonius-Laertes, Ghost-Hamlet sequence. Shakespeare seems to have missed none of the tensions, none of the ambivalence, in this crucial relationship. But can it be regarded as the fundamental theme of the play?

My objection to Jones's interpretation is that it reduces the motivation of the play to the emotional drives of the Oedipus complex. This overworks that complex, and takes us too far from the play itself. Thus part of the point of the Polonius-Laertes, Ghost-Hamlet analogy is the comic similarity and the tragic difference between the insights of Hamlet and Polonius; and this tension cannot be reduced to the Oedipus complex. The Oedipus complex does not account for the fact that Hamlet, besides being a son, is also a dispossessed prince; nor that Claudius, besides being a father symbol, is also the actual ruler of the state. But the actual movement of the play—to say nothing of its ultimate meaning—depends upon such objective facts and values as these.

Jones has studied the changes and elaborations which Shakespeare made in the Hamlet story, with its very ancient mythic roots, transforming it from what was perhaps a simple revenge motif into something much deeper. Jones thinks that the "deeper" theme which Shakespeare unconsciously felt was the son's desire to kill his father and possess his mother; and that the elaborations and variations he made were disguises of the theme which really held him. But the elaborations Shakespeare made could equally well be understood as due to his extremely critical and skeptical bent; his need to criticize one version of his theme by means of another analogous one.

In short, the analogous stories, situations, and relationships in *Hamlet* point, not to the Oedipus complex, but to the main action or underlying theme of the play. And in that the emotional tensions of the Oedipus complex are only one element. The disease which is killing Denmark does not have a purely psychological explanation and cure, and the attempt to understand and destroy it has a moral as well as an emotional content. The religious, cultural, moral values of the tradition are at stake in this action; and the play as a whole has dimensions which cannot be completely understood if one thinks of it in these psychological terms, in abstraction from the theater in which it was formed.

A study of the interwoven plots of *Hamlet* points to the underlying theme, the main action of the play as a whole. But it does not quite enable us to understand Hamlet's shifting motives; and it does not throw much light upon the rhythms, the spectacular effects, and the rise and fall of tension, in the play considered as a performance before an audience. If we are to come a little closer to the play as play, it is necessary to consider the whole idea of the theater which Shakespeare used and assumed in his audience; for this theater offered means of "imitating the action" which cannot be subsumed under the art of plot-making as it is generally understood.

HAMLET AS RITUAL AND IMPROVISATION

If one could see a performance of *Hamlet,* uncut, unbroken by intermissions, and employing the kind of simple make-believe which Shakespeare, with his bare stage, must have intended, we should find much to enthrall us besides the stories themselves. The stories, of course, start at once, and are felt continuously as working themselves out: fate, behind the scenes, makes, from time to time, its sudden pronouncements. But on-stage, the music and the drums and the marching of royal and military pageantry, are directly absorbing, and they assure us that something of great and general significance is going on. From time to time the stage is emptied; the pageantry is gone; the stories seem to be marking time—and Hamlet emerges, alone, or with one or two interlocutors. Sometimes he suffers his visions before us; sometimes he makes jokes and topical allusions; sometimes he spars with his interlocutors like the gag-man in a minstrel show, or the master of ceremonies in a modern musical.

The scenes of pageantry are all civic or military or religious rituals; the changing of the guard, the formal assembling of the court of Denmark; the funeral of Ophelia. Though they all have their relevance to the interwoven stories of the play and to the discordant purposes of the various characters, their chief function is to show forth the main action or underlying theme, at various stages in its development. At these ritual moments the plot-lines are, as it were, gathered together; the issues are held in suspension, and we are reminded of the traditional social values in which all have some sort of stake.

Hamlet's monologues, and his nimble exchanges with Polonius or Rosencrantz and Guildenstern, his "topical allusions" to drunkenness or to the state of the theater, make a very different kind of theatrical appeal. He steps out of the narrative course of the play, out of the "world of Denmark" which is the basic postulate of the make-believe, refers directly to the parallels between "Denmark" and the England of his audience. From one point of view Shakespeare seems to be counting on the inherent dramatic and theatrical interest which this character has apart from the story—permitting him, like the first violin in a concerto, a cadenza on his own, after which we are returned to the matter in hand. From another point of view, Hamlet's "improvized" moments are carried by our confidence in him as "chief reflector": we look to him, as to the ritual scenes, to show us the underlying theme of the whole.

Both the ritual and the improvisational elements in *Hamlet* are essential— as essential as the stories—in the structure of the whole. The Elizabethan theater, at once as frankly "theatrical" as vaudeville, and as central to the life of its time as an ancient rite, offered Shakespeare two resources, two theatrical "dimensions" which the modern naturalistic tradition of serious drama must try, or pretend, to do without. In the table on the following page I have shown the chief ritual and the chief improvisational scenes in relation to the main parts of the plot.

If one thinks over the succession of ritual scenes as they appear in the play, it is clear that they serve to focus attention on the Danish body politic and its hidden malady: they are ceremonious invocations of the well-being of so-

THE PARTS OF THE PLOT	RITUAL SCENES	IMPROVISATIONAL ENTERTAINMENT
The Prologue	Act I, sc. 1 The changing of the Guard Act I, sc. 2 Claudius' First Court	
The Agons—development of conflicting purposes of various characters; contrasts of their stories; "purposes mistook"; indecision and fighting in the dark		Act I, sc. 4 Hamlet's sermon on drunkenness (in Denmark and/or England) Act II, sc. 2 Hamlet exchanges wisecracks with Polonius, Rosencrantz, Guildenstern, and the players. Act III, sc. 2 Hamlet's charge to the players—his opinions on the art of acting.
The Climax, Peripety, and Recognitions; all narrative strands brought together	RITUAL AND ENTERTAINMENT Act III, sc. 2 The performance of Hamlet's play is both rite and entertainment, and shows the Prince as at once clown and ritual head of the state.	
The Pathos or "sparagmos," both of the state and the individuals, leading to the epiphany or "collective revelation" of the general disease. (Cf. Toynbee's "schism in the state and schism in the soul")	Act IV, sc. 5 Ophelia's Madness is a mock ritual, a mixture of false and lewd marriage, and false and savage funeral; refers also to the funeral of Hamlet's father and Gertrude's false marriage. Alternates with rebellion in the state.	
The Epiphany, or Final Vision of the underlying truth of the action	Act. V, sc. 1 Ophelia's funeral. A "maimed rite" but a real death. Act V, sc. 2 The duel between Hamlet and Laertes. This duel is surrounded with all the ceremonies of Claudius' Court, like the players' scene, and Claudius' other loud and drunken celebrations; but every element in it is false or mistaken: a mockery of invocation; and it eventuates in death, and "resurrection" in the shape of Fortinbras, who, now that Claudius' regime is gone, can appear with his new faith and hope.	Act V Hamlet jokes and moralizes with the Gravedigger and Horatio. He feels like the gag-man and the royal victim in one. Gravedigger corresponds to Polonius.

ciety, and secular or religious devices for securing it. As the play progresses, the rituals change in character, from the dim but honest changing of the guard, through Ophelia's mock rites, to the black mass of Claudius' last court. And it appears that the improvisational scenes bear a significant and developing relationship to the rituals. In general, they throw doubt upon the efficacy of the official magic, as when Hamlet refuses to take Claudius' first court at its face value; yet even the most cutting ironies of Hamlet do not disavow the mystery which the rituals celebrate, or reject the purposes that inform them.

The rituals, the stories, and the improvisations together make the peculiar rhythm of *Hamlet* as a performance. Denmark is shown as waiting, as it were, in the darkness of its ineffective ceremonies and hollow communal prayers while the infection, "mining all within," divides every man in secret from every other and bursts forth, from time to time, in savage but brief and ineffective fights.

But before examining the sequence of rituals, with its center in the players scene, it is necessary to endeavor to support the view that the Elizabethan theater had, in fact, this ritual aspect: that Shakespeare's audience, like that of Sophocles, was prepared to accept his play not only as an exciting story but as the "celebration of the mystery" of human life.

THE GLOBE THEATER AND THE FESTIVAL OF DIONYSOS

The main evidence (apart from the play itself) for taking *Hamlet* as a species of ritual drama, is provided by recent studies which show that a great deal of the religious culture of the Middle Ages was still alive in Shakespeare's time. Tillyard's *The Elizabethan World Picture,* for example, makes this clear. Mr. Tillyard quotes Hamlet's famous speech on man: "What a piece of work is a man: how noble in reason; how infinite in faculty; in form and moving how express and admirable; in action how like an angel; in apprehension how like a god; the beauty of the world, the paragon of animals." —"This has been taken," Mr. Tillyard explains, "as one of the great English versions of Renaissance humanism, an assertion of the dignity of man against the asceticisms of medieval misanthropy. Actually it is in the purest medieval tradition: Shakespeare's version of the orthodox encomia of what man, created in God's image, was like in his prelapsarian state and of what ideally he is still capable of being. It also shows Shakespeare placing man in the traditional cosmic setting between the angels and the beasts. It is what the theologians had been saying for centuries." And Mr. Tillyard proceeds to show that most of the "world picture which the Middle Ages inherited" was still tacitly assumed by the Elizabethans: "an ordered universe arranged in a fixed system of hierarchies but modified by man's sin and the hope of his redemption."

The Elizabethan stage itself, that central mirror of the life of its times, was a symbolic representation of this traditional cosmos: it was thus taken both as the physical and as the metaphysical "scene" of man's life. Mr. Kernodle has shown this in detail in his illuminating study, *From Art to Theater*. He traces the genealogy of the symbolic façade of the Elizabethan stage house back through street pageantry to painting and to the architecture of tombs and altars; and thence to the arcade screen of the Greek tragic theater itself. "More than an arrangement of side doors and inner and upper stages, that façade was itself a symbol of castle, throne, triumphal arch, altar, tomb"—in short, an all-purpose, eminently practicable setting, implying the constant elements in the Elizabethan world picture, yet flexible enough to serve the shifting make-believe of the actors. Over the whole was a permanent canopy, painted to represent the heavens, a vault literally "fretted with golden fire."

The symbolic character of this stage seems to imply a conception of the theater akin to that of ritual: the celebration of the mystery of human life. This stage and its drama did not, it is true, develop directly from the Mass; it developed from the secular theater of the Middle Ages and, as Mr. Kernodle shows, from royal and civic pageantry. But in the Renaissance the monarchy and its rites was taking over some of the religious significance of the church and its rites. The pope tended to be superseded by the prince as vicar, or "type" of Christ, the pageantry and ceremony of the church by the pageantry and ceremony of the national state. The Tudor monarch was the symbol, and the visible center of the traditional world order, so that Donne could write, on the death of Prince Henry:

> Of Weight one Centre, one of Greatness is,
> And Both my Centres feel this Period.

The role of the monarch in Shakespeare's time (and in his plays) was thus very close to that of Sophocles' Oedipus or Creon: he was at once ruler, high priest, and father of the community. And the ceremonies which Shakespeare and Hamlet's Danes engaged in—whether obviously religious, like the funeral, or more secular, like the Court—were taken as celebrating and securing the welfare of the whole, of the monarchy, and of the "lives of many" that depended on it.

The Elizabethan theater may thus be regarded as the heir of the Greek tragic theater with its ritual basis. The Elizabethan cosmos is still that of the great tradition, which the Middle Ages inherited from the city state. The physical stage itself is symbolic in the same way as the tragic stage of the

Greeks; and the ritual component in its drama has similar deep and general meanings.

This does not mean, of course, that Shakespeare's audience, or even Shakespeare himself, could have expounded this genealogy and these parallels. If the tradition was alive in Shakespeare's time, it was as a "habit of thought and feeling" rather than as an explicit and integrated philosophy. But Shakespeare seems to have felt the essential elements of this great "theater" as alive still; to have assumed that his audience would respond to them, and to have based his dramaturgy upon them.

If Shakespeare's theater is thus akin to the theater of Sophocles, their drama should be composed on similar principles: appealing in both cases to ancient and publicly accepted values and modes of understanding, rather than preaching, inventing, and arguing in the manner of modern drama. And the comparison should throw some light on both.

The themes of *Oedipus* are, from many points of view, strikingly similar to those of *Hamlet*. Oedipus gave his name to that "complex" to which, as we saw, Ernest Jones reduces *Hamlet*. Whatever one may think of this reduction, it is clear that in both plays a royal sufferer is associated with pollution, in its very sources, of an entire social order. Both plays open with an invocation of the well-being of the endangered body politic. In both, the destiny of the individual and of society are closely intertwined; and in both the suffering of the royal victim seems to be necessary before purgation and renewal can be achieved.

But my purpose here is not to attempt an extended comparison of the two plays; it is, rather, to contrast the structural principles of these two ritual dramas, one from the beginnings of the tradition, the other from the end, at the very brink of the modern world.

The extraordinary unity and clarity of *Oedipus,* in comparison with *Hamlet,* is perhaps due to the fact that it is closer to the form, purpose, and occasion (the Festival of Dionysos) of its ritual source than *Hamlet,* in the Globe Theater, is to its ritual sources. Oedipus is the one and obvious protagonist, his story the literal subject of the play. He is the diagrammatic royal scapegoat, a marked man, from the first. And the parts of the play, which show the stages of his destruction, correspond very closely to the stages of the ancient ritual sacrifice.

In *Hamlet* it is as though every one of these elements had been elaborated by a process of critical analysis. Hamlet himself, though a prince, is without a throne; though a sufferer for the truth, he can appear in public as a mere infatuated or whimsical youth. We have seen how many ironic parallels Shakespeare provides to his story—and to this I may add that it takes both Hamlet and Claudius to represent the royal victim of the tradition. Though the play has the general shape of the tragic rhythm, and the traditional parts of the plot, each part is presented in several ironically analogous versions. The prologue is in three scenes of contrasting moods. The agon is so complicated that the very purposes of the antagonists are critically seen as false, hidden, or "mistook." It takes all of Act v to represent the epiphany, the final vision of death, from all the angles that Shakespeare knows.

Even the ritual process itself is, in *Hamlet,* directly dramatized: i.e., presented in a tragic, ironic light. There are no rituals in *Oedipus:* Oedipus is a ritual. But Hamlet has an extremely modern and skeptical, a Pirandellesque, theatricality as well; Shakespeare plays with the basis of his own make-believe. Sophocles uses the tragic theater with its ritual basis to mirror human life directly. Shakespeare uses the Elizabethan theater in the same way; but at the same time he has another mirror—his own and Hamlet's supermodern awareness—in which the making of the ritual is itself ironically reflected.

Oedipus moves, as it were, straight to its end, in clear figures of the tragic rhythm. But in *Hamlet* there is also a movement of ironic analysis, represented by the analogous versions of the main theme which the interwoven plots embody, and by Hamlet's monologues and wry jokes: improvisations which are beside the story of the play, in closer relationship to the audience. But though Shakespeare thus sees the ritual order of Claudius' Denmark as it were from without, he does not, like Euripides, simply satirize the values and the order of the traditional religion: the movement of analysis is corrected from time to time by a synthesis (a funeral or a Court scene) in which the main theme of the play, and the interdependence of all the dramatis personae, is reaffirmed. These rituals in *Hamlet* are not simply absurd, as a Euripidean *deus ex machina* is absurd; they are rather tragic failures, like Claudius' private attempt to pray: "Words without thoughts never to heaven go." In spite of the ironic device of the double plot, and the deeper irony of the Pirandellesque improvisation (Is all the world a stage or the stage life itself?) Shakespeare also clings to the conception of the theater as ritual.

RITUAL AND IMPROVISATION:
HAMLET'S PLAY AS THE CENTER

Shakespeare's theater, because of its ancient roots and its central place in society, permitted the development of ritual drama—or at least a drama which had this dimension as well as others. In the structure of *Hamlet* the rituals, as distinguished from the plots, serve to present the main action at various points in its development. Shakespeare uses them in much the same way in which Henry James used his "social occasions" to present the main theme of *The Awkward Age.* The structure of *Hamlet* could be described in Henry

James's words: "A circle consisting of a number of small rounds disposed at equal distance about a central object. The central object was my situation, my subject in itself, to which the thing would owe its title, and the small rounds represented so many distinct lamps, as I liked to call them, the function of each of which would be to light up with all due intensity one of its aspects. ... I revelled in this notion of the Occasion as a thing by itself." That is the important point: the social rite or occasion is taken as a thing by itself; it enables the author to assemble his dramatis personae in a wider light than any of their individual intelligences could provide. If my analysis of *Hamlet* is correct, the rituals (though they have deeper meanings than James's social gatherings) are also "occasions" of this kind: lamps lighting the rottenness of Denmark (the basic situation of the play) and the many-sided action which results, at various points in its course, and in various aspects.

In the table showing the relation of the plot to the ritual scenes and the improvisations, the players' scene is at the center. It has a ritual aspect, it is Hamlet's most ambitious improvisation, and it is the climax and peripety of the whole complex plot-scheme. If one can understand this scene, one will be close to grasping Shakespeare's sense of the theater, and his direct, profoundly histrionic dramaturgy.

The prologue contains two rituals, the changing of the guard and Claudius' first court. The changing of the guard is conducted by the honest and simple-minded soldiers, in perfect good faith: the welfare of the state is conceived in the most obvious and acceptable terms, and with the solemnity and authority of the military function. The motives of the soldiers are not impugned; and the only ironic angle we get on this scene is due to the arrival of the Ghost, which clearly suggests that the military rite is not an appropriate means for dealing with the actual danger. Claudius' court, on the other hand, is conducted by the new King; and here we feel (both in the light of Hamlet's disabused view of Claudius, and in the light of the visit of the Ghost) that there is something false about Claudius' discharge of the royal function. Together the two scenes establish the fact of danger and the common concern with the threatened welfare of the state. But they throw ironic lights upon each other. The point of view of the regime is in conflict with that of the simple soldiers. Neither the soldiers nor the regime have the magic for dealing with the Ghost; and it appears that the rituals of the state in general are false or mistaken.

The many conflicts, which the prologue presents as it were in suspension, are further developed (though without coming to direct issue) during the rest of the first act, the second act, and the first scene of Act III. Then (bringing the climax, peripety, and recognition) comes Hamlet's improvised ritual, the players' scene. Hamlet, as the "chief reflector," the widest consciousness in literature, as Henry James called him, is aware of what the soldiers see, of what Claudius sees, and of what the Ghost sees, and he is torn by all the conflicts implicit in these partial values and myopic vested interests. His "ritual occasion" is thus an answer to both rituals in the prologue; and at the same time (because he has also seen what the Ghost sees) it is an answer to, and a substitute for, the inadequate or false ritual order of Denmark. It is itself a "ritual" in that it assembles the whole tribe for an act symbolic of their deepest welfare; it is false and ineffective, like the other public occasions, in that the Danes do not really understand or intend the enactment which they witness. It is, on the other hand, not a true ritual, but an improvisation—for here the role of Hamlet, as showman, as master of ceremonies, as clown, as night-club entertainer who lewdly jokes with the embarrassed patrons—Hamlet the ironist, in sharpest contact with the audience on-stage and the audience off-stage, yet a bit outside the literal belief in the story: it is here that this aspect of Hamlet's role is clearest. But notice that, if Hamlet is the joking clown, he is also like those improvising Old Testament prophets who, gathering a handful of dust or of little bones, or a damaged pot from the potter's wheel, present to a blind generation a sudden image of their state. It is in the players' scene that the peculiar theatricality of *Hamlet*—ritual as theater and theater as ritual; at once the lightest improvisation and the solemnest occasion—is most clearly visible.

What then is the image, the parable, the "fear in a handful of dust," which Hamlet thus places—with all the pomp of court and all the impudence of the night-club entertainer—in the very center of the public consciousness of Denmark?

The most detailed analysis I know of the players' scene is Mr. Dover Wilson's, in his excellent book, *What Happens in Hamlet.* The reader is referred to that study, and to its companion-piece, Granville-Barker's book on *Hamlet,* for a discussion of the theatrical problems which the scene presents and for an understanding of the complexity of the scene as a whole, wherein the focus of the audience's attention is shifted from Hamlet (the "central reflector") to Horatio, to the Queen, to Ophelia, to the King—as though the play-within-a-play were being lighted from many angles by reflection from many mirrors. My purpose here is only to describe Hamlet's play itself, in order to show how it reveals the malady of the regime in all its ambiguity, mystery, and spreading ramifications. For this little play is indeed an all-purpose mousetrap—and it catches more than the conscience of the King.

First of all the play presents the hidden crime (the murder of a king and the more or less incestuous theft of his queen and his throne) upon which, as in *Oedipus,* all the threads of the interwoven plots depend. It is the presentation of this literal fact which has the immediate effect upon the innocent bystanders of the court and upon the innocent groundlings in the audience, though in Hamlet's violent view none are innocent. Because the security of the regime and the purposes of its supporters depend either upon ignorance or concealment, the public representation of the crime is itself an act of aggression, Hamlet's attack, the turning-point in the story. This attack reaches the guilty Claudius first, Gertrude second, Polonius third; then Laertes and Ophelia. And at length it clears the way for Fortinbras, the new faith and the new regime.

But though the fact of murder, incest, and usurpation is clearly presented, the time of the murder—is it still to come?—is vague; and the dramatis personae in the playlet are shifted about in such a way as to leave the identity of the criminal in question, and so to spread the guilt. The actual crime was that of Claudius; but in the play the guilty one is nephew to the King. This could mean (as Polonius and Gertrude seem to think) a direct threat by Hamlet to Claudius; it also means that Hamlet (who had admitted to himself a "weakness and melancholy" which makes him subject to devilish solicitations, and who had assured Ophelia, that "I am myself indifferent honest, yet I could accuse me of such things it were better my mother had not borne me") had granted Claudius, in advance, that he too is at least potentially guilty. Neither Hamlet nor Shakespeare seems to rule out a Freudian interpretation of the tangle; Hamlet comes close to representing himself as the diagrammatic son of the Oedipus complex, killing the father and possessing the mother. Yet his awareness of such motivations lifts the problems from the level of pathology to that of drama; he sees himself, Claudius, Denmark, the race itself, as subject to greeds and lusts which the hypocritical façade of the regime guiltily conceals.

Thus the literal meaning of the playlet is the fact of the crime; but the trope and the anagoge convey a picture of the human in general as weak, guilty, and foolish: the deepest and most sinister version of the malady of Claudius' regime in Denmark. This picture should emerge directly from the staging of the playlet before the corrupt and hypocritical court, under the inspired and triumphant irony of the regisseur-prince. The whining of pipes, the parade of mummers, the wooden gestures of the dumb-show, the tinkle of the rhymes, should have the magical solemnity of a play-party or children's singing-game ("London bridge is falling down"). Yet because of the crimes represented, this atmosphere is felt as unbearably weak and frivolous, a parody of all solemn rites. If this playlet invokes the magic potency of the theater ("the play's the thing") it does so with as much despairing irony as love. The staging is crude and childish: Hamlet's actors vainly take things into their own hands, and the court audience is as condescendingly unperceptive (until the scandal dawns on them) as any cynical crowd at a Broadway opening.

Hamlet's audience on-stage (and perhaps off-stage as well) misses the deeper meanings of his play. Yet he and his author have put it as simply as possible in the weary couplets of the Player-King. The Player-King seems to stand for Hamlet's father, and thus for the Ghost; and he speaks in fact with the clarity but helplessness (in this world) of the dead—addressing the frivolous Player-Queen without much hope of understanding. Since he is Hamlet's puppet, he speaks also for Hamlet, and since he is the King, he stands also for Claudius. Claudius, in the course of the play, will gradually acquire a helplessness like that of the Ghost; a faithlessness and an indecision like that of Hamlet. It is the function of the Player-King to state as directly as possible that gloomy and fatalistic sense of human action which is the subject of the play, and which all the various characters have by analogy.

The way to show this in detail would be to study the action of each character and to show what frivolity and gloomy faithlessness they have in common, but this would take too long. The point may be briefly illustrated by juxtaposing a few utterances of Hamlet and Claudius with analogous couplets of the Player-King:

HAMLET   There's a divinity that shapes our ends,
Act V   Rough-hew them how we will.
Scene 2

             Was't Hamlet wronged Laertes? Never Hamlet:
             . . . . .
             . . . . Hamlet denies it.
             Who does it then? His madness.

CLAUDIUS   My stronger guilt defeats my strong intent:
Act III   And, like a man to double business bound,
Scene 3   I stand in pause where I shall first begin,
             And both neglect.

Act IV   Not that I think you did not love your father,
Scene 7   But that I know love is begun by time,
             And that I see, in passages of proof,
             Time qualifies the spark and fire of it.
             There lives within the very flame of love
             A kind of wick or snuff that will abate it,
             And nothing is at a like goodness still,
             For goodness, growing to a plurisy,

[359]

Dies in his own too much. That we would do,
We should do when we would, for this "would" changes
And hath abatements and delays as many
As there are tongues, are hands, are accidents;
And then this "should" is like a spendthrift sigh,
That hurts by easing.

PLAYER   Our wills and fates do so contrary run
KING   That our devices still are overthrown,
Our thoughts are ours, their ends none of our own.

What to ourselves in passion we propose,
The passion ending, doth the purpose lose.

Purpose is but the slave to memory
Of violent birth, but poor validity.

The speeches of Hamlet and Claudius which I have quoted come late in the play, when both of them gain a deathly insight into their destinies—the hidden and uncontrolled springs of their own and others' actions. Even Claudius sees so deeply at this moment that he gets the sense of human action which all the characters have by analogy. His speech to Laertes (Act IV, scene 7) is, moreover, both made more ironic and more general by being addressed to Laertes in order to deceive him into a course which is contrary to his deepest purposes and best interests. As for Hamlet, his sense of pathos, of the suffering of motivations beyond our understanding or control, does not save him from violent outbursts any more than that of Claudius does. Shakespeare usually grants his victims a moment of great clarity when it is too late—and then shows them returning, like automatons, to "ravin down their proper bane" and die.

But the chief point I wish to make here is that the Player-King presents very pithily the basic vision of human action in the play, at a level so deep that it applies to all the characters: the guilty, the free, the principals, the bystanders, those in power and the dispossessed. This vision of course comes directly from the crime of Claudius and the other "accidental judgments, casual slaughters, purposes mistook" (as Horatio describes them when summing up for Fortinbras) upon which the complicated plot depends; yet this generalized vision is more terrible than any of the particular crimes, and much more important for understanding Hamlet's motivation. To this point I shall return later.

The immediate effect of Hamlet's play comes by way of the concrete scandal which brings the climax and peripety of the narratives. The presentation of the play is Hamlet's attack; it succeeds; it convicts Claudius' regime, and "the lives of many" that depend upon it, of impotence and corruption. After that revelation all is lost (just as Macbeth is lost after the banquet scene)—and the desperate devices of the King and Laertes, the brief folly of Polonius, and the unimpeded progress of Fortinbras, in the healthy rhythm of the march, are seen as clearly fated or doomed.

For this reason also the "rituals" which follow the players' scene have a different quality from those which precede it. Since the regime has lost its manna—been "shown up"—the rituals in Acts IV and V, marking the stages of the collective pathos and epiphany, are clearly presented as mad or evil. Ophelia's mad ritual presents the "sparagmos" or tearing asunder of the individual and society at once ("schism in the state and schism in the soul"); mingling marriage and funeral, lewdness and prettiness, love and destruction to the accompaniment of plotting and rebellion. Ophelia's funeral is a real death but a "maimèd rite"; the duel between Hamlet and Laertes is ostensibly a ritual and actually a murder. With the assembling of the court and the royal family for the duel, the picture of Claudius' regime (the collective revelation of his black masses) is complete.

In the succession of "ritual scenes" with its center and climax in Hamlet's little play, it is obvious that Hamlet himself plays a central role. In the two rituals of the prologue he is, like the audience, a mere puzzled and troubled bystander. After the hidden struggles of Act I, II, and III, he presents, with his play, his own black mass, his own parody of a rite. He does not appear for the "tearing asunder" of Ophelia's madness, for this marks the pathos of the regime, and of the lives that depend directly on it; and his life (wherever it may be) has already withdrawn from all loyalty to Claudius' Denmark. But he returns to record Ophelia's truncated funeral in his cold, spent, but clear awareness; and to take his fated role in the duel at the end. I have endeavored to study the rituals as marking the progress of the "play as a whole"; but it is evident that in the play, and in the order of the rituals, Hamlet himself is both chief "agonist" and central "reflector." With this in mind it is possible to offer an interpretation of the role of Hamlet in relation to Shakespeare's idea of the theater, and the traditional social values which the play assumes.

AN INTERPRETATION OF THE ROLE OF HAMLET

> For, by the image of my cause, I see
> The portraiture of his.

Oedipus, as I have pointed out, starts out as the hero, the triumphant human adequate to rule, and ends, like Tiresias, a scapegoat, a witness and a sufferer for the hidden truth of the human condition. The play starts with the conflict and contrast between Oedipus and Tiresias, shows the steps of Oedipus' dismemberment, and ends when he is blind and all-seeing and helpless, as Tiresias was in the beginning. Hamlet is apparently thought of as undergoing a similar transformation, from hero to scapegoat, from "the expectancy and rose of the fair state" to the distracted, suffering witness and victim of Act v. But this development is not neatly laid out for him according to a publicly understood series of struggles: he feels his way toward it, not with public sanction but against the faithless worldliness of the Danes. It is not until Act v that his martyr-like destiny "feels right" to him.

We see him in the first three acts of the play as a puzzled and, as it were, unconvinced hero and prince. He knows that "the times are out of joint" and that he is born to set them right; he knows that the Prince should be moved by honor and ambition: but he cannot reconcile this worldly code with his sense of evil in Denmark nor with the otherworldly solicitations of his Ghost-father. From Corneille to Dryden the ethical values of "honor" will be taken as sufficient basis for the drama of human life; but Hamlet's sense of his own and Denmark's condition contradicts this simplified philosophy. When he looks at Laertes, that "noble youth," he envies him— envies, at least, his simple and honorable motivations. When he looks at Fortinbras, he envies him the ability to risk his own and other lives for honor—"even for an eggshell." If he could accept this code, he would feel that the murder of Claudius would heal the schism in his own soul and in society; but just as his sense of evil preceded his knowledge of Claudius' literal guilt, so he cannot believe that the literal punishment of Claudius (an eye for an eye) will cure the damage he has done. And so his drama becomes far deeper than a simple revenge play.

If Hamlet is not content with the simple soldierly code of honor, it is because he sees too deeply and skeptically into that cosmic setting of human life which Shakespeare's theater symbolically represented. He sees beyond the tiny human involvements of the foreground to the social order indicated by the stage house façade and, above that, to the order in the stars implied by the canopy over his head. This is especially clear in his first scene with Rosencrantz and Guildenstern (Act II, scene 2). It is in this scene that he makes the great speech on Man which Tillyard quotes as an exposition of the traditional ordered universe. But the speech ends bitterly: "And yet, to me, what is this quintessence of dust?"

Though Hamlet accepts this order, he does not know where he belongs in it; he is not even sure which way is up. He would have felt the force of that remark of Heracleitus which Eliot uses as epigraph to *Burnt Norton*: "The way up and the way down are one and the same." His intellect plays over the world of the religious tradition with an all-dissolving irony like that of Montaigne in the *Apologie de Raimond Sebonde:* a truly double-edged irony, for he can neither do with nor do without the ancient moral and cosmic order.

That is why he has a despairing fellow-feeling for Rosencrantz and Guildenstern. He knows them for little trimmers, neither for God nor for the Devil, but "for themselves," like the dim figures in Dante's Limbo: "indifferent children of the earth," "Fortune's privates," as they call themselves. He is himself anything but indifferent, yet he does not at that moment know how to care, and so feels himself, like them, lost between "greatness" and the chill of mere bodily "weight" and utter faithlessness at the bottom of the universe. Thus he is troubled with "bad dreams":

GUIL. Which dreams, indeed, are ambition, for the very substance of the ambitious is but the shadow of a dream.

HAM. A dream itself is but a shadow.

ROS. Truly, and I hold ambition of so airy and light a quality that it is but a shadow's shadow.

HAM. Then are our beggars bodies, and our monarchs and outstretched heroes the beggars' shadows. Shall we to the court? for, by my fay, I cannot reason.

Hamlet draws the deduction which troubles *him,* but not Rosencrantz and Guildenstern: if ambition like Fortinbras' is illusory, what, in Denmark, is to show us the way, and prevent us from taking the "shadow as a solid thing"?

It would be an exaggeration to say that Hamlet envies these two as he envies Fortinbras and Laertes. But his fellow-feeling for them—call it sympathy, or a sense of the analogy between them, or seeing their cause as mirroring his—comes, like his envy, from the fact that he himself is lost. Until the success of his play, Hamlet feels his over-quick sympathy as a weakness, and covers it up with murderous sarcasm. On his return from England, he has accepted it, and in Act v his abnormally quick sympathy has acquired some of the quiet of the vision integrated and lived-up-to, some of the breadth of charity.

What has intervened is chiefly the presentation of his play. When the players come, and do a speech for Hamlet, he envies *them;* but at this time it turns out that he has found a real clue to his own action. He cannot act like a simple soldier but he can employ the theater in an equally dangerous, and far more significant, project. He can use it as a trap for the conscience of the King, and at the same time as a test of his own and the Ghost's vision. Thus empirically, or improvisationally, feeling his way through the concrete

elements of his situation, he finds his own proper line of action, and a use of
the theater very much like that which two other autobiographical characters
of Shakespeare make of it.

The two other characters who use the theater in this way are the Duke
in *Measure for Measure* and Prospero in *The Tempest*. These two plays are,
of course, very different from each other and from *Hamlet*. But the analogies
between the three dispossessed rulers, and their attempts to purify the spiritual atmosphere of their societies by means of significant shows, are close
enough to throw a good deal of light on the nature of the role of Hamlet.

The "Duke of dark corners" is dispossessed and anonymous much as
Hamlet is, even though he himself had rejected the official role of ruler. His
theatricality consists in casting Angelo and Claudio and Isabella for tragic
roles, and then moving about behind the scenes like a nervous regisseur, to
make sure that the moral of the drama is clear, and yet that the real tragedy
does not go too far. The play he arranges is almost a practical joke; yet, like
Hamlet's play, it both tests and reveals a wider and healthier vision of human
society than Vienna publicly accepts. And by this means he proposes to
substitute the rule of charity for Angelo's blind and univocal conception of
Mosaic justice. *Measure for Measure* has been called a problem comedy, and
it has, in fact, a discursive clarity, a kind of modern intellectuality, quite unlike *Hamlet*. But with this reservation, the Duke as regisseur-prince is very
closely akin to Hamlet in that role.

The Tempest has neither the analytic naturalism of *Hamlet* nor the
"thesis" quality of *Measure for Measure*. It partakes of the qualities of myth,
of Medieval allegory, and of dream; as though Shakespeare's mind, at the
end of his career, were in that state which Dante knew, in the early morning,
at the threshold of the Mount of Purgatory:

> Canto ix: *e che la mente nostra, peregrina / più dalla carne e men da'
> pensier presa, / alle sue vision quasi è divina.*

> When our mind, wandering farther from the flesh and less caught by
> thought, is in its visions almost prophetic.

The basic donné of the play is the magic of Prospero. And hence the
shows with which he purges the worldly exiles from Milan can be close to
the very idea of such shows. Mr. Colin Still (in *The Timeless Theme*) has
traced in them many ancient ritual themes. It is in this play that Shakespeare comes to terms with his own imaginative power as a wielder of the
theater—indicating its use in the service of truth, and its limitations as a
means of salvation. For at the end, when Prospero has demonstrated both
the magic power of the theater and its use, he buries his book and staff and

prays for grace. He has a ripeness and a clarity and a power which Hamlet lacks, but for that very reason he helps one to see what Hamlet, with his play, was trying to do.

Hamlet, more than either the Duke or Prospero, is defenseless and uninstructed in the midst of life; and if he stumbles on the theater as a means of realizing his vision and his anonymous being, he does not clearly understand what he has accomplished. When the King rises after the play, Hamlet takes his success with almost childish pleasure: "Would not this, sir, and a forest of feathers, if the rest of my fortunes turn Turk with me, with two Provincial roses on my razed shoes, get me a fellowship in a cry of players, sir?" The delight is, of course, partly ironic; moreover he has still to confirm his success with his mother and the King. Even after those two interviews he is puzzled and tormented; he does not really feel that he has done his part, borne his witness, taken his stand, until he returns from England. By that time his testimony has had its effect: the regime is wounded beyond repair, and he himself is doomed.

In Act v, while he records in the graveyard the vision of death—literal death and the death of society, to the accompaniment of the clowns' heartless equivocations—and finally suffers the truncated funeral of Ophelia—he feels that his role, all but the very last episode, has been played. He is still uncertain what this will be, still feels that it must include the killing of Claudius: "Is't not perfect conscience to quit him with this arm?" His personal hatred for the King is sharp as ever; but he is content, now, to let the fated end come as it will. "It will be short: the interim is mine; and a man's life's no more than to say 'one'." He feels, I think, whether he or his author would put it so or not, that he is ready to take the consequences of his revelation, to suffer for that truth: "Thou wouldst not think how ill's all here about my heart; but it is no matter. . . . It is such a kind of gain-giving as would perhaps trouble a woman. . . . The readiness is all." One could say that he feels the poetic rightness of his own death. One could say, with Ernest Jones, that because of his Oedipus complex he had a death-wish all along. Or one could say that his death was the only adequate expiation for the evil of Denmark, according to the ancient emotional logic of the scapegoat; or one could say that only by accepting death to prove it could the truth of his vision be properly affirmed.

However one may interpret it, when his death comes it "feels right," the only possible end for the play. Horatio makes music for his going-off like that which accompanies Oedipus' death at Colonnus: "Good night, sweet prince, and flights of angels sing thee to thy rest." And Fortinbras treats him like one of those honor-seekers that had puzzled him all along, as though in his career the hero had somehow been subsumed in the martyr: "Let four captains bear Hamlet, like a soldier, to the stage." We are certainly intended to feel that Hamlet, however darkly and uncertainly he worked, had discerned the way to be obedient to his deepest values, and accomplished some sort of purgatorial progress for himself and Denmark.

I am aware that this interpretation of the role of Hamlet is open to the same sort of objections as all other interpretations; there is no substitute for the direct knowledge which a good performance of the play would give. But I think that Shakespeare, in writing the play, was counting on such a performance, and upon the willing make-believe of his audience and his performers. The elements of the Tudor monarchy, of the emblematic stage of the Globe, and of the traditional cosmos they stood for, were accepted for the purposes of the play as real; and within the concrete elements of this scene the role of Hamlet has its own logic.

ANALOGOUS ACTION: AN INTERPRETATION OF THE PLAY

> For goodness, growing to a plurisy,
> Dies in his own too much.

The remark of the King, which he uses as a warning to Laertes, and which I have used to describe Hamlet's over-quick and over-subtle sympathy, applies also to Shakespeare's principles of composition in the play as a whole. Shakespeare's sense of analogy is perhaps too productive, burgeoning too richly in all directions, as though the dramatic life he had got hold of gave him more instances than he needed. Yet it is my belief that the life itself, the germ, the "unity" is there, however overlaid with elaborations and confusingly illumined from many directions.

Miss Caroline Spurgeon discerned this underlying life, quite accurately, as a result of her studies of the metaphors in the play: "To Shakespeare's pictorial imagination," she writes, "the problem in *Hamlet* is not predominantly that of the will and reason, of a mind too philosophic or a nature temperamentally unfitted to act quickly: he sees it pictorially *not as the problem of an individual at all,* but as something greater and even more mysterious, as a *condition* for which the individual himself is apparently not responsible, any more than the sick man is to blame for the infection which strikes and devours him, but which, nevertheless, in its course and development, impartially and relentlessly annihilates him and others, innocent and guilty alike. That is the tragedy of *Hamlet,* and it is perhaps the chief tragic mystery of life."

Miss Spurgeon offers a kind of scientific proof of her view of the play by showing that the predominant metaphors are those of disease. An analysis of the play as the imitation of action gives the same result. The action of the play as a whole is "to identify and destroy the hidden imposthume which is endangering the life of Denmark." But because the source of infection is hidden, and there is no general agreement about its nature or location, the action of the play is predominantly in the passive mode—the suffering of forces not controlled or understood, rather than the consistent drive of an intelligible purpose. *Hamlet* is, like *The Cherry Orchard,* in its essential structure an "ensemble pathos," broken from time to time by the spasmodic moves of one or two of the characters.

This action is realized in many analogous ways in the contrasted characters. Claudius, who identifies the health of Denmark with the safety of his own corrupt regime, and therefore merely wishes to hold what he has, gradually comes to feel that the imposthume which poisons the communal life and his own is Hamlet: "for like the hectic in my blood he rages." Polonius, the chief figure in the comic sub-plot, also identifies the health of the body politic with the status quo; and for him the dis-ease is only the normal but troublesome fires of youth: Laertes' appetite for drabbing and gambling, Hamlet's infatuation for Ophelia—both to be cured by a judicious mixture of discipline and indulgence, which his age and experience can easily concoct.

Gertrude and Ophelia (like other women pictured by Shakespeare) define their actions and their beings only with reference to their men; and since they both have a stake in the regime, and at the same time in the rebellious Hamlet, they suffer the worst of the disease itself. In the economy of the play, they are symbols and measures of the health of the body politic— glamorous signs of what might have been, and torn and dishonored images of what is.

Hamlet himself, as we saw, comes the closest to seeing the whole range of the disease, as it spreads from the immediate guilt of Claudius to ruin all dependent lives. And we have seen that the adequate response to the rotten-ness of Denmark, as he sees it, is not a simple, purposive course of action, but a bearing-witness and a suffering-for-the-truth.

The characters have not only analogous objects of their actions, they all act in a similar way, indirectly. Polonius has his "windlasses" and his "assays of bias." Claudius acts only through intermediaries: Polonius, Rosencrantz and Guildenstern, Laertes. Ophelia acts as the puppet of her father, and Hamlet by means of his symbolic play. The Gravedigger speaks in equivocations, and Osric in such a "yesty collection" of ornamental clichés that he is barely comprehensible.

In defining the action of the play as a whole, the one underlying "essence" which the actions of the various characters "adumbrate" in their different ways, the character of Claudius is all important—not because he sees more, or realizes a deeper life, but because as head of the state he is, *de facto,* the one center of "weight" and of "greatness." As Tudor monarch, father, king, and high-priest—the massy wheel upon which the lives of the many depend— he makes, so to speak, the spiritual weather in Denmark. It is his particular kind of spiritual night—his motionless worldly presence, like a wall; his gratified lust ("fat weed on Lethe wharf," "things rank and gross in nature") —which defines the action in *Hamlet.* In such a nonconducting atmosphere, all purposes are short, hidden, and mistook, and they soon sink into frightened or oblivious stagnation. As long as he rules, "Denmark is a prison," "one of the worst" of the world's many confines, closed away from Dante's "dolce mondo."

From this point of view, Claudius' place in the economy of the play is like that of Macbeth in his play: Shakespeare thinks of the usurper in both cases as defining the "scene" and thereby the action of the play. Macbeth is in his moral being quite unlike Claudius; and he produces a different action and a different rhythm in the play as a whole. Macbeth is like a man running down-hill to escape himself: however fast he goes, "the pauser, reason," is still with him. In his depraved career he lays an irrational and obsessive basis for all human thought and intercourse; hence every action is paradoxical and unnatural. Even the peripety, when Macduff, Malcolm, and Ross are forced to take action against Macbeth, is realized as a tissue of denials and paradoxes. The final assault upon the castle is (in spite of its healthy marching rhythm) unreasonable and unnatural too. The wood moves, the leader is unborn of woman, and the soldiers are sustained by the super-rational, the miraculous blessings and graces that hang about King Edward's throne.

Mr. Kenneth Burke has pointed out that "action" may be defined in terms of "scene." This is one of the principles of composition in the *Divine Comedy:* human actions are presented in an orderly succession of scenes which concretely realize and define them. But Dante's tremendous subject was human life and action in general, while the subject of a Shakespearean tragedy is, more immediately, human action under a particular regime, or at a particular historic moment. His dramatis personae are seldom seeking salvation directly, but rather trying to realize a human life in a concrete society. That is why an analysis like Miss Spurgeon's is so suggestive, and takes one so far toward an understanding of the play as a whole—much further, for example, than the attempt to rationalize Hamlet's character, as though Shakespeare had been writing a drama of the individual will and reason only.

Yet there are dangers in an analysis based on metaphor. Such an analysis leaves *Hamlet* at the level of the romantic lyric, as though its "logic" were a logic of feeling only, and its principles of composition those of "association and contrast," as Mr. Burke calls them. Such an analysis works better for *Tristan* than for *Hamlet,* for it leaves out the substantial elements (the beings of the individual characters, the stable elements in the traditional cosmos) which underlie the associated or contrasted *qualities* of their lives, the "atmosphere" or feeling tone of the play. Miss Spurgeon's lyrical or subjective or qualitative analysis needs to be supported and extended by a more realist analysis, one based for instance on the four levels of Medieval symbolism.

According to this system, the analogous actions of the characters in their attempts to destroy the hidden disease of Denmark would constitute the "trope" or moral meaning of the play. The rottenness of the regime itself, from which they all suffer, could be called the "allegory," for it refers to a particular moment in history when a corrupt regime falsifies the life of the community. We have seen that in *Hamlet,* as in *Macbeth,* Shakespeare takes this historic moment as defining his subject. But Shakespeare is no Spenglerian determinist; in spite of his worldly focus, his preoccupation with social order, and his feeling for the "divine sanction" of kingship, he places Claudius' Denmark in a wider setting; and this "placing" of Claudius' regime is the anagoge, the meaning of the play in relation to ultimate values.

Miss Spurgeon records the fact that there is in *Hamlet* a series of images contrasting with those of disease and darkness; and, indeed, from the first we are made to feel that the condition of the Danes is not the human condition *überhaupt* but only a particular version of it. Ophelia's description of Hamlet, "What a noble mind is here o'erthrown," contrasts his present plight with what she feels to be his natural role: "the expectancy and rose of the fair state." Hamlet's description of his father, in his terrible interview with his mother, has a similar effect—to make us feel that a natural and divinely sanctioned order has been betrayed and lost. And in his famous speech on "man, the paragon of animals," though the context gives it depths of irony, Hamlet unrolls the traditional moral order as both good and true though he has somehow lost a vital relation to it. But it is chiefly in Act v that Claudius' regime is seen for what it is, brought to its temporal end, and placed in a wider and therefore truer scene.

Act v unrolls for us, first of all, a picture of Denmark after it has been torn asunder, its deathliness or its nonentity laid as it were flat and open to the eye of the audience and the eyes of Hamlet. The vision, as usual in Shakespeare, is firmly based upon the most concrete sensory impact (like the darkness of Act I, scene 1) and proceeds then to elaborate ever wider and more complex perspectives. The basic sensual impression is the brutal digging up of skulls; then comes the solemn-joyful equivocating of the clowns—a denial of all meaning, the end result of Claudius' falsity. With this goes a series of hints of social disorder: the dead receive no respect; the professions, especially law, are laughably helpless; "the age is grown so picked that the toe of the peasant comes so near the heel of the courtier, he galls his kibe." As for the courtiers, we shall presently have Osric: "He did comply with his dug before he sucked it." Osric corresponds to Rosencrantz and Guildenstern, a more shameless hypocrite and time-server, much as the clowns correspond to Polonius in their complacent irrelevancy but speak in equivocations where Polonius, less deathly, merely rationalizes upon false premises.

From this opening impression of literal death and meaninglessness in many forms comes the funeral of Ophelia, the "maimèd rite." I have already pointed out its place in the succession of rituals. It is full of cross-references: to the funerals of Hamlet the first and Polonius; to Gertrude's corrupt marriage; to the marriage of Ophelia and Hamlet, which never occurred; and to Ophelia's mad mixture of funeral and marriage.

The second scene of Act v, with the duel between Hamlet and Laertes, shows the denouements of all the intrigues in the play: Polonius is avenged by Laertes; Laertes, like Hamlet, falls victim to Claudius' deceits; Gertrude follows Ophelia; Hamlet kills the King at last, and Fortinbras finally appears upon the Danish scene, the new faith and hope which Claudius no longer prevents. But these events, which literally end the narratives in the play, and bring Claudius' regime to its temporal end, tell us nothing new but the fact: that the sentence, which fate or providence pronounced long since, has now been executed. It is the pageantry, the ceremonial mummery, in short the ritual character of this last scene which makes us feel it as the final epiphany, the showing-forth of the true nature of Claudius' regime.

The staging of this scene is parallel to that of Claudius' first court (Act 1, scene 2) and to that of the players' scene. It is the last time we see all the dramatis personae gathered to celebrate the social order upon which they all depend. But whereas we saw Claudius' first court as smooth, plausible, almost majestic, and ostensibly devoted to guarding the welfare of all the subjects, we see this last court, all in mourning, for the deathtrap it is. The vision of Claudius' Denmark which Hamlet's play presented as a parable, is now brilliantly and literally visible. As soon as we glimpse it with this literal clarity, it is gone like a bad dream, and we are returned, with the healthy rhythms of young Fortinbras, to the wider world of the order of nature, with the possibility at least of divine sanction.

Thus the "placing" of the play follows immediately upon the completion of its action. Fortinbras is the agent; and in the scheme of the whole the role of Fortinbras, though it is very economically developed, is of major importance.

Hamlet, Prince of Denmark: The Analogy of Action

I have already pointed out that Fortinbras' story is one of the variations on the son-father theme. When we first hear of Fortinbras he, like Hamlet (and later, Laertes) is trying to avenge a dead and dishonored father. Like Hamlet, he has an uncle who stands *in loco parentis*. Like Laertes, he is a simple and noble youth, expending his high spirits upon the worldly code of "honor," yet at the same time he is a "good child," obedient to age—so that when his uncle tells him to, he is quite willing to turn his martial ambitions from the Danes to the Poles. But unlike both Hamlet and Laertes he does not live under Claudius' shadow: his obedience is not (like Laertes' obedience to Claudius) misplaced—and his life works itself out (as we hear) in a region free of the Danish infection.

Thus the role of Fortinbras, in *Hamlet,* corresponds to those of Malcolm, Macduff, and King Edward in *Macbeth*. Like them, he is felt as a constant, though off-stage, threat to the corrupt regime. Like them, he does not appear in the flesh until after the peripety and, though we feel his approach, does not enter Denmark until Claudius is gone. Like Malcolm and Macduff, he has his own version of the main action of the play. He moves and fights in the dark as much as his contemporaries, Hamlet and Laertes; but his darkness is not the artificial shadow of Claudius but the natural darkness of inexperience. He confronts it with a kind of sanguine natural faith, "exposing all that's mortal and unsure even for an eggshell"—as he could not (Laertes' example is there to prove it) in Denmark. That is why he cannot enter Denmark until the end. In the same way, in *Macbeth,* we are not ready for Macduff's and Malcolm's reception of Grace until Macbeth and his Queen have reached the nightmarish stalemate of the banquet scene. When the avengers appear before Macbeth's castle, they show him that there is another way to "outrun reason"; and when Fortinbras comes in at the end, he places the action we have seen in Denmark, both with reference to the wider world from which he comes, and with reference to his healthier version of "the fight in the dark," the "quest for the unseen danger." Fortinbras' darkness of natural faith is the last variation, this time in a major key, which Shakespeare plays upon his great theme.

This does not mean that Fortinbras, either in his character or in his vision, provides an answer to Hamlet's "problem"—nor does it mean that his example is intended to show that the experience of the play was simply illusory. This experience was "real," just as Dante's experience of Hell was real—though this is the region of low ceilings, and of those who have lost the good of the intellect. Hamlet sees a great deal that Fortinbras will never see; but Hamlet, who has his own limited being, is defined by it, and by the spiritual realm in which he moves; and this is not all of life. Fortinbras does not de-

stroy, he "places" the action of the play by suddenly revealing a new analogue of this action. The effect, once more, is not to provide us with an intellectual key, an explicit philosophy, but to release us from the contemplation of the limited mystery of Denmark by returning us to the wider mystery
of life in the world at large.

Thus it seems to me that the elements of Shakespeare's composition (like
those of Sophocles and Dante before him) are not qualities, like those of the
romantics with their logic of feeling, not abstract concepts, like those of the
dramatists of the Age of Reason, with their clear and distinct moral ideas,
but beings, real people in a real world, related to each other in a vast and
intricate web of analogies.

I know that analogy is a very difficult concept to use with accuracy. I have
endeavored to raise some of the questions connected with it in the Appendix.
At this point I merely wish to point out that the anagoge, or ultimate meaning of the play, can only be sought through a study of the analogical relationships within the play and between the world of Denmark and the traditional cosmos. There are the analogous actions of all the characters, pointing
to the action which is the underlying substance of the play. There are the
analogous father-son relationships, and the analogous man-woman relationships. There are the analogous stories, or chains of events, the fated results of
the characters' actions. And stretching beyond the play in all directions are
the analogies between Denmark and England; Denmark and Rome under
"the mightiest Julius"; Hamlet's stage and Shakespeare's stage; the theater
and life. Because Shakespeare takes all these elements as "real," he can respect
their essential mystery, not replacing them with abstractions, nor merely exploiting their qualities as mood-makers, nor confining us in an artificial world
with no exit. He asks us to sense the unity of his play through the direct perception of these analogies; he does not ask us to replace our sense of a real
and mysterious world with a consistent artifact, "the world of the play."

If Shakespeare's Hamlet is realist in the tradition represented by Sophocles
and Dante, if he composes by analogy rather than by "qualitative progression" or "syllogistic progression," then the question of *Hamlet* as an artistic
success appears in a different light. Because it is rooted in an ancient tradition, and in a theater central to its culture, it is not only a work of art, but
a kind of more-than-individual natural growth, like the culture itself, and
Shakespeare is not so much its inventor as its god-like recorder: "Cuando
amor spira, vo significando." The question is not whether the subject Shakespeare intends is there, but whether it is there in too bewildering a richness
and complexity. The besetting sin of the Renaissance, as Pico foresaw, was
an overindulgence in the imagination as it discerns analogies of every kind.
M. Gilson has explained how even Bonaventura could abuse his gift for

analogizing, losing at times the distinction between real analogy and the superficial correspondences which his faith led him to see. And Mr. Scott Buchanan in *Poetry and Mathematics* asks the suggestive question, at what point in history, and by what process, was the clue to the vast system of Medieval analogies lost, the thread broken, and the way cleared for the centerless proliferations of modern culture?

Of this question too Shakespeare seems to have been prophetically aware. Like Hamlet, he felt, perhaps, too wide a sympathy, too precise a scruple. His endless sense of analogical relationships, though a good, *could* "grow to a plurisy." And *Hamlet* can be regarded as a dramatization of the process which led, in the Renaissance, to the modern world and its fragmentary theaters.

HAMLET AND THE MODERN THEATER

Mr. Eliot remarked that the age of Shakespeare "moved toward chaos"; and he noted that Shakespeare's theater (compared, say, with Racine's) had no consistent and clear conventions which might have prevented it from degenerating into naturalism, sensationalism, or editorializing. If Shakespeare had an "idea of the theater" it was a very comprehensive and many-sided one which, to be realized at all, was obliged to comprehend many discordant elements in precarious and hidden harmony. Or you may say, if you take the view that he "succeeded," that his notion of the theater was so deep that it foresaw, as it were in significant relationship, the more limited dramatic genres which were to develop later.

Mr. Mark Van Doren noted, about *The Tempest*, that "any set of symbols, moved close to this play, lights up as in an electric field." *Hamlet* has the same mysterious property. Most dramas that were written since Shakespeare, when moved close to *Hamlet*, are themselves illumined, and seem to offer the clue to the interpretation of Shakespeare's great work.

If there is an exception to this observation, it is the drama of rationalism. Racine's masterpieces have a kind of consistency and explicit unity which is utterly foreign to Shakespeare. If the rationalism of the next age is foreseen at all in *Hamlet*, it is in the role of Polonius, with his faith in logic, his feeling for the neat antithesis and the triumphant demonstration, and his rhythms of speech—for, though he speaks in blank verse, his sense of language suggests the heroic couplet.

But the romantics took *Hamlet* for their own; and a generation later most critics thought that the greatness of the play lay in its naturalistic truth to nature—and when they criticized it, they objected that Shakespeare was less photographic than Ibsen. In our own time, Pirandello's desperate theatricality is seen as having been anticipated by Hamlet the *improvisateur*.

The age of Shakespeare "moved toward chaos," and the great mirror of his theater was broken into fragments. But it lasted long enough to give us the last image of western man in the light of his great tradition.

C E R V A N T E S

[*1547–1616*]

CERVANTES'S READERS INCREASE AND THE VOLUME OF PRAISE SWELLS, BUT MANY
questions about *Don Quixote* remain unsettled. Eric Auerbach maintains in
Mimesis that we must take Cervantes' declared intention literally: he writes
to make fun of medieval romances. Miguel de Unamuno, perhaps the most
famous Spanish writer in this century to deal with Cervantes, finds a more
complicated struggle between illusion and fact. Indeed, he makes Don
Quixote an archetype of Spanish character, and all Spaniards his fellows.

The question Américo Castro deals with in this essay is of the highest importance: how did *Don Quixote* become possible? Never before had people
so streamed into a book, nor had a writer so dramatized the conflict between
aspiration and circumstance. Castro seeks "the irreducible literary essence of
Don Quixote." A vast amount of learning about the Renaissance is employed
to support this conclusion: "Before Cervantes it had not been possible organically to harmonize the expression of the imaginary or fictitious and the concrete, contemporary experience of the character without falling into moral-
izations or grotesque farce." The remainder of Castro's essay makes this
massive and simple point in enough ways to enable us to respond not simply
with assent, but with understanding.

"Incarnation in Don Quixote" appears in a memorial volume, *Cervantes
Across the Centuries,* celebrating the four hundredth anniversary of the
writer's birth in 1547. Dr. Castro is Professor Emeritus of Spanish at Princeton.

From *Cervantes Across the Centuries,* Angel Flores and M. J. Benardete, eds. Copyright 1947 by The Dryden Press, Inc. Reprinted by special permission of The Dryden
Press, Inc.

AMÉRICO CASTRO

The Orientation of Style

THE BASIC THEME OF *Don Quixote* IS LIFE AS A PROCESS CREATIVE OF ITSELF —the onrush of incitements (the written or spoken word, love, wealth, possibilities of amusement, etc.) into the river bed of the life of each individual. The previously given—immutable, objectified realities confronted with the rushing current of life—does not play an essential role in the most important literary work of Spain. The *Entremés de los romances* and the traditional disturbances occasioned by the reading of chivalric novels enter here only to serve that fundamental theme. The style of *Don Quixote* rests on the assumption that all reality is something transitory, "transient," something that is inundated by effluvia emanating from some individual life, or that is already stylized in literature. The consciousness of feeling oneself living is the foundation upon which this oscillating world of constant flux finds stability. Don Quixote feels himself Don Quixote, and later, Alonso Quijano ("I was Don Quixote, and I am now Alonso Quijano the Good."). Sancho is conscious of being an irreducible naked person, a firm channel for the most varied fluid currents.

Years ago I attempted to interpret *Don Quixote* with excessively Occidental norms, and I believed that Cervantes was interested on occasion in determining the nature of the reality that lies behind the fluctuation of appearance. But the problem of logical truth or error does not preoccupy the author; it is rather a question of showing that reality is always an aspect of the experience of the person who is living it. As I pointed out in *El pensamiento de Cervantes,* Cervantes undoubtedly was familiar with the question often debated in Renaissance poetics as to the difference between poetic (universal) truth and historical (particular) truth. But the innovation of *Don Quixote* consists in its establishing as true what is authentically interlaced with a vital experience, and not what is determined by a cognitive process. Consequently, all that is implicit in the effective life of someone (a literary character or an actual person), and all that is connected with the creative, well-articulated intention of the poet-novelist is true.

When the author begins to give life, in elusive style, to the fluid figure of Don Quixote, he says that ascertaining whether his name was Quijada, Quesada, or Quejana "is of but little importance to our tale; it will be enough not to stray a hair's breadth from the truth in the telling of it"—from the truth, or rather from the proper fluidity of the artistic process, which has become real as a "value," and not as an objectified entity or an extraliterary reality. It is for this reason that Sancho's wife is called in different ways, and that at the end of the book, the gentleman from La Mancha is called Quijano, and not any of the three names mentioned at the beginning. Such minor discrepancies are not oversights or careless slips, but the result of the fact that what seems to exist here does not matter very much. This technique may be conceived as the antithesis of the naturalism of the nineteenth-century novelist. In one of the cases brought before Sancho during his governorship, the law says that if someone "swears truly, he shall be allowed to pass, but if falsely, he shall . . . be put to death for it by hanging on the gallows . . . ." Truth here means veracity—truthfulness.

Don Quixote asks the enchanted head ". . . was that which . . . happened to me in the cave of Montesinos the truth or a dream?" and the answer is: ". . . there is much to be said; there is something of both in it." In that adventure we are given, in effect, the truth about dreams, and also about him who lives the episode and about those who relive it in their own manner upon hearing it recounted. Such disparate phenomena are articulated in the vital experience of time, which is here an index of the extreme limits within which, as with a shuttle, the style of this novel is being woven. The atemporal time of the poetic illusion (*Amadís,* etc.) would then be in the same relation to time felt as an actual factor as is the supreme limit of ascending aspiration (Dulcinea), to the most abject extremes of that which is poetically scorned (Maritornes).

The adventure of the cave of Montesinos is fitted into precise terms of space and time: "They had let down the hundred fathoms of rope," till they could not give Don Quixote any more; ". . . they waited about half an hour, at the end of which time they began to gather in the rope again with great ease and without feeling any weight, which made them fancy Don Quixote was remaining below; . . . Sancho wept bitterly, and hauled away in great haste in order to settle the question. When, however, they had come, as it seemed, to rather more than eighty fathoms, they felt a weight . . ." They pull out the Knight, who eats heartily with Sancho and the Cousin, and then the author begins his tale: "It was about four in the afternoon when the sun, veiled in clouds, with subdued light and tempered beams, enabled Don Quixote to relate, without heat or inconvenience, what he had seen in the cave of Montesinos to his two illustrious hearers . . ." Aside from the heat, which could have been avoided by any of the conventional devices so frequent in *Don Quixote,* it is just to think that a soft light would be more suitable than the dazzling sun of La Mancha for the story of what has been lived between the sunrays of imaginative poetry and the twilight of implacable criticism ever prone to attack it. Montesinos and the Knight converse about the events narrated in the ballad or "romance"; Montesinos took out the heart of his friend Durandarte to take it to the Lady Belerma, not with a dagger, but with "a burnished poniard sharper than an awl." The epic figure steps out of his nebulous poetic context and reveals himself to us as living his own story, and thus he can enter into the lives of those who are outside the sphere of illusion. Sancho observes immediately (now that Montesinos is made accessible to him) that "that poniard must have been made by Ramón de Hoces the Sevillan." And Don Quixote replies—with half of him outside the realm of fantasy"—that "it could not have been by that poniard maker . . . because Ramón de Hoces *was a man of yesterday,* and the affair of Roncesvalles, where this mishap (*desgracia*—a word of *today* and vulgar) occurred, *was long ago."* Montesinos marvels that "though I know it to be as sure as day that Durandarte ended his life in my arms . . . how comes it that he now moans and sighs from time to time, as if he were still alive?" Durandarte thus passes from the eternal present of his poetic existence into the "now" in which we are living. It would not suffice to think that this is merely an attempt to achieve a comic or grotesque effect, because our laughter or smile upon reading these pages is not like that which bursts forth upon reading the strophes of Boiardo, Pulci, or Ariosto, in which we feel the rational criticism of these poets. Cervantes creates his unique scene by making the living experience of atemporal time flow into that of actual time, just as Don Quixote enters into Sancho, and Sancho into Don Quixote, in the integration of their reciprocal fluid lives. Literary creation is here a closed, absolute world, wholly self-sufficient, and into which the reasoning of the author is not heterogeneously injected.

Montesinos lives his own enchantment: " . . . the sage Merlin has been keeping us enchanted here these many years; and although more than five hundred have gone by, not one of us has died . . . " Upon passing into the *time of "now,"* the character finds himself at the beginning of the seventeenth century, and calculates the date on which he changed from a "person" to a "personage"—in the eleventh century—the epoch of the Cid and of Alphonse VI, which was the limit of the epic-historic horizon of the Spaniard of those days. The accuracy of such a belief is not what concerns us; the essential fact is that Montesinos feels himself a man encased between a *yesterday* and a *today,* and an eternal atemporal entity, all at the same time. The eternal Montesinos is integrated into the temporalized Montesinos, just as is the Knight of the Rueful Countenance into the person invited by Sancho to satisfy his most elemental needs; in the same way the poetic dagger of the ballad becomes the poniard of Ramón de Hoces; the song of the farm laborer of El Toboso merges with the discordant noise of his plow as it drags along the ground; and the Dulcinea of quixotic dreams takes form in the cave of Montesinos as a Dulcinea who sends one of her companions to ask her lover to lend her "half a dozen reals . . . on this *new* dimity petticoat that I have here." And this is Don Quixote, and not Sancho, who tells it.

The living experience of time, in consequence, is organically articulated with the total structure of *Don Quixote:* "I can not understand, Señor Don Quixote," remarked the Cousin here, "how it is that your lordship, in such a short space of time as you have been below there, could have seen so many things, and said and answered so much." "How long is it since I went down?" asked Don Quixote. "Little better than an hour," replied Sancho. "That can not be," returned Don Quixote, "because night overtook me while I was there, and day came, and it was night again three times; so that, *by my reckoning,* I have been three days in those remote regions beyond our ken." Sancho thinks that "as everything that has happened to him is by enchantment, maybe what *seems to us an hour would seem three days and nights there."*

The difference in the estimation of time, expressed in terms of "what seems to be," is founded upon the same vital criterion that permits the object that shines on the barber's head to be at one time the helmet of Mambrino, and again, an ordinary shaving basin. One might say then that all this is pure, arbitrary relativism or capricious fantasmagoria; but if that were so, *Don Quixote* would not be the immortal work that it is. The vacillation of this dance of semblances acquires solidity, not as a logical reality, but as an existential value that impresses itself on us. The reality of the style of *Don Quixote* lies in a vital articulation of its values; beliefs, be they what they may, are made acceptable to us to the degree that they are held and lived, by those who interweave them with their existence. Instead of being logically arbitrary, they become vitally valid, and we accept them, not as a farce or an amusement, but as one accepts all that appears authentic. Our esteem, our artistic enjoyment, and lastly, our conviction proceed from the self-assurance, from the integrity of all those who speak and live in these pages. The fundament for the "truth" of the three days spent by Don Quixote in the cave, and the hour of waiting spent by Sancho, is embedded in the total, well-integrated structure of human existence, which Cervantes imposes as a necessity, and not as an arbitrary caprice. *Don Quixote* is a beautiful piece of architecture, a well-harmonized symphony of meaningful manifestations of life the value and existence of which are mutually interdependent. The literary character is split into a person who "lives" his literary existence, and those who approach him, live, in their turn, in this double dimension. From this stems the incalculable influence of *Don Quixote* upon the modern novel, which arose during the Romantic period, and in which the central characters are not only what they portend to be but also a poetic projection of themselves (good Père Goriot of Balzac is a manufacturer of vermicelli and a reincarnation of the imprudent and despairing King Lear; Julien Sorel of Stendhal's *Le rouge et le noir,* is the boy from the the the lumber sawmill, and also a projection of the hero of the *Mémorial de Sainte Hélène;* etc.).

These living experiences of values do not postulate any objective conclusion (such as Calderón's "man's greatest crime is having been born . . . For all of life is a dream, and dreams are but dreams"). Instead we find ourselves before a polarity which is integrated into the forms of life: flight toward the supreme and descent toward the depths. This way of living manifests itself and finds "realization" in such a polar existence upon being projected into inexhaustible perspectives. Cervantes did not confront the epic world with the purpose of objectifying it in comedy, gay diversion, or morality. For the epic and all the other forms serve here as incitements aimed at nurturing the polarized current that flows between the creative "eros" and the absence of "eros." *Don Quixote* was neither written against books of chivalry nor was it *not* written against them. In formulating the question this way, we are focusing upon the work from a logical, rational category that does not fit it at all. Don Quixote's *raison d'être* is found exclusively in his will for heroism, his noble courtesy, and in his infinite goodness, all of which are evident in the very process of his existence. Don Quixote is bolstered by his faith in the values that man creates, sustains, and diffuses with his very life. The book is a great repertory, as I have already said, of axiological themes, always lived with maximal tension—and from this arises its fascinating beauty.

The foregoing discussion could be illustrated with a brief examination of the subject that I would entitle "jests turn to earnest." When Knight and Squire begin their wanderings along the byroads of the world, they act as an incitement upon all who observe them or deal with them; thus they become the object of jest, respect, pity, anger, or of an indifferent, vague curiosity. Sancho is very variously reflected as he affects the lives of his master, his wife, and his daughter, of Tome Cecial, Ricote, the Duke and Duchess, the duenna Rodríguez, the ecclesiastic, etc.—just as Don Quixote, the island, Clavileño, Dorotea, etc., produce many varied reactions and opinions in Sancho. The same phenomenon occurs with regard to the amusing or cruel jokes so frequent in this work, especially in Part II, wherein the author forgets his vacillations of the First. These episodes owe a great deal to the burlesque tradition of Italian literature, which was so familiar to Cervantes. But the Italian themes of farce and skepticism were generally one-dimensional, their character was not modified by the moralizing glosses that were at times superimposed upon them. The situations in *Don Quixote* are different. There is nothing more "farcical" than the episodes that occur during the ephemeral governorship of Sancho. One night he is taken on a patrol of the island, for the purpose of finding more comic material with which to fill the idle vacuum in the existence of his Lorship, the Duke. But note that while the night patrol invents fictitious tasks, there is one among them that is different; a beautiful young girl has escaped from her home in company with her brother, in order to break the monotony of their secluded existence; they come upon the night patrol, which is not at all a laughing matter to them, but a very serious predicament. The lovely maiden confesses her mischief: "I longed to see the world, or at least the town where I was born." She had received word of an outside world unknown to her: "When I heard them talking of bull-fights taking place, and of jousts, and of the acting of plays, I asked my brother, who is a year younger than myself, to tell me what sort of things these were, and many more that I had never seen; he explained them to me as well as he could, but the only effect was to *kindle in me a still stronger desire to see them.*" This beautiful and bold victim of boredom bears within her the germ of a Madame Bovary. But this is not what interests us now. The governor's chief waiter and taster—an opaque figure in the droll comedy of the night watch—remains as if enchanted upon observing the beauty of this girl: "The maiden's beauty had made a deep impression on the head-carver's heart, and again he raised his lantern for another look at her." The "incited" now incites. The following night was a sleepless one for the poor head-carver: " . . . so full were his thoughts of the face and air and beauty of the disguised damsel." Mocking? Serious? In the last analysis, the idea that hordes of enchanters wander about spying on our slightest movements is not really so absurd.

Let us recall the colossal battle between Don Quixote and the lackey Tosilos in which the latter renounces the combat in order really to marry the ruined daughter of the duenna Rodríguez. The Duke "was amazed and extremely angry at it" (which is not in jest either), while the girl declares her preference for being "the lawful wife of a lackey rather than the cheated mistress of a gentleman." Let us mention as the ultimate example (among the various that could be employed here) the episode of the enchanted head in the home of Don Antonio Moreno, who had to put an end to a game that provided him with so much amusement, *for fear* "it might come to the ears of the watchful sentinels of the faith . . . " that is, the Holy Office of the Inquisition. " . . . the inquisitors . . . commanded him to destroy it up and have done with it." Jokes, pranks, and farce are included within the polarity that governs this style, and they rise up and topple down just as do islands, castles, shepherd's huts; Dulcinea, the coarse farm girl, and Don Quixote and Alonso Quijano the Good!

M I L T O N

[*1608–1674*]

SHAKESPEARE'S REPUTATION HAS NEVER BEEN SERIOUSLY QUESTIONED; MILTON'S has been vulnerable to shifts in taste. The eighteenth century thought it could do no better than imitate Milton's music; the twentieth century found his music one-keyed, his personality uncongenial, his ideas remote and fanatic. He was toppled from a lofty eminence, like his own Satan, by the "new critics" who found John Donne more to their taste. Lately the balance has been righted and he stands among the first poets in English. The force of his personality and his imagination overcome parochial objection; his style now overpowers even those who, like Eliot and Pound, once felt "he wrote no language," as Johnson said. We can discover his genius not only in the greatest epic in the language, but also in his elegies and lyrics.

William Hazlitt takes Milton's absorption in his political milieu as a point of departure for discussion of *Paradise Lost*. Every age discovers the poet it wants to find; the measure of the great poet is that he be various enough to support all the separate inquiries. Hazlitt's essay was written in 1818.

WILLIAM HAZLITT

On Shakespeare and Milton

SHAKESPEARE DISCOVERS IN HIS WRITINGS LITTLE RELIGIOUS ENTHUSIASM, AND an indifference to personal reputation; he had none of the bigotry of his age, and his political prejudices were not very strong. In these respects, as well as in every other, he formed a direct contrast to Milton. Milton's works are a perpetual invocation to the Muses; a hymn to Fame. He had his thoughts constantly fixed on the contemplation of the Hebrew theocracy, and of a perfect commonwealth; and he seized the pen with a hand just warm from the touch of the ark of faith. His religious zeal infused its character into his imagination; so that he devotes himself with the same sense of duty to the cultivation of his genius, as he did to the exercise of virtue, or the good of his country. The spirit of the poet, the patriot, and the prophet, vied with each other in his breast. His mind appears to have held equal communion with the inspired writers, and with the bards and sages of ancient Greece and Rome;

> Blind Thamyris, and blind Maeonides,
> And Tiresias, and Phineus, prophets old.

He had a high standard, with which he was always comparing himself, nothing short of which could satisfy his jealous ambition. He thought of nobler forms and nobler things than those he found about him. He lived apart, in the solitude of his own thoughts, carefully excluding from his mind whatever might distract its purposes or alloy its purity, or damp its zeal. "With darkness and with dangers compassed round," he had the mighty models of antiquity always present to his thoughts, and determined to raise a monument of equal height and glory, "piling up every stone of lustre from the brook," for the delight and wonder of posterity. He had girded himself up, and as it were, sanctified his genius to this service from his youth. "For after," he says, "I had from my first years, by the ceaseless diligence and care of my father, been exercised to the tongues, and some sciences as my age could suffer, by sundry masters and teachers, it was found that whether aught was imposed upon me by them, or betaken to of my own choice, the style by certain vital signs it had, was likely to live; but much latelier, in the private academies of Italy, perceiving that some trifles which I had in memory, composed at under twenty or thereabout, met with acceptance above what was looked for; I began thus far to assent both to them and divers of my friends here at home, and not less to an inward prompting which now grew daily upon me, that by labour and intense study (which I take to be my portion in this life), joined with the strong propensity of nature, I might perhaps leave something so written to after-times as they should not willingly let it die. The accomplishment of these intentions, which have lived within me ever since I could conceive myself anything worth to my country, lies not but in a power above man's to promise; but that none hath by more studious ways endeavoured, and with more unwearied spirit that none shall, that I dare almost aver of myself, as far as life and free leisure will extend. Neither do I think it shame to convenant with any knowing reader, that for some few years yet, I may go on trust with him toward the payment of what I am now indebted, as being a work not to be raised from the heat of youth or the vapours of wine; like that which flows at waste from the pen of some vulgar amourist, or the trencher fury of a rhyming parasite, nor to be obtained by the invocation of Dame Memory and her Siren daughters, but by devout prayer to that eternal spirit who can enrich with all utterance and knowledge, and sends out his Seraphim with the hallowed fire of his altar, to touch and purify the lips of whom he pleases: to this must be added industrious and select reading, steady observation, and insight into all seemly and generous arts and affairs. Although it nothing content me to have disclosed thus much beforehand; but that I trust hereby to make it manifest with what small willingness I endure to interrupt the pursuit of no less hopes than these, and leave a calm and pleasing solitariness, fed with cheerful and confident thoughts, to embark in a troubled sea of noises and hoarse disputes, from beholding the bright countenance of truth in the quiet and still air of delightful studies."

So that of Spenser:

> The noble heart that harbours virtuous thought,
>   And is with child of glorious great intent,
> Can never rest until it forth have brought
>   The eternal brood of glory excellent.

Milton, therefore, did not write from casual impulse, but after a severe examination of his own strength, and with a resolution to leave nothing undone which it was in his power to do. He always labours, and almost always succeeds. He strives hard to say the finest things in the world, and he does say them. He adorns and dignifies his subject to the utmost: he surrounds it with every possible association of beauty or grandeur, whether moral, intellectual, or physical. He refines on his descriptions of beauty; loading sweets on sweets, till the sense aches at them; and raises his images of terror to a gigantic elevation, that "makes Ossa like a wart." In Milton, there is always an appearance of effort: in Shakespeare, scarcely any.

Milton has borrowed more than any other writer, and exhausted every source of imitation, sacred or profane; yet he is perfectly distinct from every other writer. He is a writer of centos, and yet in originality scarcely inferior to Homer. The power of his mind is stamped on every line. The fervour of his imagination melts down and renders malleable, as in a furnace, the most contradictory materials. In reading his works, we feel ourselves under the influence of a mighty intellect, that the nearer it approaches to others, becomes more distinct from them. The quantity of art in him shews the strength of his genius: the weight of his intellectual obligations would have oppressed any other writer. Milton's learning has the effect of intuition. He describes objects, of which he could only have read in books, with the vividness of actual observation. His imagination has the force of nature. He makes words tell as pictures.

> Him followed Rimmon, whose delightful seat
> Was fair Damascus, on the fertile banks
> Of Abbana and Pharphar, lucid streams.

The word *lucid* here gives to the idea all the sparkling effect of the most perfect landscape.

And again:

As when a vulture on Imaus bred,
Whose snowy ridge the roving Tartar bounds,
Dislodging from a region scarce of prey,
To gorge the flesh of lambs and yeanling kids
On hills where flocks are fed, flies towards the springs
Of Ganges or Hydaspes, Indian streams;
But in his way lights on the barren plains
Of Sericana, where Chineses drive
With sails and wind their cany waggons light.

If Milton had taken a journey for the express purpose, he could not have described this scenery and mode of life better. Such passages are like demonstrations of natural history. Instances might be multiplied without end.

We might be tempted to suppose that the vividness with which he describes visible objects, was owing to their having acquired an unusual degree of strength in his mind, after the privation of his sight; but we find the same palpableness and truth in the descriptions which occur in his early poems. In *Lycidas* he speaks of "the great vision of the guarded mount," with that preternatural weight of impression with which it would present itself suddenly to "the pilot of some small night-foundered skiff": and the lines in the *Penseroso,* describing "the wandering moon,"

Riding near her highest noon,
Like one that had been led astray
Through the heaven's wide pathless way,

are as if he had gazed himself blind in looking at her. There is also the same depth of impression in his descriptions of the objects of all the different senses, whether colours, or sounds, or smells—the same absorption of his mind in whatever engaged his attention at the time. It has been indeed objected to Milton, by a common perversity of criticism, that his ideas were musical rather than picturesque, as if because they were in the highest degree musical, they must be (to keep the sage critical balance even, and to allow no one man to possess two qualities at the same time) proportionably deficient in other respects. But Milton's poetry is not cast in any such narrow, commonplace mould; it is not so barren of resources. His worship of the Muse was not so simple or confined. A sound arises "like a steam of rich distilled perfumes"; we hear the pealing organ but the incense on the altars is also there, and the statues of the gods are ranged around! The ear indeed predominates over the eye, because it is more immediately affected, and because the language of music blends more immediately with, and forms a

more natural accompaniment to, the variable and indefinite associations of
ideas conveyed by words. But where the associations of the imagination are
not the principal thing, the individual object is given by Milton with equal
force and beauty. The strongest and best proof of this, as a characteristic
power of his mind, is, that the persons of Adam and Eve, of Satan, &c. are
always accompanied, in our imagination, with the grandeur of the naked
figure; they convey to us the ideas of sculpture. As an instance take the following:

> He soon
> Saw within ken a glorious Angel stand,
> The same whom John saw also in the sun:
> His back was turned, but not his brightness hid;
> Of beaming sunny rays a golden tiar
> Circled his head, nor less his locks behind
> Illustrious on his shoulders fledge with wings
> Lay waving round; on some great charge employ'd
> He seem'd, or fix'd in cogitation deep.
> Glad was the spirit impure, as now in hope
> To find who might direct his wand'ring flight
> To Paradise, the happy seat of man,
> His journey's end, and our beginning woe.
> But first he casts to change his proper shape,
> Which else might work him danger or delay
> And now a stripling cherub he appears,
> Not of the prime, yet such as in his face
> Youth smiled celestial, and to every limb
> Suitable grace diffus'd, so well he feign'd:
> Under a coronet his flowing hair
> In curls on either cheek play'd; wings he wore
> Of many a colour'd plume sprinkled with gold,
> His habit fit for speed succinct, and held
> Before his decent steps a silver wand.

The figures introduced here have all the elegance and precision of a Greek
statue; glossy and impurpled, tinged with golden light, and musical as the
strings of Memnon's harp!

Again, nothing can be more magnificent than the portrait of Beelzebub:

> With Atlantean shoulders fit to bear
> The weight of mightiest monarchies:

Or the comparison of Satan, as he "lay floating many a rood," to "that sea beast,"

> Leviathan, which God of all his works
> Created hugest that swim the ocean-stream!

What a force of imagination is there in this last expression! What an idea it conveys of the size of that hugest of created beings, as if it shrunk up the ocean to a stream, and took up the sea in its nostrils as a very little thing? Force of style is one of Milton's greatest excellences. Hence, perhaps, he stimulates us more in the reading, and less afterwards. The way to defend Milton against all impugners, is to take down the book and read it.

Milton's blank verse is the only blank verse in the language (except Shakspeare's) that deserves the name of verse. Dr. Johnson, who had modelled his ideas of versification on the regular sing-song of Pope, condemns the *Paradise Lost* as harsh and unequal. I shall not pretend to say that this is not sometimes the case; for where a degree of excellence beyond the mechanical rules of art is attempted, the poet must sometimes fail. But I imagine that there are more perfect examples in Milton of musical expression, or of an adaptation of the sound and movement of the verse to the meaning of the passage, than in all our other writers, whether of rhyme or blank verse, put together, (with the exception already mentioned). Spenser is the most harmonious of our stanza writers, as Dryden is the most sounding and varied of our rhymists. But in neither is there any thing like the same ear for music, the same power of approximating the varieties of poetical to those of musical rhythm, as there is in our great epic poet. The sound of his lines is moulded into the expression of the sentiment, almost of the very image. They rise or fall, pause or hurry rapidly on, with exquisite art, but without the least trick or affectation, as the occasion seems to require.

The following are some of the finest instances:

> His hand was known
> In Heaven by many a tower'd structure high;—
> Nor was his name unheard or unador'd
> In ancient Greece: and in the Ausonian land
> Men called him Mulciber: and how he fell
> From Heaven, they fabled, thrown by angry Jove
> Sheer o'er the chrystal battlements; from morn
> To noon he fell, from noon to dewy eve,
> A summer's day; and with the setting sun
> Dropt from the zenith like a falling star

On Lemnos, the Aegean isle: thus they relate,
Erring.

                      But chief the spacious hall
Thick swarm'd, both on the ground and in the air,
Brush'd with the hiss of rustling wings. As bees
In spring time, when the sun with Taurus rides,
Pour forth their populous youth about the hive
In clusters; they among fresh dews and flow'rs
Fly to and fro: or on the smoothed plank,
The suburb of their straw-built citadel,
New rubb'd with balm, expatiate and confer
Their state affairs. So thick the airy crowd
Swarm'd and were straiten'd; till the signal giv'n,
Behold a wonder! They but now who seem'd
In bigness to surpass earth's giant sons,
Now less than smallest dwarfs, in narrow room
Throng numberless, like that Pygmean race
Beyond the Indian mount, or fairy elves,
Whose midnight revels by a forest side
Or fountain, some belated peasant sees,
Or dreams he sees, while over-head the moon
Sits arbitress, and nearer to the earth
Wheels her pale course: they on their mirth and dance
Intent, with jocund music charm his ear;
At once with joy and fear his heart rebounds.

I can only give another instance, though I have some difficulty in leaving off.

        Round he surveys (and well might, where he stood
So high above the circling canopy
Of night's extended shade) from th' eastern point
Of Libra to the fleecy star that bears
Andromeda far off Atlantic seas
Beyond the horizon: then from pole to pole
He views in breadth, and without longer pause
Down right into the world's first region throws
His flight precipitant, and winds with ease
Through the pure marble air his oblique way
Amongst innumerable stars that shone

> Stars distant, but nigh hand seem'd other worlds;
> Or other worlds they seem'd or happy isles, &c.

The verse, in this exquisitely modulated passage, floats up and down as if it had itself wings. Milton has himself given us the theory of his versification—

> Such as the meeting soul may pierce
> In notes with many a winding bout
> Of linked sweetness long drawn out.

Dr. Johnson and Pope would have converted his vaulting Pegasus into a rocking-horse. Read any other blank verse but Milton's,—Thomson's, Young's, Cowper's, Wordsworth's,—and it will be found, from the want of the same insight into "the hidden soul of harmony," to be mere lumbering prose.

To proceed to a consideration of the merits of *Paradise Lost,* in the most essential point of view, I mean as to the poetry of character and passion. I shall say nothing of the fable, or of other technical objections or excellences; but I shall try to explain at once the foundation of the interest belonging to the poem. I am ready to give up the dialogues in Heaven, where, as Pope justly observes, "God the Father turns a school-divine"; nor do I consider the battle of the angels as the climax of sublimity, or the most successful effort of Milton's pen. In a word, the interest of the poem arises from the daring ambition and fierce passions of Satan, and from the account of the paradisaical happiness, and the loss of it by our first parents. Three-fourths of the work are taken up with these characters, and nearly all that relates to them is unmixed sublimity and beauty. The two first books alone are like two massy pillars of solid gold.

Satan is the most heroic subject that ever was chosen for a poem; and the execution is as perfect as the design is lofty. He was the first of created beings, who, for endeavouring to be equal with the highest, and to divide the empire of heaven with the Almighty, was hurled down to hell. His aim was no less than the throne of the universe; his means, myriads of angelic armies bright, the third part of the heavens, whom he lured after him with his countenance, and who durst defy the Omnipotent in arms. His ambition was the greatest, and his punishment was the greatest; but not so his despair, for his fortitude was as great as his sufferings. His strength of mind was matchless as his strength of body; the vastness of his designs did not surpass the firm, inflexible determination with which he submitted to his irreversible doom, and final loss of all good. His power of action and of suffering was equal. He was the greatest power that was ever overthrown, with the strongest will left to resist or to endure. He was baffled, not confounded. He stood like a tower; or

> As when Heaven's fire
> Hath scathed the forest oaks or mountain pines.

He was still surrounded with hosts of rebel angels, armed warriors, who own him as their sovereign leader, and with whose fate he sympathises as he views them round, far as the eye can reach; though he keeps aloof from them in his own mind, and holds supreme counsel only with his own breast. An outcast from Heaven, Hell trembles beneath his feet, Sin and Death are at his heels, and mankind are his easy prey.

> All is not lost; th' unconquerable will,
> And study of revenge, immortal hate,
> And courage never to submit or yield,
> And what else is not to be overcome,

are still his. The sense of his punishment seems lost in the magnitude of it; the fierceness of tormenting flames is qualified and made innoxious by the greater fierceness of his pride; the loss of infinite happiness to himself is compensated in thought, by the power of inflicting infinite misery on others. Yet Satan is not the principle of malignity, or of the abstract love of evil—but of the abstract love of power, of pride, of self-will personified, to which last principle of all other good and evil, and even his own, are subordinate. From this principle he never once flinches. His love of power and contempt for suffering are never once relaxed from the highest pitch of intensity. His thoughts burn like a hell within him; but the power of thought holds dominion in his mind over every other consideration. The consciousness of a determined purpose, of "that intellectual being, those thoughts that wander through eternity," though accompanied with endless pain, he prefers to nonentity, to "being swallowed up and lost in the wide womb of uncreated night." He expresses the sum and substance of all ambition in one line. "Fallen cherub, to be weak is miserable, doing or suffering!" After such a conflict as his, and such a defeat, to retreat in order, to rally, to make terms, to exist at all, is something; but he does more than this—he founds a new empire in hell, and from it conquers this new world, whither he bends his undaunted flight, forcing his way through nether and surrounding fires. The poet has not in all this given us a mere shadowy outline; the strength is equal to the magnitude of the conception. The Achilles of Homer is not more distinct; the Titans were not more vast; Prometheus chained to his rock was not a more terrific example of suffering and of crime. Wherever the figure of Satan is introduced, whether he walks or flies, "rising aloft incumbent on the dusky air," it is illustrated with the most striking and appropriate images: so that we see it always before us, gigantic, irregular, portentous, uneasy, and disturbed—but dazzling in its faded splendour, the clouded ruins of a god. The deformity of Satan is only in the depravity of his will; he has no bodily deformity to excite our loathing or disgust. The horns and tail are not there, poor emblems of the unbending, unconquered spirit, of the writhing agonies within. Milton was too magnanimous and open an antagonist to support his argument by the bye-tricks of a hump and cloven foot; to bring into the fair field of controversy the good old catholic prejudices of which Tasso and Dante have availed themselves, and which the mystic German critics would restore. He relied on the justice of his cause, and did not scruple to give the devil his due. Some persons may think that he has carried his liberality too far, and injured the cause he professed to espouse by making him the chief person in his poem. Considering the nature of his subject, he would be equally in danger of running into this fault, from his faith in religion, and his love of rebellion; and perhaps each of these motives had its full share in determining the choice of his subject.

Not only the figure of Satan, but his speeches in council, his soliloquies, his address to Eve, his share in the war in heaven, or in the fall of man, shew the same decided superiority of character. To give only one instance, almost the first speech he makes:

> Is this the region, this the soil, the clime,
> Said then the lost archangel, this the seat
> That we must change for Heaven; this mournful gloom
> For that celestial light? Be it so, since he
> Who now is sov'rain can dispose and bid
> What shall be right: farthest from him is best,
> Whom reason hath equal'd, force hath made supreme
> Above his equals. Farewel happy fields,
> Where joy for ever dwells: Hail horrors, hail
> Infernal world, and thou profoundest Hell,
> Receive thy new possessor: one who brings
> A mind not to be chang'd by place or time.
> The mind is its own place, and in itself
> Can make a Heav'n of Hell, a Hell of Heav'n.
> What matter where, if I be still the same,
> And what I should be, all but less than he
> Whom thunder hath made greater? Here at least

[393]

We shall be free; th' Almighty hath not built
Here for his envy, will not drive us hence:
Here we may reign secure, and in my choice
To reign is worth ambition, though in Hell:
Better to reign in Hell, than serve in Heaven.

The whole of the speeches and debates in Pandemonium are well worthy of the place and the occasion—with Gods for speakers, and angels and arch-angels for hearers. There is a decided manly tone in the arguments and sentiments, an eloquent dogmatism, as if each person spoke from thorough conviction; an excellence which Milton probably borrowed from his spirit of partisanship, or else his spirit of partisanship from the natural firmness and vigour of his mind. In this respect Milton resembles Dante, (the only modern writer with whom he has any thing in common) and it is remark-able that Dante, as well as Milton, was a political partisan. That approxi-mation to the severity of impassioned prose which has been made an objec-tion to Milton's poetry, and which is chiefly to be met with in these bitter invectives, is one of its great excellences. The author might here turn his philippics against Salmasius to good account. The rout in Heaven is like the fall of some mighty structure, nodding to its base, "with hideous ruin and combustion down." But, perhaps, of all the passages in *Paradise Lost,* the description of the employments of the angels during the absence of Satan, some of whom "retreated in a silent valley, sing with notes angelical to many a harp their own heroic deeds and hapless fall by doom of battle," is the most perfect example of mingled pathos and sublimity.—What proves the truth of this noble picture in every part, and that the frequent complaint of want of interest in it is the fault of the reader, not of the poet, is that when any interest of a practical kind takes a shape that can be at all turned into this, (and there is little doubt that Milton had some such in his eye in writing it,) each party converts it to its own purposes, feels the absolute identity of these abstracted and high speculations; and that, in fact, a noted political writer of the present day has exhausted nearly the whole account of Satan in the *Paradise Lost,* by applying it to a character whom he considered as after the devil, (though I do not know whether he would make even that exception) the greatest enemy of the human race. This may serve to shew that Milton's Satan is not a very insipid personage.

Of Adam and Eve it has been said, that the ordinary reader can feel little interest in them, because they have none of the passions, pursuits, or even relations of human life, except that of man and wife, the least interesting of all others, if not to the parties concerned, at least to the by-standers. The preference has on this account been given to Homer, who, it is said, has left very vivid and infinitely diversified pictures of all the passions and affections, public and private, incident to human nature—the relations of son, of brother, parent, friend, citizen, and many others. Longinus preferred the *Iliad* to the *Odyssey,* on account of the greater number of battles it contains; but I can neither agree to his criticism, nor assent to the present objection. It is true, there is little action in this part of Milton's poem; but there is much repose, and more enjoyment. There are none of the every-day occurrences, contentions, disputes, wars, fighting, feuds, jealousies, trades, professions, liveries, and common handicrafts of life; "no kind of traffic; letters are not known; no use of service, of riches, poverty, contract, succession, bourne, bound of land, tilth, vineyard none; no occupation, no treason, felony, sword, pike, gun, nor need of any engine." So much the better; thank Heaven, all these were yet to come. But still the die was cast, and in them our doom was sealed. In them

> The generations were prepared; the pangs,
> The internal pangs, were ready, the dread strife
> Of poor humanity's afflicted will,
> Struggling in vain with ruthless destiny.

In their first false step we trace all our future woe, with loss of Eden. But there was a short and precious interval between, like the first blush of morning before the day is overcast with tempest, the dawn of the world, the birth of nature from "the unapparent deep," with its first dews and freshness on its cheek, breathing odours. Theirs was the first delicious taste of life, and on them depended all that was to come of it. In them hung trembling all our hopes and fears. They were as yet alone in the world, in the eye of nature, wondering at their new being, full of enjoyment and enraptured with one another, with the voice of their Maker walking in the garden, and ministering angels attendant on their steps, winged messengers from heaven like rosy clouds descending in their sight. Nature played around them her virgin fancies wild; and spread for them a repast where no crude surfeit reigned. Was there nothing in this scene, which God and nature alone witnessed, to interest a modern critic? What need was there of action, where the heart was full of bliss and innocence without it! They had nothing to do but feel their own happiness, and "know to know no more." "They toiled not, neither did they spin; yet Solomon in all his glory was not arrayed like one of these." All things seem to acquire fresh sweetness, and to be clothed with fresh beauty in their sight. They tasted as it were for themselves and us, of all that there ever was pure in human bliss. "In them the burthen of the mystery, the heavy and the weary weight of all this unintelligible world, is lightened." They stood awhile perfect, but they afterwards fell, and were driven out of Paradise, tasting the first fruits of bitterness as they had done of bliss. But their pangs were such as a pure spirit might feel at the sight—their tears "such as angels weep." The pathos is of that mild contemplative kind which arises from regret for the loss of unspeakable happiness, and resignation to inevitable fate. There is none of the fierceness of intemperate passion, none of the agony of mind and turbulence of action, which is the result of the habitual struggles of the will with circumstances, irritated by repeated disappointment, and constantly setting its desires most eagerly on that which there is an impossibility of attaining. This would have destroyed the beauty of the whole picture. They had received their un-looked-for happiness as a free gift from their Creator's hands, and they submitted to its loss, not without sorrow, but without impious and stubborn repining.

> In either hand the hast'ning angel caught
> Our ling'ring parents, and to th' eastern gate
> Led them direct, and down the cliff as fast
> To the subjected plain; then disappear'd.
> They looking back, all th' eastern side beheld
> Of Paradise, so late their happy seat,
> Wav'd over by that flaming brand, the gate
> With dreadful faces throng'd, and fiery arms:
> Some natural tears they dropt, but wip'd them soon;
> The world was all before them, where to choose
> Their place of rest, and Providence their guide.

MOLIÈRE

[*1622–1673*]

MOLIÈRE WROTE FOR A SOCIETY IN WHICH SOCIAL STATUS WAS FIXED—CONCENTRIC circles around the pinnacle occupied by the Sun King, Louis the Fourteenth. Molière's audience was drawn from the nobility and the upper bourgeoisie, and acutely aware of the mere step which separates some classes, the gulfs which divide these from others, and the anomalous spectacles that occur when an individual tries to shift from one role to another. Such a society furnishes a perfect paradigm for dramatic conflict; one has but to imagine the consequences of misconceiving one's role to have abundant material for comedy, as Molière does in *Le Médecin Malgré Lui* and *Le Bourgeois Gentilhomme*. The modern audience cannot comprehend these conditions without cultivating its historical imagination. But this does not end the difficulty. Molière's intelligence makes full use of the presumptions of the aristocracy which so highly composed his audience: the audience of shared experience and settled expectations. Such people can dispense with ideas; they make us feel lumpish because they know just how things go in a social world.

It is commonly thought that Molière constructs his plays in such a way as to exhibit a central figure with a bee in his bonnet and hold him up to the scorn of people who know how ridiculous all extremes are. But he is not content with curbing the demonic energies of a Scapin, or unmasking the wicked Tartuffe. In *Le Misanthrope* he exhibits the inadequacy of the voices of accommodating reasonableness so often heard in his plays. He creates a social malcontent who will not accommodate himself. We know that Alceste is often wrong—as cruel or blind in his way as the world he opposes—yet we cannot happily consign him to the limbo of ridicule.

Martin Turnell lessens our difficulties by extended quotations which keep the poetic texture of the play before us. He succeeds in making us see that Molière's dramatic form is the vehicle of poetic assertion, precise as poetry is precise, dramatic not simply because persons encounter one another, but because Molière's lines give their encounter a formal resonance expressive of psychological attitudes; it is a counterpoint of psychic gestures contrived with exquisite economy and subtlety.

Mr. Turnell works for the BBC, and has written many books about French literature.

MARTIN TURNELL

Le Misanthrope

*L*e *Misanthrope* IS BY COMMON CONSENT THE GREATEST OF MOLIÈRE'S PLAYS, but attempts to discover the nature of its peculiar excellence have some-times led critics into unprofitable paths. The Romantic critics found in it the main support for their theory of "the tragic Molière"; Ramon Fernandez, the stern champion of "philosophical criticism," has spoken of "cette comédie où le principe même de la comédie est mis en péril"; and a German writer has used it to propound a theory of "the diabolical element in great com-edy."[1] These theories have one factor in common. They suggest that the *Misanthrope* is in some way "deeper," more "profound," more "serious" than Molière's other works, overlooking perhaps the fact that comedy is essen-tially a serious activity.[2] Compare it with *Tartuffe* and the dangers of such a criterion are at once apparent. It is not difficult to see in what sense the

---

[1] Curt Sigmar Gutkind in *Molière und das Komische Drama* (Halle, 1928). It is only fair to add that the point is not unduly stressed and that the chapter on the *Misanthrope* seems to me to be the best study of the play that I have come across in any language.

[2] How little this has been understood in France, where the distinction between tragedy and comedy is much more definite than in England, can be seen from Brunetière's "*Le Misanthrope* and *Tartuffe* are already middle-class tragedies which Molière tried

Misanthrope and *Tartuffe* are more "serious" than *les Femmes savantes* or *l'Avare,* but we should be on very uncertain ground in claiming that the *Misanthrope* is more serious than *Tartuffe.* Indeed, it would be less difficult to prove the contrary. *Tartuffe* has obvious affinities with primitive comedy. The most striking of them is the sacrificial element. Tartuffe is the scapegoat whose chastisement provides a release for the audience's primitive desires and emotions, and Molière knew very well what he was about when he under-lined the sexual propensities of his victim. The play appeals to some of the deepest, though not the most admirable, of human instincts, and it has a ferocity which is unparalleled in Molière's work. "My opinion of *Tartuffe,*" wrote Baudelaire in his diary, "is that it is not a comedy, but a pamphlet." This is an over-statement, but it helps us to understand the limitations of that masterpiece and the superiority of the *Misanthrope.*

The *Misanthrope* in the seventeenth century was the connoisseur's play and a contemporary described it with felicity as "une pièce qui fait rire dans l'âme." Its pre-eminence lies not in greater depth or profundity, but in a greater variety of tone, a wider social reference, more complex and more delicate shades of feeling. It is one of the most personal of Molière's plays. *Tartuffe* was a magnificent onslaught on a narrow, vindictive puritanism which had all but succeeded in driving comedy from the stage. The *Misan-thrope* was written during a personal crisis and is certainly coloured by Molière's own domestic difficulties. We must be careful not to read too much into the play, but those critics who have found its laughter "sad" are on the right track; there is no doubt that personal suffering helped to give Molière the astonishing insight into the human heart which he displays in the *Misan-thrope* and which contributes to its richness and maturity.[3]

"He did not set out to write a comedy full of incidents," said Visé in a commentary which is believed to have been published with Molière's ap-proval, "but simply a play in which he could speak against the manners of the age."

There is one striking difference between the *Misanthrope* and Molière's other plays. He does not confine himself to the study of the psychology of an individual seen against the background of a stable society. His irony is turned

---

in vain to fit into the framework of comedy." ("Les Époques de la Comédie de Molière" in *Études critiques sur l'histoire de la littérature française,* VIII, 3ième ed., Paris, 1922, pp. 116-17.)

[3] When the play was originally produced, Alceste was played by Molière, Célimène by his wife, Éliante by his mistress and Arsinoé by Mlle du Parc who had repulsed his advances!

on society as well as on Alceste, and the play ends, as we shall see, not with the restoration of order, but with something that is very like a mark of interrogation.

The theme is presented by means of a triple conflict—the conflict between Alceste and social convention, Alceste and justice, Alceste and Célimène. It is the constant shifting of the focus from one to the other and the way in which Molière plays on our divided sympathies that give the *Misanthrope* its variety, so that it calls for a greater effort of attention from the reader than any of the other comedies.

Mr. L. C. Knights has suggested that a close examination of the tone and intention of each line in the first scene is the best way of discovering how the play as a whole should be read. The opening scene is so carefully constructed and the theme stated with such clarity and force that almost everything which follows is a development of hints and suggestions contained in it.

PHILINTE Qu'est-ce donc? Qu'avez-vous?
ALCESTE (*assis*) Laissez-moi, je vous prie.
PHILINTE Mais encor, dites-moi, quelle bizarrerie . . .
ALCESTE Laissez-moi là, vous dis-je, et courez vous cacher.
PHILINTE Mais on entend les gens, au moins, sans se fâcher.
ALCESTE Moi, je veux me fâcher, et ne veux point entendre.
PHILINTE Dans vos brusques chagrins je ne puis vous comprendre,
Et, quoique amis, enfin, je suis tout des premiers . . .
ALCESTE (*se levant brusquement*)
Moi, votre ami? Rayez cela de vos papiers.
J'ai fait jusques ici profession de l'être;
Mais après ce qu'en vous je viens de voir paraître,
Je vous déclare net que je ne le suis plus,
Et ne veux nulle place en des cœurs corrompus.

The play opens as usual on a note which sounds uncommonly like farce, but the intention is serious. There is something wrong with Alceste and most of the play is devoted to discovering what it is. It makes his behaviour so unreasonable that he becomes incomprehensible to the tolerant and reasonable Philinte. The violent tone is characteristic of Alceste and an understanding of it leads to an understanding of the *motifs* behind it. The *cacher* and the *brusques chagrins* are important clues—the unobtrusive stage direction, *se levant brusquement*, illustrates the close connection between word and gesture in Molière—and their recurrence in the play emphasizes the closeness of its texture.

The dialogue that follows explains the origin of Alceste's *chagrin*, but before examining it in detail, I wish to jump eighty lines and look at the next use of the word:

ALCESTE   Mes yeux sont trop blessés, et la cour et la ville
            Ne m'offrent rien qu'objets à m'échauffer la bile;
            J'entre en une humeur noire, en un chagrin profond,
            Quand je vois vivre entre eux les hommes comme ils font . . .
PHILINTE   Ce chagrin philosophe est un peu trop sauvage.
            Je ris des noirs accès où je vous envisage . . .

It is clear that for Alceste the *humeur noire* and the *chagrin profond* are a matter of deadly seriousness, but it is also clear from the change of tone and the ironical *chagrin philosophe* that they have a different value for Philinte, for the ordinary, reasonable man. It is characteristic of the peculiar ambiguity of the play, and of Philinte's place in it, that we feel doubtful at this point whether the *chagrin* is or is not a laughing matter. There is still room for doubt when he goes on four lines later:

      Non, tout de bon, quittez toutes ces incartades.
      Le monde par vos soins ne se changera pas;
      Et puisque la franchise a pour vous tant d'appas,
      Je vous dirai tout franc que cette maladie,
      Partout où vous allez, donne la comédie . . .

Philinte drops the tone of easy banter and proceeds to give a serious warning. The *chagrin* is now described as *cette maladie* and we are meant to take the word at its face value, but it is still a *maladie* which in the eyes of the world *donne la comédie*. There is a conflict of values. The *chagrin* has a different significance for different individuals. The doubt lies in deciding what importance should be attached to the respective valuations of Alceste, Philinte and *le monde*. Are they all right or all wrong, or partly right and partly wrong?

This doubt is really the crux of the whole play, and it is interesting to glance at the use of this and similar words—the *désert* and the *endroit écarté* —in other contexts:

     1. Têtebleu! ce me sont de mortelles blessures
       De voir qu'avec le vice on garde des mesures;
       Et parfois il me prend des mouvements soudains
       De fuir dans un *désert* l'approche des humains.

                           (i. i.)

2. C'est que jamais, morbleu! les hommes n'ont raison,
   Que *le chagrin contre eux* est toujours de saison ...

(II. iv.)

3. Elle tâche à couvrir d'un faux voile de prude
   Ce que chex elle on voit *d'affreuse solitude.*

(*Célimène of Arsinoé,* III. iii.)

4. Allez-vous en la voir, et me laissez enfin
   Dans ce petit coin sombre, avec *mon noir chagrin.*

(v. i.)

5. Pourvu que votre cœur veuille donner les mains
   Au dessein que j'ai fait de fuir tous les humains,
   Et que dans mon *désert,* où j'ai fait vœu de vivre,
   Vous soyez, sans tarder, résolue à me suivre ...

(v. iv.)

6. Trahi de toutes parts, accablé d'injustices,
   Je vais sortir d'un *gouffre* où triomphent les vices,
   Et chercher sur la terre *un endroit écarté,*
   Où d'être homme d'honneur on ait la liberté.

(v. iv.)

It is tempting but dangerous to compare Alceste's *chagrin* with Pascal's vision of *l'abîme* or even with Baudelaire's *spleen,* because in doing so we run the risk of serious misinterpretation. Alceste is painfully conscious of his perplexity and frustration, but it is evident from these examples that his attitude is a *personal* one. It does not spring from a vision which transcends the deceptive appearances of everyday life. It is largely negative, is directed *contre* [*les hommes*]; and in the fourth example, where he caricatures himself, he seems for a moment to be aware that there is something a little absurd about his *chagrin.* There is a burlesque note, too, in the fifth and sixth examples. Alceste strikes a pose. He renounces the world and goes off to play at being a "man of honour" in the "desert." Now the "desert" is both objective and subjective, and it has certain affinities with Arsinoé's *affreuse solitude* which are suggested by a passage in M. Mauriac's interesting essay on the play:

In a world where a decent man and a Christian has so many reasons if not for protest, at least for examining his own conscience, Alceste only attacks the most harmless practices, those "lies" which do not take anyone in but which are necessary if social life is to go on at all. He is indignant over slanders which only affect people indirectly, which do not penetrate the hidden vices and merely provoke laughter. In a world where injustice is rife, where crime is everywhere, he is up in arms against trivialities. He feels no horror

[402]

for what is really horrible—beginning with himself. All his attacks are directed to things outside himself; he only compares himself with other people in order to demonstrate his own superiority.[4]

M. Mauriac's criticism of Alceste seems to me to be unduly severe and there is, perhaps, a tendency to simplify the issues; but it does illuminate one side of his character. A good deal of his *chagrin contre les hommes* springs from a psychological need to distract his attention from his own sense of frustration, from "what is horrible" in his own nature, and in this he is representative of the society that he is attacking. For all the characters on whom Molière turns his irony are in a greater or lesser degree aware of their own interior emptiness, of an *affreuse solitude* from which they are trying to escape. This explains their restless activity, their desperate preoccupation with gossip and *galanterie*. While the struggle to escape from themselves by losing themselves in the world of minor social events is one of the principal themes of the play, it must be emphasized that Molière's study of their vacancy and fatuity is not a tragic one. The *Misanthrope* is pre-eminently a comedy; it is not a *tragédie bourgeoise* in the manner of *l'Éducation sentimentale*.

It is time to turn to a consideration of the individual characters and their place in the pattern of the play, and to the sources of Alceste's *chagrin*. His first long speech is a denunciation of social convention:

> Je vous vois accabler un homme de caresses,
> Et témoigner pour lui les dernières tendresses;
> De protestations, d'offres et de serments
> Vous chargez la fureur de vos embrassements;
> Et quand je vous demande après quel est cet homme,
> A peine pouvez-vous dire comme il se nomme;
> Votre chaleur pour lui tombe en vous séparant,
> Et vous me le traitez, à moi, d'indifférent.
> Morbleu! c'est une chose indigne, lâche, infâme,
> De s'abaisser ainsi jusqu'à trahir son âme;
> Et si par un malheur j'en avais fait autant,
> Je m'irais, de regret, pendre tout à l'instant.

---

[4] As a corrective to this, compare Stendhal's view of Alceste: "His mania for hurling himself against whatever appears odious, his gift for close and accurate reasoning and his extreme probity would soon have led him into politics or, what would have been much worse, to an objectionable and seditious philosophy. Célimène's salon would at once have been compromised and soon have become a desert. And what would a coquette find to do in a deserted salon?" (*Racine et Shakespeare*, II ed., P. Martino, Paris, 1925, p. 177.)

The tone of nervous exasperation, the taste for extremes, signified by *accabler, dernières tendresses, fureur de vos embrassements,* and the piled up adjectives rising to a crescendo—*indigne, lâche, infâme*—is peculiar to Alceste, and there is an obvious disproportion between the language used and the "most harmless practices" which he is attacking. He uses precisely the same tone in speaking of his lawsuit and his love affairs:

> Quoi! contre ma partie on voit tout à la fois
> L'honneur, la probité, la pudeur, et les lois;
> On publie en tous lieux l'équité de ma cause,
> Sur la foi de mon droit mon âme se repose;
> Cependant je me vois trompé par le succès:
> J'ai pour moi la justice, et je perds mon procès!
> Un traître, dont on sait la scandaleuse histoire,
> Est sorti triomphant d'une fausseté noire!
> Toute la bonne foi cède à sa trahison!
> Il trouve, en m'égorgeant, moyen d'avoir raison!
> Le poids de sa grimace, où brille l'artifice,
> Renverse le bon droit et tourne la justice!

> J'ai ce que sans mourir je ne puis concevoir;
> Et le déchaînement de toute la nature
> Ne m'accablerait pas comme cette aventure.
> C'en est fait . . . Mon amour . . . Je ne saurais parler.

The uniformity of tone shows that he reacts in precisely the same way to three different situations, that he places the same valuation on his campaign against convention, his lawsuit and his love affair. There is certainly a connection between the three, but they are very far from being of the same importance. His cult of sincerity is a fetish. If his principles were adopted, social intercourse would come to an end, and it is perhaps because he is a threat to a brittle society that his attitude is unpopular. There is more to be said for his other preoccupations. Philinte admits that he has a grievance over the unfortunate lawsuit, and Célimène confesses that she has treated him badly. But though they sympathize with him, they are at one in protesting against the violence of his denunciation and the extravagance of his remedies. "I agree with all you say," remarks Philinte,

> . . . je tombe d'accord de tout ce qu'il vous plaît:
> Tout marche par cabale et par pur intérêt;
> Ce n'est plus que la ruse aujourd'hui qui l'emporte,

> Et les hommes devraient être faits d'autre sorte.
> *Mais est-ce une raison que leur peu d'équité*
> *Pour vouloir se tirer de leur société?*[5]

In short, Alceste's attitude betrays a confusion of values, an extraordinary lack of discrimination, which alone would make him ludicrous. Minor mishaps are the pretext for wild generalizations about human nature; the perfidy of a shallow, frivolous society woman assumes the proportions of a universal catastrophe in his disordered imagination, and his denunciation peters out in a strangled cry:

> C'en est fait . . . Mon amour . . . Je ne saurais parler.

The more we study his pronouncements, the more evident it becomes that his attitude is the reverse of disinterested. When he declares:

> Je veux qu'on soit sincère, et qu'en homme d'honneur
> On ne lâche aucun mot qui ne parte du cœur

we may feel that though this is a counsel of perfection, it is not altogether unreasonable. A few lines later, however, his real objections to the insincere enthusiasm with which people greet one another emerge very clearly:

> Je refuse d'un cœur la vaste complaisance
> Qui ne fait de mérite aucune différence;
> Je veux qu'on me distingue, et, pour le trancher net,
> L'ami du genre humain n'est point du tout mon fait.

There is a strong element of vanity in his protests. He is determined that people shall be made to distinguish *him* from his fellows, and the lines betray a sense of insecurity, a need of psychological affirmation. When Philinte suggests in the first scene that he should visit some of the judges who will try his suit, he refuses angrily:

> Non; j'ai résolu de n'en pas faire un pas.
> J'ai tort ou j'ai raison.

The second line is a curious illustration of the rigidity of Alceste's mind which prevents any compromise with society; but it is interesting for another

---

[5] Italics mine.

reason. It has not always been understood by contemporary readers who have felt that his attitude is commendable and have compared it favourably with Célimène's assiduous "touting" in *her* lawsuit. Now it must be remembered that in the seventeenth century the practice of visiting one's judges was universal and was not regarded as being in any way improper. The explanation of Alceste's refusal is to be found in his reaction to Philinte's suggestion that he should appeal against the decision when he loses his case:

> Non; je veux m'y tenir.
> Quelque sensible tort qu'un tel arrêt me fasse,
> Je me garderai bien de vouloir qu'on le casse:
> On y voit trop à plein le bon droit maltraité,
> Et je veux qu'il demeure à la postérité
> Comme une marque insigne, un fameux témoignage
> De la méchanceté des hommes de notre âge.
> Ce sont vingt mille francs qu'il m'en pourra coûter;
> Mais pour vingt mille francs j'aurai droit de pester
> Contre l'iniquité de la nature humaine,
> Et de nourrir pour elle une immortelle haine.

These are not the words of a fighter or a reformer. Alceste is convinced that there has been a miscarriage of justice; but instead of trying to set it right, he is delighted at the loss of his suit because he feels that it gives him a *right* to fulminate against human nature, and this right seems cheap at twenty thousand francs. This is characteristic of his general behaviour. He is always on the lookout for some abuse that he can attack or someone with whom he can pick a quarrel, and the slightest excuse is sufficient to set the machinery of excited denunciation in motion. "Quoi!" cries the horrified Philinte,

> Quoi! vous iriez dire à la vieille Emilie
> Qu'à son âge il sied mal de faire la jolie,
> Et que le blanc qu'elle a scandalise chacun?

ALCESTE Sans doute.

PHILINTE A Dorilas, qu'il est trop importun,
> Et qu'il n'est, à la cour, oreille qu'il ne lasse
> A conter sa bravoure et l'éclat de sa race?

ALCESTE Fort bien.

This suggests that his attitude is to a certain extent *voulu*. While it is true that denunciation is a form of self-indulgence, a substitute for *action,* this

does not exhaust the question. It is noticeable that in most of the plays the
honnête homme treats this heated denunciation as the danger point. It is the
point at which the normative influence of society ceases to be effective and
the comic character's hysterical mood may well lead to some desperate act.
It is for this reason that Philinte's warnings are nearly always directed
against Alceste's *tone* and not against what he says. Now Alceste's violence
deserves a closer examination than it has perhaps received. In some of the
lines lifted from *Dom Garcie de Navarre* Alceste denounces Célimène's
perfidy:

> Que toutes les horreurs dont une âme est capable
> A vos déloyautés n'ont rien de comparable;
> Que le sort, les démons, et el Ciel en courroux
> N'ont jamais rien produit de si méchant que vous.

Again:

> Je ne suis plus à moi, je suis tout à la rage:
> Percé du coup mortel dont vous m'assassinez,
> Mes sens par la raison ne sont plus gouvernés,
> Je cède aux mouvements d'une juste colère. . . .

At such moments we have the illusion that we are listening to a Cornelian
tirade, but it is an illusion. Alceste is not, even at these moments, a tragic
figure. His denunciation, though undeniably serious, belongs peculiarly to
comedy, and there is an interesting passage at the beginning of the play
which helps us to appreciate why this is so:

> Non, je ne puis souffrir cette lâche méthode
> Qu'affectent la plupart de vos gens à la mode;
> Et je ne hais rien tant que les contorsions
> De tous ces grands faiseurs de protestations,
> Ces affables donneurs d'embrassades frivoles,
> Ces obligeants diseurs d'inutiles paroles,
> Qui de civilités avec tous font combat,
> Et traitent du même air l'honnête homme et le fat.

What is striking about these lines is a curious air of unreality, the sense
that we are watching a Punch-and-Judy show. This is no accident. The violence and the jerkiness have a different function here. The focal word is
contorsions and it colours the rest of the passage. The element of caricature

is deliberate. This is not abstract denunciation of real people; it is society as it appears to Alceste. We feel ourselves looking at it through his eyes and seeing a world of grinning, gesticulating marionnettes, going through their grotesque performance as some unseen showman pulls the strings. For Alceste's violence leads to a state of hysteria—Molière's word for it is *emportement*—in which the actual world is transformed into a comic nightmare, reminding us a little oddly of a Disney cartoon. The nightmare is in Alceste's mind, and the contrast between his distorted outlook and unreasonable behaviour and the humdrum world in which he lives makes him at once a comic and a moving figure. Our response to this passage, and indeed to the whole play, is a balance between two impulses which superficially appear to exclude one another—the impulse to laugh at Alceste's absurdity and the impulse to pity the obvious waste of his gifts. The art of the comic writer depends on preserving this nice balance between two apparently contradictory emotions, on the continual switch from one set of feelings to another and back again without ever allowing the balance to tip over to the extremes of tragedy or farce. There are moments when he takes us to the brink of tragedy. George Dandin will go to the edge of the water and will stand there gazing at his own reflection, wondering whether to throw himself in or not; but in the end he will turn his back on it and return slowly homewards, will return to the cultivation of his farm and to the problem of finding a *modus vivendi* with his impossible wife—as Molière himself did. In the same way, Alceste reaches the point at which reason totters, but he too will retreat into the world of words and harmless denunciation. It is not the least of the dramatist's achievements that he establishes this feeling of confidence in his audience and convinces us that it will be so.

It is the failure to understand this that has led to many of the attempts to turn the *Misanthrope* into a tragedy. Fernandez, for example, has suggested that in the course of the play Alceste's character undergoes a radical change and that the man who departs for the "desert" as the curtain falls is no longer the same man as the fiery reformer of Act i. The change is supposed to lie in the collapse of the will. It is an entertaining theory, but I can find no evidence for it in the text of the play. It is true that Alceste is always using expressions of great determination—"Je veux qu'on me distingue," "Je veux m'y tenir"—but, as I have already suggested, there is no real volition behind the words which are a sort of smoke screen used to hide a complete absence of determination. The Alceste of Act v is identical with the Alceste of Act i. His *physical* exile is the logical outcome of the *psychological* exile—the retreat into a private world—which is studied with such profound insight in the course of the play.

I stress this point because Fernandez' theory seems to me to rest on a misunderstanding of Molière's method of presentation in this play. Alceste is constructed partly by direct statement and partly by his action on other characters. Certain essential traits are presented in the opening scene and driven home by deliberate repetition all through the play. Once he has sketched the outlines, Molière proceeds to fill in the details. A series of impressions of Alceste as he appears to other characters is superimposed one on another. These impressions add to our knowledge both of Alceste and of the other characters. They are not always in agreement and sometimes, as we shall see, they qualify or contradict one another. This is a point of considerable importance and it is one of the things that force the reader to follow the dialogue with such minute care, to decide what weight must be attributed to the constant shift and change of tone.

This brings us to a consideration of Philinte's role in the play. In one of the central passages he declares:

> Il faut, parmi le monde, une vertu traitable;
> A force de sagesse on peut être blâmable;
> La parfaite raison fuit toute extrémité,
> Et veut que l'on soit sage avec sobriété.
> Cette grande roideur des vertus des vieux âges
> Heurte trop notre siècle et les communs usages;
> Elle veut aux mortels trop de perfection :
> Il faut fléchir au temps sans obstination,
> Et c'est une folie à nulle autre seconde
> De vouloir se mêler de corriger le monde.
> J'observe, comme vous, cent choses tous les jours,
> Qui pourraient mieux aller, prenant un autre cours;
> Mais, quoi qu'à chaque pas je puisse voir paraître,
> En courroux, comme vous, on ne me voit point être;
> Je prends tout doucement les hommes comme ils sont,
> J'accoutume mon âme à souffrir ce qu'ils font;
> Et je crois qu'à la cour, de même qu'à la ville,
> Mon flegme est philosophe autant que votre bile.

We recognize this passage, which recalls Cléante's plea for a devotion which is *humaine* and *traitable,* as the familiar statement of Molière's positives. It is also a good example of the patterned movement of his verse. It is not a mere catalogue of "the great abstractions." There are life and warmth in his *sagesse, parfaite raison* and *sobriété.* They have behind them centuries of European civilization which is vividly felt. The *roideur des vieux âges* underlines the peculiar and disabling rigidity of Alceste's outlook and, at the same time, reflects a delicate appreciation of the graciousness of contemporary civilization which exists in spite of human imperfection. The passage closes on a personal note; precept merges into practice and one becomes aware of the urbanity and good sense of the civilized man. Philinte's tone is intended to act as a foil to Alceste's, to moderate his transports. When Alceste cries

> Et parfois il me prend des mouvements soudains
> De fuir dans un désert l'approche des humains,

Philinte replies:

> Mon Dieu, des mœurs du temps mettons-nous moins en peine,
> Et faisons un peu grâce à la nature humaine.

The sharp *soudains-humains* creates a sense of physical constriction and the relief provided by *peine-humaine* is palpable. The *grâce* and the *douceur* prolong the process on the logical plane. It is not without significance, however, that Philinte's attempts to moderate Alceste's transports are seldom successful. The very gentleness of tone seems to heighten his exasperation, and he reserves some of his bitterest shafts for his friend. In these exchanges his tactics vary and he is decidedly *rusé*. When he retorts:

> Mais ce flegme, monsieur, qui raisonne si bien,
> Ce flegme pourra-t-il s'échauffer de rien?

raisonne is balanced against *s'échauffer*. He feels instinctively that *flegme* puts the brake on his *emportement* and he tries to discredit it by suggesting that it is an excuse for tolerating injustice. There is a curious eagerness to brush aside obstacles. The verse stumbles and almost comes to a halt over the repeated *flegme,* then moves breathlessly forward to the word *s'échauffer* which is sufficient to set the machinery of denunciation in motion.

"Je sais," he begins with icy politeness in another place,

> Je sais que vous parlez, monsieur, le mieux du monde;
> En beaux raisonnements vous abondez toujours;
> Mais vous perdez le temps et tous vos beaux discours.
> La raison, pour mon bien, veut que je me retire:
> Je n'ai pas sur ma langue un assez grand empire;
> De ce que je dirais je ne répondrais pas,
> Et je me jetterais cent choses sur les bras.

[410]

In order to keep up the appearance of rational behaviour, he pretends that his proposal to retire to the desert is a reasoned one, but there is a world of difference between the *beaux raisonnements* attributed to Philinte and Alceste's *raison*. "Reason" ceases to be universal and becomes a private and very misleading label that he attaches to the demon which is driving him into the desert. The last three lines are double-edged. It is because he is unreasonable and not because society is unreasonable that he is likely to find himself in trouble if he remains where he is.

I have already spoken of the peculiar ambiguity of the play and of Philinte's place in it. In the *Misanthrope* there is a skilful modification of the pattern of Molière's comedies which becomes more subtle and more varied. Although Philinte is certainly Molière's spokesman in many places and certainly helps to provide the background of reason and sanity which contributes largely to the poise of the play, his role is a shifting one. We do not feel, as we do with Cléante, that the whole of the play is behind his words, and the explanation is to be found in Éliante's observations on Alceste in Act IV. Sc. i:

> Dans ses façons d'agir il est fort singulier;
> Mais j'en fais, je l'avoue, un cas particulier,
> Et la sincérité dont son âme se pique
> A quelque chose en soi de noble et d'héroïque.
> C'est une vertu rare au siècle d'aujourd'hui,
> Et je la voudrais voir partout comme chez lui.

Éliante is the only wholly sympathetic character in the play. It would not be accurate to say that she represents Molière's own point of view more completely than Philinte, but her role is of the first importance. In the *Misanthrope,* as in *Tartuffe,* Molière felt the need of two spokesmen; but the function of Éliante and Philinte goes beyond that of Dorine and Cléante. Dorine and Cléante complete one another, but Éliante qualifies the role of Philinte and it is this that gives the play a mellowness which is unique in Molière's work. For Éliante's words display a fresh attitude towards the comic hero. Arnolphe, Harpagon and Orgon (in spite of his conversion to a *dévotion traitable*) are and remain completely unsympathetic; but Alceste awakens the sympathies of the audience to a degree which is exceptional in seventeenth-century and indeed in all comedy.

Éliante minimizes Alceste's peculiarities and by placing the emphasis on his "rare virtue" she corrects Philinte. Alceste is not a buffoon in the same sense as Molière's other comic characters. There is always a foundation of good sense behind his criticisms and, in spite of their exaggeration, this is true of his attacks on convention. In the scene where Oronte's sonnet is criticized, which is significantly placed immediately after the exposition of the principal theme of the play in Scene i, his good taste and sound judgment obviously compare favourably with Philinte's flattery. There is a less obvious but more impressive example towards the end of the play when, after commiserating with Alceste on the loss of his lawsuit, Philinte proceeds to expound the virtues of his own philosophy:

> Tous ces défauts humains nous donnent dans la vie
> Des moyens d'exercer notre philosophie;
> C'est le plus bel emploi que trouve la vertu;
> Et si de probité tout était revêtu,
> Si tous les cœurs étaient francs, justes et dociles,
> La plupart des vertus nous seraient inutiles . . .

Philinte's logic may be unexceptional, but is not the attitude that he is defending in danger of becoming abstract and unreal? Is there not a gap between life and thought, a gap which can only be closed by the more human and more generous approach of Éliante? Does not his attitude overlook the fact that the ordinary man is not a mere logician and that "the exercise of our philosophy" cannot impose order on the tangled feelings and desires which Molière perceived as clearly as Racine? The neat maxims which appealed so much to the reasonable seventeenth century are useless in solving the central problem of the play—the conflict between what Gutkind calls with true Teutonic violence "the pert, frivolous, fickle, coquettish young widow and Alceste, the heavy-blooded man who is eaten up by his passion and who is fighting for his love."

The conclusion seems to me to be unmistakable. In this play Molière criticizes his own standards. The urbanity and moderation of the *honnête homme* are felt to be insufficient. When Éliante speaks of "quelque chose en soi de noble et d'héroïque," she is referring to the potentialities of Alceste's character; but these potentialities are prevented from realizing themselves by his lack of balance and his impatience of all restraint. His virtues are converted into negation, into the *haines vigoureuses* of one passage and the *immortelle haine* of another; his violence leads him away from the world of common experience into a world of private mania where, deprived of the normative influence of society, he thunders against wildly exaggerated abuses in the void. This makes him a comic figure, but it is the consciousness of his potential virtues and of his profound humanity which gives the play its peculiar resonance.

The triple conflict represents the three points of contact between Alceste and society. The continual switching from one to the other and back again enables Molière to present both Alceste and society in a perpetually changing light until, as the play moves towards its climax, the three blend and give it its cumulative force. The direct conflict with convention underlines Alceste's absurdity and prevents comedy from turning into tragedy; the lawsuit redresses the balance and seems at times to justify his violence; the affair with Célimène is the richest and most serious of all and in a way contains them both. Alceste's rage over convention and his lawsuit is the point at which he separates himself from his fellow men and his love affair is the point at which he rejoins them. It stands for normality; it is the side of his character by which (in Mauriac's words) "il nous devient fraternel." "Je m'étonne, pour moi," remarks Philinte:

> Je m'étonne, pour moi, qu'étant, comme il le semble,
> Vous et le genre humain si fort brouillés ensemble,
> Malgré tout ce qui peut vous le rendre odieux,
> Vous ayez pris chez lui ce qui charme vos yeux;
> Et ce qui me surprend encore davantage,
> C'est cet étrange choix où votre cœur s'engage.
> La sincère Eliante a du penchant pour vous,
> La prude Arsinoé vous voit d'un œil fort doux:
> Cependant à leurs vœux votre âme se refuse,
> Tandis qu'en ses liens Célimène l'amuse,
> De qui l'humeur coquette et l'esprit médisant
> Semble si fort donner dans les mœurs d'à présent.

Alceste replies at once, with his curious mixture of arrogance and perspicacity, that he has no illusions about the shortcomings of Célimène:

> Non, l'amour que j'ai pour cette jeune veuve
> Ne ferme point mes yeux aux défauts qu'on lui treuve,
> Et je suis, quelque ardeur qu'elle m'ait pu donner,
> Le premier à les voir, comme à les condamner.
> Mais, avec tout cela, quoi que je puisse faire,
> Je confesse mon faible, elle a l'art de me plaire;
> J'ai beau voir ses défauts, et j'ai beau l'en blâmer,
> En dépit qu'on en ait, elle se fait aimer;
> Sa grâce est la plus forte, et sans doute ma flamme
> De ces vices du temps pourra purger son âme.

Célimène's importance is twofold. She is the complete representative of the society that Alceste and through him Molière is attacking. When some of her retainers tell Alceste that he should blame her and not them for the spiteful remarks that she is making about acquaintances and friends, he retorts acutely:

> Non, morbleu! c'est à vous; et vos ris complaisants
> Tirent de son esprit tous ces traits médisants.

Part of his problem is to "convert" Célimène, to carry her away from the vicious circle in which she lives; but the problem remains unsolved because of Alceste's eccentricity, because he can only convert her by transporting her into his own world, by carrying her off with him into the "desert" to which he eventually retires. What distinguishes him from Molière's other characters is an extraordinary insight into his own feelings. There are moments when he suddenly forgets his grievances against society, drops the tone of violent denunciation and sees himself as he really is—not a reformer, but a man sadly perplexed by his passion for a woman who is unworthy of him. It is at such moments that we become aware of his immense superiority over the brittle society that is trying to laugh him out of criticisms which are felt to be a threat to it:

> PHILINTE Pour moi, si je n'avais qu'à former des désirs,
>   La cousine Éliante aurait tous mes soupirs.
>   Son cœur, qui vous estime, est solide et sincère,
>   Et ce choix plus conforme était mieux votre affaire.
> ALCESTE Il est vrai: ma raison me le dit chaque jour;
>   Mais la raison n'est pas ce qui règle l'amour.

In the last two lines *raison* is used in its normal sense, which is not the sense of

> La raison, pour mon bien, veut que je me retire.

Célimène stands for the tangled feelings and desires which, as I have already suggested, the seventeenth century tried in vain to enclose in its neat formulas. It is at this point that the "systems" of both Alceste and Philinte break down. The obstinate fanaticism of the one and the philosophical maxims of the other are alike impotent to solve the problems of life. For in this play Molière explores regions in which conventional formulas have no validity, and the insight with which he does so gives the *Misanthrope* its

exceptional place in French comedy. Nor must we overlook the irony of
solide et sincère which is echoed later in the play by Alceste's

> Enfin, quoi qu'il en soit, et sur quoi qu'on se fonde,
> Vous trouvez des raisons pour souffrir tout le monde.

Alceste, Célimène and Éliante form a triangle. Alceste places himself at a
point outside society; Célimène is entirely absorbed in it; Éliante occupies an
intermediate position. She is of society, but is wholly uncontaminated by it.
*Alceste's contact with the world of common experience is seen to be inter-
mittent.* He is continually rebounding from its polished surface into the
world of his private mania. The victory of either Alceste or Célimène in the
tug-of-war would fail to solve the problem. For Alceste the only solution, the
only way back to the norm of sanity and common sense, lies in marriage
with Éliante and he refuses it. This is true of nearly all the characters in
their different ways. They are all looking for something *solide et sincère,* for
some philosophy on which to base their lives, but they meet with disappointment at every turn. Custom, justice and love prove equally hollow and unreal
and they suddenly find themselves face to face with the void.

A large part of the play is thus taken up with the tug-of-war between
Alceste and Célimène as each tries to draw the other into his or her own
sphere. Célimène is shallow and frivolous but she too is dimly conscious of
her shortcomings, and it is only because she is not beyond redemption that
she provides Alceste with an adequate foil. From time to time the glitter and
polish of the exchanges between them are disturbed by a deeper note:

ALCESTE   Mais moi, que vous blâmez de trop de jalousie,
           Qu'ai-je de plus qu'eux tous, madame, je vous prie?
CÉLIMÈNE   Le bonheur de savoir que vous êtes aimé.

This note only occurs at rare intervals. Célimène's normal tone bears a
marked similarity to Philinte's. She answers Alceste's over-wrought declarations either in a mood of light banter or with mild surprise which lowers the
tension:

ALCESTE   Morbleu! faut-il que je vous aime!
           Ah! que si de vos mains je rattrape con cœur,
           Je bénirai le Ciel de ce rare bonheur!
           Je ne le cèle pas, je fais tout mon possible
           A rompre de ce cœur l'attachement terrible;
           Mais mes plus grands efforts n'ont rien fait jusqu'ici

Et c'est pour mes péchés que je vous aime ainsi.
CÉLIMÈNE   Il est vrai, votre ardeur est pour moi sans seconde.
ALCESTE   Oui, je puis là-dessus défier tout le monde.
Mon amour ne se peut concevoir, et jamais
Personne n'a, madame, aimé comme je fais.
CÉLIMÈNE   En effet, la méthode en est toute nouvelle,
Car vous aimez les gens pour leur faire querelle;
Ce n'est qu'en mots fâcheux qu'éclate votre ardeur,
Et l'on n'a jamais vu un amour si grondeur.
ALCESTE   Mais il ne tient qu'à vous que son chagrin[6] ne passe.
A tous nos démêlés coupons chemin, de grâce,
Parlons à cœur ouvert, et voyons d'arrêter . . .

This illustrates very well the constant change of tone. Alceste begins in a mood of deadly seriousness. The turns and twists of the dialogue reflect the turns and twists of the trapped animal—"the heavy-blooded man who is eaten up by his passion and who is fighting for his love"—to escape the *attachement terrible,* and recalls ironically Philinte's

> Cependant à leurs vœux votre âme se refuse,
> Tandis qu'en ses liens Célimène l'*amuse.*

For Alceste's struggle is no laughing matter, and the gravity of Célimène's

> Il est vrai, votre ardeur est pour moi sans seconde

shows that she is impressed in spite of herself, is faced with something which is outside her experience. But when Alceste continues in the same tone, her mood changes and she comments lightheartedly on the "new method" of making love. The reference to his notorious ill-humour not only lowers the tension of the scene, it brings Alceste back to his usual level—the comic figure who is at odds with society. The relief, however, is only momentary, and the scene closes with something that sounds like a cry for mercy. "Coupons chemin, de grâce"—Alceste's arrogance vanishes and he knows he has been defeated in the encounter.

With Act II. Sc. ii the work of exposition is complete. The stage is cleared and Molière brings his batteries to bear on the procession of vain, empty,

---

[6] This use of the word *chagrin* illustrates the way in which, as I have already said, Alceste's love affair "contains" the conflict with convention and justice.

frivolous courtiers who have nothing better to do than engage Célimène in malicious chatter or attend some small function at Court.

ACASTE   A moins de voir Madame en être importunée,
              Rien ne m'appelle ailleurs toute a journée.
CLITANDRE   Moi, pourvu que je puisse être au petit couché,
              Je n'ai point d'autre affairs où je sois attaché.

It is noticeable that almost every word uttered by these people about their friends or in the bitter exchanges between themselves is double-edged. It returns like a boomerang to the speaker. Acaste remarks complacently:

> Parbleu! je ne vois pas, lorsque je m'examine,
> Où prendre aucun sujet d'avoir l'âme chagrine.

The implication is that the game of self-deception is so successful, that he is so shallow and empty, that he is incapable of perceiving his shortcomings or experiencing the torment which infects Alceste. This becomes clearer in the brilliant portrait of the fop which emerges innocently as the speech continues:

> Pour le cœur, dont sur tout nous devons faire cas,
> On sait, sans vanité, que je n'en manque pas,
> Et l'on m'a vu pousser, dans le monde, une affaire
> D'une assez vigoureuse et gaillarde manière.
> Pour de l'esprit, j'en ai sans doute, et du bon goût
> A juger sans étude et raisoner de tout,
> A faire aux nouveautés, dont je suis idolâtre,
> Figure de savant sur les banes du théâtre,
> Y décider en chef, et faire du fracas
> A tous les beaux endroits qui méritent des Has.
> Je suis assez adroit; j'ai bon air, bonne mine,
> Les dents belles surtout, et la taille fort fine.
> Quant à se mettre bien, je crois, sans me flatter,
> Qu'on serait mal venu de me le disputer.
> Je me vois dans l'estime autant qu'on y puisse être,
> Fort aimé du beau sexe, et bien auprès du maître.
> Je crois qu'avec cela, mon cher Marquis, je crois
> Qu'on peut, par tout pays, être content de soi.

The small, flat words contrast with the solemnity of the performance. When he uses a word like *vigoureuse* the thin, mincing lilt of the line robs

[417]

it of its power and gives it a grotesque air. When we come to the *juger sans étude,* there is a note of fatuity which is heightened by the eulogy of his teeth and his waist which are given the same importance as his skill as a critic. And with a final pirouette he turns to survey the admiring world of his peers. The brittle, artificial style reflects the poverty of experience of all these people.

One of the best demonstrations of the vigour and subtlety of Molière's style occurs in the great scene between Célimène and Arsinoé which is one of the high-lights of the play. Thus Célimème:

> Oui, Oui, franche grimace;
> Dans l'âme elle est du monde, et ses soins tentent tout
> Pour accrocher quelqu'un, sans en venir à bout.
> Elle ne saurait voir qu'avec un œil d'envie
> Les amants déclarés dont une autre est suivie;
> Et son triste mérite, abandonné de tous,
> Contre le siècle aveugle est toujours en courroux.
> Elle tâche à couvrir d'un faux voile de prude
> Ce que chez elle on voit d'affreuse solitude,
> Et, pour sauver l'honneur de ses faibles appas,
> Elle attache du crime au pouvoir qu'ils n'ont pas.
> Cependant un amant plairait fort à la dame,
> Et même pour Alceste elle a tendresse d'âme;
> Ce qu'il me rend de soins outrage ses attraits,
> Elle veut que ce soit un vol que je lui fais,
> Et son jaloux dépit, qu'avec peine elle cache,
> En tous endroits, sous main, contre moi se détache.

The more one studies Molière's style, the more impressed one is by its concrete particularity. It is possible to argue, as some critics have done, that his prose is superior to his verse and that the alexandrine was on occasion too rigid an instrument for his purpose. This may be true, but it can be seen in this play that the verse registers the changing expressions of his characters with remarkable vividness and that, without seeming to do so, the words do an immense amount of work. Words almost invariably issue in action and the actions of the characters mirror conflicting feelings. There was nothing absurd or discreditable about the *métier de prude* in the seventeenth century. A prude was simply an austere and rather puritanical woman; it was only later that the word acquired its present-day suggestion of affectation and insincerity. Molière's prudes, however, are all "false prudes" and they are used as negative symbols—as symbols of a hypocritical rejection of the life of the senses in which Molière himself believed so firmly. So it is here. *Grimace* sets the tone of the passage and it is sufficient to give us a picture of the stiff, puritanical old maid, trying to hide her lack of success behind a mask; but it is a *franche grimace,* a mask which hides nothing and simply draws attention to her hypocrisy. For in spirit she belongs to the world of Célimène and Acaste, accepts its values and does her best to "hook" or "angle" for a husband. We see the prude stretching out her hand furtively, but she misses the mark. She is left looking enviously at the procession of gallants who pass her by, without so much as a glance, in the train of some other beauty. She is the withered old maid—this is the cruel sense of *triste mérite*—completely abandoned in a world, in an age, in which favours are only too lightly distributed. The *faux voile de prude* reinforces the *franche grimace,* makes it more explicit, more pictorial. It is a veil which she puts between herself and the world, a veil which she uses vainly to cover the *affreuse solitude,* the terrible, consuming sexual frustration of the ageing spinster. But her deception extends further than that. It is used to conceal her intrigues and it is also a weapon which she uses to attack other women who are more successful than herself. The hand which is stretched out, pathetically, to "hook" a gallant is now stretched out to stab Célimène as a relief to her bitterness. The image of the "veil" is caught up and developed in the encounter between Célimène and Arsinoé which follows. Célimène is pretending to quote some unfavourable comments on Arsinoé's deportment which she has overheard in someone's drawing-room:

> A quoi bon, disaient-ils, cette mine modeste,
> Et ce sage dehors que dément tout le reste?
> Elle est à bien prier exacte au dernier point;
> Mais elle bat ses gens et ne les paye point.
> Dans tous les lieux dévots elle étale un grand zèle;
> Mais elle met du blanc et veut paraître belle.
> Elle fait des tableaux couvrir les nudités;
> Mais elle a de l'amour pour les réalités.

The procedure is the same as in the earlier passage. We see life going on simultaneously on different sides of a "veil," the contrast between the public and private life of a false prude. The *mine modeste* is the mask which hides, or is intended to hide, an interior disorder. She is exact in carrying out her religious duties; we see her sink to her knees and rise to her feet in church; but behind the locked doors of her house, the pious gestures merge into the savage rise and fall of the whip as she thrashes her servants. She gives alms, but has no money to pay her servants their just wages. She is the centre of attention at the cenacle where the pious meet, ostentatiously crossing herself; but in the fastness of her boudoir the pious gestures are replaced by the hand painting the face in a vain effort to repair its *triste mérite*. The last two lines are one of the glories of the play. The prude solemnly hangs a veil over some heavy classical painting of nude figures to hide them from a shocked world, but it is another subterfuge, another attempt to hide her own frustration. The *réalités* convey an extraordinary sense of hot, guilty intimacy, a morbid brooding over the intimate details of sexual relations, and the spiteful Célimène is only too conscious of the bitterness of the shaft.

I have dwelt on these passages not only because of their intrinsic merits, but also because the image of the "veil" and the "mask" explains the intention behind the play. It is to an even greater extent than *Tartuffe* a comedy of unmasking, but the unmasking is a game in which author and characters all take part. Alceste tries to abolish conventional politeness because he feels that it encourages insincerity and prevents him from seeing into the human heart. He attacks his opponent in the lawsuit because he is accepted at his face value and is able to secure an unjust decision:

> Au travers de son *masque* on voit à plein le traître;
> Partout il est connu pour tout ce qu'il peut être,
> Et ses roulements d'yeux et son ton radouci
> N'imposent qu'à des gens qui ne sont point d'ici.

In another place:

> . . . on devrait châtier sans pitié
> Ce commerce honteux de *semblants d'amitié*.

Célimène is busy stripping the mask from Arsinoé and from other members of her circle in order to reveal their hypocrisy and absurdity, but at the end of the encounter with Arsinoé she makes a far more damaging admission than she realizes:

> Madame, on peut, je crois, louer et blâmer tout,
> Et chacun a raison suivant l'âge ou le goût.
> Il est une saison pour la galanterie;
> Il en est une aussi propre à la pruderie.
> On peut, par politique, en prendre le parti,
> Quand de nos jeunes ans l'éclat est amorti:

[420]

Cela sert à couvrir de fâcheuses disgrâces.
Je ne dis pas qu'un jour je ne suive vos traces:
L'âge amènera tout, et ce n'est pas le temps,
Madame, comme on sait, d'être prude à vingt ans.

For here Molière himself takes a hand. The fragile prettiness of the verse reflects the fragile values by which Célimène lives. She accepts them absolutely and uncritically, and the future holds out little for her beyond Arsinoé's own fate.

The characters enter wholeheartedly into the game of unmasking which reaches its climax with the reading of Célimène's letter in the last Act; but as with Arsinoé they only do it as a distraction, as a means of "veiling" their own interior emptiness from themselves.

Now the game is of the utmost seriousness when played by Alceste and Célimène. They are doubtful about their feelings for one another. Alceste *thinks* that he is madly in love with Célimène, but the very violence of his protestations betrays an element of doubt. He is not at all sure that she loves him, and he sets to work to find out because it distracts him from his doubts about his own feelings. The play enters on its last phase when Arsinoé undertakes to prove to Alceste that Célimène is not in love with him:

Oui, toute mon amie, elle est et je la nomme
Indigne d'asservir le cœur d'un galant homme,
Et le sien n'a pour vous que de feintes douceurs.

Alceste bridles at this:

Cela se peut, madame: on ne voit pas les cœurs;
Mais votre charité se serait bien passée
De jeter dans le mien une telle pensée.

The "on ne voit pas les cœurs" is a defence mechanism: it describes exactly what Alceste wants to know and directs his attention uncomfortably back to his own doubts. The damage is done in spite of his protests:

Non; mais sur ce sujet, quoi que l'on nous expose,
Les doutes sont fâcheux plus que toute autre chose;
Et je voudrais, pour moi, qu'on ne me fît savoir
Que ce qu'avec clarté l'on peut me faire voir.

[421]

Arsinoé gleefully undertakes the job—on condition that he goes home with her:

> Là je vous ferai voir une preuve fidèle
> De l'infidélité du cœur de votre belle;
> Et si pour d'autres yeux le vôtre peut brûler,
> On pourra vous offrir de quoi vous consoler.

She is extremely successful in giving Célimène away, but not in replacing her. In the last two acts Molière rings the changes so rapidly, the feelings are so complex, that one is doubtful whether "comic," "moving" or "horrible" is the proper description of some of the scenes.

> The whole misfortune of Alceste [writes M. Mauriac] of that Alceste who is in all of us, lies in a psychological need of the absolute that we bring to love which is the most relative of human feelings. Alceste angrily brushes aside all false appearances; he is determined to advance on firm ground into this *pays du Tendre* which is essentially the home of fickleness and change; and it is precisely because it is the home of fickleness and change that it is the domain of Célimène."

Alceste's

> Non; j'ai résolu de n'en pas faire un pas.
> J'ai tort ou j'ai raison,

of which I have already spoken, has its parallel in the story of his love affair. When he remarks

> Plus on aime quelqu'un, moins il faut qu'on le flatte:
> A ne rien pardonner le pur amour éclate,

his *pur amour* is the absolute love described by Mauriac, the absolute necessity of fixing his love in a formula and compelling the loved one to conform to it. It is here that he fails with Célimène. He feels that he is in the *domaine du mouvant,* that the ground is shifting under his feet, threatening to plunge him into chaos at any moment. When he discovers the letter to Oronte, he loses all control over himself; the whole universe rocks:

> . . . le déchaînement de toute la nature
> Ne m'accablerait pas comme cette aventure.

Éliante comes to the rescue with her moderate and reasonable

Avez-vous, pour le croire, un juste fondement?

recalling the *solide et sincère* and the desperate hunt for a sound foundation
of earlier scenes. This produces an extraordinary reaction in Alceste who suddenly sees in her a refuge against the devouring doubt. "You must avenge
me, madame," he cries. "Avenge you, but how?"

> En recevant mon cœur.
> Acceptez-le, madame, au lieu de l'infidèle;
> C'est par là que je puis prendre vengeance d'elle.

When we recall that Éliante is Alceste's one chance of salvation, we can
appreciate the grimness of Molière's irony here.

It becomes clearer as the play draws towards its conclusion that Célimène
is a means to an end, that Alceste's chief preoccupation is deliverance from
his own obsession, is a need to achieve a startling success to rehabilitate himself in the eyes of the world and to make himself feel that he is rooted in
society:

> Ah! rien n'est comparable à mon amour extrême,
> Et, dans l'ardeur qu'il a de se montrer à tous,
> Il va jusqu'à former des souhaits contre vous.
> Oui, je voudrais qu'aucun ne vous trouvât aimable,
> Que vous fussiez réduite en un sort misérable,
> Que le Ciel, en naissant, ne vous eût donné rien,
> Que vous n'eussiez ni rang, ni naissance, ni bien,
> Afin que de mon cœur l'éclatant sacrifice
> Vous pût d'un pareil sort réparer l'injustice,
> Et que j'eusse la joie et la gloire, en ce jour,
> De vous voir tenir tout des mains de mon amour.

This shows to what extent Alceste lives in a private world, how impossible
it is to prevent the "quelque chose en soi de noble et d'héroïque" from being
swamped and destroyed by his eccentricities. For he is obliged to invent a
situation, in which he can repair imaginary injustices by imaginary sacrifices,
to convince himself not merely of the reality of his own feelings, but of his
very existence.

While Alceste is hunting desperately to discover some sure foundation in
the *domaine du mouvant*, Célimène is clinging no less tenaciously to her

shifting, changing world. For her whole existence depends on maintaining a state of doubt—doubt about her own feelings, doubt in the minds of her retainers about her feelings for them. When Alceste and Oronte deliver their ultimatum—"Choose between us two"—it is she who assumes the role of a trapped animal, or perhaps of the trapped butterfly, struggling desperately to avoid a commitment:

> Mon Dieu! que cette instance est là hors de saison,
> Et que vous témoignez, tous deux, peu de raison!
> Je sais prendre parti sur cette préférence,
> Et ce n'est pas mon cœur maintenant qui balance:
> Il n'est point suspendu, sans doute, entre vous deux,
> Et rien n'est si tôt fait que le choix de nos vœux.
> Mais je souffre, à vrai dire, une gêne trop forte
> A prononcer en face un aveu de la sorte:
> Je trouve que ces mots, qui sont désobligeants,
> Ne se doivent point dire en présence des gens;
> Qu'un cœur de son penchant donne assez de lumière,
> Sans qu'on nous fasse aller jusqu'à rompre en visière;
> Et qu'il suffit enfin que de plus doux témoins
> Instruisent un amant du malheur de ses soins.

Finally, when she can no longer avoid making a choice, she discovers that she does not love Alceste enough to follow him into his desert, and his vanity is too great to allow of any compromise:

> La solitude effraye une âme de vingt ans;
> Je ne sens point la mienne assez grande, assez forte,
> Pour me résoudre à prendre un dessein de la sorte . . .

I have already spoken of the differences between the *Misanthrope* and Molière's other plays. When the curtain comes down on the *École des femmes, Tartuffe, l'Avare* and *les Femmes savantes,* the audience is left in no doubt about the author's intentions. It is able to "determine . . . exactly what attitude is broken down and what takes its place." In *Tartuffe* religious mania is satirized, a criminal is brought to book and the play closes with the triumph of society.

The same cannot be said of the *Misanthrope.* Molière has richly fulfilled his intention of speaking *contre les mœurs de siècle*; but the doubt, which is an integral part of our experience, persists. We are, perhaps, able to determine what attitude is broken down, but it is less easy to decide what takes its place. It is idle to pretend that order is re-established and that a chastened buffoon is brought back to the norm of sanity. At the close of the play society, in the persons of Célimène and her retainers, leaves by one exit and Alceste abandons society by another, leaving an empty stage. The line that echoes in the mind is not profession of belief, but a profession of complete disbelief, is not Philinte's

La parfaite raison fuit toute extrémité,

but Alceste's

Mais la raison n'est pas ce qui règle l'amour.

Indeed, so far from ending in another triumph for *la parfaite raison,* it is *la parfaite raison* which dissolves into Alceste's

Mes sens par la raison ne sont plus gouvernés.

Ramon Fernandez seems to put his finger on the point when, in the course of his stimulating but highly erratic study of Molière, he remarks that Molière lived in an age of intellectual scepticism. For when one considers the play as a whole, it is difficult not to feel that Molière had come to share Alceste's own scepticism. The *honnête homme* no doubt contributes to the poise of each of the plays in which he appears, but his urbane, polished discourses never succeed in converting anyone; and even in *Tartuffe* conversion is brought about by a sudden change of situation—the intervention of the "great Prince"—and not by Cléante. In the *Misanthrope,* more than in any of the other plays, the *honnête homme* is a symbolical figure and Molière is particularly careful to avoid the appearance of imposing a solution. The most that he does is to suggest that a blending of the virtues of Philinte and Éliante may have some bearing on the complicated situation which he has created. In no other play does he reveal such variety and complexity of feelings, but in no other does he show such reluctance to judge the individual or so marked a tendency to call in question all accepted standards and formulas. It is a masterly exploration of the motives behind social behaviour; feelings are tracked down, as surely as in Racine, to the moment of their formation; but judgment on them is suspended. There is in truth no formal ending to the play. The catharsis lies in the clarifying of our feelings, in the perception that social adjustment is a personal matter where in the last resort no facile slogan or philosophical system can help us; and the "message," if we must have one, is that we must have the courage to create our own "order," whatever the cost, instead of yielding to the temptation of an easy escape.

S P I N O Z A

[*1632–1677*]

So closely articulated is Stuart Hampshire's book on Spinoza that it may seem improper to print only part of it. Yet this excerpt, two-thirds of the chapter "Freedom and Morality," offers the reader more than whole volumes on Spinoza. The reader will here gain a notion of the shape of Spinoza's entire philosophy through Hampshire's discussion of but one part of it. What is of first importance here is Spinoza's moral intention: to teach us that we can be free only through submission to the order of things as they are in God and nature (*Deus sive Natura*)—a nature of which our nature is but a mode.

Stuart Hampshire is a Fellow of All Souls College, Oxford.

From *Spinoza* by Stuart Hampshire, 1951, by permission of Penguin Books.

STUART HAMPSHIRE

Spinoza

W E ARE ALREADY PREPARED, AND PERHAPS EVEN COMPELLED, TO ADMIT THAT relatively elaborate patterns of behaviour—e.g. the behaviour of animals and of sleepwalkers—can be explained in physical terms, without any appeal to faculties of will or judgement; even in our ordinary, common-sense terminology, behaviour may be in most observable respects indistinguishable from so-called purposive behaviour without being called purposive in any sense which excludes physical explanation. Once this is admitted, there remains no *a priori* justification for drawing a line, and for excluding the possibility of description and explanation in physical terms, at any particular point on the scale of complication; we may in our commonsense descriptions fall back on the terminology of will and purpose, simply because purely physical explanations and descriptions are not yet in fact available; the use of these words "will" and "purpose" confesses that we do not in fact generally possess clear and adequate ideas of causes; they are confessions of ignorance, which philosophers, conspicuously Descartes, have erected into metaphysical dogmas grounded on logical principle. The strength and originality of this argument is the recognition, both as against Descartes and as against seventeenth-century materialists such as Hobbes and Gassendi, of the possible, but still unimagined, complication of physical structures and physical laws. It is the importance of so stressing the almost unlimited complexities of physical structures which most clearly emerges in all recent discussions of the relations of mind and body against the background of twentieth-century scientific knowledge. Descartes, and the rationalists and materialists of his own age (and even up to the present day), conceived matter or the extended world as essentially simple in structure, and as governed in its motions by essentially simple geometrical principles, or by essentially simple mechanical laws. The paradigm of a physical system was a piece of clockwork; only that part of human behaviour which could be described and explained by the use of concepts which are also applicable to clockwork could be regarded as explicable in physical terms; in so far as human behaviour cannot be assimilated to the behaviour of clockwork, no explanation which is clear and intelligible can be looked for; the prevailing assumption was that only more or less simple mechanical systems—and the physiologist must exhibit the human body as such a system—can be regarded as intelligible physical systems. Thus the dichotomy—a person as a machine regulated by causal laws or a person as a free and causally inexplicable spiritual substance—persisted long after Descartes; throughout the two following centuries a materialist was someone who tried to show that human thought and behaviour can be analysed into more or less simple mechanical patterns. In the last fifty years, physicists have abandoned the more simple mechanical models as essential to all physical explanation, and have admitted vast complexities of structure of an unmechanical kind, not only in the study of the human brain, but in other branches of biology and physiology; Spinoza's argument has again become important. Any scientist or philosopher must to-day be prepared to admit that "no one has yet been taught by experience what the body is capable of doing merely from the laws of Nature alone, in so far as Nature is considered as purely physical" (*Ethics Pt.* III. *Prop.* II. *Note*). This must be left an open question; and there can be no *logical,* but only empirical, grounds for closing it; and certainly no general conclusions can be based on our present ignorance of the powers and structure of the human brain and body.

Spinoza's theory of *conatus,* of desire and will, is designed to show the full implications of admitting the possibility of complete causal explanation of human behaviour. He has so defined these basic terms that it follows logically that all men pursue their own pleasure in accordance with the necessary laws of Nature; they necessarily pursue pleasure, not in the sense that they always in fact deliberate about what will give them most pleasure and then choose to act accordingly, but in the sense that their so-called choices, and their pleasures, can always be explained as arising from the *conatus* of

the organism, its tendency to self-maintenance and self-preservation. Anything of any kind may accidentally be a source of pleasure or of increased
vitality, or of pain and of decreased vitality; the reaction depends on the
psycho-physical condition of the organism at a particular time. In so far as
the idea of a particular external cause comes to be associated in my mind
with a sense of pleasure or increased vitality, I can be said to love the thing
taken to be the external cause, and I will consider the thing good; whatever
comes to be associated in my mind with pain or a sense of depressed vitality,
I can be said to hate and will consider bad. The succession of ideas which
constitutes my mind is, as explained in the last chapter, normally governed
by laws of association; one idea calls up another because they have occurred
together in the past, or because similar ideas have occurred together in the
past. By the agency of these laws of association in the imagination, the whole
complex system of our desires and aversions is formed. Whatever becomes
associated in our mind with something which is associated with pleasure,
itself becomes an object of desire; and this association of ideas may proceed to any degree of complication. Thus objects which, considered in themselves, are not the direct or primary causes of pleasure or pain in me, may
indirectly become associated with pleasure or pain.

Pleasure, pain and desire are taken by Spinoza as the primary passions in
terms of which all the other passions or emotions are to be defined. They
are passions, not only in the popular sense of the word, but also in his technical sense; in ordinary life (special conditions will be described later) they
arise, as described, from the *passive* association of ideas; in so far as they
arise from the passive association of ideas, they are by definition "confused"
perceptions, in which the mind is not aware of the causes of its ideas. In
experiencing these passions, we are merely reacting to external causes; our
conscious life is proceeding at the level of sense-perception and imagination,
and not at the level of logical thought or active intellect. When in ordinary
life we enjoy and pursue, hate and avoid various kinds of things, the ideas
constituting our minds are "inadequate," and the judgements we make about
these things unscientific; for these ideas or judgements exhibit only the inter-
actions between our bodies and other parts of nature, and do not show the
true causes of the modifications of our body; the ideas accompanying these
modifications of the body "indicate the actual constitution of our own body
rather than that of the external bodies" (*Ethics Pt.* II. *Prop.* XVI. *Coroll.*
II); but they exhibit neither the nature of our own bodies nor of external
bodies adequately, in their proper place in the order of causes in nature.
These are the grounds of Spinoza's famous distinction between active and
passive emotion, the first of his contributions to the theory of conduct; the
distinction derives directly from the epistemological distinction between

imagination (inadequate ideas) and intellect (true and adequate ideas). There is nothing in Spinoza's vocabulary which exactly corresponds to the ordinary distinction between "feeling an emotion" and "thinking"; as his doctrine is that every modification of the body involves at the same time having an idea, every kind and phase of consciousness involves having an idea, including even the mere experiencing of an emotion. The word *affectus,* although it comes the nearest to the word "emotion" in the familiar sense, represents the whole modification of the person, mental and physical. The "affection" is a passion (in Spinoza's technical sense) in so far as the cause of the modification or "affection" does not lie within myself, and it is an "action" or active emotion in so far as the cause does lie within myself; this is another way of saying that any "affection," of which the mental equivalent is not an adequate idea, must be a passive emotion; for an adequate idea is an idea which follows necessarily from the idea which preceded it. I am active in so far as I am thinking logically, that is, in so far as the succession of ideas constituting my mind is a self-contained and self-generating series; I am passive, in so far as my succession of ideas can only be explained in terms of ideas which are not members of the series constituting my mind; for in this latter case the ideas constituting my mind must be, at least in part, the effects of external causes. My ordinary hates and loves, desires and aversions, succeed each other without any internal logical connexion between the ideas annexed to them.

This argument is at first difficult to grasp because we do not now use the word "cause" as Spinoza and other philosophers of his time used it; it is strange to us to identify *the cause* of a certain idea in my mind with the *logical ground* from which this idea can be deduced; but the distinction between active and passive emotions, and indeed the whole of Spinoza's moral theory, depends upon this identification. To re-state: I experience an active emotion, if and only if the idea which is the psychical accompaniment of the "affection" is logically deducible from the previous idea constituting my mind; only if it is so deducible, can I be said to have an adequate idea of the cause of my emotion. If the idea annexed to the emotion is not deducible from a previous idea in my mind, it follows that the emotion or "affection" must be the effect of an external cause, and that I am in this sense passive in respect of it. As the ideas constituting my mind are the psychical equivalents of the modifications of my body, I can only have adequate knowledge of the causes of those of my "affections" which are not the effects of external causes. If the cause of the "affection" is external to me, it follows that it involves an inadequate idea, and the converse must also be true; therefore, to say that the cause of the modification is external to me is *equivalent* to saying that it involves incomplete knowledge and an inadequate idea. In so far as I am a free agent, unaffected by external causes, I necessarily have adequate or scientific knowledge, and the converse must also be true; only the intelligent man can (logically) be free, and only the free man can (logically) be intelligent. But human beings, as finite modes, cannot in principle be *completely* free and unaffected by external causes; human freedom must be a matter of degree. Spinoza's method in the last three parts of the *Ethics* is to contrast the actual and normal conditions of human servitude with the humanly unattainable ideal of permanent and perfect freedom.

In his survey of the normal conditions of our emotional life, Spinoza attempts to define the ordinarily recognized emotions in terms of his primary "affections"—pleasure, pain and desire. There had been several previous attempts to systematize the vocabulary of the emotions; and such systems of definitions were generally conceived as explanations of the "essence" or "true nature" of the various emotions. But in Spinoza's design, the names of the emotions—jealousy, anger, fear, envy and so on—are not in themselves taken to be important, nor are his definitions primarily intended to enlighten us as to the "true nature" of each particular emotion named in the common vocabulary. It is one of the first principles of his logic, throughout nominalistic, that definitions of the abstract, general terms of ordinary language cannot yield genuine knowledge; it is nonsense to talk of the essence of jealousy common to your jealousy and to mine. He strongly insists (*Ethics Pt.* III. *Prop.* LV. *Note* I) that the joy of one man is essentially different from the joy of another, although the common name is properly applicable to them both; the difference between the two experiences depends on the particular nature ("actual essence") of the particular individuals involved, and this in turn depends on their particular situations in Nature. To understand the two experiences is to situate each of them in the chain of causes in Nature as a whole; it is useless to inquire into the vague similarities which the common abstract name represents. The catalogue of the emotions, and Spinoza's analyses of them in terms of pleasure, pain and desire, serve mainly to show that the emotions can be understood and interpreted on his principles, and as ultimately arising from the *conatus,* the tendency to self-preservation, which is common to all things in Nature, human or inhuman; secondly, the catalogue serves to exhibit in convincing detail the varieties of human servitude and unreason. The emotions which we ordinarily distinguish—ambition, lust, pity, pride, anger, and many others—are shown to be differentiated only by the way in which the primary passions of pleasure, pain and desire are evoked. In our ordinary experience of this whole range of emotions, we are "agitated by contrary winds like waves of the sea, waver and are unconscious of our issue and our fate"

(*Ethics Pt*. III. *Prop*. LIX. *Note*); this is one of the very few uses of rhetorical metaphor in Spinoza's writing; to him, as to Montaigne, man in his normal condition is essentially *chose ondoyante,* pathetically unstable and unreasonable. The list of the emotions at the end of Part III of the *Ethics,* although mainly intended to illustrate the manifold complications of desire and its objects, contains many acute psychological observations, for example, on the natural alternation between love and hatred of the same person. Spinoza, in his detached and impersonal style, notices the twists and perversities of human feeling and behaviour more closely than most of the philosopher-psychologists of his age; he is conspicuously less schematic and crude than Hobbes, and is nearer to the great French moralists in his calm pessimism. The many philosophers who have tried to show the varieties of human feeling and behaviour as deducible from a primary urge towards pleasure and self-preservation have generally over-simplified the varieties of human behaviour; they have made men appear more starkly rational and self-seeking than they are. Spinoza was not in this sense rationalistic, and allows for the literally infinite varieties of human folly and helplessness: literally infinite, because the pleasures and pains of each individual are essentially different, depending on his individual constitution and his position in Nature. In emphasizing the helpless irrationality of normal human loves and hates, desires and aversions, and their entire independence of conscious thought and purpose, Spinoza is once again nearer to modern psychology than to the commonplace psychology of his contemporaries; he is certainly less shallow than Descartes, who seemed uninterested in the less conscious sources of human weakness; he rejects the facile optimism of Descartes' appeals to will and reason. In order to understand the reactions of any individual, we must attend, not to his own statements about his feelings and motives, but, first, to his particular physical constitution and, secondly, to the trains of unconscious association and habit which have been established by his particular experiences. Any individual's own accounts of his motives and behaviour will be what we now call rationalizations; he will give plausible reasons for feeling and behaving in certain ways, but these reasons, expressed in terms of deliberate choices and decisions, will not give the true causes of his reactions. The ordinary man in his rationalizations will speak as if his desires and aversions were determined by the properties of external objects; if he really is an ordinary and not a philosophical man, he will not see his desires and aversions as determined by his own constitution and past experience, until these causes are pointed out to him.

The transition from the normal life of passive emotion and confused ideas to the free man's life of active emotion and adequate ideas must be achieved, if at all, by a method in some respects not unlike the methods of modern psychology; the cure, or method of salvation, consists in making the patient more self-conscious, and in making him perceive the more or less unconscious struggle within himself to preserve his own internal adjustment and balance; he must be brought to realize that it is this continuous struggle which expresses itself in his pleasures and pains, desires and aversions. Hatred and love, jealousy and pride, and the other emotions which he feels, can be shown to him as the compensations necessary to restore loss of 'psychical energy.' There is an evident parallel between Freud's conception of *libido* and Spinoza's *conatus;* the importance of the parallel, which is rather more than superficial, is that both philosophers conceive emotional life as based on a universal unconscious drive or tendency to self-preservation; both maintain that any frustration of this drive must manifest itself in our conscious life as some painful disturbance. Every person is held to dispose of a certain quantity of psychical energy, a counterpart (for Spinoza at least) of his physical energy, and conscious pleasures and pains are only reflexions of the relatively uninhibited expression and frustration of this energy. Consequently, for Spinoza no less than for Freud, moral praise and blame of the objects of our particular desires, and of the sources of our pleasure, are irrelevant superstitions; we may as reasonably praise or condemn people for having the physical allergies and tastes which they do have. According to both Freud and Spinoza, it is the first error of conventional moralists to find moral and *a priori* reasons for repressing our natural energy, our *libido* or *conatus;* they both condemn puritanism and asceticism in strikingly similar tones and for roughly similar reasons. Asceticism is only one expression among others of the depression of vitality and the frustration of the *libido* or *conatus;* however we may deceive ourselves, our feelings and behaviour, even what we distinguish as self-denial, can always be explained as the effects of causes which are independent of our conscious will. Consequently both Spinoza and Freud represent moral problems as essentially clinical problems, which can only be confused by the use of epithets of praise and blame, and by emotional attitudes of approval and disapproval. There can in principle be only one way of achieving sanity and happiness; the way is to come to understand the causes of our own states of mind. Vice, if the word is to be given a meaning, is that diseased state of the organism, in which neither mind nor body function freely and efficiently. Vice, in this sense, always betrays itself to the agent as that depression of vitality which is pain; vice and pain are necessarily connected, as are virtue and pleasure; this is another way of saying that, in Spinoza's sense of the word, "virtue is its own reward." Pleasure, in this primary sense of the felt tone of efficiency of the organism, is distinguished by Spinoza from mere local stimulation, which he calls "titillation" (*titillatio*). When we ordinarily speak of pleasure or pleasures, we are referring only to these temporary and partial stimulations; and because of this use of the word it appears paradoxical to assert a necessary connexion between virtue and pleasure; but in this context pleasure (*laetitia*) is contrasted, as the organism's sense of entire well-being, with pleasure in the more common sense of a temporary excitement. This contrast between a sense of total well-being and a mere temporary stimulation has a long philosophical history from Plato onwards; perhaps it corresponds to something in our experience which is reflected in the ordinary association of the words "happiness" (*laetitia*) and "pleasure" (*titillatio*). But I suspect that all such precise labelling and classifying is irrelevant for anyone who would really explore the varieties of human experience.

Other points of comparison could profitably be found between the two great Jewish thinkers, Freud and Spinoza, each so isolated, austere and uncompromising in their own original ways of thought. The points of detailed resemblance between them follow from their common central conception of the *libido* or *conatus,* the natural drive for self-preservation and the extension of power and energy, as being the clue to the understanding of all forms of personal life. Neither crudely suggested that all men consciously pursue their own pleasure or deliberately seek to extend their own power; but both insisted that people must be studied scientifically, as organisms within Nature, and that only by such study could men be enabled to understand the causes of their own infirmity. Consequently both have been attacked for insisting on an entirely objective and clinical study of human feeling and behaviour. Lastly, there is a similarity, evident but more difficult to make precise, in the grave, prophetic, scrupulously objective tone of voice in which they quietly undermine all the established prejudices of popular and religious morality: there is the same quietly ruthless insistence that we must look in every case for the natural causes of human unhappiness, as we would look for the causes of the imperfections of any other natural object; moral problems cannot be solved by appeals to emotion and prejudice, which are always the symptoms of ignorance. They have both provoked the hatred which visits anyone who would regard man as a natural object and not as a supernatural agent, and who is concerned impassively to understand the nature of human imbecility, rather than to condemn it. In reading Spinoza it must not be forgotten that he was before all things concerned to point the way to human freedom through understanding and natural knowledge.

FREEDOM AND MORAL STANDARDS

Our normal life is a series of agitations and "fluctuations" of the mind reflecting the manifold influences to which we are subject in the unceasing modifications of Nature; we feel pains, pleasures, and desires, and experience a flow of complicated and ambivalent emotions. We naturally associate these agitations, in our confused ideas, with external persons and objects as their causes. Spinoza points out that we are trained and conditioned as children to hate some things and to love others, and to associate the ideas of some things with pain and of others with pleasure. By habit and association we come to call some things good and other things bad; we call things good, in one common use of the word, if the idea of them, as a result of something in our past experience, causes us pleasure, and if they have become, consciously or unconsciously, objects of desire. As human beings are generally similar to some degree in their psycho-physical structure and are generally subjected to roughly similar external influences, there must in fact be some things which most normal men generally desire or enjoy; the things which are generally the objects of normal appetites, or the idea of which is normally associated with pleasure, are called good, in this quasi-objective sense of the word; those things, of which the idea is in fact generally depressing to normally constituted men, are called bad in this sense. Spinoza can allow that the moral epithets "good" and "bad" are popularly and intelligibly used in this quasi-objective sense; so far they have the same use as words like "pleasant" or "admirable"; they indicate the appetites and repugnances of the user, or what happen to be the tastes of most normal men. But it is important to notice that in this popular use the epithets must not be interpreted as referring to the intrinsic properties of the things or persons called good or bad; they refer rather to the constitution and reactions of the persons applying the epithets. But there is a natural extension of this popular use of the words "good" and "bad." We naturally come to speak of "normal" men and the "normal" constitution of man; in talking of "man" in the abstract, we are led to form a universal notion, or vague composite image, of what a man should be, or of the type or model of a man. We are then inclined to think of this type or ideal of a man as we think of an ideal house or an ideal theatre; objects which are created by human beings with a definite purpose, artifacts such as houses or theatres, can properly be said to conform more or less closely to a norm or ideal of what a house should be; we can judge how far any particular house satisfies the purposes for which houses in general are designed. But we are led into confusion when, having formed an abstract universal notion of a natural kind, we come to think of this universal notion as representing the ideal or perfect specimen of the natural kind; we form in this way a general notion of what a man should be, as we form a general notion of what a house should be; and we think of men, as of houses, as more or less perfect in so far as they conform to the ideal. The misleading implication in this way of thinking is that human beings, and other natural kinds, are designed with a purpose. To

[436]

say of a house that it is imperfect in some respect is to make a statement to which a definite meaning can be attached by an objective test; the statement is tested by a comparison of the actual house with what was projected in the design of it. To say of a man that he is imperfect in some respect looks as if it were to make a statement which is testable by the same procedure, and which looks as if it had a similarly definite sense; but this is wholly misleading, since we must not suppose that human beings, or any other natural objects, have been designed for any purpose; consequently it makes no sense to think of them as fulfilling, or failing to fulfil, a purpose or design. In thinking of particular men as in some respect perfect or imperfect, or as (in this sense) good or bad specimens of their kind, we can only be comparing them with some abstract general notion which has formed itself in our minds of what a man should be; and this general notion has no objective significance, but arises only out of our own particular associations; it can be no more than an arbitrary projection of our own tastes, interests and experience. Whenever we hear natural objects discussed as though they were artifacts, we have the most sure evidence of theological superstition; Spinoza will not allow any mention of design or of final causes in the study of Nature.

Spinoza's destructive analysis of the basis of ordinary moral judgements, and of the standards which they imply, follows directly from the basic propositions of his logic. (1) The properties of everything within Nature are deducible from the necessary laws of self-development of Nature as a whole; if something appears to us imperfect or bad, in the sense of "not what it should be," this is only a reflection of our ignorance of these necessary laws. If we understood the necessary principles on which the individual nature of particular things depends, we would thereby understand the part which various things play in the whole system. Philosophically speaking, all finite things within Nature are imperfect, simply in the sense that they are finite things within Nature, which alone is complete and perfect; but they all fit perfectly into the system, and could not possibly be other than they are. (2) All general, classificatory terms, distinguishing different natural kinds, are confused images, formed as the effect of an arbitrary association of ideas, and do not represent the real essences of things. To understand the nature of anything is to fit it into the system of causes and effects of which it is a part; all qualitative classifications are subjective and arbitrary. (3) To think of things or persons as fulfilling, or failing to fulfil, a purpose or design is to imply the existence of a creator distinct from his creation; this is a demonstrably meaningless conception. Repudiating the whole traditional logic of classification, and with it the Aristotelian search for the real essences of natural kinds, Spinoza must repudiate the conception of final causes, which was an integral part of this traditional logic. Such phrases as "the essential nature of man" and "the purpose of human existence" are phrases which survive in popular philosophy and language only as the ghosts of Aristotelianism, and can have no place in a scientific language. Popular and traditional morality is largely founded on such surviving pre-scientific and confused ideas. In ordinary moral praise and condemnation, we necessarily imply a reference to some standard or ideal of what a person should be, or assume some end, purpose or design in human existence.

Considered scientifically and in the light of systematic knowledge, nothing can be said to be in itself morally good or bad, morally perfect or imperfect; everything is what it is as the consequence of necessary laws; to say that some-one is morally bad is, in popular usage, to imply that he could have been better; this implication is always and necessarily false, and is always a reflexion of incomplete knowledge. Spinoza can allow no sense in which "good" and "bad" can be applied to persons which is not also a sense in which the words are applicable to any other natural objects, whether brutes or things. It is this disturbing contention which is the core of the metaphysical issue between determinism and free-will, and this issue we must now consider.

The phrases *"morally* good" and *"morally* bad" and their equivalents have generally been used, at least in Europe, in such a way as implicitly to dis-tinguish human beings from animals and inanimate objects. It is part of the force of the word "moral" that only human beings can significantly be judged as morally good or bad, because only human beings can be said to deliberate and to choose; what distinguishes human beings, as the possible subjects of *moral* judgements, is that in general it makes sense (although it is often false) to say of a human being that he could have acted in some differ-ent way if he had chosen. It was Spinoza's "hideous hypothesis," and the only part of his philosophy which immediately became generally famous, that this criterion of distinguishing human beings as exercising rational will and choice is mere superstition; it is a superstition which must be rejected as we advance up the scale of natural knowledge. He did not deny, and no philo-sophical determinist could plausibly deny, that, as language is ordinarily used, we do in fact speak of persons, as opposed to animals and inanimate objects, as being free to choose between alternative courses of action. But his determinism cannot be refuted by the type of argument which philosophers to-day are apt to use in attacking such metaphysical theses—namely, by an appeal to such standard uses of language; for he is criticizing, and giving reasons for criticizing, the ordinary uses of language as superstitious, and as reflexions of inadequate ideas or pre-scientific thinking. He is maintaining that we will necessarily abandon the notion of freedom of choice as our knowledge and understanding of Nature, and of human nature as part of Nature, increase; and this is a more formidable thesis. The argument of a metaphysical determinist such as Spinoza seems simple and compelling. As we progressively acquire more and more scientific knowledge of the behaviour and reactions of human beings, more and more of their actions are shown to be deducible from laws of nature; this is a mere tautology, since by "scientific" knowledge we simply mean the explanation of events as deducible from laws of nature. If a human action is shown to be deducible from a law of nature, that is, is exhibited as the effect of a cause, there is at least one sense in which we must say that the agent could not in this case have acted otherwise, or that no alternative action was possible; and if no alternative action was in this sense possible for him, it seems unreasonable to allow a sense to saying that he could have acted otherwise if he had chosen. Therefore, as our psychological and physiological knowledge of human actions and reactions increases, the range of human actions of which we can reasonably say "an alternative action was possible," or "he could have acted otherwise," necessarily diminishes; this seems to amount to saying that any statement of the kind "an alternative action was possible," or "he could have acted otherwise," is necessarily a sign of the incompleteness of our scientific knowledge, or an expression of our present state of ignorance: and this was precisely Spinoza's contention.

He expresses this simple and formidable argument elliptically and in his own terminology, using his basic logical distinction between adequate ideas, which are logically necessary propositions, and inadequate ideas, which are contingent propositions, or propositions which could (logically) be false. In so far as we have adequate knowledge, we understand someone's actions as the necessary effect of a cause; in so far as our ideas are inadequate, the action is represented in our thought as contingent and uncaused. In Spinoza's logic the discovery of the cause of some event is the discovery of the grounds from which the occurrence of the event could be logically deduced; these grounds themselves will in their turn be shown to follow from some higher-order premises, and the event will gradually be fitted into the single deductive system which is God or Nature conceived under the attribute of thought; as our knowledge grows, every human action becomes one necessary link in the infinite chain of causes. "Men think themselves free, in so far as they are conscious of their volitions and desire, and are ignorant of the causes by which they are disposed to will and desire . . ." Superstition is by definition ignorance of causes; when we do not know the cause of something, we superstitiously accept some explanation in terms of the purpose or end for which the thing was done; superstition is belief in final causes. At the most primitive level of superstition, we explain the fall of a stone from a roof as the result of God's will to kill someone; but, as our physical knowledge increases, we discard such supernatural explanations of physical events in terms of final causes, and in terms of acts of will, in favour of purely scientific explanations. But in respect of human actions, involving a more complicated structure of causes, we are still generally in a state of primitive ignorance of causes, and we are therefore content to describe most human behaviour in terms of inexplicable acts of will; such popular, pre-scientific accounts of human behaviour are necessarily displaced by explanations in terms of causes as our knowledge increases, and as the confused ideas of the imagination are replaced by adequate ideas of the intellect; such pre-scientific accounts of personality are characteristic of the lower grades of knowledge (*experientia vaga*), and are naturally reflected in the familiar uses of common-sense language; it is the responsibility of the philosopher to show their inadequacy when judged by those standards of genuine knowledge which we all implicitly recognize. But a philosopher must expect to meet bitter sentimental resistance from those whose desires and fears, loves and hates, are tied to the primitive superstitions which represent persons as free and uncaused causes. Admittedly passages can be found in the *Ethics* which, when quoted (as they so often are) out of their context, give the impression that Spinoza was denying that there is anything to be found in our experience corresponding to the notions of "will" or "choice." Such a denial would be plainly absurd; but it is certainly not a necessary consequence of his determinist argument; and he did not (I think) intend it. He need not, and (I think) did not, deny that we are in fact often conscious of a state which we describe as "choosing between alternatives" or "deciding by an act of will to do what we do not want to do"; we are often in a state of "fluctuation of mind" (*fluctuatio animi*), and from this state some decision, often with a peculiar sense of effort, finally emerges. His contention is only that, in giving a coherent, rational account of human actions in terms of their causes, "will" and "choice," as psychological phenomena, have no special place; they are just one mode of consciousness among others, one set of ideas among others in the sequence which constitutes our mind. Yet, at the common-sense, pre-scientific level, we talk as if conscious acts of will or deliberate choice in themselves constitute adequate *explanations* of human action, because we are conscious of acts of will and choice, but not of their causes. Such pseudo-explanations mention the agents' conscious purposes, but not the ultimate and true causes of his action, and therefore are inadequate as explanations; for they do not exhibit actions as deducible from the necessary features of the natural order, but as merely contingent, and as the effects of the "free" choices of individuals. But individuals, being finite modes within Nature, cannot be "free," in the sense that their actions are uncaused or self-determined; they only appear free to the ignorant, as the falling of the stone appears free to the ignorant; the only differences in this respect between the person and the stone lie in the comparative complication of the causes, and in the fact that a person is conscious of his own states in a sense in which a stone is not. The individual person's consciousness of his own needs and strivings (*appetitus*) is reflected in his consciousness as desire (*cupiditas*). But the desire, which is associated with his pursuit of particular ends, is no more than the reflexion in idea of his total state, which itself is determined by a variety of external and internal causes; we can therefore adequately explain his pursuit of particular ends only in terms of these causes, and not *vice versa*.

Determinism, so ruthlessly stated, is no longer widely accepted, as it was by many untheological thinkers in the nineteenth century; an effort of imagination is now required in order to reconstruct the intellectual conditions in which it seemed generally plausible. The simple faith of Laplace in the theoretical possibility of a complete explanation of every state of the universe is now generally represented as logically absurd. Determinism in this extreme form seems plausible only at a time when the possibilities of *complete* scientific explanation are accepted as absolutely *unlimited*. If it is accepted that a *single* form of scientific explanation is, or must be, in principle applicable to every thing or event in the universe, whatever their qualitative differences and however great their complexity, then it will seem reasonable to reject much of the common-sense language which we ordinarily apply to the choices and decisions of human beings; for the apparent implication of this language, as it is ordinarily used, is that forms of explanation which are applicable to the behaviour of animals and physical things are *in principle* inapplicable to the behaviour of human beings; we seem ordinarily to take it for granted that the type of explanation accepted in physics or biology must be, in kind and in principle, radically different from the kinds of explanation which can be given of rational human behaviour. The idioms of personal description in common language are inherited from periods in which a systematic psychology, parallel with the other natural sciences, was not yet envisaged; they seem to descend from the age of magic; this at least is the thought of a scientific optimist. In the heroic, pioneering and confident phase of modern science, extending roughly from Galileo to Einstein, this last surviving barrier is naturally challenged, and the possibility is envisaged of a single language of science, which will be complete and unlimited in its application; and just this programme of removing the barrier between human choices and the motions of the animal and physical world is the thesis of determinism. Such confident visions of a single system or language of science are less prominent to-day, partly because the actual development of the sciences in the last fifty years has not been generally in accordance with the simple programme originally envisaged; the various sciences have not in fact tended to conform to a single, simple pattern of mechanical explanation and have not in fact shown a single set of intuitively evident mathematical notions to be sufficient for all purposes. Some of the accepted patterns of physical explanation have been called in question as having only a restricted and not a universal application, and new and more complicated types of theory have been adopted for some purposes. Theoreticians of science are no longer inclined to speak so confidently of a single system of natural law in terms of which all natural events might in principle be explained. They are inclined rather to envisage a variety of overlapping systems of different types, each of which is found appropriate to some specific purpose and in some limited contexts. Consequently metaphysical determinism, of which Spinoza was the most uncompromising proponent, no longer seems such an acute issue to philosophers and moralists; early optimism about the construction of a unified and all-embracing language of science has been, at least temporarily, overclouded; and it now seems questionable whether simple and definite causal explanations of human choices and decisions, explanations not substantially different in type from physical explanations, are likely to emerge from the study of psychology; this is at least considered an open question, which it is wise, as a principle of method, to leave open. Certainly we will always try to establish some systematic theory of human behaviour; but one cannot dogmatically forecast what form the theories will take, or to what degree they will conflict with our ordinary pre-scientific descriptions of human conduct.

These, roughly summarized, are the historical factors which explain why Spinoza's dogmatic determinism is now generally rejected. But the arguments cannot be brushed aside merely on the grounds that, as Spinoza stated them, they depend on his metaphysical thesis of the unity of Nature as a causal system; for the kernel of his argument can (I think) still be re-stated so as to be independent of his metaphysical premise. Spinoza as metaphysician asserts that Nature *must* be conceived as a completely intelligible, infinite and self-contained causal system; any other conception of it can be shown to be logically self-contradictory. But a determinist may reject this inference from the logical coherence of Spinoza's definitions to the nature of reality, and yet may still use the argument that *in proportion as* our scientific knowledge, or knowledge of causes, increases, we necessarily abandon the primitive conception of human beings as free and self-determining in their choices; he may admit that our scientific knowledge may never in fact be complete, or he may even admit that there can be no sense in speaking of complete scientific knowledge. But he might still maintain that we think of human beings as self-determining and free agents, to be distinguished in this respect from all other things in Nature, only in so far as we are ignorant of the causes of their behaviour, and in so far as our scientific knowledge is incomplete. In support of his thesis he can point to the fact that, as soon as we do come to understand the causes of a particular kind of human behaviour, we do generally cease to regard people as, in the normal sense, morally responsible for the type of behaviour now causally explained; we do in fact cease to apply purely moral epithets to them as responsible agents. When the behaviour now causally explained is what was formerly regarded as morally wicked, we come to regard it as the symptom of a disease, curable, if at all, by the removal of its causes; expressions of moral disapproval come to seem useless and irrelevant. As psychology in its various branches progresses, the sins and wickedness of free agents come to be regarded as the diseases of patients; the line drawn in our common-sense speech and thought between a disease or pathological condition, for which the sufferer is not responsible, and wickedness, which the agent could have avoided, is gradually effaced in one case after another; young criminals are reclassified as juvenile delinquents, whose antisocial behaviour can be cured by the appropriate treatment, but cannot usefully and reasonably be blamed, with the purely moral implications which formerly attached to such blame; the very words—"anti-social" in place of "bad," "delinquent" in place of "criminal" and so on—show the gradual erosion of the old common-sense attitude, as scientific knowledge advances. At the level of common-sense, a Spinozist may argue, we adjust our moral attitudes haphazardly, regarding people as free agents whenever we happen to be ignorant of the causes of their actions. But the scientist-philosopher, who tries before all things to achieve intellectual consistency in his thinking, cannot be content with the illogicalities of ordinary usage; he can demonstrate to himself that the range of actions which he can regard as avoidable progressively contracts as scientific knowledge advances; and, secondly, that ordinary usage provides no constant and objectively justifiable principle by which he can distinguish avoidable and morally blameworthy actions from other natural events. As a philosopher, he is conscious of our actual present state of relative ignorance, and he can envisage the possibility of an indefinite advance in the understanding of the causes of human behaviour, whether or not in any particular case the causes have in fact been discovered, or are likely soon to be discovered. According to Spinoza, we know *a priori,* and can prove, that human knowledge must at all stages be limited and incomplete; otherwise it would cease to be human knowledge and would become divine knowledge. But equally we know *a priori* what ignorance is and what complete knowledge would be, for we could not otherwise distinguish, as we do, between adequate and inadequate knowledge; we are able to recognize the inadequacy of our present scientific knowledge in respect of human behaviour, and we can envisage the possibility of our knowledge becoming progressively less inadequate; and this is precisely what the philosopher is doing in maintaining the determinist thesis.

Throughout all his writing, whether on political, religious or purely ethical subjects, Spinoza is constantly pleading, in opposition to traditional theology and respectable opinion, for a purely naturalistic and scientific study of all aspects of human thought and behaviour; he is constantly insisting that emotional and moral attitudes, which can only be the reflections of our subjective desires and fears, must obstruct us in understanding the causes of our unhappiness and folly, and so must obstruct us in the pursuit of wisdom. If we would improve human beings, we must study the natural laws of their behaviour as dispassionately as we would study the behaviour of trees and horses. In the twentieth century this thesis, although not always combined with belief in strict determinism, is very familiar in theory, though still uncommon in practice; in the nineteenth century it earned for Spinoza the admiration of Flaubert and of many others, who in their time more easily foresaw the necessity of a natural history of human religion, and of moral codes and social structures. But in the seventeenth century, which was still throughout Europe predominantly an age of belief in supernatural causes, a purely naturalistic approach to human affairs was terrifying, and to the ordinary dilettante (as Spinoza's correspondence shows) was almost unintelligible. Spinoza, alone of the great figures of that age, seems somehow to have anticipated modern conceptions of the scale of the universe, and of man's relatively infinitesimal place within the vast system; in Descartes and in Leibniz, and in most of the literature of the age, one is still in various ways given the impression of a Universe in which human beings on this earth are the privileged centre around whom everything is arranged, almost, as it were, for their benefit; whatever their professed doctrine, almost everyone still implicitly thought in terms of a man-centred universe, although Pascal also, in some moments of conflict, had this inhuman vision of human beings as not especially significant or distinguished parts of an infinite system, which seems in itself vastly more worthy of respect and attention than any of our transitory interests and adventures. To Spinoza it seemed that men can attain happiness and dignity only by identifying themselves, through their knowledge and understanding, with the whole order of nature, and by submerging their individual interests in this understanding. I suggest—and this is no more than speculative interpretation—that it is this aspect of Spinoza's naturalism, the surviving spirit of Lucretius against a greater background of knowledge, which most shocked and baffled his contemporaries and successors, and which seemed the most "hideous" feature of "the hideous hypothesis."

WISDOM AND THE LIFE OF THE FREE MAN

We can be said to be free in so far as we have a clear and distinct idea of the causes of our own states, physical and mental; to have this adequate knowledge of causes necessarily involves a more complete knowledge of Nature as a whole. In so far as we acquire more knowledge of Nature, and therefore of ourselves as parts of Nature, we necessarily cease to desire, love and hate particular things, and we cease to be in any way affected by the particular things and persons around us; for these loves and hates arise by the association of ideas out of our ignorance of the true causes of our pleasures and pains. The free and wise man therefore feels morally and emotionally neutral towards the particular things and persons around him, both because he understands why they are what they are and why they cannot be otherwise, and because he no longer ignorantly sees them as the true causes of his own pleasures and pains. The free man's pleasures must be generated spontaneously, as the consciousness of his own free activity and not as the effects of external causes. The greater the real activity and vitality of his body, the greater the real activity and vitality of his mind; and the converse is also necessarily true. In so far as a person is functioning freely and is uninhibited by external causes, he will necessarily be in a state of pleasure (*laetitia*), since pleasure in this sense is the reflexion of the vitality of the whole person. It follows that the wise and free man will avoid pain and all the so-called virtues of asceticism; his aim will necessarily be *"bene agere ac laetari"*—"to act well and to rejoice." Spinoza, so austere in his personality and life, repudiates all the values of self-sacrifice and self-denial and the gloomier, more unnatural Christian virtues, such as humility, repentance, and remorse; "there cannot be too much joy: it is always good: but melancholy is always bad" (*Ethics Pt.* IV. *Prop.* XLII). Pain, and the painful emotions (e.g. hatred, envy, fear), are always and necessarily signs of weakness, or of lack of freedom; they are reflexions of some inhibition of vitality by external causes; particular pleasures in the narrow sense (*titillatio*) may be excessive, as upsetting the balance and well-being of the whole organism; but pleasure in the sense of conscious well-being and enjoyed activity is the characteristic of the free or intelligent man's life; to act well is fully to enjoy oneself, and fully to enjoy oneself is to act well. Suffering, guilt, and remorse are morbid symptoms, and virtue is sanity and health. Anything which is an aid to the development of knowledge and intelligence, and is therefore an aid to power and freedom, is necessarily good for the individual, and is to be pursued in the interests of self-preservation; anything which obstructs knowledge is self-destructive, "bad" in the only quasi-objective sense of the word, as diminishing the freedom and vitality of the individual. Social and political instability and personal rivalries clearly interfere with that independence and detachment which the free man requires for the pursuit of knowledge. The free man has therefore every interest in upholding the necessary conventions of a peaceful society. Spinoza argues, as so many moralists have argued, that in so far as our desires, loves and hates are not directed towards particular things and persons around us, we are not involved in conflicts with other persons; the happiness of the free man, which is the free exercise of his understanding, is essentially uncompetitive, and requires from others only peacefulness and respect for law and order. The free man, so far from being competitive, has a positive interest in promoting the happiness and intellectual emancipation of his neighbours; and this must be part of Spinoza's theoretical justification of his own lifework. In so far as the members of any society are governed by passive emotions, there must necessarily arise conflicts of interest in the society which must threaten the free man and his self-preservation and self-advancement in knowledge. It is therefore the direct interest of the enlightened and the free man to work (as Spinoza himself methodically did work) to emancipate his fellow-citizens from superstition and ignorance and from the blind hatreds which superstitions engender. "Whatever helps to maintain the common society of men, or whatever brings it about that men live together in peace and agreement, is useful, and, on the other hand, what produces discord in the state, is bad" (*Ethics Pt*. IV. *Prop*. XL). The happy, wise, and free man (and no one can qualify for one of these three titles without qualifying for the others) is incapable of hating his fellow men, and will, like a Christian, repay hatred, rage and contempt with love; but the reason for this secular saintliness is simply a superior prudence. Hatred is in itself disagreeable and bad, and the wise man knows that the reciprocation of hatreds must produce a greater hatred. The true philosopher will be uninfluenced by fear and hope, and unaffected by the superstitious fears and hopes of the anthropomorphic religions, with their futile imaginations of jealous personal Gods allotting rewards and punishments. He will know that "virtue is its own reward," in the strict sense that the best life is necessarily the happiest life; the intrinsic satisfactions of the free mind are the most lasting and secure. As free men, we do not need to be bribed, by the hope of rewards or the fear of punishments, like children; no external sanction is needed in addition to the supreme inner satisfaction which arises from a rational peace of mind. Spinoza writes with disgust and contempt of the appeal of conventional religious morality to supernatural rewards and punishments, as being appeals which are essentially squalid and unworthy of adult intelligence. He had, of course, been criticized, as most secular and humane moralists have been, on the grounds that, by denying the possibility of a personal God acting as moral umpire and prize-giver, he was undermining morality and opening the way to chaos and debauch. In his contemptuous letters of reply he allowed himself to be less unimpassioned than anywhere else in his extant writings.

"A free man thinks of nothing less than of death, and his wisdom is a meditation not of death but of life" (*Ethics Pt.* IV. *Prop.* LXVII). This famous sentence emerges directly from the argument and is certainly not rhetorical ornament. The strict proof provided is very simple: "A free man, that is, one who lives according to the dictate of reason alone, is not led by the fear of death (*Ethics Pt.* IV. *Prop.* LXIII), but directly desires what is good (*Coroll.* of same *Prop.*), that is (*Ethics Pt.* IV. *Prop.* XXIV), to act, to live, and preserve his being on the basis of seeking what is useful to him. And therefore he thinks of nothing less than of death, but his wisdom is a meditation of life. *Q.E.D.*" (*Ethics Pt.* IV. *Prop.* LXVII. *Dem.*). The free man is wholly absorbed in the development and exercise of his own powers of mind and body, and is always aware of his status as a finite mode of Nature. As he becomes less and less affected by passive emotions, and in proportion as his knowledge increases, he becomes more and more identified in his own mind with the whole process of Nature: the order of his ideas approximates more and more closely to the order of ideas which constitutes God's thought; he becomes progressively detached from his particular interests as a particular person interacting with a particular environment, and he comes to view all things *sub specie aeternitatis.* His real happiness (*beatitudo*) consists in this contemplation of the whole machinery and system of Nature, and in reflecting within his own mind the whole intellectual order of things. Pain and evil cannot affect him, unless his understanding is imperfect, and unless he is affected by external causes which he does not fully understand. The wise man, pursuing, as all men must pursue, his own preservation and happiness, removes every obstruction to the development of his own understanding; he will need mutual aid, friendship and an ordered society, and he will do what is necessary to promote them. Ideally he requires a community of these secular saints, of disinterested philosopher-scientists bound together by "the love which acknowledges as its cause freedom of mind" (*Ethics Pt.* IV. *Appendix, Section* XIX); but, the human condition being always imperfection, he will have to accept and sustain the compromise of a system of law and punishment, which for perfectly wise men would be unnecessary. A wise man is still only a man, and therefore only relatively wise and (by definition) not perfect or all-powerful; he cannot be wholly free, rational, and self-contained. "Human power is greatly limited and infinitely surpassed by the power of external causes, and therefore we do not have absolute power of adapting things which are outside for our use. But we shall bear with equanimity those things which happen to us and which are contrary to what our interest demands, if we are conscious that we have done our duty and cannot extend our actual power to such an extent as to avoid these things, and further, that we are a part of Nature as a whole, and we follow its order. If we understand this clearly and distinctly, that part of us which is called our understanding or intelligence, that is, the best part in us, will entirely acquiesce in this, and will strive to persist in this acquiescence. For in so far as we understand, we can desire nothing other than what is necessary, and we cannot entirely acquiesce in anything other than the truth" (*Ethics Pt.* IV. *Appendix* XXXII). In so far as we are intelligent, frustration and the restless emotions cannot occur, because, realizing the necessity of our position, we have no image of how things might be otherwise, and we therefore have no unsatisfied desires and ambitions. We acknowledge, not (as Leibniz suggested) that all is for the best in the best of all possible worlds, but that all must be as it is in the only possible world. The characteristic virtues of the free man, who thus resolutely sees things as they are and who takes an active pleasure in understanding the infinite concatenation of causes, are strength of mind (*fortitudo*) and nobility (*generositas*); nobility is a form of disinterestedness, not unlike Aristotle's supreme virtue of magnificence (*megaloprepeia*), and is a rational disdain of particular interests and of small worldly calculations. Spinoza carefully distinguishes the strength of mind of the free man from the virtues of stoicism; it is not an exercise of will, but rather the intellectual virtue of confronting the facts impassively, without sentiment and without the intrusion of subjective fears and hopes; it is the virtue of objectivity, an acquiescence in the rationally ascertained truth, however personally disagreeable the truth may seem; for any other attitude to experience must seem to the free man merely stupid and childish, like the attitude of someone who kicks a chair because it causes him to stumble.

S W I F T

[*1667–1747*]

THE POET, SATIRIST, TORY PAMPHLETEER, DEFENDER OF IRELAND, AND DEAN OF
St. Patrick's in Dublin is now so identified with Gulliver that we are in danger of losing sight of Jonathan Swift. Dr. Leavis here addresses himself to
Swift's greatness as a writer. He does not discuss *Gulliver's Travels,* not even
the fourth part on the Houyhnhnms, because (he says) it exhibits too fully
Swift's taste for "negation." Gulliver's disgust for man is indeed overwhelming, but it is a generic, not simply a personal, disgust. The book fascinates
and repels because it embraces feelings that we all hesitate to acknowledge;
as Freud says, "Negation is a way of taking account of what is repressed."
The ideal essay on Swift, then, would analyze Swift's success in putting before us what *we* wish to negate. Nevertheless, Leavis' strategy gives the
reader what he needs first and foremost; a way of considering Swift's extraordinary mastery of English.

Dr. Leavis, formerly University Reader in English at Cambridge, is a
critic of international reputation.

F . R .   L E A V I S

The Irony of Swift

SWIFT IS A GREAT ENGLISH WRITER. FOR OPENING WITH THIS TRUISM I HAVE A reason: I wish to discuss Swift's writings—to examine what they are; and they are (as the extant commentary bears witness) of such a kind that it is peculiarly difficult to discuss them without shifting the focus of discussion to the kind of man that Swift was. What is most interesting in them does not so clearly belong to the realm of things made and detached that literary criticism, which has certainly not the less its duties towards Swift, can easily avoid turning—unawares, and that is, degenerating—into something else. In the attempt to say what makes these writings so remarkable, reference to the man who wrote is indeed necessary; but there are distinctions. For instance, one may (it appears), having offered to discuss the nature and import of Swift's satire, find oneself countering imputations of misanthropy with the argument that Swift earned the love of Pope, Arbuthnot, Gay, several other men and two women: this should not be found necessary by the literary critic. But the irrelevancies of Thackeray and of his castigator, the late Charles Whibley— irrelevancies not merely from the point of view of literary criticism—are too gross to need placarding; more insidious deviations are possible.

The reason for the opening truism is also the reason for the choice of title.

The Irony of Swift

To direct the attention upon Swift's irony gives, I think, the best chance of dealing adequately, without deviation or confusion, with what is essential in his work. But it involves also (to anticipate an objection) a slight to the classical status of *Gulliver's Travels*, a book which, though it may represent Swift's most impressive achievement in the way of complete creation—the thing achieved and detached—does not give the best opportunities for examining his irony. And *Gulliver's Travels,* one readily agrees, hasn't its classical status for nothing. But neither is it for nothing that, suitably abbreviated, it has become a classic for children. What for the adult reader constitutes its peculiar force—what puts it in so different a class from *Robinson Crusoe*—resides for the most part in the fourth book (to less extent in the third). The adult may re-read the first two parts, as he may *Robinson Crusoe,* with great interest, but his interest, apart from being more critically conscious, will not be of a different order from the child's. He will, of course, be aware of an ingenuity of political satire in *Lilliput,* but the political satire is, unless for historians, not very much alive to-day. And even the more general satire characteristic of the second book will not strike him as very subtle. His main satisfaction, a great deal enhanced, no doubt, by the ironic seasoning, will be that which Swift, the student of the *Mariner's Magazine* and of travellers' relations, aimed to supply in the bare precision and the matter-of-fact realness of his narrative.

But what in Swift is most important, the disturbing characteristic of his genius, is a peculiar emotional intensity; that which, in *Gulliver,* confronts us in the Struldbrugs and the Yahoos. It is what we find ourselves contemplating when elsewhere we examine his irony. To lay the stress upon an emotional intensity should be matter of commonplace: actually, in routine usage, the acepted word for Swift is "intellectual." We are told, for instance, that his is pre-eminently "intellectual satire" (though we are not told what satire is). For this formula the best reason some commentators can allege is the elaboration of analogies—their "exact and elaborate propriety"—in *Gulliver.* But a muddled perception can hardly be expected to give a clear account of itself; the stress on Swift's "intellect" (Mr. Herbert Read alludes to his "mighty intelligence") registers, it would appear, a confused sense, not only of the mental exercise involved in his irony, but of the habitually critical attitude he maintains towards the world, and of the negative emotions he specializes in.

From "critical" to "negative" in this last sentence is, it will be observed, a shift of stress. There are writings of Swift where "critical" is the more obvious word (and where "intellectual" may seem correspondingly apt)—notably, the pamphlets or pamphleteering essays in which the irony is instrumental, directed and limited to a given end. The *Argument Against Abolishing Christianity* and the *Modest Proposal,* for instance, are discussible in the terms in which satire is commonly discussed: as the criticism of vice, folly or other aberration, by some kind of reference to positive standards. But even here, even in the *Argument,* where Swift's ironic intensity undeniably directs itself to the defence of something that he is intensely concerned to defend, the effect is essentially negative. The positive itself appears only negatively—a kind of skeletal presence, rigid enough, but without life or body; a necessary pre-condition, as it were, of directed negation. The intensity is purely destructive.

The point may be enforced by the obvious contrast with Gibbon—except that between Swift's irony and Gibbon's the contrast is so complete that any one point is difficult to isolate. Gibbon's irony, in the fifteenth chapter, may be aimed against, instead of for, Christianity, but contrasted with Swift's it is an assertion of faith. The decourously insistent pattern of Gibbonian prose insinuates a solidarity with the reader (the implied solidarity in Swift is itself ironical—a means to betrayal), establishes an understanding and habituates to certain assumptions. The reader, it is implied, is an eighteenth-century gentleman ("rational," "candid," "polite," "elegant," "humane"); eighteen hundred years ago he would have been a pagan gentleman, living by these same standards (those of absolute civilization); by these standards (present everywhere in the stylized prose and adroitly emphasized at key points in such phrases as "the polite Augustus," "the elegant mythology of the Greeks") the Jews and early Christians are seen to have been ignorant fanatics, uncouth and probably dirty. Gibbon as a historian of Christianity had, we know, limitations; but the positive standards by reference to which his irony works represent something impressively realized in eighteenth-century civilization; impressively "there" too in the grandiose, assured and ordered elegance of his history. (When, on the other hand, Lytton Strachey, with a Gibbonian period or phrase or word, a "remarkable," "oddly" or "curious," assures us that he feels an amused superiority to these Victorian puppets, he succeeds only in conveying his personal conviction that he feels amused and superior.)

Gibbon's irony, then, habituates and reassures, ministering to a kind of judicial certitude or complacency. Swift's is essentially a matter of surprise and negation; its function is to defeat habit, to intimidate and to demoralize. What he assumes in the *Argument* is not so much a common acceptance of Christianity as that the reader will be ashamed to have to recognize how fundamentally unchristian his actual assumptions, motives and attitudes are. And in general the implication is that it would shame people if they were made to recognize themselves unequivocally. If one had to justify this irony according to the conventional notion of satire, then its satiric efficacy would be to make comfortable non-recognition, the unconsciousness of habit, impossible.

The Irony of Swift

A method of surprise does not admit of description in an easy formula. Surprise is a perpetually varied accompaniment of the grave, dispassionate, matter-of-fact tone in which Swift delivers his intensities. The dissociation of emotional intensity from its usual accompaniments inhibits the automatic defence-reaction:

> He is a Presbyterian in politics, and an atheist in religion; but he chooses at present to whore with a Papist.
> What bailiff would venture to arrest Mr. Steele, now he has the honour to be your representative? and what bailiff ever scrupled it before?

Or inhibits, let us say, the normal response; since "defence" suggests that it is the "victim" whose surprise we should be contemplating, whereas it is our own, whether Swift's butt is Wharton or the atheist or mankind in general. "But satire, being levelled at all, is never resented for an offence, by any, since every individual makes bold to understand it of others, and very wisely removes his particular part of the burden upon the shoulders of the World, which are broad enough and able to bear it." There is, of course, no contradiction here; a complete statement would be complex. But, actually, the discussion of satire in terms of offence and castigation, victim and castigator, is unprofitable, though the idea of these has to be taken into account. What we are concerned with (the reminder is especially opportune) is an arrangement of words on the page and their effects—the emotions, attitudes and ideas that they organize.

Our reaction, as Swift says, is not that of the butt or victim; nevertheless, it necessarily entails some measure of sympathetic self-projection. We more often, probably, feel the effect of the words as an intensity in the castigator than as an effect upon a victim: the dissociation of animus from the usual signs defines for our contemplation a peculiarly intense contempt or disgust. When, as sometimes we have to do, we talk in terms of effect on the victim, then "surprise" becomes an obviously apt word; he is to be betrayed, again and again, into an incipient acquiescence:

> *Sixthly.* This would be a great Inducement to Marriage, which all wise Nations have either encouraged by Rewards, or enforced by Laws and Penalties. It would increase the Care and Tenderness of Mothers towards their Children, when they were sure of a Settlement for Life, to the poor Babes, provided in some Sort by the Publick, to their annual Profit instead of Expence; we should soon see an honest Emulation among the married Women, *which of them could bring the fattest Child to the Market.* Men would become as *fond* of their Wives, during the Time of their Pregnancy, as they are now of their *Mares* in Foal, their *Cows* in Calf, or *Sows* when they are ready to farrow, nor offer to beat or kick them (as is too *frequent* a Practice) for fear of a Miscarriage.

[453]

F. R. Leavis

The implication is: "This, as you so obligingly demonstrate, is the only kind of argument that appeals to you; here are your actual faith and morals. How, on consideration, do you like the smell of them?"

But when in reading the *Modest Proposal* we are most engaged, it is an effect directly upon ourselves that we are most disturbingly aware of. The dispassionate, matter-of-fact tone induces a feeling and a motion of assent, while the burden, at the same time, compels the feelings appropriate to rejection, and in the contrast—the tension—a remarkably disturbing energy is generated. A sense of an extraordinary energy is the general effect of Swift's irony. The intensive means just indicated are reinforced extensively in the continuous and unpredictable movement of the attack, which turns this way and that, comes now from one quarter and now from another, inexhaustibly surprising—making again an odd contrast with the sustained and level gravity of the tone. If Swift does for a moment appear to settle down to a formula it is only in order to betray; to induce a trust in the solid ground before opening the pitfall.

"His *Tale of a Tub* has little resemblance to his other pieces. It exhibits a vehemence and rapidity of mind, a copiousness of images, a vivacity of diction, such as he afterwards never possessed, or never exerted. It is of a mode so distinct and peculiar, that it must be considered by itself; what is true of that, is not true of anything else he has written." What Johnson is really testifying to here is the degree in which the *Tale of a Tub* is characteristic and presents the qualities of Swift's genius in concentrated form. "That he has in his works no metaphors, as has been said, is not true," says Johnson a sentence or two later, "but his few metaphors seem to be received rather by necessity than choice." This last judgment may at any rate serve to enforce Johnson's earlier observation that in the *Tale of a Tub* Swift's powers function with unusual freedom. For the "copiousness of images" that Johnson constates is, as the phrase indicates, not a matter of choice but of essential genius. And, as a matter of fact, in this "copiousness of images" the characteristics that we noted in discussing Swift's pampleteering irony have their supreme expression.

It is as if the gift applied in *Gulliver* to a very limiting task—directed and confined by a scheme uniting a certain consistency in analogical elaboration with verisimilitude—were here enjoying free play. For the bent expressing itself in this "copiousness" is clearly fundamental. It shows itself in the spontaneous metaphorical energy of Swift's prose—in the image, action or blow that, leaping out of the prosaic manner, continually surprises and disconcerts the reader: "such a man, truly wise, creams off Nature, leaving the sour and the dregs for philosophy and reason to lap up." It appears with as convincing a spontaneity in the sardonic vivacity of comic vision that characterizes the

[454]

narrative, the presentment of action and actor. If, then, the continual elaborate play of analogy is a matter of cultivated habit, it is a matter also of cultivated natural bent, a congenial development. It is a development that would seem to bear a relation to the Metaphysical fashion in verse (Swift was born in 1667). The spirit of it is that of a fierce and insolent game, but a game to which Swift devotes himself with a creative intensity.

> And whereas the mind of man, when he gives the spur and bridle to his thoughts, does never stop, but naturally sallies out into both extremes of high and low, of good and evil, his first flight of fancy commonly transports him to ideas of what is more perfect, finished, and exalted, till, having soared out of his own reach and sight, not well perceiving how near the frontiers of height and depth border upon each other, with the same course and wing he falls down plump into the lowest bottom of things, like one who travels the east into the west, or like a straight line drawn by its own length into a circle. Whether a tincture of malice in our natures makes us fond of furnishing every bright idea with its reverse, or whether reason, reflecting upon the sum of things, can, like the sun, serve only to enlighten one half of the globe, leaving the other half by necessity under shade and darkness, or whether fancy, flying up to the imagination of what is highest and best, becomes overshort, and spent, and weary, and suddenly falls, like a dead bird of paradise, to the ground. . . .

One may (without difficulty) resist the temptation to make the point by saying that this is poetry; one is still tempted to say that the use to which so exuberant an energy is put is a poet's. "Exuberant" seems, no doubt, a paradoxical word to apply to an energy used as Swift uses his; but the case is essentially one for paradoxical descriptions.

In his use of negative materials—negative emotions and attitudes—there is something that it is difficult not to call creative, though the aim always is destructive. Not all the materials, of course, are negative; the "bird of paradise" in the passage above is alive as well as dead. Effects of this kind, often much more intense, are characteristic of the *Tale of a Tub,* where surprise and contrast operate in modes that there is some point in calling poetic. "The most heterogeneous ideas are yoked by violence together"—and in the juxtaposition intensity is generated.

"Paracelsus brought a squadron of stink-pot-flingers from the snowy mountains of Rhaetia"—this (which comes actually from the *Battle of the Books*) does not represent what I have in mind; it is at once too simple and too little charged with animus. Swift's intensities are intensities of rejection and negation; his poetic juxtapositions are, characteristically, destructive in intention, and when they most seem creative of energy are most successful in spoiling,

[455]

reducing and destroying. Sustained "copiousness," continually varying, and concentrating surprise in sudden local foci, cannot be represented in short extracts; it must suffice here to say that this kind of thing may be found at a glance on almost any page:

> Meantime it is my earnest request that so useful an undertaking may be entered upon (if their Majesties please) with all convenient speed, because I have a strong inclination before I leave the world to taste a blessing which we mysterious writers can seldom reach till we have got into our graves, whether it is that fame, being a fruit grafted on the body, can hardly grow and much less ripen till the stock is in the earth, or whether she be a bird of prey, and is lured among the rest to pursue after the scent of a carcass, or whether she conceives her trumpet sounds best and farthest when she stands on a tomb, by the advantage of a rising ground and the echo of a hollow vault.

It is, of course, possible, to adduce Swift's authority for finding that his negations carry with them a complementary positive—an implicit assertion. But (*pace* Charles Whibley) the only thing in the nature of a positive that most readers will find convincingly present is self-assertion—*superbia*. Swift's way of demonstrating his superiority is to destroy, but he takes a positive delight in his power. And that the reader's sense of the negativeness of the *Tale of a Tub* is really qualified comes out when we refer to the Yahoos and the Struldbrugs for a test. The ironic detachment is of such a kind as to re-assure us that this savage exhibition is mainly a game, played because it is the insolent pleasure of the author: "demonstration of superiority" is as good a formula as any for its prevailing spirit. Nevertheless, about a superiority that asserts itself in this way there is something disturbingly odd, and again and again in the *Tale of a Tub* we come on intensities that shift the stress decisively and remind us how different from Voltaire Swift is, even in his most complacent detachment.

I propose to examine in illustration a passage from the *Digression Concerning the Original, the Use, and Improvement of Madness in a Commonwealth* (i.e., Section IX). It will have, in the nature of the case, to be a long one, but since it exemplifies at the same time all Swift's essential characteristics, its length will perhaps be tolerated. I shall break up the passage for convenience of comment, but, except for the omission of nine or ten lines in the second instalment, quotation will be continuous:

> For the brain in its natural position and state of serenity disposeth its owner to pass his life in the common forms, without any thought of subduing multitudes to his own power, his reasons, or his visions, and the more he shapes his understanding by the pattern of human learning, the less he is inclined to form parties after his particular notions, because that instructs him in his

private infirmities, as well as in the stubborn ignorance of the people. But when a man's fancy gets astride on his reason, when imagination is at cuffs with the senses, and common understanding as well as common sense is kicked out of doors, the first proselyte he makes is himself; and when that is once compassed, the difficulty is not so great in bringing over others, a strong delusion always operating from without as vigorously as from within. For cant and vision are to the ear and the eye the same that tickling is to the touch. Those entertainments and pleasures we most value in life are such as dupe and play the wag with the senses. For if we take an examination of what is generally understood by happiness, as it has respect either to the understanding or to the senses, we shall find all its properties and adjuncts will herd under this short definition, that it is a perpetual possession of being well deceived.

Swift's ant-like energy—the business-like air, obsessed intentness and unpredictable movement—have already had an effect. We are not, at the end of this instalment, as sure that we know just what his irony is doing as we were at the opening. Satiric criticism of sectarian "enthusiasm" by reference to the "common forms"—the Augustan standards—is something that, in Swift, we can take as very seriously meant. But in the incessant patter of the argument we have (helped by such things as, at the end, the suggestion of animus in that oddly concrete "herd") a sense that direction and tone are changing. Nevertheless, the change of tone for which the next passage is most remarkable comes as a disconcerting surprise:

> And first, with relation to the mind or understanding, it is manifest what mighty advantages fiction has over truth, and the reason is just at our elbow; because imagination can build nobler scenes and produce more wonderful revolutions than fortune or Nature will be at the expense to furnish. . . . Again, if we take this definition of happiness and examine it with reference to the senses, it will be acknowledged wonderfully adept. How sad and insipid do all objects accost us that are not conveyed in the vehicle of delusion! How shrunk is everything as it appears in the glass of Nature, so that if it were not for the assistance of artificial mediums, false lights, refracted angles, varnish, and tinsel, there would be a mighty level in the felicity and enjoyments of mortal men. If this were seriously considered by the world, as I have a certain reason to suspect it hardly will, men would no longer reckon among their high points of wisdom the art of exposing weak sides and publishing infirmities—an employment, in my opinion, neither better nor worse than that of unmasking, which, I think, has never been allowed fair usage, either in the world or the playhouse.

The suggestion of changing direction does not, in the first part of this passage, bring with it anything unsettling: from ridicule of "enthusiasm" to ridicule of human capacity for self-deception is an easy transition. The reader, as a matter of fact, begins to settle down to the habit, the steady drift of this irony, and is completely unprepared for the sudden change of tone and reversal of attitude in the two sentences beginning "How sad and insipid do all objects," etc. Exactly what the change means or is, it is difficult to be certain (and that is of the essence of the effect). But the tone has certainly a personal intensity and the ironic detachment seems suddenly to disappear. It is as if one found Swift in the place—at the point of view—where one expected to find his butt. But the ambiguously mocking sentence with which the paragraph ends reinforces the uncertainty.

The next paragraph keeps the reader for some time in uneasy doubt. The irony has clearly shifted its plane, but in which direction is the attack going to develop? Which, to be safe, must one dissociate oneself from, "credulity" or "curiosity"?

> In the proportion that credulity is a more peaceful possession of the mind than curiosity, so far preferable is that wisdom which converses about the surface to that pretended philosophy which enters into the depths of things and then comes gravely back with informations and discoveries, that in the inside they are good for nothing. The two senses to which all objects first address themselves are the sight and the touch; these never examine further than the colour, the shape, the size, and whatever other qualities dwell or are drawn by art upon the outward of bodies; and then comes reason officiously, with tools for cutting, and opening, and mangling, and piercing, offering to demonstrate that they are not of the same consistence quite through. Now I take all this to be the last degree of perverting Nature, one of whose eternal laws is to put her best furniture forward. And therefore, in order to save the charges of all such expensive anatomy for the time to come, I do here think fit to inform the reader that in such conclusions as these reason is certainly in the right; and that in most corporeal beings which have fallen under my cognisance the outside hath been infinitely preferable to the in, whereof I have been further convinced from some late experiments. Last week I saw a woman flayed, and you will hardly believe how much it altered her person for the worse.

The peculiar intensity of that last sentence is, in its own way, so decisive that it has for the reader the effect of resolving uncertainty in general. The disturbing force of the sentence is a notable instance of a kind already touched on: repulsion is intensified by the momentary co-presence, induced by the tone, of incipient and incompatible feelings (or motions) of acceptance. And that Swift feels the strongest animus against "curiosity" is now beyond all doubt. The natural corollary would seem to be that "credulity," standing ironically for the "common forms"—the sane, socially sustained, common-sense illusions—is the positive that the reader must associate himself with and rest on for safety. The next half-page steadily and (to all appearances) unequivocally confirms this assumption:

> Yesterday I ordered the carcass of a beau to be stripped in my presence, when we were all amazed to find so many unsuspected faults under one suit of clothes. Then I laid open his brain, his heart, and his spleen, but I plainly perceived at every operation that the farther we proceeded, we found the defects increase upon us in number and bulk; from all of which I justly formed this conclusion to myself, that whatever philosopher or projector can find out an art to sodder and patch up the flaws and imperfections of Nature, will deserve much better of mankind and teach us a much more useful science than that, so much in present esteem, of widening and exposing them (like him who held anatomy to be the ultimate end of physic). And he whose fortunes and dispositions have placed him in a convenient station to enjoy the fruits of this noble art, he that can with Epicurus content his ideas with the films and images that fly off upon his senses from the superficies of things, such a man, truly wise, creams off Nature, leaving the sour and the dregs for philosophy and reason to lap up.

Assumption has become habit, and has been so nourished that few readers note anything equivocal to trouble them in that last sentence: the concrete force of "creams off," "dregs" and "lap up" seems unmistakably to identify Swift with an intense animus against "philosophy and reason" (understood implicitly to stand for "curiosity" the anatomist). The reader's place, of course, is with Swift.

The trap is sprung in the last sentence of the paragraph:

> This is the sublime and refined point of felicity called the possession of being well-deceived, the serene peaceful state of being a fool among knaves.

What is left? The next paragraph begins significantly: "But to return to madness." This irony may be critical, but "critical" turns out, in no very long run, to be indistinguishable from "negative." The positives disappear. Even when, as in the Houyhnhnms, they seem to be more substantially present, they disappear under our "curiosity." The Houyhnhnms, of course, stand for Reason, Truth and Nature, the Augustan positives, and it was in deadly earnest that Swift appealed to these; but how little at best they were anything solidly realized, comparison with Pope brings out. Swift did his best for the Houyhnhnms, and they may have all the reason, but the Yahoos have all the life. Gulliver's master "thought Nature and reason were sufficient guides for a reasonable animal," but nature and reason as Gulliver exhibits them are curiously negative, and the reasonable animals appear to have nothing in them to guide. "They have no fondness for their colts or foals, but the care they take in educating them proceeds entirely from the dictates of reason." This freedom from irrational feelings and impulses simplifies other matters too: "their language doth not abound in variety of words, because their wants and passions are fewer than among us." And so conversation, in this model society, is simplified: "nothing passed but what was useful, expressed in the fewest and most significant words . . ." "Courtship, love, presents, jointures, settlements, have no place in their thoughts, or terms whereby to express them in their language. The young couple meet and are joined, merely because it is the determination of their parents and friends: it is what they see done every day, and they look upon it as one of the necessary actions of a reasonable being." The injunction of "temperance, industry, exercise, and cleanliness . . . the lessons enjoined to the young ones of both sexes," seems unnecessary; except possibly for exercise, the usefulness of which would not, perhaps, be immediately apparent to the reasonable young.

The clean skin of the Houyhnhnms, in short, is stretched over a void; instincts, emotions and life, which complicate the problem of cleanliness and decency, are left for the Yahoos with the dirt and the indecorum. Reason, Truth and Nature serve instead; the Houyhnhnms (who scorn metaphysics) find them adequate. Swift too scorned metaphysics, and never found anything better to contend for than a skin, a surface, an outward show. An outward show is, explicitly, all he contends for in the quite unironical *Project for the Advancement of Religion,* and the difference between the reality of religion and the show is, for the author of the *Tale of a Tub,* hardly substantial. Of Jack we are told, "nor could all the world persuade him, as the common phrase is, to eat his victuals like a Christian." It is characteristic of Swift that he should put in these terms, showing a complete incapacity even to guess what religious feeling might be, a genuine conviction that Jack should be made to kneel when receiving the Sacrament.

Of the intensity of this conviction there can be no doubt. The Church of England was the established "common form," and, moreover, was Swift's church: his insane egotism reinforced the savagery with which he fought to maintain this cover over the void, this decent surface. But what the savagery of the passage from the *Digression* shows mainly is Swift's sense of insecurity and of the undisguisable flimsiness of any surface that offered.

The case, of course, is more complex. In the passage examined the "surface" becomes, at the most savage moment, a human skin. Swift's negative horror, at its most disturbing, becomes one with his disgust-obsession: he cannot bear to be reminded that under the skin there is blood, mess and entrails; and the skin itself, as we know from *Gulliver,* must not be seen from too close. Hypertrophy of the sense of uncleanness, of the instinct of repulsion, is not uncommon; nor is its association with what accompanies it in Swift. What is uncommon is Swift's genius and the paradoxical vitality with which this self-defeat of life—life turned against itself—is manifested. In the *Tale of a Tub* the defeat is also a triumph; the genius delights in its mastery, in its power to destroy, and negation is felt as self-assertion. It is only when time has confirmed Swift in disappointment and brought him to more intimate contemplation of physical decay that we get the Yahoos and the Struldbrugs.

Here, well on this side of pathology, literary criticism stops. To attempt encroachments would be absurd, and, even if one were qualified, unprofitable. No doubt psychopathology and medicine have an interesting commentary to offer, but their help is not necessary. Swift's genius belongs to literature, and its appreciation to literary criticism.

We have, then, in his writings probably the most remarkable expression of negative feelings and attitudes that literature can offer—the spectacle of creative powers (the paradoxical description seems right) exhibited consistently in negation and rejection. His verse demands an essay to itself, but fits in readily with what has been said. "In poetry," he reports of the Houyhnhnms, "they must be allowed to excel all other mortals; wherein the justness of their similes and the minuteness as well as exactness of their descriptions are, indeed, inimitable. Their verses abound very much in both of these. . . ." The actuality of presentment for which Swift is notable, in prose as well as verse, seems always to owe its convincing "justness" to, at his least actively malicious, a coldly intense scrutiny, a potentially hostile attention. "To his domesticks," says Johnson, "he was naturally rough; and a man of rigorous temper, with that vigilance of minute attention which his works discover, must have been a master that few could bear." *Instructions to Servants* and the *Polite Conversation* enforce obviously the critical bearing and felicity of Johnson's remark.

A great writer—yes; that account still imposes itself as fitting, though his greatness is no matter of moral grandeur or human centrality; our sense of it is merely a sense of great force. And this force, as we feel it, is conditioned by frustration and constriction; the channels of life have been blocked and perverted. That we should be so often invited to regard him as a moralist and an idealist would seem to be mainly a witness to the power of vanity, and the part that vanity can play in literary appreciation: *saeva indignatio* is an indulgence that solicits us all, and the use of literature by readers and critics for the projection of nobly suffering selves is familiar. No doubt, too, it is pleasant to believe that unusual capacity for egotistic animus means unusual distinction of intellect; but, as we have seen, there is no reason to lay stress on intellect in Swift. His work does indeed exhibit an extraordinary play of mind; but it is not great intellectual force that is exhibited in his indifference to the problems raised—in, for instance, the *Voyage to the Houyhnhnms*—by his use of the concept, or the word, "Nature." It is not merely that he had an Augustan contempt for metaphysics; he shared the shallowest complacencies of Augustan common sense: his irony might destroy these, but there is no conscious criticism.

He was, in various ways, curiously unaware—the reverse of clairvoyant. He is distinguished by the intensity of his feelings, not by insight into them, and he certainly does not impress us as a mind in possession of its experience.

We shall not find Swift remarkable for intelligence if we think of Blake.

G O E T H E

[*1749–1832*]

THOSE WHO MUST READ *Faust* IN TRANSLATION WILL APPRECIATE ERICH HELLER'S use of *Hamlet,* a play with which we are all familiar, in discussing Goethe's attitude toward tragedy. In Heller's view the "unassimilable contrariety" in things did not exist for Goethe. He could not, for example, comprehend the situation of a man like Hamlet, for whom the wellspring of action had been tainted, who could have counted himself king of infinite space were it not for his bad dreams. But Heller does more than reveal Goethe's limitations; he also shows the fruitful polarity in Goethe's temperament, the antithesis between the public man and his "daimon," his creative self. The Herr Geheimrat, so much a part of the little court at Weimar and so fond of coins, medals, and "dull drawings," made way for the genius within.

Goethe's humanism, "his intuitive certainty that knowledge can only be true as long as it is not in excess of man's feelings," is exemplary for succeeding generations. In his scientific investigations, "he resigns himself, as he says, on reaching the *Urphänomen,* that is, at the boundaries of humanity." Happily, this heroic humanism is, as Heller insists, the quality of the greatest of German lyric poets.

Erich Heller teaches at University College, Swansea, South Wales.

From *The Disinherited Mind* by Erich Heller, 1952. Reprinted by permission of Bowes & Bowes Publishers Ltd. Published in the United States by Farrar, Straus & Cudahy.

ERICH HELLER

Goethe and the Avoidance of Tragedy

In 1797, AFTER A LAPSE OF SEVEN YEARS FOLLOWING THE PUBLICATION OF THE *Fragment: Faust,* and more than twenty years after the completion of the first draft of the dramatic poem, the *Urfaust,* Goethe announced in a letter to Schiller (June 22nd) that, finding himself in a state of acute unrest, he was preparing, as a kind of spiritual sedative, to take up *Faust* once more and to retreat "into that world of symbols, ideas and mists" (June 24th). He begged his friend "to think it over in a sleepless night," and to tell him what he would expect of the whole work and, as it were, "interpret, as a true prophet, his [Goethe's] own dreams" (June 22nd). Goethe must have known that he would arouse some uneasiness in Schiller's methodical mind when he added: "As the various parts of the poem can be treated in different modes if only they fall in with the spirit and the tone of the whole, and as, moreover, this creation is subjective in kind, I shall be able to work at it in odd free moments now and then." Schiller's reply was as prompt as it was suggestive of misgivings. "With all its poetic individualism," he said, "this play cannot escape the demand for symbolic significance. . . . The duality of human nature and the unsuccessful striving for a reconciliation in man between what is divine and what is physical—this is something one cannot lose sight of;

[464]

and just because the story tends towards shrillness and formlessness one does not wish to be arrested within the subject itself, but to be guided by it towards ideas. In brief, the claims made upon *Faust* are at the same time philosophical and poetical, and in whatever direction you may turn, the very nature of the subject will impose upon you a philosophical treatment, and the imagination will have to put up with a period of employment in the service of an idea" (June 23rd).

It is, once again, the issue raised by *Naive und sentimentalische Dichtung.* In that essay, which had appeared in the preceding year, Schiller defended the workings of his own reflective genius against the overpowering spontaneity of Goethe's. This time, Schiller seems to imply, Goethe will have to leave behind the state of innocence, submitting himself to a more complex, more philosophically disciplined inspiration. If it appeared to Schiller that in *Werther,* in *Tasso,* a miraculously preserved innocence, a poetic imagination of almost terrifying integrity, had told the story of a world divided and coming to grief—as though the genius of the tree in Paradise had opened its mouth to announce to the world the news of the Fall—then the continuation of that record could only come from the creature that had eaten the apple. For the hero of *Faust* was no longer the kind of person that Werther was, or Egmont, or Tasso, or Iphigenie, who are all profoundly "naïve"—the word to be understood with its German connotations. One might be tempted to apply to them Pascal's reflection that "the heart has reasons of which the reason knows nothing," were it not for the fact that Pascal meant *reasons* of the heart (Hölderlin had them), tools of the highest *understanding* of the world, whereas Werther, Egmont, Tasso and even Iphigenie, live, with regard to the world, in a state of fundamental incomprehension, varying between the raptures of bliss ("himmelhoch jauchzend") when the heart, wholly immaculate, to use Iphigenie's phrase, enjoys itself, and the agonies of woe ("zu Tode betrübt") when the uncomprehended world interferes. *They do not know*—in the sense in which knowledge means the knowledge of good and evil; they live, not beyond, but before that fatal rift, and thus reflect an essential characteristic of their creator's genius and sensibility. Here is at least one of the roots of Goethe's uniqueness within the European tradition, a uniqueness revealed in achievement as well as in failure. This also accounts for the extremes of Goethe worship (mostly inside Germany) and Goethe rejection (mostly outside Germany, and by critics of the stature of, for instance, Irving Babbitt, Ortega y Gasset, George Santayana, T. S. Eliot).

Any criticism of Goethe requires the utmost tact. Not only is the man so immense—and nothing is more difficult in criticism than to keep alive at every moment that sense of proportion which the very difference in level between creativeness and critical judgment demands; criticism is, alas, an

unaristocratic habit, easily tempted into a false intimacy, in praise and negation alike—but also so much of the perennial discussion about Goethe is so
massively wrongheaded, and so passionate, that it has filled the atmosphere
around him with an abundance of electrical charges, making it all too easy
to produce short circuits. I am saying this because I wish to speak of a limitation in Goethe's range of awareness and of a defect in his sensibility, and because I believe, paradoxically enough, that this limitation lies in the very
boundlessness of his genius, and the defect in the inexhaustible richness of
his sensitivity. It would be preposterous to derive the standards for an assess-
ment of Goethe's achievements from anywhere else but the great classics of
European civilization. Yet it would be futile to seek a place for him in a pattern determined by Homer, or Sophocles, or Virgil, or Dante, or Shakespeare.
His range is too wide, and his gifts too universal ever to find full realization
in one type of work alone, and his genius too diffused ever to concentrate on
a single exemplary, classical achievement; and while in scope he is too vast
ever to represent the character of an age, the mode of his imagination, its
susceptibilities and idiosyncrasies, partake, at the same time, too definitely of
the unresolved problems of the late eighteenth century for him easily to be
acknowledged as being for all times and all places. With regard to Goethe's
position within his own nation, it is very revealing that it could be said with
some justice—as it was said immediately after the Second World War by Karl
Jaspers—"that we came face to face with experiences in which we had no
inclination to read Goethe, but took up Shakespeare, or the Bible, or Aeschylus, if it was possible to read at all."

What was the nature of the experience in the face of which Goethe offered
no help? It was the very kind of experience before which Goethe himself
always proved helpless: the exposure to the manifestations of evil and sin.
"The mere attempt to write tragedy might be my undoing," he once said,
and it was the truth—at least for the greatest part of his life. Among his
dramas there are three dramatic poems which, more than any other dramas
he wrote, established his fame: *Iphigenie, Tasso, Faust.* All of them are potential tragedies, indeed so much so that one may feel that the tragic conclusion could only be avoided at the price of complete artistic conclusiveness.
They show a moving and yet unsatisfactory reluctance of mind and imagination to accept the rule of the road leading to the very centre of human destiny. This is not to imply that in that very centre there dwells, inescapably,
tragedy. But once a man is compelled to penetrate to that central point in
all seriousness, then there is only one region left that stretches, for the European, beyond tragedy. Beyond Hamlet and the rest that is silence, there
stands only Prospero:

[466]

And my ending is despair
Unless I be reliev'd by prayer,
Which pierces so that it assaults
Mercy itself, and frees all faults.

And frees all faults; the German translation of this is: *Alle menschliche Gebrechen,* which, we are told by Goethe, are redeemed by "pure humanity," of which Iphigenie is the embodiment.

Anyone who has ever come under the spell of Goethe's *Iphigenie* knows its power to persuade, to convince and to move. There seems to be no doubt that it is poetically true. But which aspect of poetic truth do we mean? The same that applies to *Antigone* or *King Lear?* No, certainly not. *Iphigenie* is lyrically, but not dramatically true, which is as much as to say that it has the truth of a vision of what life and the world could be if they corresponded to what is best in a great and good soul. It is dramatically not true because the objective world which is the scene of the play is not real enough to offer serious resistance to the realization of that vision. In other words, there is no real evil in that world. All the evil inherent in the mythological pattern taken over from the Greeks is considerably reduced in stature so as to lose an essential degree of reality. The reality of evil asserts itself poetically on only three occasions, which are scattered about the play like three erratic blocks in the gentle groves of human kindness: Iphigenie's story of the horrible deeds perpetrated in her family, Orestes' account of the murder of his mother with the rage of madness that follows, and the *Parzenlied* (the song of the goddesses of Fate). For the rest—and it is all but the whole play—the inexorable hardness of the Greek myth is dissolved into the softer substance of the goodness of human nature.

From the opening monologue of the first act onwards we are sure that, unless the poem were to become grossly incongruous, Iphigenie could not seriously be asked to perform, or indeed seriously consider, human sacrifices, let alone the sacrifice of her own brother. And the much-discussed question of the "cure" of Orestes reveals, through the very wording of the question as suggested by the play, the surprising shift of emphasis from what was once, and is again, the centre of the problem, to a more humane periphery. Cure? Of what? Of a temporary fit of madness? For surely there is no "cure" for the murder of a mother. There is, for the Greeks, only the supreme sacrifice to atone for it, or else the direct intervention of the gods to lift the curse—which is, in spite of all the fundamental differences, nearer the Christian repentance and the forgiving grace than the administering of pure humanity. If the curse on the house of Tantalus and the deed of Orestes are to be taken as real—as real, say, as the murder committed by Macbeth—then Goethe's solution is not dramatically true. We simply have to discard the reality of curse and murder—and, indeed, this oblivion is granted to us by the lyrically soothing climate of Arcadian Tauris itself—we have to accept curse and murder as mythological names for a less spectacular kind of guilt, and finally allow a more vaguely general state of spiritual restlessness to assume the place of any articulate guilt if we are to remain convinced of the effectiveness of a purely human redemption.

Schiller's dramatic instinct sensed this defect of Goethe's Orestes; in criticizing him in terms of purely dramatic considerations, he yet pointed to the profounder issue when he wrote to Goethe (January 22nd, 1802): "Orestes is the most doubtful figure of the drama. There is no Orestes without Furies; and when the cause of his condition does not strike the senses but lies hidden in his mind and emotions, his is too long and monotonous an agony—without an object. Here we are up against one of the limitations of modern drama as compared with ancient tragedy. I wish you could think of a remedy; but bearing in mind the economy of the play, I do not think it likely that you will; for you have indeed done everything that is possible without gods and spirits."

I have said that the theme of *Iphigenie* would lend itself to, indeed invite, a tragic treatment. The reply that the play of Euripides, from whom the story is borrowed, is not a tragedy either would be beside the point, for it is too obvious that Goethe's heroine is a person totally different from Euripides' Iphigenia. Yet there is one Greek tragedy which, in situation and aspects of the main character, is related to Goethe's *Iphigenie:* the *Antigone* of Sophocles. In both plays it is a loving sister who has determined in her soul to abide by the divine law as it is given to her, and to remain, as Antigone says, "imprisoned in the fear of the gods," and thus to defy all worldly power and the rules of common sense. In both plays the conflict involves death—or, at least, potentially death—not merely for the one who is so madly resolved, but for those whom she loves as well: in *Antigone* for Ismene, perhaps, the sister, and for Haemon, the lover, and in *Iphigenie* for Orestes, the brother, and Pylades, the friend. In the one play as much as in the other, the heroine is bound by bonds of gratitude to him whom she has decided to disobey; in both plays the king has provided a home for the child of a cursed race after her great tribulations. For Antigone as well as for Iphigenie it is not merely the wish for full moral realization of her own character that inspires her deed, but the hope of redeeming the guilt of ancestors. Moreover, in both plays the king is finally moved to revoke his own law and to yield to an overriding commandment. Thus it is through the contrast between Sophocles' *Antigone* and Goethe's *Iphigenie* (and not in comparison with the play of Euripides, where such problems never enter) that one can see most clearly the limitations of the Iphigenie faith.

These limitations might be artistically irrelevant were the play not such that its subject could not be dealt with on the level which Goethe set himself, without implicitly giving a comprehensive vision (a vision, not a discussion) of the ultimate nature of the moral problem involved. Also one cannot state these limitations by simply drawing attention to the tragic ending of *Antigone* and the happy solution of *Iphigenie*. But perhaps one can bring home the point that matters by saying that Iphigenie would not do what she does—or rather, would not be what she is—if her vision of life really comprehended the possibility of her having to put her brother to death; whereas Antigone, whether or not she is to die herself and bring death to others, *is* the realization of the truth that the triumph of divine law may involve at every point disaster in terms of human aspirations. In other words, there is in Goethe's *Iphigenie* an incongruity between the radicalism with which the moral problem is posed, and the certainly lovable gentleness of the spiritual nature that has to carry it. The *dramatic* flaw of Goethe's other great poetic drama, *Torquato Tasso*—lyrically as supremely successful as *Iphigenie*—is that the spiritual excitement of the hero is in excess of the moral facts of his situation, while in *Iphigenie* the moral situation outweighs the spiritual stature of the protagonist. It is because in the dramatic order of things natures like Iphigenie must not be made to encounter such situations (which could only crush them without affording them even the semblance of spiritual triumph) that, in this case, the moral problem is identical with the problem of dramatic integrity.

At the root of this problem there is not merely the time-honoured and, in this form, interminable antithesis between the belief in the fundamental goodness and the dogma of the essential corruption of the human heart. Not one of the characters of *Antigone* is "bad." If Creon were a wicked man there would still be catastrophe, but no tragedy. For both Greeks and Christians it is not in terms of morality that the moral problem can be solved. Once more, it is not the belief in man's readiness to be persuaded and moved into goodness that limits the spiritual scope of Goethe's *Iphigenie*. The uneasiness springs from a different question, which is, I think, implicitly answered by Goethe; the question: what would happen to the human spirit if all human goodness were of no avail on this earth, as happens to be the case in *Antigone?* Would the ending be despair then, or a faith beyond despair? The light and the beauty which emanate from Iphigenie have their source in her (or Goethe's) conviction that in the final reckoning such questions will not be asked. Yet as it happens, Iphigenie actually does ask the question. From the depth of her conflict she implores the gods that good should prevail on the shores of Tauris, that they should save her and thus *"save their image in her soul."* In other words, the image of the gods in Iphigenie's soul is such that it would be undone by catastrophe and her faith would crumble. But this is an extraneous and somewhat illegitimate consideration; it would be better to say that Iphigenie simply embodies the belief that the gods cannot fail her by contradicting her own convictions of what is good and necessary. Thus she stands for the impossibility of tragedy. Antigone, on the other hand, knowing that she is to die and lamenting her fate, asks on which right of the gods she might have trespassed. Why should she in her wretchedness still raise her eyes to the heavenly powers? "My lot was godlessness received in exchange for piety. But if this is good before the gods then I shall suffer, and in suffering come to know my sin."

If it can be said that Goethe's limitations have their origin in the apparently limitless scope of his genius, then what is meant is his *genius,* not his talents; on the contrary, he always used his talents to defend himself against his genius. In the deployment of his extrapoetic talents he often seems to insist stubbornly on a playfully cultivated mediocrity. This we can see at work in his unsophisticated taste for rather dull drawings, in his "classical" preoccupation with the most uninspired examples of Roman sculpture, in his preferring Zelter's innocuous music to Beethoven's and, above all, in the all but philistine pedantry betrayed by his endless collecting, cataloguing, describing and displaying of all manner of objects, documents and instruments. People lacking in a sense of humour have often blamed Goethe for so irresponsibly scattering his interests and wasting his time. Their insatiable desire for still more and still greater poetry is sadly frustrated by the Herr Geheimrat's habits of painstaking theatrical management and time-squandering mineralogical meticulousness.

Yet there is, of course, in all seriousness something puzzling in those radical defensive manoeuvres of Goethe, and I think that only by understanding them as necessary defences can one hope to arrive at some comprehension of Goethe's genius. Only then may one see a little more clearly why his lyrical achievements should have been so truly incomparable, his embarrassment in the face of tragedy so conspicuous, the moral solutions offered by some of his works such anti-climaxes that Irving Babbitt could speak of them as "sham solutions," and, incidentally, his science so aggressively anti-Newtonian. It may also help to explain why his greatest work, *Faust,* had to remain so ambiguous (and I mean an ambiguity falling short of the essential ambiguity of all great art, an ambiguity not in terms of unresolvable paradox, but of plain contradiction)—so ambiguous that throughout the message-ridden German nineteenth century it could, with the support of what were quite unambiguous quotations, be interpreted as the high-poetical celebration of restlessly active striving and of a freedom that resides in conquest; whereas now, with the ethos of action and aggrandizement deflated, and again with quite unequivocal support from the text, it

[470]

can be shown to proclaim the hope in the inscrutable workings of divine grace which may descend upon the greatest sinner.

Critics have always tried to account in various ways for Goethe's more baffling waverings and uncertainties. Some say that at times he jeopardized his genius by occupying himself with the wrong things; others, that he allowed himself too easily to get entangled in the wrong emotions. Yet it is difficult to be convinced by the standards such critics apply in their assessments of what was "right" for Goethe. Is it what Ortega y Gasset calls the "realized *Existenz*" of Goethe the man? This might only have been attained by the sacrifice of Goethe the poet. Or is it the idea of contented equilibrium and psychological balance which Barker Fairley's *Study of Goethe* appears to put forward? But surely this therapeutic approach is most unbecoming for the literary critic, who would soon be out of his job if poets decided to accept for the conduct of their lives the rules of mental health. To say that Goethe was pathologically introspective in his youth is to say that we should be prepared to dispense with *Werther* and the original design of *Faust;* and to imply that Frau von Stein was bad for Goethe is equal to holding that it would have been just as well if Goethe had not written *Iphigenie* or *Tasso* or *Erhabner Geist, du gabst mir, gabst mir alles* or *Warum gabst du uns die tiefen Blicke.* This kind of criticism implicitly pretends to possess the secret of an ideal pattern of creative life which, had it only been adopted by Goethe, would have made him into a still greater poet and a better and happier man.

The paradox of limitations caused by universality, with which Goethe confronts us, originates in a violent clash between the nature of Goethe's genius and his historical situation. In the spiritually barren climate of eighteenth- and nineteenth-century society, amidst that vanity fair of conflicting values and self-contradictory aspirations, a genius apparently so chaotic and yet so profoundly organized as that of Goethe's will easily seem to itself (and to others) to be something almost monstrous, demonic, extra-human—in fact, the spirit of *Nature* itself. And this is what, set up against the spiritual character of his age, Goethe's genius was. If Goethe is not a *European* classic, this is due to the fact that his society was lacking in a fundamentally accepted and generally valid spiritual mould in which alone a classic can be cast.

In spite of all the unavoidable cleavages, disharmonies, animosities and antagonisms which are the perennial lot of human beings and human societies, there is a possibility—and this possibility is called culture when it is realized—of a community of men living together, and maybe fighting one another, in a state of tacit agreement on what the nature and meaning of human existence really is. This unity will then show itself to be at work beyond, or beneath, or despite all differences of actually proclaimed beliefs and articulate opinions. Such must have been the society for which the performances of the tragedies of Aeschylus and Sophocles were national celebrations; such were wide stretches of what we rather vaguely call the Middle Ages; such were, to judge by their artistic creations, the days of the Renaissance and of Elizabeth. The age of Goethe, however, was not of this kind. Its true representatives were the twin creatures of spiritual chaos: rationalism and romanticism, the one abhorring, the other worshipping the irrational aspect of man. In the absence of a genuine supranatural order human beings were thrown back on their purely naturalistic resources, with analytical sceptical reason on the one hand, and disorganized emotions on the other. Pascal's reasons of the heart degenerated into sheer emotionalism, which was mistaken for spirituality, and Plato's reason of understanding into the crudest empiricism, which prided itself upon its "realistic" outlook. In vain had Kant fought his lonely battle. Those who came after him, the great philosophers of the age of Goethe, who, of course, felt and knew the disaster that had befallen the spirit, raised their arbitrary, "exciting," "interesting" metaphysical towers above the heads of a society that had become Babel in its mutual incomprehension.

Into such a situation there was born a genius who, more than any other of his time (with the possible exception of Blake), seemed to have been sent to fill with precious life whatever order of the spirit, whatever tradition he may have found upon his arrival—as Sophocles had done with the religious tradition of Greece, and Dante with the scholastic order of the Middle Ages. But, alas, "the day was so absurd and confused," as Goethe himself put it in his last letter to Wilhelm von Humboldt, and his genius, being a perpetual source of light to the world, had itself to grope in darkness. What, I think, is correct in Ortega y Gasset's and—in some measure—Karl Jasper's thesis of Goethe's *Existenz* having remained unfulfilled is the fact that his own genius was an unending puzzle to him. For the very nature of this genius deprived Goethe of that particular kind of historical sense, that intuitive grasp of the historical character of his age and his own position in it, which Schiller had and, above all, Hölderlin, who wrote:

> *. . . Indessen dünket mir öfters*
> *Besser zu schlafen, wie so ohne Genossen zu seyn,*
> *So zu harren und was zu thun indess und zu sugen,*
> *Weiss ich nicht und wozu Dichter in dürftiger Zeit?*

. . . Meanwhile, it seems to me often,
Better to slumber than live without companions, like this,
So to linger, and know not what to begin or to utter,
Or, in such spiritless times, why to be poet at all?

Goethe too knew that question, and there were periods in his life when he actually did answer it in the negative and all but behaved accordingly. But for him the question was not an historical one; not "why to be poet at all in spiritless times," but solely whether he himself *was* a poet. True, he once wrote (and just when he was about to resume his work on *Faust*): "We are compelled to step out of our century if we wish to work according to our convictions" (to Schiller, November 25th, 1797); but such statements are extremely rare. Unaware of the deeper historical perspective of his situation, he merely perceived through his own agonies and through his spontaneous hostility towards almost all and everything that represented the spiritual character of his century—its rationalism, its romanticism, its unnatural hysterias, its cold empiricism, its idealistic philosophies, its tempestuous music—that there was a gulf fixed between what he himself was in his inmost being and the world in which he lived as a citizen. Yet, unlike Hölderlin, he would not allow his genius to burden and destroy him with the historical mission of poetic prophet-martyr. He continually tried to "do the duty of the day" by seeking a compromise between opposition and collaboration. Within his genius (which is never the whole man) he was undivided, in the sense in which a genuine pattern of nature and spirit fused, or any vital religious and cultural order, is undivided; but in the absence of any such valid order of human life outside himself he came to identify the inner order, inherent in his genius, with the spirit of nature itself.

"Unnatural," in the mouth of Goethe, was one of the strongest invectives. "Diese verdammte Unnatur!" he exclaimed, faced with the productions of Kleist, and Kleist was judged. Thus pantheism, God in nature, became his natural religion, and Spinoza his chosen prophet. "This philosopher," he wrote in a letter to Jacobi (June 9th, 1785), "does not prove the being of God; God is being. And if others, because of this, blame him as an atheist, then I feel like praising him as *theissimum*, indeed *christianissimum*." In the same letter, however, he confesses, in a rather touchingly ingenious fashion, that he had never read systematically what the philosopher wrote (if he had, there is reason to think that he would occasionally have felt rather sadly disappointed): "My way of living and thinking does not permit it. But whenever I cast a glance into his books, I believe I understand him, that is, he never seems to be self-contradictory, and I can derive from him something that affects my own feelings and doings in a very salutary

[473]

manner." How amazingly self-assured was Goethe's conviction that he represented, as it were, nature in her own right! And what a wonderful intimacy with all the disguises of the godhead is displayed in the following lines (from a very much later letter to Jacobi, January 6th, 1813): "With all the manifold facets of my being, one way of thinking is not sufficient for me; as a poet and artist I am a polytheist, but a pantheist as a student of Nature, and either belief I hold with equal determination. And if I need a divinity for my personal being, my moral existence—well, this need too is promptly catered for."

Goethe, having to express the whole order of spirit and nature through his own genius, was limited in the performance of such an impossible duty by the absence of anything corresponding to that order within the society to which he belonged. Goethe's genius is miraculously "natural" and "uncivilized," in the sense that he has no support from a society civilized in the mould of the spirit that was his. And this is why, as a member of this society which had so little use for his genius, he could be so amazingly "civilized," often to the point of cold formality and embarrassed stiffness, and even to the point of saying that he would rather commit an act of injustice than tolerate disorder. And this is also why his genius seems so boundless and its limitations, at the same time, so striking; for within his own contemporary situation such genius as his hovers perpetually on the precarious dividing-line between greatness and excess. (His counterpart, in the sphere of political genius, was Napoleon.) In the absence of a tradition to feed and educate his genius, the umbilical cord between it and nature was, as Goethe himself once put it, never severed.

Schiller, while admiring this fascinating spectacle of an undivided poetic nature, yet ceaselessly strained to play the part of midwife. In the letters about *Faust,* and still more in the correspondence about *Wilhelm Meister,* he makes the ever-renewed and ever-frustrated attempt to civilize, educate and discipline what seemed to him a too luxurious production of genius. Yet he was bound to fail, in spite of the fact that he had a profounder understanding of Goethe than anyone else. In one of the very first letters he wrote to him (August 23rd, 1794) he said that if Goethe had been born a Greek or in any other civilization where he would have been surrounded by "an exquisite nature and an ideal art," his struggle "would have been shortened or even been superfluous." At least in the creation of certain types of work—*Faust* and *Wilhelm Meister* for instance—Goethe, he thought, ought to resign himself to the rigours of a more philosophical discipline. It was no good. Ideas were not embodied in the society of his time, and in the abstract terms of philosophical speculation Goethe had no use for them. He had to *see* and feel them; but when he did see and feel them they became so real to him that he was even surprised that to others they appeared to be mere "ideas."

The impression that Goethe's genius is "wholly nature" is partly due to an optical illusion caused by the refraction in the medium of a "spiritless time" where the spiritual had ceased to be incarnate, having evaporated into vague abstractions. The anaemic and artificial civilization of his day drove Goethe again and again into a realm where the "real thing" could be found. This is why Italy was such a revelation to Goethe. There, set up against a clearer sky and the memory of a clearer realization of the human destiny, he found a vision of life in which nature and humanity were merged in a "natural civilization."

It would be inadequate to the point of idiocy to approach Goethe in a moralizing fashion; but there is no reason why one should not see that, with such a predominance of nature within him and such a lack of civilized tradition around him, he had to fail when faced with the tragic or religious aspect of the moral problem as it is inherent in the very plots of both *Iphigenie* and *Faust*. No human being can come to grips with such a problem unaided by tradition and traditional teaching. As it happened, within the "tradition" of Goethe's day it was precisely this problem that had been deformed and dwarfed beyond recognition. The practical, "lived" side of it was indeed, after all is said (and said with great affection) about Fräulein von Klettenberg and other beautiful souls, too pietistically mediocre ever really to mean anything to Goethe; and its philosophical side too speculative, abstract and metaphysical not to be discarded by Goethe's passion for "reality." In the spiritual climate of the eighteenth and the beginning of the nineteenth centuries the terror of a man's exposure to the need for ultimate moral or religious decisions could not be creatively grasped, either on the level of Greek tragedy or on that of undiluted Christianity, or indeed even on the level of that unique encounter of both which took place in the Elizabethan drama. And Goethe was of his age in failing to grasp it in either of these spheres.

We have seen what happened in his dealings with a classically tragic subject; how he missed the meaning of the cross of Christianity is best illustrated by that passage from *Wilhelm Meisters Wanderjahre* where he "draws a veil over this suffering" just because he "reveres it so deeply," and because he "regards it as a damnable insolence to expose the agonies of the saint to the sun which had hidden its face when an infamous world obtruded upon it this sight." (It happened to be Weimar where an American commandant very wisely decreed that Hitler's electorate in what was once Goethe's city were to be shown the horrors of Buchenwald concentration camp.) And summing up the meaning of *Hamlet*, Goethe defines it as the tragedy of a man who was too weak to carry the burden of his mission. Stating the problem in terms of strength and weakness, he once more fails to be impressed by the moral aspect of *Hamlet* and the all-pervasive, all-corroding power of evil, the "morbid" preoccupation of Elizabethan tragedy. For to be able to perceive and creatively to articulate this problem, that is, to form a vision of it rather than to discuss it, presupposes a theology underlying, however dispersedly, the picture of reality that an age possesses; and this is something different from a philosophy of nature and from even the highest human wisdom. Goethe's genius soared gloriously above the flat expanses of contemporary religious sentimentality and mediocre morality, in triumphant opposition to all puritan gloom, moral suspicion and tearful piety, asserting that life, whatever it be, is good and beautiful: "wie es auch sei, das Leben, es ist gut," and

> *Ihr glücklichen Augen,*
> *Was je ihr gesehn,*
> *Es sei wie es wolle,*
> *Es war doch so schön!*

It is this finality in his assertion of life that makes it possible to claim for Goethe the position of the greatest lyrical genius of Europe. But though it is *his* final assertion, it is not ultimate. It indeed transcends all sorrows of Werther, Tasso and Ottilie, and endless conflicts most deeply felt and suffered. But would it transcend, one wonders, tragedy fully realized? And only there is the place of an ultimate "Es ist gut."

Under such auspices what was to become of a dramatic plot in which a man enters into a contract with the Devil, signing away, on certain conditions, the fate of his soul? What was to become of *Faust?* One may well ask. It took Goethe, all in all, sixty years to decide, or rather to decide that he would not quite decide. Certain things, however, the play decided for him. For instance, that it would, being Goethe's, become a lyrical masterpiece. There is no greater and no more varied lyrical poetry to be found within the German language. And more: *Faust* became a pageant of the human spirit on its voyage throughout the ages. An extraordinary wealth of mythological creatures, Teutonic, Greek, Christian, populate the scene, all testifying to their creator's inexhaustible imaginative power. And still more: the hero of the play was to become the representative of a whole epoch of history, its lust for knowledge, for power over nature, its intellectual and emotional instability, its terrible failure in love, humility and patience. And still more: the first part of the play, dominated by what is usually called the

Gretchen tragedy, was to bring out most movingly the undoing, by the Faustian manoeuvres, of what was left in the world of simplicity of heart, devotion of love and innocence of feeling. This part of what is, after all, called the tragedy of Faust, developed by its own momentum into a poetic and dramatic achievement so immaculate that it will, I think, for ever hold its place by the side of what is great in the literature of the world—and this precisely because in its design it is not, in the traditional sense, tragic but lyrical. It is what might have become of the play *Hamlet* if Ophelia and not the Prince of Denmark were to be its protagonist. In other words, Goethe may have succeeded in creating a new genre: sentimental tragedy, or the tragedy of human *feelings*: Werther, Gretchen, Ottilie. What he could not write was the tragedy of the human *spirit*. It is here that the tragedy of Faust fails and becomes illegitimately ambiguous, because there is for Goethe in the last analysis no specifically *human* spirit. It is fundamentally at one with the spirit of nature. Hence it is He, the Spirit of Nature, or the Spirit of Earth, not God or the Devil, who holds in his hands the final decision over Faust's bliss or damnation. Had He, when He appeared to Faust in the first scene of the play, not rejected him, neither God in Heaven nor the Devil in Hell would have had a chance. And one of the only two scenes in which Faust really regrets that he has committed himself to his satanic company is the great monologue *Wald und Höhle*:

> *Erhabner Geist, du gabst mir, gabst mir alles . . .*
>
> Oh thou great Spirit, thou has given me all . . .

when it appears that this Spirit did not crush him after all.

There are in this vast display of demons great and small only two that affect Faust demonically; certainly not God, who is a jovial old gentleman, enlightened and rather commonplace in some of his utterances ("Ein guter Mensch, in seinem dunklen Drange, Ist sich des rechten Weges wohl bewusst," which really means not more than that a good man will not altogether go astray; a conviction not so difficult to hold that it would need a divinity to persuade one), and certainly not Mephistopheles, a Voltairean spirit, with whom Faust is from the very beginning on terms of great familiarity. Goethe himself, in a conversation with Eckermann (March 2nd, 1831), has denied him all demonic properties: "He is altogether too negative," he said, and has explicitly stated in the play itself that he is of lesser rank than the Spirit of Earth. But the two which teach Faust what a real demon is are the Earth Spirit and the Mothers, the innermost spirits of nature and life. They represent the demonic element in Goethe's genius. It is in union with this element that Faust seeks his happiness from beginning to end, or *almost* to the very end, and not in the realization of a specifically human spirit. And Faust has been in contact with those demons before Mephistopheles enters the scene. This contact means black magic, and Faust is a magician when the curtain rises. It is this that reduces the *dramatic* stature of Mephistopheles to all but nil, and not the rather naïve consideration that Goethe has forestalled all dramatic tension in this respect by making, in the Prologue, the Lord himself, a sure winner, as it were, party to the wager. All that Mephistopheles can do for Faust is to give him a hand in a job of which he already knows the essential tricks of the trade. And throughout the play the Devil performs hardly any magical feats with which one would not willingly credit the magician himself who had already succeeded in establishing contact with the spirit of life.

All this would be rather irrelevant if it were not at the centre of the essential ambiguity of *Faust*—the most striking outcome of Goethe's avoidance of tragedy. What does Faust *really* expect of Mephistopheles? Still more magic? No; but contentment, rest, peace; to be able to say to the moment: "Verweile doch, du bist so schön." [Stay, thou art so fair.] In other words, life is good. True, this is preceded by Faust's contemptuous identification of such a state with self-complacency. But it is the words themselves, not what leads up to them, which become the condition of the wager. And their poetic truth gives the lie to the preamble. They are made of the same stuff as "Es sei, wie es wolle, Es war doch so schön!" And this the devil is to provide? The very same devil whom Faust, a few scenes later, when he has found temporary peace in the company of the Spirit of Nature, knows to be the spirit responsible for

> *So tauml' ich von Begierde zu Genuss*
> *Und im Genuss verschmacht' ich nach Begierde*

> Thus I tumble from desire to fulfilment
> And in fulfilment I crave for more desire

for ever destroying that very peace which communion with the Spirit of Nature gives him. With the Devil defined as the spirit of negation and unrest, this becomes indeed a very strange condition meaning in fact that the Devil is to have Faust if Faust ever escapes the Devil.

What, on the other hand, is the condition of the wager between the Lord and Mephistopheles?

> *Zieh diesen Geist von seinem Urquell ab*

> Drag this spirit away from the very source of his life

The Lord, that is, challenges Mephistopheles to alienate Faust from the springs of life, to uproot him. If he succeeds, Faust will be his. This sounds more like "Deprive him of all peace, if indeed you can" than "Make him contented with the moment." And in the end, when Faust, anticipating this peace and contentment, blinded by anxiety, deluded into the belief that the great work of colonization has begun while, in actual fact, the busy noise is merely the sound of shovels digging his own grave, utters the fatal words, in the face of a vision so totally unconvincing in its meagre guilt-burdened town-and-country-planning bliss that one cannot but agree with Mephistopheles that it is the emptiest moment of his life, then the Devil is cheated of his apparently well-deserved prey by the feeble trick of a future tense ["Im Vorgefühl von solchem hohen Glück"], and by the intervention of divine grace called down upon him by the only human love Faust ever received and experienced.

How is this? Faust has indeed promised that he would content himself, even anticipated the enjoyment of peace ["Geniess' ich jetzt . . ."] in his vision of the contented future. He has satisfied the Devil who has never been found wanting in the shrewd judgment of any situation, and is, having faithfully renounced his programme of eternal striving, carried into Heaven in reward for his determination to strive eternally:

> *Wer immer strebend sich bemüht,*
> *Den können wir erlösen.*

> It is the struggling, striving man
> Whom we are free to save.

What is at the root of such confusion, which has indeed defeated four generations of interpreters of *Faust,* and, if we are to trust Eckermann's report, Goethe's own faculties as a commentator? It would be tempting to relegate it to the place where many an impenetrable mystery is stored, were it not for the persistent suspicion that we are faced here not so much with a genuine poetic paradox as with a plain contradiction. It is the inevitable contradiction of the undedicated mind and heart. In Faust's world there are no real loyalties to be realized and no real commitments to be broken. Both his eternal striving and his desire for peace are merely the extreme stations of his mind and heart in their never-ending voyage of self-exploration. His "tragedy" is that he is incapable of tragedy. For tragedy presupposes the belief in an external order of things which is indeed incomplete without the conformity of the human soul, but would be still more defective without the soul's freedom to violate it. Yet Faust's dilemma is different. His "two souls" are merely the one soul divided in itself because it knows of no independent external reality to which it is related as a free agent. Faust is in every essential respect Goethe's *alter ego,* the embodiment of that part of his self which remained unprotected by his apparently fondest trust and belief: that he belonged to Nature as her most precious possession. Faust, outside this zone of safety, is therefore torn between the belief in a world to which, strive as he may, he has no access whatever, and the belief in himself as the creator of his own world. Thus the spiritual extremes of his existence are not guilt and atonement, but despair and titanism. It is a situation unresolvable in tragedy.

Nature is fundamentally innocent, and Goethe's genius is in communion with Nature. Hence there can be, for Goethe, no catharsis, only metamorphosis. It is never with the spirit of a transcendent God or with the spirit of Man that Goethe's potentially tragic heroes are reunited after their dramatic crises. When the crisis is over, they are at one again with the spirit of Nature. They are not purified in a tragic sense, not raised above their guilt through atonement, but enter, as it were, a biologically, not morally, new phase of life, healed by oblivion and restored to strength through the sleep of the just. This is what happens to Orestes, and what happens to Faust at the beginning of Part II. Both put down their cup of Lethe and burst into magnificent praises of Nature. But such, clearly, could not have been the conclusion of Faust. He had to be saved or damned, for Heaven and Hell had become involved by virtue of the legendary pattern. But it is *only* by virtue of the legendary pattern that they have become involved at all. For the world of Faust is only just Christian enough to have room for purgatory. It is a purgatory suspended between two half unreal spheres. Hence "Mephistopheles must only half win his wager," and Faust be "only half guilty," as Goethe himself put it in a letter which looks forward to the play's "most serene conclusion" when "the old Lord may exercise his privilege of mercy."

What is Faust's sin? Restlessness of spirit. What is Faust's salvation? Restlessness of spirit. The confusion lies in a perpetual criss-crossing of restless strivings of different qualities: the striving for peace, and the striving for sensation; or, to put it differently, and in terms of the quality of the contentment sought, the striving for that peace that passeth all understanding, and the striving for a state of calm, an "enough" which is merely a state of emotional exhaustion. What the heavenly powers mean by that striving which carries its own salvation must surely be different from the striving the goal of which Faust hopes to achieve with the help of black magic and the Devil. Yet these two kinds of striving perpetually get into each other's way throughout the poem, and the entanglement is at its worst in the crucial last scene of Faust's life when his desire for doing good and for the realization of his humanity within its decreed limits is inextricably bound up with the delusion and madness of titanism. Of these two strivings the one desires the attainment of the superman, the alchemist heightening of all human faculties, whereas the other aims at renunciation and resignation to the simple state of man. The first is the native element of Goethe's genius, the second the longing of Goethe's moral existence.

> *Könnt' ich Magie von meinem Pfad entfernen,*
> *Die Zaubersprüche ganz und gar verlernen,*
> *Stünd ich, Natur, vor dir ein Mann allein,*
> *Da wär's der Mühe wert, ein Mensch zu sein.*

(Could I forget my sorcery, and ban my magic, stand, stripped of it utterly, oh Nature, face to face with thee, it would be worth while then to be a man.)

This outcry of Faust's, towards the end of the play when he is visited by *Sorge*—and this is the second place where Faust is prepared to renounce the Devil—reveals perhaps Goethe's deepest secret. To cut the umbilical cord joining him with Nature and her magic power, not to remain what he once called "a magic oyster over which there pass mysterious waves," to be face to face with Nature and escape the fate of Proteus—this only would be human happiness. Over and over again he sought deliverance from his genius in work, in the practical jobs of everyday life, through Wilhelm Meister's, through Faust's solution, and so desperately that as a man of fifty he confessed to Schiller (January 6th, 1798) that he owed it to him if he had learned to "look at the manysidedness of my own inner being with more justice. . . . *You* have made me a poet again which I had all but ceased to be." Such was the nature of his genius and the character of his age that the spirit could only live at the expense of life, and life only at the expense of the spirit. Thus the meaning of creative genius as well as the meaning of doing the sober work of the day, inwardness as well as action, had to remain puzzles to each other, anonymous, undefined strangers. They never met in a common dedication and could not be at peace with each other because they knew no will other than their own. And at such distance from "la sua volontate è nostra pace" neither divine comedy nor human tragedy can be written.

It was impossible for Goethe to accept this situation, and impossible, by the very nature of things, to solve it. Hence his perpetual oscillation between the precarious magic of the inner communion with the deep where the Earth Spirit dwells, and the moral determination to reconcile himself to the cruder demands made on human existence by society, with the emphasis of approval shifting to and fro between the two: Egmont and Oranien, Tasso and Antonio, Prometheus and *Grenzen der Mensch-heit,* elective affinities and legal bonds. Was harmony ever to be achieved? The answer may be found in the ambiguity of *Faust.*

WORDSWORTH

[*1770–1850*]

WORDSWORTH'S CELEBRATION OF NATURE AND ITS POWERS IN "TINTERN ABBEY" once had a much simpler and more apprehensible meaning for his readers than it now has. We are likely to be perplexed by Wordsworth's faith that nature can assure us of anything humanly significant. But the author of *The Prelude: or the Growth of a Poet's Mind* had a profound sense of the psychological conditions of growth, and we have only to read that poem, or the "Ode" which is the subject of this essay, to discover that Wordsworth is our fellow in the quest for identity, for self-awareness. The difference between us is suggested by Wordsworth's assertion in *The Prelude* that the poet is a "Power" who takes possession of a world. That world is the world of nature, of politics, of human community, which Wordsworth felt assured was the scene of human growth. In the measure that we lack that assurance, our quest for identity, our multiplicity of strategies for discovering our inmost selves, will not carry us far.

Lionel Trilling is Professor of English at Columbia and is widely known as author and critic.

LIONEL TRILLING

The Immortality Ode

CRITICISM, WE KNOW, MUST ALWAYS BE CONCERNED WITH THE POEM ITSELF. But a poem does not always exist only in itself: sometimes it has a very lively existence in its false or partial appearances. These simulacra of the actual poem must be taken into account by criticism; and sometimes, in its effort to come at the poem as it really is, criticism does well to allow the simulacra to dictate at least its opening moves. In speaking about Wordsworth's "Ode: Intimations of Immortality from Recollections of Early Childhood," I should like to begin by considering an interpretation of the poem which is commonly made. According to this interpretation—I choose for its brevity Dean Sperry's statement of a view which is held by many other admirable critics—the Ode is "Wordsworth's conscious farewell to his art, a dirge sung over his departing powers."

How did this interpretation—erroneous, as I believe—come into being? The Ode may indeed be quoted to substantiate it, but I do not think it has been drawn directly from the poem itself. To be sure, the Ode is not wholly perspicuous. Wordsworth himself seems to have thought it difficult, for in the Fenwick notes he speaks of the need for competence and attention in the reader. The difficulty does not lie in the diction, which is simple, or even in the syntax, which is sometimes obscure, but rather in certain contradictory statements which the poem makes, and in the ambiguity of some of its crucial words. Yet the erroneous interpretation I am dealing with does not arise from any intrinsic difficulty of the poem itself but rather from certain extraneous and unexpressed assumptions which some of its readers make about the nature of the mind.

Nowadays it is not difficult for us to understand that such tacit assumptions about the mental processes are likely to lie hidden beneath what we say about poetry. Usually, despite our general awareness of their existence, it requires great effort to bring these assumptions explicitly into consciousness. But in speaking of Wordsworth one of the commonest of our unexpressed ideas comes so close to the surface of our thought that it needs only to be grasped and named. I refer to the belief that poetry is made by means of a particular poetic faculty, a faculty which may be isolated and defined.

It is this belief, based wholly upon assumption, which underlies all the speculations of the critics who attempt to provide us with explanations of Wordsworth's poetic decline by attributing it to one or another of the events of his life. In effect any such explanation is a way of *defining* Wordsworth's poetic faculty: what the biographical critics are telling us is that Wordsworth wrote great poetry by means of a faculty which depended upon his relations with Annette Vallon, or by means of a faculty which operated only so long as he admired the French Revolution, or by means of a faculty which flourished by virtue of a particular pitch of youthful sense-perception or by virtue of a certain attitude toward Jeffrey's criticism or by virtue of a certain relation with Coleridge.

Now no one can reasonably object to the idea of mental determination in general, and I certainly do not intend to make out that poetry is an unconditioned activity. Still, this particular notion of mental determination which implies that Wordsworth's genius failed when it was deprived of some single emotional circumstance is so much too simple and so much too mechanical that I think we must inevitably reject it. Certainly what we know of poetry does not allow us to refer the making of it to any single faculty. Nothing less than the whole mind, the whole man, will suffice for its origin. And such was Wordsworth's own view of the matter.

There is another unsubstantiated assumption at work in the common biographical interpretation of the Ode. This is the belief that a natural and inevitable warfare exists between the poetic faculty and the faculty by which we conceive or comprehend general ideas. Wordsworth himself did not believe in this antagonism—indeed, he held an almost contrary view—but Coleridge thought that philosophy had encroached upon and destroyed his own powers, and the critics who speculate on Wordsworth's artistic fate seem to prefer Coleridge's psychology to Wordsworth's own. Observing in the Ode a contrast drawn between something called "the visionary gleam" and something called "the philosophic mind," they leap to the conclusion that the Ode is Wordsworth's conscious farewell to his art, a dirge sung over departing powers.

I am so far from agreeing with this conclusion that I believe the Ode is not only not a dirge sung over departing powers but actually a dedication to new powers. Wordsworth did not, to be sure, realize his hopes for these new powers, but that is quite another matter.

As with many poems, it is hard to understand any part of the Ode until we first understand the whole of it. I will therefore say at once what I think the poem is chiefly about. It is a poem about growing; some say it is a poem about growing old, but I believe it is about growing up. It is incidentally a poem about optics and then, inevitably, about epistemology; it is concerned with ways of seeing and then with ways of knowing. Ultimately it is concerned with ways of acting, for, as usual with Wordsworth, knowledge implies liberty and power. In only a limited sense is the Ode a poem about immortality.

Both formally and in the history of its composition the poem is divided into two main parts. The first part, consisting of four stanzas, states an optical phenomenon and asks a question about it. The second part, consisting of seven stanzas, answers that question and is itself divided into two parts, of which the first is despairing, the second hopeful. Some time separates the composition of the question from that of the answer; the evidence most recently adduced by Professor de Selincourt seems to indicate that the interval was two years.

The question which the first part asks is this:

> Whither is fled the visionary gleam?
> Where is it now, the glory and the dream?

All the first part leads to this question, but although it moves in only one direction it takes its way through more than one mood. There are at least three moods before the climax of the question is reached.

The first stanza makes a relatively simple statement. "There was a time" when all common things seemed clothed in "celestial light," when they had "the glory and the freshness of a dream." In a poem ostensibly about immortality we ought perhaps to pause over the word "celestial," but the present elaborate title was not given to the poem until much later, and conceivably at the time of the writing of the first part the idea of immortality was not in Wordsworth's mind at all. Celestial light probably means only something different from ordinary, earthly, scientific light; it is a light of the mind, shining even in darkness—"by night or day"—and it is perhaps similar to the light which is praised in the invocation to the third book of *Paradise Lost*.

The second stanza goes on to develop this first mood, speaking of the ordinary, physical kind of vision and suggesting further the meaning of "celestial." We must remark that in this stanza Wordsworth is so far from observing a diminution of his physical senses that he explicitly affirms their strength. He is at pains to tell us how vividly he sees the rainbow, the rose, the moon, the stars, the water and the sunshine. I emphasize this because some of those who find the Ode a dirge over the poetic power maintain that the poetic power failed with the failure of Wordsworth's senses. It is true that Wordsworth, who lived to be eighty, was said in middle life to look much older than his years. Still, thirty-two, his age at the time of writing the first part of the Ode, is an extravagantly early age for a dramatic failure of the senses. We might observe here, as others have observed elsewhere, that Wordsworth never did have the special and perhaps modern sensibility of his sister or of Coleridge, who were so aware of exquisite particularities. His finest passages are moral, emotional, subjective; whatever visual intensity they have comes from his response to the object, not from his close observation of it.

And in the second stanza Wordsworth not only confirms his senses but he also confirms his ability to perceive beauty. He tells us how he responds to the loveliness of the rose and of the stars reflected in the water. He can deal, in the way of Fancy, with the delight of the moon when there are no competing stars in the sky. He can see in Nature certain moral propensities. He speaks of the sunshine as a "glorious birth." But here he pauses to draw distinctions from that fascinating word "glory": despite his perception of the sunshine as a glorious birth, he knows "That there hath past away a glory from the earth."

Now, with the third stanza, the poem begins to complicate itself. It is *while* Wordsworth is aware of the "optical" change in himself, the loss of the "glory," that there comes to him "a thought of grief." I emphasize the word "while" to suggest that we must understand that for some time he had been conscious of the "optical" change *without* feeling grief. The grief, then, would seem to be coincidental with but not necessarily caused by the change. And the grief is not of long duration, for we learn that

> A timely utterance gave that thought relief,
> And I again am strong.

It would be not only interesting but also useful to know what that "timely utterance" was, and I shall hazard a guess; but first I should like to follow the development of the Ode a little further, pausing only to remark that the reference to the timely utterance seems to imply that, although the grief is not of long duration, still we are not dealing with the internal experiences of a moment, or of a morning's walk, but of a time sufficient to allow for development and change of mood; that is, the dramatic time of the poem is not exactly equivalent to the emotional time.

Stanza IV goes on to tell us that the poet, after gaining relief from the timely utterance, whatever that was, felt himself quite in harmony with the joy of Nature in spring. The tone of this stanza is ecstatic, and in a way that some readers find strained and unpleasant and even of doubtful sincerity. Twice there is a halting repetition of words to express a kind of painful intensity of response: "I feel—I feel it all," and "I hear, I hear, with joy I hear!" Wordsworth sees, hears, feels—and with that "joy" which both he and Coleridge felt to be so necessary to the poet. But despite the response, despite the joy, the ecstasy changes to sadness in a wonderful modulation which quite justifies the antecedent shrillness of affirmation:

> —But there's a Tree, of many, one,
> A single Field which I have looked upon.
> Both of them speak of something that is gone:
> The Pansy at my feet
> Doth the same tale repeat.

And what they utter is the terrible question:

> Whither is fled the visionary gleam?
> Where is it now, the glory and the dream?

Now, the interpretation which makes the Ode a dirge over departing powers and a conscious farewell to art takes it for granted that the visionary gleam, the glory, and the dream, are Wordsworth's names for the power by which he made poetry. This interpretation gives to the Ode a place in Wordsworth's life exactly analogous to the place that "Dejection: An Ode" has in Coleridge's life. It is well known how intimately the two poems are connected; the circumstances of their composition makes them symbiotic. Coleridge in his poem most certainly does say that his poetic powers are gone or going; he is very explicit, and the language he uses is very close to Wordsworth's own. He tells us that upon "the inanimate cold world" there must issue from the soul "a light, a glory, a fair luminous cloud," and that this glory *is* Joy, which he himself no longer possesses. But Coleridge's poem, although it responds to the first part of Wordsworth's, is not a recapitulation of it. On the contrary, Coleridge is precisely contrasting his situation with Wordsworth's. As Professor de Selincourt says in his comments on the first version of "Dejection," this contrast "was the root idea" of Coleridge's ode. In April of 1802 Wordsworth was a month away from his marriage to Mary Hutchinson, on the point of establishing his life in a felicity and order which became his genius, while Coleridge was at the nadir of despair over his own unhappy marriage and his hopeless love for Sara, the sister of Wordsworth's fiancée. And the difference between the situations of the two friends stands in Coleridge's mind for the difference in the states of health of their respective poetic powers.

Coleridge explicitly ascribes the decay of his poetic power to his unhappiness, which worked him harm in two ways—by forcing him to escape from the life of emotion to find refuge in intellectual abstraction and by destroying the Joy which, issuing as "a light, a glory, a fair luminous cloud," so irradiated the world as to make it a fit object of the shaping power of imagination. But Wordsworth tells us something quite different about himself. He tells us that he has strength, that he has Joy, but still he has not the glory. In short, we have no reason to assume that, when he asks the question at the end of the fourth stanza, he means, "Where has my creative power gone?" Wordsworth tells us how he made poetry; he says he made it out of the experience of his senses as worked upon by his contemplative intellect, but he nowhere tells us that he made poetry out of visionary gleams, out of glories, or out of dreams.

To be sure, he writes very often about gleams. The word "gleam" is a favorite one with him, and a glance at the Lane Cooper concordance will confirm our impression that Wordsworth, whenever he has a moment of insight or happiness, talks about it in the language of light. His great poems are about moments of enlightenment, in which the metaphoric and the literal meaning of the word are at one—he uses "glory" in the abstract modern sense, but always with an awareness of the old concrete iconographic sense of a visible nimbus.[1] But this momentary and special light is the subject matter of his poetry, not the power of making it. The moments are moments of understanding, but Wordsworth does not say that they make writing

---

[1] We recall that in *The Varieties of Religious Experience* William James speaks of the "hallucinatory or pseudo-hallucinatory luminous phenomena, *photisms,* to use the term of the psychologists," the "floods of light and glory," which characterize so many moments of revelation. James mentions one person who, experiencing the light, was uncertain of its externality.

poetry any easier. Indeed, in lines 59-131 of the first book of *The Prelude* he expressly says that the moments of clarity are by no means always matched by poetic creativity.

As for dreams and poetry, there is some doubt about the meaning that Wordsworth gave to the word "dream" used as a metaphor. In "Expostulation and Reply" he seems to say that dreaming—"dream my time away"—is a good thing, but he is ironically using his interlocutor's depreciatory word, and he really does not mean "dream" at all. In the Peele Castle verses, which have so close a connection with the Immortality Ode, he speaks of the "poet's dream" and makes it synonymous with "gleam," with "the light that never was, on sea or land," and with the "consecration." But the beauty of the famous lines often makes us forget to connect them with what follows, for Wordsworth says that gleam, light, consecration, and dream would have made an "illusion," or, in the 1807 version, a "delusion." Professor Beatty reminds us that in the 1820 version Wordsworth destroyed the beauty of the lines in order to make his intention quite clear. He wrote:

> and add a gleam
> Of lustre known to neither sea nor land,
> But borrowed from the youthful Poet's Dream.

That is, according to the terms of Wordsworth's conception of the three ages of man, the youthful Poet was, as he had a right to be, in the service of Fancy and therefore saw the sea as calm. But Wordsworth himself can now no longer see in the way of Fancy; he has, he says, "submitted to a new control." This seems to be at once a loss and a gain. The loss: "A power is gone, which nothing can restore." The gain: "A deep distress hath humanized my Soul"; this is gain because happiness without "humanization" "is to be pitied, for 'tis surely blind"; to be "housed in a dream" is to be "at distance from the kind" (i.e., mankind). In the "Letter to Mathetes" he speaks of the Fancy as "dreaming"; and the Fancy is, we know, a lower form of intellect in Wordsworth's hierarchy, and peculiar to youth.

But although, as we see, Wordsworth uses the word "dream" to mean illusion, we must remember that he thought illusions might be very useful. They often led him to proper attitudes and allowed him to deal successfully with reality. In *The Prelude* he tells us how his reading of fiction made him able to look at the disfigured face of the drowned man without too much horror; how a kind of superstitious conviction of his own powers was useful to him; how, indeed, many of the most critical moments of his boyhood education were moments of significant illusion; and in *The Excursion* he is quite explicit about the salutary effects of superstition. But he was interested in dreams not for their own sake but for the sake of reality. Dreams may *perhaps* be associated with poetry, but reality *certainly* is; and reality for Wordsworth comes fullest with Imagination, the faculty of maturity. The loss of the "dream" may be painful, but it does not necessarily mean the end of poetry.

And now for a moment I should like to turn back to the "timely utterance," because I think an understanding of it will help to get rid of the idea that Wordsworth was saying farewell to poetry. Professor Garrod believes that this "utterance" was "My heart leaps up when I behold," which was written the day before the Ode was begun. Certainly this poem is most intimately related to the Ode—its theme, the legacy left by the child to the man, is a dominant theme of the Ode, and Wordsworth used its last lines as the Ode's epigraph. But I should like to suggest that the "utterance" was something else. In line 43 Wordsworth says, "Oh evil day! if I were sullen," and the word "sullen" leaps out at us as a striking and carefully chosen word. Now there is one poem in which Wordsworth says that he was sullen; it is "Resolution and Independence."

We know that Wordsworth was working on the first part of the Ode on the 27th of March, the day after the composition of the rainbow poem. On the 17th of June he added a little to the Ode, but what he added we do not know. Between these two dates Wordsworth and Dorothy had paid their visit to Coleridge, who was sojourning at Keswick; during this visit Coleridge, on April 4, had written "Dejection: an Ode," very probably after he had read what was already in existence of the Immortality Ode. Coleridge's mental state was very bad—still, not so bad as to keep him from writing a great poem—and the Wordsworths were much distressed. A month later, on May 3, Wordsworth began to compose "The Leech-Gatherer," later known as "Resolution and Independence." It is this poem that is, I think, the timely utterance.[2]

"Resolution and Independence" is a poem about the fate of poets. It is also a poem about sullenness, in the sense that the people in the Fifth Circle are said by Dante to be sullen: " 'Sullen were we in the sweet air, that is gladdened by the sun, carrying lazy smoke within our hearts; now lie sullen here in the black mire!' This hymn they gurgle in their throats, for they can-

---

[2] I follow Professor Garrod in assuming that the "utterance" was a poem, but of course it may have been a letter or a spoken word. And if indeed the "utterance" does refer to "Resolution and Independence," it may not refer to the poem itself—as Jacques Barzun has suggested to me, it may refer to what the Leech-gatherer in the poem says to the poet, for certainly it is what the old man "utters" that gives the poet "relief."

not speak it in full words"[3]—that is, they cannot now have relief by timely utterance, as they would not on earth. And "sullenness" I take to be the creation of difficulties where none exist, the working of a self-injuring imagination such as a modern mental physician would be quick to recognize as a neurotic symptom. Wordsworth's poem is about a sudden unmotivated anxiety after a mood of great exaltation. He speaks of this reversal of feeling as something experienced by himself before and known to all. In this mood he is the prey of "fears and fancies," of "dim sadness" and "blind thoughts." These feelings have reference to two imagined catastrophes. One of them— natural enough in a man under the stress of approaching marriage, for Wordsworth was to be married in October—is economic destitution. He reproaches himself for his past indifference to the means of getting a living and thinks of what may follow from this carefree life: "solitude, pain of heart, distress, and poverty." His black thoughts are led to the fate of poets "in their misery dead," among them Chatterton and Burns. The second specific fear is of mental distress:

> We Poets in our youth begin in gladness;
> But thereof come in the end despondency and madness.

Coleridge, we must suppose, was in his thoughts after the depressing Keswick meeting, but he is of course thinking chiefly of himself. It will be remembered how the poem ends, how with some difficulty of utterance the poet brings himself to speak with an incredibly old leech-gatherer, and, taking heart from the man's resolution and independence, becomes again "strong."

This great poem is not to be given a crucial meaning in Wordsworth's life. It makes use of a mood to which everyone, certainly every creative person, is now and again a victim. It seems to me more likely that it, rather than the rainbow poem, is the timely utterance of which the Ode speaks because in it, and not in the rainbow poem, a sullen feeling occurs and is relieved. But whether or not it is actually the timely utterance, it is an autobiographical and deeply felt poem written at the time the Ode was being written and seeming to have an emotional connection with the first part of the Ode. (The meeting with the old man had taken place two years earlier and it is of some significance that it should have come to mind as the subject of a poem at just this time.) It is a very precise and hardheaded account of a mood of great fear and it deals in a very explicit way with the dangers that beset the poetic

---

[3] The Carlyle-Wicksteed translation. Dante's word is *"tristi"*; in "Resolution and Independence" Wordsworth speaks of "dim sadness." I mention Dante's sinners simply to elucidate the emotion that Wordsworth speaks of, not to suggest an influence.

life. But although Wordsworth urges himself on to think of all the bad things that can possibly happen to a poet, and mentions solitude, pain of heart, distress and poverty, cold, pain and labor, all fleshly ills, and then even madness, he never says that a poet stands in danger of losing his talent. It seems reasonable to suppose that if Wordsworth were actually saying farewell to his talent in the Ode, there would be some hint of an endangered or vanishing talent in "Resolution and Independence." But there is none; at the end of the poem Wordsworth is resolute in poetry.

Must we not, then, look with considerable skepticism at such interpretations of the Ode and suppose without question that the "gleam," the "glory," and the "dream" constitute the power of making poetry?—especially when we remember that at a time still three years distant Wordsworth in *The Prelude* will speak of himself as becoming a *"creative* soul" (book xii, line 207; the italics are Wordsworth's own) despite the fact that, as he says (book xii, line 281), he "sees by glimpses now."

The second half of the Ode is divided into two large movements, each of which gives an answer to the question with which the first part ends. The two answers seem to contradict each other. The first issues in despair, the second in hope; the first uses a language strikingly supernatural, the second is entirely naturalistic. The two parts even differ in the statement of fact, for the first says that the gleam is gone, whereas the second says that it is not gone, but only transmuted. It is necessary to understand this contradiction, but it is not necessary to resolve it, for from the circuit between its two poles comes much of the power of the poem.

The first of the two answers (stanzas v-viii) tells us where the visionary gleam has gone by telling us where it came from. It is a remnant of a pre-existence in which we enjoyed a way of seeing and knowing now almost wholly gone from us. We come into the world, not with minds that are merely *tabulae rasae,* but with a kind of attendant light, the vestige of an existence otherwise obliterated from our memories. In infancy and childhood the recollection is relatively strong, but it fades as we move forward into earthly life. Maturity, with its habits and its cares and its increase of distance from our celestial origin, wears away the light of recollection. Nothing could be more poignantly sad than the conclusion of this part with the heavy sonority of its last line as Wordsworth addresses the child in whom the glory still lives:

> Full soon thy Soul shall have her earthly freight,
> And custom lie upon thee with a weight,
> Heavy as frost, and deep almost as life!

Between this movement of despair and the following movement of hope there is no clear connection save that of contradiction. But between the question itself and the movement of hope there is an explicit verbal link, for the question is: "Whither has *fled* the visionary gleam?" and the movement of hope answers that "nature yet remembers/What was so *fugitive.*"

The second movement of the second part of the Ode tells us again what has happened to the visionary gleam: it has not wholly fled, for it is remembered. This possession of childhood has been passed on as a legacy to the child's heir, the adult man; for the mind, as the rainbow epigraph also says, is one and continuous, and what was so intense a light in childhood becomes "the fountain-light of all our day" and a "master-light of all our seeing," that is, of our adult day and our mature seeing. The child's recollection of his heavenly home exists in the recollection of the adult.

But what exactly is this fountain-light, this master-light? I am sure that when we understand what it is we shall see that the glory that Wordsworth means is very different from Coleridge's glory, which is Joy. Wordsworth says that what he holds in memory as the guiding heritage of childhood is exactly not the Joy of childhood. It is not "delight," not "liberty," not even "hope"—not for these, he says, "I raise/The song of thanks and praise." For what then does he raise the song? For this particular experience of childhood:

> . . . those obstinate questionings
> Of sense and outward things,
> Fallings from us, vanishings;
> Blank misgivings of a Creature
> Moving about in worlds not realised.

He mentions other reasons for gratitude, but here for the moment I should like to halt the enumeration.

We are told, then, that light and glory consist, at least in part, of "questionings," "fallings from us," "vanishings," and "blank misgivings" in a world not yet *made real,* for surely Wordsworth uses the word "realised" in its most literal sense. In his note on the poem he has this to say of the experience he refers to:

> . . . I was often unable to think of external things as having external exist-
> ence, and I communed with all that I saw as something not apart from, but
> inherent in, my own material nature. Many times while going to school have
> I grasped at a wall or tree to recall myself from this abyss of idealism to the
> reality. At this time I was afraid of such processes.

He remarks that the experience is not peculiar to himself, which is of course true, and he says that it was connected in his thoughts with a potency of spirit which made him believe that he could never die.

The precise and naturalistic way in which Wordsworth talks of this experience of his childhood must cast doubt on Professor Garrod's statement that Wordsworth believed quite literally in the notion of pre-existence, with which the "vanishings" experience is connected. Wordsworth is very careful to delimit the extent of his belief; he says that it is "too shadowy a notion to be recommended to faith" as an evidence of immortality. He says that he is using the idea to illuminate another idea—using it, as he says, "for my purpose" and "as a poet." It has as much validity for him as any "popular" religious idea might have, that is to say, a kind of suggestive validity. We may regard pre-existence as being for Wordsworth a very serious conceit, vested with relative belief, intended to give a high value to the natural experience of the "vanishings."[4]

The naturalistic tone of Wordsworth's note suggests that we shall be doing no violence to the experience of the "vanishings" if we consider it scientifically. In a well-known essay, "Stages in the Development of the Sense of Reality," the distinguished psychoanalyst Ferenczi speaks of the child's reluctance to distinguish between himself and the world and of the slow growth of objectivity which differentiates the self from external things. And Freud himself, dealing with the "oceanic" sensation of "being at one with the universe," which a literary friend had supposed to be the source of all religious emotions, conjectures that it is a vestige of the infant's state of feeling before he has learned to distinguish between the stimuli of his own sensations and those of the world outside. In *Civilization and Its Discontents* he writes:

> Originally the ego includes everything, later it detaches from itself the outside world. The ego-feeling we are aware of now is thus only a shrunken vestige of a more extensive feeling—a feeling which embraced the universe and expressed an inseparable connection of the ego with the external world. If we may suppose that this primary ego-feeling has been preserved in the minds of many people—to a greater or lesser extent—it would co-exist like a sort of counterpart with the narrower and more sharply outlined ego-feeling of maturity, and the ideational content belonging to it would be precisely the notion of limitless extension and oneness with the universe—the same feeling as that described by my friend as "oceanic."

---

[4] In his *Studies in the Poetry of Henry Vaughan,* a Cambridge University dissertation, Andrew Chiappe makes a similar judgment of the quality and degree of belief in the idea of pre-existence in the poetry of Vaughan and Traherne.

This has its clear relation to Wordsworth's "worlds not realised." Wordsworth, like Freud, was preoccupied by the idea of reality, and, again like Freud, he knew that the child's way of apprehension was but a stage which, in the course of nature, would give way to another. If we understand that Wordsworth is speaking of a period common to the development of everyone, we are helped to see that we cannot identify the vision of that period with his peculiar poetic power.

But in addition to the experience of the "vanishings" there is another experience for which Wordsworth is grateful to his childhood and which, I believe, goes with the "vanishings" to make up the "master-light," the "fountain-light." I am not referring to the

> High instincts before which our mortal Nature
> Did tremble like a guilty Thing surprised,

but rather to what Wordsworth calls "those first affections."

I am inclined to think that with this phrase Wordsworth refers to a later stage in the child's development which, like the earlier stage in which the external world is included within the ego, leaves vestiges in the developing mind. This is the period described in a well-known passage in Book II of *The Prelude,* in which the child learns about the world in his mother's arms:

> Blest the infant Babe,
> (For with my best conjecture I would trace
> Our Being's earthly progress), blest the Babe,
> Nursed in his Mother's arms, who sings to sleep,
> Rocked on his Mother's breast; who with his soul
> Drinks in the feelings of his Mother's eye!
> For him, in one dear Presence, there exists
> A virtue which irradiates and exalts
> Objects through widest intercourse of sense.
> No outcast he, bewildered and depressed:
> Along his infant veins are interfused
> The gravitation and the filial bond
> Of nature that connect him with the world.
> Is there a flower, to which he points with hand
> Too weak to gather it, already love
> Drawn from love's purest earthly fount for him
> Hath beautified that flower; already shades
> Of pity cast from inward tenderness
> Do fall around him upon aught that bears

Unsightly marks of violence or harm.
Emphatically such a Being lives,
Frail creature as he is, helpless as frail,
An inmate of this active universe:
For feeling has to him imparted power
That through the growing faculties of sense,
Doth like an agent of the one great Mind
Create, creator and receiver both,
Working but in alliance with the works
Which it beholds.—Such, verily, is the first
Poetic[5] spirit of our human life,
By uniform control of after years,
In most, abated or suppressed; in some,
Through every change of growth and of decay
Pre-eminent till death.

The child, this passage says, does not perceive things merely as objects; he first sees them, because maternal love is a condition of his perception, as objects-and-judgments, as valued objects. He does not learn about a flower, but about the pretty-flower, the flower that-I-want-and-that-mother-will-get-for-me; he does not learn about the bird and a broken wing but about the poor-bird-whose-wing-was-broken. The safety, warmth, and good feeling of his mother's conscious benevolence is a circumstance of his first learning. He sees, in short, with "glory"; not only is he himself not in "utter nakedness" as the Ode puts it, but the objects he sees are not in utter nakedness. The passage from *The Prelude* says in naturalistic language what stanza v of the Ode expresses by a theistical metaphor. Both the *Prelude* passage and the Ode distinguish a state of exile from a state of security and comfort, of at-homeness; there is (as the *Prelude* passage puts it) a "filial bond," or (as in stanza x of the Ode) a "primal sympathy," which keeps man from being an "outcast . . . bewildered and depressed."

The Ode and *The Prelude* differ about the source of this primal sympathy of filial bond. The Ode makes heavenly pre-existence the source, *The Prelude* finds the source in maternal affection. But the psychologists tell us that notions of heavenly pre-existence figure commonly as representations of physical prenatality—the womb is the environment which is perfectly adapted to its inmate and compared to it all other conditions of life may well seem like

---

[5] The use here of the word "poetic" is either metaphorical and general, or it is entirely literal, that is, it refers to the root-meaning of the word, which is "to make"—Wordsworth has in mind the creative nature of right human perception and not merely poetry.

[497]

"exile" to the (very literal) "outcast."[6] Even the security of the mother's arms, although it is an effort to re-create for the child the old environment, is but a diminished comfort. And if we think of the experience of which Wordsworth is speaking, the "vanishings," as the child's recollection of a condition in which it was very nearly true that he and his environment were one, it will not seem surprising that Wordsworth should compound the two experiences and figure them in the single metaphor of the glorious heavenly pre-existence.[7]

I have tried to be as naturalistic as possible in speaking of Wordsworth's childhood experiences and the more-or-less Platonic notion they suggested to him. I believe that naturalism is in order here, for what we must now see is that Wordsworth is talking about something common to us all, the development of the sense of reality. To have once had the visionary gleam of the perfect union of the self and the universe is essential to and definitive of our human nature, and it is in that sense connected with the making of poetry. But the visionary gleam is not in itself the poetry-making power, and its diminution is right and inevitable.

That there should be ambivalence in Wordsworth's response to this diminution is quite natural, and the two answers, that of stanzas v-viii and that of stanzas ix-xi, comprise both the resistance to and the acceptance of growth. Inevitably we resist change and turn back with passionate nostalgia to the stage we are leaving. Still, we fulfill ourselves by choosing what is painful and difficult and necessary, and we develop by moving toward death. In short, organic development is a hard paradox which Wordsworth is stating in the discrepant answers of the second part of the Ode. And it seems to me that those critics who made the Ode refer to some particular and unique experience of Wordsworth's and who make it relate only to poetical powers have forgotten their own lives and in consequence conceive the Ode to be a lesser thing than it really is, for it is not about poetry, it is about life. And having made this error, they are inevitably led to misinterpret the meaning of the "philosophic mind" and also to deny that Wordsworth's ambivalence is

---

[6] "Before born babe bliss had. Within womb won he worship. Whatever in that one case done commodiously done was."—James Joyce, *Ulysses*. The myth of Eden is also interpreted as figuring either childhood or the womb—see below Wordsworth's statement of the connection of the notion of pre-existence with Adam's fall.

[7] Readers of Ferenczi's remarkable study, *Thalassa*, a discussion, admittedly speculative but wonderfully fascinating, of unconscious racial memories of the ocean as the ultimate source of life, will not be able to resist giving an added meaning to Wordsworth's lines about the "immortal sea/Which brought us hither" and of the unborn children who "Sport upon the shore." The recollection of Samuel Butler's delightful fantasy of the Unborn and his theory of unconscious memory will also serve to enrich our reading of the Ode by suggesting the continuing force of the Platonic myth.

sincere. No doubt it would not be a sincere ambivalence if Wordsworth were really saying farewell to poetry, it would merely be an attempt at self-consolation. But he is not saying farewell to poetry, he is saying farewell to Eden, and his ambivalence is much what Adam's was, and Milton's, and for the same reasons.[8]

To speak naturalistically of the quasi-mystical experiences of his childhood does not in the least bring into question the value which Wordsworth attached to them, for, despite its dominating theistical metaphor, the Ode is largely naturalistic in its intention. We can begin to see what that intention is by understanding the force of the word "imperial" in stanza vi. This stanza is the second of the four stanzas in which Wordsworth states and develops the theme of the reminiscence of the light of heaven and its gradual evanescence through the maturing years. In Stanza v we are told that the infant inhabits it; the Boy beholds it, seeing it "in his joy"; the Youth is still attended by it; "the Man perceives it die away,/And fade into the light of common day." Stanza vi speaks briefly of the efforts made by earthly life to bring about the natural and inevitable amnesia:

> Earth fills her lap with pleasures of her own;
> Yearnings she hath in her own natural kind,
> And even with something of a Mother's mind,
> And no unworthy aim,
> The homely Nurse doth all she can
> To make her Foster-child, her Inmate Man,
> Forget the glories he hath known,
> And that imperial palace whence he came.

"Imperial" suggests grandeur, dignity, and splendor, everything that stands in opposition to what, in *The Excursion,* Wordsworth was to call "littleness." And "littleness" is the result of having wrong notions about the nature of man and his connection with the universe; its outcome is "deadness." The melancholy and despair of the Solitary in *The Excursion* are the signs of the

---

[8] Milton provides a possible gloss to several difficult points in the poem. In stanza viii, the Child is addressed as "thou Eye among the blind," and to the Eye are applied the epithets "deaf and silent"; Colderidge objected to these epithets as irrational, but his objection may be met by citing the brilliant precedent of "blind mouths" of "Lycidas." Again, Coleridge's question of the propriety of making a master *brood* over a slave is in part answered by the sonnet "On His Being Arrived at the Age of Twenty-three," in which Milton expresses his security in his development as it shall take place in his "great Task-master's eye." Between this sonnet and the Ode there are other significant correspondences of thought and of phrase; there are also correspondences to the Ode in the sonnet "On His Blindness."

deadness which resulted from his having conceived of man as something less than imperial. Wordsworth's idea of splendid power is his protest against all views of the mind that would limit and debase it. By conceiving, as he does, an intimate connection between mind and universe, by seeing the universe fitted to the mind and the mind to the universe, he bestows upon man a dignity which cannot be derived from looking at him in the actualities of common life, from seeing him engaged in business, in morality and politics.

Yet here we must credit Wordsworth with the double vision. Man must be conceived of as "imperial," but he must also be seen as he actually is in the field of life. The earth is not an environment in which the celestial or imperial qualities can easily exist. Wordsworth, who spoke of the notion of imperial pre-existence as being adumbrated by Adam's fall, uses the words "earth" and "earthly" in the common quasi-religious sense to refer to the things of this world. He does not make Earth synonymous with Nature, for although Man may be the true child of Nature, he is the "Foster-child" of Earth. But it is to be observed that the foster mother is a kindly one, that her disposition is at least quasi-maternal, that her aims are at least not unworthy; she is, in short, the foster mother who figures so often in the legend of the Hero, whose real and unknown parents are noble or divine.[9]

Wordsworth, in short, is looking at man in a double way, seeing man both in his ideal nature and in his earthly activity. The two views do not so much contradict as supplement each other. If in stanzas v-viii Wordsworth tells us that we live by decrease, in stanzas ix-xi he tells us of the everlasting connection of the diminished person with his own ideal personality. The child hands on to the hampered adult the imperial nature, the "primal sympathy/Which having been must ever be," the mind fitted to the universe, the universe to the mind. The sympathy is not so pure and intense in maturity as in childhood, but only because another relation grows up beside the relation of man to Nature—the relation of man to his fellows in the moral world of difficulty and pain. Given Wordsworth's epistemology the new relation is bound to change the very aspect of Nature itself: the clouds will take a somber coloring from an eye that hath kept watch o'er man's mortality, but a somber color is a color still.

There is sorrow in the Ode, the inevitable sorrow of giving up an old habit of vision for a new one. In shifting the center of his interest from Nature to man in the field of morality Wordsworth is fulfilling his own conception of the three ages of man which Professor Beatty has expounded so well. The

---

[9] Carlyle makes elaborate play with this idea in his account of Teufelsdröckh. . . . The fantasy that their parents are really foster parents is a common one with children, and it is to be associated with the various forms of the belief that the world is not real.

shift in interest he called the coming of "the philosophic mind," but the word "philosophic" does not have here either of two of its meanings in common usage—it does not mean abstract and it does not mean apathetic. Wordsworth is not saying, and it is sentimental and unimaginative of us to say, that he has become less a feeling man and less a poet. He is only saying that he has become less a youth. Indeed, the Ode is so little a farewell to art, so little a dirge sung over departing powers, that it is actually the very opposite—it is a welcome of new powers and a dedication to a new poetic subject. For if sensitivity and responsiveness be among the poetic powers, what else is Wordsworth saying at the end of the poem except that he has a greater sensitivity and responsiveness than ever before? The "philosophic mind" has not decreased but, on the contrary, increased the power to feel.

> The clouds that gather round the setting sun
> Do take a sober colouring from an eye
> That hath kept watch o'er man's mortality;
> Another race hath been and other palms are won.
> Thanks to the human heart by which we live,
> Thanks to its tenderness, it joys, and fears,
> To me the meanest flower that blows can give
> Thoughts that do often lie too deep for tears.

The meanest flower is significant now not only because, like the small celandine, it speaks of age, suffering, and death, but because to a man who is aware of man's mortality the world becomes significant and precious. The knowledge of man's mortality—this must be carefully noted in a poem presumably about immortality—now replaces the "glory" as the agency which makes things significant and precious. We are back again at optics, which we have never really left, and the Ode in a very honest fashion has come full circle.

The new poetic powers of sensitivity and responsiveness are new not so much in degree as in kind; they would therefore seem to require a new poetic subject matter for their exercise. And the very definition of the new powers seems to imply what the new subject matter must be—thoughts that lie too deep for tears are ideally the thoughts which are brought to mind by tragedy. It would be an extravagant but not an absurd reading of the Ode that found it to be Wordsworth's farewell to the characteristic mode of his poetry, the mode that Keats called the "egotistical sublime" and a dedication to the mode of tragedy. But the tragic mode could not be Wordsworth's. He did not have the "negative capability" which Keats believed to be the source of Shakespeare's power, the gift of being able to be "content with half-knowledge," to give up the "irritable reaching after fact and reason," to remain "in uncertainties, mysteries, doubts." In this he was at one with all the poets of the Romantic Movement and after—negative capability was impossible for them to come by and tragedy was not for them. But although Wordsworth did not realize the new kind of art which seems implied by his sense of new powers, yet his bold declaration that he had acquired a new way of feeling makes it impossible for us to go on saying that the Ode was his "conscious farewell to his art, a dirge sung over his departing powers."

Still, was there not, after the composition of the Ode, a great falling off in his genius which we are drawn to connect with the crucial changes the Ode records? That there was a falling off is certain, although we must observe that it was not so sharp as is commonly held and also that it did not occur immediately or even soon after the composition of the first four stanzas with their statement that the visionary gleam had gone; on the contrary, some of the most striking of Wordsworth's verse was written at this time. It must be remembered too that another statement of the loss of the visionary gleam, that made in "Tintern Abbey," had been followed by all the superb production of the "great decade"—an objection which is sometimes dealt with by saying that Wordsworth wrote his best work from his near memories of the gleam, and that, as he grew older and moved farther from it, his recollection dimmed and thus he lost his power: it is an explanation which suggests that mechanical and simple notions of the mind and of the poetic process are all too tempting to those who speculate on Wordsworth's decline. Given the fact of the great power, the desire to explain its relative deterioration will no doubt always be irresistible. But we must be aware, in any attempt to make this explanation, that an account of why Wordsworth ceased to write great poetry must at the same time be an account of how he once did write great poetry. And this latter account, in our present state of knowledge, we cannot begin to furnish.

S T E N D H A L

(HENRI BEYLE)

[*1783–1842*]

STENDHAL'S *Le Rouge et le Noir* IS A NOVEL OF POST-NAPOLEONIC FRANCE.
Julien Sorel, the hero, seeks opportunities for heroic action in the church
("black," as are its vestments), and in the army ("red," as are its uniforms).
He bursts through the rotten fabric of prevailing institutions and dies a character in a legend of his own making, demonstrating that, failing heroic
achievement, men of great powers turn on themselves and those who love
them. *The Red and the Black* depicts Julien as mercilessly as the world he
encounters; Stendhal's capacity to balance oppositions, to modulate ideas
with other ideas, interests Jacques Barzun most in the following essay.

Barzun finds certain figures especially congenial, among them Samuel
Butler, Walter Bagehot, Bernard Shaw, and Stendhal. All have an awareness
that the life of the mind is a matter of confrontations: of one time with
another, of an idea with its opposite, of a current cliché with a historical
fact. Perhaps the sympathy with which Barzun enters into Stendhal's gay
heroism is a historian's tribute to a writer who dealt with nineteenth-century
society in terms that seem ever more clairvoyant.

Jacques Barzun is Provost and Professor of History at Columbia
University.

Stendhal on Love

THE PURITAN IMPULSE HAS SURELY FAILED AND DIED IN OUR ENGLISH-SPEAK-ing lands when we see that an author highly esteemed for two great novels—and a Frenchman at that—can find no readers for a book entitled *De l'Amour*.

This indifference suggests that either the title is a misnomer or that its contents do not titillate. The first reason is to be looked into; the second holds. Some might even say, after slogging through Stendhal's book, that the author denies us every satisfaction; he flouts our conception of man and society as well as our idea of the way a serious work should be composed. If it were adequately dull or the least bit salacious or subtly flattering to our modern ego, *On Love* would long since have been taken up by the choruses of graduate research, and thanks to them every literate person would now know six phrases from it—in short, possess the book thoroughly, as times go.

Being the book it is, *On Love* has appeared in English twice, each time on both sides of the Atlantic, without attracting many more readers than when the little-known author first brought out the original in Paris in 1822. There may be some excuse for the reception of the translation prepared "under the supervision of C. K. Scott-Moncrieff," for it is pretty poor. But the earlier version by Philip and Cecil Sidney Woolf is excellent and deserves the repute it never obtained.

It deserved it because, as Stendhal knew and said, this work of theory which preceded all his novels throws light on them and on his mind, on his age and that which followed—the period 1880-1900-1935 to which he kept addressing himself, in despair of being heard by his own. Today, *On Love* seems very new and very old, and is correspondingly difficult to interpret steadily. Like Stendhal himself it baffles all those who do not understand in a flash what elements have gone into its making—into the making of so singular a man as its author, who seems to belong to every century beginning with the eighteenth. No eclectic compound but a true element, and yet not a blind force, he was what he professed to be, a logician of the emotions. But his own, which he freely exhibits, suggest by turns those of the Enlightened Voltaire, of the Romantic Byron, and of any sardonic modern you may choose. We rather expect the unique genius to be more of a piece.

These seemings explain why Stendhal has never been and is not now popular, even though Hollywood has bought an option on *The Red and the Black,* one wonders from whom. Here and in England, it is mainly writers and professional thinkers who form the little band of his admirers. As a lucky consequence, he has been spared both vogue and cult; there is no need of either when the textual scholarship which justifies a cult is being provided in France by a group of competent *beylistes.*[1]

Still, one could wish that the interest of the Anglo-American public went beyond *The Red and the Black* and *The Charterhouse of Parma,* so that it might be better prepared for Stendhal himself. Not long ago the reviewers of his so-called *Private Diaries* were reduced to calling him an enigma. Several lost their temper on finding the touted author "egotistical and weak"; and one disposed of him with the phrase "improbable genius." When Criticism turns defeatist or petulant it should promptly search itself to find the exposed nerve that has been touched. The truth is that Stendhal and the modern image of the self bear a close resemblance; and even when he is clearly more fortunate or, as some think, inherently superior, he does not grow less congenial. One reason is that, like his Alpine neighbor Berlioz, he never puts on "side." So there is no need to fight, or fight shy, but simply to come nearer and look within.

---

[1] Their appellation, derived from Stendhal's real name, Henri Beyle, follows his custom of referring to his moral attitude as *le beylisme,* rather than *le Stendhalisme* as might have been expected.

Love is, to be sure, an impossible subject. Everyone is bound to think himself an authority upon it, though at best able to speak for only half the constituency; and what is worse, the ruling assumption about love is that it remains ever itself, one of Nature's constants, defying history as easily as it does convention. So we are all uncommonly tempted to dismiss as ignorant or perverse any report at variance with our impressions. These prejudices are fatal to Stendhal. No one can find merit in his long, meandering, and over-allusive essay who is not willing to do two things—translate ideas across the frontier of time and draw up a fair balance sheet of similarity and difference between our convictions and his.

He shares, for example, our pretensions to scientific detachment. He does not simply describe or discuss, he *studies* love and he concludes, soberly, that it is a disease. He means that love is oddly external to ourselves, an obsession, a force independent of our will, and yet related to our aggressiveness. Freud comes to mind when Stendhal writes: "Cruelty is only an ailing affection. Power comes next to love in making us happy only because it makes us believe that we can *command* affection." These and other observations soon persuade us that *De l'Amour* stands on the modern side of the Sexual Revolution, the great change in moral axioms which took place toward the end of the nineteenth century and vindicated at long last the postulates of such Romantics as Blake, Stendhal, Gautier, and Schopenhauer. Coming after Montesquieu, Diderot and Rousseau, Stendhal is of them all the one who most boldly and shockingly recorded the truths of sexuality. Most notable is his account of the lustful adoration he felt as a child for his mother and the jealous hatred with which he pursued his father all his life.[2]

We love Stendhal for this, no doubt, but are then put off by his apparent worship of love itself. Love is a disease, love is folly, it makes the cleverest man ridiculous, but Stendhal also believes it is the delight *and the merit* of superior minds. He relates a typically foolish love illusion in a young girl, and adds: "This is what people of low intelligence would call one of the absurdities of love." For his own part (as for Molière) it is the absurdities that are the purest reason. He declares: "Love has always been for me the greatest of all concerns, or rather, the only one." We shake our heads over this and explain it away as the unfortunate sequel, precisely, of the broken love-affair with the mother. She died when Stendhal was seven, and he was brought up in the worst manner possible by a timid, ugly, repressed father and a beautiful but shrewish and bigoted aunt. His numerous "victories of love" in later life never, we suppose, assuaged his hunger; and so he never became one of those well-adjusted organisms approved by later textbooks.

---

[2] This "confession" does not occur in *De l'Amour* but in the autobiography, *La Vie de Henri Brulard*, Chapter 3.

All this is plausible. But Stendhal cannot be psychologized out of his competence about love. His observations still have upon them the bloom of original genius, and however we interpret his reports on the direct experience of passion, we cannot say he is either taken in or a willing dupe. On the contrary, he shows many of the traits our century admires: factuality, self-mockery, intense curiosity, distrust of appearances, hatred of the crowd as well as of bourgeois ideals, addiction to art, contempt for politics, and a sense of rivalry toward women, mixed with zeal for their equality. Other tendencies in him will fill the opposite side of the ledger and perhaps baffle us again. Meanwhile Stendhal's style testifies to his being one of us: that sharp, jerky prose is the fit instrument for puncturing every sort of sentimentality, for making new opinions stick with barbs. So stern an analyst abhors rhetoric—that is, every rhetoric but that of terseness—and he knows why: "I dared," he says in explaining the failure of *De l'Amour,*

> to despise the fashionable style; I saw the literary beginner wholly bent on avoiding the unrhythmical close of his sentences or the ugly succession of sounds. But at the same time he never hesitated to change any and every detail in matters that are hard to express. Voltaire himself is afraid of things that are hard to express. Now my *Essay on Love* could be of value only through the number of small nuances of feeling which I begged the reader to verify in his own recollections—if he was lucky enough to have any.

The attempt to outdo Voltaire in sharpness and fidelity to fact often makes Stendhal obscure. But when he is successful it produces the *raccourci,* or short-circuiting of feeling and idea which is his hallmark: "People who are happy in love are profoundly attentive, which to a Frenchman means profoundly sad." That is all—no context. The unaccustomed reader wonders, What is hidden here? The three ideas seem to lack liaison. But one need not go very far to discover that whatever Stendhal has to say about love leads to every other subject he has ideas upon. Though he nowhere expounds it systematically, he calls the whole "my system." Its structure shows up like bone shadow in all the author's didactic or reflective works, and when the light is seen behind the shadow it illuminates the asides and obscurities in the novels.

The principle of the system is what we should call today irony or dialectic —the deep-rooted intimacy of opposites. We have already seen Stendhal pointing out not the two aspects of love, sublime and ridiculous, but their oneness. The subject has endless ramifications in which the irony persists: "There is no doubt that it is pure folly for a man to expose himself to passion-love. But sometimes the remedy works too effectively. Young American girls are so penetrated and fortified with reasonable ideas that love, the flower of life, has in that country deserted youth." *What* remedy? we want to know. Why "passion-love"—as if there were some other kind? And by what authority does Stendhal pretend to speak about American girls? Well, the "remedy" is the impulse to shrink from folly, the determination to avoid ridicule by reason. Rejecting the remedy, Stendhal is surely not one of us. But pursuing his own reason he argues that the avoidance of ridicule destroys the "miracle of civilization" by which in well-born souls lust begets love.

To miss love is for him to lose one's reason for being—which is a very strong reason indeed. And there are consequences that go beyond the individual. The absence of love in the United States illustrates for him the difference between a good government and a good society, between security and happiness. As a liberal, Stendhal admires American freedom and ascribes it to the citizens' control over their government—reversing the European order. But that same benevolent government becomes a hypocritical agent of moral oppression when the society devotes itself to being sensible and avoiding trouble at all costs. It should remember to devote itself to the pursuit of happiness and avoid boredom. "What strengthens my conjecture," adds Stendhal, "is the total lack of artists and writers. The United States have not yet given us a tragic scene, a picture, or a life of Washington." Thus do we pass from the cure of love's foolishness in young girls to the deficient culture of free states.

If only Stendhal had loved literary order as much as he did simplicity! All the fine small steps of the demonstration, which are really there, would appear in their proper place and rout dissent. Nobody then could question the seriousness of the system, despite its improbable classifications of love and its formulas drawn from botany and mineralogy—passion-love, crystallization, and the rest. But alas, Stendhal preferred to anticipate Proust and mirror the stream of his consciousness. Like Montesquieu, who is one of his great unrecognized models, his mind scorned the sweaty logic of the treatise-maker. And for all we know, he enjoyed undermining the tiresome generality about classical form in great French writers: Montesquieu, Diderot, and Stendhal confirm the lesson of Rabelais and Montaigne that form is secondary to substance. In short, there is no help for it: after the first few pages Stendhal's views must be acquired, as he himself acquired them, from the natural progress of his thought: "I ruminate incessantly on what interests me; by dint of looking at it from different *mental positions,* I end by seeing something new in it and *I change its aspect.*"

But what of passion-love? It is the highest of four types of love, born of different kinds of temperament, upbringing, and social milieu. The other three are: the purely physical, the love that springs from vanity, and the love ruled by good taste within a confined social circle.[3] Having distinguished

---

[3] The descending order of worth in Stendhal's eyes is: *l'amour-passion, l'amour-goût, l'amour physique, l'amour de vanité.*

four kinds, Stendhal admits that there may be infinite mixtures and grada-tions. It is the dominant quality in each that interests him, and particularly the character of the passionate. This is the strongest and noblest, being the one in which what Stendhal calls Crystallization is most evident and power-ful. The term comes by analogy from the effect of dipping a twig into a saline spring so that the branch later comes out sparkling as with diamonds. In love, crystallization endows its object with compelling perfections as a result of centering attention and projecting desire upon one person. The lower kinds of love disclose inferior powers of mind and heart, and presum-ably a duller crystallization, but it occurs throughout the scale. If this suggests that Stendhal puts highest the love that breeds the greatest amount of illusion, the answer is, "Quite so." But illusion here is not synonymous with untruth. The bespangled twig is real; it is more beautiful than the bare bough, and for this we single it out and prolong our interest in it. Nor does crystallization take place at will, or upon any chance object. It comes as a mystery and a boon, for it demands all that a man can muster of thought and emotion, re-turning it to him in the perfected form of the intensely desirable and uniquely beautiful beloved. As in art, not even the clear perception of faults diminishes the truth of beauty. This is why love is the source of man's highest happiness, and hence the real folly is to avoid its apparent folly.

Such is the reason of Romantic love. It is, as Yeats says, a discipline: "Each divines the secret self of the other, and refusing to believe in the mere daily self, creates a mirror where the lover or the beloved sees an image to copy in daily life." This presupposes a secret self worth mirroring, and if Stendhal is able—as we no longer are—to build on passion-love a social and cultural ideal, it is because unlike the twentieth-century skeptic he has encountered noble souls. We—or some among us—believe rather that by "adjusting" the love "function," we can *regulate* the aggressive impulses. The "behavioral scien-tist" is the clock-maker writ large, as is shown by his frequent reference to what makes people tick. As against this, Stendhal continues to speak of "qualities of mind and heart," to which he accords absolute importance. These qualities are supreme because, precious as is the transient happiness they afford to man in love, they also serve the next best agencies of happiness, which are society and art. The junction of Stendhal's three great themes—love, art, and the good life—results from his belief that spontaneity is their common source. To take joy in living is to be conscious of free activity. It follows that hypocrisy is the worst vice. On this premise Stendhal can sketch in a few strokes a casual utopia which without this clue might seem inconse-quential: "In my opinion a man ought to be a passionate lover and at the same time should carry life and animation into every company where he hap-pens to be. This universal gaiety, moreover, this art of pleasing everybody, ought not to rest on the art of flattering everybody's tastes and weaknesses.

... The amenity I desired [as a youth] was the pure joy of Shakespeare in his comedies, the charm that reigned at the court of the exiled duke in the forest of Arden."

The curious thing is that this proponent of passion, who pursued with Shakespearean images the vision of its flowering in a cultivated society akin to Rabelais's *Abbaye de Thélème,* was not only the most caustic recorder of love's antics (whether in himself or in his fictional heroes), but also a strong adherent to the theory of mind's physical causation. The names of Cabanis, Condillac and Destutt de Tracy recur in his pages to help him explain character traits by climate and physiology.

At this point "the system" will certainly seem inconsistent, but only if one supposes that all its elements are equally Stendhal's conclusions about life. Some, it is clear, are instruments—for example the materialist physiology just mentioned, which serves to deflate religious and sentimental make-believe. But what is real and how do we ascertain this? The self-consciousness, mocking and anxious by turns, which makes Stendhal seem so close to us, is the method for testing what experience and imagination wantonly propose. As for the desire to explore the world for its yield of reality, that is simply the business of life for Romanticist genius.

De l'Amour is in consequence none of the things it might be supposed to be or to resemble—a manual for seducers, a medley of aphorisms and autobiography, a confusion of psychology with fiction, a clumsy liberal pamphlet by a man with a grudge against his country. It is about love, and its title is no misnomer. But the subject is so ruminated upon that its aspect changes and the volume is nothing less than a discourse on civilization. Its three themes Stendhal could never disentangle because their union defined for him the final cause of man. And though his acuteness delighted to transfix minute nuances of feeling, he was an enemy to the specialism that might have found his trinity irrelevant when he defended Romantic art in *Racine and Shakespeare,* described his childhood, in *Henry Brulard,* or "chronicled 1830" in *The Red and the Black*. His inclusive and anthropological outlook may make us impatient by its lack of form, but it is not so alien to our ways of thought that we need to excuse it. All we need do is identify it. Read *De l'Amour,* then, as the prolegomenon to Stendhal's other works and also to Freud's *Civilization and Its Discontents.*

Granting that Stendhal's "system" has value for its frequent extraordinary shortcuts among ideas, it is nonetheless tempting to reject the man as "improbable." Here is a writer visited with the stroke of genius to represent in a novel the battle of Waterloo as a hoax: an actual eyewitness does not see, cannot know what is going on. A great battle is a pure construct after the fact. Yes: Tolstoy only had to expand the brilliant notion. But Tolstoy was consistent, whereas the same Stendhal who debunked Waterloo revered Napoleon and wrote two books about him.

Then Stendhal makes an axiom of his belief that the prime condition of virtue is strength. Nietzsche read this and never forgot the revelation. But our early apostle of the Third Morality tells us repeatedly that his happiest moments were those of tender reverie, of giving way to tears, of "charming visions of the beautiful that still haunt me at fifty-two." Again, in all his writings we discover that what Stendhal hates next to hypocrisy is pedantry; he knows that sociability and wit are killed by fact-grubbing, the virtue par excellence of his bourgeois and our democratic century. But this same aristocrat is fanatical about noting down the *petit fait vrai,* to the point where there is little left for Proust to do in the way of minuteness. And to make matters worse, Stendhal is a liar, mystifier, and plagiarist, who as he writes spends half hours wondering whether the truth is in him. At least once he confesses that all his life it has been his "idea, not reality" that he saw. In the novels—to pursue the indictment—he exalts ambition, high manners, and the play of cultivated wits. But after self-searching he admits that he despises power and loves only simplicity. His hierarchy of loves puts the physical and the vainglorious as the two lowest kinds, but his diaries show him scheming for "victories" indifferently over chambermaids and great ladies.

Art, finally, was for him the quasi-religion it has since become for many; he was among the first to make philosophy out of music. But he does not accord music or the other arts the autonomy we have come to expect; he uses them cavalierly as texts to remind him of his emotional pretexts. He foretells and half-codifies the esthetics of his age, demanding that all the arts be expressive, dramatic, untrammeled, and above all modern. But while he acts as guerrilla and ground-clearer for Romanticism, he struggles to keep the lyrical out of his writing and ridicules in Chateaubriand and others the "beautiful visions" akin to his own.

These contrasts are too great to be explained by irony and too deliberate to be ascribed to the hybrid culture of his formative years—from the Terror to Waterloo. He was, to be sure, twenty years older than Hugo, Berlioz, and Delacroix, but that need not have caused the precursor of their artistic philosophy to appear so completely contradictory. If the age was all-compelling, why did Stendhal revolt against both the old and the new in it? In keeping with his theories of heredity and environment, he liked to attribute his rebellion to his birth in Dauphiné and his maternal ancestors of supposedly Italian origin: he was a passionate man, he must necessarily be as little of a Frenchman as possible. Having been to Milan as a soldier of seventeen, he forever after deemed himself an Italian, and from his thirty-seventh year began to fashion the epitaph which ultimately read: *"Arrigo Beyle, Milanese: visse, amò, scrisse."*[4] The race-and-climate men are free to enjoy their usual acrobatics over Stendhal's family origins. He gives them the lie himself when he refers to the "Spanish ideas" that he learned from his other, well-loved aunt; and again to the influences of Rousseau's *Nouvelle Héloïse,* which he says made him a man of integrity, and to Shakespeare and the *Edinburgh Review,* which, like Cabanis and Destutt, strengthened his love of concreteness and independence of public opinion.

The "Spanish ideas," it need hardly be said, are those of pride, honor, and magnanimity. Stendhal follows a tradition as old as Tacitus in assigning the traits he admires to foreign nations, with a view to castigating his own. His aim in all these vagaries is to show up the pettiness and futility of contemporary French culture. But since Stendhal was bred on French authors and formed in late adolescence by Paris manners, he could no more divest himself of certain French habits of thought than he could stamp out his simple and sincere patriotism. The first cause of his seeming inconsistency, then, lies in his being through and through a cultural critic, perhaps the first with an unlimited program. He does not merely preach English ways, like Voltaire, or a new morality and religion, like Blake. He fights in his loneliness on every battlefield—foreign versus French, post-Napoleonic versus old régime, artistic versus Philistine, the comic spirit versus the lyrical, the scientific versus the theological. Stendhal is, in other words, the first Nietzschean personality on the Continent, the counterpart of Blake and Hazlitt and Byron combined; and like Nietzsche's, his inchoateness appears as incoherence.

But it is not enough to account for a critic's inconsistencies by pointing to those present in the world he surveys. We must also allow for the psychological fact that we are always ready to forgive contradiction in those who are bitter and angry. Their animus, if it is at all congenial, begets its counterpart in us and suspends judgment. Thus we accept the chaotic fulminations of Léon Bloy or Rimbaud, the *Chants de Maldoror* and *Ubu Roi,* with an indulgent regard for their authors' being in a passion and superior to logic. Stendhal, it appears, talks a great deal about passion but never shows himself mastered by it. Rather, he is secretive about it, as in his pseudonyms, mystifying as in the "codes" of his diaries, private to the point of prudery. Everywhere he makes us emulate his coolness and we judge his ideas with the quizzicalness that his malicious style invites. Here is the characteristic self-management which insinuates that he needs no help or indulgence from us:

[4] "Henri Beyle, a Milanese: he lived, he loved, he wrote."

I recommend to most people born in the North to skip the present chapter. It is an obscure dissertation on a few phenomena having to do with the orange tree, a tree that grows (or attains its full growth) only in Italy and Spain. To be intelligible elsewhere, I should have *minimized* the facts. And that is what I should infallibly have done had I entertained for a moment the idea of writing a book meant to please generally. But Providence having denied me literary talent, I have meant only to describe, with all the churlishness of science, but also with all its exactness, certain facts of which my stay in the land of the orange tree has made me an involuntary witness.

Stendhal elaborates the irony, catches himself at it and adds: "Since this sincere statement might look like pride, I join to it the following reflexion." This is his famous remark about books being nothing else than lottery tickets. The winning ones are those posterity reprints. "Until then each of us, having written as best he could what seems to him true, hardly has any excuse for making fun of his neighbor—unless the mockery is amusing, in which case he is always justified, especially if he writes like Courier to Del Furia."[5]

Only after this self-conscious preamble do we reach the orange tree, which symbolizes the effects of passion-love. The orange tree is no more credible to Northerners than love to cold natures. But where is Stendhal's own passion? Neither in the preamble nor in the churlish exactitude of science, which goes on to speak as follows: the lover waiting for nightfall and a sight of his beloved

> looks at his watch every instant. He is delighted when he has managed to make ten minutes go by without a glance at it. The hour so long awaited finally strikes and when he is at her door, ready to knock, he would be glad not to find her in. Only by reflecting on it later would this be distressing. In a word, the waiting to see her produces an unpleasant effect. That is one of the things that make good people say that love is out of its mind. What happens is that the imagination is violently pulled away from delightful daydreams, every step of which yields happiness, and is brought back to severe reality.

The further result is to make the lover say things foolish or insincere to his beloved, or to keep away for fear of saying them. "When I first knew love, this strangeness I felt within made me suppose that I did not love." He would therefore plunge into talk. "The amount of stupidity I have uttered during the last two years in order not to keep my mouth shut reduces me to

---

[5] *On Love*, "Trip to an Unknown Land," Chapter 24. The allusions, as elsewhere in Stendhal, are purposely obscure. Did he not warn us about his obscurity?

despair when I think of it. This fact should make very clear to women the difference between passion-love and gallantry, between a loving soul and a prosaic one."

These extracts probably suggest to the discerning that here is a new literary genre, which ought to be called "passion science." For wrestling within Stendhal are those same two souls, loving and prosaic, imaginative and skeptical. His "method" has but one purpose—to verify the intimations of desire by "prose"; and thus, on occasion, he is not incapable of mere gallantry, of vanity-love or mere lust. Like Samuel Butler, also reared in a loveless province, what Stendhal fears is self-deception. This compels them alike to be double men. To the historical critic their lives will suggest how Romantic irony and two-sidedness ends as the modern temper. But in Stendhal (and rarely among us) the goal of self-consciousness is to achieve candor, not safety. He acknowledges whatever impulses he finds in himself—generous, heroic, vain, or abject, and sees that this leaves character to be made by choice, a choice uncontrolled by the fear of ridicule but guided by the pursuit of happiness. This is a trustworthy guide because the passionate heart and fastidious mind cannot be happy harboring lies or plotting a course by low cunning.

Rejecting these arts, superior natures paradoxically achieve happiness by perpetually risking it. They develop the habit of willing: "To will is to have the courage of exposing oneself to trouble; to expose oneself in this way is to take a chance, to gamble. Some who have been soldiers [Stendhal himself] cannot live without this risk. This is what makes them intolerable in family life." Note at the end the seeming irrelevance which is really a "short-circuit." In its flash of light, Stendhal's famous motto, "To live dangerously," appears as the fundamental criticism leveled by nineteenth-century genius at bourgeois existence. From time to time in the century the critique changes its stance: Byron the rebel, Gautier the sensualist, Baudelaire the dandy, Blake the visionary, Hazlitt the revolutionist, Carlyle and Ruskin the moral prophets, Flaubert the impassive realist, Nietzsche the antichrist, Shaw the socialist —all are taking a pose to say, "Trade, prudence, and the prosaic are death; passion, poetry, and the risks of wars are enhancers of life." The military mood is metaphorical—no need to be a soldier in the field to live dangerously. Speaking out in a drawing room shows equal courage in the face of a similar risk—as Stendhal often found to his cost. And a declaration of love, when it is not trifling, exemplifies the clear hazards of the will: it endangers the happiness of creatures consumable by passion.

It would be a mistake to see in Stendhal's references to the "victories of love" a further extension of the military metaphor, or worse, the conventional cliché expressive of the woman's "surrender," which leaves her "fallen" and the man conceited. This stage conception, though dimly truthful, argues in both lovers a preoccupation with vanity. Passion-love may well be felt as *mutual* conquest and defeat, though this will depend on manners and individual character. But the true Stendhalian idea of victory applies elsewhere, namely, to the conquest of the social self by Eros. Sexual passion is aggressive inwardly also, undoing the work of habit and self-control, and even dissolving the natural identity in the spasm of union. Unless this is seen as a miracle, not a mishap to be avoided, the essence of passion is not understood and its power of bestowing happiness is nullified. Love diminished may still afford pleasure, but it cannot justify itself as the chief concern of a civilized life. For while transforming lust into love, civilization has hedged the person with defenses (shame, vanity, and the rest) which are inimical to simple happiness. A complicated happiness—the only one possible—entails the deliberate primitivism of seeking to possess through love the "secret self" divined by Yeats, that is to say by the man of imagination.

Passion-love is thus the mainspring of that more general desire for the primitive which is common to high civilizations; and Stendhal, therefore, unmasks hypocrisy for the same reason that his master Rousseau struck at convention: both seek the irreducible substance of life in the burning core of emotion. Both are saying, not "Back" but "Forward to Nature." Or to put it still differently, if they could enter into our modern "healthy" attitude toward sex (as we call it), they would borrow another of our quaint terms and call it "unrealistic," contending that to take love as "a function" degrades it to something less courageous even than lust; while in overlooking passion's effect on the senses and the mind, we ignore its creation of a new and induplicable state, which is intimacy.

There are reasons, of course, why we cannot follow Stendhal's vision of love and happiness, no matter how much we agree with his estimate of prudent and prudish convention. The Sexual Revolution freed our tongues on the subject of sex, but the Industrial Revolution and democracy seem to have frozen our hearts and limbs for love's risks. What was still possible for Stendhal to feel and to act out is no longer open to us. He saw that love and art both required leisure, and whether in Paris or in Milan he enjoyed his fair share of it. No able man today, not even a rich able man, could lead such a life as his. Leisure has vanished while hobbies have increased and time has shrunk. Stendhal noticed the beginnings of agitated living, which in Paris reduced still further the scope allowed by the tyranny of ridicule. But in Italy leisure remained for music and love; spirit and instinct were given room, which enabled the privileged to live luckily and acquire "recollections."

One benefit preserved another. Though the women Stendhal knew were not educated precisely as he would have wished, many had the worldliness

and wit, the manners and the self-esteem, which made their social role a
charming spectacle and their intimacy the revelation of a secret self. This
self might in the end turn out stupid, vain, deceitful, or dully ambitious, but
the voyage of discovery afforded charming compensations. These decorative
obstacles to victory are not likely to be matched today by their modern
equivalents in the form of domesticated neuroses. Technicalities and bourgeois seriousness kill conversation just as home therapy kills love. Nor can
one imagine on the boudoir tables of the women whose salons Stendhal fre-
quented a "self-help" volume such as the one entitled *Conditioned Love: the
art of winning and holding a man's love,* which we are told is "written for
the woman who is neither beautiful nor ugly, neither brilliant nor stupid. It
recognizes the problems and limitations of the ordinary woman."[6] To this
Stendhal would very likely say that woman should be brilliant if unable to be
beautiful, and that if the sum of life is no more than an addition of problems,
the problems themselves had better not be dwelt on, but evaded or annihi-
lated. Otherwise life turns into social work, with oneself the sad case.

But to use such disparate words is to draw unfair comparisons, as if an age
or a man could translate chosen modes of conceived happiness into another's.
What today we should call the subjective element, meaning the quality of
personal and social imagination, determines the amount of reality—hence of
joy—to be found in the objects of desire. Contrast Baudelaire's imagination
of love with Stendhal's and the range of possible difference appears even in
two men who were partly contemporary. To the younger, love is a sinister
fraud: "Love greatly resembles an application of torture or a surgical operation. . . . Do you hear these sighs—preludes to a shameful tragedy—these
groans, these screams, these rattling gasps? . . . The human face . . . speaks
here only of an insane ferocity relaxing into a kind of death. . . . For my part,
I say the sole and supreme pleasure in Love lies in the absolute knowledge of
doing *evil*." And again: "In Love, as in nearly all human affairs, a satisfactory
relationship is the result of a misunderstanding. This misunderstanding constitutes pleasure. The man cries: Oh, my angel! The woman coos: Mamma!
Mamma! And these two imbeciles are persuaded that they think alike!"

Baudelaire, to put it mildly, brings to the climaxes of passion a suspicious
spirit. Yet not more suspicious than Stendhal's with whom he shares the
dandiacal attitude, the hatred of vulgarity, and the hunger for *esprit* in all
social intercourse. But whereas Stendhal keeps his hope, faith, and charity,
Baudelaire has given up; he is quite certain that "Woman is the antithesis

---

[6] By the mid-century, Hawthorne had noted this depressing transformation: "We
seldom meet with women, nowadays and in this country, who impress us as being
women at all—their sex fades away and goes for nothing in ordinary intercourse."
The Blithedale Romance (1852) in *Complete Novels* (1937), 448.

of the Dandy. Therefore she should inspire horror. Woman is hungry, and she wants to eat; thirsty, and she wants to drink. . . . Woman is *natural,* that is to say abominable. Thus she is always vulgar; the opposite, in fact, of the Dandy." And he ponders: "Why does the man of parts prefer prostitutes to society women, although they are equally stupid? Find this out."

No one can do Baudelaire's research for him, but one may in passing question his last generality and go on to suggest that in the interval since Stendhal, certain of the necessary ingredients of love had disappeared from society as well as from the soul of the Dandy. One episode in *Lucien Leuwen,* Stendhal's last novel, shows the disenchanting effect of a woman's stupidity on a man who could be drawn by her charms of person. But her stupidity might well pass for cultivated mind in times when distinctions of class, breeding, and education have all but disappeared. And the hero, who has elsewhere been rebuffed by a prude, neither rails nor flings himself into the arms of the nearest prostitute, but departs for other loves, of which the last is idyllic. In short, to Lucien the possibility of choice enabled the heart to receive the messages of the mind without distorting them or its own impulse. Unexasperated, the Will remains simple.

This accounts for our amazement in reading Stendhal. How could so clever a man stay so naïve? And knowing himself naïve, how could he refrain from using his cleverness to hide the naïveté? With half his wit any of us could do this so it would never show. Stendhal was content to see through all the ruses and stupidities of high and low, was brought to despise the corrupt, sodden, and brutish, without letting contempt corrode his soul. "Having been frank, others' contempt will not touch me. At most, it will be said that I attach too much importance to what I am saying. In an hour, I myself shall laugh at the sentence I have just written. But I shall probably not erase it; it seemed to me true as I wrote it, and the man who is roused by the sight of a great deed is worth the man about town who is reined in to a strict watch over himself by the presence of cold hearts."

To Stendhal, the tricks of getting along were as vulgar as are to us the tricks of getting on. Accordingly—so Sainte Beuve tells us—he often fought fashionable vulgarity with its own weapons, by being deliberately crude. Clearly, he was not forgetting how vulgar the preoccupation with vulgarity can be: the genteel will not speak of money, drains, or death, and will do their utmost to conceal the fact that they are eating—doubtless feeling with Baudelaire that it is abominably natural. Stendhal preferred to turn his scornful gaze on affectation, the frivolous form of hypocrisy. All classes, he thought, were tainted with these three vices, and he could only pin his hopes on a "literary aristocracy," which he knew hardly existed.

The gap between him (or for that matter, Beethoven) and Baudelaire is thus measured by the opportunity that remained to a Romanticist of accepting himself. Stendhal's social and private torments, real as they were, left him scope for his dialectical play; unlike Baudelaire, he made good his claim to the society of the happy few and enjoyed their attractive surroundings. He did not have to battle a nameless misery from hall bedrooms, and hence never thought of himself as an "imbecile" pursuing the evil deception of sex. He took the risk of passion whenever it offered, and his ironic smile seems to say to us: "Jump in! The icy waters of experience can chill almost anything except the lifelong fever of love." The modern Baudelairized ego replies: "But love is hard, Mr. Beyle!" To which Stendhal's rejoiner must be: "Nonsense! Love is either easy or impossible."

If Stendhal had made that remark, he would have forestalled Shaw's same words on the subject of art, and reminded us of his own belief that art and love grow from one stem. They express alike the energy of the self, originally unconscious and undirected, later made conscious in art and directed to its object in love. The cycle is completed through action: after hearing a duet by Cimarosa "my heart will perceive fresh nuances in the spectacle of love thwarted by ambition. . . . At once, whatever may be *vulgar* in the story of the poor lovers whom I meet in society will vanish and I shall be softened. I shall owe this delightful moment, and perhaps the good deed that it will inspire, to Cimarosa. . . . Dry characters will make fun of my tears, but I have long since resigned myself: we are all ridiculous to one another. Shall I go and attempt to change myself because my neighbor differs from me?"

This aside in his advocacy of Shakespeare hints of the difference between Stendhal's fiction and ours. His novels, like the "good deed" adumbrated above, are the work of an autonomous person (to use David Riesman's term) who prefers to be and to feel agreeable. Like Montesquieu, Stendhal rejects "the delight of false afflictions." His outlook is, once again, predominately erotic, which does not mean the pursuit and possession of mistresses, but the capacity to embrace—in both the literal and figurative senses. His art, like his life and his "system," shows what Eros can beget. When today critics examine the condition of the novel, they usually report, first, that it is unwell; and second, that its ailment is due to the complexity of the outside world and the exhaustion of the psychological vein. This may correctly define the symptoms, but it does not explain why that complexity baffles and why we are tired of poking about in the modern psyche. The answer may simply be our lack of love, of comprehensive embrace. Whether this begins with the public or with the writer would be hard to say, but its effect is unmistakable. Stendhal is an expert witness on the point. Already in 1824 he reproved the public of Paris for "its distrust of everything, its complete absence of beliefs and passions, its habit of lying and fear of being compromised, the dull melancholy of its young. . . ." And he concluded that for such a public no great art can be composed.

Yet Stendhal was no less melancholy by nature than the contemporary youths of twenty—half his age—already were by habit. He reacted against his own gloom because he had found that when he despised anything he could not attend to it, could not satisfy his curiosity about it. This is an observation he returns to again and again: "I had lost," he says on one occasion,[7] "the habit of intense and extreme attention, because I was usually thinking only of things I held in contempt." The phenomenon is not hard to understand, for contempt is a self-regarding, protective emotion, which by dismissing its object dismisses any risk it may entail for oneself. Now the prevailing wish of novelists today is to make contempt disclose the true nature of reality. The few who have chosen love and acceptance, like Thomas Wolfe, have done it with bravado and achieved bathos; to avoid which, D. H. Lawrence seasoned his novels of love with a savage animosity more akin to vituperation than to criticism. And this has become, in other hands, the stridency of the hard-boiled. It is not alone in tough murder stories that the "point of view" may objectively be described as swinish.

The middle voice is that of the professional cynic, often incarnated by Mr. Somerset Maugham, whose wide popularity today almost reunites the unpretentious reader with the intelligentsia, on the basis, doubtless, of a common trait. It is instructive to compare a scene of self-consciousness and derision in him and in Stendhal. Here is Lucien Leuwen—a modified self-portrait of Stendhal:

> Over the billiard table Lucien began talking almost incessantly. His gaiety increased as the success of his heavy commonplaces made him quite forget the embarrassing necessity of paying court, by paternal order, to Madame Grandet. At first his sallies were really too hackneyed, and he amused himself by making fun of his own words. It was barbershop wit—anecdotes heard everywhere, stories from the newspaper.
>
> "She is a mass of absurdities," he thought, "but she is nevertheless accustomed to a certain standard of wit. Anecdotes will 'go down,' but preferably those that are a little less trite; heavy remarks, but on delicate subjects—on Racine's sweetness as compared with Virgil's, on the Italian tales from which Shakespeare took his plots—never any quick, pointed sallies: they would pass unnoticed. But the same rule does not hold true for glances, especially when

---

[7] The time he refers to is also significant: his return from Moscow in Napoleon's routed army.

one is very much in love." And he contemplated with barely disguised admiration Madame Grandet's charming attitudes.

"God! What would Madame de Chasteller say if she could see one of these glances of mine? I must forget her to be happy here," he murmured to himself. And he brushed aside this fatal thought, but not before emotion had darkened his eyes.

And here is Mr. Maugham's partial representative, the *déclassé* Dr. Saunders in *The Narrow Corner*:

> He was perhaps a cynic, and his withers were unwrung at many of the misfortunes that affect men, but he had a peculiar feeling for youth, perhaps because it promised so much and lasted too short a time, and it seemed to him that there was in the bitterness it experiences when reality breaks upon its illusions something more pathetic than in many graver ills. . . . It was amusing, to begin with, in an island of the Malay Archipelago, to come across a trader who knew Shakespeare well enough to say long passages by heart. The doctor could not but look on it as a somewhat tiresome accomplishment. He wondered idly if Erik was a good business man. He was not very fond of idealists. It was difficult for them in this workaday world to reconcile their professions with the exigencies of life, and it was disconcerting how often they managed to combine exalted notions with a keen eye to the main chance.

At other moments in the novel, this sullenness that is pleased with itself is made enviable to the modern ego by flattering its hope of strength: "The doctor chuckled. It diverted him to think of that rascal making shrewd use of the decent feelings of others to go his crooked, nasty way. . . ." And elsewhere: "Dr. Saunders found the situation faintly humorous. . . . There is a futility about it that gratifies the sense of irony."

These sentimentalities—by which I mean feelings adopted without their consequences—betray that permanent fear which Stendhal's "Spanish ideas" of heroism would not permit. Whereas Lucien's uncomfortably divided soul inspires him with "gaiety," Dr. Saunders rises only to our boasted "sense of humor"—the faintly humorous at that—which is a device to obviate risk. To feel tender for youth because "the loss of its illusions is more pathetic than graver ills" is to feel not outgoing affection but retrospective self-pity. For the shock of discovering that the objects of our love are weak and unworthy should be topped by the surprise that they can give so much delight—were it only to the senses. The more pitiless our judgment, the more extraordinary the fact becomes. It is all in how we "take" what we are pleased to call reality.

The place where for any man the road forks is the point where self-will and skepticism meet. Sensibility coupled with intellect soon prove to any man of parts that it is foolish to go charging ahead in a world full of traps and false appearances. But the self, bent on some mad goal, says: "I will!" Depending on circumstance, on the force of the positive and the negative impulse, on the power of an emotion one degree higher than fear or desire, the temperament is forged. Santayana tells us in *Scepticism and Animal Faith*: "It was the fear of illusion that originally disquieted the honest mind, congenitally dogmatic, and drove it in the direction of scepticism." This is doubly relevant because it shows the sophisticated, "scientific" origin of the fear, and because Santayana's own character of arrogant timidity authorizes him to speak for the negative. Stendhal too was a mass of sensibilities; his very skin was uncommonly liable to bruising. But when he came to the crossroads, he forced his mind to acknowledge once for all the external folly of the ego and its internal rightness: "The passions and the arts are but the attaching of a ridiculous importance to some small thing." Having said this he was free to judge each small thing for its worth to him. And he might have added, in Emerson's words: "Take the egotism out and you castrate the benefactors."

Yet this no longer holds of many a modern ego, whose egotism seems to have worked inward against itself, to the detriment of happiness, which may be deemed little, and of art, which is much. The late George Orwell, for example, a man to whom no thinking person can refuse a large measure of respect, has told in *Why I Write* how the absence of political purpose deprived his early fiction of any merit. He "wrote lifeless books and was betrayed into purple passages, sentences without meaning, decorative adjectives and humbug generally." Though the blemishes were actually unimportant, being often found in great art, the humbug was fatal, and came from lack of passion—that resolving passion which Orwell came to feel about politics and nothing else. Political purpose displaced in him the false shame and sophomoric posturing which one finds depressingly recorded in the titles of so many works of the last thirty years, including Orwell's *Keep the Aspidistra Flying*.

Elsewhere, Orwell explains this wormlike stance by the sense of failure he acquired in school, and the accompanying humiliation and snobbery that poisoned his adult years. But nearly all artists and writers begin by finding life a torment compounded of a fraud—Byron and Stendhal no less than Orwell and Maugham—so sensitivity is no excuse. The real difficulty of life begins with the need to control the recoil, while the fatal flaw in literature comes from not knowing how to live with one's feelings. We talk a great deal today about tension, as we do about its tone, which is irony, and we desire both; but being ourselves ill-committed, we accept a sort of articulate paralysis for the live pull of opposites. When these truly exist and serve the imagination they must be equally accepted, not suppressed singly or together.

For a man can create only out of what he feels, not out of what he thinks he ought to feel. Yet modern literature is ridden by one-sided imperatives drawn from amputated experience and it dictates certain feelings as well as the absence of others. Like Baudelaire about sex, it cannot get over certain perceptions. And by a curious interplay of cultures, these perceptions hold sway over us by virtue of our attachment to that same French tradition which Stendhal was already combating in *Racine and Shakespeare*—a social tradition of taste and sophistication enforced by public opinion through ridicule. What democracy has done is to enlarge the salon into an invisible arena where none the less the fear of ridicule compels every artist to be *au fait*. This means—as in Paris in 1824 and since—being distrustful, cold, skeptical, fearful, and melancholy. These are the reagents applied today whenever some rash adventurer in passion is to be purged of his "romanticism."

In keeping with this practice, Mr. Maugham finds *The Red and the Black* "sadly imperfect," and would like, in addition to other emendations, to retain only the first half. The second is "sheer romanticism" because, one gathers, the motives and actions of Mlle de la Mole are not convincing. Believing in her and loving her no doubt require "Spanish ideas," not because she is noble or good, but because she is heroic and what Stendhal would call *romanesque* —novel-like. One has to admit that nowadays fiction is the one place where nobody acts "like people in novels"—anything but that! And, appropriately, Mr. Maugham's *Notebook* shows the limitations imposed by this rage for skepticism. Sketch after sketch recorded in it relies on the formula of pretension unmasked: the teetotaler always turns out to be a secret drinker. Not that this lessens the writer's respect for goodness—only his belief in it and the power to paint it. Mr. Maugham deeply admires the creation of Alyosha Karamazov and of Stendhal's Mme de Rénal, and he says he tried twice to portray credible goodness, but "it was too difficult for me to cope with and I never wrote it."

We may surmise that here again the democratic situation makes art difficult: the sense of goodness depends on love, and love is undemocratic because it marks a preference; it creates privilege and demands privacy. We tolerate it in the very young, but the proper adult emotion is envy, which secures equality. The trouble is that in so doing envy undermines candor, which is essential to art. It was candor that saved Stendhal from being ruined by his hatred of his father and his native Grenoble. It was candor that enabled him to give himself away in *De l'Amour*. It is his candor that shocks and irritates the reviewers of his private diaries, incapable as they are of restraining judgment while they invade this privacy. Candid with himself, Stendhal could write for his own eyes, like a code, the peculiar English phrases that his editor derides, knowing that *he* wouldn't let himself be caught that way. Most of us would feel the same: with everyone watching, we cannot *afford* candor. And this of necessity affects the art we read or write. When idea overcomes feeling and technical apprehension shackles freedom, every impulse emerges as either "cagey" or "corny" and is chosen accordingly. By degrees the storyteller turns into our familiar figure, the nonfiction novelist: he is full of intelligence, "insights," and talent, but his every story is mere exposition, a stillborn child. To create illusion, it would seem, the writer must be in some way illuded himself—and willingly, like a man in love.

This is not to say that with a little effort warmed over with the breath of love, our novelists could produce a new *Charterhouse, Cousin Betty,* or *Golden Bowl.* It means only that we should not attribute the slow suicide of the novel altogether to external causes, as if Stendhal and Balzac's world, or James's, had been delightfully simple, yet filled with living models whose souls were wonderfully rich for artistic purposes. No, these writers had to do something to earn their greatness, they worked on themselves to prevent the freezing of the genial current. Stendhal in his diary used to refer to his unamiable father as "The Bastard" but refused this heredity for himself. Seeing in his earliest surroundings "everything that is irretrievably mean and base, everything that is hostile to the slightest impulse of generosity," he did not fight by imitating but by differing.

From the age of seven he wanted to write comedies like Molière's, to become the comic bard who would finally dispossess the tragic rhetorician. But Molière's "bourgeois details" reminded him too much of his unhappy life and he shunned their observation at the cost of losing experience. A dreadful dilemma; and to the end of his days, he felt, experience would disappoint him: "What!" he kept exclaiming, "Is *that* all it is?" Yet he concluded: "I have had no reason to complain of my destiny; on the contrary, I have reason to congratulate myself upon it." He gives us here the measure of his closeness and of his distance; he is nobody's fool, but loves himself well enough to stand being his own; which saves him.

This is what it means to be a man of imagination. The complete grasp of the real eludes us all, but the imaginative are in the end the least deceived. Balzac, we know, was so completely under the spell of his vision that he believed in the actuality of his characters—as well he might, seeing that they were projections of his own intense being. Their part as sinister emblems of the society he was criticizing did not lessen his attachment to them. As Taine pointed out apropos of the diabolical Madame Marneffe, *"Balzac aime sa Valérie";* and Nordau was exemplifying the truth that fiction must be fictional in order to seem real when he called the visionary Balzac "the first Buddhist in Europe." Nor should we suppose that the refinement of the novel beyond the evocative power of Balzac and the dissecting skill of Stendhal changed the terms on which art is gained. James was as skeptical as

Stendhal before him and Maugham or Santayana after: "I am by nature more in dread of any fool's paradise, or at least of any bad misguidedness, than in love with the idea of a security proved." Yet what recipe did he offer for the novel when, on the eve of the nineties, he was asked to yield his secret to a conference of writers? His answer was to brush all formulas aside:

"There are no tendencies worth anything but to see the actual or the imaginative, which is just as visible, and to paint it. I have only two little words for the matter remotely approaching to rule or doctrine; one is life and the other freedom. Tell the ladies and gentlemen, the ingenious inquirers, to consider life directly and closely, and not to be put off with mean and puerile falsities, and be conscientious about it. It is infinitely large, various, and comprehensive. Every sort of mind will find what it looks for in it, whereby the novel becomes truly multifarious and illustrative."

Since every sort of mind finds what it looks for, we may read our psychograph in the contemporary alternatives to "the novel of fiction," the genre which down to Proust accepted as an aid the trappings of romance (in Hawthorne's sense), while finding its subject in the desire for women and money which has ruled storytelling from *The Iliad* to *The Wings of the Dove.* The later alternatives are familiar: the novel of dream and fantasy, which proffers simplicity and induces nostalgia; the novel of public events, which by accurate horrifying restores our confidence in our fears; the novel of pure exotic information, or Baedeker in dialogue; the novel of allusion—the You-know-how-it-is of Kiplingesque origin, now based on no common tribal lore but on a common bookshelf; the novel of myth and symbol, experimental in form and often psychiatric in concern which, in the words of a qualified anthologist, "illuminates the neuroses of our time"; the novel of archeological reconstruction, hitched to an acknowledged past—Dr. Faustus or Eternal Rome; finally the novel which buttresses with proper names and improper acts some little thought too immature to appear nakedly by itself in an essay. And shortly, perhaps, we shall be adding the latest thing from France, patterned after the work of Pierre Gascar, whose theme is "the tragic absence of communication between man and the animals."

The common element in this variety is slavish dependence on fact. Fact has adorned the novel as far back as *Robinson Crusoe,* but with us it has usurped the first place. When we are assured that in Mr. Tolkien's epic fairy tale, *The Fellowship of the Ring,* the geology has been carefully devised and is perfectly possible; or when the unfailingly vigilant *New Yorker* bothers to note with pleasure the discrepancies of fictional age and season in "Our Forgetful Authors," we glimpse the pedantic mind of the public hunting for howlers and insisting on fiction's clinging to fact for verisimilitude.

For this too Stendhal must bear a part of the blame. He loved and hated pedantry and fell into it, like ourselves, from the democratic expectation of being asked for proof. The habit in him is sometimes ludicrous: "I had a loathsome time from seven to seventeen, but since my crossing of the Saint-Bernard pass (2,491 metres above sea level), I have had no reason to complain." The allusion here is to his first trip to Italy where he found the latitude for love. The opposite, the need to prove, came from his belief that logic, reason, and fact would undermine the principle of authority and thus doom the classical-monarchical order. Romanticism (as Proust later remarked) was the natural ally of liberal democracy. Unfortunately, liberalism brought with it bourgeois manners, which were cold and dull and ill at ease outside factuality. For a novelist the dilemma could only be resolved by balancing the pleasures of exactitude with those of the imagination. There was no guaranty that latercomers would know how to mix them, and Stendhal himself was uncertain about his own performance. Writing in the margins of his *Charterhouse* in 1840, he remarks: "I think I notice that this style fatigues the attention through not giving enough details easy to understand. It must be made easy for women of thirty, and even amusing if possible."

Flaubert was similarly caught between his erudition and observation, on the one hand, and his lyricism, on the other. The first drafts of *Madame Bovary* demonstrate that his whittling down to verifiable fact often resulted in the loss of remoter and more valuable perceptions. We are entitled to think that the character of Pellerin, in *L'Education Sentimentale*, speaks some of his creator's doubts: "Leave me alone with your hideous reality! What does it mean, anyway, reality? Some see black, others blue, and the multitude sees dull. . . . The care for external truth is a sign of our contemporary degradation; art is turning into an old wheeze lower than religion in point of poetry and lower than politics in point of self-interest."

We are not yet at the concluding stage, and no one can predict who will see what is all about us that no one yet sees, and will magically make it visible through words. A hundred years ago, George Eliot opened *De L'Amour* and was struck by the drama and conciseness of the short story, "Ernestine, or the Birth of Love," which is one of the dozen appendages of the book. Though fifteen years dead, Stendhal was an unknown name. Yet his perceptive reader across the channel had found in him that substance without which narrative does not crystallize into fiction. Here is how the tale begins, in Stendhal's clearest voice and with the simplicity of forgotten times:

A woman of great mind and some experience was maintaining one day that love is not born so suddenly as people say. "It seems to me," said she, "that I discern seven altogether distinct stages in the birth of love;" and to prove her point she related the following story. It was in the country; the rain came down in torrents; we were only too glad to listen.

The story is severely moral. Ernestine loves and, after some jealous incertitude, is loved in return. But circumstances punish the lover for his abandonment, just then, of a mistress approaching middle age. He asks for Ernestine's hand, but she is "married off to an elderly lieutenant-general who was very rich and had been decorated several times." Those are the last words. Artificial? Romantic? Yes. But not sentimental, for Stendhal was seeing and saying what he chose, amusing himself with what his life proves he truly loved, and caring not at all for what you and I may think. He had taken out his lottery ticket, labeling it *De l'Amour,* and saying to himself:

One is always right to feel as one feels and to find beautiful what gives one pleasure.

MELVILLE

[*1819–1881*]

THE DISCOVERY AND DEFINITION OF THE IMAGINATIVE ACCOMPLISHMENT OF OUR nineteenth-century writers has taken place within the last forty years. The consideration of major figures initiated by D. H. Lawrence's *Studies in Classic American Literature* in 1923, and carried foward by Constance Rourke's *American Humor: A Study of the National Character* in 1931, became lively with the appearance of F. O. Matthiessen's *American Renaissance* in 1941. Matthiessen's work was most effective when least historical; he was best when describing the process by which the passionate concerns of Hawthorne, Melville, and Whitman found formal expression. The work of Richard Chase has a large and explicit historical intention: he wishes to revive and pursue the appraisal of American qualities, strengths, and weaknesses which was begun in the second decade of our century by Randolph Bourne and the youthful Van Wyck Brooks.

Constance Rourke employed the term "American Narcissus" to describe the lonely figures of American myth. The same idea has a central place in Chase's analysis of *Moby Dick*: "Solipsisms, hypnotic self-regard, imprisonment within the self—these themes have absorbed American novelists. The Concord transcendentalism, of which Melville was very much aware and whose sensibility he in many ways shared, was a philosophy—or rather an ethical poetry—of the self. The idea of the image reflected in the mirror or in water appeals as strongly to Melville as to Hawthorne, and like Hawthorne he uses this literary convention to point up the dangers of an exaggerated self-regard."

The American poetry of the self has often been written in almost total disregard of the claims of institutions, family, and manners—the very things which are largely the subject of nineteenth-century European novels. The tendency of Melville to define the human condition in general, and without regard to these boundaries, may explain the recent enthusiasm for our literature on the Continent. Americans were exposed earlier to the bleak wind of existential thought, which was not really felt in Europe before the 1920's, and had no wide repercussions until after the second World War.

Richard Chase is Professor of English at Columbia.

R I C H A R D   C H A S E

Melville and Moby-Dick

MELVILLE'S IMAGINATION ORIGINATES IN HIS POWERFUL SENSE OF THE IRRA-tionality and contradictoriness of experience. His essay on Hawthorne, written in the summer of 1850 while he was composing *Moby-Dick,* gives us a clear impression of this imagination at the high point of its power. We find that what most moves Melville in Hawthorne's tales (for he is reviewing *Mosses from an Old Manse*) is not only their "Shakespearean" profundity, their fine comedy, and power of fantasy but especially their mingling of light and dark. "For in spite of all the Indian-summer sunlight on the hither-side of Hawthorne's soul," Melville writes, "the other side—like the dark half of the physical sphere—is shrouded in a blackness, ten times black." Melville speculates that "this great power of blackness" derives from "that Calvinistic sense of Innate Depravity and Original Sin, from whose visitations, in some shape or other, no deeply thinking mind is always and wholly free." Reading Hawthorne's tales, Melville writes, "You may be witched by his sunlight—transported by the bright gildings in the skies he builds over you; but there is the blackness of darkness beyond."

As everyone notices, Melville's essay has as much to do with the qualities of his own imagination as with Hawthorne's. They share many perceptions, to be sure. But Hawthorne put his finger on the essential difference when, after briefly renewing his acquaintance with Melville in Liverpool in 1856, he remarked that although Melville talked endlessly and eloquently of the ultimate dilemmas of truth and belief, he could neither believe "nor be comfortable in his disbelief." Having very little of the aloof, contemplative skepticism of Hawthorne, and being unable to discover any philosophical or religious synthesis he could believe in, Melville became a kind of alien wanderer in the world of the imagination, seeking a truth that should be at once a truth of reason and a truth of art. As a thinker, Melville was an inspired amateur, with an agonized and troublesome yen (as Hawthorne seems to have felt) for posing insoluble problems. As an artist, Melville was again the inspired amateur, who despite his great native gifts (perhaps the greatest ever given to an American) never developed a firm novelistic or poetic sense of things. He had little patience with the quotidian demands of the art of the novel or the poem; he had little power of invention; he showed none of Hawthorne's understanding of the quality and scope of his own imagination. His goal was the highest; no one short of Shakespeare would do as the ideal. His career as a writer was bound to be precarious and desperate, the results fragmentary and uneven.

It seems generally agreed that the voyages of Melville's heroes in his early books—*Typee* (1846), *Omoo* (1847), *Mardi* (1849), *Redburn* (1849), *White Jacket* (1850), and *Moby-Dick* (1851)—are, in one sense, quests for truth. That the quest is conceived as both rational and aesthetic is suggested by *Mardi,* where the voyage to sea expands, is arbitrarily transformed rather, into an allegorical-symbolic fantasy in which the truth-seeking philosopher Babbalanja asserts the view that ideally the poet and the philosopher have the same mission. The vision of truth Taji, the questing hero of the book, longs for will be one that is gained simultaneously, as it were, by rational and aesthetic means. Unfortunately, Taji does not succeed, and at the end he is shown sailing further into the problematical seas, having left a world which strikes him as being the abode of unreason and ambiguity, a world symbolized by the wraith-like creature called Yillah (the princess of light) and by the sinister Hautia (the queen of darkness).

Although Melville never, even in his last years, ceased to protest and resist the necessity of remaining skeptical, he had got hold of such truth as was to come to him, by the time he had finished *Mardi* and *White-Jacket.* This truth is that man lives in an insolubly dualistic world, that his profoundest awareness does not transcend the perception of his paradoxical situation, caught as he is between apparently eternal and autonomous opposites such as good and evil, heaven and hell, God and Satan, head and heart, spirit and matter. Only in *Moby-Dick* (among his longer works) does Melville's imagination provide a metaphor adequate to his darkly skeptical view. In the white whale, and the tremendous actions he sets off, the polarities that preoccupy Melville are for once magnificently expressed. And although this fortunate conjunction of the philosophic and the poetic does not produce a truth that transcends Melville's radical skepticism, it does produce a work of art which is so far the grandest expression of the American imagination.

But even as Melville's imagination achieved its great feat the spectacle of disaster is powerfully before us. In Ahab the reason and the aesthetic sense pull apart. Ahab has had his humanities, as we are told. He is still drawn to the aesthetic, the intuitive, the poetic experience. He still has some of the "low enjoying power" as well as the "high perception," and he still has fellow feeling and natural piety (the phrases I have quoted here are from Chapter 37, "The Sunset," which contains an important soliloquy by Ahab). But gradually his intellect is drawn apart from whatever might nourish, harmonize, and symbolize it, and in its isolation, it grows willful, obsessive, and finally suicidal. Except for the narcissism that makes a mad allegorist of Ahab, he is blind to all the imaginative versions of reality that his own mind or that of others may offer to him.

There is, unhappily, a good deal of Ahab in Melville, and, on the evidence of *Pierre* and *The Confidence Man,* we conclude that Melville, after *Moby-Dick,* faced a deeply stultifying dilemma. He saw that to write at all one had to assume that reason and the aesthetic sense, the high perception and the low enjoying power, must lead at some point to the same synthesis. Yet for Pierre the provisional syntheses offered by the aesthetic sense fail to satisfy the intellect's thirst for absolute truth or to modify its perception of irreconcilables. Thus the rational and the aesthetic are at once incompatible and mutually indispensable. This is of course a paralyzing dilemma, if you allow it to become one, and Melville did. In a more highly organized mind, or a more serenely contemplative mind, or a mind richer in its aesthetic sense, this dilemma is not an impasse, but merely one of the large facts of experience, to be treated like any other fact. But for Melville the dilemma was almost fatal; it suggested to him, as to his Pierre, that aesthetic perception was mere illusion and that rational perception was an alien activity, doomed to monomania and nihilism.

Thus both *Pierre* (1852) and *The Confidence Man* (1857) are studies of man caught among "the ambiguities" (as the subtitle of *Pierre* says). *Pierre* is a melodrama of incest and suicide, showing man crushed by the contradictions involved in his attempt to live a moral and creative life, whereas *The Confidence Man* is a comedy of appearance and reality, showing the absurdity of man's attempts to attribute meaning and value to a world in which these can have no ground or status.

[530]

Not until *Billy Budd* (except in some of his poems) does Melville seem to give us a sense of ambiguities resolved and irreconcilables reconciled—for in *Billy Budd*, Melville finds some comfort in the idea that, beyond the special illusion of unity a work of art provides, irreconcilables may perhaps be absorbed in history or in legend. But this is a matter that may be better discussed at the end of the present chapter.

How Moby-Dick Was Written

The scope and tone of *Moby-Dick* appear to have changed while Melville was writing it. Just what the changes were, and what induced them, is the subject of much interesting scholarship. For our purposes, certain plausible speculations by George R. Stewart, in an essay called "The Two Moby-Dicks," will suffice.

With the exception of the fanciful *Mardi*, Melville's first five books had been based partly on personal experience. The first book, *Typee*, told a somewhat romanticized story of the author's actual sojourn in the Marquesas Islands after he deserted the whaling ship Acushnet, on which he had sailed some months previous. Mr. Stewart conjectures that in its original conception *Moby-Dick* was to be another of Melville's quasi-autobiographical travelogues, this time recounting his adventures on the Acushnet up to the time of his leaving the ship in the Marquesas. As he wrote, however, the story took on ever new possibilities for him, and these possibilities finally crystallized into a whole new conception of the book. Having already substantially completed the writing of the story as he first conceived it, however, the author did not start entirely afresh but included all or most of the original version, with varying degrees of revision, in the book as we now have it.

Thus we may suppose that Chapters 1–15, in which after various adventures Ishmael and Queequeg arrive in Nantucket, are substantially as they were in the original version. Chapters 16–22, concerning the preliminaries to sailing, belong to the original version, but with considerable rewriting. Chapters 23 to the end constitute the new version of the book, with the exception of certain passages which appear to have been salvaged and interpolated from the original version.

Something like this undoubtedly happened, and it accounts for certain inconsistencies in the book. For example, the fact that the Pequod appears to head for Cape Horn but actually, without sufficient reason for the change, rounds the Cape of Good Hope, that the Pequod is said sometimes to have a wheel and other times a whale-bone tiller, that Stubb is called both third and second mate (although Melville settles on the latter), and so on. More remarkable is the virtual disappearance of some of the characters who figure largely in the opening chapters. Queequeg, to whom we have been introduced in much detail, becomes merely one of the harpooners. Bulkington, although apparently destined for some heroic role, is dismissed with a poetic epitaph. Ishmael himself all but disappears as a character and as the observer becomes hardly more than the voice of the omniscient author. Ahab, perhaps originally conceived as one more portrait in Melville's gallery of tyrannical and irritable captains, becomes a great, doomed hero. The language itself, rather jocose and colloquial at first, becomes opulent with metaphor, simile, and oratorical flourishes.

What caused this flowering of Melville's genius cannot, of course, be known. But figuring prominently in the miracle must be his rereading of Shakespeare during the time he was working on the book. The influence of *Lear* and *Macbeth* is felt as one beholds Ahab and listens to his speeches and soliloquies. The language and metaphor of Shakespeare make themselves strongly felt in *Moby-Dick,* though not, we observe, in the earlier chapters. Probably it occurred to Melville, as he paused in the process of writing, that two factual narratives about whaling which he had read might be woven into his narrative—one concerning the ramming and sinking by a whale of the Nantucket ship Essex, another concerning a monstrous white whale called Mocha Dick. It is probable too that he discovered that the legends, tall tales, and folklore of whaling could be more than embellishments to his narrative; they could be for him what other bodies of folklore had been for Homer, Virgil, or Camoens (an author of whom Melville was fond)—the materials of an epic. Finally, one may suppose that partly under the influence of Hawthorne he saw that Ahab might be not only a quasi-Shakespearean hero, doomed by an inordinate pride or tragic ignorance, but also the protagonist in a kind of Puritan inner drama, a drama of the mind in its isolation and obsession. For if Ahab is akin to Shakespeare's heroes, he is more so to such Hawthorne characters as Chillingworth, the pattern of whose life also became, in Hawthorne's phrase, "a dark necessity."

The reason one is interested in the process by which *Moby-Dick* evolved from a travelogue to the complex book it is is that as readers we often seem to share Melville's excitement as he and we make new discoveries—as we push farther into the unknown and find metaphors and formulations that make the unknown knowable. Melville thought of art as a process, as an emergent, ever creative, but never complete metaphor. Thus he makes his imaginary poet in *Mardi* triumphantly exclaim, in reference to the epic he has written, "I have created the creative!" In taking the view that a work of art is not a completed object but is an imperfect form which should be left only potentially complete, Melville is much closer to Whitman than to Hawthorne.

And what he says about the technical whaling sections of *Moby-Dick* applies as well to the whole book.

It was stated at the outset, that this system would not be here, and at once, perfected. You cannot but plainly see that I have kept my word. But I now leave my Cetological System standing thus unfinished, even as the great Cathedral of Cologne was left, with the crane still standing upon the top of the uncompleted tower. For small erections may be finished by their first architects; grand ones, true ones, ever leave the copestone to posterity. God keep me from ever completing anything. This whole book is but a draught— nay, but the draught of a draught. Oh, Time, Strength, Cash, and Patience!

Moby-Dick, like the cathedral with the crane on its tower, allows us to see— in fact insists that we shall see—some of the machinery by which it was built, some of the processes of construction. Two passages may be quoted in this connection. The first was presumably interpolated in Chapter 16 and sounds, as Mr. Stewart suggests, like something one might as soon expect to find in a novelist's notebook as in his novel. Melville seems almost to be arguing himself into believing that a tragic hero might be made out of a Nantucket whaleman, especially if he spoke in the Quaker manner:

So that there are instances among [the Nantucketers] of men, who, named with Scripture names—a singularly common fashion on the island—and in childhood naturally imbibing the stately dramatic thee and thou of the Quaker idiom; still, from the audacious, daring, and boundless adventure of their subsequent lives, strangely blend with these unoutgrown peculiarities, a thousand bold dashes of character, not unworthy of a Scandinavian sea-king, or a poetical Pagan Roman. And when these things unite in a man of greatly superior natural force, with a globular brain and a ponderous heart; who has also by the stillness and seclusion of many long night-watches in the remotest waters, and beneath constellations never seen here at the north, been led to think untraditionally and independently; receiving all nature's sweet or savage impressions fresh from her own virgin voluntary and confiding breast, and thereby chiefly, but with some help from accidental advantages, to learn a bold and nervous lofty language—that man makes one in a whole nation's census—a mighty pageant creature, formed for noble tragedies. Nor will it at all detract from him, dramatically regarded, if either by birth or other circumstances, he have what seems a half wilful overruling morbidness at the bottom of his nature. For all men tragically great are made so through a certain morbidness. Be sure of this, O young ambition, all mortal greatness is but disease.

In this passage we join in the discovery of ideas that were to produce Ahab.

In Chapter 14, "Nantucket," we participate in the process by which an epic emerges—namely, by the transmutation of the central facts about the life of a culture into poetry by means of the accretion of folklore, legend, and myth. The wave-like amplification and building-up, followed by the lyric subsidence at the end, is characteristic of Melville's imagination and is similar to the action of the book as a whole, as well as to various sections of it. One may be pardoned, then, for including here a long quotation:

Nantucket! Take out your map and look at it. See what a real corner of the world it occupies; how it stands there, away off shore, more lonely than the Eddystone lighthouse. Look at it—a mere hillock, and elbow of sand; all beach, without a background. There is more sand there than you would use in twenty years as a substitute for blotting paper. Some gamesome wights will tell you that they have to plant weeds there, they don't grow naturally; that they import Canada thistles; that they have to send beyond seas for a spile to stop a leak in an oil cask; that pieces of wood in Nantucket are carried about like bits of the true cross in Rome; that people there plant toadstools before their houses, to get under the shade in summer time; that one blade of grass makes an oasis, three blades in a day's walk a prairie; that they wear quicksand shoes, something like Laplander snowshoes; that they are so shut up, belted about, every way inclosed, surrounded, and made an utter island of by the ocean, that to their very chairs and tables small clams will sometimes be found adhering, as to the backs of sea turtles. But these extravaganzas only show that Nantucket is no Illinois.

Look now at the wondrous traditional story of how this island was settled by the red-men. Thus goes the legend. In olden times an eagle swooped down upon the New England coast, and carried off an infant Indian in his talons. With loud lament the parents saw their child borne out of sight over the wide waters. They resolved to follow in the same direction. Setting out in their canoes, after a perilous passage they discovered the island, and there they found an empty ivory casket,—the poor little Indian's skeleton.

What wonder, then, that these Nantucketers, born on a beach, should take to the sea for a livelihood! They first caught crabs and quohogs in the sand; grown bolder, they waded out with nets for mackerel; more experienced, they pushed off in boats and captured cod; and at last, launching a navy of great ships on the sea, explored this watery world; put an incessant belt of circumnavigations round it; peeped in at Behring's Straits; and in all seasons and all oceans declared everlasting war with the mightiest animated mass that has survived the flood; most monstrous and most mountainous! That Himmalehan, salt-sea Mastodon, clothed with such portentousness of unconscious power, that his very panics are more to be dreaded than his most fearless and malicious assaults!

And thus have these naked Nantucketers, these sea hermits, issuing from their ant-hill in the sea, overrun and conquered the watery world like so many

Alexanders; parcelling out among them the Atlantic, Pacific, and Indian oceans, as the three pirate powers did Poland. Let America add Mexico to Texas, and pile Cuba upon Canada; let the English overswarm all India, and hang out their blazing banner from the sun; two thirds of this terraqueous globe are the Nantucketer's. For the sea is his; he owns it, as Emperors own empires; other seamen having but a right of way through it. Merchant ships are but extension bridges; armed ones but floating forts; even pirates and privateers, though following the sea as highwaymen the road, they but plunder other ships, other fragments of the land like themselves, without seeking to draw their living from the bottomless deep itself. The Nantucketer, he alone resides and riots on the sea; he alone, in Bible language, goes down to it in ships; to and fro ploughing it as his own special plantation. *There* is his home; *there* lies his business which a Noah's flood would not interrupt, though it overwhelmed all the millions in China. He lives on the sea, as prairie cocks in the prairie; he hides among the waves, he climbs them as chamois hunters climb the Alps. For years he knows not the land; so that when he comes to it at last, it smells like another world, more strangely than the moon would to an Earthman. With the landless gull, that at sunset folds her wings and is rocked to sleep between billows; so at nightfall, the Nantucketer, out of sight of land, furls his sails, and lays him to his rest, while under his very pillow rush herds of walruses and whales.

An Epic Romance

This term is perhaps the inevitable one for Melville's great book. But *Moby-Dick* is extremely impure art; it is a hybrid, one of the most audacious, surely, that have ever been conceived. As Melville himself exclaims at one point, "I try everything. I achieve what I can."

The partly romanticized travelogue-novel which the book was apparently first intended to be still contributes its considerable realism and wealth of detail to the whole. And of course those admonitory critics who are always telling us that *Moby-Dick* is just a good whaling yarn and should be discussed only as such seem at first to have their point. But the realistic sea-going novel as practiced by Melville and by Cooper, Smollett, Marryat, and Dana, whose example Melville followed, is not a particularly interesting form, exciting as it is to read. Although *Moby-Dick* contains many novelistic elements—of character, panorama, scene, and action—it has fewer that repay study than, for example, *The Scarlet Letter*. If we are to follow Melville's imagination, we have to go afield from the sea-novel, although we always come back to it as we read.

As was suggested earlier, in discussing allegory and symbol, *Moby-Dick* is in one sense a symbolist poem. It contains also strong melodramatic, if not fully tragic elements. It is certainly in one sense a comic work. And some passages, such as appear in the inconceivably beautiful chapters called "The Funeral," "The Pacific," "The Dying Whale," and "The Symphony," are sheer lyric.

One does not detract from the book in saying that it has a "made-up" quality, that it is a good deal "put together," and is very much a piece of literary fabrication. In view of this one has trouble associating it quite so readily with the epic imagination of the Bronze Age and the Age of the Vikings as Newton Arvin does in his book on Melville (which is, however, at least through the chapter on *Moby-Dick,* much the best book).

As an epic, *Moby-Dick* follows in some ways the universal convention to which it belongs. It celebrates, that is, customs, techniques, occupations, ideals, and types of heroic humanity which are characteristic of the culture in which they appear. Given the culture Melville is expressing, what would we expect him to include in his epic? We must have heroes, nobility, and these will be the heroes of the American nineteenth century—hunters, exploiters, captains of industry (for Ahab *is* one of these, and the Pequod is a beautifully efficient factory for the production of whale oil). What skills and preoccupations will be stressed? Not the martial skills of the *Iliad,* nor the political and moral skills of the *Aeneid,* nor the theological and political prowess of *Paradise Lost,* but the techniques of subduing nature—and thus the descriptions, as loving and detailed as that of Achilles's shield in the *Iliad,* of the ship, the whale boats, and all their intricate apparatus. But although superficially resembling the *Odyssey, Moby-Dick* lacks, among other things, the rich observation of *ethos,* of ways of life, real and fabulous, which we find in Homer's poem. The *Odyssey* is extremely sophisticated about manners and morals and is actually more novelistic than *Moby-Dick.*

In a democratic epic such as *Moby-Dick* avowedly is we would expect a celebration of the ideals of equality and brotherhood, on the one hand, and individualism, on the other. The ideal masculine attachment here is not the hierarchic relation of Achilles and Patroclus, tender as that is, but the perfect fraternal equality of persons of different race. Thus Ishmael and Queequeg join the much discussed company of Natty Bumppo and Chingachgook, Huck Finn and Jim. The different ideal of individualism is expressed in the ready derring-do and self-respecting unconventionality of all the main figures. And Ahab becomes, as the "dark necessity" of the story sets in, a heightened example of independent man, as if Melville were out to test some of the extreme implications of the dominant Emersonian creed of self-reliance.

As is suggested by the passage about Nantucket, quoted above, the raw material for the great metaphors of Melville's epic is "American humor"— that is, the body of folk sayings, jokes, and tall tales that had formed by

Melville's time a reservoir of legendary materials on which he could draw. The story of the white whale is of course in itself a very tall tale and, in the manner of the tale teller, Melville adduces a considerable number of fancies and rumors about Moby-Dick's almost supernatural powers. One finds frequent references to semilegendary early heroes, like George Washington, Andrew Jackson, Franklin. The main characters, even Ahab, behave and speak sometimes like the humorous, boastful frontiersmen and canny, canting, mystical Yankee peddlers who figured in the oral legend and on the popular stage of Melville's time.

The native legends, which Melville was the first important writer to use with any fullness, are unusual in the history of the world by being predominantly humorous. The humor, as Constance Rourke has shown, oscillates rather wildly between extremes, being on the one hand boasting, oratorical, even megalomaniac and on the other meditative, soliloquizing, oddly indirect, covert, and sad. It is characteristically oral, even after being incorporated into so literary, so *written* a book as *Moby-Dick*. For Melville presents his story to us as if he felt the necessity of talking us, and himself, into accepting it. He does not accredit it by saying that the Muse told it to him. He assumes, rather, the guise of the salesman and the showman. In the very first chapter we find that whereas a hero of another epic might attribute his turn of fortune to Hera or Zeus, Ishmael regards himself as a sort of bit player in an extravaganza produced by "those stage managers, the Fates"—showmen who, as we may think more than once in reading *Moby-Dick,* resemble P. T. Barnum, rather than Zeus.

And, doubtless, my going on this whaling voyage, formed part of the grand programme of Providence that was drawn up a long time ago. It came in as a sort of brief interlude and solo between more extensive performances. I take it that this part of the bill must have run something like this:
"*Grand Contested Election for the Presidency of the United States.*
"WHALING VOYAGE BY ONE ISHMAEL.
"BLOODY BATTLE IN AFGHANISTAN."
Though I cannot tell why it was exactly that those stage managers, the Fates, put me down for this shabby part of a whaling voyage, when others were set down for magnificent parts in high tragedies, and short and easy parts in genteel comedies, and jolly parts in farces—though I cannot tell why this was exactly; yet, now I recall all the circumstances, I think I can see a little into the springs and motives which being cunningly presented to me under various disguises, induced me to set about performing the part I did, besides cajoling me into the delusion that it was a choice resulting from my own unbiased freewill and discriminating judgment.

The brash, vaunting tone of "American humor" is heard throughout *Moby-Dick,* as in the episode (to take but one example out of a hundred) in which Stubb bedevils and hoodwinks the master of the French ship Rosebud.

Yet the most beautiful pages in *Moby-Dick* are those in which the insistent, though often disembodied voice of Ishmael takes on the flowing, meditative tone of introspection and revery. Thus at the end of Chapter 35 we have Ishmael on the masthead. He is so engrossed in his own thoughts that he forgets to watch for whales, meriting the reproach that "Whales are scarce as hen's teeth whenever thou art up there." But then with an abrupt but not disconcerting change from this jocose beginning we follow Ishmael's flow of consciousness as he "takes the mystic ocean at his feet for the visible magic of that deep, blue, bottomless soul, pervading mankind and nature; and every strange, half-seen, beautiful thing that eludes him; every dimly-discovered, uprising fin of some undiscernible form, seems to him the embodiment of those elusive thoughts that only people the soul by continually flitting through it." Then nearly losing consciousness under the spell of the fantasy, he imagines himself in a moment of panic dropping with a shriek into the sea. And Melville winds up the chapter, as he often does, with a moral based on an elaborate analogy: "Heed it well, ye Pantheists!" "American humor," with its sense of violence and the precariousness of life, is aware of ranges of reality unsuspected by "pantheists"—or by the Emersonian transcendentalists Melville may have in mind when in describing the "mystic ocean" into which Ishmael gazes he makes it resemble the Oversoul.

To pursue the method suggested in Constance Rourke's *American Humor* (for that is what I have been doing in the above paragraphs) is to discover the legendary materials of Melville's epic of whaling. It gives us some insight into the origins of the great images, persons, and actions of the book. It is even a way of understanding some of the author's leading attitudes about life. It gives us, above all, the sense of the genial, the humane, and the creative. And if it does not show up all that is apprehended by what Ahab calls the "high perception," it does make us feel the natural, the aesthetic texture of life that appeals to the "low enjoying power." Perhaps only Mark Twain and Faulkner have known as well as Melville how to capture in their stories the variegated musings of the folk humor, and how to play these off against actions whose meaning is abstract and universal.

THE MEANING OF MOBY-DICK

If we think of the dramatic action involving Ahab and the pursuit of the whale, isolating this in our minds from the almost encyclopedic context in which it occurs, we are conscious of a meaning, even of a didactic purpose.

Just what the meaning is has been the subject of much speculation. Undoubtedly the first step towards understanding *Moby-Dick* is to observe what is really very obvious: it is a book about the alienation from life that results from an excessive or neurotic self-dependence. Melville has conceived of his moral fable in a way which makes *Moby-Dick* distinctly a book of its time and place and allies it intimately with the work of other American writers. As Newton Arvin demonstrates, there is some reason to think of Ahab as guilty of *hybris,* in the Greek sense, or of excessive pride, in the Christian sense; but there is more reason to think of him as guilty of or victimized by a distorted "self-reliance." An alternative to Ahab's suicidal course is proposed by the author. But since Mr. Arvin explains this in a way which seems generally to confirm the view of the American imagination as we are attempting to understand it in the present book, let us listen to him. Mr. Arvin begins by saying that "the alternative to Ahab's egotism" is not the Greek "ideal of 'nothing too much'" nor the Christian ideal of "a broken and contrite heart." Rather, he says,

> On one level it is an intuition that carries us beyond morality, in the usual sense, into the realm of cosmic piety; on the usual ethical level, however, it is a strong intuition of human solidarity as a priceless good. Behind Melville's expression of this, one is conscious of the gravity and the tenderness of religious feeling, if not of religious belief; it came to him in part from the Christian tradition in which he had been nurtured. The form it took in him, however, is no longer specifically Christian; as with Hawthorne and Whitman, it was the natural recoil of a sensitive imagination, enriched by the humanities of romantic idealism, against the ruinous individualism of the age. It is Melville's version of Hawthorne's "magnetic chain of humanity," of Whitman's "manly attachment"; so far, it is an essentially humanistic and secular principle.

The only caveat that needs to be added to these words is that the "intuition of human solidarity as a priceless good" is stronger in Melville and Whitman than in Hawthorne and that for all of them "human solidarity" means not a settled social order but a more or less unstable idyllic relationship, a personal and ideal sharing of the human fate among people temporarily brought together by chance or by a common purpose. The intuition of solidarity tends to come to American writers only when the solidarity is precarious and doomed by the passing of time or by the mere anarchic instinct of the individual. And so the American novel is full of idealized momentary associations—Natty Bumppo and his companions, Hawthorne's Blithedalers, Ishmael, Queequeg and the crew of the Pequod, Huck Finn and Nigger Jim on their raft, or—that classic example of the instability and mixed motives that characterize united action among Americans—the Bundren family in Faulkner's *As I Lay Dying*. Even such relatively stable social orders as that of the Bostonians described in James's *The Europeans* or that of the New Yorkers in Edith Wharton's *Age of Innocence* have to regroup themselves and suffer a good deal of agony in order to put up a united front against the foreigner who, in each novel, threatens invasion.

But to take up Mr. Arvin's argument again, one notes, in carrying it a step further, that the moral action of *Moby-Dick* is not strictly tragic or Christian. It is an action conceived as taking place in a universe of extreme contradictions. There is death and there is life. Death—spiritual, emotional, physical—is the price of self-reliance when it is pushed to the point of solipsism, where the world has no existence apart from the all-sufficient self. Life is to be clung to, if only precariously and for the moment, by natural piety and the ability to share with others the common vicissitudes of the human situation. These are the clear alternatives.

What must be remembered is that this is a melodramatic view of things. Strictly speaking, both Greek and Christian tragedy offer an ideal of catharsis or redemption—forms of harmonious life that come about *through* death. It is this life through death that Ishmael seems to have been given in the Epilogue, when he alone is saved by the coffin-life-buoy. But is this really a catharsis, a redemption, a rebirth? The momentary sense of harmony and joy is all too easily dispelled by the chilly gloom, the final despair, of the last words. "On the second day, a sail drew near, nearer, and picked me up at last. It was the devious-cruising Rachel, that in her retracing search after her missing children, only found another orphan."

For Melville there is little promise of renewal and reward after suffering. There is no transcendent ground where the painful contradictions of the human dilemma are reconciled. There is no life *through* death. There is only life *and* death, and for any individual a momentary choice between them. What moves Melville most powerfully is the horror that is the violent result of making the wrong choice. He is moved too by the comic aspect of the spectacle, the absurdity of such a creature as man, endowed with desires and an imagination so various, complex, and procreative yet so much the prisoner of the cruel contradictions with which, in his very being, he is inexorably involved. Finally, he is moved by the blissful, idyllic, erotic attachment to life and to one's ideal comrades, which is the only promise of happiness.

Solipsism, hypnotic self-regard, imprisonment within the self—these themes have absorbed American novelists. The Concord transcendentalism, of which Melville was very much aware and whose sensibility he in many ways shared, was a philosophy—or rather an ethical poetry—of the self. The idea of the image reflected in the mirror or in the water appeals as strongly to Melville as to Hawthorne, and like Hawthorne he uses this literary convention to point up the dangers of an exaggerated self-regard, rather than, as Whitman and Emerson loved to do, to suggest the vital possibilities of the self. At the very beginning of *Moby-Dick* we are shown "crowds of water-gazers" who are "posted like silent sentinels" around the shores of Manhattan and are "fixed in ocean reveries." And then, says Melville, amplifying his effect with his usual semi-humorous parody of learning, there is the still deeper "meaning of that story of Narcissus, who because he could not grasp the tormenting, mild image he saw in the fountain, plunged into it and was drowned. But that same image, we ourselves see in all rivers and oceans. It is the image of the ungraspable phantom of life; and this is the key to it all."

This last statement is tantalizing and although it sounds a little offhand, like a too facile way to end a paragraph, it also sounds and *is* important. For the book is to offer the alternative of Narcissus. One may, like Ahab, look into the water, or into the profound and ultimately unknowable abyss of nature, and see only one's own image or an ungraspable phantom, a white whale which is only a projection of self. Or, like Ishmael or Starbuck, one may see one's own image but in a context of life and reality which is *not* one's self. To be Ahab is to be unable to resist the hypnotic attraction of the self with its impulse to envelop and control the universe. To be Ishmael is to be able at the last minute to resist the plunge from the masthead into the sea one has with rapt fascination been gazing at, to assert at the critical moment the difference between the self and the not-self. To be Starbuck is to understand what the white whale might mean to a man like Ahab but to insist "with the stubbornness of life" that the whale is merely "a dumb brute" to seek vengeance on which is "blasphemous" and "madness."

Chapter 99, "The Doubloon," tells us much about the meaning of *Moby-Dick*. The doubloon is a gold coin Ahab has nailed to the main mast. It is to be won by whoever first sights the white whale. Ishmael describes the coin in detail (if indeed Ishmael can be called the narrator at this point; he is always ostensibly the narrator but in much of the latter part of the novel he is not *felt* as such). The coin is from Ecuador. "So this bright coin came from a country planted in the middle of the world, and beneath the great equator, and named after it; and it had been cast midway up the Andes, in the unwaning climate that knows no autumn." In the ambiguous symbolism of the coin, involving three mountains crowned respectively with a flame, a tower, and a crowing cock, we see "the keystone sun entering the equinoctial point at Libra" (the Scales). Without worrying over the rather labored symbolism, we note that for author-Ishmael the coin represents the equator, the dividing line in a dualistic world. From the point of view of the equator, there are in human destiny two grand alternatives: the self-absorption which leads to isolation, madness, and suicide, or the imperfect but more or less objective perceptions of the world which allow one to cling to life. All this is shown in the procession of the main figures of the drama as each in turn meditates momentarily on the coin.

Ahab soliloquizes thus:

> the firm tower, that is Ahab; the volcano, that is Ahab; the courageous, the undaunted, and victorious fowl, that, too, is Ahab; all are Ahab; and this round gold is but the image of the rounder globe, which, like a magician's glass, to each and every man in turn but mirrors back his own mysterious self.

The others respond to the symbolism of the coin in their different ways, but each is free of Ahab's imprisonment. Starbuck sees the symbolism of the ordinary pious Christian life. Stubb is reminded of his *carpe diem* philosophy, his jolly acceptance of life and death. Flask, even less imaginative, sees simply a gold coin that, as he pauses to calculate, would buy nine hundred and sixty cigars. The Manxman, a primitive soothsayer, sees merely a vague doom. Fedallah, the Parsee harpooner Ahab has smuggled aboard, sees the fire worshiped in his religion. Pip, rather reminiscent of of King Lear's fool, expresses with a theological despair, one may think, the impossibility of seeing anything, the impossibility of knowledge. To him it is not only Ahab who is imprisoned within the self; it is in the nature of man to seek but not to find, to look but not to see. Thus he mutters: "I look, you look, he looks; we look, ye look, they look." Little Pip is Melville's Christian caveat. As we are told in "The Castaway" (Chapter 93), Pip "saw God's foot upon the treadle of the loom, and spoke it; and therefore his shipmates called him mad. So man's insanity is heaven's sense. . . ." Heaven's sense may be glimpsed by visionaries, Melville concedes, but it cannot be brought to bear on such actions as are reported in *Moby-Dick*.

As a symbol the whale is endlessly suggestive of meanings. It is as significant and manifold as Nature herself, and, of course, that is the point. Like nature the whale is paradoxically benign and malevolent, nourishing and destructive. It is massive, brutal, monolithic, but at the same time protean, erotically beautiful, infinitely variable. It appears to be unpredictable and mindless; yet it is controlled by certain laws. The chapter on "The Whiteness of the Whale" is a *tour de force* of learning and ingenuity such as Melville liked to get off. It remains, however, rather inert, and like some of the excessively extended chapters on cetology, or the interpolated story of the Town-Ho, it forces us to step outside the action of the book in order to take in a sort of sideshow at a moment when we are all for getting on with the main event. Still the idea of the whale's whiteness is indispensable. Whiteness is the paradoxical color, the color that involves all the contradictions Melville attributes to nature. It signifies death and corruption as readily as virginal purity, innocence, and youth. It has the advantage of being, from one point of view, the color that contains all colors, whereas from another point of view, it suggests a *tabula rasa* which may be imaginatively endowed with significance according to the desire or obsession of him who beholds it. It also readily suggests the sense of the uncanny or the preternatural out of which mythic and religious ideas are formed.

As Melville writes:

> Is it that by its indefiniteness it shadows forth the heartless voids and immensities of the universe, and thus stabs us from behind with the thought of annihilation, when beholding the white depths of the milky way? Or is it, that as in essence whiteness is not so much a color as the visible absence of color, and at the same time the concrete of all colors; is it for these reasons that there is such a dumb blankness, full of meaning, in a wide landscape of snows—a colorless, all-color of atheism from which we shrink?

These rhetorical questions help us to understand what Melville has in mind. Yet the most memorable passages about the whiteness of the whale are in other chapters where Melville the unsurpassable poet lays aside the rather awkward philosophizings that encumber portions of his book. The essential voice of Melville is to be heard in the half humorous, subtly erotic lyric tone which is peculiar to *Moby-Dick*:

> A gentle joyousness—a mighty mildness of repose in swiftness, invested the gliding whale. Not the white bull Jupiter swimming away with ravished Europa clinging to his graceful horns; his lovely, leering eyes sideways intent upon the maid; with smooth bewitching fleetness, rippling straight for the nuptial bower in Crete; not Jove, not that great majesty Supreme! did surpass the glorified White Whale as he so divinely swam.

But we should not think Melville a very great poet if he had not written passages like the following (from "The Funeral," Chapter 69):

> The vast tackles have now done their duty. The peeled white body of the beheaded whale flashes like a marble sepulchre; though changed in hue, it has not perceptibly lost anything in bulk. It is still colossal. Slowly it floats more and more away, the water round it torn and splashed by the insatiate sharks, and the air above vexed with rapacious flights of screaming fowls, whose beaks are like so many insulting poniards in the whale. The vast white headless phantom floats further and further from the ship, and every rod that it so floats, what seem square roods of sharks and cubic roods of fowls, augment

the murderous din. For hours and hours from the almost stationary ship that hideous sight is seen. Beneath the unclouded and mild azure sky, upon the fair face of the pleasant sea, wafted by the joyous breezes, that great mass of death floats on and on, till lost in infinite perspectives.

The point of these remarks on "the meaning of *Moby-Dick*" will have been missed unless it is seen that they attribute a less manifold meaning to the book than is sometimes attributed to it. The symbols are manifold and suggestive; the epic scope is opulent; the rhetoric is full and various; the incidental actions and metaphors are richly absorbing. The meaning is profound. But at the same time it is narrow. The issues, as opposed to the states of mind and feeling they generate, are all simplified; they are abstracted and compressed to a degree incompatible with the broader reach, the more comprehensive concreted significance of greater poems like *King Lear, The Divine Comedy,* or *The Iliad.* These poems bring to the given facts of human destiny a universal tragic conception of their meaning. Melville's mind, no less profound in its intuitive sense of life, is nevertheless comparatively narrow and abstract. In this as in its incomparable discoveries of language, its appropriation of new subject matters, and its opening out of new aesthetic experience, *Moby-Dick* is at once the most startling and the most characteristic product of the American imagination.

D O S T O E V S K Y

[*1821–1881*]

IN RECENT YEARS CRITICISM HAS OFFERED TWO IMAGES OF DOSTOEVSKY. ONE makes him the prëeminent novelist of inner turmoil and contradiction; the other emphasizes his extraordinarily full and dramatic account of his society. We tend to split novels into these two kinds: Dostoevsky makes it plain that the one without the other makes for an impoverished idea of the novel. V. S. Pritchett suggests that we tend to think that psychology dissolves complexity. He writes: "The value of psychological analysis to the novel lay for Dostoevsky in its latent dramatic quality." In Dostoevsky characters who suffer profound internal divisions are by that very fact deeply engaged with others; we are prone to emphasize their isolation from some imposed (and quite evanescent) standard of normality.

The reader is warned that R. P. Blackmur, one of the most accomplished American critics, sometimes writes as if for himself. Certain connectives are left out. Read manfully on; you will find yourself dancing to his tune, which renders the characteristic strategy of Dostoevsky perfectly.

Reprinted by permission of R. P. Blackmur.

R . P . B L A C K M U R

Crime and Punishment:
A Study of Dostoevsky's Novel

*C*rime and Punishment HAS UPON MOST READERS AN IMPACT AS IMMEDIATE and obvious and full as the news of murder next door; one *almost* participates in the crime, and the trivial details become obsessively important. It has besides a secondary impact, by which, as one feels it, one discovers that one has been permanently involved in the nature of the crime: one has somehow contributed to the clarification of the true residual nature of crime in general through having contributed to the enactment of this crime in particular. It is the feeling of this impact that leads us to say our powers of attention have been exhausted. But there is a third and gradual impact, which comes not only at the end but almost from the beginning to the end creating in us new and inexhaustible powers of attention. This is the impact of what Dostoevsky meant by punishment. The three impacts are united by the art of the novelist, and they are felt simultaneously. It is only that we are not aware at the time of the triple significance, and must, when it does transpire, rebuild it analytically. Thus we may come to estimate what it is that we know—what it is that has been clarified in the history of Raskolnikov which we had known all along in ourselves without being aware of it; we estimate our own guilt.

A crime is above all an act against the institutions of human law, custom, or religion; and there is a sense in which any act may be understood as criminal, for if the institution cannot be found against which it is committed, then it may be called an anarchic act—against some institution that has not yet come to exist, but which will exist because of the crime. This notion comes from putting Rousseau's dusty vision in reverse. If, as Rousseau thought for one inspired moment, the evils of living come mostly from human institutions, it is as likely true, though not as inspired, that our institutions arise out of the evil that we do. It is LaForgue who has said it best, and without any but poetic logic to blister his cry:

> *Allez, stérile ritournelles!*
> *La Vie est vraie et criminelle!*

This cry of LaForgue represents the lyric sense that must inhabit every criminal who truly imagines his crime, if only for a flash, *before* he commits it to act. What the criminal imagines afterwards is another thing and we shall come to it. Here it is the crime only that has been imagined, and the promise of liberation in the cry within.

So it is with Raskolnikov. If we feel his case in terms of the LaForgue lines we can understand both the motivation of his crime and the external logic of most of his conduct afterwards. It is the story of *Crime and Punishment* at the level of its immediate impact. We are very near it; it is the murder that only by some saving accident we did not ourselves commit—as we did not make a million, win a race, or conquer Europe, all the things it is still not impossible to do, and which, because we have not done them, may yet tempt us to murder. Between temptation and deed there is no distance at all in symbolic meaning. With that symbolic strength in mind, the story of Raskolnikov becomes not only possible but probable, and, as we attend it, not only probable but proved. Let us look and see.

How easy it is to believe that this young, handsome, proud, and sensitive boy might be drawn *first of all* to the possibility of murder as the way out of an intolerable situation. It is the situation of poverty, debt, starvation, shabbiness, sickness, loneliness; for Raskolnikov has reached such a stage of privation that even thought has become a luxury—a kind of luxurious hallucinated hysteria; an extremity in which only the rashest dream seems a normal activity. It is the situation of the sponge, too, for Raskolnikov has come to depend on his mother and sister for help they cannot afford to give, for help they can give only by prostituting themselves in marriage and servile relationships. The sponge who is aware that he is a sponge is in an awkward situation; the pride of his awareness deprives him of the use of the exactions he makes;

and that is how it is with Raskolnikov, as he lies in his attic committing symbolic murder. He deceives himself, proudly, that he has conceived murder to symbolise his mother's and sister's freedom as well as his own. He lends his dark motive the external colour of a good deed, and then identifies the colour with the motive, and forgets what the murder, dark within him, really is. But to starve and be a sponge, that is not all Raskolnikov has to put up with in his pride; he is in the situation, too, of the proud man of intellect who has as yet done nothing and who is afraid that there will be nothing for him to do unless he invents it. Not only can he do nothing for his poverty or for his family, he is in the terrible position of being unable to do anything for himself. Such is his pride, that none of the ordinary things men do will be enough; and such is his pride, too, that none of the things ordinary people— his mother, his sister, his forgotten friends—can do for him are tolerable to him; he is the man for whom no one can do anything. Deeper still, he is that part of all men which cannot be touched, but which must create an image of itself in some extraordinary deed, some act against ordinary people and against the ordinary part of himself. The extraordinary wells within him and inundates the ordinary self with its fever. And in that fever, which never leaves him while we know him, the possibility of murder becomes the necessity of murder.

What is fully imagined as necessary has goodness and freedom at the very heart of its horror, a sentiment which may be interpreted in different ways, having to do either with the tearing down of order or with the envelopment of disorder, or, finally, with the balancing of several disorders so as to form an order. At the level of immediate impact, Raskolnikov's story is concerned with the tearing down of order; that is the melodrama which carries us along and exhausts our attention. What Dostoevsky does to that story, the immense clarification of secret life and intimate impulse which he brings to it, composes the secondary impact of the story, and brings us to the second stage where the disorder brought about in the first stage is enveloped by the created personality of Raskolnikov. Actually, the two processes go on at once, in the sense that no matter how far into the second stage Dostoevsky leads us, the first stage is never left behind, but is rather always present, a frame of action and image, to carry the significance of the second stage. This is to say that Dostoevsky never fails of the primary task of the novelist; if his story seems for the moment to have been left behind, it is only that in reality it has got ahead of us, and when we catch up we see how much has been done without our noticing it. The story of the Crime is blended with the clarification of the Punishment; the actor creates the role which expresses the nature and significance of his deed; Raskolnikov, in the end, becomes the product of his crime, but still depends on it to command our attention.

That is how Dostoevsky envelops the disorder consequent upon Raskolnikov's attempt at the destruction of order. With the third possibility, whereby the imagination not only envelops disorder—our substantial chaos—in a created personality, but proceeds to balance the sense of several disorders—the tensions of chaos—against each other so as to form a new order; with this possibility Dostoevsky has little to do. It is not that he was necessarily unequal to the task, but the nature, source, and direction of his insights did not lead him to undertake it. His view of necessity was simpler, and his sense of possibility more simplified, than the task would require; his vision was that of the primitive Christian, and that vision was so powerful within him that it blinded him to everything else. To him the edge of the abyss of sin was the horizon of salvation by faith, and suffering was the condition of vision. Sin was the Crime, and the suffering created by faith was the Punishment.

If we push the operation of this insight one step further, it becomes evident that the act of life itself is the Crime, and that to submit, by faith, to the suffering of life at the expense of the act is to achieve salvation—or, if you like a less theological phrase, it is to achieve integration or wholeness of personality. It is only dramatically true that the greater the sin the greater the salvation, and it is only arbitrarily true that any one act is sinful more than another act or than all acts. The crime of Raskolnikov, and its punishment in created suffering, could have been as great if he had never stirred from his room, if only the novelist's imagination could have conceived them. But the imagination requires images, as vision requires fables and thought requires formulas, before conceptions can be realised; which is to say that the faculties of men are not equal to their needs except by the intervention of symbols which they discover rather than create, and which they discover best of all in stories of violence, or of the sense of violence, or of the promise of violence.

So we watch, with the immediate attention which discovers meaning, the process of Raskolnikov trying to make a hero—a complete man—of himself by committing a foul and frivolous murder. Any animal might strike another down without need when the odour of blood is thick, and it means nothing. But we are shown how much this murder of an old and malevolent pawnbroker, ripe with death, as Raskolnikov says, ripe as a louse, is not meaningless but huge with meaning. The meaning begins with the stench of Petersburg, the stench of the detailed plans, the stench of pothouses, the pervading sense of the filthy possibilities of the human heart, and the glittering eyes of the victim peering through the slit of the door. The meaning grows more meaningful, irretrievably meaningful, when in the second chapter we are exposed to Marmeladov in the stinking tavern and hear his confession of drunken humiliation and of what it has brought upon Katerina his wife in the way of sickness and shame and anger and hairpulling, and brought upon his daughter too, in her glad submissive acceptance of the humiliation of prostitution. It is impossible to *say* how this adds to the richness of Raskolnikov's motive, but like the general images of stench and violence and drunkenness, it is impossible not to *know,* and very precisely, how much it does add. Let us say that it exposes Raskolnikov, and through him the reader, to a kind of dead-level human degradation in terms of images which revolt him as he assents to them.

At any rate they fit him—for the purposes of the story—they fit him to see as further degradation the events which his mother's letter reports to him. Before he opens the letter we see his cluttered mind in his sleazy room trying to work around the idea of a "fortune all at once"; and in the letter he reads how indeed that is precisely what Douania his sister is about to get by selling herself to Luzhin. Douania has permitted herself or has been driven to do just the practical, ordinary thing which Raskolnikov, the extraordinary man, is unable to do, and which—as it is being done for *him*—is the more intolerably humiliating to him. Her marriage is like the prostitution of Sonia. Thinking of it, Hamlet-like, the idea of the murder rediscovers itself most naturally in his mind, and he finds that he had *felt beforehand* that it would come back; it has begun to acquire a kind of reality quite independent of him except that it requires to be completed.

Your ordinary novelist might well have now proceeded to the completion of the deed, but Dostoevsky saw deeper into the nature of the deed and knew that it required further preparation, so that it might be as ripe as the victim. Raskolnikov goes out for a breath of air and to escape the pressure of his dilemma. But there is no escape, except from one level of intensity to a deeper level. Walking on the boulevard the double pressure of Sonia and of Douania springs upon him in the shape of the drunken young girl, with the torn dress, and indecorous posture, evidently just seduced and then discarded, who is being pursued by the plump gentleman. In his shabby and dishevelled pride, and with his uprooted and irresolute mind he first attempts to save the girl and then gives it up as a bad job; he revolts against his revulsion, reminding himself of the percentage theory of vice whereby "a certain number" are bound to go that way, and resolves forthwith to go see Razumihin, that simpleton of a man who takes things as they are. But again he changes his mind; he cannot see Razumihin till after "It." The image of the debauched girl has set the murder to pursuing him still more closely. He contrives for himself, as he thinks, an escape in the green islands of the Neva, where there is no stench, no drunkenness, no human filth. The human filth is stronger. He first buys himself a glass of vodka, and then walks out exhausted, turning aside on the way home and falls asleep in the bushes, where a dream assaults him with a fresh image of the little sorrel horse beaten to death because it cannot pull all humanity. In the dream he rushes to kiss the bleeding face of the horse as it dies, and at that moment wakes. The moment of waking is the nearest he comes to renouncing his crime before committing it, and it is the nearest, too, that he comes to realising its nature before the event. "It was as though an abscess that had been forming for a month past in his heart had suddenly broken. Freedom, freedom! He was free from that spell, that sorcery, that obsession!" He had reached the point which Shakespeare, in his own play of Crime and Punishment, *Measure for Measure,* calls the point where the two prayers cross, where, in the human heart, good and evil are created in the one gesture.

It was coincidence, you will remember, that decided the event. Raskolnikov happened to hear, on his way home, that the old pawnbroker would be left alone at seven the following evening, and he heard it at precisely the moment that he had given up the idea of the murder, when he had, in fact, begun again to use his reason and will. But the other thing had grown in him like a disease, and feeding on the coincidence, was able to destroy his will and reason, that is to say his sense of propriety in the social order. It may be observed, for those who carp at the use of coincidence as belittling the probabilities, that on the contrary the use of coincidence in art, like the sense of it in life, heightens the sense of inevitability; for coincidence is the artist's way of representing those forces in us not ourselves. Coincidence, properly dealt with, creates our sense of that other self within us whom we neither can ever quite escape nor quite meet up with.

In this case it is the perfected chain of coincidence, upon which Dostoevsky lavishes so many pages, that builds up the murder so that it is a kind of separate being existing between Raskolnikov and his victim. As he climbs the stairs, he feels that Alyona Ivanovna ought to be ready for him, ready to be murdered, for he feels that the murder is somewhere between them, other than either, but equally accessible to both. It was in the nature of Dostoevsky's insight to see always that the actor and the patient are both implicated in the deed, and that they are joined by it. The actor, in this case, has more consciousness than the patient of the implication; in *The Idiot* it is the other way round, and Myshkin, the patient, is shown as more conscious, or more representative, of the deeds that are done to him than the doers of the deeds can possibly be. In *Crime and Punishment,* it is Sonia who is perhaps the counterpart of Myshkin, for to her all deeds happen whether the doers realise it or not, and they happen, moreover, completely. It is perhaps because Raskolnikov is the other sort, the sort who requires of a deed that before it is credible or fully significant he must do it himself. He does not believe in the murder until he has done it, and not altogether even then. Constantly it slips away, a thing he realises that he has forgotten, or a thing he has to re-enact, to emphasise, and so a thing that tends to lose its meaning except as he identifies himself with it; whereas to Sonia, once she has learned of it, once she has submitted herself to the idea of it in him, she has no doubts about it and it is entirely meaningful. Nothing herself, Sonia is able to contain everything; while Raskolnikov, who must be everything himself, can contain nothing for long. Dante would have known how to punish him, looking for a mirror through an eternal hell; but Dostoevsky has rather to transform him in order to save him, or more accurately to show him as about to be saved in Sonia's eyes.

But he is not transformed for a long time, never permanently in the book; never can he leave the murder which fixed him, nor the images of which it was made: the images of stench, poverty, drunkenness, vanity, sick-hunger, lechery, and intellectual debauchery, through which the murder comes to be a deed in being, with the double power of invocation and growth. At first, indeed, he forgets it for the images and the sickness which went with it, and when he wakes to it he finds that instead of feeling it behind him it has somehow got ahead of him and he is driven to catch up to it. Instead of freedom, power, completeness, he is more at loss than ever, and more incoherent, there are only "scraps and shreds of thought," suspicions, excitements, alarms, and fresh temptations to extraordinary declarations of himself. This is, of course, the first phase of the Punishment for the Crime, that having striven by the crime to reach a complete solution of his incomplete life, he should find himself not only less complete than ever and more wayward but actually perilously incoherent, with a personality on the verge of dissipation. He lives in a haunted vertigo, into which for the time he can evoke only the shrieking phantoms of rage and dread. He is in the position, so humiliating to his continuing pride, where he is completely powerless as the perfectly good man, as powerless as Sonia. There is nothing he can yet see to do for himself, and nothing any longer that he can do for others. When the police send for him about his IOU which his landlady had sold, he feels himself possessed by "a gloomy sensation of agonising, everlasting solitude and remoteness," and knows that it will never be possible for him to appeal to anyone in any circumstance of life. There is a sense in which Dostoevsky might have stopped at this point, for he had put Raskolnikov on the path at the end of which lay the meaning of his Crime as Punishment. For as in the Christian psychology no man may complete himself in deed, so the meaning of a deed can never be completed within the history of the man who enacts it. Only the judgment completes either the man, or his deed, or his meaning.

But both the deed and the meaning can continue in their course of meaningfulness. The growth of meaning is infinite. At the moment he feels his agonising solitude form consciously within him he hears the police discuss the murder; that is, it is given to him from outside for the first time, and as not his murder, but as an object in no one's possession; at once he is driven to confess, to seize it for his own, but a combination of the fumes of paint and the pang of creation cause him to faint. When he comes to, he goes out leaving a strange impression and a potent silence behind him.

Out of that strangeness and silence grows the pursuit-game which occupies the rest of the book, for Raskolnikov, having decided that suspicions may have been roused about him from his peculiar conduct, begins playing a complicated and eccentric game, or rather a set of games. He pursues the police, eggs the police on to pursue him, and himself both pursues the murder, the acknowledgment of it, and denies it whenever he comes face to face with it. The result of all this rash, tortuous, and vain activity is that he creates such an image of the murder that at last it overwhelms him. He plays his hands so that others play to him. In the event, there is nothing for anyone to believe about him except the extraordinary reality of the murder. He could not have made more certain of his arrest and imprisonment had that been his entire object. Only he delayed it, played with it, encouraged it to develop, in order to get the full savour of it and of himself.

First he rouses unconscious suspicions in Razumihin, then in Zossim—of the doctor in whom the suspicions may have been quite conscious, for he looked at Raskolnikov "curiously" whenever there was opportunity, and especially after that scene where Raskolnikov himself first realises the murder in a parallel and arbitrary image which brims and trembles as you look at it. It is that image which comes when Raskolnikov lies abed listening to the doctor and Razumihin talk of the murder, and how a house-painter has been mixed up in it. Nastasya, who is present, bursts out that Lizaveta was murdered, too.

"Lizaveta," murmured Raskolnikov hardly audibly.
"Lizaveta, who sold old clothes. Didn't you know her? She used to come here. She mended a shirt for you, too."
Raskolnikov turned to the wall where in the dirty, yellow paper he picked out one clumsy, white flower with brown lines on it and began examining how many petals there were in it, how many scallops in the petals and how many lines on them. He felt his arms and legs as lifeless as though they had been cut off. He did not attempt to move, but stared obstinately at the flower.

It is so that the murder is brought home by the housemaid's first mention of the other and incidental murder of Lizaveta. We feel what passed in Raskolnikov's mind, and feel it as if it passed in his face, and in his hands, too: quite as if he had plucked the scalloped petals of the clumsy white flower off the wallpaper. Razumihin, who was simple, may have seen nothing, but the doctor, looking at this dissenting soul, surely saw what Raskolnikov saw in the flower even if he could not then have named it. The blankest or the most conventional image is, as Dostoevsky knew, the best to hold the deepest symbol if only there is enough tension present when it is named. It is only another instance of this device that when Raskolnikov is about to go into the bar where he meets and gives himself away to Zametov, he first sees a good many drunken women, some of forty and some of seventeen, almost all of whom "had blackened eyes." Raskolnikov, who had gone out to end *this,* as he put it to himself, reflects upon this bevy with blackened eyes and pocked cheeks, that even the worst life is precious.

> "Only to live, to live and live! Life, whatever it may be! . . . How true it
> is; Good God, how true! Man is a vile creature! . . . And vile is he who calls
> him vile for that," he added a moment later.

Whereupon he proceeds to risk his life, to make it precious, by playing like Hamlet on Rosencrantz and Guildenstern, upon the suspicious nerves of Zametov the police clerk as he drank tea in a restaurant. This scene, like the two great scenes with Porfiry, and like the last scene with Svidrigailov, shows Raskolnikov clinging with a kind of ultimate shuddering tenacity to his original proud role of the extraordinary man, the role of Napoleon within the little man, and clinging the more desperately because in the act of playing it he sees the role is false, the role of the condemned man whose life is thereby sweet.

What else happens at the same time, the history of the growth of the Punishment along with the realisation of the Crime, is of course present in these scenes, but it has been instigated in other scenes—those with his mother and sister and Luzhin and Razumihin and the Marmeladovs; and it is perfected in other scenes still, those with Sonia especially, though these scenes might well be lifeless and pointless without their counterparts with Porfiry and Svidrigailov. There is a synergy—a working together and back and forth —between these counterparts much as there is a synergy between the two parts, the proud, self-willed part and the meek, submissive part of Raskolnikov's character. This working together takes place, and the resultant unity is seen, not because there is any logical or organic connection between the parts, but because, quite to the contrary, the conflicting elements are dramatised in association, in parallels that, as they say, never actually meet except as opposites. The more nearly they seem to be forced into meeting, the more disparate they actually show themselves to be. The fusion, if it can be called a fusion, is in the dramatic *product* of the conflicting elements, not of the elements themselves.

It is something along these lines, I think, that the theory of the "doubles" in Dostoevsky must be approached, and this whether we think of single characters or of whole books and the doubleness of the conflicts within either. Let us look at Raskolnikov, who is usually thought of as a typical Dostoevsky Double. He is self-willed and will-less, he is proud and he becomes humiliated, he loves Sonia and hates her at the same moment, he is fond of Razumihin and cannot tolerate him, he is on the edge both of confession and of anathema all along, he is good to the point of giving all that he has and evil to the point of taking life; and in short there is neither certainty nor limit to any of his moods or acts; any role is dominant for the moment to another role that may at once take its place because it has been really dominant underneath. But he is not these roles in turn, he is the product of all their playing taken together. In any pair, the one may be taken as the idea of the other, and the other the reality of the idea, and the only alternation is as to which, at a given moment, is idea and which reality. The relation is rather like that between the idea of murder and the image of the white flower on the wallpaper, where we can reverse it and say it is the relation between the idea of the flower and the image of the murder. What we get is a kind of steady state precariously maintained between the conflicting elements. The balance tips, but it recovers in the act of tipping. We should feel it as we feel similar physiological states in the body—only as the disturbance and forward drive of life—were it not that the language itself and Dostoevsky's taste for seeing the opposite to every presented element have together a tendency to formularise pure types, and then to ignore for the moment what does not exemplify the type. What happens is, by language and its dialectic mode, that Dostoevsky's imagination arrests, for the maximum possible amount of attention, the moments when the balance does tip from love to hate, from pride to humiliation, from idea to deed, from image to tension, and by the arrest, by the attention which is bent upon the moment of arrest, we see how the one in each case fecundates the other. We seem to see deeply what they make together by seeing wilfully what they are apart.

By a little progress of this notion, we can say that Raskolnikov is balanced in turn against the other characters in this novel, and that the other characters and their stories make something with Raskolnikov which is quite different from anything found in them as types, though there would be no product of their whole conflict if there was not a great deal that was living within each type, from Razumihin to Porfiry to Svidrigailov to Sonia, and all the rest. As illustration, let us take first the Marmeladov family, and consider by what astonishing luck it was that Dostoevsky thought of putting them into the history of Raskolnikov and the punishment of his crime. They were to have been, the whole little crowd of them, a novel all to themselves called "The Drunkards," a novel showing, no doubt, all the ills and humiliations that can come from the head of a poor family who has given over to heavy drinking. The luck is that Dostoevsky had them all going, with past and present and future, when Raskolnikov happened to meet old Marmeladov in the tavern and heard his humiliating confession with such apparently inexplicable sympathy. The truth is that he has something deeply in common with him, and again that Marmeladov has something which he has not yet but which he must have. What they have in common comes out when Marmeladov says that he has *nowhere to turn* except to his sick and somewhat crazy wife. Raskolnikov sees that it is not Marmeladov the good-natured drunk that turns, but Marmeladov humiliated, on hands and knees, with his hair pulled, Marmeladov in the mud which he Raskolnikov has not yet reached, but will reach in good time. Man grows used to everything, the scoundrel, says Raskolnikov, and adds: But what if he is not a scoundrel?

The scene is something like the great scenes in Dickens, caricature by direct observation, with the differences that Dostoevsky—and this is perhaps the way Dostoevsky himself read Dickens—replaces zest of observation for its own sake with the severity of attention that is based upon zeal, and replaces the anguish of social consciousness with the dignity of religion. Marmeladov, like Micawber, is able to represent much beyond himself because he is something of a buffoon; he can talk and act for talking and acting's sake; and he can be honest, and let himself go, just to see what will happen; he can see himself at his worst in order to be at his best. And so he does; he produces, to show himself at his utmost, and for the sake of Raskolnikov, for the sake of this new strange novel in which he unconsciously finds himself, the character and personality of Sonia, whom Raskolnikov needs as complement and salvation, and whom the novel needs for mechanics and plot. And not Sonia only, he also produces, by just the agency of his being, scenes in which all manner of things which bear on the novel can take place. His death, his funeral, the lyric insanity of Katerina his wife and her death-dance in the streets, all these are provided with new and enrichened context by the accidental meeting in the tavern of the *distrait* Raskolnikov and the drunken buffoon Marmeladov. And not only Marmeladov himself, but each of his family, as he precipitates their fates through his drunkenness and buffoonery, add to the context of Raskolnikov's growing fate.

Together they furnish him with his own opposite. As he is the person who above all must act, they are the persons who must be acted upon. He is the criminal, and they are the victims, victims generally and all the way through in much the same way that the old pawnbroker was in Raskolnikov's eyes "ripe" to be murdered. No degradation is too great for the old drunkard who has nowhere to turn; you have only to put fresh degradation in his way and he will take it up with gusto. Katerina, too, eager to find insult in everyone's speech, in his absence or in his presence, imagines insult and injury upon herself at every opportunity. The children, even, with their illness and their rags cannot be treated except with brutality. And as for Sonia, she is not only eager and willing, she fairly demands further humiliation. By prostituting herself, this thin, bird-like creature, almost without a body, shows herself as inviting at best further depravity; for surely no one not depraved, no one not desiring to sack the *last* citadel of integrity, would have any use for her. Sonia had to come from such a family, for only out of the experience of such utter humiliation could her own perfect humility grow. As they are damned so she is blessed, by the enormous shift in significance caused by the shift of a single syllable. It is Gide, who knew Dostoevsky well, who observed that where humility opened the gates of heaven, humiliation opened those of hell. Sonia's blessedness is built upon the bottomlessness of their hell. She accepts, and makes into inner strength, a worse stage of the experience which tore them apart.

Thus, as Raskolnikov comes into contact with Marmeladov and his wife, as he probes them with his intellect, they absorb his sense of himself into a kind of private hell, an abyss beyond soundings, quite off the continental shelf of consciousness which his intellect, however demoniac, can reach. But Sonia, and this is the secret of her personality, can no more be penetrated by Raskolnikov's intellect than her soul can be ravished through the degradation of her body. That is her attraction as a prostitute: that she cannot be prostituted in anything that she has to offer; and that is her power over Raskolnikov, the power of perfect submissiveness which in another place Dostoevsky calls the greatest power in the world: it is the power that he cannot attain by any deed, but that can be attained by imitation, by suffering what she has suffered. It is the power of her suffering, the happiness of it, that not so much overcomes him as it infects or fecundates him. For he is not overcome, though it is promised that he will be; he fights back, the very feeling of her goodness, his very sense of the stigma of her faith, aggravates his pride and the intellectual structure upon which his pride is built, so that when he goes to her for comfort and strength he finds that he has to torture her, and to repel her at every level. The love he feels for her is also and simultaneously hate, and there is no difference between the emotions as he feels them, only as he intellectually knows what they are. And this is an example of the profound psychological rightness of Dostoevsky's judgment, for surely it takes only a pause for judgment to see that as hate or pride is the burden Raskolnikov carries so love or humility is the *burden* of Sonia's life. If she feels his burden as love and accepts it as of nature, he must feel the burden of her love as intolerable. He is indeed a kind of Prodigal Son who finds the love with which he is welcomed the very burden from which he ran away in the first place. It was not of Sonia that he made the following remark but thinking of her and just before seeing her, so it fits all the more: "Oh, if only I were alone and no one loved me and I too had never loved anyone! *Nothing of all this would have happened.*"

It will be remembered that earlier in the book Razumihin has explained to Douania that her brother is perhaps a person incapable of love. Razumihin may have meant only that Raskolnikov is a lonely fellow, but he was literally right as well; no one can be said to love who does not feel as acceptable the burden of love in return, and who does not feel, too, that in loving someone positively, he is imposing the most difficult of human burdens. Sonia knows this in herself, by intuition directed inwards as well as outwards, as a condition of her being, and it is to that double burden that she submits.

Like the crime which existed *between* the old pawnbroker, so between Sonia and Raskolnikov there exists her intuition of love, which she feels so strongly that he *must* know, that gradually by a contagion from her understanding he does know it. It is a love, this unassailable love of the unsmirchable prostitute, that has nothing to do with sex. Not that it might not have been sexual, and even might have taken the means of a kind of ultimate lechery of the spirit, and still have been within the Christian insight, but that Dostoevsky was unable ever to create a character or a mood which showed more than the most superficial aspects of sexual awareness. His people were not eunuchs or in any way deprived of sex but they were born without it. It is love *manqué* that Dostoevsky deals with, love *malgré-lui;* and it is for this reason perhaps that Dostoevsky is able to show love as pure spiritual renunciation. That is why, too, in what was to others the romantic fancy of purity in a prostitute, he sees a kind of exorbitant and omnivorous reality: a true dramatic enactment of the idea of purity. That is why, again, he so often concerns his characters with the idea of debauching young girls, girls before puberty, in whom sex as anyone else would have understood it would not have ripened, so that the debauchery would be of the actor alone.

If these remarks help explain the character and power of Sonia who is of the character of the saint, they help with the others as well, most particularly with the riddle of Svidrigailov, to whom we shall come in a moment for his own sake, but whom now we shall consider in his relation with the character of Douania, Raskolnikov's sister. This young lady is painted as all abloom with normality; she and her mother belong in Dostoevsky's long gallery of simple, intelligent, sincere, generous, impulsive, and dependably decent women, young and old, of whom there are samples in almost every one of his novels—as, to give but one example, Mme. Epanchin and her daughter Aglaia in *The Idiot*. Always they serve the same purpose, to act as foils or background for the extraordinary actions of distorted or driven individuals, such as Raskolnikov and Myshkin. They preserve their identity and their normal responsiveness through every form of violence and disorder; it is their normality which, by contrast, promotes the meaningfulness of the good and bad angels, the light and the dark angels, whose actions make the stories. Nothing in themselves but attractive types, they come to life in terms of the protagonists.

In *Crime and Punishment* they represent the normal conduct from which Raskolnikov departs; they represent the order of society which he tears down and envelops; it is them, their lives, to whom he gives meaning. In the same way Luzhin, the bourgeois on the make, and Lebetziatnikov the nihilist reformer, are caricatures, the one malicious and the other kindly, of normal types of eccentricity within the ordered society which produces at its extremes the super-egotist Raskolnikov and the super-reformer Sonia. But these figures gather part of their meaning from the driven, demoniac, "secret" character of Svidrigailov, the lecher of women and debaucher of souls: the mysterious figure whose evil is concentrated in what is asserted to be, but never shown, his intense and overweening sexuality. As an example of sexual behaviour, Svidrigailov is incredible. Sex is Dostoevsky's symbol for a diabolic, destructive power, which he can sense but cannot measure, and which he cannot otherwise name. This aspect of the Svidrigailov type of figure is Dostoevsky's attempt to explain, to dramatise and invoke a force which he does not seem ever to have understood but which he knows must exist. It is a lonely, awkward, proud sort of power, hovering always on the brink of suicide; it is haunted and haunting; it is the power of the "Other" thing, the other self, the dark side of the self, the substance and drive of that secret world in us which the devil creates, the power which in conventional life—the life which we mostly live—we successfully ignore, so that we tend to estimate its presence in others rather than in ourselves— as if others were our othermost selves. Thus Douania's soul had been imperilled by Svidrigailov's attempt to seduce her, and imperilled precisely by Svidrigailov's technique, which he outlines to Raskolnikov, of assaulting her through purity. He has caused her purity, not her baser emotions but her purity, somehow to desire him, and she had been rescued, in the first instance, in the nick of time: by the confusion, in Marfa Petrovna's eyes, of her purity with her lust. Raskolnikov understands well enough what the risk is—that his sister may be contaminated, that her decency may somehow come to absorb the temptation which Svidrigailov affords her in the new terms of his generosity. What he does not understand is the means by which the contamination, the trespass, will take place, which is by the frustration of violence on Douania's part when in the lonely room with the locked door, she tries so hard to shoot him. She is left by the desperate effort—by the fruitless tumescence of her spirit—in a very ambiguous state, which the story of Raskolnikov's Crime and Punishment did not have time to develop. One is not sure whether in that scene Douania has absorbed something from Svidrigailov, or whether Svidrigailov has absorbed what he wanted from Douania. Something has passed between them, at any rate, which leaves Svidrigailov either done for or contented, either vastated or fully occupied. In either case his remaining hours are justified—his visit to his little girl fiancée and his farewell present, the adventure in the hotel-room, the mouse in the bed, the five-year-old girl whose smile turns in his dream to a harlot's grin, the dream of the flood, which is to say the coming of judgment, and the suicide at dawn. We feel that the enigma of Svidrigailov has either been solved beyond our understanding or that it did not really exist—quite the problem of the devil. At any rate, his function has been fulfilled for every-one but Raskolnikov.

His relations to Raskolnikov have gone beyond those with the others, in both scope and intent, however much they may depend for their actuality upon the others. For Svidrigailov is a foil for the whole story. He comes be-fore the crime, in a way induces the crime to come into being, is the first to perceive the crime, and in a way *finishes* the crime without (since he does not have Raskolnikov's luck in finding Sonia) reaching the punishment. He *is* Raskolnikov in simpler perspective, he is Raskolnikov's other self, a mirror of being into which Raskolnikov never quite dares to look. He is the mystery of Raskolnikov's other self. The sense of him is symbolic, as it always is with mystery. Because he is a mystery beforehand, and exhibits himself mysteri-ously and providentially, he gathers meaning as he goes along, but not too clearly. He has the advantage of being not well understood, the figure grasped at but not caught, whom we are always about to understand. In fact we have frequently the sense of understanding him perfectly until we stop to query what it is we understand, when we find only that he represents precisely that secret life within us which drives us into incomprehensible actions. Like the character of Stavrogin in *The Possessed,* of whom Dostoev-sky says in his notes that he was not *meant* to be understood, but was meant rather to be a reservoir of the portentous, the possible, the mysterious, he is the symbolic clarification of that which cannot be expressed other than symbolically. He is the promise upon which we lean, knowing that it cannot be kept. He recedes like the horizon that follows us, only when we look.

Perhaps we may say that Svidrigailov envelops the disorder brought about by Raskolnikov's crime by imaging a kind of order which we cannot reach but which is always about to overwhelm us. He is a symbol of the mystery of the abyss, and it is a great witness to the depth of Dostoevsky's imagination that he is able to create in the flesh, with eyes too blue and flesh too youthful, such figures at will.

It is no less a test of Dostoevsky's skill—not his depth but his skill—that he is able to employ the one remaining major character in the book without, as it were, creating him at all. I mean, of course, that thirty-five-year-old roly-poly of the disengaged intellect called Porfiry, that man whose life, as he insists to Raskolnikov, is already finished, who has no other life to live, and nothing to do with what remains to him but probe and prance intellectually. Porfiry is so much a victim of moral fatigue that he is beneath every level of being but that of intellectual buffoonery. He represents order; he understands desire, ambition, all forms of conduct, but he knows nothing of the sources and ends of conduct, except that he can catch at them, in the midst of the game of the drowning man which he plays so long and so skilfully, like so many straws that only just elude his dancing fingers. But he is unreal, except as an agency of the plot, something to make the wheels go round; he is a fancy of the pursuing intellect whom Raskolnikov must have invented had he not turned up of his own accord. As Svidrigailov and Sonia between them represent the under-part, and the conflict in the under-part, of Raskolnikov's secret self, so Porfiry represents the maximum possible perfection of the artificial, intellectual self under whose ministrations Raskolnikov *reasons* himself into committing his crime, and who therefore is the appropriate instrument for driving him to the point of confessing it. It is Porfiry, who has no morals and no faith, who is all the proud game of intellect, who whenever he comes to sack Raskolnikov leaves him in a state of collapse, just as it is either Svidrigailov or Sonia who gives him strength. Porfiry knows what he must do, and can point it out to him in the example of the peasant who came forward to take the suffering of the crime upon his guiltless shoulders, he knows all the intellect can know, and perhaps knows that it must collapse, but he cannot push Raskolnikov over the brink, because he knows it only conventionally, by rote. He understands the Crime, because he represents that against which it was committed, and knows with what it was committed, but he cannot touch the Punishment, the completion of the Crime, because it must take place in a region of the soul beyond his grasp, the region which reason, argument, all the armament of order only clutter up and from which they must be swept, the region where the assumption of guilt by all that is innocent within the self takes place through the submission of the sinful, acting self to the faithful, waiting self, which waits, in Dostoevsky's primitive Christian insight, only to be created.

I think we have touched both upon the elements that go to make up the obvious and immediate impact of Raskolnikov's crime and its consequences in action, and upon the elements which as we understand them as exhibited in the various characters leave us all—not Russians, not fanatics of humiliation, not the distorted shadowy figures of Dostoevsky's novel alone, but all of us without exception—deeply implicated in the nature of the Crime. A word remains with which to fasten upon the nature of the Crime an indication of the nature of the Punishment. I do not know that there is a word ready to hand, for we have fallen quite out of the way of thinking in insights and images with the simple, direct intensity which was Dostoevsky's second nature. We lack the anterior conviction, the conviction before we begin to think, with which Dostoevsky mastered the relationship of man to God. But at least in saying that, we state Dostoevsky's major and abiding theme. To punish Raskolnikov, to bring him to retribution, to atonement, Dostoevsky had only to create his relationship to God, and to show at the same time how that relationship sprang from the nature of man as a creature of God quite apart from the structure of human society as an institution of men's minds. Dostoevsky believed that as Christ the innocent one took upon himself the suffering of all the innocent ones in the world, and so redeemed them along with the guilty, so the individual man has in him an innocent part which must take on the suffering caused by the guilty part. As he saw it, in our crime we create our guilt. Perhaps the commonplace example of false arrest will begin to make an analogue for what he meant. Which of us, falsely arrested, would not at once begin to assess his guilt, even for the crime which brought about the false arrest? And you would assess this guilt the more clearly because you were aware of the haphazard, the hazarded, character of your innocence. Similarly, the depth of your guilt would be measured by the depth of your faith, which would then, if you had imagination enough, transform you.

It should be emphasized that it was transformation, not reformation, that Dostoevsky envisaged. Reformation would have dealt with the mere guilty act against society. Transformation, through suffering, is alone able to purge the guilt of being.

Finally, we may draw some comparisons, in this search for means of clarifying the nature of Dostoevsky's notion of punishment, from recent history in our own country. When Mooney was released from his generation of false imprisonment, it soon turned out that he had no symbolic dignity, but represented rather a mere miscarriage of institutional justice; and so with the Scottsboro boys; so, too, with Dreyfus in the last century, for Dreyfus had no dignity. But if we think of Sacco and Vanzetti, does there not arise within us at once a sense that their great and terrifying symbolic dignity is due to Vanzetti, having assumed, with profound humility, the whole devastating guilt of the industrial society which killed him? Whether Vanzetti was innocent or guilty in law has become an irrelevant question. But the guilt which his last words and letters, his last conduct, somehow expiated, which was our guilt, remains permanently in question; for Vanzetti, like Raskolnikov, showed himself in the humiliation of his punishment, in humble relation to God.

HENRY JAMES

[1843–1916]

THE BEST CRITICAL MINDS OF THE LAST TWO GENERATIONS HAVE CELEBRATED THE qualities of Henry James. The present essay continues and builds upon their efforts, but with a difference. Many readers have pointed to what Dorothy Van Ghent calls "the profound identity of the aesthetic and the moral" in James, but no one else has put this perception to such precise use. The need to do so has been apparent in the bulk of James criticism, to which this stricture of Jacques Barzun's all too often applies: "To the historical critic, every attempt to deal with art as if it were pure or capable of being freed from circumstance will seem rather an attempt at self-deception, a round-about means of securing privacy and a little irresponsibility." James' belief that American moral spontaneity—or spiritual generosity—must order the imaginative accomplishments of Europe is fundamental.

On the continent, the notions of a virgin about the moral grandeur of life could hardly be considered material for a novel. But to James, Isabel Archer is no nubile chit; she is the American Girl, a priestess of growth, of possibility, indeed, of cultural salvation. But her widening perspective turns out to be a narrowing one; she is too ignorant, too self-absorbed, to accomplish her American mission.

The greatness of *The Portrait of a Lady* depends upon James' questioning Isabel Archer's authority, as he does not question that of Milly Theale and Maggie Verver, an index of the rampant Americanism of *The Wings of the Dove* and *The Golden Bowl*.

Professor Van Ghent is presently at the City College of New York.

DOROTHY VAN GHENT

On The Portrait of a Lady

To go from Hardy's *Tess* to James's *The Portrait of a Lady* is to go from Stonehenge to St. Peter's and from a frozen northern turnip field, eyed hungrily by polar birds, to the Cascine gardens where nightingales sing. Though both books concern the "campaign" of a young woman—a campaign that, expressed most simply, is a campaign *to live*—a greater difference of atmosphere could scarcely be imagined nor of articulation of what it means *to live*. The gaunt arctic birds in *Tess* have witnessed, with their "tragical eyes," cataclysms that no human eye might see, but of which they retain no memory. The birds offer a symbol of Tess's world: a world inimical to consciousness, where one should have no memory (Tess's fatal error is to remember her own past), where the eye of the mind should remain blank, where aesthetic and moral perceptivity is traumatic. The nightingales that sing to Isabel Archer and her lover in the "grey Italian shade" also offer a symbol of a world: they are the very voice of memory, of an imperishable consciousness at once recreating and transcending its ancient, all-human knowledge. It is to the tutelage of the European memory that Isabel Archer passionately surrenders herself in her campaign *to live,* that is, to become conscious; for, in James's world, the highest affirmation of life is the development of the subtlest and most various consciousness. In doing so, she must—like the girl in the barbarous legend of the nightingale, who, likewise in a foreign land, read an obscene crime in the weaving of a tapestry—come into knowledge of an evil which, in its own civilized kind, is as corrupting and implacable as that in the old tale. But consciousness here, as an activity nourished by knowledge, transcends the knowledge which is its content: and this too is in analogy with the ancient symbolic tale, where knowledge of evil is transcended, in the very doom of its reiteration, by the bird's immortal song.

The Portrait is not, like *Tess,* a tragedy, but it is as deeply informed with the tragic view of life: that tragic view whose essence is contained in the words, "He who loses his life shall find it," and "Except a corn of wheat fall into the ground and die, it abideth alone: but if it die, it bringeth forth much fruit." We associate tragic seriousness of import in a character's destiny with tension between the power of willing (which is "free") and the power of circumstances ("necessity") binding and limiting the will; and if either term of the tension seems lacking, seriousness of import fails. Apparently, no two authors could be at further antipodes than James and Hardy in the respective emphases they place on these terms. In Hardy, the protagonist's volition founders at every move on a universally mechanical, mysteriously hostile necessity; it is only in Tess's last acts, of blood sacrifice and renunci-ation of life, that her will appallingly asserts its freedom and that she gains her tragic greatness. In James's *Portrait,* and in his other novels as well, the protagonist appears to have an extraordinarily unhampered play of volition. This appearance of extraordinary freedom from the pressure of circum-stances is largely due to the "immense deal of money" (the phrase is taken from an early page of *The Portrait*) with which James endows his world— for, in an acquisitive culture, money is the chief symbol of freedom. The vague rich gleams of money are on every cornice and sift through every vista of the world of *The Portrait,* like the muted gold backgrounds of old Persian illuminations; and the human correlative of the money is a type of character fully privileged with easy mobility upon the face of the earth and with magnificent opportunities for the cultivation of aesthetic and intellec-tual refinements. It is by visualizing with the greatest clarity the lustrously moneyed tones of the James universe that we make ourselves able to see the more clearly what grave, somber shapes of illusion and guilt he organizes in this novel. The tension between circumstances and volition, "necessity" and "freedom," is demonstrated at the uppermost levels of material opportunity where, presumably, there is most freedom and where therefore freedom becomes most threatening—and where necessity wears its most insidious dis-guise, the disguise of freedom.

In following the previous studies, the reader will perhaps have been im-pressed with the fact that the novel as a genre has shown, from *Don Quixote* on, a constant concern with the institutions created by the circulation of money and with the fantasies arising from the having of it, or, more espe-cially, the not having it; a concern not always so direct as that of *Moll Flanders* and *Vanity Fair,* but almost inevitably implicit at least, expressed in indirect forms of aspiration and encitement to passion. As the definitively middle-class literary genre, the novel purchased its roots in a money-con-scious social imagination. The wealth shining on the James world is a kind of apogee of the novel's historical concern with money, showing itself, in

The Portrait, as a grandly sweeping postulate of possession: as if to say, "Here, now, is all the beautiful money, in the most liberating quantities: what ambition, what temptation, what errors of the will, what evil, what suffering, what salvation still denote the proclivities of the human even in a world so bountifully endowed?"

The "international myth" that operates broadly in James's work, and that appears, in this novel, in the typical confrontation of American innocence and moral rigor with the tortuosities of an older civilization, gives its own and special dimension to the moneyed prospect. James came to maturity in a post-Civil War America euphoric with material achievement. In terms of the Jamesian "myth," American wealth is now able to buy up the whole museum of Europe, all its visible "point" of art objects and culture prestige, to take back home and set up in the front yard (we need look no further, for historical objectification of this aspect of the "myth," than to William Randolph Hearst's epic importation of various priceless chunks of Europe to California). If the shadows of the physically dispossessed—the sweat and the bone-weariness and the manifold anonymous deprivation in which this culture-buying power had its source—are excluded from James's money-gilded canvas, the shadow of spiritual dispossession is the somber shape under the money outline. We are not allowed to forget the aesthetic and moral impoverishment that spread its gross vacuum at the core of the American acquisitive dream—the greed, the obtuse or rapacious presumption, the disvaluation of values that kept pace to pace with material expansion. James's characteristic thematic contrasts, here as in other novels, are those of surface against depth, inspection against experience, buying power against living power, the American tourist's cultural balcony against the European abyss of history and memory and involved motive where he perilously or callously teeters. In *The Portrait,* the American heroine's pilgrimage in Europe becomes a fatally serious spiritual investment, an investment of the "free" self in and with the circumstantial and binding past, a discovery of the relations of the self with history, and a moral renovation of history in the freedom of the individual conscience. It is a growing of more delicate and deeper-reaching roots and a nourishment of a more complex, more troubled, more creative personal humanity. It is, in short, what is ideally meant by "civilization," as that word refers to a process that can take place in an individual.

The postulate of wealth and privilege is, in revised terms, that of the second chapter of Genesis (the story of Adam in the garden)—that of the optimum conditions which will leave the innocent soul at liberty to develop its potentialities—and, as in the archetype of the Fall of Man, the postulate is significant not as excluding knowledge of good and evil, but as presenting a rare opportunity for such knowledge. It is the bounty poured on Isabel Archer (significantly, the man who gives her the symbolical investiture of money is a man who is fatally ill; significantly, also, she is under an illusion as to the giver) that makes her "free" to determine her choice of action, and thus morally most responsible for her choice; but it is the very bounty of her fortune, also, that activates at once, as if chemically, the proclivity to evil in the world of privilege that her wealth allows her to enter—it is her money that draws Madame Merle and Osmond to her; so that her "freedom" is actualized as imprisonment, in a peculiarly ashen and claustral, because peculiarly refined, suburb of hell. Isabel's quest had, at the earliest, been a quest for happiness—the naïvely egoistic American quest; it converts into a problem of spiritual salvation, that is, into a quest of "life"; and again the Biblical archetype shadows forth the problem. After eating of the fruit of the tree of knowledge of good and evil, how is one to regain access to the tree of life?

The great fairy tales and saints' legends have identified life with knowledge. For the fairy-tale hero, the fruit of the tree of life that is the guerdon of kingdom is the golden fleece or the golden apples that his wicked stepmother or usurping uncle have sent him in quest of; and to achieve the guerdon he must go through all tormenting knowledge—of serpents, floods, fire, ogres, enchantment, and even of his own lusts and murderous capacities. The ordeal of the heroes of saints' legends is also an ordeal of knowledge of evil, and the guerdon is life. As do these ancient tales, *The Portrait* identifies life with the most probing, dangerous, responsible awareness—identifies, as it were, the two "trees," the tree of the Fall and the tree of the Resurrection. The heroine's voluntary search for fuller consciousness, leads her, in an illusion of perfect freedom to choose only "the best" in experience, to choose an evil; but it is this that, by providing insight through suffering and guilt, provides also access to life—to the fructification of consciousness that is a knowledge of human bondedness. At the very end of the book, Caspar Goodwood gives passionate voice to the illusion of special privileges of choice and of a good to be had by exclusion and separateness: he says to Isabel,

"It would be an insult to you to assume that you care for . . . the bottomless idiocy of the world. We've nothing to do with all that; we're quite out of it . . . We can do absolutely as we please; to whom under the sun do we owe anything? What is it that holds us, what is it that has the smallest right to interfere . . .? The world's all before us—and the world's very big."

Isabel answers at random, "The world's very small." What attitude of mind takes her back to Rome, back to old evil and old servitude, is not described; we know only that she does go back. But it is evident that she does so because the "small" necessitous world has received an extension, not in the horizontal direction of imperial mobility that Caspar Goodwood suggests, but an invisible extension in depth, within her own mind—an extension into the freedom of personal renunciation and inexhaustible responsibility. The knowledge she has acquired has been tragic knowledge, but her story does not stop here, as it would if it were a tragedy—it goes on out of the pages of the book, to Rome, where we cannot follow it; for the knowledge has been the means to "life," and having learned to live, she must "live long," as she says. It is only the process of the learning that the portrait frame itself holds.

The title, *The Portrait,* asks the eye to see. And the handling of the book is in terms of seeing. The informing and strengthening of the eye of the mind is the theme—the ultimate knowledge, the thing finally "seen," having only the contingent importance of stimulating a more subtle and various activity of perception. The dramatization is deliberately "scenic," moving in a series of recognition scenes that are slight and low-keyed at first, or blurred and erroneous, in proportion both to the innocence of the heroine and others' skill in refined disguises and obliquities; then, toward the end, proceeding in swift and livid flashes. For in adopting as his compositional center the growth of a consciousness, James was able to use the bafflements and illusions of ignorance for his "complications," as he was able to use, more consistently than any other novelist, "recognitions" for his crises. Further, this action, moving through errors and illuminations of the inward eye, is set in a symbolic construct of things to be seen by the physical eye— paintings and sculptures, old coins and porcelain and lace and tapestries, most of all buildings: the aesthetic riches of Europe, pregnant with memory, with "histories within histories" of skills and motivations, temptations and suffering. The context of particulars offered to physical sight (and these may be settings, like English country houses or Roman ruins, or objects in the setting, like a porcelain cup or a piece of old lace draped on a mantel, or a person's face or a group of people—and the emphasis on the visual is most constant and notable not in these particulars, extensive as they are, but in the figurative language of the book, in metaphors using visual images as their vehicle) intensifies the meaning of "recognition" in those scenes where *sight* is *insight,* and provides a concrete embodiment of the ambiguities of "seeing."

In James's handling of the richly qualitative setting, it is characteristically significant that he suggests visual or scenic traits almost always in such a way that the emphasis is on *modulations of perception in the observer.* The "look" of things is a response of consciousness and varies with the observer;

the "look" of things has thus the double duty of representing external stimuli, by indirection in their passage through consciousness, and of representing the observer himself. For instance, when Ralph takes Isabel through the picture gallery in the Touchett home, the "imperfect" but "genial" light of the bracketed lamps shows the pictures as "vague squares of rich colour," and the look of the pictures is Isabel's state at the moment—her eager and innately gifted sensibility and her almost complete ignorance, her conscious orientation toward an unknown "rich" mode of being that is beautiful but indeterminate. Let us take another example from late in the book. Directly after that conversation with Madame Merle when Isabel learns, with the full force of evil revelation, Madame Merle's part in her marriage, she goes out for a drive alone.

> She had long before this taken old Rome into her confidence, for in a world of ruins the ruin of her happiness seemed a less unnatural catastrophe. She rested her weariness upon things that had crumbled for centuries and yet still were upright; she dropped her secret sadness into the silence of lonely places, where its very modern quality detached itself and grew objective, so that as she sat in a sun-warmed angle on a winter's day, or stood in a mouldy church to which no one came, she could almost smile at it and think of its smallness. Small it was, in the large Roman record, and her haunting sense of the continuity of the human lot easily carried her from the less to the greater. She had become deeply, tenderly acquainted with Rome: it interfused and moderated her passion. But she had grown to think of it chiefly as the place where people had suffered. This was what came to her in the starved churches, where the marble columns, transferred from pagan ruins, seemed to offer her a companionship in endurance and the musty incense to be a compound of long-unanswered prayers.

Here the definition of visible setting—churches and marble columns and ruins, and comprehending all these, Rome—though it is full, is vague and diffuse, in the external sense of the "seen"; but in the sense that it is a setting evoked by Isabel's own deepened consciousness, it is exactly and clearly focused. It is Rome *felt,* felt as an immensity of human time, as a great human continuum of sadness and loneliness and passion and aspiration and patience; and it has this definition by virtue of Isabel's personal ordeal and her perception of its meaning. The "vague squares of rich colour" have become determinate.

The theme of "seeing" (the theme of the developing consciousness) is fertile with ironies and ambiguities that arise from the natural symbolism of the act of seeing, upon which so vastly many of human responses and decisions are dependent. The eye, as it registers surfaces, is an organ of aesthetic experience, in the etymological sense of the word "aesthetic," which is a word deriving from a Greek verb meaning "to perceive"—to perceive through the senses. James provides his world with innumerable fine surfaces for this kind of perception; it is a world endowed with the finest selective opportunities for the act of "seeing," for aesthetic cultivation. But our biological dependence upon the eye has made it a symbol of intellectual and moral and spiritual perception, forms of perception which are—by the makers of dictionaries—discriminated radically from aesthetic perception. Much of James's work is an exploration of the profound identity of the aesthetic and the moral. (In this he is at variance with the makers of dictionaries, but he has the companionship of Socrates' teacher Diotima, as her teaching is represented by Plato in the *Symposium*. Diotima taught that the way to spiritual good lay through the hierarchies of the "beautiful," that is, through graduations from one form of aesthetic experience to another.) Aesthetic experience proper, since it is acquired through the senses, is an experience of *feeling*. But so also moral experience, when it is not sheerly nominal and ritualistic, is an experience of *feeling*. Neither one has reality— has psychological depth—unless it is "felt" (hence James's so frequent use of phrases such as "felt life" and "the very *taste* of life," phrases that insist on the feeling-base of complete and integrated living). Furthermore, both aesthetic and moral experience are nonutilitarian. The first distinction that aestheticians usually make, in defining the aesthetic, is its distinction from the useful; when the aesthetic is converted to utility, it becomes something else, its value designation is different—as when a beautiful bowl becomes valuable not for its beauty but for its capacity to hold soup. So also the moral, when it is converted to utility, becomes something else than the moral— becomes even immoral, a parody of or a blasphemy against the moral life (in our richest cultural heritage, both Hellenic and Christian, the moral life is symbolically associated with utter loss of utility goods and even with loss of physical life—as in the Gospel passage, "Leave all that thou hast and follow me," or as in the career of Socrates, or as in Sophocles' *Antigone*). Moral and aesthetic experience have then in common their foundation in feeling and their distinction from the useful. The identity that James explores is their identity in the most capacious and most integrated—the most "civilized"—consciousness, whose sense relationships (aesthetic relationships) with the external world of scenes and objects have the same quality and the same spiritual determination as its relationships with people (moral relationships). But his exploration of that ideal identity involves cognizance of failed integration, cognizance of the many varieties of one-sidedness or one-eyedness or blindness that go by the name of the moral or the aesthetic, and of the destructive potentialities of the human consciousness when it is one-sided either way. His ironies revolve on the ideal concept of a spacious integrity of feeling: feeling, ideally, is *one*—and there is ironic situation when feeling is split into the "moral" and the "aesthetic," each denying the other and each posing as *all*.

There is comic irony in Henrietta Stackpole's moral busybodyness as she flutters and sputters through Europe obtaining feature materials for her home-town newspaper, "featuring" largely the morally culpable un-Americanism of Europeans to serve her readers as a flattering warning against indulgence in the aesthetic. Henrietta is a stock James comedy character, and she is essential. Without Henrietta's relative incapacity to "see" more than literal surfaces, the significant contrast between surface and depth, between outward and inward "seeing," between undeveloped and developed consciousness, would lose a needed demonstration. (But let us say for Henrietta that, like Horatio in *Hamlet,* she is employed by the dramatist for as many sorts of purposes as his scenes happen to demand; when a foil of obtuseness is wanted, Henrietta is there, and when a foil of good interpretive intelligence or plain charitable generosity is wanted, Henrietta is also there. She is the type of what James technically called the *ficelle,* a wholly subordinate character immensely useful to take in confidences from the principals and to serve other functions of "relief"—"relief" in that sense in which the lower level of a relievo provides perspective for the carved projections.) In Mrs. Touchett, what appears at first as the comic irony of absolute aesthetic insensitivity accompanied by a rugged moral dogmatism ("she had a little moral account-book—with columns unerringly ruled and a sharp steel clasp—which she kept with exemplary neatness") becomes at the end of the book, with her son's death, the tragic irony of that kind of ambiguous misery which is an inability to acknowledge or realize one's own suffering, when suffering is real but the channels of feeling have become nearly atrophied by lack of use. At the midday meal, when Isabel and Mrs. Touchett come together after the night of Ralph's death,

> Isabel saw her aunt not to be so dry as she appeared, and her old pity for the poor woman's inexpressiveness, her want of regret, of disappointment, came back to her. Unmistakably she would have found it a blessing to-day to be able to feel a defeat, a mistake, even a shame or two. [Isabel] wondered if [her aunt] were not even missing those enrichments of consciousness and privately trying—reaching out for some aftertaste of life, dregs of the banquet; the testimony of pain or the old recreation of remorse. On the other hand perhaps she was afraid; if she should begin to know remorse at all it might take her too far. Isabel could perceive, however, how it had come over her dimly that she had failed of something, that she saw herself in the future as an old woman without memories. Her little sharp face looked tragical.

Mrs. Touchett's habitual moralistic denial of feeling as an aesthetic indulgence has left her deserted even by herself, even by her love of her son, even by memory, even by suffering. She is stranded in a morality that is tragically without meaning.

In Madame Merle and Osmond the ironies intrinsic to James's theme receive another turn. Madame Merle first appeals to Isabel's admiration by her capacity for "feeling"—for that kind of feeling to which the term "aesthetic" has been specially adapted in common modern use: feeling for the arts, the sensuous perceptivity underlying the arts, and, by extension, feeling for the finer conventions of manners as "arts of living." (Madame Merle "knew how to feel . . . This was indeed Madame Merle's great talent, her most perfect gift.") At Gardencourt, when she is not engaged in writing letters, she paints (she "made no more of brushing in a sketch than of pulling off her gloves") or she plays the piano (she "was a brave musician") or she is "employed upon wonderful tasks of rich embroidery." (The presentation is just a bit insidious, not only because of Madame Merle's so very great plasticity in going from one art to another, but also in the style of the phrases: the suggestion of conventional fluidity in the comparison of her ease in painting with the ease of "pulling off her gloves," the word "brave"—an honorific word in certain places, but carrying here the faintest note of bravado—and the word "employed," suggesting, as it reverberates, Madame Merle's not disinterested professional aestheticism.) Her senses are active and acute: walking in the English rain, she says,

> "It never wets you and it always smells good." She declared that in England the pleasures of smell were great . . . and she used to lift the sleeve of her British overcoat and bury her nose in it, inhaling the clear, fine scent of the wool.

Just how acute her perceptions are is shown never more clearly than in that scene in which she learns of the distribution of property after Mr. Touchett's death, occurring in Chapter 20 of Volume I. Mrs. Touchett has just told her that Ralph, because of the state of his health, had hurried away from England before the reading of the will, in which Isabel had been left half of the fortune accruing to him. With this news, Madame Merle "remained thoughtful a moment, her eyes bent on the floor," and when Isabel enters the room, Madame Merle kisses her—this being "the only allusion the visitor, in her great good taste, made . . . to her young friend's inheritance." There are no other signs than these (and the episode is typical of James's minor "recognition scenes") of just how quickly and acutely Madame Merle's senses—her perception, her intuition—have functioned in apprising her of the possibilities of exploitation now opened, and in apprising her also of the fact that Ralph is the real donor of Isabel's fortune, a fact of which Isabel herself remains ignorant until Madame Merle viciously informs her. Madame Merle's feeling for situation is so subtly educated that she needs but the slightest of tokens in order to respond. And yet, with a sensitivity educated so exquisitely and working at such high tension she is morally insensible—or almost so; not quite—for, unlike Osmond, whose damnation is in ice where the moral faculty is quite frozen, she still has the spiritual capacity of those whose damnation is in fire, the capacity to know that she is damned.

Madame Merle and Osmond use their cultivated aestheticism for utility purposes—Madame Merle, to further her ambition for place and power; Osmond, to make himself separate and envied. Their debasement of the meaning of the aesthetic becomes symbolically vicious when it shows itself in their relationships with people—with Isabel, for instance, who is for them an object of virtu that differs from other objects of virtu in that it bestows money rather than costs it. This is the evil referred to by Kant in his second Categorical Imperative: the use of persons as means—an evil to which perhaps all evil in human relationships reduces. In the case of Madame Merle and Osmond, it has a peculiar and blasphemous ugliness, inasmuch as the atmosphere of beauty in which they live—beauty of surroundings and of manners—represents the finest, freest product of civilization and is such, ideally, as to induce the most reverential feeling for people as well as for things. Isabel first appeals to Osmond as being "as smooth to his general need of her as handled ivory to the palm": it is an "aesthetic" image suggesting his fastidiousness but, ironically, suggesting at the same time his coarseness—for while ivory, like pearls, may be the more beautiful for handling, "handled ivory" might also be the head of a walking stick, and it is in some sort as a walking stick that he uses Isabel. An extension of the same figure, without the aesthetic and with only the utilitarian connotation, indicates Osmond's real degeneracy: Isabel finally realizes that she has been for him "an applied handled hung-up tool, as senseless and convenient as mere wood and iron." But the evil is not one that can be isolated or confined; it is automatically proliferative. Morally dead himself, incapable of reverence for the human quality in others, Osmond necessarily tries to duplicate his death in them, for it is by killing their volition that he can make them useful; dead, they are alone "beautiful." He urges upon Isabel the obscene suggestion that she, in turn, "use" Lord Warburton by exploiting Warburton's old love for herself in order to get him to marry Pansy; and Osmond can find no excuse for her refusal except that she has her private designs for "using" the Englishman. But it is in Osmond's use of Pansy, his daughter, that he is most subtly and horribly effective. He has made her into a work of art, the modeling materials being the least artful of childish qualities—her innocence and gentleness; and he has almost succeeded in reducing her will to an echo of his own. The quaint figure of Pansy, always only on the edge of scenes, is of great structural importance in the latter half of the book; for she shows the full measure of the abuse that Isabel resists, and it is to nourish in her whatever small germ of creative volition may remain—to salvage, really, a life—that Isabel returns to Rome and to Osmond's paralyzing ambiance.

The moral question that is raised by every character in the book is a question of the "amount of felt life" that each is able to experience, a question of how many and how various are the relationships each can, with integrity, enter into. Or, to put the matter in its basic metaphor, it is a question of how much each person is able to "see," and not only to see but to compose into creative order. The moral question, since it involves vision, feeling, and composition, is an aesthetic one as well. Madame Merle and Osmond are blind to certain relations: "I don't pretend to know what people are meant for," Madame Merle says, ". . . I only know what I can do with them." Mrs. Touchett is blind to certain others. Let us stop for a moment with Henrietta Stackpole's comic crudity of vision, for the "eye" is all-important, and the ranges of vision really begin with an eye like that of Henrietta. It is "a peculiarly open, surprised-looking eye." "The most striking point in her appearance was the remarkable fixedness of this organ."

> She fixed her eyes on [Ralph], and there was something in their character that reminded him of large polished buttons—buttons that might have fixed the elastic loops of some tense receptacle: he seemed to see the reflection of surrounding objects on the pupil. The expression of a button is not usually deemed human, but there was something in Miss Stackpole's gaze that made him, a very modest man, feel vaguely embarrassed—less inviolate, more dishonoured, than he liked.

Henrietta, with her gregariously refractive button-sight, has also "clearcut views on most subjects . . . she knew perfectly in advance what her opinions would be." Henrietta's is the made-up consciousness, the pseudo consciousness, that is not a process but a content hopelessly once and for all given, able to refract light but not to take it in. (We can understand Henrietta's importance, caricatural as she is, by the fact that she is the primitive form of the pseudo consciousness which Madame Merle and Osmond, in their so much more sophisticated ways, exhibit: theirs too is the made-up consciousness, a rigidified content, impervious and uncreative.) The Misses Molyneux, Lord Warburton's sisters, have "eyes like the balanced basins, the circles of 'ornamental water,' set in parterres, among the geraniums." Let us note that the figure is drawn from an "aesthetic" arrangement, that of formal gardens—and in this sense has directly opposite associations to those of Henrietta's buttons (presumably very American, very *useful* buttons). The Misses Molyneux's eyes, like Henrietta's also merely reflect surrounding objects, and reflect more limitedly, far less mobily; but the image is significant of certain kinds of feeling, of "seeing," that Henrietta is incapable of, and that have derived from ancient disciplines in human relationships—contemplative feeling, reverence, feeling for privacy and for grace. Extremely minor figures such as these, of the buttons and the basins, are pregnant with the extraordinarily rich, extraordinarily subtle potentialities of the theme of "seeing" as an infinitely graduated cognizance of relations between self and world.

In this book, the great range of structural significance through figurative language is due to the fact that whatever image vehicle a figure may have—even when the image is not itself a visual one—the general context is so deeply and consistently characterized by acts of "seeing" that every metaphor has this other implied extension of meaning. For example, a very intricate and extensive symbolic construct is built on a metaphor of opening doors. Henrietta, Ralph says, "walks in without knocking at the door." "She's too personal," he adds. As her eyes indiscriminately take in everything that is literally to be seen, so she walks in without knocking at the door of personality: "she thinks one's door should stand ajar." The correspondence of eyes and doors lies in the publicity Henrietta assumes (she is a journalist): her eye is public like a button, and responds as if everything else were public, as if there were no doors, as if there were nothing to be seen but what the public (the American newspaper public) might see without effort and without discomfort. In James's thematic system of surfaces and depths, "sight" is something achieved and not given, achieved in the loneliness of the individual soul and in the lucidity of darkness suffered; privacy is its necessary stamp, and it cannot be loaned or broadcast any more than can the loneliness or the suffering. "I keep a band of music in my ante-room," Ralph tells Isabel.

> "It has orders to play without stopping; it renders me two excellent services. It keeps the sounds of the world from reaching the private apartments, and it makes the world think that dancing's going on within."

The notation has its pathos through Ralph's illness. Isabel "would have liked to pass through the ante-room . . . and enter the private apartments." It is only at the end, through her own revelations of remorse and loss, that those doors open to her.

The ironic force of the metaphor of doors, as it combines with the metaphor of "seeing," has a different direction in the crucial scene in Chapter 51 of the second volume—one of the major "recognition scenes" in the book, where Isabel sees Osmond's full malignancy, a malignancy the more blighting as it takes, and sincerely takes, the form of honor, and where Osmond sees unequivocally the vivid, mysterious resistance of a life that he has not been able to convert into a tool. Isabel comes to tell him that Ralph is dying and that she must go to England. She opens the door of her husband's study without knocking.

> "Excuse me for disturbing you," she said.
>
> "When I come to your room I always knock," he answered, going on with his work.
>
> "I forgot; I had something else to think of. My cousin's dying."
>
> "Ah, I don't believe that," said Osmond, looking at his drawing through a magnifying glass. "He was dying when we married; he'll outlive us all."

Osmond is here engaged in an activity representative of a man of taste and a "collector"—he is making traced copies of ancient coins (the fact that it is an act of tracing, of copying, has its own significance, as has the object of his attention: coins). What he "sees" in the situation that Isabel describes to him is quite exactly what he sees in the fact that she has opened the door without knocking: a transgression of convention; and what he does not see is the right of another human being to feel, to love, to will individually. Further, what he appallingly does not see is his dependence, for the fortune Isabel has brought him, on the selfless imagination of the dying man, Ralph; or, even more appallingly (for one can scarcely suppose that Madame Merle had left him ignorant of the source of Isabel's wealth), what he does not see is any reason for the moral responsibility implied by "gratitude," a defect of vision that gives a special and hideous bleakness to his use of the word "grateful," when he tells Isabel that she has not been "grateful" for his tolerance of her esteem for Ralph. The metaphor of the "doors" thus goes through its changes, each associated with a depth or shallowness, a straightness or obliquity of vision, from Henrietta's aggressive myopia, to Ralph's reticence and insight, to Osmond's refined conventionalism and moral astigmatism.

Let us consider in certain other examples this reciprocity between theme and metaphor, insight and sight, image and eye. Isabel's native choice is creativity, a "free exploration of life," but exploration is conducted constantly—vision is amplified constantly—at the cost of renunciations. It is in the "grey depths" of the eyes of the elder Miss Molyneux, those eyes like the balanced basins of water set in parterres, that Isabel recognizes what she has had to reject in rejecting Lord Warburton: "the peace, the kindness, the honour, the possessions, a deep security and a great exclusion." Caspar Goodwood has eyes that "seemed to shine through the vizard of a helmet." He appears always as an armour-man: "she saw the different fitted parts of him as she had seen, in museums and portraits, the different fitted parts of armoured warriors—in plates of steel handsomely inlaid with gold." "He might have ridden, on a plunging steed, the whirlwind of a great war." The image is one of virility, but of passion without relation, aggressive energy without responsibility. The exclusions implied by Caspar's steel-plated embrace are as great as those implied by the honor and the peace that Lord Warburton offers; and yet Isabel's final refusal of Caspar and of sexual possession is tragic, for it is to a sterile marriage that she returns.

Architectural images, and metaphors whose vehicle (like doors and windows) is associated with architecture, subtend the most various and complex of the book's meanings; and the reason for their particular richness of significance seems to be that, of all forms that are offered to sight and interpretation, buildings are the most natural symbols of civilized life, the most diverse also as to what their fronts and interiors can imply of man's relations with himself and with the outer world. Osmond's house in Florence has an "imposing front" of a "somewhat incommunicative character."

> It was the mask, not the face of the house. It had heavy lids, but no eyes; the house in reality looked another way—looked off behind . . . The windows of the ground-floor, as you saw them from the piazza, were, in their noble proportions, extremely architectural; but their function seemed less to offer communication with the world than to defy the world to look in . . .

(One notes again here the characteristic insistence on *eyes* and *looking*.) The description, perfectly fitting an old and noble Florentine villa, exactly equates with Osmond himself, and not only Isabel's first illusional impression of him —when it is his renunciatory reserve that attracts her, an appearance suggesting those "deeper rhythms of life" that she seeks—but also her later painful knowledge of the face behind the mask, which, like the house, is affected with an obliquity of vision, "looked another way—looked off behind." The interior is full of artful images; the group of people gathered there "might have been described by a painter as composing well"; even the footboy "might, tarnished as to livery and quaint as to type, have issued from some stray sketch of old-time manners, been 'put in' by the brush of a Longhi or a Goya"; the face of little Pansy is "painted" with a "fixed and intensely sweet smile." Osmond's world, contained within his eyeless house, is "sorted, sifted, arranged" for the eye; even his daughter is one of his arrangements. It is a world bred of ancient disciplines modulating through time, selection and composition, to the purest aesthetic form.

[578]

[Isabel] carried away an image from her visit to his hill-top . . . which put on for her a particular harmony with other supposed and divined things, histories within histories . . . It spoke of the kind of personal issue that touched her most nearly; of the choice between objects, subjects, contacts—what might she call them?—of a thin and those of a rich association . . . of a care for beauty and perfection so natural and so cultivated together that the career appeared to stretch beneath it in the disposed vistas and with the ranges of steps and terraces and fountains of a formal Italian garden . . .

The illusion is one of a depth and spaciousness and delicacy of relationships, an illusion of the civilized consciousness.

But while Osmond's world suggests depth, it is, ironically, a world of surfaces only, for Osmond has merely borrowed it. The architectural metaphor shifts significantly in the passage (Chapter 42 of Volume II) in which Isabel takes the full measure of her dwelling. "It was the house of darkness, the house of dumbness, the house of suffocation."

She had taken all the first steps in the purest confidence, and then she had suddenly found the infinite vista of a multiplied life to be a dark, narrow alley with a dead wall at the end. Instead of leading to the high places of happiness . . . it led rather downward and earthward, into realms of restriction and depression where the sound of other lives, easier and freer, was heard as from above . . .

"When she saw this rigid system close about her, draped though it was in pictured tapestries . . . she seemed shut up with an odour of mould and decay." Again the architectural image changes its shape in that passage (quoted earlier in this essay) where Isabel takes her knowledge and her sorrow into Rome, a Rome of architectural ruins. Here also are depth of human time, "histories within histories," aesthetic form, but not "arranged," not borrowable, not to be "collected"—only to be *lived* in the creative recognitions brought to them by a soul itself alive. The image that accompanies Ralph through the book—"his serenity was but the array of wild flowers niched in his ruin"—gains meaning from the architectural images so frequent in the Roman scenes (as, for instance, from this:

[Isabel] had often ascended to those desolate ledges from which the Roman crowd used to bellow applause and where now the wild flowers . . . bloom in the deep crevices . . .)

Whereas Osmond's forced "arrangements" of history and art and people are without racination, blighting and lifeless, Ralph's "array of wild flowers" is rooted, even if precariously rooted in a ruin; it is a life *grown,* grown in history, fertilized in the crevices of a difficult experience. The metaphor is another version of St. John's "Except a corn of wheat fall into the ground and die, it abideth alone; but if it die, it bringeth forth much fruit." Isabel, still seeking that freedom which is growth, goes back to Osmond's claustral house, for it is there, in the ruin where Pansy has been left, that she has placed roots, found a crevice in which to grow straightly and freshly, found a fertilizing, civilizing relationship between consciousness and circumstances.

F R E U D

[*1856–1939*]

THE APPEARANCE OF PHILIP RIEFF'S BOOK IS EVIDENCE THAT WE CAN NOW take account of Freud's work as a cultural event. Previously, we sought to make such immediate use of it for therapy or for personal liberation that we did not see its historical meaning. The "second Copernican revolution" which stripped us of the last vestiges of faith in man's independence of the causal order went too deep to be absorbed very quickly. Rieff believes that we should now address ourselves to the issue of moral consequences, using "moral" in its widest sense: what sort of life style, not necessarily related to Freud's own intentions, has proved compatible with our new awareness of ourselves? Rieff's conclusions here ring oddly like a description, not so much of the effect of Freud on us, as of something we had all been taking for granted as the way things go in our time. The question as to the part played by Freud himself in producing the cultural conditions Rieff describes must be left to the reader to determine.

Philip Rieff has taught at the Universities of Pennsylvania and California.

PHILIP RIEFF

The Emergence of
Psychological Man

The important thing is not to be cured but to live with one's ailments.

ABBÉ GALIANI TO MADAME D'ÉPINAY

IN A DISTINCTIVELY INTIMATE WAY, PSYCHOANALYSIS DEFENDS THE PRIVATE MAN against the demands made by both culture and instinct. Freud begins where G. E. Moore leaves off in the famous last chapter of *Principia Ethica* that declares personal affections and artistic pleasures the only true goods in our experience. The private man needs to know how to defend his affections, for the most personal are the most easily spoiled. Psychoanalytic pedagogy is intended for the student weak in the understanding of the limited possibilities in life. Freud belongs, therefore, among those great teachers who have taken everyone as their potential subject. Seen in psychoanalytic depth, no man knows himeslf so well that he cannot learn something of fundamental importance from this novel enterprise in re-education. Freud speaks for the modern individual, elaborating his sense of separateness from the world and from even the most beloved objects in it. Such careful and detailed concentration on the self as Freud encourages may more often produce pedants of the inner life than virtuosi of the outer one. Yet, in default of other cures,

[582]

egotism suits the age, and Freud's is only one of the most successful, and certainly the most subtle, of contemporary ideologies of self-salvation.

Calculation, Newman said, has never made a hero; but calculation can make the unheroic healthier. The essentially secular aim of the Freudian spiritual guidance is to wean away the ego from either a heroic or a compliant attitude to the community. Here Freud differed not only from the physicians of established faiths—Catholic or other—but also from the propagandists of secular faiths, those socialists and other radicals still essentially engaged in absorbing the individual into the community. He was not impressed by the clerical strategy of confirming faith by strengthening the individual's identification with the community. Whatever flush of interior health rises on first being received back into any community of belief after the sickness of alienation is quite temporary, Freud held. The old faiths have themselves produced the sickness they still seek to cure. The psychoanalytic physician cannot therefore direct the patient to seek relief by joining "the catholic, protestant, or socialist community." What is needed is to free men from their sick communities. To emancipate man's "I" from the communal "we" is "spiritual guidance" in the best sense Freud could give to the words.

Yet he also treated the neurotic as a social dilemma, as one unable to relate himself effectively to the established community. The prevailing image of psychoanalysis as reintegrating the neurotic, making him again a constructive member of society, must be studied very closely, for this does not signify that the patient gives his assent to the demands society makes upon his instinctual life; on the contrary, the successful patient has learned to withdraw from the painful tension of assent and dissent in his relation to society by relating himself more affirmatively to his depths. His newly acquired health entails a self-concern that takes precedence over social concern and encourages an attitude of ironic insight on the part of the self toward all that is not self. Thus the psychoanalyzed man is inwardly alienated even if he is often outwardly reconciled, for he is no longer defined essentially by his social relations. Psychoanalysis as a science carries an authentic alienating implication, from the breaking of the bondages of the past (advocated on the therapeutic level) to the critical appraisal of moral and religious beliefs (on the level of theory). Freud found contemptible Dostoevski's religious and political conservatism, despite his admiration for the writer's insights and experiences in the depths.[1]

---

[1] Freud notes that "after the most violent struggles to reconcile the instinctual demands of the individual with the claims of the community," Dostoevski "landed in the retrograde position of submission both to temporal and spiritual authority, of veneration both for the Tsar and for the God of the Christians, and of a narrow Russian nationalism—a position which lesser minds have reached with smaller effort." Indeed the point of Freud's essay on Dostoevski, from which I am quoting, is not to examine Dostoevski's

His own insights into the depths did not lead him to advocate a return to them, nor to new justifications for authoritarian codes of conduct. Rather, a less ambivalent freedom from authority is perhaps the more important motif of his doctrine, one in which authority is all the more secure.

This variety of belief in freedom makes itself felt most strongly in Freud's denial that psychoanalysis does criticize society or that it has any "concern whatsoever with . . . judgments of value." Psychoanalysis neither needs nor desires "to create a *Weltanschauung* of its own." As a branch of science, subscribing to the scientific view of the world, psychoanalysis intends to be no doctrine but only a method: "the intellectual manipulation of carefully verified observations" and the denial that any knowledge can be obtained from "intuition or inspiration." Here the rational method—working upon the irrational unconscious, which Freud conceived of as undercutting the "proud superstructure of the mind"—itself bespeaks a pre-eminent value. It is only just, when speaking of Freud, to speak of the humanism of his science. For after all his affirmations of the irrational, he reserves a possibility for rationality and freedom in science—understanding—itself, particularly in the method of treatment he devised: the creation of representative thought-art which, when interpreted, eases the patient's obsessions. On the one hand, then, Freud does advocate a rational reconciliation to social and cultural authority, granting that authority itself will under criticism become more reasonable; on the other hand, Freudianism supplies through its therapeutic stratagems and theoretical insights the means for a modest but nonetheless significant liberation.

Freud's emancipative intent first expressed itself in his method of treatment. By waiving the restrictions of conventional logic and prudery, the therapeutic hour provides the patient with a model refreshment. It puts an end to decorum, providing a private time in which anything may be said—indeed, in which the patient is encouraged to say everything. The analytic meeting is designed as an oasis in the desert of reticence in which the patient lives; it is much like those artificial ruins thoughtfully placed in eighteenth-century English formal gardens for the pleasure of those who wished to wander imaginatively from the beaten path.

From the patient's standpoint, the novelty of the therapeutic situation lies at once in its unique freedoms and in the accessibility of a final figure of

artistic endowment but to find out why he changed positions—why he "threw away the chance of becoming a teacher and liberator of humanity and made himself one with their gaolers" (*Coll. Papers* V, 223). Thus, subtly, Dostoevski is identified with the position of the Grand Inquisitor.

authority. Revived facts and new fancies are definitively received by one who has contracted to be the most sympathetic of all possible listeners. The therapist listens, comprehends, does not condemn; in return, the patient has an obligation to the therapist (not a mere invitation from him) to tell all he knows in order to be told all he does not know. Talking is the patient's work. And it is hard work. Patients eager to cooperate with the analyst fail nonetheless to tell their stories with therapeutic adequacy, because, as Freud says, they consider

> them too unimportant, too stupid, too indiscreet, and so on. There are many who never learn to apply the basic rule because their fear of losing control is too great, and before they can give expression to anything they must examine it to see exactly what it is.

A lifetime has been spent learning to be tactful, to achieve reticence, to avoid outbursts of emotion, to do what is proper or expedient rather than what is impulsive. All this has to be unlearned for successful free association.

Properly conducted, the analytic colloquy should be unpredictable; ideally, communication takes place between the unconscious of the analyst and that of the patient, avoiding the self-consciousness of ordinary conversations. Both analyst and patient are to relax and let the associations flow, depending as much as possible on the eruption of unpremeditated thoughts on the part of the patient, and of unscheduled interpretations on the part of the analyst. Normally our talk is selective, and not just for reasons of social propriety; it is selective in order to be efficient. Efficiency is the aim of most discourse, from the ordinary effort of rational explanation (in which one looks for some isolated cause or set of causes for an event) to the extremes of polemic and caricature (in which a few relevant considerations are stressed and others eliminated). But the Freudian treatment is characterized by its deliberate anti-efficiency. It is based on a technique for suppressing just that impulse which is normative in thought and talk when we try to cast strong light on something—the impulse to leave out, to cast other things in shadow. Rational thought, because it is selective, is not therapeutically useful. The verbal precipitates of selective thinking remain extremely valuable for self-understanding, but precisely because they are, like symptoms, guides for interpretations in terms of the interests or intentions behind them. No language is ordinary. The simplest cues may introduce the most complex roles.

The anti-efficiency of the Freudian therapy appears clearly in the extraordinary leisure with which it is conducted. Unlike the journalistic representation of events, which achieves a perfection of efficiency through its emphasis on speed, compression, and straightforwardness, the development of a psychoanalytic patient's thought takes time because he is adjured to disregard all selectivity.[2] The extreme leisureliness of therapy finds its correlate in a theory of mind—in particular, Freud's theory of what he deemed the crucial part of the mind, the unconscious. The timelessness and indifference to logic with which the unconscious operates are echoed in the leniency of the psychoanalytic interview. For practical reasons—lack of time and money—an individual psychoanalysis may be terminated.[3] Theoretically, however, there is no end of answering. At the very least, the analysis cannot be brief. Freud likened the treatment to the play *Oepidus,* from which he drew so much in another and more famous connection. Like the drama of Sophocles, psychoanalysis has its "cunning delays" in order to prolong the inquiry and thus raise the pitch of cathartic excitement. This is necessary and to be desired, for the good of the patient. "Psychological changes only come about very slowly; if they occur quickly and suddenly it is a bad sign," Freud says elsewhere.

Another quality of the Freudian liberation is the interest taken in emotional recollection itself. Freud sees the therapy as withdrawing the patient from the world of "hard reality," with which he has been unable to cope—though this withdrawal is only temporary, and its purpose is to return him more realistically equipped to that very reality. During this period of therapeutic withdrawal, however, Freud sanctions all the tabooed language and the shady topics which are conventionally proscribed. Memory, daydream, fantasy are what the patient is to deal in. He has total freedom to recall. The patient tries to recapture his childhood and the nightlife of dreams and sexuality; it is chiefly this material which is analyzed, according to the emancipative dialectic, just because it is not freely discussed in the ordinary daytime world.

Memory has a peculiar and central place in Freudian theory. It is constraining, since by remembering our bondages to the past we appreciate their enormity; but it is also, Freud believed, liberating, since by remembering we understand the terrors and pleasures of the past and move toward mastering them. The tabooed thoughts are accredited, raised to the status of momentous and decisive causes, by Freud's theory of personality, not only because they are explained as part of an inexorable sequence of development, but because the patient's attention is focused on them. In therapeutic explanation the taboos dominant since childhood tend to be weakened. Even though the aims and activities of childhood have to be suppressed, superseded by "reality," a

---

[2] We see this procedure aesthetically exploited in *Finnegans Wake,* which Joyce wrote in a poly-language of puns, attempting to recreate words in acordance with the symbolic overtones, or "free imagery," that hover about their edges.

[3] Freud insisted that analysis was "really interminable" no matter how regularly "in practice analyses do come to an end" (*Coll. Papers* V, 316-57).

science which so values the importance of these things is plainly a liberating one.

This helps explain Freud's special interest in dreams, which he interpreted as contemporaneous fragments of the superseded child life. Dreams themselves, as Freud saw, have an ambiguously emancipative role. They indicate a kind of freedom, because they take place when there is a "slackening in the strength of the resistance." He imagined sleep as the de-individualized play time of the instincts, when we cast off the burden of being individuals and vent our gross infantile wishes and anxieties in dreams. In sleep all persons become for that brief respite ciphers of identical emotions, differentiated only secondarily by constitution and traumatic accent. On the other hand, dreams are a kind of betrayal, too, because the analyst (representing the outer world) uses them to pry out the patient's secrets. On the whole, however, Freud conceded that the dream was a sanctuary for the free play of the psyche. We cannot be held responsible, Freud argues, for the thoughts expressed in our dream life. Night thoughts are not our own, in the moral proprietary sense, but belong to that other self which summons us thereby to account for our day lives.

Talk is therapeutic in itself. By talking about the instincts, Freud says, we do not cause the instinctual demand to disappear—this "is impossible and not even desirable"—but we do accomplish a " 'taming' of the instinct." Through talking about sexuality, we can control it, so that the healthy man can choose to express his sexual appetite and yet not be irrationally driven by it. Self-mastery being a function of self-consciousness, by making sexual desires conscious, says Freud, we gain mastery over them to a degree no system of repression can possibly equal. Talk—language—is the essential medium of consciousness, and therefore the essential means of liberation.[4]

In psychoanalysis the individual learns to break through reticence and engage himself in a sort of confessional probing, heretofore limited to conventicle life. Freud's scientific frankness has been one of the supplementary corrosives applied to the encrusted official languages of European high culture.[5]

---

[4] Compare Marx: "All forms and products of consciousness cannot be dissolved by mental criticism, by resolution into 'self-consciousness' or transformation into 'apparitions,' 'spectres,' 'fancies,' etc., but only by the practical overthrow of the actual social relations which gave rise to this idealistic humbug" (*German Ideology* [New York, 1947], pp. 28-29).
[5] Out of the Vienna of Freud's lifetime came two other great critics of official languages: the brilliant literary and social critic Karl Kraus and the great and difficult philosopher Ludwig Wittgenstein. The difference is that Wittgenstein, as a critic of philosophical language, ultimately preached a verbal quietism, saying, "Whereof one cannot

That the new freedom is first of all linguistic is expressed, as I have noted earlier, in Freud's own insistence on using the word "sexual" where he might more accurately have said "erotic." To make "concessions to faint-heartedness" seemed to Freud an acceptance of that extraordinary dishonesty which lies dangerously near ordinary civility: "One gives way first in words, and then little by little in substance too." Such concessions had exhausted the older moral vocabularies. Civilization being necessarily hypocritical, a certain terminological vulgarity, Freud calculated, was a moral imperative and a positive value. The new psychology used the plain style to debunk the inno-cence of childhood, the nobility of religious feelings, the objectivity of great art. It is the reaction of a naturalist doctrine, faced with the exhausted data of ethics. Nietzsche made the point concisely:

> A psychologist today shows his good taste (others may say his integrity) in this, if in anything, that he resists the shamefully moralized manner of speak-ing which makes all modern judgments about men and things slimy.

If psychology was to be the philosophy of the future, as Nietzsche anticipated, it would have to avoid the verbal mannerisms of older moral speculations.

To be sure, one characteristic of eras of moral reform is that it becomes necessary to revise the terminology inherited from previous epochs, to with-draw the predicate of goodness from certain motives and attribute it to others. Freud's theoretical frame and clinical data converge to transmute the standard terms of ethical discourse. His zeal as a scientist leads him to a certain effron-tery of expression, in which a spade is called a spade and very black. But be-hind this effrontery is a kind of philosophic disappointment. In the useful terms of Jeremy Bentham, Freud's dyslogy signifies the deterioration of a eulogy—that is, his clinical intention is to convince man how uncivilized he remains ("men have no business to exclude themselves [from the] animal kingdom"), in the light of his exaggerated claim to have overcome his in-stincts through civilization.

Freud's advocacy of honesty is not to be understood merely as a reaction against hypocrisy. Certainly it is not to be identified with sensationalism; Freud is very reserved. The subject of sex must be handled in "dry and direct" prose, as a commonplace element in everyday life. The frankness of psychoanalysis represents a conquest of sexuality by the prosaic and com-munal understanding of science, rather than by the lyrical and private under-standing of the individual. Freud's attitude toward sexuality must not be

---

speak, one must be silent," while Freud, as a critic of moral language, advocated a verbal catharsis, whose motto might be "Whereof one cannot speak, one must say everything."

mistaken for romantic frankness. Actually, in his attempt to cleanse the language of sexuality of its romantic elements we see one aspect of Freud's aseptic rationalism.

So congenial was the stance of an emancipator that Freud could not cope with the victory that was his during the last period of his life. As he tried to ward off the easy assent of patients as itself a tactic of resistance, so Freud could not acknowledge the extent to which his own views actually had vanquished the prudery against which they were aimed. He had been prepared for a prolonged struggle of ideas: like the sick individual, he wrote, the sick society is "bound to offer us resistance." Despite his general thesis that in modern times there is a crisis in the system of cultural authority, Freud never underestimated the power of religion and repression. The great Father-God had never died, despite the uninterrupted succession of voices crying out the good news.

In the matter of prudery, however, Freud's voice was actually in harmony with a swelling nineteenth-century chorus. The inhibitions which he thought characteristic of civilized society we see as one of those brief periods of contraction in the general expansion of pleasure that had been in progress since the eighteenth century set Western culture on its course of revolt against Christian ascetic standards of conduct. Even the curious Victorian period, when religion came back into fashion as the most somber moralism, was never without its contradictions. It was in 1865 that one of Freud's favorite authors, Dickens, introduced Mr. Podsnap, with his abhorrence of anything that might bring a blush to the cheek of a young person. But in the same decade another writer whom Freud greatly admired, Zola, was publishing such frank exposures of natural impulse as *Earth* and *Fecundity*. By the 1920s, when Freud came into vogue, talk as well as literature could be improper and still respectable. Freud's reputation as an emancipator arose during the period of reaction against a Victorian prudery long since on the defensive and retreating. From our perspective, much of his culture-criticism fails precisely to grasp the unrepressiveness of modern culture. Public morals today, far from fitting the criteria of prudery against which Freud spoke out, are permissive, at least in terms of ease of verbal acknowledgement; images of sexuality in popular entertainment and commodities advertising are displayed straightforwardly; official mores, while never congruent with actual practice, are themselves hardly so hypocritical or so restrained as he described them. Freud was overimpressed, it now appears, with the monolithic repressiveness of culture, and unable to perceive that our own culture might become highly permissive in the sphere of private, sexual morals—the better to enforce its public repressions. The combination of a repressive political order with a permissive moral order is not unheard of in human history. And indeed, today's automatic political repressions parody the Freudian description of *private* repressive culture.

How much does the decline of prudery invalidate Freud's critique? If, as it may appear, Freud and the movement of which he is a part have already largely accomplished their emancipative task, from what now can Freud liberate us?

One persuasive answer to this question would diminish its relevance. Perhaps, as so many post-Freudians suggest, the extreme sexual repression of the Victorian era, now eased, was responsible for the role which Freud attributed to sexuality in the causation of the neuroses. Sexuality acquired a pre-eminence in his account, that is, not merely because he correctly perceived its importance, but because of the repressive method of handling its manifestations within the family during the Victorian period. Nowadays the conflict between instinct and institution may be secondary to that between the values of competition and cooperation. The Protestant ethic lingers, but it is very doubtful that it in any way dominates the expression of Western energies. The man of ambition is still with us, as in all times, but now he needs a more subtle initiative, a deeper capacity to manipulate the democracy of emotions, if he is to maintain his separate identity and significantly augment it with success. Pick up almost any post-Freudian book on our emotional condition and you will find this theme. Karen Horney's *The Neurotic Personality of Our Time* prematurely examines William H. White's *Organization Man* with his defenses cracked. Erich Fromm's *Escape from Freedom* finds American specification in David Riesman's *The Lonely Crowd*. The sexual problems of the neurotic competing for some ephemeral kudos in mid-century Manhattan are very different from the problems of the neurotic in turn-of-the-century Vienna.[6] History changes the expression of neurosis even if it does not change the underlying mechanisms. If Freud may be accused of biologizing the ambivalences by which all societies are constituted, the post-Freudians may sociologize them too much. The question of reconciling these biologizing and sociologizing tendencies in depth psychology has scarcely been settled, nor even fully explored. Till it is, we had better trust Freud's cheerless intuitions into the duality of all

[6] This is well illustrated in the most elaborate and most important of all Freud's clinical histories, the case of the "Wolf Man." When this patient, a wealthy young Russian, later became destitute, he was far from acquiring a new neurosis of the competitive-status type; rather, as Freud notes sarcastically, the old one was dissolved by the new, objective pressures.

human feeling, thought, and action—whatever the style that prevails in a given historical period.

There are good reasons why sexuality is for Freud the one really profound subject matter, the demands of the instincts the most fundamental demands. A science that recognizes the instincts is a basic science, examining not this social system or that but the system of civilization as a formed thing in itself. Freud has made the greatest single contribution to the understanding of civilization—not merely to the understanding of our own. The incomparable significance of sexual life is that, "while art, religion, and the social order originated in part in a contribution from the sexual instincts," civilization is also permanently opposed by sexuality. "Woe, if the sexual instincts should be set loose! The throne [of civilization] would be overturned and the [ultimate] ruler trampled under foot." Yet, even in his cautious approach to sexuality as a scientific subject, Freud advanced the long-established assault on the repressions.

Sexuality has shown, for Freud and related figures of his century, a revolutionary potential somewhat diminished by the newer permissiveness in manners and speech which has followed Freud—and owes greatly to him. The idea of a sexual revolution is not new. In the late eighteenth and early nineteenth centuries, sexuality became the subject of the most advanced art and politics. The critical philosophy of industrial civilization, first put forth by Fourier and the Saint-Simonians, and after them in the literature of the "young Germans," based itself on a deliberately anti-Christian eroticism. The sexual rebellion that was linked with socialism, before the conservative Karl Marx broke the connection on the pejorative word "utopian," was closer to being genuinely revolutionary—i.e., a revolt from below—than we now can grasp, accustomed as we are by Marxism and its counterfeits to revolutions run by reason—i.e., from above. The goal of the sexual revolution was never a harmonious, classless society, but rather happier individuals freed from a false reverence for the general advantage of society. The great writers on sex, from de Sade to Lawrence, were less interested in society than in the individual, pressing in varying degrees for the freedom of the individual against the burdens of social morality.[7]

In the immediately pre-Christian period, when the antique world was suffering its own exhaustion, the utopian yearning had been toward something higher, for it was a period of erotic satiety and the needs of the flesh were

---

[7] For de Sade and Lawrence sexuality itself provides a utopian possibility. They assert masculine sexuality as the basis of a revolution against the prevailing feminine social order—this especially militates against political radicalism, since sex becomes an alternative to politics. Thus a new generation of Freudian-trained conservatives is rising in America. The doctrine of the revolutionary possibilities of sex is the positive side of the psychoanalytic reduction of the political radical to a special case of the neurotic.

only too well attended. In the post-Christian era—that is, the last hundred years or more—rebellion has chiefly been in the name of the flesh. The theme of liberation from a repressiveness more serious than that of any merely political regime was everywhere in the haunted air of the nineteenth century— in an acutely sexed literature, in a value philosophy (Schopenhauer's) that by its interest in "values" questioned their validity, in strange political and religious movements that in the name of the future claimed to go deeper than politics and religion. With Nietzsche's *Beyond Good and Evil* the sustained attack on spiritual love and the glorification of a humanity free to live in a more sensual way came to its philosophical completion. In literature the revolutionary erotic intention emerged in the assertion of Hellenism against Hebraism, of beauty as the real object of piety—an assertion made first perhaps by Schiller, in the name of the glory that was Greece. Heine, whom Freud revered, had also taken up the indignation against a civilization too long under the shadow of the Law, and called for a rehabilitation of the flesh against the body-despising values of Christianity. In England, Swinburne watched the decline of energy and adopted an accusing tone: "Thou hast conquered, O pale Galilean; the world has grown grey from thy breath." In France, around the same time, Gautier wrote against the "Christian contempt for what is shapely and incarnate." Love was examined with a steady and detailed ferocity by literary men and philosophers, until with Freud it entered into the twentieth century under more persuasive auspices —as a science.

Yet Freud has none of the enthusiasm that characterizes the antinomian temper. Civilization, because of its discontents, was the basic problem of his psychological science. The cry for liberty did come from the instinctual depths, but Freud heard it with the cautious attention of a physician attending an eminent but dangerous patient. Sexuality for him is a force that permanently prevents any utopian transforming of the social order. Freud held no hope of transforming civilization. On the contrary, the great utopian possibility—insofar as he held to any—is whether repressive civilization can permanently tame the instincts. He took the traditional position of assuming a conflict between man's animal and spiritual nature—the spiritual being a residual quality in the transforming process of repressive civilization.

Freud felt that the sexual scarcity characteristic of all civilizations (embodied in such institutions as monogamy) concentrated a certain surplus aggressiveness in the unconscious. A freer sexuality—a juster distribution of libido, the fundamental wealth of civilization—would lower the cost of civilization itself. Such an increase of sexual rations might go far toward resolving the nervousness of modern civilized behavior. But thus to widen the range of gratification, to relocate the problem of desire in the historical variety of "objects," fails to resolve the psychological problem. Man creates his own scarcity; the aesthetic mechanics of satisfaction themselves make gratification chimerical. Any notion that Freud's doctrine of scarce satisfaction in some way reflects the economic doctrine of scarcity representative of the best social thought in his era is to render trivial Freud's point. His use of a quasi-economic metaphor to discuss sexuality gives no warrant for treating the insight frozen into this metaphor as dated. Nature still seeks a state of balance. Freud's is a theory of the equilibrium toward which the emotional life tends after every disturbance. Sexuality is subject no less completely to Freud's first law of the emotions than any other element of human existence. Only one way lies open to escape the dissatisfactions inherent in every satisfaction, and that is to grow equable. When the inner life is not easily disturbed it has achieved what is to Freud as nearly ideal a condition as he can imagine. There is something Oriental in the Freudian ethic. The "Nirvana principle" crops up, now and again, in his later writings, intimating what is entailed in mastering the balances of nature.

Short of Nirvana, if sexuality could conceivably cease to trouble man, his destructive instincts would trouble him more. His dualism allowed Freud to maintain simultaneously a psychological version of the classical liberal and radical rationalist dream, that once civilization had reached a certain level of technological productivity (read "reality adequacy") and "consumption" (read "satisfactions") the miseries of its earlier stages would drop away, and a psychological version of the equally powerful religious idea—with the redemption fantasy stripped to a minimum faith in reason. In the therapeutic encounter, reason and unreason unite to create a third force capable of mediating between the clashing instincts. But the instincts cannot be taught to abide each other; their fusion creates tension and the possibility of abrupt reversals. Besides, were aggression merely a response to the frustration of some sexual or social need, it could be resolved, or at least ameliorated, by a specifically social reform of the conditions of frustration. But an aggression that is built in, due to the presence of a "death instinct,"[8] cannot be entirely manipulated, let alone abolished. According to this view, civilization can never resolve its nervousness, for the principle of ambivalence, more than that of integration, characterizes human nature and society. Happiness can never be achieved by the panaceas of social permissiveness or sexual plenitude. Order can never be achieved by social suppression or moral rigor. We

---

[8] There is a significant parallel in Freud's idea, advanced in the *Three Essays*, of a primal repression prior to social inhibitions, which is set off by the instinctual process itself.

are not unhappy because we are frustrated, Freud implies; we are frustrated because we are, first of all, unhappy combinations of conflicting desires. Civilization can, at best, reach a balance of discontents.

Here is no Swinburnian romance of free sexuality versus the moral law. Rather, Freud takes the romance out of sexuality, for romance is dependent upon taking the repressions for granted, in fact on their remaining entirely unconscious, so that they may be broken only at the price of guilt. The Freudian attitude, on the other hand, no longer takes them for granted, and therefore can no longer take sexuality as a static ideal, even against the present crippling incapacities of our erotic lives. Freud might seem to be suggesting an expansive erotic ideal. But any future sensual permissiveness is rendered suspect by what he asserts about the expansive erotic life of the past. Freud not only feared that sexual freedom might entail undesirable sacrifices in culture; he thought it itself a transient accomplishment. Love is not a final solution for Freud, but a therapeutic one. He acknowledged that the establishment of a repressive code (such as Christianity) might under certain circumstances (as during the satiety of pagan culture) prove beneficent, like an artificially induced scarcity which revives consumption after a long period of overproduction. Therefore he was confident only of his analysis of our crippled condition, never of his prognosis. As a psychologist of fulfillment, Freud predicts disappointment: he sees the social value of repression, the complex nature of satisfaction. It is only in the therapeutic context—which is, after all, not life—that he rejects repression.

Freud was not hopeful; nor was he nostalgic. Retrospectively, he treasured no pagan or primitive past. He looked forward to no radically different future. Pagan antiquity had encouraged too much sensual pride and demonstrated the erotic illusion no less fully than Christianity, by encouraging spiritual pride, had demonstrated the ascetic illusion. Freud disdained permissiveness as much as asceticism; both falsely resolved the essential dualism in human experience, that very dualism between mind and flesh that produces the misery of the human condition. What man suffers from finally is no more the supremacy of spirit over flesh than of flesh over spirit; it is the dualism that hurts. Freud's own attitude toward a variety of historical dualisms, including Christianity, was always respectful, for he considered that they were but versions of a more fundamental dualism in the nature of man and in the cosmos. For this reason he never seriously entertained any utopian aspiration. Indeed, his own theory "had always been strictly dualistic and had at no time failed to recognize, alongside the sexual instincts, others to which it ascribed force enough to suppress the sexual instincts." This dualism Freud described as between "sexuality" and the "ego instincts"; later he distinguished two polar instincts, love and death.[9] Whatever the terminology, it is important to see that—unlike the Christian or rationalist consciousness—Freud denies any permanent healing of the "derangement of communal life," of the struggle between individual interest and the economy of social demands, of the antagonism between binding and destructive forces in individual and group life. The most one can win against the eternal dualisms is a rational knowledge of their effects upon one's own life.

Perhaps it might be more accurate to see depth psychology not as an emancipation of sex but as an enfranchisement. Freud recognized that in fact the silent vote of the psychic world never had been silent. He is the Bentham of the unenfranchised unconscious; what he brought into the realm of legitimacy, he also brought to responsibility. If one cannot educate the ruled, then one must educate the rulers. This very aim, to educate the ruling ego, is a sure mark of Freud's classical liberalism. By enfranchising the ineducable populace of sexuality, Freud seeks to bring it into responsible relations with the ruling power. To the liberal political tradition, with its belief that the "two nations" could be brought together, Freud offered a supporting parallel in psychological and moral theory, for he desired, as far as possible, to bring the instinctual unconscious into the rational community. For this new art of compromise a new kind of specialist is needed, one who can take a destiny apart and put it back together again in a slightly more endurable shape.

Freud gives us two types of insight into the aesthetic dimension of life—art both formal and informal: the first into what I shall call its "expressive" function, and the second, its function as "self-mastery." Once we admit that a dream, poem, or symptomatic act is an "expression," there is inevitably the

---

[9] Freud thought that his version of these polar forces, which he called *Eros* and *Thanatos* and nominated as the "primal instincts," had restored the cosmology of Empedocles ("Analysis Terminable and Interminable," *Coll. Papers* V, 347-350). But what he ascribes to Empedocles is common property of the whole school of transitional thinkers passing out of the mythic stage into philosophy—Anaximander, Empedocles, Heraclitus, Parmenides, and finally Plato. Actually, among these neo-mythic cosmologies, Freud's version more resembles Anaximander's than it does that of Empedocles. (I follow here the account of Cornford in *From Religion to Philosophy*, p. 65.) "Anaximander was more purely rational than many of his successors. In later systems—notably in those of Parmenides and Empedocles—mythical associations and implications [of the love-hate, attraction-repulsion polarity] which [Anaximander] has expurgated, emerge again. In particular, we can discern that the prototype of all opposition or contrariety is the contrariety of *sex*." As late as Plato's *Timaeus*, a sexual character still clings to the great contrarieties, Form (father) and Matter (mother).

notion of "something" that is forced out by a pressure from within. Of course the idea that the emotions exert a psychic pressure whose expression acts therapeutically is as old as the advice about not keeping sorrow "in" but crying it "out." The Romantic poets constantly testified to the serviceability of art with respect to easing the private, and especially the sexual, passions. Rousseau confessed that *La Nouvelle Héloïse* originated in the compulsive daydreams in which he compensated for his frustrations as a lover, and Goethe observed that his youthful erotic disappointments transformed themselves into *The Sorrows of Young Werther,* which he wrote in four weeks "almost unconsciously, like a somnambulist." He felt "as if after a general confession, once more happy and free, and justified in beginning a new life."

But how does the venting of painful emotions perform this therapeutic service? In giving Freud's answer to this question, we must note the difference between his immature and mature pronouncements on art. The earlier Freud was too inclined to take the expressive function at face value, as itself curative in the way that a confession cures—in other words, as a cathartic. But as he gradually replaced the cathartic method of treating patients with the analytic, Freud's view of self-expression as basically cathartic in value was replaced by the idea that art has the function of self-mastery as well. Again, one can look to the Romantics for an anticipation of Freud's insight. The critic William Hazlitt, author of the most anguished erotic confession in English literature, the *Liber Amoris,* describes in proto-Freudian terms the capacity of art to master, by objectifying, the chaotic press of emotion.

> This is equally the origin of wit and fancy, of comedy and tragedy, of the sublime and the pathetic. . . . The Imagination, by thus embodying and turning them to shape, gives an obvious relief to the indistinct and importunate cravings of the will. . . . We do not wish the thing to be so; but we wish it to appear such as it is. For knowledge is conscious power; and the mind is no longer, in this case, the dupe, though it may be the victim of vice or folly.

It is not important to inquire whether Freud read Hazlitt, but rather to note the similarity between this fairly sophisticated version of the Romantic theory of art and Freud's development of the same concept in the second chapter of *Beyond the Pleasure Principle* (1920). In the context of a discussion of children's play, which he saw implicitly as art, Freud writes:

> It is clear that in their play children repeat everything that has made a great impression on them in real life, and that in doing so they abreact the strength of the impression and, as one might put it, make themselves masters of the

situation. . . . The child passes over from the passivity of the experience to the activity of the game.

The artistic play and artistic imitation carried out by adults has essentially the same motive as the play of children, except that, unlike children's play, it is directed at an audience. That this adult play does

> not spare the spectators (for instance, in tragedy) the most painful experiences and can yet be felt by them as highly enjoyable . . . is convincing proof that, even under the dominance of the pleasure-principle, there are ways and means enough of making what is in itself unpleasurable into a subject to be recollected and worked over in the mind.

The shift from expression to self-mastery as the function of play—and, by extrapolation, of art—suggests a new interpretation of catharsis.

We may compare Freud's notion of catharsis with Aristotle's. Aristotle had described catharsis as a kind of homeopathic inoculation of dangerous sentiments, through mimetic representation, in order to effect their discharge and thereby restore sentiment to bearable levels. Freud also meant by catharsis a discharge of emotion. But there are several major differences. First, whereas Aristotle was describing the experience of an audience witnessing a public spectacle, the Freudian idea of catharsis, as taking place in the privacy of the therapeutic session, united actor and audience in one person, the suffering patient; the actor is his own audience. Extended to art, this notion makes the relevant catharsis the one which the artist effects upon himself. Second, Aristotle offers no criterion for judging what the dangerous emotions are that need discharge, except to indicate that they are those which have undergone a certain excessive accumulation and must be drained off. Breuer's notion of catharsis appears to be no more than this; but in reality more is involved, as Freud was to make clear. A catharsis cannot take place with any emotion which is vented, but only with emotions toward which the patient had previously been too passive; and these emotions can be characterized even further: they involved the original feature of inhibition or repression.

In an important sense, therefore, treatment itself has an aesthetic aim: to allow the patient an expression that has been in principle repressed. The poles of the analytic situation are repression and that which remains to be expressed. Thus the Freudian analysis is focused upon an aesthetic problem —that of expression: as if we would all be artists, if only what we have to express could be free from repression. It is in this sense that the notion of a man's being natively artistic is central to Freud.

Catharsis, as the therapeutic expressiveness at which Freud understood treatment to be aiming, was, so to say, a powerful expression—itself memorable because its purpose was to empty a given memory. But Freud was dissatisfied with a merely powerful expressiveness because, although strong, it was not permanent. Catharsis remained caught within the dialectic of transience which characterizes the aesthetic process, as opposed to the intellectual one.[10] In consequence, Freud shifted toward a second therapeutic aim, which was an expression rather more *clear* than powerful. This shift comprises the difference between knowledge, which is at once an expression and a comprehension of the expression (analysis), and direct, acted-out, expressive presentation, which is not necessarily self-comprehending.[11] The cathartic method, as Freud says, "presupposed that the patient could be hypnotized, and was based on the widening of consciousness that occurs under hypnosis." When Freud gave up hypnosis, this "widening of consciousness" which had made possible the "liberating" of emotion was sacrificed. But the gain, Freud thought, was entirely worth while. Hypnosis had enabled the patient to evade the task of gaining insight into his mental conflicts. More permanently curative than to evacuate an emotion would be to understand it; for the patient gained control not through the emptying but through the understanding of an emotion.

Thus, in therapy, Freud moved from the cathartic to the analytic explanation. Similarly, his view of art passed beyond the merely cathartic. The work of art remains, in all Freud's writings, a way which the artist has of responding to his own emotional burdens. But ways differ, even in the Freudian interpretation. In one view, the work of art is a safety valve, a form of exhibitionism, in which the tension accumulated by private motives is drained off in public display; but in another view, the work of art is, more positively, a means of achieving emotional stability—not weakness but self-mastery. This more sophisticated view of the artist, as having a unique activeness, is broached in a passage in the essay "The Uncanny" (1919), where Freud writes:

In the main we adopt an unvarying passive attitude towards real experience and are subject to the influence of our physical environment. But the storyteller has a peculiarly directive influence over us; by means of the moods he can put us into, he is able to guide the current of our emotions, to dam it up in one direction and make it flow in another . . .

---

[10] Cf. the essay "On Transience" (1915) (*Coll. Papers* V, 79-82).
[11] Note that the technique of "psycho-drama" is a reversion from analysis to catharsis. The history of therapeutic debate since Freud describes a full circle back to catharsis.

In this second view—equally compatible with Freud's main views and closer to the truth about art, I think—the work of art is not merely a form of acceding to one's feelings; it may also be considered a means of asserting them.

Art—like intellectual activity, joking, or fun—"opens up sources of pleasure or enjoyment in our emotional life." In his essay "Psychopathic Characters on the Stage" (c. 1906), Freud analyzes the drama as a means of offering the members of the audience the pleasure of identifying themselves with the hero. And the hero, in Freud's view, is always a rebel. So enjoyment of art means vicarious, or safe, rebellion—i.e., rebellion against the divine order or against society. Drama allows the spectator to imagine himself as a "great man," and to give way freely "to such suppressed impulses as a craving for freedom in religious, political, social, and sexual matters." Even if the identifications promoted by art are illusory, the illusion, Freud implies, can express a critical truth about the human condition. He is usually understood to have held that art takes one farther away from, not closer to, reality. But, in this interpretation, art brings one closer to reality by releasing, as need occasions, either the rebel and blasphemer or the pietist in us all.

What I have said of art applies as well to Freud's analysis of wit. On the one hand, humor may be pictured as a certain disguised expression of deep feeling, dodging past the sentries posted to guard against more serious expressions of the same feeling. Joking, like dreams, represents an overthrow of the mind's order and integrity. On the other hand, Freud emphasized the socially subversive tendency of joking—the significance of wit as a rebellion against authority, and of jokes as themselves an unmasking of public morality. Each of us, wrote Freud, has at times admitted the attractiveness, even the justice, of a life in which one would take what pleasure one can

> and has reproached our system of morality for knowing only how to make claims upon us without reimbursing us. Since we can no longer lend credence to the ideas of a hereafter in which all former renunciations are supposed to be rewarded by gratification . . . *carpe diem* becomes the first admonition.

Much joking is in the service of the exhibitionistic, aggressive, cynical, and skeptical tendencies, giving cautious notice

> that the wishes and desires of man have a right to make themselves perceptible next to our pretensions and inconsiderate morality. . . . As long as the art of healing has not succeeded in safeguarding our lives, and as long as the social organizations do not do more towards making conditions more agreeable, just so long cannot the voice within us which is striving against the demand of

morality be stifled. Every honest person finally makes this admission—at least to himself.

This analysis of joking may be extended to all types of fantasy. Fantasy may be considered not only as an escape from reality but also, more positively, as a mental reservation "reclaimed from the encroachment of the reality principle," i.e., from conformity to social demands, in which the person allows himself to seek pleasure unreasonably and asocially. In sexuality, and in the products of fantasy (dreams, wit, and art) a refuge from society is created. At the same time, these activities defy society and triumph over it; they are a mode of blasphemy.

Freud's entire concern with the psychic symptom—the art of the neurotic will—has this same duality, between a conformist and a subversive meaning. On the one hand, our symptomatic life is characterized by the sublimation of feeling; on the other hand, in the more aggressive productions of wit and in the moral recklessness of dreams and in the vicarious rebellion of art, it is riotously expressive of the unclaimed possibilities of our emotional life.

In thus seeing art and humor not only as sublimations but as projections, and therefore a kind of self-treatment, Freud's view of art as always being an escape from reality takes on a double edge, a profound implication of the nascent effort to change reality. It follows that there is no progress in art. Only in art

has the omnipotence of thought been retained in our own civilization. . . .
In art alone it still happens that man, consumed by his wishes, produces something similar to the gratification of these wishes, and this playing, thanks to artistic illusion, calls forth effects as if it were something real.

Reality being characterized by the progressively intensifying repressive forces of civilization, art remains behind to fulfill the permanent patterns of aspiration which have been canceled out either by the rational knowledge of reality (which comes with civilization) or by the repressive necessities of civilization itself.

Though we may doctor Freud's view in order to interpret expression as a form of self-mastery, it remains too closely tied to the *use* of art to make such an interpretation entirely acceptable. He did not believe that art—or the play of children—could be the product of superabundance and spontaneity. In Freud's view, everything in the psyche is produced for use. Play itself is a practical effort. Thus he says: "Children's play, too, is made to serve this purpose of completing and thus, as it were, annulling a passive experience by active behavior." And art, too, is practical. Both in Freud's early view, that art ministers to the evacuatory need, or in his more sophisticated view, that art is a form of self-manipulation, a self-conquest of the emotions by expelling them, art is accounted for by its utility in the psychic economy. This, it is worth noting, is a feature of the most famous of all views of art as catharsis that preceded Freud's. F. L. Lucas has convincingly argued, in his splendid little book entitled *Tragedy,* that Aristotle's *Poetics* should be read as a reply to the moralizing dispraise of art by Plato. Plato had said that art encourages men to be hysterical and uncontrolled, to which Aristotle replied that poetry makes people less, not more, emotional by giving them a periodic and healthy outlet to their feelings. Against Plato's attack on art, Aristotle offered only a medical defense (the doctrine of catharsis), much as a moderate Puritan might have tried to show that wine was healthy and dancing good exercise. But we do not drink for health or dance for exercise. Nor do we go to tragedies to get rid of emotions, but rather to feel them more abundantly; to banquet is not to be purged.

The shortcomings of Freud's utilitarian view of mental symptoms may be seen clearly in his treatment of the dream-life. He sees only the dream at work, disfiguring the disguising dangerous emotions in order to protect the dreamer's sleep and/or to fulfill a wish.[12] The dream is just another mold into which the dream-thoughts have been poured. It is this disregard of the form of the dream as mere trappings that prevents Freud from seeing the play aspect of the dream; for play is basically a *form* rather than a content: it depends upon a certain arrangement and articulation of emotion in time, employing images and speech—in other words, upon conventions. Freud's interest—a vital one—is in elucidating the inner meaning of these conventions; he is not interested in the phenomenon of the conventionalization of meaning itself. If he were, he would see that what may be liberating in the dream is not only the fact that certain suppressed contents are allowed expression but the very fact that the sleeper's emotion is dramatized, i.e.,

---

[12] In *The Interpretation of Dreams* Freud speaks of the dream as either a compromise disfigurement of morally reprehensible thoughts which would, if directly expressed, shock the dreamer out of sleep; or, more simply, an imaginary enactment of needs and obligations which disturb the dreamer's sleep. (E.g., we are thirsty and dream that we drink; or, we have an early appointment and, wishing to remain in bed, dream that we are already there.) In the case of art the imputation is similarly passive: the artist wards off the destructiveness of his neurotic conflict by unburdening himself in publicly acceptable fantasies. The work of art thus guards the neurosis in a twofold sense: it stabilizes rather than resolves it (having become a useful part of the artist's psyche, it is unlikely to be abandoned), but at the same time it tends to prevent the neurosis from getting any worse.

played, in a dream. The dream is based on a certain imagination of reality (i.e., its conversion into images). Dreams arise not only out of tension and distress and unfulfillment, but also out of a spontaneous pleasure in the mind's activity. Freud says as much, in the passage already quoted:

> When our psychic apparatus does not actually act in search of some urgently needed gratification, we let this apparatus itself work for pleasure gain. We attempt to gain pleasure from its very activity.

But this suggestion is not developed in Freud's writings. For the most part he gives the impression that dreams are to be understood in terms of their utility—that their use is to help express anxieties which cannot otherwise be communicated.

On the cultural significance of the neurotic character, Freud is entirely explicit. Neurotics are rebels out of weakness rather than strength; they witness to the inadequacies of cultural restraint. But they are unsuccessful rebels, for they pay too high a price for their revolt, and ultimately fail, turning their aggressions against themselves. Instead of being repressed and turned inward as the neurotic is, the normal personality is active and outgoing. Expedient normal attitudes lead to some active achievement in the outer world. The brisk managerial ego of the normal personality devotes itself to aggression against the environment, to the practical use of objects; it does not fixate upon them. As Freud put it elsewhere: neurotic anxiety comes from a libido which has "found no employment"; therefore, the dream, like work, has a "moralizing purpose." Again, the economic metaphor discloses Freud's ideal of health as well: a fully employed libido.

In a brilliant passage Freud describes the normal attitude toward reality as one combining the best features of neurotic and psychotic attitudes:

> Neurosis does not deny the existence of reality, it merely tries to ignore it; psychosis denies it and tries to substitute something else for it. A reaction which combines features of both these is the one we call normal or "healthy"; it denies reality as little as neurosis, but then, like a psychosis, is concerned with effecting a change in it.

Thus the neurotic character is the unsuccessful protestant of the emotional life; in him inwardness becomes incapacity. The normal character continues to protest, Freud implies, but is "not content . . . with establishing the alternation within itself." Thus, in Freud's conception of the normal man, there is a certain echo of the Romantic idea of genius—the ideal man who attains to the self-expression that other men, intimidated by convention, weakly forgo.

As the passage just quoted suggests, Freud did not draw a sharp line between the concepts of normal and neurotic. His dictum that "we are all somewhat hysterical," that the difference between so-called normality and neurosis is only a matter of degree, is one of the key statements in his writings. Its meaning is threefold.

First, it declassifies human society, creating an essential democracy within the human condition. Even the Greek tragedy—the most aristocratic context—was leveled out by Freud; the unique crime of the tragic hero becomes an intention in every heart, and in the most ordinary of plots, the history of every family. Misfortune is not an exceptional possibility, occasioned by rare circumstances or monstrous characters, but is the lot of every person, something he has to pass through in his journey from infancy to old age. The aristocratic bias of the "heroic" myth is replaced, in Freud, by the democratic bias of the "scientific" myth: Oedipus *Rex* becomes Oedipus Complex, which all men live through. It is because of the suppressed tragedies of everyday life that men respond so fully to the more explicit tragedies on the stage. But this does not mean that Freud proposed a genuinely tragic view of life; he was much too realistic for that. Ordinary men compromise with their instinctual longings and become neurotic; the tragic hero, because he suffers and dies, must be presumed to have carried out his wishes in a way forbidden to most men.

Secondly, to say that all men are neurotic means to imply an injunction to tolerance. At least Freud's discovery that the commonplace is saturated with the abnormal, the pathological—that psychopathology no longer deals with the exception but with the ordinary man—does something to alter established habits of moral judgment. It lightens the heavier burdens of guilt and responsibility, for many offenses can be made to appear smaller if perceived in sufficient depth.

Third, and more important, this conception of neurosis reveals the essentially ethical nature of Freud's idea of normality. Normality is not a statistical conception, for the majority is no longer normal. Normality is an ethical ideal, pitted against the actual abnormal. By another name, normality is the negative ideal of "overcoming"—whatever it is that ought to be overcome. Being essentially negative, normality is an ever-retreating ideal. An attitude of stoic calm is required for its pursuit. No one catches the normal; everyone must act as if it can be caught. Nor can the psychological man forget himself in pursuit of the normal, for his normality consists of a certain kind of self-awareness. Not least of all, the analysts themselves, Freud thought, needed to return to analysis every few years to renew their knowledge of themselves.

The psychological ideal of normality has a rather unheroic aspect. Think of a whole society dominated by psychotherapeutic ideals. Considered not from the individual's but from a sociological point of view, psychoanalysis is an expression of a popular tyranny such as not even de Tocqueville adequately imagined. Ideally, the democratic tyranny which is the typical social form of our era will not have a hierarchy of confessors and confessants. Rather, as I have pointed out in Chapter Nine, everyone must be a confessant, everyone must aspire to be a confessor. This is the meaning of the psychoanalytic re-education Freud speaks of. In the emergent democracy of the sick, everyone can to some extent play doctor to others, and none is allowed the temerity to claim that he can definitively cure or be cured. The hospital is succeeding the church and the parliament as the archetypal institution of Western culture.

What has caused this tyranny of psychology, legitimating self-concern as the highest science? In part, no doubt, it is the individual's failure to find anything else to affirm except the self. Having lost faith in the world, knowing himself too well to treat himself as an object of faith, modern man cannot be self-confident; this, in a negative way, justifies his science of self-concern. Though the world is indifferent to him, the lonely ego may here and there win something from it. For the rectitude and energetic naïveté of the man who was the ideal type during the middle-class, Protestant phase of American culture, we have substituted the character traits of husbanded energy and finessed self-consciousness. The Frank Merriwell of a psychological culture will not, like the moral athlete of Protestant culture, turn his reveries into realities. Rather, he will be mindful to keep realities from turning into reveries.

In this age, in which technics is invading and conquering the last enemy —man's inner life, the psyche itself—a suitable new character type has arrived on the scene: the psychological man. Three character ideals have successively dominated Western civilization: first, the ideal of the political man, formed and handed down to us from classical antiquity; second, the ideal of the religious man, formed and handed down to us from Judaism through Christianity, and dominant in the civilization of authority that preceded the Enlightenment; third, the ideal of the economic man, the very model of our liberal civilization, formed and handed down to us in the Enlightenment. This last has turned out to be a transitional type, with the shortest life-expectancy of all; out of his tenure has emerged the psychological man of the twentieth century, a child not of nature but of technology. He is not the pagan ideal, political man, for he is not committed to the public life. He is most unlike the religious man. We will recognize in the case history of psychological man the nervous habits of his father, economic man: he is anti-heroic, shrewd, carefully counting his satisfactions and dissatisfactions, studying unprofitable commitments as the sins most to be avoided. From this immediate ancestor, psychological man has constituted his own careful economy of the inner life.

The psychological man lives neither by the ideal of might nor by the ideal of right which confused his ancestors, political man and religious man. Psychological man lives by the ideal of insight—practical, experimental insight leading to the mastery of his own personality. The psychological man has withdrawn into a world always at war, where the ego is an armed force capable of achieving armistices but not peace. The prophetic egoist of Western politics and Protestant Christianity who, through the model with which he provided us, also laid down the lines along which the world was to be transformed, has been replaced by the sage, intent upon the conquest of his inner life, and, at most, like Freud, laying down the lines along which those that follow him can salvage something of their own. Turning away from the Occidental ideal of action leading toward the salvation of others besides ourselves, the psychological man has espoused the Oriental ideal of salvation through self-contemplative manipulation. Ironically, this is happening just at the historic moment when the Orient, whose westernmost outpost is Russia, has adopted the Occidental ideal of saving activity in the world. The West has attempted many successive transformations of the enemy, the world. It now chooses to move against its last enemy, the self, in an attempt to conquer it and assimilate it to the world as it is. For it is from the self that the troublesome, world-rejecting ideal of the religious man came forth.

Freudianism closes off the long-established quarrel of Western man with his own spirit. It marks the archaism of the classical legacy of political man, for the new man must live beyond reason—reason having proved no adequate guide to his safe conduct through the meaningless experience of life. It marks the repudiation of the Christian legacy of the religious man, for the new man is taught to live a little beyond conscience—conscience having proved no adequate guide to his safe conduct through life, and furthermore to have added absurd burdens of meaning to the experience of life. Finally, psychoanalysis marks the exhaustion of the liberal legacy represented historically in economic man, for now men must live with the knowledge that their dreams are by function optimistic and cannot be fulfilled. Aware at last that he is chronically ill, psychological man may nevertheless end the ancient quest of his predecessors for a healing doctrine. His experience with the latest one, Freud's, may finally teach him that every cure must expose him to new illness.